London Guide

**THE MOST COMPREHENSIVE
GUIDE TO LONDON**

CONTENTS

Nicholson

An Imprint of HarperCollins*Publishers*

A Nicholson Guide

© Nicholson 1996

First published 1967
Fifteenth edition 1996

River Maps by Dominic Beddow, Draughtsman Maps

London Maps
© Nicholson, generated from the
Bartholomew London Digital Database

London Underground Map by kind
permission of London Regional Transport
LRT Registered User No 96/1496

All other maps
© Nicholson

Nicholson
An Imprint of HarperCollins*Publishers*
77-85 Fulham Palace Road
Hammersmith
London W6 8JB

Great care has been taken throughout this book to be accurate,
but the publishers cannot accept responsibility for any errors or
their consequences.

Printed in Hong Kong

ISBN 0 7028 3154 9

67/15/2718

SYMBOLS AND ABBREVIATIONS

A	Access/Mastercard/Eurocard
Ax	American Express
Dc	Diners Club
V	Visa/Barclaycard

Average prices for a three-course meal for one without wine but including
VAT (these prices are for guidance only):

£	£10.00 and under
££	£10.00-£20.00
£££	£20.00-£30.00
£££+	£30.00 and over

Reserve – advisable to reserve

L	lunch
D	dinner
🍺	bar food
	open all day 11.00-23.00 Mon-Sat,
	12.00-14.30 & 19.00-22.30 Sun (as a minimum; may be
	open all day)
(M)	membership required

Opening times

Many places are closed on Xmas Day, New Year's Day and Good Friday,
and opening times are subject to change, so it is advisable to check first.

Sightseeing

British Travel Centre   4 **D3**
12 Lower Regent St SW1. Personal callers only. British Tourist Authority Information Centre, incorporating the American Express Travel Service Office, British Rail ticket office and a bureau de change. Details on where to go throughout the UK. Book a room, coach trip or theatre ticket; buy plane or train tickets, hire a car; all under one roof. Also regular exhibitions, videos, travel bookshop and gift shop. *OPEN 09.00-18.30 Mon-Fri, 10.00-16.00 Sat & Sun (09.00-17.00 Sat in May-Sep only).*

City of London Information   5 **D2**
Centre
St Paul's Churchyard EC4. 0171-606 3030. Information and advice with specific reference to the 'Square Mile'. Free literature. Essential to get monthly Diary of Events which lists a big choice of free entertainment in the City. *OPEN May-Sep 09.30-17.00 Mon-Sun; Oct-Apr 09.30-17.00 Mon-Fri, 09.30-12.30 Sat.*

Guildhall Library   5 **D2**
Aldermanbury EC2. 0171-332 1868. Provides historical information about London. *OPEN 09.30-17.00 Mon-Sat, Limited sections OPEN 09.30-17.00 Sat.*

London Tourist Board   7 **B1**
Information Centre
Victoria Station Forecourt SW1. (0839) 123456. Travel and tourist information for London and England. Most languages spoken. Also instant hotel reservations, theatre and tour bookings, sales of guide books, maps and gifts. *OPEN Apr-Oct 08.00-19.00 Mon-Sun; Nov-Mar 08.00-19.00 Mon-Sat, 08.00-16.00 Sun.*

Other LTB information centres at:
Point of Arrival
Heathrow Central Tube Station
Heathrow Terminal 3
Liverpool Street Station EC2   5 **F1**
Inner London
107a Commercial St SE1
Hays Galleria, Tooley St SE1   5 **F4**
46 Greenwich Church St SE10
44 Duncan St N1   2 **D3**
Lewisham Library, 366 High St SE13
Selfridges, 400 Oxford St W1   4 **B2**
Outer London
The Atrium, Civic Centre, York St, Twickenham, Middx
Library, Townley Rd, Bexleyheath, Kent

Library, 14 High St, Uxbridge, Middx
Civic Centre, Station Rd, Harrow, Middx
Hall Place, Bourne Rd, Bexley, Kent
Katharine St, Croydon, Surrey
Old Town Hall, Whittaker Av, Richmond, Surrey
24 The Treaty Centre, High St, Hounslow, Middx
Town Hall, High Rd, Ilford, Essex

London Transport Travel
Information Centres
London Transport information 0171-222 1234 *(24 hrs)*. London Transport offices for enquiries on travel (underground and buses). Free maps of the underground and bus routes, plus information leaflets in French, German and English. *OPENING times vary. Phone for details.*

Euston Tube Station   1 **F4**
Hammersmith Bus Station
Heathrow Central Tube Station
King's Cross Tube Station   1 **G3**
Liverpool Street Station   5 **F1**
Oxford Circus Tube Station   4 **D2**
Piccadilly Circus Tube Station   4 **E3**
St James's Park Tube Station   4 **D5**
Victoria British Rail Station   7 **B1**
Waterloo International Terminal   5 **A5**

Scottish Tourist Board   4 **E4**
19 Cockspur St SW1. 0171-930 8661. Tourist leaflets and information on mainland Scotland and the islands. *OPEN for leaflets and information May-Sep 09.00-18.00 Mon-Fri (to 18.30 Thur), 10.00-17.00 Sat (Jun-Sep only); Oct-Apr 09.30-17.30 Mon-Fri (to 18.30 Thur). OPEN 09.30-17.00 Mon-Fri all year for bookings.*

Wales Tourist Board   4 **D3**
12 Lower Regent St W1. 0171-409 0969. Leaflets and information for the visitor to Wales. *OPEN 09.00-18.30 Mon-Fri, 10.00-16.00 Sat & Sun (09.00-17.30 Sat in Jun-Sep only).*

London numbers are prefixed with 0171- or 0181- depending on area; central London numbers are 0171- and Greater London 0181-. Codes can be checked with the operator (dial 100) or Directory Enquiries (dial 192); telephone directories and The Code Book also have full details. If dialling from London to an exchange elsewhere, you must find the code of the exchange. The codes are listed in The Code Book or the operator (dial 100) will tell you. If you are using a public telephone in London it will almost certainly be a push-button one. You will need 10p, 20p, 50p or £1 coins. The coins must be inserted before you can dial but if you do not get through the money will be refunded when you replace the receiver. It is best to use smaller denominations as percentages of larger ones will not be refunded. More and more public telephones take phonecards as a form of payment. British Telecom phonecards can be bought in denominations from 20 units (£2.00) to 200 units (£20.00). Mercury phones accept only Mercury phonecards or credit cards (A.Ax.Dc.V.). Phonecards are obtainable from newsagents, chemists and post offices.

Emergency calls Dial 999 and ask for police, fire or ambulance service.
Directory enquiries 192 for all British addresses.
Transfer charge (collect) calls or difficulty in getting through to a number – 100 for the operator.
International calls You can dial direct to many countries. Codes are listed in *The Code Book* or ask the operator.

Viewpoints

Get a fresh perspective on London by looking down on it from a tall building or a natural high point. There are many places which command a view of almost the entire metropolis, and from them you can appreciate its sheer magnitude.

Alexandra Palace
On Muswell Hill N22. About 250ft (76.3m). View from the terrace over north London, Kent, Surrey, Essex and Hertfordshire.
Eltham Park SE9
View of central London. Best view from the ornamental pond.
Hampstead Heath NW3
Constable's famous view of London. Good vantage points are Whitestone Pond and Parliament Hill.
Heathrow Airport
Roof of Queen's Building, Heathrow, Middx. 0181-745 5259. Aircraft continuously landing and taking off. *OPEN 09.00-½ hr before dusk.*
Highgate Archway N6
From the top you see the whole of London laid out before you.
Jack Straw's Castle
North End Way NW3. 0171-435 8885. Lunch and dinner in the restaurant at 450ft (137m) with long views across London to the distant Kentish hills. *LD Reserve. Last orders 22.00 Mon-Sat, 21.00 Sun.*

Kenwood House
Hampstead La NW3. 0181-348 1286. Panorama of almost the whole of London. View from the gazebo by the coach house. *OPEN summer 10.00-18.00, winter 10.00-1600.*
London Hilton   **4 B4**
22 Park La W1. 0171-493 8000. 'Windows Piano Bar' at 320ft (97.6m). Lift. Fine views over Hyde Park, Buckingham Palace and Mayfair.
Monument   **5 E3**
Monument St EC3. 0171-626 2717. Magnificent view from the top, but it is 202ft (61.5m) high and there are 311 stairs to climb! *Closed for renovation at time of going to press; due to re-open Easter 1996.*
Point Hill
Blackheath SE10. View from the docks in the east to Alexandra Palace in the north and the City and Westminster in the west.
Pole Hill
Chingford E4. The high point of Epping Forest. View towards the river and of Shooters Hill south of the river.
Primrose Hill NW8   **1 B2**
At 206ft (61.7m) high gives fine views over London. A helpful table identifies some of London's most prominent landmarks.
St Paul's Cathedral   **5 D2**
Ludgate Hill EC4. 0171-248 2705. Magnificent view from the Golden Gallery of the City, the Wren churches, the Tower and London Pool. 355ft (108.2m), 530 steps. *OPEN 08.30-16.15 Mon-Sat. Charge.*
Shrewsbury Park SE18
View of the river, the docks to the north and east along the river towards Tilbury.
Tower Bridge SE1   **5 G4**
0171-407 0922. Breathtaking views of London and the Thames from high walkways. *OPEN Apr-Oct 10.00-18.30 Mon-Sun; Nov-Mar 10.00-17.15 Mon-Sun. Last admission 1hr 15 mins before closing time. CLOSED B. hols. Charge.*
Westminster Cathedral   **7 C1**
Ashley Pl, off Victoria St SW1. 0171-798 9055. View over Westminster and the Thames from the top of 273ft (83.3m) campanile. Lift usually *OPEN Apr-Sep 06.45-20.00 Mon-Sun. Charge.*

Daily ceremonies and events

Pageantry

These are the main ceremonies which occur throughout the year. Phone the London Tourist Board on (0839) 123456 for details of events on the day you want to go.

Ceremony of the Keys   5 **G3**
Tower of London, Tower Hill EC3. 0171-709 0765. The Chief Warder of the Yeomen Warders, with an escort of the Brigade of Guards, locks the West Gates, the Middle Tower and Byward Tower. One of the oldest continuous military ceremonies in the world. *21.40 Mon-Sun, by written application to the Governor of the Tower well in advance, enclosing sae.*

Changing of the Guard   4 **D5**
Buckingham Palace SW1. Takes place inside the palace railings (in *summer* the crowd makes it impossible to see much). An alternative is to see the Guards on their way from Chelsea or Wellington Barracks; phone the London Tourist Board to find out which they are leaving from on the day you are going. *Mon-Sun in summer, alternate days in winter.* Leave Chelsea Barracks at *10.45* or Wellington Barracks at *11.00*. Palace ceremony *11.30*.

St James's Palace SW1   4 **D4**
A detachment of the Buckingham Palace Guard comes here. Guards change *11.15 (days as above)*.

Whitehall SW1   4 **F4**
Horse Guards Pde SW1. Changing of the Queen's Life Guard mounted on splendid horses. Guards leave Hyde Park Barracks *10.28* Mon-Sat, *09.28* Sun. Ceremony *11.00* Mon-Sat, *10.00* Sun.

Windsor Castle
Windsor, Berks. (01753) 868286. The Queen's out of town and favoured residence. Changing of the Guard at *11.00-11.30*. *Days vary, phone for details.* A military band enlivens the pageant.

Speakers' Corner: A remaining vestige of the British tradition of free speech is this institution of impromptu discourses by unknown orators, usually on religion or politics. At Speakers' Corner (Marble Arch corner of Hyde Park (4 **A3**), usually on *Sun*). Also Lincoln's Inn Fields (4 **G2**) and Tower Hill (5 **G3**) *Mon-Fri lunchtime*.

Feeding the pigeons: In Trafalgar Square (4 **F4**) – a famous tradition. You will soon be accosted by touts who want to sell you bird-seed and photographs of yourself covered in pigeons.

The following list presents not only the most important annual events but also some of the more obscure London

customs in order to cover as wide a field as possible. For exact days, times and places, where not given, and to find out whether or not there is a charge, contact one of the centres given under 'Tourist information'.

Chinese New Year   4 **E3**
Gerrard St W1. Papier-mâché dragons, the lion dance and firecrackers bring Chinatown to life. *Jan or Feb.*

International Boat Show   6 **A3**
Earl's Court Exhibition Centre, Warwick Rd SW5. 0171-385 1200. The latest pleasure craft, yachts and equipment. The largest boat show in Europe. *Early Jan.*

January sales
Most London stores have stock-clearing sales after Christmas. Some fantastic bargains, but they go quickly – the real fanatics camp outside the stores the night before the sale starts to be first in the queue – and there are always big crowds. Start *early Jan.*

Lord Mayor of Westminster's New Year's Day Parade
One of the largest parades in Europe with some 7000 performers, from marching bands to colourful floats. Starts at *12.30* on Piccadilly (4 **D4**) and ends at Hyde Park (4 **A4**).

Model Engineer Exhibition
Olympia Exhibition Centre, Hammersmith Rd W14. 0171-603 3344. Model cars, trains, planes, boats. *Late Dec/Early Jan.*

Royal Epiphany Gifts   4 **D4**
Chapel Royal, St James's Pl, Marlborough Rd SW1. Picturesque ceremony, when two 'Gentlemen Ushers' offer gold, frankincense and myrrh on behalf of the Queen. *6 Jan 11.30. Admission by ticket only.*

Spring Stampex   2 **C2**
Business Design Centre, 52 Upper St N1. 0171-359 3535. National stamp exhibition. Contact the British Philatelic Centre 0171-490 1005 for details. *Late Jan. Also hold Autumn Stampex late Sep-early Oct.*

Holiday on Ice
Wembley Arena, Wembley, Middx. 0181-900 1234. Pantomime on ice. *Early Feb.*

International Performance   6 **A3**
Motor Show
Earl's Court Exhibition Centre, Warwick Rd SW5. 0171-385 1200. *Mid Feb.*

Road Racing & Superbike Show
Alexandra Pavilion, Alexandra Palace & Park N22. 0181-365 2121. *Early Feb.*

Great Spitalfields 5 **G1**
Pancake Day Race
Old Spitalfields Market, Brushfield St E1. 0171-287 0907. Watch various teams running with frying pans, tossing their pancakes as they go.

March

Chelsea Spring Antiques 6 **E3**
Fair
Chelsea Old Town Hall, King's Rd SW3. All exhibits pre-date 1870. 0171-351 1980. *Mid Mar.*

Classic Car Show
Alexandra Palace, Alexandra Park N22. 0181-365 2121. Classic car display and auction, car parts jumble stall. *Late Mar.*

Daily Mail Ideal Home 6 **A3**
Exhibition
Earl's Court Exhibition Centre, Warwick Rd SW5. 0171-385 1200. Full of new and interesting gadgets. Very popular and always crowded. *Mid Mar.*

John Stow Memorial Service 5 **F2**
Church of St Andrew Undershaft, St Mary Axe EC3. The Lord Mayor attends this commemoration of London's first historian and places a new quill pen in the hand of Stow's statue. *Sun in Mar or Apr, 11.30.*

Oranges & Lemons Service 5 **A2**
St Clement Danes, Strand WC2. 0171-242 8282. After a special service, oranges and lemons are distributed to children while the traditional tune is played on handbells. *Late March.*

Oxford v Cambridge Boat Race
River Thames, Putney to Mortlake. University boat race over four miles. View from the banks of the river or one of the bridges. Get there early for a good view. *Sat afternoon in Mar or Apr.*

Royal Film Performance
A selected film gets royal patronage in aid of charity. Celebrities and glitter at one of the big cinemas. *No fixed date.*

Sailboat
Alexandra Palace N22. (01703) 629962. Britain's largest exhibition of dinghies and small sailing craft. *No fixed date.*

St David's Day
Windsor, Berks. Leeks given to the Welsh Guards. Generally attended by the Duke of Edinburgh. *1 Mar.*

St Patrick's Day
Pirbright, Surrey. Shamrocks given to the Irish Guards by Her Majesty the Queen Mother. *17 Mar.*

April

Annual Spital Sermon 5 **D2**
St Lawrence Jewry, Gresham St EC2. 0171-600 9478. Governors of the two great hospitals, Christ's and Bridewell, attend with the Lord Mayor, sheriffs and aldermen. *Coincides with the first meeting of the Court of Common Council.*

Butterworth Charity 5 **C1**
St Bartholomew-the-Great, Smithfield EC1. 0171-606 5171. Presentation of hot-cross buns, traditionally to 'poor widows', now to children. *Good Fri before 10.30 service.*

Easter Procession & Carols 4 **F6**
Westminster Abbey SW1. 0171-222 5152. *Easter Sun.*

Easter Show 6 **F5**
Battersea Park SW11. Colourful carnival – fairground, side stalls, various stage acts. *Easter Sun.*

London Harness Horse Parade 1 **C4**
Regent's Park NW1. Fine horses and carts; brewers' vans and drays on parade. Judging *starts at 09.45* followed by a procession twice round the Inner Circle *at about 12.00. Easter Mon.*

The London Marathon
The famous 26-mile race starting *09.30* at Greenwich Park SE10 and Blackheath SE3 and finishing at Westminster Bridge SW1 (4 **F5**). For information ring 0171-620 4117. *Late Apr.*

Tower of London Church 5 **G3**
Parade
Tower of London, Tower Hill EC3. 0171-709 0765. The Yeomen Warders in state dress are inspected, and parade before and after morning service on *Easter Sun, 11.00. Also Whit Sun & Sun before Xmas.*

May

Beating the Bounds 5 **F3**
0171-488 4772. From All-Hallows-by-the-Tower to St Dunstan's, Idol Lane EC3. The boundaries of the parishes of London were once proclaimed by a special ceremony. Now the pupils of St Dunstan's School march from All-Hallows, carrying sticks to beat the boundary marks around the Tower of London, one of which is in the Thames! The Lord Mayor usually attends the service at *17.00* at All-Hallows. Every third year the Tower of London yeomen meet the beaters at about *19.00* for some good-natured jeering! *Ascension Day.*

Chelsea Flower Show 6 **F3**
Royal Hospital Grounds, Chelsea SW3. 0171-834 4333 (*24-hr information line*

0171-828 1744). Superb flower displays. *For 4 days late May*.

FA Cup Final
Wembley Stadium, Wembley, Middx. 0181-900 1234. The climax of the English football season. *Late Apr/early May*.

Festival for Mind, Body & Spirit   7 D1
The New Hall, Royal Horticultural Society Halls, Greycoat St SW1. Development of human consciousness and natural health. Includes astrology, alternative medicine, healing, animal welfare, ecology, spiritual development, personal growth and the psychic arts. Demonstrations, consultations, lectures and performance arts. Contact 0171-938 3788 for information. *Late May*.

Glyndebourne Festival Opera Season
Glyndebourne, nr Lewes, E. Sussex. (01273) 812321. Opera lovers don evening dress and flock from town to hear superlative singing, and sup on the lawn if the summer air is clement. *Late May-mid Aug*.

Open-air Art Exhibitions
Victoria Embankment Gardens WC2 (4 **F4**) (next to Embankment underground station). Artists and their work on exhibition. *2-14 May; Aug, Mon-Sat*. The Terrace, Richmond Hill, Richmond, Surrey. Run by Richmond Art Group. Fine views from terrace. *May or Jun 10.00-20.00 Sat & Sun*. Royal Av, King's Rd SW3 (6 **F3**). *May-Oct 11.00-18.00 Sat*. The Green Park side of Piccadilly (4 **C4**), where a multitude of street artists set up their pictures against the railings. And along Bayswater Rd, outside Kensington Gardens and Hyde Park (3 **D3**). *Every Sun morning*.

Putney & Hammersmith Amateur Regattas
Rowing regattas make exciting watching from the banks of the Thames. Contact the Amateur Rowing Assn (ARA) for information 0181-748 3632. *Late Apr/early May*.

Rugby League Challenge Cup Final
Wembley Stadium, Wembley, Middx. Contact Rugby Football League. (0113) 262 4637. *Late Apr/early May*.

Rugby Union Cup Final
Twickenham Rugby Football Ground, Whitton Rd, Twickenham, Middx. 0181-892 8161. *Early May*.

Samuel Pepys   5 F3
Commemoration Service
St Olave's, Hart St EC3. 0171-488 4318. The Lord Mayor lays a wreath on Pepys' monument. *Late May or early Jun*.

Antiquarian Book Fair   2 A5
Hotel Russell, Russell Sq WC1. (01763) 248400. International fair with books, documents, musical scores. *Late Jun*.

Beating the Retreat   4 F4
Horse Guards Parade SW1. 0171-839 5323. Military display of marching and drilling bands. Trumpeters, massed bands and pipe and drums. Some floodlit performances. *Jun*.

The Derby
Epsom Racecourse, Surrey. (01372) 726311. World-famous flat horserace. *Early Jun*.

Election of Sheriffs of the   5 D2
City of London
Guildhall EC2. 0171-606 3030. Lord Mayor and Aldermen in a colourful ceremony. Posies are carried traditionally to ward off 'the plague'. *Midsummer's Day (unless it falls on a Sat or Sun)*.

Founder's Day   7 A3
Royal Hospital, Chelsea SW3. 0171-730 0161. Chelsea pensioners parade in their colourful uniforms for inspection, sometimes by royalty. *Early Jun*.

The Garter Ceremony
Service attended by the Queen at St George's Chapel, Windsor, preceded by a colourful procession with the Household Cavalry and Yeomen of the Guard. Ceremony dates from 14thC. *Mon afternoon of Ascot week (usually 3rd week in Jun)*.

Greenwich Festival
SE10. Multi-arts programme at various historic venues, and street performances in Cutty Sark Gardens. Incorporates Greenwich Dance Festival. Phone 0181-305 1818 for details. *Early-mid Jun*.

Kenwood Lakeside Concerts
Kenwood House, Hampstead La NW3. 0171-973 3427. Bookings: 0171-413 1443. Classical concerts beside Kenwood Lake on Hampstead Heath performed by some of the most famous orchestras in the world. Often end with spectacular firework displays. *Sat evenings Jun-Sep. Charge*.

Lord's Test Match
Lord's Cricket Ground, St John's Wood Rd NW8. Ring 0171-289 8979 for tickets, 0171-286 8011 for information on state of play. *Jun or Jul*.

Royal Ascot Races
(01344) 22211. A fashionable society event where the hats often attract more attention than the horses. The Queen and other members of the royal party travel the course in open carriages before the race. *Jun*.

Spitalfields Festival 5 **G1**
Christchurch, Commercial St E1. 0171-377 0287. Classical music concerts, *lunchtimes and evenings. Jun.*

Summer Art Exhibition 4 **D3**
Royal Academy, Burlington House, Piccadilly W1. 0171-439 7438. Aspiring Cézannes and Hockneys enter their works to be admired, selected and hopefully bought! *Jun-mid Aug.*

Trooping the Colour
The route is from Buckingham Palace SW1 (4 **D5**) along the Mall (4 **D5**) to Horse Guards Parade (4 **F4**), then to Whitehall (4 **F4**) and back again. Pageantry at its best for the Queen's official birthday. *11.00, Sat nearest 11 Jun.*

Westminster Dance Week
Performances, workshops and participatory events, including free performances in Victoria Embankment Gardens (4 **F4**). Phone 0171-798 1906 for details. *Early Jun.*

Wimbledon Lawn Tennis Championships
All England Lawn Tennis & Croquet Club, Church Rd SW19. 0181-946 2244. 'Wimbledon Fortnight', the world's most famous championship. *Last week Jun & 1st week Jul.*

July

City of London Festival
0171-377 0540. Held in the Barbican, the Tower of London, Mansion House, the City's livery halls, St Paul's Cathedral, many fine churches and the City's open spaces. Concerts, opera, exhibitions, poetry, drama, dance, jazz and street events. *Three weeks in Jul.*

Doggetts Coat & Badge Race
The Thames, London Bridge (5 **E3**) to Chelsea (7 **B4**). 0171-626 3531. Rowing race for Thames Watermen, originated in 1715. Sometimes called the 'Watermen's Derby'. *Late Jul.*

Henley Royal Regatta
Henley-on-Thames, Oxon. (01491) 572153. Steeped in tradition; rowing and socialising side by side. *Early Jul.*

Proms (Henry Wood 3 **E5**
Promenade Concerts)
Royal Albert Hall, Kensington Gore SW7. 0171-589 8212. Concerts of classical music. Ticket qualification system for famous 'Last Night' celebrations. *Late Jul-Sep.*

Richmond Festival
Amateur and professional performing and visual arts. Venues include Richmond Theatre, Orange Tree Theatre, Richmond Green, the Thames. 0181-332 0534. *Mid Jul.*

Royal Tournament 4 **F4**
Earl's Court Exhibition Centre, Warwick Rd SW5. 0171-385 1200. Impressive military spectacle with marching displays and massed brass bands. *Two weeks mid Jul.*

Royal Tournament March Past 4 **F4**
Horse Guards, Whitehall SW1. Colourful parade by all troops taking part in the Royal Tournament. *Sun before Tournament.*

Strollerthon
Sponsored 'stroll' through the city centre, for children's charities. Street entertainments en route. Phone 0171-232 2255 for details. *Mid Jul.*

Swan Upping
Starts: Sunbury Lock *09.00-09.30.* Ownership of the swans on the Thames is divided between the Dyers Company, the Vintners Company and the Sovereign. Each *Jul* a census of the swans on the reaches up to Abingdon is taken, and the cygnets are branded by nicking their beaks. No fixed date. Phone 0171-236 1863 to find out exactly where the fleet is at any one time.

August

Notting Hill Carnival 3 **B4**
Ladbroke Grove and Notting Hill W11. 0181-964 0544. West Indian carnival with colourful floats, steel bands and dancing in the streets. *B.hol Sun & Mon.*

September

Battle of Britain Week 4 **F6**
Thanksgiving service at Westminster Abbey SW1. 0171-222 5152. Also Biggin Hill Flying Display. *Early Sep.*

Chelsea Autumn Antiques 6 **E3**
Fair
Chelsea Old Town Hall, King's Rd SW3. 0171-352 3619. *For ten days mid Sep.*

Christ's Hospital March
Founded by Edward VI as a hospital for orphans. 'Bluecoats' (the distinctive long coats which the boys wear date from this time) march through the City. *St Matthew's Day; on or near 21 Sep.*

Election of Lord Mayor of 5 **D2**
London
Procession from the church of St Lawrence Jewry, Gresham St EC2, to

the Guildhall EC2. 0171-606 3030. *Michaelmas Day, 29 Sep.*

Last Night of the Proms 3 **E5**
Royal Albert Hall, Kensington Gore SW7. 0171-589 8212. The culmination of the Proms concerts. Traditional rousing performance of *Land of Hope and Glory*. Tickets by qualification system only. *15 Sep or nearest Sat.*

London to Brighton Walk 4 **F5**
Starts Westminster Bridge SW1. Originated in 1903. *Early Sep, 07.00.*

October

Annual Full Tidal Closure
Thames Barrier, Unity Way SE18. 0181-854 1373. The annual closing of the Thames Barrier. See the huge barriers lifting out of the water.

Costermonger's Harvest Festival 4 **F3**
St Martin-in-the-Fields, Trafalgar Sq WC2. 0171-930 1862. Service attended by the Pearly Kings and Queens in their colourful regalia. *15.00, first Sun in Oct.* Regular evening concerts *all year round.*

Daily Mail International Ski Show 6 **A3**
Olympia Exhibition Centre, Hammersmith Rd W14. 0171-603 3344. Holiday kit for the keen skier. *Late Oct.*

Her Majesty's Judges & Queen's Counsels Annual Breakfast 4 **F6**
After a service at Westminster Abbey there is a procession to the House of Lords for the opening of the Law term. *1 Oct.*

Horse of the Year Show
Wembley Arena, Wembley, Middx. 0181-902 8833. Fine show jumping. *Early Oct.*

Quit-Rent Ceremony 5 **B2**
The Queen's Remembrancer receives the Quit-rent of a bill-hook, a hatchet, six horseshoes and 61 nails for two holdings from the Comptroller and the City Solicitor: an annual ceremony since 1234. *Tickets from the Chief Clerk to the Queen's Remembrancer, Room 118, Royal Courts of Justice, Strand WC2.*

Trafalgar Day Service & Parade 4 **F4**
Trafalgar Sq WC2. 0171-928 8978. Organised by the Navy League. *Sun nearest Trafalgar Day 21 Oct.*

November

Admission of the Lord Mayor Elect 5 **D2**
Guildhall, Gresham St EC2. 0171-606 3030. The Lord Mayor takes office. Colourful ceremony including handing over of insignia by former Lord Mayor. *Fri before Lord Mayor's show (second Fri in Nov).*

Christmas Lights 4 **D2**
Regent St and Oxford St W1. Festive illuminations to attract Christmas shoppers. Best seen *from 16.00 onwards. Late Nov-6 Jan (12th Night).*

Christmas Parade
0171-938 7402. New large-scale event featuring purpose-built floats parading through the West End. *Last Sun in Nov.*

Guy Fawkes Night
Anniversary of the Gunpowder Plot of 1605. Private and public firework displays throughout London. *Evening, 5 Nov.*

London to Brighton Veteran Car Run 4 **B5**
Hyde Park Corner W1. Cars leave here for Brighton. Colourful event with contestants in period costume. Commemorates the anniversary of Emancipation Day. *08.00, 1st Sun in Nov.*

Lord Mayor's Procession & Show
The newly elected Lord Mayor is driven in his state coach from the Guildhall (5 **D2**) to the Law Courts (5 **A2**) to be received by the Lord Chief Justice. The biggest ceremonial event in the City. *2nd Sat in Nov.*

Remembrance Sunday 4 **F5**
Poppies sold in the streets to raise money for ex-servicemen. Service at the Cenotaph, Whitehall SW1 with a salute of guns. *11.00, 2nd Sun in Nov.*

Royal Smithfield Show 6 **A3**
Earl's Court Exhibition Centre, Warwick Rd SW5. 0171-385 1200. Exhibition of agricultural machinery, supplies and services. Also livestock. *Late Nov.*

State Opening of Parliament
The Queen, in the Irish state coach, is driven from Buckingham Palace (4 **D5**) to the House of Lords (4 **F5**). A royal salute is fired from St James's Park. *Early Nov.*

December

Carol Services 4 **F6**
Westminster Abbey, Broad Sanctuary SW1. 0171-222 7110. Carol services on 26, 27 & 28 Dec.

Carol Singing   **4 E4**
Trafalgar Sq WC2. Recorded on tape. *Early evening from about 14 Dec*.

Christmas Tree   **4 E4**
Trafalgar Sq WC2. Norwegian spruce donated each year by the citizens of Oslo. Brightly lit *from 16.00*. Carol singing round the tree. *Mid Dec-6 Jan (12th Night)*.

New Year's Eve   **4 E4**
Trafalgar Sq WC2. Singing of 'Auld Lang Syne' by massed crowds – also dancing around the fountains (now usually protected behind screens).

Tower of London Church   **5 G3**
Parades
Tower Hill EC3. 0171-709 0765. The Yeomen Warders in state dress are inspected and parade before and after morning service on the *Sun before Xmas, 11.00. Also Easter Sun & Whit Sun*.

Watchnight Service   **5 D2**
St Paul's Cathedral, Ludgate Hill EC4. 0171-248 2705. *22.00-24.00, 31 Dec*.

London tours

London tours: by coach

Sightseeing tours, usually on double-decker buses or coaches. Some take several hours and the passengers stay on the bus listening to a commentary which is often translated into a number of different languages. Others take the whole day, and include guided tours of various sights, plus lunch. The London Tourist Board Information Centre, Victoria Station Forecourt SW1 (7 **B1***) sells tickets for a selection of sightseeing tours; alternatively you can telephone the organisations direct to reserve seats.*

Big Bus Company
Waterside Way SW17. 0181-944 7810. Tours on open-top double-decker buses with live commentary by London Tourist Board approved guides. Depart *every ½ hr Mon-Fri, every 15 min Sat, Sun & B.hols*, from Speakers' Corner, Park Lane W1 (4 **A3**), outside Ritz Hotel, Piccadilly W1 (4 **D4**) and outside Royal Westminster Hotel, Buckingham Palace Rd SW1 (7 **B1**); take *90 mins*. Stopper Tour (with 14 optional stopping points) valid for 24 hrs: tours leave Royal Westminster Hotel *Apr-Sep 08.50-16.50 Mon-Sun every 15 min (Oct-Mar to 15.50, every ½ hr)*.

Docklands Tours
London Docklands Visitor Centre, 3 Limeharbour, Isle of Dogs E14. 0171-512 1111. *2-hr* tours of Docklands accompanied by guides of your choice. See

restored wharves and warehouses, conservation areas, historic buildings, magnificent waterside views. Audio-visual presentation in Visitor Centre *45 mins prior to departure. Group bookings in advance*.

Evan Evans   **1 B2**
136 Wigmore St W1. 0171-930 2377. Operates a variety of tours; full day, morning, afternoon, plus a *2½-hr* general drive around the capital and *30-min* cruise on the Thames. Also extended tours out of London.

Frames Rickards   **1 G5**
11 Herbrand St WC1. 0171-837 6311. *Morning* and *afternoon* tours of the City and the West End, *evening* 'Ghosts & Ghouls' tour following the trail of Jack the Ripper. Tours to Windsor, Stratford-upon-Avon and many other tourist destinations.

Golden Tours   **7 B2**
4 Fountain Sq, 123-151 Buckingham Palace Rd SW1. 0171-233 7030. Range of *full-day, morning, afternoon* and *evening* tours, covering most of London's attractions, from East End pubs to the Tower of London and the National Gallery. Some tours include stopovers for a walk, museum visit or refreshments. *Phone for details*.

Harrods   **6 F1**
Sightseeing Tours Dept, Harrods, Knightsbridge SW1. 0171-730 1234. The Mercedes Benz B10 undoubtedly provides the most luxurious coach tour of London. The tour takes *2 hrs*. Taped commentary in eight languages, plus refreshments served by multi-lingual stewardesses. Harrods also operate tours to Stratford-upon-Avon and Blenheim Palace. Ticket reservations and information: 0171-581 3603.

London Pride Sightseeing
Ensign Bus Services, Albright Industrial Estate, Ferry La, Rainham, Essex. (01708) 631122. London Docklands and Greenwich tours leave from Lower Regent Street SW1 (4 **E3**) *every hr 09.30-16.00 Mon-Sun (Sat, Sun & B.hols only in winter)*. Grand Tour of London 'hop-on-hop-off' service leaves Coventry Street W1 (4 **E3**) for *90 min* tours ending in Lower Regent Street.

Original London Sightseeing Tours
London Coaches, Jew's Row SW18. Information: 0171-877 1722. Round London tours in traditional double-decker buses, some of which are open-topped.

Star Safari
Full day and *afternoon* tours taking in the lives and lifestyles of the rich and famous with commentary by guides who will give you an insight into London and its glitterati. Tours depart from the Forum Hotel SW7 (6 **C2**), Victoria Station Tourist

Information Centre SW1 (7 **B1**) and the Strand WC2 (4 **F3**). Details and bookings on (01932) 854721.

London tours: by helicopter

Cabair Helicopters
Elstree Aerodrome, Borehamwood, Herts. 0181-953 4411. *½-hr* sightseeing trips over London. *Sun by appointment only.*

CB
Biggin Hill Airport, Biggin Hill, Kent. (01959) 540633. Helicopter flights over London. Any size of group catered for. *By appointment only.*

London tours: by horse & carriage

The London Omnibus Company
36 Hazon Way, Epsom, Surrey. (01372) 727153. Rides on a restored Victorian double-decker horsebus, with the driver and conductor in period costume. Pick-up outside the London Transport Museum, Covent Garden WC2 (4 **F3**) *11.30-13.30* for *15 min* circuit around Covent Garden, or *13.30-15.30* for *40 min* tour taking in Trafalgar Square, Whitehall, Parliament Square and Westminster Abbey. *Phone above number to book in advance.*

London tours: by private guide

The Guild of Guide Lecturers   5 **D5**
52D Borough High St SE1. 0171-403 1115. This is the professional association for Tourist Board Registered Guides, with over 1000 trained members, all specialists in their subjects and speaking more than 35 languages between them. The Guild compiles an annual list of Registered Guides.

The London Tourist Board   7 **B1**
(Guides Dept)
26 Grosvenor Gdns SW1. 0171-730 3450. Can provide assistance in finding registered guides.

The following companies all use registered guides:
British Tours   4 **C2**
6 South Molton St W1. 0171-629 5267. Wide variety of individual tours throughout London and surrounding areas with qualified driver/guides.

Go-By-Guides Ltd
17 Woodfield, Parkhill Rd NW3. 0171-722 7506. Sightseeing tours by private car accompanied by trained driver/guides. *Half, full and multi-day* tours.

London Docklands Development Corporation
Group and individual tours organised in the London Docklands area. *For details and prices phone 0171-512 1111.*

Tour Guides Ltd   4 **B2**
57 Duke St W1. 0171-495 5504. Tourist Board registered guides will escort individuals or groups on car, coach or walking tours. *24 hr service.*

London tours: walking

Canal Walks
Inland Waterways Association, 114 Regent's Park Rd NW1. Two walks along the Regent's Canal starting from Camden Town tube station, then either west to Little Venice or east to the City Road Basin. Other walks. *Phone 0171-624 3978 to book.*

Citisights of London
213 Brooke Rd E5. 0181-806 4325. Archaeologists and historians working in association with the Museum of London provide a series of walks and tours concerning the history and archaeology of London. *Phone 0171-624 3978 to book.*

Historical Walks of London
3 Florence Rd, South Croydon, Surrey. 0181-668 4019. Wide variety of walks from *A City in the Blitz* to *Jack the Ripper Murder Trail.* Last about *2 hrs* and take place regardless of weather or numbers. *Mon-Sun.*

The Londoners Historic Pub Walks
3 Springfield Av N10. 0181-883 2656. Discover some of the links with London's past with visits to four or five of its famous pubs. Different route *each week.* From Temple tube station *19.30 Fri.*

London Wall Walk   5 **D1**
Museum of London, London Wall EC2. 0171-600 3699. Devised by the Museum of London, this is the best way to see the Roman and medieval city walls. The route takes about *1-2 hours* to complete and in that time you'll cover about 2 miles (3.2km) of London's streets. Buy the booklet *Roman Wall Walk* from the museum shop to set you on the right trail.

The Original **London Walks**
PO Box 1708 NW6. 0171-624 3978. Meet at various tube stations for stimulating walks through London lasting *1½ to 2 hrs.* A choice of more than 80 walks including *Dickens' London, Ghosts of the City* and *Jack the Ripper haunts.* Also pub walks. *Phone for details.*

Silver Jubilee Walkway
Buy a booklet from the London Tourist Board Information Centre (7 **B1**) or follow the paving stones marked with Jubilee

THE RIVER THAMES

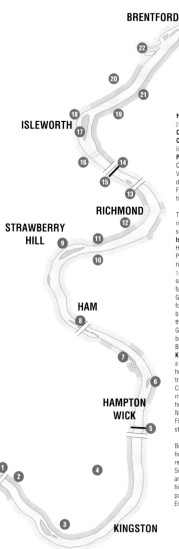

BRENTFORD

KEW

MORTLAKE

ISLEWORTH

STRAWBERRY HILL

RICHMOND

HAM

HAMPTON WICK

KINGSTON

NORTH BANK

2 **Hampton Court Palace** is bordered by 3 **Hampto Court Park**. Embarking at Barge Walk, by 1 **Hampto Court Bridge**, you can get a good idea of what travel ling to London was like for royal residents. 4 **Bush Park** used to be enclosed as part of the Hampto Court estate; it was opened to the public by Quee Victoria in 1838. Hampton Wick, to the left, is a resi dential area. Around the bend lies 8 **Teddington Lock** From here, going towards London, the Thames is tidal.

Twickenham, past Strawberry Hill, offers beautiful riverside settings. The path of the river is dotted with several willow-covered islands, among them 9 **Eel Pie Island**. The **Twickenham Ferry** 11 runs from the Boat House to Ham House. 12 **Marble Hill House**, an 18thC Palladian villa, looms gracefully from its spaciou riverside park. Through Richmond (see south bank) is 16 **Richmond Lock and Footbridge**, with good river side walks. Isleworth, by 17 **Isleworth Eyot**, became a fashionable place to live in the 18thC. Vincent var Gogh taught here and used the Thames as the subjec for his first paintings. 18 the **London Apprentice** pub built around 1741, is part of a charming setting with the 15thC tower of All Saint's Church and severa Georgian houses. 20 **Syon House** set in Syon Park behind wooded banks to the north and the Roya Botanic Gardens to the south. Heading towards 21 **Kew Bridge** is Brentford. 22 **The Grand Union Canal** a direct link to Birmingham, still joins the Thames here, although it is no longer busy with commercia traffic. Past Kew Bridge, the residential area o Chiswick is fronted by 26 **Strand-on-the-Green**, a riverside path with pubs and several notable 18thC houses, once home to famous residents including Nancy Mitford, William Morris and Dylan Thomas Flooding was common here at high tide until the con struction of the Thames Barrier.

Boats moored at the riverside gardens of grand 18thC houses on 31 **Chiswick Mall** are a continuing reminder of the wealthy riverside village it once was. Similar houses line the banks along 32 **Upper Mall** and 33 **Lower Mall**, where there are several popular historic pubs — the Blue Anchor, the Dove (whose past imbibers include Nell Gwynne, Graham Greene and Ernest Hemingway), the 17thC Old Ship — and several

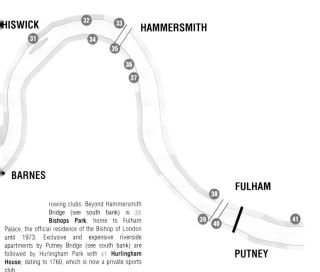

CHISWICK

31 32 33 HAMMERSMITH

34 35

36

37

BARNES

FULHAM

38

39 40

41

PUTNEY

rowing clubs. Beyond Hammersmith Bridge (see south bank) is 38 **Bishops Park**, home to Fulham Palace, the official residence of the Bishop of London until 1973. Exclusive and expensive riverside apartments by Putney Bridge (see south bank) are followed by Hurlingham Park with 41 **Hurlingham House**, dating to 1760, which is now a private sports club.

SOUTH BANK

Behind the pretty white arches of 5 **Kingston Bridge** lies Kingston, an early fishing village, market town and royal borough with a wide range of shops and a good river frontage. Passing 6 **Stevens Eyot** and 7 **Trowlock Island**, all around is rural greenery. 8 **Teddington Lock** marks the beginning of the tidal Thames. To the east is Ham, a largely residential area with parkland bordering the river. Within the parkland is 10 **Ham House**, built in 1610 by Sir Thomas Vavasour for the Earls of Dysart. Owned by the National Trust, it has been restored to its full baroque splendour.

9 **Eel Pie Island**, now a luxury housing development accessible only by boat, once housed a noisy nightclub which played host to many of the most famous groups, including the Rolling Stones. From here the Thames enters Richmond, the only London borough with land on both sides of the Thames. Just under 13 the 18thC **Richmond Bridge**, is 14 a delightful towpath with several drinking and eating spots, among them the White Cross Hotel. Behind is Richmond, whose focal point is the river. Full of royal, historic and theatrical associations, it was named by Henry VII when he rebuilt Richmond Palace (now destroyed) in 1497. Passing 15 **Twickenham Bridge**, 16 **Richmond Lock** and 17 **Isleworth Eyot**, you will see stretches of 21 **Old Deer Park**, the former garden and park of Richmond Palace. 19 **Kew Observatory**, within the park, was built by Sir William Chambers for George III and was the Meteorological Office until 1981. The river now passes between Syon Park and 23 the **Royal Botanic Gardens**. Started in 1759 with a small area devoted to botanic collections, the gardens today are among the greatest in the world with over 25,000 plant specimens. They also contain 24 **Kew Palace**, the favourite home of Georges II and III. Kew, behind 25 **Kew Bridge**, is a mainly residential area

with a long history due to its easy access by river. The name is derived from a word meaning 'neck of land by a landing place'. Past 27 **Kew Railway Bridge** is Mortlake, where in 1619 Flemish weavers made tapestries. Along the waterfront are The Limes, several 18thC houses with gardens leading to the river. By 28 **Chiswick Bridge**, along 29 **Thames Bank**, is a cluster of attractive houses, among them Leyden House, a 15thC timber-framed building behind an 18thC façade. It is here that the annual Oxford v. Cambridge Boat Race ends.

On the edge of the loop is 30 **Barnes Terrace**, behind whose attractive ironwork façades lies delightful Barnes village. The terrace was and is a fashionable place to live; former residents include Sheridan and Gustav Holst. At the tip of Barnes is 34 **St Paul's School**, an exclusive public school founded in 1509 by the Dean of St Paul's Cathedral. Famous pupils include John Milton, Samuel Pepys, Judge Jeffreys and Edmond Halley, the astronomer. 35 **Hammersmith Bridge** was the first suspension bridge in London. The original, built 1824 by William T. Clarke, was replaced in 1883 by the present construction by Sir Joseph Bazalgette. Beyond the bridge is 36 **Harrods Repository**, a former storage depot for the great shop. 37 **Barn Elms Reservoir** is host to a variety of water-sports, plus fishing and birdwatching. Along Putney Embankment are several rowing clubs — the Oxford v. Cambridge Boat Race starts from here. By 39 **Putney Pier** are some good pubs, among them the Duke's Head and the Star & Garter. 40 **Putney Bridge** originally linked Fulham to the once farming and fishing community at Putney. Completed in 1727, the original arch spans were of such differing sizes that they presented serious difficulties for navigators and were reduced in 1870. The bridge was entirely replaced in 1882.

NORTH BANK

Under 43 **Wandsworth Bridge** and past Battersea Reach is 44 **Chelsea Harbour** with its smart shops, apartments, restaurants and marina. 46 **Chelsea Wharf** has been transformed from old warehouses into modern business units. Beyond Battersea Bridge (see south bank) is fashionable 48 **Cheyne Walk**; still a smart address, grand houses here were occupied by such famous former residents as Isambard Kingdom Brunel, Hilaire Belloc and James Whistler. Chelsea Old Church, the last resting place of Sir Thomas More, lies on its western point. 49 **Albert Bridge** is a three-span bridge built 1871 by R.M. Ordish. The bridge was strengthened in 1971 to increase traffic loads. It is particularly beautiful at night when illuminated. Beyond the bridge is 50 **Chelsea Royal Hospital**, established by Charles II for veteran soldiers. It opened in 1689, admitting 476 army pensioners. The Chelsea Flower Show is held in the grounds annually in May. Beyond Chelsea Bridge (see south bank) and behind the wharves of Pimlico and 55 **Pimlico Gardens** lies genteel residential charm. Past 57 **Vauxhall Bridge**, the first iron bridge to span the Thames, is 59 **Tate Gallery**, housing the national collection of modern and British art. It stands on the site of the Millbank Penitentiary, where criminals awaited boats to carry them downriver to be deported to Australia. Next door is 60 **Vickers Tower**, one of London's earliest glass-walled office skyscrapers (1960-63). Beyond Lambeth Bridge (see south bank) 64 the **Houses of Parliament** by Augustus Pugin and Charles Barry come into view. In 1856 the 'Great Stink' from untreated sewage in the river became so bad that canvases soaked in chloride of lime were hung at the windows to counteract the smell. Nowadays, in summer, you can see MPs on the terraces taking refreshment and entertaining their guests. 65 **Westminster Bridge** opened in 1750. The watermen of the Thames were paid £25,000 in compensation when it was built. The present structure is cast iron and was built in 1854 to a design by Thomas Page. 67 **Victoria Embankment** was created by Joseph Bazalgette in 1868 by reclaiming 37 acres (15.4ha) of mud. This made the river narrower and the water flow faster, so ending the skating era on the once frozen waters. Halfway along the Embankment are 68 **Whitehall Stairs**, once part of Whitehall Palace (destroyed by fire in 1698). Cardinal Wolsey descended these steps to be rowed to Henry

VIII at Greenwich, and in 1688 James II escaped b them from William of Orange. There are severa ships along this stretch; 69 **PS** *Tattershall Castle* once a paddle-steamer, now converted into a restau rant and bar, 73 **RS** *Hispaniola*, once a ferry on the Firth of Clyde in Scotland and now a restaurant, an 74 **TS** *Queen Mary*, a pub and functions venue 71 **Embankment Place** above Charing Cross Statior and the vaults below the station, house retail outlet and restaurants. The imposing gateway on the nort side of Victoria Embankment Gardens is 75 **Yor Watergate**, built in 1626 by Nicholas Stone as th riverside entrance to York House which once ha gardens sweeping down to the Thames. It marks th position of the north bank of the Thames before th construction of Victoria Embankment. The rooftop of 77 the **Savoy Hotel** are clearly discernible fron the river. The famous and wealthy stay here to enjo some of the best views of the Thames. It was fron one of the hotel's balconies that Claude Mone painted 18 canvases of 78 **Waterloo Bridge** Originally built in 1811 by Rennie, the bridge wa opened on the anniversary of the Battle of Waterloc The present bridge was designed by Sir Giles Gilbe Scott and was constructed in 1937-42. Near th Savoy is 76 **Cleopatra's Needle**, a 60ft (18m) hig ancient Egyptian granite obelisk brought to Londor by sea in 1878. When it was erected various article were buried beneath it for posterity — the morning newspapers, a razor, coins, four bibles in differen languages and photographs of '12 of the bes looking Englishwomen of the day'. The bronz sphinxes were added (facing the wrong way!) in 1882. 80 **Thames Sailing Barge Wilfred** at Temp Stairs is now a restaurant. 81 **Somerset Hous** stands on the site of an unfinished Renaissanc palace. Best seen from the river, its long, elegar façade is a magnificent landmark. The river onc lapped against its terraces and through rive entrances, but is now separated from it b Embankment. After a long history of roya inhabitants, it houses offices of the Inland Revenu and the Courtauld Institute Galleries. 82 **HM** *President* was once used by the Royal Naval Reserv

CHELSEA

SOUTH BANK

The once rural village of Wandsworth, named after the tributary, the River Wandle, now presents an industrial, somewhat drab scene. Past residents include Defoe, Thackeray and Voltaire. There is a good pub, 42 the **Ship**, just by Wandsworth Bridge. Several wharves and jetties along this part of the river are testiment to the days of thriving trade — Huguenot refugees settled here, making hats and dying cloth in the 18thC. In the vestry of 45, the riverside **Church of St Mary**, J.M.W. Turner sat and watched the sunsets across the river. 47 **Battersea Bridge** replaced the ferry between Chelsea and Battersea, transforming Chelsea from a village into a thriving small town. The original bridge (1771) was replaced in 1886-90 by the present one, designed by Sir

FULHAM

WANDSWORTH

now houses an educational charity. **83 Blackfriars Bridge** was built in 1760. It cost £230,000 and was mainly paid for by fines which had accumulated from men refusing the post of Sheriff. It was replaced by the present structure in 1860.

As you round the corner, you can see the dome and spire of St Paul's Cathedral and the NatWest Tower rising above the rooftops of the City. You pass under Southwark Bridge (see south bank) and then **London Bridge**, with the towering monoliths of the City behind. Originally a wooden construction built by the Romans, it was replaced with a stone one in the 12thC which carried houses, shops and the heads of traitors on spikes. It has been replaced

many times and in 1971 the granite construction by Rennie (1832) was shipped off to Lake Havasu City, Arizona. The present bridge dates from 1973. 91 **Fishmongers' Hall** is dedicated to the Worshipful Company of Fishmongers, one of the 96 City Livery companies. On the other side of London Bridge is 93 **Monument**, a 202ft (61.5m) high Doric column commemorating the Great Fire of London. Along this stretch and set back from the river is 94 **Watermen's Hall**, founded by the watermen of London, who once operated all water transport. They had the monopoly on passenger carriage until the arrival of hackney coaches, sedan chairs and more bridges, which obviated the need for ferries. The company is still active.

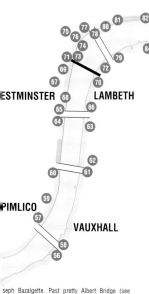

impressive **Lambeth Palace**, the official London residence of the Archbishop of Canterbury since 1197. 63 **St Thomas's Hospital**, named after Thomas à Becket, originally had strict rules; patients were only fed if they went daily to chapel and no person could be admitted for the same disease twice! Florence Nightingale established her nursing school here. On the other side of Westminster Bridge (see north bank) is 66 **County Hall**, a massive edifice designed in 1911 for the Greater London Council (abolished in 1986). Partly converted into luxury flats, there are plans to turn the rest — including 2100ft (640m) river frontage — into a hotel and leisure complex. 70 **Hungerford Railway Bridge** has excellent views from its footbridge and next to it is 72 the **South Bank Centre** with the Royal Festival Hall, RFH2 (Queen Elizabeth Hall), RFH3 (Purcell Room), National Film Theatre and, nestling behind, the Hayward Gallery, complete with colourful neon sculpture. Past Waterloo Bridge (see north bank) is 79 the **National Theatre** with the Museum of the Moving Image beside it. 84 **Gabriel's Wharf** is a lively market, the south bank's answer to Covent Garden. 85 The art deco **'OXO' Tower** contains an unusual mixture of community housing, shops, workshops, cafés and offices.

From 87 **Bankside** are fine views of St Paul's Cathedral and the City. Wren lodged at No.49 while his cathedral and city were being built after the Great Fire of 1666. Dominated by 88 **Bankside Power Station** — soon to become the Tate Gallery of Modern Art — there are riverside walks here and 86 the **Anchor**, an historic pub with strong smuggling connections, built in 1770. Nearby is the reconstructed Shakespeare's Globe, now holding regular performances. 89 the first **Southwark Bridge**, built in 1814, was the largest bridge ever built of cast iron. It was replaced 1912-21 by the present steel structure. Just before London Bridge (see north bank) is 90 the schooner **Kathleen & May**, moored in St Mary Overy Dock. It is the last surviving three-masted, topsail, trading schooner. In the Pool of London is the vast 95 **HMS Belfast**, the last survivor of the Royal Navy's World War II cruisers. Behind it is 96 the **London Bridge City** development, incorporating Hay's Galleria, an elegant shopping and leisure complex.

seph Bazalgette. Past pretty Albert Bridge (see north bank) lies 52 **Battersea Park**, with 51 the striking **London Peace Pagoda**, dedicated to world peace. 53 **Chelsea Bridge** was built in 1858 by Thomas Page. It was entirely replaced in 1934 by another suspension bridge (Rendel, Palmer and Tritton). 54 **Battersea Power Station**, currently disused, is a remarkable landmark that may soon be developed for office and leisure use. Industrial areas now loom on the banks with busy Nine Elms Lane, on which stands 56 **New Covent Garden Market**, moved in 1974 from its central London site. Beyond Vauxhall Bridge (see north bank) is 57 **Vauxhall Cross**, a ten-storey glass office block rising in layers from the bank of the Thames, built to house government offices. 61 **Lambeth Bridge** (1861) was once the only place where it was possible to cross the river with a coach and horses. It was replaced by the present bridge in 1929. Past the bridge you can see 62 the Tudor gatehouse of

NORTH BANK

97 the **Tower of London** looks solid and forbidding; it is easy to imagine the terror of the criminals as they were brought downriver through Traitors' Gate to await their fate. Elizabeth I would have had a particularly distressing arrival seeing the head of her mother, Anne Boleyn, on a spike at the gate. Today it is a lot safer to disembark and explore London's oldest medieval fortress. **98 Tower Bridge** was completed in 1894. Designed by Sir Horace Jones and John Wolfe-Barry, this dramatic Victorian-Gothic stucture opens to allow tall ships to pass. Each section of the double-bascule drawbridge weighs over 1000 tonnes but can be raised in under two minutes. Stretching from Tower Pier to Beckton (off map) is London's Docklands. The area has undergone massive change from a thriving commercial port through closure to regeneration. The London Docklands Development Corporation (LDDC) was set up in 1981 to create a 'new city for the 21stC' with riverside apartments, shops, restaurants and offices. **99** **St Katharine's Dock** was the first of the docks to be rejuvenated. Built on 23 acres (9.5ha), the original docks were closed down in 1968. Five years later an £80 million building scheme was begun which included **100** the **Tower Thistle Hotel** and the **World Trade Centre**. The magnificent warehouses have been restored and now house shops, apartments, offices, restaurants, a yacht club and marina. Visiting cruisers nestle alongside resident yachts and barges. The Dickens Inn is a popular drinking spot. Wapping is a mainly residential area with a good selection of pubs including **104** the **Prospect of Whitby**, dating from the reign of Henry VIII and once known as the Devil's Tavern, such were its associations with thieves and smugglers. Next door is **106** the **Town of Ramsgate** with an equally grisly past, where convicts were chained in cellars at the inn before deportation to Australia. By the pub are **105 Wapping Old Stairs** where Colonel Blood was caught trying to escape with

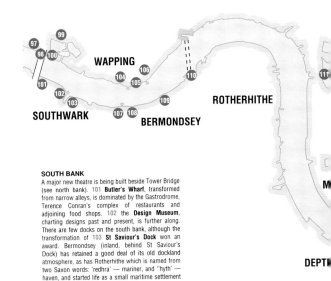

WAPPING

SOUTHWARK

ROTHERHITHE

BERMONDSEY

DEPT[

M

SOUTH BANK

A major new theatre is being built beside Tower Bridge (see north bank). **101** **Butler's Wharf**, transformed from narrow alleys, is dominated by the Gastrodrome, Terence Conran's complex of restaurants and adjoining food shops. **102** the **Design Museum**, charting designs past and present, is further along. There are few docks on the south bank, although the transformation of **103 St Saviour's Dock** won an award. Bermondsey (inland, behind St Saviour's Dock) has retained a good deal of its old dockland atmosphere, as has Rotherhithe which is named from two Saxon words: 'redhra' — mariner, and ''hyth'' — haven, and started life as a small maritime settlement along the river. By **107 Cherry Garden Pier**, where a ship sounds her horn if she needs Tower Bridge opened, and from where J.M.W. Turner painted *The Fighting Témeraire*, is **108** the historic **Angel** pub. It dates from the 15thC with part of the inn built on piles over the river. Trapdoors in the floor were once used by smugglers and 'Hanging' Judge Jeffreys reportedly sat here watching pirates being hanged at Execution Dock opposite (now moved downstream to Blackwall). **109** the **Mayflower** pub, a 17thC inn, was renamed to commemorate the sailing of the Pilgrim Fathers' boat, the *Mayflower*, carrying pilgrims to America in 1620. It is still the only inn licensed to sell stamps to British and foreign sailors. **110 Rotherhithe Tunnel**, built 1904-8

by Sir Maurice Fitzmarice, is still used as a thoroughfare. The top of the tunnel is 48ft (14.5 m) below the high water mark to allow for large ships passing above. Old warehouses and former ship-building yards line the banks as far as **114** Deptford Creek where the Royal Dock was built in 1513 for Henry VI's navy. It was here that Elizabeth I visited Sir Francis Drake's ship the *Golden Hind* and from here Capt Cook's *Discovery* set sail. Deptford is still used by some big cargo ships. Greenwich is rich in nautical history. Here, in dry dock, are the *Cutty Sark*, the only surviving tea-clipper, and Sir Francis Chichester's t[

e Crown Jewels. Shadwell, behind Wapping, was nce densely populated with watermen, lightermen nd sailors. Captain James Cook stayed here in etween his three Pacific explorations. Limehouse, amed after its lime kilns, was originally a ship-uilding centre and was where the first Chinese sailors et up their community. Later, hounded out by British eamen, they moved away and are now only emembered by a few street names (Pekin, Nankin, anton) and restaurants. The Isle of Dogs, so called ecause it was once the royal kennel, was uninhabited ntil 111 **West India Docks** were built in 1800. At ne northernmost strip of these waters is 112 **Canary Wharf**, an 80-acre (35ha) development with shops, ffices, apartments, restaurants, gardens and water-ont promenades. It is also home to the tallest build-ng in the United Kingdom, One Canada Square, which tands 50 storeys high, at 800ft (244m), and ominates the skyline for miles around. The West ndia Docks are also the site of 113 **Billingsgate Fish Market**, which was originally based near London Bridge. Millwall provides good opportunities to see smart, colourful riverside apartments next to old hous-ing. Wherever you go, the high tracks of the Docklands Light Railway rise unexpectedly behind houses and between streets. At the tip of the Isle of Dogs, at 115 **Island Gardens**, is 116 the **Greenwich Foot Tunnel**, built 1902 for pedestrians only. From the Island Gardens are excellent views of Wren's Royal Naval College set off by Greenwich Park. From Greenwich you can take a river trip to the Thames Barrier (see south bank) via the vast docks (off map) Royal Victoria, Royal Albert and King George V, the last to be built in 1921. With immense resources for cargo and passengers, the docks enjoyed prime importance until closure in the early 1970s. They were later transformed into an airstrip (London City Airport) and a centre for watersports. The river here is peppered with wharves and jetties, a reminder of the days of merchants and constant cargo deliveries.

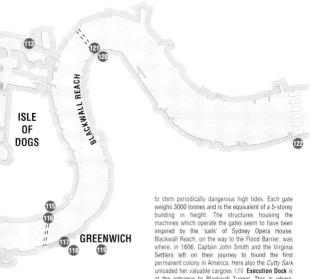

ISLE OF DOGS

BLACKWALL REACH

GREENWICH

etch *Gipsy Moth IV*. Right by Greenwich Pier is Sir hristopher Wren's beautiful baroque building, 117 he **Royal Naval College**, which will be auctioned during 996. Behind it are 118 the **National Maritime Museum** and, on its hilltop setting within Greenwich ark, 119 the **Old Royal Observatory**, home of the reenwich Meridian. From here it is a short boat ride o 122 the Thames Flood Barrier, best seen from the ver. Rounding the bend, the steel fins rise up from ne water. Completed in 1982, it is the world's largest novable floor barrier and is designed to swing up om the river bed and create a stainless steel barrage to stem periodically dangerous high tides. Each gate weighs 3000 tonnes and is the equivalent of a 5-storey building in height. The structures housing the machines which operate the gates seem to have been inspired by the 'sails' of Sydney Opera House. Blackwall Reach, on the way to the Flood Barrier, was where, in 1606, Captain John Smith and the Virginia Settlers left on their journey to found the first permanent colony in America. Here also the *Cutty Sark* unloaded her valuable cargoes. 120 **Execution Dock** is at the entrance to Blackwall Tunnel. This is where, until the late 19thC, the bodies of convicted pirates were hung in iron cages until three tides had washed over them. A warning to all passing sailors! 121 the **Blackwall Tunnel** was built in 1897 by Sir Alexander Binnie. There are now two tunnels; the second opened in 1967. One is for northbound traffic, the other for southbound traffic. Queen Elizabeth II Bridge (off map) was opened in 1991 to ease the traffic through Dartford Tunnel; it is used by southbound vehicles. It is the largest bridge of its type in Europe, with twin towers rising nearly 450ft (130m) above the Thames and a total length of nearly two miles.

crowns. This pedestrian trail takes you across London from Leicester Square (4 **E3**) to Tower Hill (5 **G3**).

Streets of London
16 The Grove N3. 0181-346 9255. Guided walking tours with regular programme of scheduled tours, regardless of weather. Themes include *Dickens' London* and *History of London*. Also private tours for clubs, societies, schools etc.

River trips

The Thames is a fascinatingly beautiful river, never more so than as it passes through London. One of the best ways of appreciating the city is to take a boat trip. The buildings which line the banks range from decrepit warehouses to palaces, conjuring up a whole host of historic, artistic and literary associations. Daily services run from the piers listed below, but travellers may board at any of the other piers en route. It is important to note that times vary according to the tides and the weather and it's always advisable to telephone for details here. The London Tourist Board provides an excellent recorded River Trips Information Service on (0839) 123432.
NB: always check times of return boats at the pier on arrival.

Downriver services

Charing Cross Pier 4 **F4**
Victoria Embankment WC2. 0171-839 3572. Trips to the Tower *(20-min journey)* and Greenwich *(50-min journey)* every 30 mins between 10.30-16.00 Apr-Oct; every 45 mins between 10.30-15.00 Nov-Mar. 2-hr luncheon cruise 12.45 Sun only; all year.

Greenwich Pier
Return services to Charing Cross Pier *(45-min journey)*, Tower Pier *(30-min journey)* and Westminster Pier *(45-min journey)*. Phone the individual piers for details.

Tower Pier 5 **F4**
0171-488 0344. Trips to Greenwich *(30-min journey)* every 20 mins 11.00-17.00 in summer *(departures every 40 mins from 11.00 in winter)*. Ferry to HMS Belfast *(5 mins)* every 15 mins in summer only.

Westminster Pier 4 **F5**
Victoria Embankment SW1. 0171-930 4097. Trips to the Tower *(30-min journey)*

every 20 mins 10.30-16.00 and to Greenwich *(40-min journey)* every half hour 10.30-16.00; all year. Special trips to the Thames Flood Barrier *(1¼ hrs each way)* 10.00, 11.15, 12.40, 13.45 & 15.15 Apr-Oct. Disco cruises *19.00 Fri & 20.00 Sat; all year.*

Upriver services

Run from Westminster Pier only, all services call at Putney Embankment.

Westminster Pier 4 **F5**
Victoria Embankment SW1. Westminster Passenger Services operate boat trips during *summer only* to Putney *(30-min journey)*, Kew *(1½-hr journey)*, Richmond *(2-hr journey)* and Hampton Court *(3-4-hr journey)*. Phone 0171-930 2062 for departure times.
There are local services to Hampton Court from Richmond and Kingston *(Easter-Sep)*. Phone 0181-546 2434 for details.

Upper Thames

Salter Bros
Follybridge, Oxford. (01865) 243421. Salter's steamers run from Oxford-Abingdon, Reading-Henley, Maidenhead-Windsor and Windsor-Staines; *May-Sep Mon-Sun*. Private hire available. *Phone for details.*

Canal trips

Canal Water Bus 1 **D1**
London Waterbus Co, Camden Lock Pl NW1. 0171-482 2550. Boat leaves from Little Venice stopping at the zoo and continuing to Camden Lock. *Apr-Sep 10.00-17.00 Mon-Sun; Oct 10.30-15.45 Mon-Sun; Nov-Mar 10.30-15.45 Sat & Sun.* Also run Limehouse trips which explore the architecture and industrial history of London's quiet canalways; *May-Oct 09.30-18.00 some Sats.*

Jason's Trip 3 **C1**
Opposite 60 Blomfield Rd W9. 0171-286 3428. The traditional narrowboat *Jason* leaves Little Venice for 1½-hr return trip, with commentary, through Regent's Park and zoo to Camden Lock. Disembark to look round the craft shops if you like, or the market at weekends. Refreshments. Depart *Apr, May & Sep 10.30, 12.30 & 14.30; Jun-Aug 10.30, 12.30, 14.30 & 16.30.* Private parties of all kinds can be booked. *Phone for details.*

Jenny Wren Cruises   **1 D1**
250 Camden High St NW1. 0171-485 4433. 1½-hr round trips along Regent's Canal passing the zoo and Little Venice. Up to four tours a day Feb-Nov Mon-Sun. Also longer and evening trips. Also runs *My Fair Lady*, a cruising restaurant, for dinner cruise evenings *20.00-23.00 Tue-Sat, & Sun lunch 13.00-15.30.*

Charter boats

Boat Enquiries
43 Botley Rd, Oxford. (01865) 727288. Will arrange cruiser and narrowboat hire in England.

Catamaran Cruisers   **4 F4**
Charing Cross Pier, Victoria Embankment WC2. 0171-987 1185. Can be hired for private parties or business functions. Disco, dinner dance and cabaret cruises. *Phone for details.*

Inland Waterways Association   **1 B2**
114 Regent's Park Rd NW1. 0171-586 2556. Publish the *Inland Waterways Guide* with general details of holidays and hire boats.

Thames Luxury Charters
3 The Mews, 6 Putney Common SW15. 0181-780 1562. *Daytime* and *evening* cruises. Fully licensed launches with dancing space, including *The Elizabethan*. Embark at various piers *by arrangement*.

Woods River Services
PO Box 177 SE3. 0171-481 2711. Modern all-weather passenger launches. *Silver Barracuda* – 230-passenger. *Silver Bonito* – 199-passenger, for guided tours. *Silver Dolphin* – 90-passenger. Fully-fitted dancefloor, film projector and licensed bar. Private charter only. Luncheon cruise once a *month*.

Day trips from London

Every era, from prehistoric times, has altered, and left its mark on, the English landscape. Ancient heath and moorland contrast with stately gardens and manor houses. Centuries mingle in the architecture along village streets. The ruins of a Norman or Tudor castle are not far from a Victorian cathedral or 14thC parish church. The 19thC pleasure-dome in Brighton is a short drive away from thatched cottages in Sussex and hop fields in Kent. The English countryside is a constantly changing, often magical land-scape – well worth exploring. All the places listed below are easily accessible on a day trip from London.
For information about train, coach and bus services out of London see 'Tourist information' and 'Transport in London'.

Ashdown Forest, E. Sussex
Excellent walking. High sandy country of heather and bracken with wind-blown pine trees, silver birch and beech in the valleys. 'Winnie-the-Pooh' country. Start from Crowborough, Hartfield, Forest Row or Three Bridges. London 30 miles (A22).

Bath, Avon
A delightful Georgian town rich in architectural detail such as the dramatic sweeping curve of Ionic columns which forms the Royal Crescent. Lots of museums including the Roman Baths and Pump Room. Natural hot springs bubbling out of the ground and the bathing complex, built when it was the Roman town of Aquae Sulis, are still very visible. Good shopping and lots of charming cafés and restaurants. Train 1½ hrs. London 107 miles (M4).

Battle, E. Sussex
Site of the famous battle of 1066. An abbey, which William the Conqueror had vowed to build should he win the battle, is now in ruins but the Gateway still stands on Battle Hill. Opposite this is the 12thC church of St Mary. London 56 miles (A21).

Brighton, E. Sussex
Known as 'Little London by the Sea', this once poor fishing village has been a lively, bustling seaside resort ever since the Prince Regent set up his court in the fabulous Oriental-domed Pavilion. Fashionable shops, Regency terraces, good pubs and restaurants, cockle stalls, fairs and sport of all kinds. Five miles of beach and a magical Victorian pier. Train 1 hr. London 48 miles (A23).

Cambridge, Cambs
A great university city of spires, mellow colleges and riverside meadows, bordering the Cam. The famous 'Backs' and the lovely bridges are best seen by hiring a punt. The 20 or so colleges date from the 13thC onwards including Trinity by Wren, King's by James Gibbs and the modern Queen's by Basil Spence. The city contains the superb Fitzwilliam Museum, the notable Botanic Garden and some fine churches. Train 1½ hrs. London 55 miles (M11).

Canterbury, Kent
Pleasant, old, walled city on the river Stour, dominated by the magnificent

Gothic cathedral, containing the shrine of Thomas à Becket (murdered 1170) and the tomb of the Black Prince. Good local museum in West Gate. Train 1½ hrs. London 56 miles (M2).

Chichester, W. Sussex
An old Roman city walled by the Saxons and graced by its beautiful 12thC cathedral. Now mostly Georgian in character. Fine 16thC Butter Cross, a medieval Guildhall and modern Festival Theatre, built 1962. Excellent harbour for sailing. Train 1½hrs. London 63 miles (A3, A286).

The Chilterns
A 40-mile-long ridge of chalk hills with fine views. Open downs, wheat fields, magnificent beech woods and charming villages. Start from Henley, Great Missenden, Stokenchurch, Wendover or Whipsnade. London 20-30 miles (M1 or M40).

Colchester, Essex
England's first Roman city, with many visible remains: the city wall, a Mithraic temple, and arches, windows and doorways built from Roman bricks. Norman relics include Colchester Castle (now housing a museum) and the ruins of the church of St Botolph. There is a small harbour and an oyster fishery. The famous 'Colchester Oyster Feast' takes place every year, about 20 Oct. Train 1 hr. London 52 miles (A12).

Cotswolds
A beautiful area west of London with buildings constructed from Cotswold stone and towns and villages full of Tudor and Jacobean architecture. Stow-on-the-Wold has a fine market place and Bourton-on-the-Water holds many delights. There's also the Wildlife Park at Burford, Blenheim Palace and Sudeley Castle. Gloucester and Cheltenham are two cities on the edge of the Cotswolds which are worth a visit. London 50-100 miles (M4).

Devil's Punchbowl, Surrey
A vast and impressive bowl scooped out of the high open hills. Good views. Start from Haslemere or Hindhead. Train 1 hr. London 30 miles (A3).

Henley-on-Thames, Oxon
Situated on a very pretty part of the Thames and most famous for the Regatta, held in early Jul. The arched bridge was built in 1786. In St Mary's churchyard are 16thC almshouses and a rare unspoilt 15thC timber-framed building – the Chantry House. The Regatta is held on the straight mile of the river downstream from the bridge. Train 1 hr. London 36 miles (A4).

The North Downs
An outcrop of high chalk hills with magnificent views over the Weald of Kent. The Pilgrim's Way runs along the south face of the hills. Farming country with open beech and oak woods, pleasant villages and pubs. Start from Dorking, Box Hill, Woldingham or Otford. London 15-20 miles (A24, A23 or A21).

Oxford, Oxon
A university city of spires and fine college buildings on the Thames and the Cherwell and dating from the 13thC. The Sheldonian Theatre by Wren, the Radcliffe Camera by Gibbs and the 15thC Bodleian Library are particularly notable. Visit also the famous old Botanic Garden and the Ashmolean Museum. Train 1½ hrs. London 65 miles (A40).

Portsmouth
Old, historic battleships and new, modern warships lie side by side at Portsmouth's Naval Base, which has been the home of the Royal Navy since Henry VII first founded the Royal Dockyard. The Royal Naval Museum is also here. Train 1½hrs. London 77 miles (A3).

Salisbury & Stonehenge, Wiltshire
Salisbury is famous for its 13thC cathedral, apparently built where a random arrow was fired. Its spire is the highest in England. The town is rich in medieval architecture. Cathedral Close boasts the most interesting buildings such as the Bishop's Palace and the King's House. The market square is dominated by 600-year-old Poultry Cross. Stonehenge is 10 miles away and the best British example of groups of ancient stone circles known as Druid's Circles. Estimated that it took 30 million years to come about, but what it was originally erected for is still a mystery. Ringed by perimeter fence but still good views. London 90 miles (A30, A303). Charge.

The South Downs
Grassy slopes and ridges which follow the Sussex coast ending in high chalk cliffs by the sea. The steep escarpments face the North Downs across the Weald. The South Downs Way follows 80 miles of ancient paths where Stone Age man grazed sheep 5000 years ago. The section from Bramber to Washington (6½ miles) is particularly pleasant. London 45 miles (A24).

Southend-on-Sea, Essex
Traditionally the Cockney's weekend seaside resort. Fun-fairs and every sort of entertainment and attraction. Visit Westcliff-on-Sea nearby and Shoeburyness for cockle-beds, boats and paddling. Train 1 hr. London 40 miles (A127).

Stratford-upon-Avon, Warks
The birthplace of William Shakespeare (1564-1616). The town is still Elizabethan in atmosphere with overhanging gables and timbered inns. Visit the playwright's birthplace in Henley Street, his house at New Place, Anne Hathaway's cottage and the museum and picture gallery. The Shakespeare Memorial Theatre in Waterside is thriving and progressive. Train 2½ hrs. London 90 miles (A40, A34).

Thames Estuary
Unusual and sometimes tough walking along the tidal sea wall. Not everyone's cup of tea; it can be cold, windy or foggy. Take binoculars and wrap up well. Thousands of sea birds, a constant traffic of ships and the lonely marshes. Romantic and isolated but you have to be able to absorb the odd oil refinery or factory and accept that commerce is part of it all. Start from Cliffe, Higham or Gravesend in Kent, Tilbury or Mucking in Essex. London 20-25 miles (A2 or A13).

Winchester, Hants
The ancient Saxon capital of England set among lovely rolling chalk downland. The massive, square-towered Norman cathedral, with its superb vaulted Gothic nave, contains the graves of King Canute, Izaac Walton and Jane Austen. The 'round table of King Arthur' is in the remains of the Norman castle. Train 1½ hrs. London 65 miles (A30).

Great houses, castles and gardens near London

England's country houses and their gardens have been loved and written about for nearly 400 years; even the socialist reformer H.G. Wells said of them: 'It is the country house that has opened the way to human equality.' The country house represents a blending of many strands in English history: rural life, great architecture, landscaping, collecting, pride and patronage.
Not that they, any more than other buildings, are unaffected by social and economic change; less than half of the 5000 stately homes reckoned to have been standing in 1920 have survived to the present day. Fortunately, however, not only have many of the most splendid examples been preserved but, thanks to organisations such as the National Trust and English Heritage, a number of these
are open to the public. Those listed here are some of the great country houses within a 70-mile radius of London, dating from the 11th to the 19thC. Each property has been selected as being characteristic of its period; many were designed by such famous architects as Inigo Jones, Christopher Wren and Robert Adam. The gardens and parks were laid out by various inspired landscape gardeners including Sir John Vanbrugh, William Kent, Capability Brown and Humphry Repton. Almost without exception they contain great richness of interior decoration and ornament, and often famous collections or works of art.

Arundel Castle
Arundel, W. Sussex. (01903) 882173. An imposing feudal stronghold set among the beech woods of the South Downs, overlooking the tidal river Arun. First part built in 1070, it has been the seat of the Dukes of Norfolk and Earls of Arundel for the last 700 years. Largely restored in 1890 by the 15th Duke. Paintings by Van Dyck, Holbein and Gainsborough; important collection of portraits of the Howard family. London 58 miles (A29). *OPEN Apr-Oct 12.00-17.00 Mon-Fri & Sun (CLOSED Sat). Last admission 1 hr before closing. Charge.*

Audley End
Saffron Walden, Essex. (01799) 522842. A great Jacobean mansion standing mellow and serene in its park near the road to Cambridge. Imposing as it now is, Audley End was once three times its present size. Built 1605-14, it served for a while as a royal country palace. In 1721 Vanbrugh demolished two thirds of the building. Fine state rooms – some decorated by Robert Adam, others 19thC neo-Jacobean. London 40 miles (A11). House *OPEN Easter-Sep 12.00-17.00 Wed-Sun & B.hol Mon.* Grounds *OPEN Easter-Sep 10.00-17.00 Wed-Sun & B.hol Mon. Charge.*

Blenheim Palace
Woodstock, Oxon. (01993) 811325. A great classical-style ducal palace built 1705-22 by Sir John Vanbrugh. The estate was given by Queen Anne to John Churchill, Duke of Marlborough for his victory over Louis XIV at Blenheim in 1704. Winston Churchill was born here. Fine paintings, tapestries and furniture. The park was landscaped first by Henry Wise and later by Capability Brown in 1760, who dammed the small stream to create two great lakes, keeping

DAY TRIPS FROM LONDON

Warwick
*Warwick
Castle* ▲

Northampton

M1

Worcester ■

Stratford-
upon-Avon ■

Milton
Keynes ■

Banbury ■

M50

*Sudeley
Castle* ▲

Buckingham ■

A41

*Woburn
Abbey* ▲

Cheltenham

C
O
T
S
W
O
L
D
S

*Blenheim
Palace* ▲

Gloucester ■

*Cotswold
Wildlife
Park* ▲

Oxford ■

C
H
I
L
T
E
R
N

H
I
L
L
S

A40

Severn

M5

M4 ■ Swindon

M40

Henley ■

Bristol ■

A4

Reading ■

*Windso[r]
Castle* ▲

Bath ■

Windsor

Basingstoke ■

Guildford ■

Stonehenge ▲

A303

A30

M3

A30

A3

Winchester ■

Salisbury ■

Haslemere ■

*Petworth
House* ▲

NEW
FOREST

Southampton ■

M27

*Goodwood
House* ▲

Chichester ■

*Arunde[l]
Castle* ▲

A31

Poole ■

Bournemouth

Portsmouth ■

Dorchester ■
Weymouth

ISLE OF WIGHT

© Nicholson

Vanbrugh's original bridge. London 60 miles (A34). Palace *OPEN mid Mar-Oct 10.30-17.30 Mon-Sun. Charge.* Park *OPEN 09.00-17.00 Mon-Sun all year.*

Bodiam Castle
Robertsbridge, E. Sussex. (01580) 830436. A romantic and lovely medieval castle completely surrounded by a wide moat. A mighty fortress built 1385 as a defence for the realm. London 45 miles (A21). *OPEN Apr-Oct 10.00-17.30 Mon-Sun; Nov-Mar 10.00-½ hr before sunset Tue-Sun. Charge.*

Boston Manor House
Boston Manor Rd, Brentford, Middx. 0181-570 7728 ex5798. Jacobean mansion with park and gardens. London 8 miles. House *OPEN May-Sep 14.00-16.30 Sun only. Free.* Gardens *OPEN dawn-dusk Mon-Sun. Free.*

Buscot Park
Faringdon, Oxon. (01367) 240786. A charming late 18thC house in the Adam style. Notable for its splendid painted panels by the pre-Raphaelite painter Burne-Jones in the 'Sleeping Beauty' room. Also paintings by Reynolds, Murillo and Rembrandt. Pleasant park and lake. London 70 miles (A417). *OPEN Apr-Sep 14.00-18.00 Wed-Fri, 2nd & 4th weekends. Charge.*

Clandon Park
West Clandon, Surrey. (01483) 222482. Superb Palladian house built c1733 by the Venetian architect Leoni. Magnificent marble halls. Original wallpapers uncovered in restoration. Furniture, porcelain and needlework collections. London 25 miles (A247. Close to M25). *OPEN Apr-end Oct 13.30-17.30 Sun-Wed. CLOSED Thur & Fri. Charge.*

Claydon House
Middle Claydon, nr Buckingham. (01296) 730349. Built in 1752-68 as an ambitious effort by the 2nd Earl Verney to outdo the splendours of the Grenvilles' rival seat at Stowe. Never completed, this remaining wing contains marvellous rococo state rooms decorated by the inspired carvings of a relatively unknown craftsman called Lightfoot. The Chinese Room is notable. Family museum which includes Florence Nightingale memorabilia. Tea rooms. London 45 miles (off A413 & A41). *OPEN Apr-Oct 13.00-17.00 Mon-Wed & Sat-Sun. Charge.*

Cliveden
Nr Maidenhead, Bucks. (01628) 605069. Superbly sited in wooded grounds overlooking the Thames. An imposing and famous country house built for the Duke of Sutherland in 1850 by Sir Charles Barry, in Italian palazzo style, replacing the two previous buildings destroyed by fire. Formal gardens with fine sculpture from the Villa Borghese and temples by Giacomo Leoni. *The house is now a hotel.* London 25 miles (M4). House *(3 rooms) OPEN Apr-Oct 15.00-18.00 Thur & Sun.* Gardens *OPEN Mar-Dec 11.00-18.00 (or sunset) Mon-Sun. Charge.*

Goodwood House
Nr Chichester, W. Sussex. (01243) 774107. An 18thC house planned by James Wyatt to have eight sides, of which only three were completed. Stables by Sir William Chambers. A fine example of building in Sussex flint. Excellent paintings; some of Canaletto's London views and portraits by Van Dyck, Romney, Kneller and Reynolds. Also a particularly interesting collection of early Stubbs. Magnificent Sèvres porcelain, considered to be as fine as any in France; Gobelin tapestries; Louis XV and XVI furniture. Afternoon teas. London 60 miles (off A285 & A286). *OPEN May-Oct 14.00-17.00 Sun & Mon (& Easter Sun & Mon). Also Tue-Thur in Aug. Charge.*

Nearby at Hat Hill Copse is **Sculpture at Goodwood**, a sculpture park with evolving displays of contemporary British work. *OPEN by appt Apr-mid Nov 10.30 & 14.30 Thur-Sat. Charge. Phone* (01243) 531852.

Hall Place
Bexley, Kent. (01322) 526574. Part Tudor, part Jacobean mansion, 1540, in a park with rose garden, conservatories and fine water garden. Mansion *OPEN Apr-Oct 10.00-17.00 Mon-Sat, 14.00-18.00 Sun; Nov-Mar 10.00-18.00 Mon-Sat only. Free.* Park *OPEN every day during daylight. Free.*

Ham House
Petersham, Surrey. 0181-940 1950. Superb 17thC country house built on an 'H' plan. Lavish Restoration interior. Important collection of Stuart furniture. *OPEN 13.00-17.00 Mon-Wed, 13.00-17.30 Sat, 11.30-17.30 Sun Apr-Oct; 13.00-16.00 Sat & Sun Nov-mid Dec.* Garden *open all year. Charge.*

Hampton Court Palace
Hampton Court, East Molesey, Surrey. 0181-781 9500. Royal riverside palace built 1514 for Cardinal Wolsey with later additions by Henry VIII and Wren. Sumptuous state rooms painted by Vanbrugh, Verrio and Thornhill. Famous picture gallery of Italian masterpieces. Orangery, mellow courtyards, the 'great vine' and the maze. The formal gardens are probably among the greatest in the

world. A Tudor character is preserved in some of the plants. *OPEN Apr-Sep 09.30-18.00 Mon-Sun; Oct-Mar 10.15-18.00 Mon, 09.30-16.30 Tue-Sun. Charge.*

Hatfield House
Hatfield, Herts. (01707) 262823. A mellow and completely preserved Jacobean mansion with magnificent interior built in 1607-11 by Robert Cecil, 1st Earl of Salisbury and still the home of the Cecil family. The Tudor Old Royal Palace nearby was the home of Queen Elizabeth I. Collection of 16th, 17th and 18thC portraits, manuscripts and relics. London 20 miles (A1). For Elizabethan banquets phone (01707) 262055, *all year.* House *OPEN end Mar-mid Oct 12.00-16.00 Tue-Sat, 13.30-17.00 Sun, 11.00-17.00 B.hols. Charge.*

Hever Castle
Nr Edenbridge, Kent. (01732) 865224. 13th and 15thC moated castle once the home of Anne Boleyn who was courted here by Henry VIII. Excellent furnished rooms of the period and many fine portraits. A delightful garden and lake, landscaped by the first Viscount Astor in 1905 and containing a walled Italianate garden with statues, topiary and fountains. London 25 miles (A21). *OPEN mid Mar-early Nov 12.00-18.00 Mon-Sun* (grounds and gardens *from 11.00*). *Charge.*

Hughenden Manor
High Wycombe, Bucks. (01494) 528051. Benjamin Disraeli's country seat from 1847 until his death in 1881, altered from its original Georgian to typical mid-Victorian. Museum of Disraeli relics. Terraced garden. London 30 miles (A40). *OPEN Apr-Oct 14.00-18.00 Wed-Sun & B.hols; Mar 14.00-18.00 Sat & Sun. Charge.*

Knebworth House
Knebworth, Herts. (01438) 812661. A successful and imaginative re-creation from the original Tudor built by the 1st Lord Lytton, the Victorian novelist, in 1844. Pleasant garden with adventure playground for children. Barns Restaurant (01438) 813825. London 30 miles (A1). *OPEN Apr & Jun-Aug, Tue-Sun; May & Sep Sat & Sun;* park *OPEN 11.00-17.30,* house and garden *OPEN 12.00-17.00. CLOSED Oct-Mar. Parties by arrangement. Charge.*

Knole
Sevenoaks, Kent. (01732) 450608. A great Jacobean country house with a splendid park. The family home of the Sackvilles since 1566. The house and its interior survive intact. It is a treasure house

of robust gilded decoration and ornament, fine furniture, tapestries and paintings of 16th-18thC. Many ancient trees in the large park with a fine herd of deer (not to be fed). London 25 miles (A21). *OPEN Apr-Oct 11.00-17.00 Wed, Fri, Sat, Sun & B.hols; 14.00-17.00 Thur* (guided tours *10.00-13.00 Thur only). Charge.* Gardens *OPEN 1st Wed of month May-Sep. Charge.*

Leeds Castle
Maidstone, Kent. (01622) 765400. A beautiful castle which was traditionally a gift from the Kings of England to their Queens. The moat is in fact a lake fed by the River Len. 200 hectares of parkland include a cottage garden, the Wood Garden, greenhouses, aviaries, the Duckery and the Vineyard. Inside is a wine cellar dating to the 12thC, the Queen's Gallery, Banqueting Hall, Chapel and Seminar Room. Shop, restaurant, golf course. London 40 miles (M20). *OPEN Mar-Oct 10.00-17.00 Mon-Sun; Nov-Feb 10.00-15.00 Mon-Sun. Charge.*

Leonardslee Gardens
Lower Beeding, Horsham, W. Sussex. (01403) 891212. Overlooking the South Downs and containing ancient 'hammer ponds' from the time when the Weald was a great iron-producing area. Famous for magnolias, azaleas, rhododendrons and camellias. Lovely views and woodland walks. Wallabies and deer. No dogs allowed. Plants for sale. Restaurant. London 35 miles (M23). *OPEN Apr-Oct 10.00-18.00 Mon-Sun. Charge.*

Luton Hoo
Luton, Beds. (01582) 22955. Imposing front of original house designed by Robert Adam 1767. Altered in 1903 and interior decorated in French 18thC style. Park designed by Capability Brown. Notable for the Wernher Collection, several fine gardens, and important private collection of paintings, tapestries, English porcelain, Fabergé jewels and an unusual collection of mementoes and portraits of the Russian imperial family. London 30 miles (M1, Exit 10). *OPEN Apr-Oct 13.30-17.00 Fri-Sun & B.hols. Charge.*

Marble Hill House
Richmond Rd, Twickenham, Middx. 0181-892 5115. Perfect Palladian villa by the Thames. Built 1724-9 for Henrietta Howard, mistress of George II, with interior and furnishings in period. London 11 miles. *OPEN Apr-Oct 10.00-18.00 Mon-Sun; Nov-Mar 10.00-16.00 Mon-Sun. Free.*

Nymans Garden
Handcross, W. Sussex. (01444) 400321. One of the great gardens of the Sussex

Weald, originally designed by Colonel Messel. Consists of a heather garden, a sunken garden, a walled garden with herbaceous borders and a rose garden. The rhododendrons are features of great beauty and around the lawns are plants from foreign countries, many of which are rarely seen in England. London 40 miles (M23). *OPEN Mar-Oct 11.00-19.00 (or sunset) Wed-Sun & B.hols. Charge.*

Osterley Park House
Thornbury Rd, Osterley, Middx. 0181-560 3918. Remodelled by Robert Adam 1761-78 on an already fine Elizabethan building built round a courtyard. The magnificent interiors with furniture, mirrors, carpets and tapestry all show the elegance and richness of Adam's genius. London 11 miles. *OPEN Apr-Oct 13.00-17.00 Wed-Sat, 11.00-17.00 Sun & B.hols. Charge.* Park *OPEN all year 09.00-dusk. Free.*

Parham
Pulborough, W. Sussex. (01903) 742021. Fine Elizabethan house in a great deer park facing the South Downs, with a superb Great Hall and Long Gallery, and a good collection of portraits. Parham Church is in the grounds. London 50 miles (A24). *OPEN Apr-end Oct 14.00-18.00 Sun, Wed, Thur & B.hols; OPEN from 12.00 Jul & Aug. Charge.* Gardens *OPEN 13.00-18.00. Charge.*

Penshurst Place
Penshurst, Tonbridge, Kent. (01892) 870307. A serene medieval house set amidst flat lawns. Built 1340 and enlarged during Elizabeth I's reign. Magnificent Great Hall with carved timber roof, fine portraits of the Sidney family, early Georgian and Chippendale furniture, and a delightful formal walled garden with ponds and ancient apple trees. London 30 miles (off A21). *OPEN Apr-Oct 12.00-17.30 (last admission 17.00) Mon-Sun (grounds 11.00-18.00); OPEN Sat & Sun in Mar & Oct. Guided tours by arrangement; mornings only. Charge.*

Petworth House
Petworth, W. Sussex. (01798) 342207. An impressive 320ft-long (97.6m) house, rebuilt late 17thC and containing a range of magnificent state rooms. Famous for its splendid 'Carved Room' by the greatest carver in wood, Grinling Gibbons, and a most important collection of paintings including Van Dycks, Reynolds, many Dutch pictures and some particularly superb Turners. Fine deer park. London 50 miles (A283). *OPEN Apr-Oct 13.00-17.30 Tue-Thur, Sat, Sun & B.hols. CLOSED Tue after B.hols. Extra rooms shown Tue, Wed & Thur (except Tue following B.hols). Charge.*

Rousham
Steeple Aston, Oxon. (01869) 347110. One of the best remaining examples of the work of William Kent, carried out 1738-40. Original interior decoration, painted ceilings and furniture within the Jacobean house. Kent's delightful classic garden beside the Cherwell. 17th-century walled garden with herbaceous borders, glades and cascades, remains unaltered. London 65 miles (A423). *OPEN Apr-Sep 14.00-16.30 Wed, Sun & B.hols. Guided tours.* Garden *OPEN all year 10.00-16.30 (last admission). Charge.*

Royal Pavilion, Brighton
Old Steine, Brighton, E. Sussex. (01273) 603005. A fantastic Oriental seaside 'villa', complete with onion domes, and minarets, built for the Prince Regent (later George IV) by John Nash in 1815-22. The lavish Chinese-style state rooms are breathtaking, the original furniture has been returned from Buckingham Palace and the exemplary restorations, after years of neglect, were completed in 1991. London 45 miles (A23). *OPEN Jun-Sep 10.00-18.00 Mon-Sun; Oct-May 10.00-17.00 Mon-Sun. Charge.*

Sheffield Park Garden
Nr Uckfield, E. Sussex. (01825) 790655. Magnificent 120-acre garden laid out by Capability Brown 1775. London 43 miles (A22). *OPEN Mar 11.00-16.00 Sat & Sun, Apr-early Nov 11.00-18.00 Tue-Sun & B.Hols; late Nov-late Dec 11.00-16.00 Wed-Sun. CLOSED Mon & Tue following B.hol Mon. Last admission 1 hr before closing. Charge.*

Sissinghurst Castle
Sissinghurst, Kent. (01580) 712850. The soft red-brick remains of the walls and buildings of a once extensive Tudor manor, enchantingly transformed by the late Victoria Sackville-West and Sir Harold Nicolson into numerous enclosed walled gardens. Each is different in its character and outstandingly beautiful in its richness of flowers and shrubs. Time ticket system for gardens. No dogs. London 40 miles (A21). *OPEN Apr-Oct 13.00-18.30 Tue-Fri, 10.00-17.30 Sat, Sun & Good Friday. CLOSED Mon (inc B.hols). Charge.*

Stowe School
Stowe, nr Buckingham, Bucks. (01280) 822850. Chiefly famous for its succession of notable landscape gardeners and garden architects: Bridgeman, Vanbrugh, James Gibbs, William Kent and Capability

Brown. They produced the fine gardens, park, lake and Palladian bridges, temples and garden pavilions. London 55 miles (A413). *Phone for details of opening times. Charge.*

Strawberry Hill

Waldegrave Rd, Twickenham, Middx. 0181-744 1932. One of the earliest examples of the Gothic Revival, this romantic rococo building was converted from 'a little plaything house' (1750-76) by Horace Walpole. It now stands in the grounds of a college. *Phone for details.*

Syon House

Park Rd, Brentford, Middx. 0181-560 0881. The exterior is the original convent building of the 15thC, but the interior 1762-9 is by Robert Adam. The imaginative elegance and variety in each room is unsurpassed. Garden by Capability Brown. Additional attractions include the London Butterfly House, embroidery centre, children's adventure playground and an excellent garden centre. House *OPEN Apr-Oct 11.00-17.00 Wed-Sun & B.hol Mon. Charge.* Gardens *OPEN Apr-Oct 10.00-18.00 Mon-Sun; Nov-Mar 10.00-17.00 Mon-Sun.* Butterfly House *OPEN Mar-Nov 10.00-17.00 Mon-Sun; Dec-Feb 10.00-15.30. Charge.* Garden centre *OPEN all year 09.30-17.30 Mon-Sun.*

Uppark House

Petersfield, (01730) 825317. Beautifully simple 17thC house on the ridge of the South Downs, by William Talman 1690. Home of Emma Hamilton and H.G. Wells' mother. Faultless 18thC interiors with fine plasterwork and ceilings. London 50 miles (A3). No dogs. *Phone for opening times. CLOSED Oct-Mar. Charge.*

The Vyne

Sherborne St John, Basingstoke, Hants. (01256) 881337. Early 16thC mansion with private chapel containing original glass. A classic-style portico was added in 1654. Fine Long Gallery with 'linenfold' carving on the panels throughout its length. 18thC staircase by John Chute. London 45 miles (M3). Tea-room and shop. *OPEN Apr-Oct 13.30 (grounds from 12.30)-17.30 Tue-Thur, Sat & Sun, 11.00-17.30 B.hols (CLOSED following Tue). Last admission 17.00. Charge.*

Waddesdon Manor

Nr Aylesbury, Bucks. (01296) 651211. An extraordinary house built 1874-89 for Baron Ferdinand de Rothschild by the French architect Gabriel-Hippolyte Destailleur, in the style of a great château

in Touraine. The garden, fountains and large aviary of rare birds are enchanting. The house contains a superb collection of works of art, mostly of the 17th and 18thC. Fine French furniture, Savonnerie carpets, 18thC terracotta figures, and remarkable collections of Sèvres and Meissen porcelain. The paintings include Rubens' *Garden of Love*, eight views of Venice by Guardi, many portraits by Gainsborough and Reynolds, including the latter's *Pink Boy*, and paintings by Watteau and Boucher. London 45 miles (A41). *House OPEN 13.00-17.00 Thur-Sat, 11.00-17.00 Sun & B.hols.* Grounds, tea room and aviary *OPEN 11.00-18.00 Wed-Sun. Charge.*

Warwick Castle

Warwick, Warks. (01926) 408000. One of the finest medieval castles in the country, famed for its dungeons and peacocks. The views from the ramparts are breathtaking. Inside the castle, in private royal apartments, is a re-creation of a Royal Weekend Party which gives an insight into the former glory of the castle and its occupants. Grounds landscaped by Capability Brown. Victorian Rose Garden laid out to the original designs. Café, restaurant. London 85 miles (A41). *OPEN Apr-mid Oct 10.00-17.30 Mon-Sun; Nov-Feb 10.00-16.30 Mon-Sun.* Victorian Rose Garden *OPEN all year.*

West Wycombe Park

High Wycombe, Bucks. (01494) 524411. Georgian house rebuilt 1745-71, by Sir Francis Dashwood. Still the home of the Dashwood family, it has good furniture, painted ceilings and frescoed walls. The landscaped grounds are dotted with garden buildings, including Roman and Greek temples, a flint mausoleum and, on the opposite hill, the cave where the notorious 18thC drinking club, the Hell Fire Club, is reputed to have met. London 30 miles (A40). House and grounds *OPEN Jun-Aug 14.00-17.00 Sun-Thur. Charge.* Caves *OPEN Apr-Sep 13.00-17.00 Mon-Sun. Charge.*

Windsor Castle

Windsor, Berks. (01753) 868286. An imposing 800-year-old medieval fortress. 12thC Round Tower built by Henry II. St George's chapel is fine 16thC perpendicular. Magnificent state apartments. London 20 miles (M4). Castle precinct and state apartments *OPEN Apr-Oct 10.00-15.00 Mon-Sun; Nov-Mar 10.00-14.00 Mon-Sun. CLOSED Garter Day (2nd or 3rd Mon in Jun) and any State Visit arrival day. Charge.*

Woburn Abbey

Woburn, Beds. (01525) 290666. The Duke of Bedford's 18thC mansion, set in a fine 3000-acre (1215ha) park landscaped by Humphry Repton (part of which has been converted into a safari park). The house retains the quadrangular plan of the medieval monastery from which it also derived its site and name. Remodelling has occurred at different periods; the west front and the magnificent state apartments were done in 1747-60 by Henry Flitcroft; the south side, the lovely Chinese dairy and the orangery in 1802 by Henry Holland. Incomparable collection of pictures by Rembrandt, Van Dyck, Reynolds, Gainsborough, Holbein, and a famous group of fine Canalettos. English and French furniture, porcelain and silver. London 40 miles (M1). Abbey *OPEN Mar-Oct 11.00-16.00 Mon-Sat, 11.00-17.00 Sun & B.hols; Nov-Feb 11.00-17.00 Sat & Sun. CLOSED Nov & Dec. Charge.* Safari Park *OPEN Mar-Oct 10.00-17.00 Mon-Sun; Nov-Feb 11.00-15.00 Sat & Sun (weather permitting). Charge.* Deer Park *OPEN Mar-Oct 10.00-16.30 Mon-Sat, 10.00-16.45 Sun.*

Historic London

London's history begins in AD43 when invading Romans bridged the Thames. Around AD200 they built the London Wall (traces of which are still visible today, see entry in this chapter). This was to determine the shape of what we still call the City of London for some 1300 years. The Normans incorporated the Wall into their defences and, despite the extensive devastation and damage caused by the Great Fire of 1666, no radical replanning took place within the 'Square Mile'.

However, post-Fire London was to expand well beyond the historic City and its neighbour Westminster – originally a Saxon religious settlement and a seat of government in Norman times – absorbing in the process numerous surrounding villages which have now given their names to districts of the capital.

London's growth resulted from rising commercial importance (the City is still one of the world's major financial centres), the industrial revolution and, more recently, developing public transport which pushed new suburbs well out into the countryside.

Cities change; London has changed more than many. But despite the Blitz and decades of redevelopment, every stage of London's history, including the present, can be traced in her buildings, monuments, churches and famous houses.

Looking at history

The following entries are of important places, buildings, characteristic areas and also some elements that make London unique in its people and its history.

Abbey Mills Pumping Station

Abbey La E15. 0181-534 6717. An unusual building of cupolas and domes built in 1865 to pump the 83 miles of main sewers draining the 100 sq miles of London. This remarkable piece of drainage engineering was the work of the engineer Joseph Bazalgette and still survives intact and perfect after well over 100 years of use. Visits *by arrangement.* Maximum 15 people.

Admiralty Arch   **4 E4**

Entrance to the Mall SW1. Massive Edwardian triple arch by Sir Aston Webb 1910. Memorial to Queen Victoria.

Albany   **4 D4**

Piccadilly W1. Patrician Georgian mansion 1770-4 by Sir William Chambers. Now privately-owned residences with quiet public forecourt.

Albert Memorial   **3 E5**

Kensington Gore SW7. Gothic memorial to Prince Albert, consort of Queen Victoria, by Sir George Gilbert Scott 1872. *During restoration work, the memorial is covered. However, the adjacent Visitors' Centre houses an exhibition showing the extent and scope of the work.*

Annesley Lodge
Platts La NW3. Fine example of an Art Nouveau house by C.F.A. Voysey, built 1895.

Apsley House   4 **B5**
149 Piccadilly W1. 0171-499 5676. Robert Adam 1771-8 but altered in 1828 by Wyatt. Home of the Dukes of Wellington since 1817. Re-opened in 1995 after three years of renovations to return it to the condition in which it was known by the First Duke. Houses the Wellington Museum containing paintings, silver plate, porcelain and personal and military relics. Near-naked statue of Napoleon stands a startling 11ft (3.4m) high in the staircase well. *OPEN 11.00-17.00 Tue-Sun. Charge.*

Atlas House   5 **D2**
3 King St EC2. One of London's earliest surviving purpose-designed office buildings completed in 1836 by Thomas Hopper for the Atlas Insurance Company.

Ball Court   5 **E2**
Next to 39 Cornhill EC3. Straight out of Dickens. Simpson's chop house built in 1757.

Bank of England   5 **E2**
Threadneedle St EC2. 0171-601 5545. The vaults hold the nation's gold reserves. Outer walls are still the original design by Sir John Soane, architect to the Bank 1788-1833. Rebuilt by Sir Herbert Baker 1925-39. Museum *OPEN 10.00-17.00 Mon-Fri. CLOSED Sat & Sun. Special presentations by appt only. Free.*

Bankside   5 **D3**
Southwark SE1. Thames-side walk with fine views of St Paul's and the City across the river and 'The Anchor', historic riverside inn rebuilt c1750. Here were Shakespeare's theatres; his Globe is marked by a plaque in Park St and a working reconstruction of it, following the original designs of 1599, can be seen at Shakespeare's Globe Exhibition in New Globe Walk *(see page 61).* Number 49 Bankside is reputed to be the house in which Wren lodged while St Paul's was being built.

Bedford Park W4
Just north of Turnham Green station, the earliest planned suburb, laid out 1875-81 by Norman Shaw, who designed a number of the houses.

Belgravia SW1   7 **A1**
Thomas Cubitt converted a swamp almost level with the Thames and intersected by mud banks into the posh village of Belgravia. Draining the site, he turned its clay into bricks, built up its sub-

strata of gravel and, in 1827, started on streets, mansions and houses from designs by George Basevi, Disraeli's uncle. Cubitt died in 1856, but his firm completed Cubitt Town in Poplar, one of the great industrial parishes on the Thames.

Blackheath SE3
High, open and grassy. Bordered by 18thC houses including 'The Paragon', and the pleasant village of Blackheath.

The Blitz
Although the Docks and the City were prime targets during World War II, bombs rained all over London. The Blitz lasted for nine months beginning Sep 1940. In June 1944 a renewed assault with V1s ('Doodlebugs') began and lasted nearly a year. Later, V2 rockets arrived with such speed (3600 mph) that they were virtually invisible; the first fell at Chiswick but was heard at Westminster; another hit a New Cross Woolworth's and killed 160 people. Many Londoners spent their nights in air-raid shelters or bedded down in the tube stations. Ten thousand people could fit into Liverpool Street tube station. Over 1.5 million homes were damaged by bombing and 100,000 houses were destroyed. In the City alone, 164 out of 460 acres (66.4 out of 186.3ha) were wiped out. Historic buildings, including churches, were destroyed and damaged.

Bloomsbury Squares WC1   1 **G6**
Elegant Regency-style houses and squares: Bedford Sq, Russell Sq, Tavistock Sq etc. Many by Thomas Cubitt, mid 19thC.

Bond Street W1   4 **C3**
Fashionable high street. Originally laid out in the 1680s, it no longer has any architectural distinction, but is noted for its art dealers' galleries, fashion and quality shops.

Bridges
The tidal Thames currently has 17 bridges. Noteworthy ones in central London are:

Albert Bridge   6 **E4**
Unusual rigid chain suspension. Built by Ordish 1871-3.

Chelsea Bridge   7 **B4**
Original 1858. Rebuilt as suspension bridge by Rendel, Palmer & Tritton 1935-7.

London Bridge   5 **E4**
The site of many replacements. Wooden construction until 12thC; the famous stone bridge that followed carried houses and shops. Granite bridge built in 1832 by

Rennie was shipped off to Lake Havasu City, Arizona in 1971. Latest construction completed 1973.

Tower Bridge 5 G4
0171-378 1928. Victorian-Gothic towers with hydraulic twin drawbridge. Jones and Wolfe-Barry 1894. A permanent museum exhibition brings to life the history, human endeavour and engineering achievement which created this famous landmark. Breathtaking views of London and the Thames from the high walkways. *OPEN Apr-Oct 10.00-17.15 Mon-Sun; Nov-Mar 10.00-16.45 Mon-Sun. Charge.*

Waterloo Bridge 4 G3
Concrete. Fine design by Sir Giles Gilbert Scott 1937-42.

Westminster Bridge 4 F5
Graceful cast iron. Thomas Page 1862.

Brixton Windmill
Blenheim Gdns SW2. Elegant windmill of the tower type, built 1816. Now restored.

Buckingham Palace 4 D5
St James's Park SW1. The official London residence of the Sovereign. Originally built 1705, remodelled by Nash 1825 and Edward Blore 1830-47; refaced 1913 by Sir Aston Webb. State apartments open to the public; visitors can see most of the apartments and the Queen's Picture Gallery. State apartments *OPEN Aug & Sep 09.30-17.30 Mon-Sun. Phone 0171-930 5526 for tickets.* Queen's Gallery *OPEN 10.00-17.00 Tue-Sat & B.hols, 14.00-17.00 Sun throughout the year. Phone 0171-930 4832.*

Burlington Arcade 4 D3
Piccadilly W1. 1819 Regency shopping promenade with original shop windows. Still employs a beadle to preserve the gracious atmosphere.

Burlington House 4 D3
Piccadilly W1. Victorian-Renaissance façade on one of the great 18thC palaces. Houses the Royal Academy and various Royal Societies. *OPEN 10.00-16.00 (tours at 11.30 & 14.30).*

Cadogan Square SW1 6 F1
A typical 19thC Chelsea square of red-brick houses.

Canals
Many years before railways were built canals carried goods in and out of London. The Grand Union Canal (opened in 1800) provided a link from Brentford to the Midlands; in 1820 a direct link to the Thames dockland was completed. The Regent's Canal, once London's main artery, is still in good condition although its working days are over. At Camden, where the lock starts a 90ft (27.5m) drop to the Thames, you can see houseboats bobbing stern to stern and, occasionally, a cruising pleasure boat. Towpaths there, at Little Venice in Paddington, and a tree-lined cutting that goes through the zoo in Regent's Park, afford close-up views of the canal.

Cemeteries
Cemeteries didn't exist until the 19thC. Before that churchyards sufficed but the pressing burial needs of a rapidly expanding population caused problems of overcrowding (and sometimes cholera). Thus large non-denominational cemeteries were started. They were privately owned and designed by architects and landscape gardeners, though nowadays they are mostly overgrown. The following are notable:

Brompton 6 B4
Old Brompton Rd SW10. Classical architecture; circular central colonnade beneath which lie the catacombs.

City of London
Aldersbrook Rd E12. 200 acres (81ha) of avenues, rhododendrons and Gothic chapels and catacombs. The largest municipal cemetery in Europe.

Highgate
Swain's La N6. 0181-340 1834. Designed by Stephen Geary. The Friends of Highgate Cemetery guide visitors round the older western section: tours *Apr-Oct at 12.00, 14.00 & 16.00 Mon-Fri, on the hour 11.00-16.00 Sat & Sun; Nov & Mar at 12.00, 14.00 & 15.00 Mon-Fri, on the hour 11.00-15.00 Sat & Sun.* Thanks to their efforts much of the aggressive sycamore has been removed to allow native woodland to flourish, and wild flowers and birds abound. The eclectic assembly of 19thC society buried here includes bare-fisted prizefighter Tom Sayers, whose grave is guarded by a mastiff who attended his master's funeral in a carriage of his own; and menagerist George Wombwell, lying beneath a colossal, slumbering lion. Other funerary sculpture highlighting the Victorian way of death includes hovering angels, ivy-clad mourners making ephemeral appearances beside winding paths, and the celebrated female figure of *Religion* by Joseph Edwards, lost beneath wreathing ivy for many years. The grand Egyptian gateway leads to the Cedar of Lebanon Circle. Look out for the towering classical mausoleum to financier Julius Beer and for the occasional Gothic shrine. The eastern cemetery, resting place of George Eliot, George Holyoake (pioneer organiser

of workers' co-operatives), Herbert Spencer (sociologist and philosopher), Sir Ralph Richardson and, of course, Karl Marx is *OPEN Apr-Oct 10.00-17.00 Mon-Fri, 11.00-17.00 Sat & Sun; Nov-Mar 10.00-16.00 Mon-Fri, 11.00-16.00 Sat & Sun. CLOSED during funerals. Charge.*

Kensal Green
Harrow Rd W10. 0181-969 0152. London's first cemetery, established in 1832. Comprises 77 acres (31.1ha) of stone and marble tombs, including more free-standing mausolea than any other cemetery in England. Architectural styles trace the decline of the 'classic' and the use of the Gothic. Wilkie Collins, the two Brunels, Princess Sophia, the Duke of Sussex, Thackeray and Trollope lie here. *OPEN 09.00-17.30 Mon-Sat, 10.00-17.30 Sun (earlier closing in winter).* The Friends of Kensal Green Cemetery organise lectures and *2-hr* guided tours *Mar-Sept at 14.30 Sat & Sun; Oct-Feb at 14.00 Sun. Tour of colonnaded catacombs 1st Sun every month. Donations requested.*

Tower Hamlets
Southern Gro E3. Privately built in 1841 to provide burial ˉ space for wealthy Londoners, this Victorian cemetery has provided a superb natural habitat for a variety of wildlife since it ceased being used for burials in 1966. Gothic architecture. Cemetery tree trail.

The Cenotaph   4 **F5**
Whitehall SW1. Designed 1920 by Sir Edwin Lutyens to honour the dead of World War I. The annual service of remembrance takes place here.

Chandos House   4 **C1**
Chandos St W1. Fine Robert Adam house built 1869-70.

Charing Cross WC2   4 **F4**
The Charing Cross was the last of the stone crosses set up by Edward I to mark the funeral resting places of Queen Eleanor's body on its way to Westminster Abbey. Originally placed where Trafalgar Sq now is, it was demolished in 1647 and the statue of Charles I now stands in its place. The stone cross in the station courtyard is an 1865 replica.

Charlton House
See under Greenwich.

Charterhouse   2 **D6**
Charterhouse Sq EC1. 0171-253 9503. 14thC Carthusian monastery then a private house 1545-1611 which was converted into an almshouse and school. Now a house for 'gentlemen pensioners'. Cloister and Cell with 16thC Great Hall. *OPEN Apr-Jul. Guided tour at 14.15. Charge.*

Chelsea Royal Hospital   6 **F3**
Royal Hospital Rd SW3. 0171-730 0161. Fine, austere building. 1682 by Wren. Stables 1814-17 by Sir John Soane. Museum. *OPEN 10.00-12.00 & 14.00-16.00 Mon-Sat, 14.00-16.00 Sun. CLOSED Sun Oct-Mar. Free.*

Chiswick House
Burlington La W4. 0181-995 0508. Lovely Palladian villa built in the grand manner by 3rd Earl of Burlington 1725-30. Fine interiors and gardens by William Kent. *OPEN Apr-Sep 10.00-13.00 & 14.00-18.00 Mon-Sun; Oct-Mar 10.00-13.00 & 14.00-16.00 Wed-Sun. Charge.*

Chiswick Mall W4
17th-18thC riverside houses.

The Citadel   4 **E4**
The Mall SW1. Creeper-covered concrete. Built as a bomb-proof unit by the Admiralty 1940.

Clarence House   4 **D5**
Stable Yard Gate SW1. Mansion by Nash 1825. Now the home of the Queen Mother.

Cleopatra's Needle   5 **A3**
Victoria Embankment SW1. From Heliopolis. 1500BC. Presented by Egypt and set up next to the Thames 1878.

41-42 Cloth Fair EC1   5 **C1**
A rare domestic survivor of the Great Fire, with its two-storey bay windows of timber (forbidden in post-Fire reconstruction) much restored. Peep round the corner in Cloth Ct at the dummy window painted with a faded Victorian parlour scene.

Cock Lane   5 **C1**
Scene of the notorious 'ghost' hoax of the 18thC and once the only walk licensed for prostitutes within the City.

Cockney or rhyming slang
A particular accent and form of language still exists today which was once the common language of the people of the slums of London, particularly of the East End. To an acute ear a mere sentence at one time would reveal where in London you were born, which school your parents could afford and what your father did for a living. In addition to this very characteristic accent, the petty criminals of the City and the East End developed their own way of communicating by obscuring a dangerous word in a form of 'rhyming slang'. This in turn developed into a general misuse of most words – to the utter mystification of strangers. Instances are: 'apples and pears' for stairs, 'Lady Godiva' for fiver (£5 note); 'Cain and Abel' for table; 'Dickie dirt' for shirt – there are countless others.

College of Arms **5 D3**
Queen Victoria St EC4. 0171-248 2762. Handsome late 17thC building which houses the official records of English, Welsh and Irish heraldry and genealogy. *OPEN 10.00-16.00 Mon-Fri. Free.*

Covent Garden Market WC2 **4 F3**
Originally designed by Inigo Jones (with his St Paul's church) as a residential square in the 1630s. Market buildings dating from 1830 by Fowler. Floral Hall added in 1860 by E.M. Barry, architect of the Royal Opera House (1858). In 1974 the market moved to Nine Elms, but the area survived to become a flourishing new community, with shops, restaurants, London Transport Museum and Theatre Museum.

Crewe House **4 C4**
15 Curzon St W1. Georgian town house, 1735 by Edward Shepherd, who gave his name to Shepherd Market nearby. It was for many years the home of the Marquess of Crewe.

Croydon Palace
Old Palace Rd, Croydon, Surrey. 0181-688 3349. A 'standing house' of the Archbishops of Canterbury for over 1000 years, Croydon Palace is now a girls' school. Magnificent 15thC banqueting hall and Tudor chapel. Tours *14.00-14.30 Mon-Sat during certain school hols, Apr, May & Jul. Charge.*

Custom House **5 F3**
Lower Thames St EC3. Rebuilt many times. Admired for its classical river front by Robert Smirke.

Downing Street SW1 **4 F5**
17thC street; houses built by Sir George Downing. No. 10 is the official residence of the Prime Minister; No. 11 that of the Chancellor of the Exchequer.

Drapers Company Hall **5 E2**
Throgmorton Av EC2. City Livery Hall dating from 1667 but largely rebuilt in 1870. Fine staircase and collection of plate. For information on tours of all Livery Company Halls contact the City Information Centre, St Paul's Churchyard EC4 (**5 D2**). 0171-606 3030 ex1456.

Eltham Palace
Off Court Yd, Eltham SE9. 0181-294 2548 or 0181-294 2621 outside opening hours. 15thC royal palace until Henry VIII. Also remains of earlier royal residences. Great Hall with hammer beam roof and a very fine 15thC bridge over the moat. Guided tours of Courtauld House. *OPEN summer 10.00-18.00 Sun, Fri & Sun; winter 10.00-16.00. Charge.*

Fitzroy Square W1 **1 E5**
The south and east sides 1790-4 by

Robert Adam. Now pedestrianised with a landscaped garden.

Flamsteed House
See Greenwich: Old Royal Observatory.

Fleet Street EC4 **5 B2**
London's 'Street of Ink' associated with printing since Caxton. Most newspapers have now moved to new hi-tech offices but the association continues.

Fulham Gasometer **6 C6**
Fulham Gasworks SW6. The oldest gasholder in the world; built in 1830 by Winsor & Mindock. Diameter 100ft (30.5m), capacity 250,000 ft^3 (7075m^3). An extraordinary piece of early industrial engineering.

Fulham Palace
Fulham Palace Rd SW6. 0171-736 5821. Ex-residence of the Bishop of London. 16thC building with riverside park. Grounds *OPEN daily.* **Museum of Fulham Palace** 0171-736 3233. *OPEN Mar-Oct 14.00-17.00 Wed-Sun; Nov-Feb 13.00-16.00 Thur-Sun. Charge.*

George Inn **5 E4**
77 Borough High St SE1. 0171-407 2056. Built 1677. London's only surviving galleried inn of the kind which inspired early English theatre design. Owned by the National Trust.

Goldsmiths' Hall **5 D2**
Foster La EC2. 0171-606 7010. Pre-Victorian classical-style palazzo built in 1835 by Hardwick. Occasional exhibitions. For information on tours of all Livery Company Halls contact the City Information Centre, St Paul's Churchyard EC4 (**5 D2**). 0171-606 3030 ex1456.

Goodwin's Court **4 F3**
St Martin's La WC2. A completely intact row of bow-windowed 17thC houses.

Gray's Inn **5 B1**
High Holborn WC1. 0171-405 8164. Entrance from passage next to Cittie of York pub, 22 High Holborn. An Inn of Court since 14thC. The Hall (16thC) and 'Buildings' restored after bomb damage. Gardens were laid out by Francis Bacon. Hall *OPEN by written application to the Under Treasurer.* Gardens *OPEN 12.00-14.30 Mon-Fri. Free.*

Greenwich
Six miles downriver and associated with England's former seapower. The following are notable:

Charlton House
Charlton Rd SE7. 0181-856 3951. Perfect small red-brick Jacobean manor house on an 'H' plan, built 1607-12. Fine ceilings, staircase and some bizarre chimney-pieces. A very active community

centre. *Tours by appt, usually 1st Sat every month. Small charge.*

The Cutty Sark
King William Walk SE10. 0181-858 3445. Stands in dry-dock. One of the great sailing tea-clippers, built 1869. *Gipsy Moth IV*, the boat in which Sir Francis Chichester sailed round the world in 1966, stands in dry-dock next to the *Cutty Sark*. Both ships *OPEN Apr-Sep 10.00-17.30 Mon-Sat, 12.00-18.00 Sun; Cutty Sark also OPEN Oct-Mar 10.00-17.00 Mon-Sat, 12.00-17.00 Sun. Charge.*

National Maritime Museum
Romney Rd SE10. 0181-858 4422. Finest maritime collection of paintings, navigational instruments, costumes and weapons. A major exhibition tells the story of Nelson's epic life and death. *Twentieth Century Seapower'* is a permanent gallery illustrating seapower on a global scale with paintings, watercolours, ship models, photographs and medals. *OPEN 10.00-17.00 Mon-Sun. Charge (combined entry to Old Royal Observatory and The Queen's House).*

Old Royal Observatory
Greenwich Park SE10. 0181-858 4422. Formerly the Greenwich Observatory. Part of the National Maritime Museum and includes Flamsteed House. Designed by Wren and founded by Charles II in 1675. Astronomical and time instruments; the Meridian Line; largest refracting telescope in the UK. Most of the pioneer work in the development of astronomy and nautical navigation was done here. Houses London's only camera obscura. *OPEN 10.00-17.00 Mon-Sun. Charge.*

The Queen's House
Romney Rd SE10. 0181-858 4422. Part of the National Maritime Museum. Built by Inigo Jones, 1619-40, for the Queen of Denmark. *OPEN 10.00-17.00 Mon-Sun. CLOSED Jan. Charge.*

Ranger's House
Chesterfield Walk SE10. 0181-853 0035. 18thC red-brick villa, once home to the 4th Earl of Chesterfield. Suffolk Collection of paintings. *OPEN Easter-Sep 10.00-13.00 & 14.00-18.00 Mon-Sun; Oct-Mar 10.00-13.00 & 14.00-16.00 Wed-Sun. Charge.*

Rotunda Museum
Woolwich Common SE18. 0181-854 2242 ex3127. Pavilion by Nash 1814. Renowned museum displaying a highly impressive array of artillery starting with the 1346 Crécy bombard. *OPEN 13.00-16.00 Mon-Fri. Free.*

Royal Naval College
Greenwich SE10. 0181-858 2154. The site of the former royal palace of the Tudor sovereigns. A fine and interesting group of classical buildings by Webb 1664, Wren 1694 and Vanbrugh 1728. Chapel by James 'Athenian' Stuart 1789 and Painted Hall by Thornhill 1708. *OPEN 14.30-16.45 Mon-Sun. Free.*

Vanbrugh Castle
3 Westcombe Park Rd, Maze Hill SE3. Sir John Vanbrugh's own house 1717-26. Outside of the house can be seen – best view from east side of the park.

Guildhall   5 D2
Off Gresham St EC2. 0171-606 3030. 15thC with alterations to the façade by George Dance, 1789, and later restorations by Sir Giles Gilbert Scott. The Great Hall is used for ceremonial occasions. Medieval groined vaulting in crypts. Roman amphitheatre excavated in the courtyard *(viewing only by special arrangement).* Great Hall *OPEN 10.00-17.00 Mon-Sat. Free.* Library *OPEN 09.30-17.00 Mon-Sat. Free.* The Museum of the Clockmakers Company is contained within the library and is *OPEN 09.30-16.45 Mon-Fri. Free.*

Gunnersbury Park W3
0181-992 1612. Regency house of the Rothschilds. Museum of local history, including transport. Park. *OPEN Mar-Oct 13.00-17.00 Mon-Fri, 13.00-18.00 Sat & Sun; Nov-Feb 13.00-16.00 Mon-Sun. Park OPEN all day. Free.*

Hammersmith Mall
Upper & Lower Mall W6. Boathouses, riverside pubs and terraces of Georgian houses, including Kelmscott House, 1780, where William Morris lived and founded his printing press.

Hampstead Garden Suburb
Good pioneering suburban planning. Laid out by Sir Raymond Unwin and Barry Parker, 1907.

Hampstead Village NW3
Still very much a village of Georgian houses and alleyways. Church Row, Holly Mount and Regency houses on Downshire Hill, including Keats' House, are notable.

Highgate N6
Here you stand level with the cross of St Paul's. A village full of 18thC surprises.

Highgate Archway N6
Carries Hornsey La across Archway Rd. London's first 'flyover'. Originally built in 1813 and replaced by present structure in 1897. From the top you see the whole of London laid out before you.

Holborn Viaduct EC1   **5 C2**
William Heyward, 1869. Fine example of Victorian cast iron, and a pioneer traffic improvement scheme.

Holland House   **3 A5**
Holland Park W8. Jacobean house restored after extensive war damage and now used partly as a youth hostel and open-air theatre.

Honourable Artillery   **2 F5**
Company
Armoury House, City Rd EC1. 0171-382 1530. Victorian castellated fortress (1857) hides the Georgian (1735) headquarters of the oldest regiment in the British Army. Supplies Guard of Honour for Lord Mayor's Shows and for Royalty visiting the City. *OPEN by arrangement only. Write in advance to the Chief Executive at the above address.*

House of St Barnabas   **4 E2**
1 Greek St W1. 0171-437 1894. Early Georgian town house in Soho Square with mock-Gothic chapel, fine carvings and rococo plasterwork. Connections with Dickens and Gladstone. Now a temporary refuge for distressed women. *OPEN 14.30-16.15 Wed, 11.00-12.30 Thur. Free.*

Houses of Parliament   **4 F5**
St Margaret St SW1. 0171-219 3000. Victorian-Gothic building 1840-68 by Sir Charles Barry and A.W.N. Pugin. Westminster Hall was built in 1099 as the Great Hall of William Rufus' new palace; the roof dates from the late 14thC. *Admission to Prime Minister's Question Time by application to your MP (or embassy for foreigner visitors). Admission to debates by queueing. OPEN 10.00-14.30 Wed, 09.30-15.00 Fri, from 14.30 onwards Mon, Tue & Thur. Tours of Westminster Hall and the Palace of Westminster by application to your MP. Free.*

Hyde Park Corner SW1   **4 B5**
Consists of Constitution Arch at the top of Constitution Hill, and the Ionic screen of three classical-style triumphal arches at the entry to Hyde Park, by Decimus Burton, 1825. Admire too the Duke of Wellington's former home Apsley House, once known as 'Number One, London'.

Inns of Chancery   **5 B1**
Before the 18thC, a student of law had first to go through one of the nine Inns of Chancery then existing. They have now mostly disappeared. Staple Inn, High Holborn, remains a fine Elizabethan building. Others survive only as names: Clifford Inn, Thavies Inn and Furnival's Inn.

Jewel Tower   **4 F6**
Old Palace Yd SW1. 0171-222 2219. 14thC fragment of the old palace of Westminster. Houses *Parliament Past and Present* exhibition. *OPEN Apr-Sep 10.00-18.00 Mon-Sun; Oct-Mar 10.00-16.00 Mon-Sun. CLOSED 13.00-14.00. Charge.*

Kensington Palace   **3 C4**
Kensington Gdns W8. 0171-937 9561. Bought in 1689 by William III and altered by Wren, Hawksmoor and William Kent; attribution of the Orangery, of exceptionally fine brick, is uncertain. Queen Victoria and Queen Mary born here. State apartments and Costume Museum. *OPEN 09.00-17.00 Mon-Sat, 11.00-17.00 Sun (last admission 16.15). Charge. Closed for refurbishment until May 1996.*

Kensington Palace   **3 C4**
Gardens W8
A street of prosperous town mansions in the grand Italianate style, laid out by Pennethorne in 1843, but continued by other famous architects. No. 8a is by Owen Jones and Decimus Burton; No. 12a James Murray; Nos. 18 & 20 by Banks and Barry; No. 13 by C.J. Richardson.

Kenwood House (Iveagh Bequest)
Hampstead La NW3. 0181-348 1286. Robert Adam house and interior 1767-9. English 18thC paintings and furniture. Also fine paintings by Rembrandt, Van Dyck and Vermeer. Gardens and wooded estate of 200 acres (81ha). *OPEN Mon-Sun, Easter-Sep 10.00-18.00; Oct-Easter 10.00-16.00. Free.* Refreshments in the coach house.

Kew Palace
Kew, Surrey. 0181-332 5121. Small red-brick house in Dutch style. Built 1631. Souvenirs of George III and Queen Charlotte. *OPEN Apr-Sep 11.00-17.30 Mon-Sun. Kew Gardens OPEN 09.30 to dusk Mon-Sun. Charge.*

Lambeth Palace   **7 F1**
Lambeth Palace Rd SE1. 0171-928 8282. The London residence of the Archbishop of Canterbury since 1197. Remarkable Tudor gatehouse, fine medieval crypt. 14thC Hall with a splendid roof and portraits of archbishops on its walls. The Great Hall, which houses the library, was rebuilt in medieval style in 1633; prominent pendants and black-amoors' heads decorate its elaborate timber roof; the gloves worn by Charles I when he went to the scaffold are on display. Look out for the famous spreading fig tree, planted during Mary Tudor's

reign by the last Catholic archbishop, Cardinal Pole; for the brass plate commemorating the negligence of a gardener who put his fork through Archbishop Laud's tortoise, and for the picture of the original Nosy Parker – archbishop under Elizabeth I and the first to have no allegiance to Rome – so called because he had a big nose. *Tours (very restricted) on a Wed or Thur by written application to the Booking Secretary. Charge.*

Lancaster Gate W2 3 **E3**
Area of fine stucco houses 1865, in and around Lancaster Gate. (Queen's Gdns, Cleveland Sq and Cleveland Gdns.)

Lancaster House 4 **D5**
Stable Yd, St James's SW1. Early Victorian London town house. Lavish state apartments and painted ceilings. Used for official functions.

Law Courts 5 **B2**
Strand WC2. 0171-936 6000. Massive Victorian-Gothic building housing the Royal Courts of Justice. *OPEN to public 10.00-16.30 Mon-Fri. Over 16s only for criminal cases; over 14s for civil cases. Courts not in session Aug and Sep but open to public. Free.*

Leadenhall Market 5 **F2**
Gracechurch St EC3. Impressive Victorian glass and iron hall 1881 by Horace Jones preserving the old street pattern; on the site of the Roman basilica.

Lincoln's Inn 5 **A2**
Lincoln's Inn WC2. 0171-405 1393. An Inn of Court 17thC. New Sq, gardens, barristers' chambers and solicitors' offices. A chapel by Inigo Jones (1623), the New Hall and the 15thC Old Hall. Great Hall was built in 1845. The 'Stone Buildings' are by Sir Robert Taylor and were begun in 1774. Still has Dickensian atmosphere. *OPEN 10.00-16.00 Mon-Fri (gardens 12.00-14.30 only). CLOSED Sat & Sun. Admission to the Chapel outside these hours, and to the Hall and Library, by written application to the Treasury Office, Whitehall SW1. Free.*

Lincoln's Inn Fields WC2 5 **A2**
Seven acres (2.8ha) of gardens laid out by Inigo Jones 1618. Once a famous duelling ground. Criminals were occasionally hanged from its plane trees. Nos. 13 & 14 built 1792 by Sir John Soane. Nos. 57 & 58 built 1730 by Henry Joynes. Nos. 59 & 60 built 1640, attributed to Inigo Jones.

Little Venice 3 **D1**
W2. Artists, writers, converted barges and the Grand Union Canal.

Lloyds of London 5 **F2**
Lime St EC3. 0171-623 7100. World-famous international insurance market.
Huge dealing room in a 240ft (75m) high atrium housing the famous Lutine Bell. Viewing gallery *no longer open to the public.*

London Stone 5 **E3**
Cannon St EC4. Set into the wall of the Bank of China opposite Cannon Street station. Possibly the Roman Millarium from which all road distances were measured.

London Wall 5 **D1**
Surviving parts of the Roman and medieval wall around the old city of London can still be seen at St Alphage on the north side of London Wall EC2; St Giles Churchyard, Cripplegate EC1; Jewry St EC3 (5 **G2**); off Trinity Sq EC3 (5 **G3**); and in the Tower of London EC3 (5 **G3**).

Mansion House 5 **E2**
Walbrook EC4. 0171-626 2500. Opposite the Bank of England. Official residence of the Lord Mayor. Palladian building by George Dance 1739. Completed 1752. Sumptuous Egyptian Hall. *OPEN (to parties of 15-40 people only) Tue-Thur by written application. Free.*

Marble Arch W1 3 **G3**
Designed by John Nash, 1827, based on the Arch of Constantine in Rome. Intended to be a grand new entrance for Buckingham Palace, it wasn't until it was finished that it was discovered that the arch was too narrow for the state coach to pass through so it had to be moved to its present site. From the 14thC to 1783 this was the spot for the Tyburn Gallows, the main execution site where hangings took place watched by excited crowds.

Melbury Road W14 3 **A6**
Near Holland Park. Contains several notable houses; No. 29 William Burges' Tower House 1875-80; Nos. 8 & 31 are by Norman Shaw 1876 & 1877, and No. 14 Holland Park Rd nearby is by Philip Webb.

Metropolitan Police
In the 18thC, highway robbery on new bridges across the Thames and on roads leading from the Angel and Islington across the fields into the city, necessitated armed patrols for convoys of pedestrians. Nevertheless, the idea of a permanent police force was considered an infringement of freedom by many Londoners. The Metropolitan Police Act, 1829, was pressed into being by Home Secretary Robert Peel; thus the first policemen were known as 'Peelers' and 'Bobbies'. They carried rattles in their coat-tail pockets and police batons. In 1860 a whistle replaced the rattle. In the 20thC women were recruited. The London Bobby,

relatively the most benign cop in the world, still doesn't carry a gun on his normal duties. Riot shields have, however, been used in recent disturbances.

Monument　　　　　　　**5 E3**
Monument St EC3. 0171-626 2717. A 17thC hollow fluted column by Wren to commemorate the Great Fire of London; stands at 202ft (61.5m), a foot in height for every foot in distance from where the fire started in Pudding Lane. Magnificent view. *Closed for renovation at time of going to press; expected to re-open April 1996.*

Morden College
19 St German's Pl, Blackheath SE3. 0181-858 3365. Characteristic domestic architecture in 17thC landscaped grounds. *OPEN to specialist groups only, by written application. Free.*

Nelson's Column　　　　　**4 E4**
Trafalgar Sq WC2. 145ft (44m) high column by William Railton 1839-42. Weighs 16 tons. At the top a statue of Nelson by Baily 1843, minus his eye and arm, both lost in battle.

Old Bailey　　　　　　　**5 C2**
Old Bailey EC4. 0171-248 3277. The Central Criminal Court. On the site of old Newgate Prison. Trials open to the public. Gallery *OPEN 10.30-13.00 & 14.00-16.00 Mon-Fri. Minimum age 14 (must be accompanied by an adult until 16). Photography not permitted. Free.*

Old Operating Theatre　　**5 E4**
Museum & Herb Garret
9a St Thomas's St, London Bridge SE1. 0171-955 4791. A well-preserved early 19thC operating theatre, located in the ex-parish church and old chapel of St Thomas's Hospital (now the Chapter House of Southwark Cathedral). Owned by the Diocese of Southwark. *OPEN 10.00-16.00 Tue-Sun. Charge.*

Old Swan House　　　　　**6 F4**
17 Chelsea Embankment SW3. Late 19thC house by R. Norman Shaw.

Pall Mall SW1　　　　　　**4 D4**
Early 19thC opulence. This fine street and its surroundings express the confidence and wealth of the London of this period. Pall Mall itself contains two fine buildings by Sir Charles Barry, the Travellers' Club, 1829-32 (Italian-Renaissance revival), and his more mature Reform Club, 1837-41.

Piccadilly Circus W1　　　**4 E3**
The confluence of five major thoroughfares. Fountains and statue of Eros by Gilbert 1893, commemorating Victorian philanthropist Lord Shaftesbury.

Pimlico SW1　　　　　　　**7 C3**
Laid out by Cubitt in the 1840s as a less grand neighbour to Belgravia.

Pitshanger Manor
Mattock La W5. 0181-567 1227. 18thC country house rebuilt by Soane 1800-10 to create a Regency villa. It has a collection of Martinware pottery and is surrounded by Walpole Park. *OPEN 10.00-17.00 Tue-Sat. Free.*

Postman's Park　　　　　**5 D2**
Churchyard of St Botolph, Aldersgate EC1. Under an alcove are some remarkable tiles recording Victorian deeds of bravery (1880).

Prince Henry's Room　　　**5 B2**
17 Fleet St EC4. 0181-294 1158. From 1610; oldest domestic building in London. Named after the elder son of James I. Fine plaster ceiling and carved oak panelling. *OPEN 11.00-14.00 Mon-Sat. CLOSED Xmas, New Year, B.hols. Free. Closed for renovation at time of publication.*

Prisons
Prisons were not used for punishment until the 19thC. Before that time they were used only for debtors and for those awaiting trial. In those days the principal punishment was death or transportation to Australia and America. The industrial revolution introduced the 'hulks', prison ships moored in the Thames. In the early 19thC the government built prisons in which the most abominable conditions existed. Things gradually changed after many middle-class suffragettes and conscientious objectors were imprisoned around the time of the First World War. Prison improvement has been badly neglected in recent years so that most are now seriously overcrowded. Many of London's prisons (from the outside) are formidable and important buildings architecturally – including Brixton, Holloway, Pentonville, Wandsworth and Wormwood Scrubs.

Queen Anne's Gate SW1　　**4 E5**
Quiet, completely preserved 18thC street in its original state. Close to St James's Park. Statue of Queen Anne near No. 13.

Regent's Canal　　　　　**3 E1**
Paddington Bridge W2 to Regent's Canal Dock E14. The canal was built by James Morgan in 1820 to connect Paddington with the Thames, thus allowing goods to be shipped direct from Birmingham to the Thames by the canal network. The best way to see the canal is to take a boat trip (*see 'Canal trips'*).

Regent's Park environs　　**1 C4**
The park and the surrounding Regency architecture were planned almost entirely by John Nash, 1812-26. Particularly notable are Park Cres, Park Sq,

Cambridge Ter, York Ter and Chester Ter. Decimus Burton designed the façades of Cornwall Ter and Clarence Ter.

Regent Street　　　　4 **D3**
John Nash, asked by George IV (then Prince of Wales) to construct an artery from Carlton House to the royal country home near Regent's Park, not only designed the route for Regent Street but also most of the houses. This took many years since it was pieced together to conform with the various architectural styles along the way. Initially acclaimed, its imminent destruction was celebrated in 1927 when King George V and his Queen drove down its flower-decked length; it was then rebuilt from end to end.

Roman Bath　　　　5 **A3**
5 Strand La WC2. Disputed origin, restored in the 17thC. Not open but visible from the pathway.

Royal Exchange　　　　5 **E2**
Corner of Threadneedle St and Cornhill EC3. Completed 1884 by Tite. The third building on this site. Originally founded as a market for merchants and craftsmen in 1564, and destroyed in the Great Fire. The second building was also burnt down, in 1838.

Royal Mews　　　　4 **C6**
Buckingham Palace Rd SW1. 0171-930 4832 ex634. The Queen's horses and carriages including the Coronation coach. *OPEN Apr-Sep 12.00-16.00 Tue-Thur; Oct-Mar 12.00-16.00 Wed only. Last admission 15.30. CLOSED on royal occasions. Charge.*

Royal Opera Arcade　　　　4 **E4**
Between Pall Mall and Charles II St SW1. John Nash 1816. London's earliest arcade. Pure Regency; bow-fronted shops, glass-domed vaults and elegant lamps.

Royal Society of Arts　　　　4 **F3**
8 John Adam St WC2. 0171-930 5115. Built 1774 after the Society was founded in 1754. Fine surviving example of Adam architecture, from the original Adelphi area (now almost entirely demolished).

St James's Palace　　　　4 **D4**
Pall Mall SW1. Built by Henry VIII with many later additions. Still officially a royal residence. Ceiling of Chapel Royal possibly by Holbein. *No admission to palace. Entry to courtyards only. Free.*

St James's Street SW1　　　　4 **D4**
Celebrated for its fine shops and gentlemen's clubs since the early 18thC. Two shops still survive; Berry Bros & Rudd, wine merchants, (No.3), and Lock's the hatters (No.6). Amongst the surviving clubs are Boodle's (No.28) 1775 by J. Crunden and Brooks's (No.60) 1788 by Henry Holland.

St John's Gate　　　　2 **D5**
St John's La EC1. Once a gateway to the Priory of the Knights Hospitallers of St John of Jerusalem. Built in 1504, it is the only monastic gateway left in London. **Museum of the Order of St John**. 0171-253 6644. *OPEN 10.00-17.00 Mon-Fri, to 16.00 Sat; tours at 11.00 & 14.30 Tue, Fri & Sat. Donations welcome.*

Skinners Hall　　　　3 **E3**
8 Dowgate Hill EC4. 0171-236 5629. 17th-18thC buildings and quiet arcaded courtyard. Open days; occasional visits *by arrangement* with City Information Centre, St Paul's Churchyard EC4 (5 **D2**). 0171-332 1456.

Smithfield EC1　　　　5 **C1**
Once 'Smooth Field'. Historical site of the murder of Wat Tyler, tournaments, public executions, cattle market and the famous Bartholomew Fair. In north-east corner original Tudor gatehouse built over 13thC archway leading to Church of St Bartholomew-the-Great (*see 'Churches'*). South-east side occupied by St Bartholomew's Hospital, London's oldest hospital, founded in 1123. Gateway (1702) bears London's only statue of Henry VIII. Smithfield Market is the largest meat market in the world (10 acres – 4ha). The Italianate-style market buildings with some ornamental ironwork were designed by Horace Jones and erected between 1868 and 1899.

Soho　　　　4 **E2**
An area bounded by Regent St, Oxford St, Shaftesbury Av and Charing Cross Rd. Only a handful of peep shows and strip joints remain from its seedier days. Now full of fascinating foreign food shops, restaurants, street markets, flashing neon and nightlife of all sorts. Visit London's 'Chinatown' around Gerrard St.

Somerset House　　　　4 **G3**
Strand WC2. 0171-438 6622. On the site of an unfinished 16thC palace. By Sir W. Chambers, 1776. It used to house the register of births, marriages and deaths in England and Wales, now holds the register of divorce, wills and probate, the Inland Revenue and the Courtauld Collection. Admission only to Courtauld Institute Galleries. *OPEN 10.00-18.00 Mon-Sat, 14.00-18.00 Sun. Charge. No admission to Somerset House.*

Spitalfields E1   5 G1
This centre of silk-weaving in England was established by the influx of Flemish and French weavers in the 16th and 17thC. The industry reached its height at the end of the 18th and early 19thC when about 17,000 looms were in use and a large area of East London was dependent on these family concerns. Fournier Street is a good example of typical Dutch-style houses of the time. The industry collapsed some 100 years ago.

Stations
Some good examples of 19thC 'railway architecture':

King's Cross   1 G3
Euston Rd NW1. Functional. 1851, by Lewis Cubitt.

St Pancras   1 G4
Euston Rd NW1. Impressive glass and iron roof by Barlow & Ordish 1863-7. Victorian Gothic façade and former Midland Grand Hotel by Sir George Gilbert Scott 1868-72.

Paddington   3 E2
Praed St W2. 1850-2. 'Railway cathedral' engineering at its best by Brunel; the Gothic ornament by Wyatt and Owen Jones; the Renaissance-style hotel by Hardwick.

Stock Exchange   5 E2
Old Broad St EC2. 0171-588 2355. The home of trading in stocks and shares, where fortunes are made and lost. The public gallery closed as a result of a bomb attack in 1990; trading is now done via computer in private offices.

Strand WC2   4 F3
Once a 'Strand' – a walk along the river – bordered in Stuart times with mansions and gardens down to the Thames. Their names still survive in the streets: Bedford, Buckingham, Villiers. A major commercial thoroughfare.

The Temple   5 B3
Inner Temple, Crown Office Row EC4. 0171-797 8250. Middle Temple, Middle Temple La EC4. 0171-353 4355. Both are Inns of Court. Enter by the gatehouse, 1685, in Middle Temple La. An extensive area of courtyards, alleys, gardens and warm brick buildings. Step back into the 19thC on misty winter afternoons when the lamplighter lights the gas lamps. Middle Temple Hall 1570. The restored Temple Church is one of only four remaining early Gothic round churches built by the Templars in England. 12th-13thC. Inner Temple *OPEN 10.00-16.00 Mon-Fri by arrangement. CLOSED Sat & Sun, B.hols & legal vacations.* Middle Temple Hall *OPEN 10.00-12.00 & 14.00-16.00 Mon-Fri by arrangement. CLOSED Sat & Sun, B.hols, Aug & during examinations. Free.*

Temple of Mithras,   5 E2
Bucklersbury House
3 Queen Victoria St EC4. Originally discovered 18ft (5.5m) underground in Walbrook and moved here with other Roman relics.

Thames Tunnels
Rotherhithe to Wapping
The first tunnel under the Thames built by Sir Marc Isambard Brunel (the elder), and completed in 1843 after many deaths by accident and illness. Now used by underground trains and still a perfect feat of engineering – withstanding over 100 years of train vibration. Original tunnel can be seen at Wapping station – also stairs and handrails. **The Engine House**, Railway Av SE16, 0181-318 2489, houses the sole surviving example of a compound horizontal V steam pumping engine and a permanent exhibition.

Rotherhithe
1908. For vehicles and pedestrians.

Blackwall
1897 by Binnie. Now incorporated in a two-way system with the new tunnel, completed in 1967. For vehicles and pedestrians.

Greenwich and Woolwich
1902 and 1912. Pedestrians only.

Tower of London   5 G3
Tower Hill EC3. 0171-709 0765. A keep, a prison and still a fortress. Famous for the Bloody Tower, Traitors' Gate, the ravens, Crown Jewels, the Armouries and the Yeomen Warders. Edward I's Medieval Palace has been restored and is open to the public. *OPEN Mar-Oct 09.00-18.00 Mon-Sat, 10.00-18.00 Sun; Nov-Feb 09.00-17.00 Mon-Sat, 10.00-17.00 Sun. Charge.*

Trafalgar Square WC2   4 F4
Laid out by Sir Charles Barry 1830-40. Nelson's column (granite) by William Railton 1839-42. Statue by Baily. Bronze lions by Landseer 1868. Fountains by Lutyens. Famous for political rallies, pigeons and the excesses of New Year's Eve revellers.

The Underground
Although overground railways existed in the mid-19thC, a need for more transport in a rapidly expanding London resulted in the 'underground'. The world's first was the Metropolitan Line with 30,000 passengers taking an opening day ride (in March 1863) from Bishops Rd, Paddington to Farringdon St. The original carriages were open trucks drawn by

steam trains. The line was cut out by the 'trench' system, usually under a road, lined with brick and the street relaid on top. The Tower subway, opened in 1870, was the world's first iron-lined tube railway. A small cable-hauled car carried 12 passengers at a time from the Tower to Bermondsey. (Today, the 'tube' houses water mains.) Early underground passengers endured dimly lit carriages and windows closed against smoke. To this day two dummy housefronts in Leinster Gardens W2 puzzle passers-by. They conceal part of the street which had to be demolished for the underground and were built at the insistence of the irate local residents. Twenty-one years after the Metropolitan Line opened, the Circle Line was completed. The underground system has steadily expanded since then – there are now 11 lines (including the Docklands Light Railway).

Watermen's Hall   5 F3
18 St Mary at Hill EC3. 0171-283 2373. Adam-style front surviving from 1780. Unexpectedly beautiful amid drab surroundings. Visits arranged in *summer* through City Information Centre, St Paul's Churchyard EC4 (5 **D2**).

Whitefriars Crypt   5 B2
30 Bouverie St EC4. 14thC crypt belonging to a House of Carmelites. Discovered in 1895 and restored by the proprietors of the *News of the World* and *The Sun* when they occupied the offices above.

Whitehall SW1   4 F4
Wide thoroughfare used for ceremonial and State processions; contains the Cenotaph and several notable statues. Lined with Government offices.

Old Admiralty
1725-8 by T. Ripley. Fine Robert Adam columnar screen 1760. The New Admiralty 1887 lies behind.

Old Scotland Yard
1888. An asymmetrical building by Shaw.

War Office
1898-1907 by William Young. Victorian-baroque.

Horse Guards Parade
1750-60 by William Kent. Changing of the Guard in the forecourt daily – see 'Daily ceremonies'.

Banqueting House
0171-930 4179. 17thC Palladian-style by Inigo Jones. 1619-25. Rubens ceilings 1635. *OPEN 10.00-17.00 Mon-Sat. Charge.*

Dover House
1755-8 by Paine. Entrance screen and rotunda 1787 by Henry Holland.

Treasury
1846 by Sir C. Barry. Victorian columned façade on Whitehall. Earlier façade overlooking Horse Guards Parade 1733-6 by William Kent.

Foreign Office
Mid-Victorian palazzo-style by Gilbert Scott. Completed by Ministry of Housing 1920.

Whittington Stone
Highgate Hill N6, near junction with Dartmouth Park Hill. Milestone marking the spot where tradition says young Dick Whittington rested on his way home from London and heard Bow Bells ring out 'Turn again Whittington, thrice Lord Mayor of London', and returned to become London's most famous Mayor.

Woolwich Arsenal
Woolwich SE18. Fine example of early 18thC ordnance architecture. Sir John Vanbrugh, 1716-19. *OPEN by appt only. Free.*

York Watergate   4 F4
Watergate Walk, off Villiers St WC2. Built in 1626 by Nicholas Stone as the watergate to York House, it marks the position of the north bank of the Thames before the construction of the Victoria Embankment in 1862. The arms and motto are those of the Villiers family.

Houses of famous people

Visiting the homes of the famous has had its attractions since long before the days of tourism and mass travel. As early as the 17thC, for example, the birthplace of John Milton was one of London's most important sights; while in the next century Boswell anticipated the tourist guides and gazetteers of today by conscientiously listing all the London houses where Dr Johnson had ever lived. Only in rare cases, of course, is the house of some-one famous retained as a shrine and opened to the public. Most such houses are simply houses, and they have carried on being lived in as private homes, marked perhaps with a commemorative plaque (see next section). Below, however, is a selection of the most interesting and worthwhile of those houses that are open to the public.

Carlyle's House   6 E4
24 Cheyne Row SW3. 0171-352 7087. A fine Queen Anne house where Carlyle lived for 42 years until his death in 1881. Walled Victorian garden. *OPEN 11.00-17.00 (last admission 16.30) Wed-Sun*

and B.hols except Good Friday. CLOSED Nov-Mar. Charge.

Churchill's House
Chartwell, nr Westerham, Kent. (01732) 866368. A famous house full of recent political history. The water gardens, grounds and views of the Weald of Kent are memorable. Gardens *OPEN Apr-Oct 11.00-16.30 Tue-Thur, Sat, Sun & B.hols. CLOSED Mon, Fri & Tue following B.hol.* House *OPEN Mar & Nov 11.00-16.00 Wed, Sat & Sun. Charge.*

Darwin's House
Down House, Downe, Kent. (01689) 859119. Charles Darwin lived and worked here. Two rooms are as they were in his day and others contain exhibitions illuminating his work. Investigate the Sand Walk where Darwin pondered his theory of evolution. *OPEN 13.00-18.00 Wed-Sun. CLOSED Feb & mid-end Dec, plus every Mon (except B.hols) & Tue. Charge.*

Dickens' House   **2 B5**
48 Doughty St WC1. 0171-405 2127. Regency terrace house. Relics of Dickens' life and writings. He lived here from 1837 to 1839. Be sure to see the reconstructed drawing room. *OPEN 10.00-17.00 (last admission 16.30). CLOSED Sun & B.hols. Charge.*

Disraeli's House
Hughenden Manor, High Wycombe, Bucks. (01494) 532580. Disraeli lived here from 1847 until his death in 1881. Contains much of his furniture, pictures, books and other relics. *OPEN Apr-Oct 14.00-18.00 Wed-Sat, 12.00-18.00 Sun & B.hols; Mar 14.00-18.00 (or sunset) Sat & Sun. Charge.*

Freud Museum
20 Maresfield Gdns NW3. 0171-435 2002. This was Freud's last home from 1938-9. The museum contains a major collection of Freud's personal effects: library, correspondence, antiquities, carpets and furniture including the famous couch on which psychoanalysis was pioneered. *OPEN 12.00-17.00 Wed-Sun. Charge.*

Hogarth's House
Hogarth La, Great West Rd W4. 0181-994 6757. The 17thC country villa of William Hogarth; relics and late impressions of his engravings. *OPEN Apr-Sep 11.00-18.00 Mon & Wed-Sat; 14.00-18.00 Sun. Oct-Mar 11.00-16.00 Mon & Wed-Sat; 14.00-16.00 Sun. CLOSED Tue, first 2 weeks of Sep and last 3 weeks of Dec. Free.*

Dr Johnson's House   **5 B2**
17 Gough Sq, Fleet St EC4. 0171-353 3745. 17thC house. Relics and contemporary portraits. He lived here from 1748 to 1759. *OPEN May-Sep 11.00-17.30 Mon-Sat; Oct-Apr 11.00-17.00 Mon-Sat. CLOSED Sun & B.hols. Small charge.*

Keats' House
Wentworth Pl, Keats Gro NW3. 0171-435 2062. The poet John Keats lived here during his prolific period 1818-20. *OPEN Apr-Oct 10.00-13.00 & 14.00-18.00 Mon-Fri, 10.00-13.00 & 14.00-17.00 Sat, 14.00-17.00 Sun; Nov-Mar 10.00-17.00 Mon-Fri, 10.00-13.00 & 14.00-17.00 Sat, 14.00-17.00 Sun. Donations welcome.*

Kipling's House
Bateman's, Burwash, E. Sussex. (01435) 882302. The house, built in 1634, contains Kipling's furniture and a Kipling exhibition. The surroundings are described in *Puck of Pooks Hill* and *Rewards and Fairies*. *OPEN Apr-Oct 11.00-17.30 Sat-Wed. CLOSED Thur & Fri. Charge.*

Leighton House   **3 A6**
12 Holland Park Rd W14. 0171-602 3316. Former home of Fredric, Lord Leighton. Centre for Victorian studies and special exhibitions. Arab hall with decorations of 14th-16thC Oriental tiles. Paintings by Leighton, Burne-Jones and Millais. Watts and De Morgan pottery. *OPEN 11.00-17.30 Mon-Sat. CLOSED Sun & B.hols. Free.*

William Morris Gallery
Lloyd Park, Forest Rd E17. 0181-527 3782. 18thC house. Textiles, wallpapers, carpets, woodwork and designs by Morris, pre-Raphaelites and contemporaries, housed in Morris's boyhood home. *OPEN all year 10.00-13.00 & 14.00-17.00 Tue-Sat, 10.00-13.00 & 14.00-17.00 1st Sun in month. CLOSED Mon & B.hols. Free.*

Linley Sambourne House   **3 B5**
18 Stafford Ter W8. Home of Linley Sambourne, leading *Punch* cartoonist of the late Victorian and Edwardian eras. Unique interior reflecting artistic taste of the period. Contact the Victorian Society, 0181-994 1019. *OPEN Wed 10.00-16.00 & Sun 14.00-17.00 Mar-Oct. Parties at other times by appt. Charge.*

Shaw's Corner
Ayot St Lawrence, Welwyn, Herts. (01438) 820307. George Bernard Shaw lived here from 1906 until his death in 1950. *OPEN Apr-Oct 14.00-18.00 Wed-Sat, 12.00-18.00 Sun & B.hols. CLOSED Nov-Mar except by appt. Charge.*

Wellington Museum   **4 B5**
Apsley House, 149 Piccadilly W1. 0171-499 5676. Originally known as 'Number

One London'. Duke of Wellington's house. Built 1771-8 from designs by Robert Adam and altered 1828 by B. D. Wyatt. Contains Wellington relics, fine Spanish (Velázquez) and Dutch paintings, silver plate and porcelain. *OPEN 11.00-17.00 Tue-Sun. Charge.*

Wesley's House & chapel   2 **F5**
49 City Rd EC1. 0171-253 2262. John Wesley's possessions and personal relics. His tomb is in the chapel grounds. The chapel crypt houses a museum which tells the story of Methodism and displays Wesleyan memorabilia. *OPEN 10.00-16.00 Mon-Sat, 12.00-14.00 Sun.* (There is also a service at 11.00 on Sun, followed by lunch and a guided tour). *Small charge (free on Sun).*

Wolfe's House
Quebec House, Westerham, Kent. (01959) 562206. Mainly 17thC house where General Wolfe spent his early years. Collection of 'Wolfiana'. *OPEN Apr-Oct 14.00-17.30 Sun-Wed & Fri. CLOSED Thur & Sat. Charge.*

Commemorative plaques

Marking houses and other buildings associated with famous people or events since the now familiar blue plaques has been a feature of London's street scene since 1866. Originally on the private initiative of the Royal Society of Arts in 1901, they came under the aegis of the London County Council, later the Greater London Council. Since 1 April 1986 the plaques have been the responsibility of English Heritage. There are now nearly 400 of them, commemorating important events in the lives of architects, artists, composers, politicians, scientists, soldiers and writers. The following are some of the best known:

Adam, Robert
Lived at 1-3 Robert St, Adelphi WC2. 4 **F3**
Arnold, Matthew
Lived at 2 Chester Sq SW1.   7 **B1**
Asquith, Herbert Henry
Lived at 20 Cavendish Sq W1.   4 **C2**
Baden-Powell, Robert
Lived at 9 Hyde Park Gate SW7.   3 **D5**
Baird, John Logie
First demonstrated television at 22 Frith St W1.   4 **E2**
Baldwin, Stanley
Lived at 93 Eaton Sq SW1.   7 **A1**

Barrie, Sir James M.
Lived at 100 Bayswater Rd W2   3 **D3**
and at 1-3 Robert St, Adelphi WC2. 4 **F3**
Beardsley, Aubrey
Lived at 114 Cambridge St SW1.   7 **B3**
Bennett, Arnold
Lived at 75 Cadogan Sq SW1.   6 **F1**
Berlioz, Hector
Stayed at 58 Queen Anne St W1.   4 **C1**
Bligh, William
Commander of the *Bounty* lived at 100 Lambeth Rd SE1.   7 **G1**
Boswell, James
Lived and died on the site of 122 Great Portland St W1.   4 **C1**
Browning, Elizabeth Barrett
Lived on site of 50 Wimpole St W1   4 **C2**
and at 99 Gloucester Pl W1.   4 **A1**
Brunel, Isambard Kingdom
Lived at 98 Cheyne Walk SW3.   6 **E4**
Burne-Jones, Sir Edward
Lived at 17 Red Lion Sq WC1.   4 **G1**
Canaletto, Antonio
Lived at 41 Beak St W1.   4 **D3**
Carlyle, Thomas
Lived at 24 Cheyne Row SW3.   6 **E4**
Chamberlain, Neville
Lived at 37 Eaton Sq SW1.   7 **A1**
Chaplin, Charlie
Lived at 287 Kennington Rd SE11. 7 **G2**
Chesterton, Gilbert Keith
Lived at 11 Warwick Gdns W14.   3 **A6**
Chippendale, Thomas
and his son had their workshop near 61 St Martin's La WC2.   4 **F3**
Churchill, Sir Winston
Lived at 34 Eccleston Sq SW1.   7 **B2**
Clive of India, Lord
Lived at 45 Berkeley Sq W1.   4 **C3**
Cole, Sir Henry
Lived at 33 Thurloe Sq SW7.   6 **E2**
Conan Doyle, Sir Arthur
Lived not as you might imagine at 221b Baker St, but at 12 Tennison Rd SE25.
Constable, John
Lived at 40 Well Walk NW3.
Cook, Captain James
Lived on the site of 88 Mile End Rd E1.
Darwin, Charles
Lived on the site of 110 Gower St WC1.   1 **F5**
Defoe, Daniel
Lived on the site of 95 Stoke Newington Church St N16.
Dickens, Charles
Lived at 48 Doughty St WC1.   2 **B5**
Disraeli, Benjamin
Born at 22 Theobalds Rd WC1   2 **B6**
and died at 19 Curzon St W1.   4 **C4**
Eliot, George (Mary Ann Evans)
Lived at Holly Lodge, 31 Wimbledon Park Rd SW18 and
died at 4 Cheyne Walk SW3.   6 **E4**

Engels, Friedrich
Lived at 121 Regent's Park Rd
NW1. **1 B2**

Faraday, Michael
Apprenticed at 48 Blandford St W1. **4 B1**

Fielding, Henry
Lived at 19-20 Bow St WC2 **4 F2**
and at Milbourne House, Station Rd
SW13.

Ford, Ford Madox
Lived at 80 Campden Hill Rd W8. **3 B4**

Franklin, Benjamin
Lived at 36 Craven St WC2. **4 F4**

Franklin, Rosalind
Lived and worked at Donovan Ct,
Drayton Gdns SW10. **6 C3**

Freud, Sigmund
Lived at 20 Maresfield Gdns NW3.

Fry, Elizabeth
Lived at St Mildred's Ct, Poultry
EC2. **5 E2**

Gainsborough, Thomas
Lived at 82 Pall Mall SW1. **4 E4**

Galsworthy, John
Lived at Grove Lodge, Hampstead Gro
NW3
and at 1-3 Robert St, Adelphi WC2. **4 F3**

Garrett Anderson, Elizabeth
Lived at 20 Upper Berkeley St W1. **4 A2**

Gibbon, Edward
Lived on the site of 7 Bentinck St
W1. **4 B2**

Gibbons, Grinling
Lived at 19-20 Bow St WC2. **4 F2**

Gladstone, William Ewart
Lived at 11 Carlton House Ter SW1 **4 E4**
at 10 St James's Sq SW1 **4 E4**
and at 73 Harley St W1. **4 C1**

Handel, George Frideric
Lived and died at 25 Brook St W1. **4 C3**

Hardy, Thomas
Lived at 172 Trinity Rd SW17
and at Adelphi Ter WC2. **4 F3**

Hazlitt, William
Lived on the site of 6 Bouverie St
EC4 **5 B2**
and died at 6 Frith St W1. **4 E2**

**Hendrix, James Marshall
(Jimmy)**
Lived at 23 Brook St W1. **4 B3**

Housman, A. E.
Lived at 17 North Rd N6.

Irving, Sir Henry
Lived at 15a Grafton St W1. **4 C3**

James, Henry
Lived at 34 De Vere Gdns W8. **3 D5**

Johnson, Dr Samuel
Lived at 17 Gough Sq EC4 **5 B2**
and at Johnson's Ct, Fleet St EC4. **5 B2**

Joyce, James
Spent 1931 at 28 Campden Gro
W8. **3 B5**

Keats, John
Was born on the site of the
Swan & Hoop public house,
86 Moorgate EC2 and lived at **5 E1**
Wentworth Pl, Keats Gro NW3

Keynes, John Maynard
Lived at 46 Gordon Sq WC1. **1 F5**

Kingsley, Charles
Lived at 56 Old Church St SW3. **6 E4**

Kipling, Rudyard
Lived at 43 Villiers St WC2. **4 F4**

Kitchener of Khartoum
Lived at 2 Carlton Gdns SW1. **4 E4**

Lamb, Charles
Lived at Colebrook Cottage, 64 Duncan
Ter N1. **2 D3**

Laughton, Charles
Lived at 15 Percy St W1. **4 E1**

Lawrence, David Herbert
Lived at 1 Byron Villas, Vale of Health
NW3.

**Lawrence, T. E. ('Lawrence of
Arabia')**
Lived at 14 Barton St SW1. **7 E1**

Lear, Edward
Lived at 30 Seymour St W1. **4 A2**

Lind, Jenny
Lived at 189 Old Brompton Rd
SW5. **6 B3**

Lloyd George, David
Lived at 3 Routh Rd SW18.

Lutyens, Sir Edwin Landseer
Lived at 13 Mansfield St W1. **4 C1**

MacDonald, Ramsay
Lived at 9 Howitt Rd NW3.

Mansfield, Katherine
Lived at 17 East Heath Rd NW3.

Marconi, Guglielmo
Lived at 71 Hereford Rd W2. **3 B2**

Marx, Karl
Lived at 28 Dean St W1. **4 E2**

Maugham, W. Somerset
Lived at 6 Chesterfield St W1. **4 C4**

Millais, Sir John Everett
Lived and died at 2 Palace Gate
W8. **3 D5**

Morris, William
Lived at 17 Red Lion Sq WC1 **2 B6**
and at Kelmscott House, 26 Upper
Mall W6.

Mozart, Wolfgang Amadeus
Composed his first symphony at 180
Ebury St SW1. **7 A2**

Napoleon III
Lived at 1c King St SW1. **4 D4**

Nelson, Lord (Horatio)
Lived on the site of 147 New Bond
St W1 **4 C3**
and at 103 New Bond St W1. **4 C2**

Newton, Sir Isaac
Lived on the site of 87 Jermyn St
SW1. **4 D4**

Nicolson, Harold & Sackville-West, Vita
Lived at 182 Ebury St SW1.   7 **A2**
Nightingale, Florence
Lived and died on the site of 10 South
St W1.   4 **B4**
Palmerston, Lord (Henry John Temple)
Born at 20 Queen Anne's Gate
SW1.   4 **E5**
Lived at 4 Carlton Gdns SW1   4 **E4**
and at Naval and Military Club,
94 Piccadilly W1.   4 **D4**
Pepys, Samuel
Lived on the site of 12 & 14 Buckingham
St WC2.   4 **F3**
Pitt, William
Lived at 10 St James's Sq SW1.   4 **E4**
Pitt, William (The Younger)
Lived at 120 Baker St W1.   1 **B6**
Reynolds, Sir Joshua
Lived and died on the site of Fanum
House, 47 Leicester Sq WC2.   4 **E3**
Rossetti, Dante Gabriel
Born on the site of 110 Hallam St
W1.   1 **D6**
Lived at 17 Red Lion Sq WC1   2 **B6**
and at 16 Cheyne Wlk SW3.   6 **E4**
Ruskin, John
Lived on the site of 26 Herne Hill SE24.
Scott, Captain Robert Falcon
Lived at 56 Oakley St SW3.   6 **E4**
Shackleton, Sir Ernest
Lived at 12 Westwood Hill SE26.
Shaw, George Bernard
Lived at 29 Fitzroy Sq W1.   2 **E5**
Shelley, Percy Bysshe
Lived at 15 Poland St W1.   4 **D2**
Sheraton, Thomas
Lived at 163 Wardour St W1.   4 **E2**
Sheridan, Richard Brinsley
Lived at 14 Savile Row W1   4 **D3**
and at 10 Hertford St W1.   4 **C4**
Stephenson, Robert
Died on the site of 35 Gloucester
Sq W2.   3 **E2**
Swinburne, Algernon Charles
Lived at 16 Cheyne Walk SW3   6 **E4**
and died at 11 Putney Hill SW15.
Thackeray, William Makepeace
Lived at 16 Young St W8   3 **C5**
at 2 Palace Grn W8   3 **C5**
and at 36 Onslow Sq SW7.   6 **D2**
Trollope, Anthony
Lived at 39 Montagu Sq W1.   4 **A2**
Turner, Joseph Mallord William
Lived at 23 Queen Anne St W1   4 **C1**
and at 119 Cheyne Walk SW3.   6 **E4**
Twain, Mark (Samuel L. Clemens)
Lived at 23 Tedworth Sq SW3.   4 **F3**
Vaughan Williams, Ralph
Lived at 10 Hanover Ter NW1.   1 **B4**

Wallace, Edgar
Lived at 6 Tressillian Cres SE4.
Walpole, Sir Robert
Lived at 5 Arlington St SW1.   4 **D4**
Waugh, Evelyn
Lived at 145 North End Rd NW11.
Wells, H. G.
Lived and died at 13 Hanover Ter
NW1.   1 **B4**
Wesley, John
Lived at 47 City Rd EC1.   2 **F5**
Whistler, James Abbott McNeil
Lived at 96 Cheyne Walk SW3.   6 **E4**
Whittington, Richard ('Dick')
House of Whittington stood at 20 College
Hill EC4.   5 **D3**
'Dick' died in 1423 and was buried in
the church of St Michael Royal, College
Hill EC4.   5 **D3**
Wilberforce, William
Lived at 111 Broomwood Rd SW11
and at 44 Cadogan Pl SW1.   6 **F1**
Wilde, Oscar
Lived at 34 Tite St SW3.   6 **F4**
Wolfe, General James
Lived at Macartney House, Greenwich
Park SE10.
Wood, Sir Henry
Lived at 4 Elsworthy Rd NW3.
Woolf, Virginia
Lived at 29 Fitzroy Sq W1.   1 **E5**
Wren, Sir Christopher
Lived at 49 Bankside SE1.   5 **D3**
Wyndham, Sir Charles
Lived at 43 York Ter NW1.   1 **C5**
Yeats, William Butler
Lived at 23 Fitzroy Rd NW1.   1 **C2**

Statues

London has some 1700 outdoor statues, memorials and pieces of historic sculpture. Their subjects range from classical mythology to modern statesmen. From such a number it is only possible to suggest a selection of some of the best and most interesting, which are listed below.

Achilles   4 **B4**
Hyde Park W1. Westmacott, 1822. Erected to honour Wellington. London's first nude statue.
Alfred the Great   5 **D6**
Trinity Church Sq SE1. Origin unknown but it possibly came from Westminster Hall, in which case it dates from 1395 and is by far the oldest statue in London.
Queen Anne   5 **D2**
In front of St Paul's Cathedral EC4. After Bird, 1712. This is a copy (1886) of the original. Surrounding the Queen are

figures representing England, France, Ireland and North America.

Queen Anne   **4 E5**
Queen Anne's Gate SW1. Origin uncertain but probably by Francis Bird early 18thC; believed to have stood originally over the portico of the church of St Mary-le-Strand.

Boadicea (Boudicca)   **4 F5**
Westminster Bridge SW1. Thornycroft, unveiled 1902. Famous group showing the ancient British Queen with her daughters in her war chariot.

George Canning   **4 F5**
Parliament Sq SW1. Westmacott, 1832. Fell over while in the sculptor's studio and killed a man.

Nurse Cavell   **4 F3**
St Martin's Pl WC2. Frampton, 1920. Simple and impressive memorial to the nurse who was shot for assisting prisoners to escape during World War I.

Charles I   **4 E4**
Trafalgar Sq SW1. Le Sueur, 1633. The oldest equestrian statue in London, and one of the finest. Ordered to be destroyed during the Civil War and buried until the Restoration. It was erected on its present site between 1675 and 1677.

Charles II   **6 G3**
Royal Hospital, Royal Hospital Rd SW3. Bronze. Grinling Gibbons, 1676. King in Roman costume. The statue is wreathed in oak leaves on Oak Apple Day, 29 May.

Sir Charles Chaplin   **4 E3**
Leicester Sq WC2. John Doubleday, 1981. Bronze. Appropriately surrounded by the cinemas of Leicester Sq. Charlie Chaplin, with his characteristic cane and bowler hat, is probably still the cinema's greatest comedian.

Sir Winston Churchill   **4 F5**
Parliament Sq SW1. Ivor Roberts-Jones, 1973. Large bronze statue of one of Britain's greatest statesmen, half-facing the House of Commons.

Crimea Memorial   **4 E4**
Waterloo Pl SW1. Bell, 1859. Figures of Guards cast from melted down cannon taken in battle. A pile of actual cannons decorates the back. Memorial includes a statue of:

Florence Nightingale   **4 E4**
Waterloo Pl SW1. Waller, 1915. She is shown holding an oil lamp, whereas the famous lamp which gave her the name 'The lady with the lamp' was actually a candle lantern.

Oliver Cromwell   **4 F5**
Old Palace Yd SW1. Thornycroft, 1899. Significantly with his back turned to Parliament.

Edward VII   **4 E4**
Waterloo Pl SW1. Sir Bertram Mackennal, 1921. Memorial statue showing the King in military uniform. Bronze and Portland stone.

Queen Elizabeth I   **5 B2**
St Dunstan-in-the-West, Fleet St EC4. Originally stood over Lud Gate. Made during the queen's lifetime in 1586 by William Kerwin, it is one of London's oldest statues.

Eros   **4 E3**
Piccadilly Circus W1. Gilbert, 1893. Officially the Angel of Christian Charity. It is part of the memorial to the Victorian philanthropist Lord Shaftesbury. Made in aluminium. Fully restored in 1984 and returned in 1986 to a site just south of its original position.

George III   **4 E4**
Cockspur St SW1. Wyatt, 1836. The best statue of this king, on a fine spirited horse.

George IV   **4 E4**
Trafalgar Sq WC2. Chantrey, 1834. Rides without boots on a horse without saddle or stirrups. Originally intended for the top of Marble Arch.

George V   **4 F6**
Old Palace Yd SW1. Reid Dick, 1947.

Sir Henry Irving   **4 F3**
By the side of the National Portrait Gallery, St Martin's Pl WC2. Brock, 1910.

James II   **4 E3**
Outside National Gallery, Trafalgar Sq WC2. Grinling Gibbons, 1686. One of London's finest statues.

Dr Samuel Johnson   **5 A2**
St Clement Danes churchyard, Strand WC2. Fitzgerald, 1910.

Abraham Lincoln   **4 F5**
Parliament Sq SW1. Saint-Gaudens, 1920. Replica of the one in Chicago.

Sir Thomas More   **6 E4**
Cheyne Walk SW3. Outside parish church. Bronze of the Tudor statesman and martyr by L. Cubitt Bevis, unveiled in 1969.

Lord Nelson   **4 F4**
On column in Trafalgar Sq WC2. Baily, 1843. The statue is 17ft (5.2m) high; weighs 16 tons. Made of stone, it was hoisted into position in three pieces.

Peter Pan   **3 E4**
Kensington Gardens W2. Frampton, 1912. Charming fairy figure. Erected overnight as a surprise for the children.

Sir Joshua Reynolds   **4 D3**
Forecourt of Burlington House, Piccadilly W1. Drury, 1931.

Richard I   **4 F6**
Old Palace Yd SW1. Marochetti, 1860.

Franklin D. Roosevelt   **4 B3**
Grosvenor Sq W1. Reid Dick, 1948.

Royal Artillery Memorial   4 B5
Hyde Park Corner SW1. Jagger, 1925.
London's best war memorial, with its
great stone howitzer aimed at the Somme
where the men it commemorates lost
their lives. The bronze figures of soldiers
are possibly the finest sculptures to be
seen in London.

Captain Scott   4 E4
Waterloo Pl SW1. Lady Scott, 1915. 'Scott
of the Antarctic' modelled by his widow.

William Shakespeare   4 E3
Leicester Sq WC2. Fontana after
Scheemakers, 1740. Copy (1874) of the
memorial in Westminster Abbey for which
David Garrick is said to have posed.

Victoria Memorial   4 D5
In front of Buckingham Palace SW1.
Brock, 1911. Impressive memorial to
Queen Victoria which includes a fine
dignified figure of the queen, the best of
the many statues of her.

George Washington   4 E3
Outside National Gallery, Trafalgar Sq
WC2. Replica of the statue by Houdon in
the Capitol at Richmond, Virginia, and
presented by that state in 1921.

Duke of Wellington   5 E2
Outside Royal Exchange EC3. Chantrey,
1844. Like the same sculptor's statue of
George IV, his horse has no saddle or
stirrups and he wears no boots.

Duke of Wellington   4 B5
Hyde Park Corner SW1. Boehm, 1888.
Equestrian statue of the Duke. The
memorial is distinguished by four well-
modelled figures of soldiers in full kit. The
Duke rides his favourite horse,
Copenhagen, and he looks towards
Apsley House, in which he lived.

William III   4 E4
St James's Sq SW1. Bacon, 1807. First
proposed in 1697 but not erected until
1808. Beneath one of the horse's hooves
is the molehill over which the horse stum-
bled, killing the king.

Duke of York   4 E4
On column, Waterloo Pl SW1.
Westmacott, 1834. Cost £30,000 and
was paid for by deducting a day's pay
from every officer and man in the British
Army.

Modern outdoor sculpture

*Good modern sculpture on open view is
still rather rare in London – a reflection of
a lack of both private and public commissions – although the royal parks are
regularly used for major displays and*
*there is a permanent exhibition (with
changing exhibits) in Regent's Park
(south-east corner near Chester Gate
NW1, 1 D4). Among the best
permanently-sited pieces are:*

Michael Ayrton (1921-1974)
Postman's Park, Aldersgate EC2.
'Minotaur' expressing energy.   5 D2

Geoffrey Clark (b. 1924)
Thorn Bldg, Upper St Martin's La
WC2. Bronze relief.   4 F3

Sir Jacob Epstein (1880-1959)
Heythrop College, 11 Cavendish Sq W1.
Bronze 'Madonna and Child', 1952.   4 C2
St James's Park underground station.
Fine sculpture of 'Day and Night'.   4 E6
South of Nursery Enclosure, Hyde Park.
'Rima'.   3 F4
Edinburgh Gate, Hyde Park. 'Return of
Spring'.   3 G5

Elizabeth Frink (b. 1930)
Carlton Tower Hotel, Cadogan Sq SW1.
Beaten copper relief on façade.   6 F1

**Dame Barbara Hepworth (1903-
1975)**
John Lewis Store, Oxford St W1. Bronze
relief.   4 C2
State House, High Holborn WC1. Fine
abstract 'Meridian'.   5 A1
Hyde Park. 'Family of Man' (on indefinite
loan).   3 F4

Karin Jonzen (b. 1914)
Bassishaw Highwalk, south of London
Wall EC2. 'Beyond Tomorrow', male and
female figures.   5 D1

David Kemp (b. 1945)
Hay's Galleria, Tooley St SE1. 'The
Navigators', a kinetic sculpture in bronze
with moving parts.   5 F4

Bernard Meadows (b. 1915)
TUC Building, Great Russell St WC1.
Bronze group.   4 E2

Henry Moore (1898-1986)
Abingdon St Gdns SW1. 'Knife Edge
Two-Piece' bronze, 1967.   4 F6
Kensington Gardens SW7. 'The Arch'
overlooking the Long Water. Marble,
1980.   3 E4
Riverside House, Millbank SW1. 'Locking
Pieces' bronze in garden close to
Vauxhall Bridge.   7 E3
Time & Life Bldg, New Bond St W1.
Fine stone relief; open sculpture court-
yard.   4 C3

Walenty Pytel (b. 1941)
Parliament Sq SW1. 'Silver Jubilee
Fountain', a highly elaborate and
impressive steel sculpture.   4 F5

Michael Sandle (b. 1936)
Dorset Rise EC4. 'St George and The
Dragon'. Powerful bronze horse and
rider.   5 C2

Places of worship

In their buildings, ruins, sites and associations, London's churches and cathedrals represent nearly 1400 years of Christianity in Britain (the first St Paul's Cathedral is ascribed to the beginning of the 7thC). Norman work survives in St Helen's Bishopsgate and Westminster Abbey and at the time of the Great Fire of 1666 there were over 100 churches in the present area of the City of London, a density peculiar to English cities.

The Fire set the scene for Wren's great rebuilding programme, including St Paul's Cathedral and 50 churches, most of which have survived later demolitions and war damage. Hawksmoor and Inigo Jones were other 17th and early 18thC church designers whose work we can still admire.

The Victorians too were great church builders and the 19thC produced a wealth of new churches, many of them in the triumphant Gothic style, for Anglican and other denominations. The neo-Byzantine Westminster RC Cathedral of 1903 is outstanding.

Non-Christian religions also have their part in London's history, with synagogues as at Bevis Marks and, most recently, the Regent's Park Mosque for London's growing Islamic community. London's most important religious buildings are listed below.

Abbeys & cathedrals

St George's RC Cathedral,   **5 B6**
Southwark
Lambeth Rd (opp Imperial War Museum) SE1. 0171-928 5256. By A.W. Pugin, 1848. Spire never completed. Burnt out in last war and interior restored in 1958.

St Paul's Cathedral   **5 D2**
Ludgate Hill EC4. 0171-248 4619/2705. Wren's greatest work; built 1675-1710 replacing the previous church destroyed by the Great Fire. Superb dome, porches and funerary monuments. Contains magnificent stalls by Grinling Gibbons. Ironwork by Tijou, paintings by Thornhill and mosaics by Salviati and Sir William Richmond. *OPEN 07.15-18.00 Mon-Sun except during special services. Crypt & Ambulatory OPEN 08.30-16.15 Mon-Sat. Galleries OPEN 09.00-16.15 Mon-Sat. Charge.*

Southwark Cathedral   **5 E4**
Borough High St SE1. 0171-407 3708. Much restored. Built by Augustinian Canons but destroyed by fire in 1206.

Beautiful early English choir and retro-choir. Tower built c1520, nave by Blomfield 1894-7. Work by Comper includes the altar screen. Chapter House developed in 1988 with restaurant. *OPEN 08.30-18.00 Mon-Fri. Music recitals 13.10-13.45 Mon (organ) & Tue. Evensong at 17.30 Tue & Fri.*

Westminster Abbey   **4 F6**
(The Collegiate Church of St Peter in Westminster) Broad Sanctuary SW1. 0171-222 5152. Original church by Edward the Confessor 1065. Rebuilding commenced in 1245 by Henry III who was largely influenced by the new French cathedrals. Completed by Henry Yevele and others 1376-1506 (towers incomplete and finished by Hawksmoor 1734). Henry VII Chapel added 1503; fine perpendicular with wonderful fan vaulting. The Abbey contains the Coronation Chair, and many tombs and memorials of the Kings and Queens of England and their subjects. Starting place for pilgrimage to Canterbury Cathedral. Nave and Cloisters *OPEN 09.20-16.00 Mon-Fri, 09.00-14.00 & 15.45-17.00 Sat. Free. Services only Sun. Museum OPEN 10.30-16.00 daily. Charge. Restoration work in final stages at time of publication.*

Westminster RC Cathedral   **4 D6**
Ashley Pl SW1. 0171-834 7452. Early Christian Byzantine-style church by J.F. Bentley, 1903. The most important Roman Catholic church in England. Fine interior.

Churches & other places of worship

All Hallows-by-the-Tower   **5 F3**
Byward St EC3. 0171-481 2928. Foundations date from AD675. Audaciously restored by Lord Mottistone after bombing. Fine copper steeple. Crypt museum with Roman pavement. Brass rubbing. Organ recitals every *Thur lunchtime. Church OPEN 09.00-18.00 Mon-Fri, 10.00-17.00 Sat & Sun. Free. Crypt OPEN 10.00-16.30 Mon-Fri, 11.00-16.00 Sat, 13.00-16.00 Sun (except during services). Charge (includes taped guide).*

All Hallows London Wall   **5 F2**
83 London Wall EC2. 0171-588 3388. Rebuilt 1765-7 by Dance junior. Guild church. Charming interior.

All Saints Margaret St   **4 D2**
Margaret St W1. 0171-636 9961. Gothic Revival masterpiece. William Butterfield, 1859. Paintings by Ninian Comper. *OPEN 07.00-19.00 Mon-Sun. Free.*

All Souls Langham Place   **4 C1**
Langham Pl W1. 0171-580 4357. John

Nash, 1822-4; Nash's only church. Corinthian columns with needle spire. Restored after bomb damage. Interior refitted 1976. Exterior restored 1987-8.

Bevis Marks Synagogue **5 F2**
Heneage La (off Bevis Marks) EC3. 0171-626 1274. Avis, 1700. Fine windows. Brass chandeliers from Amsterdam.

Brompton Oratory **6 E1**
Brompton Rd SW7. 0171-589 4811. Large Italian Mannerist-style church designed by H. Gribble, 1884. Fine marbled interior and original statues from the Cathedral of Siena. Noted choral tradition. *OPEN 06.30-20.00.*

Capel Bedyddwyr Cymreig **4 D2**
30 Eastcastle St W1. Highly imaginative Welsh Baptist chapel.

Central Hall **4 E5**
Storey's Gate SW1. 0171-222 8010. 'Cathedral of Methodism' 1912 by Lanchester & Rickards, the greatest exponents of the Baroque style in Edwardian London. Listed building.

Chapel Royal of St John **5 G3**
White Tower, Tower of London EC3. The oldest Norman church in London, c1085, still retains its original pillars.

Chelsea Old Church, All Saints **6 E4**
Chelsea Embankment SW3. 0171-352 5627. Rebuilt after severe bombing. 13thC chapels, one restored by Sir Thomas More, 1528. Jacobean altar table, many historic monuments and capitals attributed to Holbein.

Christ Church Newgate St **5 D2**
Newgate St EC1. Wren, 1691. Only the tower (1704) and four walls remain.

Christ Church Spitalfields **5 G1**
Commercial St E1. 0171-247 7202. Fine church by Hawksmoor, 1714-29, partly restored. Notable tower and spire, and lofty interior. Crypt a rehabilitation centre for alcoholics. Annual international music festival in *Jun*.

Christ the King **1 F5**
Gordon Sq WC1. 0171-387 3005. Catholic Apostolic church. Cruciform, cathedral-like building by Raphael Brandon, 1853. West front and tower unfinished.

City Temple **5 C2**
Holborn Viaduct EC1. 0171-583 5532. City's Free Church, 1874, by Lockwood, restored after bombing. Only continuing Free Church in own building within the City of London.

Cole Abbey Presbyterian Church **5 D3**
Queen Victoria St EC4. 0171-248 5213. Affiliated to the Free Church of Scotland. Originally by Wren, 1671-81, and restored

with similar spire after bombing. Rich stained glass by Keith New.

Crown Court Church of Scotland, Covent Garden **4 F2**
Russell St WC2. 0171-836 5643. Longest-established Presbyterian church south of the border, dating from 1719. It was rebuilt in 1909 and is situated in the heart of London's theatreland.

Dutch Church **5 E2**
7 Austin Friars EC2. 0171-588 1684. 13thC origin, given to Dutch Protestants after the Reformation. Rebuilt 1950-3 after 1940 destruction. Part of the present structure dates from 1550. *OPEN 11.00-15.00 Mon-Thur.*

French Protestant Church **4 E2**
9 Soho Sq W1. 0171-437 5311. By Aston Webb in 1893, exterior surprisingly like an office building.

Grosvenor Chapel **4 B3**
South Audley St W1. 0171-499 1684. 'Colonial'-looking chapel built 1730. Decorations by Comper added in 1912.

The Guards Chapel **4 E5**
Wellington Barracks, Birdcage Walk SW1. 0171-414 3228. Original chapel, built 1838 was destroyed in 1944 with the loss of 121 lives. New chapel, finished 1963, is austere but complements the original surviving apse.

Holy Trinity **6 G2**
Sloane St SW1. 0171-730 7270. By Sedding in 1890. London's most elaborate church of the 'Arts and Crafts' movement.

Immaculate Conception **4 B3**
114 Mount St W1. 0171-493 7811. 1849 by J.J. Scoles. Headquarters of the British Province of the Jesuit Order.

London Central Mosque **1 A4**
146 Park Rd NW8. 0171-724 3363. A graceful building on the edge of Regent's Park, it was completed in 1978 and is the religious centre for London's Muslims.

Notre Dame de France **4 E3**
5 Leicester Pl WC2. 0171-437 9363. French Catholic church of London. First church 1865, rebuilt 1955 after bombing. Circular. Large Aubusson tapestry, mural by Jean Cocteau.

Queen's Chapel of the Savoy **4 G3**
Savoy Hill, Strand WC2. 0171-836 7221. Late perpendicular style, built 1508. Some 13th and 15thC glass.

The Queen's Chapel, St James's Palace **4 D4**
Marlborough Rd SW1. 0171-930 3007. Built by Inigo Jones, 1623. Fine restored woodwork and coffered ceiling. *OPEN (for services only) Easter-end Jul 08.30 & 11.15 Sun.*

St Alban Holborn   **5 B1**
Brooke St EC1. 0171-405 1831. Originally by Butterfield, 1859. Rebuilt by Adrian Scott after bomb damage. Soaring arches. Sculpture and huge mural by Hans Feibusch.

St Alban Wood St   **5 D1**
Wood St EC2. Wren. Only the tower remains 1697-8 (modern pinnacles).

St Andrew Holborn   **5 B2**
Holborn Circus EC4. 0171-353 3544. Largest of Wren's parish churches. 1686. Restored 1961 after bombing. Pulpit, font, organ and tomb of Thomas Coram, from the chapel of the 18thC Foundling Hospital.

St Andrew-by-the-Wardrobe   **5 C3**
Queen Victoria St EC4. 0171-248 7546. Fine City church by Wren, 1685-95. Restored 1961, after bomb damage.

St Anne Limehouse
Commercial Rd E14. 0171-987 1502. Hawksmoor, built 1712-24. Highest public clock (added 1839) in Britain after Big Ben. Organ, built for 1851 Great Exhibition, is one of finest unaltered Victorian examples in the country.

St Anne Soho   **4 E3**
57 Dean St W1. Steeple only, by Cockerell, 1802-6. The church, by Wren, was destroyed by bombing.

St Anne & St Agnes (Lutheran)   **5 D2**
Gresham St EC2. 0171-373 5566. Wren, 1676-87. Attractive church restored after bomb damage. Regular lunchtime concerts.

St Augustine Watling St   **5 D2**
Watling St EC4. Wren, 1687. Only tower remains after bombing, with new spire after the original design. Now part of cathedral choir school.

St Bartholomew-the-Great   **5 C1**
West Smithfield EC1. 0171-606 5171. The oldest church in London. Norman choir of Augustinian Priory 1123 with later Lady Chapel; unusual oriel window and the only pre-Reformation font in City. Tomb of founder, who also founded St Bartholomew's Hospital, and other fine monuments. Hogarth was christened here 1697.

St Bartholomew-the-Less   **5 C1**
West Smithfield EC1. 0171-601 8888. Inside 'Barts' hospital (serves as its parish church). Tower and west end medieval, rest rebuilt 1789 and 1823. Octagonal interior.

St Benet Church   **5 D3**
Queen Victoria St EC4. 0171-723 3104. Attractive church by Wren, 1683, on foundations dating from 1098. Brick with stone dressings. A Guild Church. Also

known as the Metropolitan Welsh Church. The Chapel of the College of Arms. Burial place of Inigo Jones.

St Botolph Aldersgate   **5 D2**
Aldersgate EC1. 0171-623 6970. Nathaniel Wright, 1788, with additions in 1831. Charming interior.

St Botolph Aldgate   **5 G2**
Aldgate High St EC3. 0171-283 1670. Rebuilt 1741-4 by Dance senior. Restored by Bentley, 1880s, and again 1966. Fine monuments. Lies north and south. Renatus Harris organ (1674). Peal of eight bells (1744). Recent large addition to the crypt, which is a centre for homeless single people.

St Botolph without Bishopsgate   **5 F2**
Bishopsgate EC2. 0171-588 1053. First recorded 1212, rebuilt 1571-2, demolished 1724. Rebuilt 1725-9 by James Gould. Baroque steeple at east end. Large churchyard. Irreplaceable stained glass was destroyed in a bomb attack in April 1993.

St Bride's Church   **5 B2**
Fleet St EC4. 0171-353 1301. Wren, 1670-84. Famous spire 1701-4. Restored after bomb damage. Fine City church.

St Clement Danes   **5 A2**
Strand WC2. 0171-242 8282. First built by the Danes, 9thC. Spire by Gibbs. Rebuilt by Wren, 1681. Destroyed in air raids 1941 and restored and rededicated in 1958 as the central church of the RAF. Bells ring 'Oranges and Lemons' occasionally. Fine moulded plaster ceiling.

St Clement nr Eastcheap   **5 E3**
Clements La, King William St EC4. 0171-283 8154. Wren, 1687. Restored by Butterfield, 1872, and by Comper, 1933. Notable 17thC woodwork and fine organ (1695).

St Columba   **6 F1**
Pont St SW1. 0171-584 2321. Church of Scotland, new building by Maufe, 1950-5, replacing destroyed Victorian one.

St Cyprian   **1 B5**
Glentworth St, Clarence Gate NW1. 0171-402 6979. Outstanding example of a complete church by Comper, in his early style. 1903. Renowned interior.

St Dunstan-in-the-East   **5 F3**
St Dunstan's Hill EC3. Only the delicately poised spire by Wren remains. 1696-1701.

St Dunstan-in-the-West   **5 B2**
Fleet St EC4. 0171-242 6027. Octagonal church by John Shaw, 1831-3. Early example of Gothic Revival restored in 1950. Fine lantern-steeple clock with

'striking jacks' from old church. Early statue of Elizabeth I from Ludgate. Orthodox chapel with icon screen brought from Antim Monastery in Bucharest. Monuments to an honest solicitor, and to a swordsman. Also Lord Mayor's sword from Battle of Culloden 1745.

St Dunstan All Saints, Stepney
White Horse Rd E1. 0171-790 4194. Mother church of East London, late 15thC. Mostly rebuilt. Fine interior. Notable Saxon crucifix.

St Edmund the King **5 E2**
Lombard St EC3. 0171-623 6970. Rebuilt by Wren, 1670-90, and lies north and south, like the pre-Fire church. Restored after slight damage in both world wars. Fine woodwork, distinctive 90ft (27.5m) steeple.

St Ethelburga-the-Virgin **5 F2**
70 Bishopsgate EC2. Site of one of London's oldest churches (15thC) which was destroyed in a bomb attack in April 1993.

St Etheldreda **5 B1**
Ely Pl EC1. 0171-405 1061. Former bishop's chapel built c1300 with possibly Roman walls in the crypt, restored in the 19thC to Catholic use. Some fine post-war glass.

St George Bloomsbury **4 F1**
Bloomsbury Way WC1. 0171-405 3044. Hawksmoor, 1730. Unusual tower modelled on the Mausoleum at Halicarnassus. Statue of George I on top of steeple, posing as St George. Six-column Corinthian portico. Classical interior.

St George Hanover Sq **4 C2**
St George St W1. 0171-629 0874. Classical church by John James, 1721-4 with 16thC Flemish glass in the east windows. Restored by Blomfield in 1894. Altarpiece of 'Last Supper' by Kent.

St George-in-the-East
Cannon Street Rd E1. 0171-709 9074. Remarkable church by Hawksmoor, 1715-23. Modern rebuilding (1964) within the bomb-ruined walls.

St George the Martyr Southwark **5 D5**
Borough High St SE1. 0171-407 2796. A Georgian building with fine ornamental plaster ceiling. 'Little Dorrit's' church. Rebuilt 1734-6 by J. Price.

St Giles Cripplegate
Fore St EC2. 0171-606 3630. 12thC church rebuilt 16thC then restored 1952 after bombing. Where Cromwell was married and contains Milton's grave. Remains of London Wall in churchyard.

St Giles in the Fields **4 E2**
St Giles High St WC2. 0171-240 2532. Flitcroft, 1731-3. Well restored 1952. Wesley's pulpit from West St Chapel is here.

St Helen Bishopsgate **5 F2**
Great St Helen's EC3. 0171-283 2231. Built 1150. Has two naves, northern originally a nunnery, southern parochial. Contains fine monuments of many City worthies, some excellent brasses and a notable organ case (Victorian). Original nun's squint.

St James **3 E3**
Sussex Gdns W2. 0171-723 8119. Rebuilt to the designs of Street, 1881. Contains an unusual stained glass memorial to Alexander Fleming showing him at work in his laboratory. The discovery of penicillin was made nearby at St Mary's Hospital.

St James Bermondsey
Jamaica Rd SE1. 0171-232 2329. A Waterloo church built by James Savage in 1825-9 in the style of a Greek temple. Four columned porticos. Has a purpose-built Bishop organ with rare manual keyboard for pedal organ. Original peal of ten bells. Golden dragon weathervane.

St James Clerkenwell **2 D5**
Clerkenwell Grn EC1. 0171-833 8947. Rebuilt 1788-92 by James Carr. Fine Wren-like steeple. Good interior. Some monuments from old church.

St James Garlickhythe **5 D3**
Garlick Hill EC4. 0171-236 1719. Fine City church by Wren, 1673-83, well-restored steeple 1717. Good ironwork and woodwork.

St James Piccadilly **4 D3**
Piccadilly W1. 0171-734 4511. Wren, 1684. Restored by Sir Albert Richardson in 1954 after serious bomb damage. Reredos and organ casing by Grinling Gibbons. Famous 'Father Smith' organ presented by Queen Mary in 1691 and brought from Whitehall Palace. Healing ministry. Major programme of concerts and lectures. Lunchtime recitals every *Wed, Thur & Fri at 13.10.* Restaurant *OPEN 10.00-19.00 Mon-Sat, 10.00-16.00 Sun. Donation requested.*

St James the Less Westminster **7 D2**
Thorndike St, Vauxhall Bridge Rd SW1. 0171-821 9865. G.E. Street, 1860; largely unaltered, its furnishings are complete. Notice the patterned brick walls.

St John Clerkenwell **2 D5**
St John's Sq EC1. 0171-253 6644. Originally a round church. Became a parish church in 1723. 15thC nave, 16thC

gate, well-preserved crypt dating from 1140.

St John Smith Sq   **7 E1**
Smith Sq SW1. 0171-222 1061. Nicknamed 'Queen Anne's Footstool'. Built by Archer, 1721-8. Gutted by fire 1742; interior re-designed. Blitzed 1941; restored to Archer's original design by charitable trust. Opened as a concert hall in 1969. Footstool Gallery has monthly exhibitions. Restaurant & gallery *OPEN 10.00-17.00 Mon-Fri. Also OPEN eves if there is a concert. Free.*

St John's Wood Church
St John's Wood High St NW8. 0171-722 4378. Thomas Hardwick, 1813. White and gold interior with carved ceilings supported by impressive Doric and Etruscan columns.

St John Waterloo Rd   **5 B4**
Waterloo Rd SE1. 0171-633 9819. Bedford, 1824. Four walls, steeple and portico remained after bombing. Restored by Ford in 1951 as part of the Festival of Britain. There was a fine reredos which has now been replaced by Hans Feibusch murals.

St Katherine Cree   **5 F2**
Leadenhall St EC3. 0171-283 5733. Rebuilt under Bishop Laud 1631 in hybrid Gothic and classical style, restored 1962. 17thC organ once played by Handel.

St Lawrence Jewry   **5 D2**
Gresham St EC2. 0171-600 9478. Wren, 1671-7. Tower and four walls remained after bombing. Restored in 1957. Replicas of steeple and original Wren ceiling. Official church of City Corporation.

St Leonard Shoreditch
119 High St E1. 0171-739 2063. Rebuilt 1736-40 by Dance senior. Fine steeple and woodwork, including the beautiful clock surround. *OPEN Mon-Fri 12.00-14.00. Free.*

St Luke Chelsea   **6 E3**
Sydney St SW3. 0171-351 7365/6. Savage, 1824. First church to be built in sumptuous style of early Gothic revival. Dickens married here.

St Magnus the Martyr   **5 E3**
Lower Thames St EC3. 0171-626 4481. Wren, 1671-87. One of Wren's finest steeples, 185ft (55.9m) high, added 1705-6. Anglo-Catholic baroque interior. Fine pulpit and furnishings.

St Margaret Lothbury   **5 E2**
Lothbury EC2. 0171-606 8330. Wren, 1686-93. Steeple 1698-1700. Fine fittings, including a 17thC open-work screen. Bust of Ann Simpson by Nollekens. Grinling Gibbons font and communion rail.

St Margaret Pattens   **5 F3**
Rood La, Eastcheap EC3. 0171-623 6630. Church by Wren, 1684-9. Fine spire 1698-1702. Canopied pews.

St Margaret Westminster   **4 F5**
Parliament Sq SW1. 0171-222 6382. Rebuilt 1486-1523 and again after repeated war damage. Splendid early 16thC east window and an excellent series of stained-glass windows by John Piper. The parish church of the House of Commons. Many distinguished marriages and burials.

St Martin-in-the-Fields   **4 F3**
Trafalgar Sq WC2. 0171-930 1862. James Gibbs, 1722-6. Famous spire and portico. Fine Venetian east window and white and gold moulded plaster ceiling. Handsome pulpit. The open space of Trafalgar Square creates a pleasing prominence for the church. Lunchtime music *13.05-14.00 Mon-Wed & Fri. Free.* Evening concerts *19.30-21.30 Thur-Sat (phone 0171-839 8362 for tickets).* Crypt *OPEN 10.00-20.00 Mon-Sat, 12.00-18.00 Sun*; gift and bookshop *OPEN 10.00-19.30 Mon-Sat, 12.00-18.00 Sun*; brass rubbing centre *OPEN 10.00-18.00 Mon-Sat, 12.00-18.00 Sun (Charge)*; craft market and gallery *OPEN 10.00-18.00 Mon-Sun.* Café *OPEN 10.00-20.00 Mon-Sat, 12.00-18.00 Sun.*

St Martin Ludgate   **5 C2**
Ludgate Hill EC4. 0171-248 6054. Wren, 1677-84, now restored. Elegant spire, fine interior, notable woodwork, *Ascension* by Benjamin West.

St Mary Abbots Kensington   **3 C5**
Kensington Church St W8. 0171-937 5136. Scott, 1872. Transitional between early-English and decorated style.

St Mary Abchurch   **5 E3**
Abchurch Yd EC4. 0171-626 0306. Wren, 1681-7. Fine ceiling by William Snow. Reredos by Grinling Gibbons.

St Mary Aldermary   **5 D2**
Watling St EC4. 0171-248 4906. Late Gothic rebuilt by Wren. Fine fan vaulting with saucer domes. Pulpit, west door and wooden sword rest by Grinling Gibbons, 1682.

St Mary-at-Hill   **5 F3**
Lovat La EC3. 0171-626 4184. Wren, 1676, tower, 1788. The interior which featured box pews and magnificent fittings has been destroyed by fire.

St Mary-at-Lambeth   **7 F1**
Beside Lambeth Palace, Lambeth Rd SE1. 0171-261 1891. Rebuilt (except tower) by P. Hardwick, 1850. The tomb of Captain Bligh (Mutiny on the *Bounty*) has been restored. Now houses the Museum of Garden History.

St Mary Islington   **2 D2**
Upper St N1. 0171-226 3400. Launcelot Dowbiggin, 1750. Restored 1956, after bomb damage. Fine baroque steeple.

St Marylebone Parish Church   **1 C5**
Marylebone Rd NW1. 0171-935 7315. Thomas Hardwick, 1813-17. Thomas Harris added the chancel in 1884. Imposing white and gold interior.

St Mary-le-Bow   **5 D2**
Cheapside EC2. 0171-248 5139. The church of 'Bow Bells' fame by Wren, 1670-83. Crypt dates from 1087. Restored by Laurence King after bomb damage. Superb steeple.

St Mary-le-Strand   **4 G3**
Strand WC2. 0171-836 3205. James Gibbs, 1714-17. A perfect small baroque church in the middle of the Strand, sadly encircled by heavy traffic. The official church of the WRNS.

St Mary Magdalen Bermondsey 5 F6
Bermondsey St SE1. 0171-232 2329. Rebuilt 1680. Charming classical interior. Gothic west end, 1830.

St Mary Somerset   **5 D3**
Upper Thames St EC4. Wren, 1694. Only the imposing eight-pinnacled tower remains.

St Mary Woolnoth   **5 E2**
Lombard St EC3. 0171-626 9701. Remarkable 1716-27 Baroque Guild Church by Hawksmoor. Church of England services on weekdays. Lunchtime relaxation sessions.

St Michael Chester Square   **7 A2**
Chester Sq SW1. 0171-730 8889. Cundy, 1846. War memorial chapel added in 1920. Fine coloured alabaster.

St Michael Paternoster Royal   5 D3
College Hill EC4. 0171-248 5202. Wren, 1694, steeple 1713. Recently restored. Dick Whittington buried here (commemorative stained-glass window). Tower used as office by The Missions to Seamen.

St Michael-upon-Cornhill   **5 E2**
Cornhill EC3. 0171-626 8841. Wren, 1677, much restored by Scott. Handsome Gothic tower added 1722. Twelve magnificent bells which are always rung on Sundays. First rate choir and organ.

St Olave Hart St   **5 F3**
8 Hart St EC3. 0171-488 4318. Originally early 13thC, on the site of a wooden church of 1080, it was enlarged in 1450. Samuel Pepys' church. Restored by Glanfield after bomb damage. Fine vestry and crypt.

St Pancras New Church   **1 F4**
Euston Rd NW1. 0171-387 8250. W. and H. Inwood, 1822. One of the finest Neo-

classical churches in Britain, it is a copy of the Erechtheion in Athens complete with caryatids and Ionic columns. The largest unsupported ceiling in England. Noted for its choir and organ recitals.

St Pancras Old Church   **1 F3**
Pancras Rd NW1. 0171-387 7301. Church with country atmosphere. Added to and transformed 1848. 4thC foundations. Saxon altar stone (AD600). Third oldest Christian site in Europe. A monument to Sir John Soane, which he designed himself, in the churchyard.

St Paul Covent Garden   **4 F3**
Covent Garden WC2. 0171-836 5221. Fine 'ecclesiastical barn' by Inigo Jones affectionately known as the 'Actors' Church'. Rebuilt by Thomas Hardwick after fire of 1795. Pleasant gardens at Bedford St entrance.

St Paul Knightsbridge   **4 B5**
32a Wilton Pl SW1. 0171-235 3460. Victorian church by Cundy, 1843. Chancel by Bodley. Rich, colourful interior.

St Peter-ad-Vincula   **5 G3**
Tower of London, Tower Hill EC3. 0171-709 0765. Much restored church built about 1512. Many historic monuments. Admission by guided tour only. Frequent tours (except in bad weather) from 09.45 Mon-Sat & Sun afternoons. Charge (included in entrance charge to Tower of London). Sun services at 09.15 & 11.00.

St Peter-upon-Cornhill   **5 E2**
Cornhill EC3. 0171-626 9483. Very fine church by Wren, 1677-87. Oldest church site in City, reputedly AD179. Organ built by Schmidt. Fine carved screen. 14th and 15thC plays performed at Xmas.

St Sepulchre Without Newgate 5 C2
Holborn Viaduct EC1. 0171-248 1660. Rebuilt in 15thC, 1667 and again in the 18th and 19thC. Tombs of Sir Henry Wood and Captain John Smith. Execution bell and the Bells of Old Bailey from the nursery rhyme. Recently closed – the building's future is uncertain at time of publication.

St Stephen Walbrook   **5 D2**
Walbrook EC4. 0171-283 4444. Masterpiece by Wren, 1672-9; steeple 1714-17. Dome, with eight arches, supported by Corinthian pillars, all beautifully restored. Directly under the dome is an intricately carved cylindrical altar in Roman travertine marble sculpted by Henry Moore. Fine fittings. Lord Mayor of London's church and the home since 1953 of 'The Samaritans' who help the suicidal and desperate.

St Vedast   **5 D2**
Foster La EC2. Founded in the Middle
Ages, rebuilt by Wren after the Great Fire
and rebuilt again following bomb damage
in 1940. Beautifully restored and cleaned
to expose parts of the old church. Grinling
Gibbons carvings.

The Temple Church   **5 B3**
Inner Temple La EC4. 0171-353 1736.
Completely restored. 12thC round nave
and 13thC choir. Fine effigies. Reredos
designed by Wren.

Modern architecture

*'Modern' architecture came relatively late
to England as compared with the USA or
Continental Europe. The 1920s and
1930s provide isolated examples, but the
1950s really set the scene, following the
1951 Festival of Britain, with post-war
reconstruction needs (both from the
intensive bombing and the growth of
London itself) creating the impetus for
massive housebuilding and town centre
redevelopment programmes. Town planning became a major new profession,
intended originally to guide development
in the public interest but, with the property
boom of the 1960s, often acting as the
willing ally of the new commercial devel-
opers with their vast schemes. Too
much in too short a time was the result.
The Barbican, London Wall, Victoria
Street South West and Commercial
Union/P & O, all described in the following
pages, show what could be done, as do
some of the schools, hospitals, new
towns and universities for which British
designers have become internationally
renowned. But much of London, as of
other cities and towns, suffered from the
uncontrolled impact of scale, height, form,
materials and building technology. With
the collapse of the property boom, however, and the growth of conservationist
pressure, both phenomena of the 1970s,
more balanced policies prevailed and
there was growing interest in the saving
and re-use of worthwhile buildings. In the
1980s a series of proposals for major new
office blocks raised controversy, and the
proponents of hi-tech and post-modern
architecture began to make their contributions to the city. Docklands was transformed by a massive building boom and
is a showplace for 1980s architecture;
gleaming office blocks and waterfront
apartments replaced disused warehouses
and derelict wharves. (These can best be
seen from the river.) The most recent*
*building designs in London reflect the
varied contemporary scene and different
ways of approaching architecture. Some
of London's most interesting and innovative buildings are listed below.*

Architectural Dialogue
West Hill House, 6 Swains La N6. 0181-
341 1371. Organise architectural tours of
London. *Phone or write for details.*

Alexandra Road Housing
Abbey Rd NW8. London Borough of
Camden Architects Dept, Neave Brown
1977. Huge new housing development in
which dwellings are stacked in stepped
terraces, like the curving contours of
artificial hills, enclosing the pedestrian
access road in the valley. Dazzling white
concrete finish, the detailing of which is of
a very high standard.

Alton West Estate (Roehampton)
Roehampton La SW15. London County
Council Architects Dept, 1956-61. One of
the earliest and most dramatic of post-
war housing schemes, mixing high and
low-rise blocks in a parkland setting in
what should have been a blueprint for
future developments.

Apollo Victoria   **7 C1**
17 Wilton Rd SW1. E. Walmsley-Lewis,
1928-9. London's first cinema built for the
'talkies', its modernistic exterior, in the
contemporary Continental horizontal
style, concealing a 'fairy palace' of an
interior. Now a theatre.

The Ark
Talgarth Rd W6. Ralph Erskine, 1989-
92. A remarkable and ambitious purpose-built office building, the shape of
which stems from the shape of the site,
bound on one side by the Hammersmith
flyover, and on the other by tube tracks.
Striking feature is the inclined façade;
the cladding comprises alternate bands
of clear and tinted triple glazing with
copper panels between floors. Internal
open terraces overlook a dramatic central atrium; this is the first building in
Europe to be treated as one room. A
glass-sided wall-climber lift travels
through the roof of the atrium to the
Summit Room which is 220ft (67m)
above London; the view sweeps from
Docklands to Heathrow. In spite of
winning several architectural awards,
the building still has vacant space.

Barbican   **5 D1**
London Wall EC2. Chamberlin, Powell &
Bon, 1955. A competition-winning city
within a city, with over 2000 flats, some in
40-storey towers, a water garden, the
restored St Giles' Church, a girls' school,
pubs, shops and an arts centre all linked

by pedestrian decks to the office towers of London Wall (see page 54).

British Telecom Tower   **4 D1**
Howland St W1. Ministry of Public Building & Works, 1964. A dramatic landmark: 580ft (176.9m) tower housing telecommunications equipment and offices. Formerly the Post Office Tower. Marked the start of a trend to high-rise buildings. No longer open to public.

Brunswick Centre   **2 A5**
Brunswick Sq WC1. Patrick Hodgkinson, 1973. A scaled-down version of the megastructure concept. Housing, step- ped upwards in the form of a ziggurat, overlooks a pleasant raised shopping plaza. Car parking out of sight below.

Bush Lane House   **5 E3**
80 Cannon St EC4. Arup Associates, 1976. An inside-out building in which the structural skeleton of stainless steel tubes is exposed, and the transparent skin suspended within a metal cage. This was a solution to the structural constraints imposed by the need to have open floor-plans, unimpeded by columns, and restrictions on foundation depth due to the presence of Cannon Street station.

Canary Wharf Tower
One Canada Sq, Canary Wharf E14. Cesar Pelli, 1988-90. At 800ft (244m) this is the tallest building in the UK. Clad in stainless steel and topped with a pyramid, the 50-storey building boasts a magnificent lobby finished in Italian and Guatemalan marble. 32 passenger lifts operate from the lobby and are the fastest in the country. Canary Wharf itself is full of elegant architecture, stately streets, well-planted squares and outdoor spaces. Used predominantly as office space; several international companies have taken up residence.

Clore Gallery   **7 E2**
Millbank SW1. James Stirling, Michael Wilford & Assoc, 1986. Housing the Turner Museum, the gallery forms a striking visual link between its two neighbours, the Tate Gallery and the Edwardian military hospital. It adopts characteristics from each – classical stonework on one side, brickwork on the other.

Commercial Union and   **5 F2**
P & O Buildings
Leadenhall St EC3. GMW Ptnrs, 1987. These buildings represent a unique occurrence in City redevelopment. The two companies, finding that they both

needed rehousing, merged to jointly hire the Gollins, Melvin, Ward Partnership to design two separate but complementary buildings. Deliberately contrasted, the tall, sheer CU building stands in an open piazza next to the smaller horizontally-emphasised P & O building and creates a striking effect.

Economist Building   **4 D4**
25 St James's St SW1. Alison & Peter Smithson, 1964-6. A very beautiful and harmonious group of buildings with its own raised piazza. The design was intended to demonstrate a general principle for the redevelopment of dense commercial areas and is a rare example of new building in an area with a traditional street pattern.

Embankment Place   **4 F4**
Charing Cross WC2. Terry Farrell, 1987-90. This massive redevelopment of Charing Cross provides 625,000 sq ft of office space, retail outlets and restaurants, as well as the conversion and revitalisation of the vaults below the station. The nine-storey building is suspended from steel arches supported by diameter concrete columns and steel sections. Within the barrel-vault roof are dormer windows, doors and a huge atrium.

Foster Olsen Building
Millwall Dock, Isle of Dogs. Norman Foster, 1970. First building in Britain to make use of special heat and light-reflecting mirror glass. Houses London Docklands Development Corporation.

Hoover Building
Perivale on the A40 just outside Central London. Wallis, Gilbert & Ptnrs, 1932. Blend of Art Deco and Modern Movement. Hoover factory until 1987; restored by Lyons, Sleeman & Hoare; now a superstore.

Lillington Gardens   **7 C2**
Vauxhall Bridge Rd SW1. Darbourne & Darke, 1968-72. Award-winning example of the low-rise, high-density public sector housing which followed the over-exploitation of the tower block. Some tenants have their own gardens.

Lloyds Building   **5 F2**
Lime St EC3. Richard Rogers Ptnrs, 1986. A new hi-tech monument in the City from the architect jointly responsible for the Pompidou Centre in Paris. This multi-faceted, 12-storey, 6-towered structure is the headquarters for the international insurance market. The huge dealing room is housed in a 246ft (75m)-high atrium.

London Bridge City   5 F4
Tooley St SE1. St Martin's Property Corporation, 1987. Includes Hay's Galleria, an elegant and lofty shopping and restaurant arcade with a barrel-vaulted glass roof, reminiscent of Victorian railway architecture or perhaps the Crystal Palace. Also includes No.1 London Bridge, an office building of pink granite, comprised of two towers – one of 12 storeys, in the form of an arch, and the other of nine storeys.

London Central Mosque   1 A4
Regent's Park, entrance by Hanover Gate NW1. Sir Frederick Gibberd & Ptnrs, 1978. Islam's aesthetic and functional needs blend with the constraints of a small and sensitive site adjacent to Nash terraces in a dramatic focus for London's Muslim community.

London Pavilion   4 E3
Piccadilly Circus W1. Chapman Taylor Ptnrs, 1988. Listed building redeveloped as a shopping and leisure complex. The elegant Neo-classical exterior remains as it was originally but two extra storeys have been added and topped with sculptures of classical maidens.

London Wall office development   5 D1
London Wall EC2. Early post-1945 comprehensive planning in a badly blitzed area. Six 18-storey office towers (interspersed with smaller blocks) laid out on the City planners' grid and among the first in Britain with all-glass curtain walling. At the north-west end of London Wall, the most recent tower stands on top of the Museum of London.

Minster Court   5 F3
Mincing La EC3. GMW Ptnrs, 1988-91. Group of three Gothic buildings surrounding a glass-roofed court. Clad in granite with pannelised curtain walling, the buildings contribute to the patchwork of forms and colours which now make up the City. Built to provide high quality office space.

Museum of London   5 D1
London Wall EC2. Powell & Moya, 1978. Highly ingenious planning. The Museum (combining the Guildhall and London Museum collections) serves as the podium for an office block and bridges London Wall to descend into a garden restaurant inside a traffic roundabout.

National Westminster Tower   5 F2
25 Old Broad St EC2. Richard Seifert, 1978-81. Extraordinarily slender, shining structure, the closeness of its vertical lines giving a pin-striped effect. Higher than Telecom Tower. Believed to be the tallest cantilevered building in the world at 600ft (183m), it gracefully dominates London's skyline. Bomb damaged in 1992 and 1993, it has now been upgraded and extended. Houses offices of the National Westminster Bank.

New Zealand House   4 E4
Haymarket SW1. Robert Matthew, Johnson-Marshall & Ptnrs, 1963. A finely modelled 15-storey glass tower on a 4-storey podium. Good material and detailing and an exciting entrance hall. A particularly interesting foil to its flamboyant Victorian neighbour – 'Her Majesty's Theatre'.

Regent's Park Zoo   1 C3
North side of Regent's Park NW1. Contains a number of interesting buildings: Gorilla House by Lubetkin & Tecton 1935; Penguin Pool by Tecton 1935; Aviary by Viscount Snowdon, Cedric Price & Frank Newby 1965-6; Elephant House by Casson, Conder & Ptnrs 1965-6; Small Mammal House by Design Research Unit 1967; Sobell Apes & Monkeys Pavilion 1972; New Lion Terraces 1976; Amphitheatre by John Toovey 1982-5; African Aviary remodelled by John S. Bonnington Ptnrs 1989-90 (previously Eastern Aviary 1863).

St Paul's Cathedral Choir School   5 D2
New Change EC4. Architects' Co-Partnership, 1967. Incorporates the surviving tower of Wren's war-destroyed St Augustine's, a good example of old blended with new and a better neighbour to the Cathedral than the office plaza to its west.

St Katharine's Dock development   5 G4
St Katharine-by-the-Tower E1. The first major bid to regenerate London's former dockland, an £80 million scheme by Taylor Woodrow following a competition in 1969. The World Trade Centre and the Tower Hotel are modern buildings by Renton Howard Wood Levin; the restored Ivory House, a 19thC warehouse, is now apartments, shops, offices, a yacht club and a restaurant.

South Bank Arts Centre   5 A4
Waterloo SE1. First came the Royal Festival Hall (Robert Matthew and Leslie Martin, London County Council Architects Dept), musical focus of the 1951 Festival of Britain which spurred the redevelopment of this run-down area.

Most recent is the Museum of the Moving Image (Avery Assoc) opened in 1988. In between came the National Theatre (Denys Lasdun) completed in 1977 with its three auditoria; the Hayward Art Gallery and the Queen Elizabeth Hall and Purcell Room (now named RFH2 and RFH3 respectively), by the Greater London Council Architects Dept. Concrete dominates.

Sudbury Town underground station
Bridgewater Rd, Wembley, Middx. Charles Holden, 1932. First in a series of modern underground stations.

Thames Flood Barrier
Unity Way, Eastmoor St SE18. This visually and technologically exciting structure is one of the most impressive examples of modern engineering in Europe. Completed in 1982, its gates swing up through 90 degrees from the river bed and create a stainless steel barrage to stem dangerously high tides which periodically threaten London. The Thames Barrier Visitor Centre houses an exhibition and presentation, illuminating the engineering feats involved in the barrier's construction. *Charge.*

Tobacco Dock
Pennington St E1. Terry Farrell, 1989. 19thC former warehouse converted into a shopping and leisure complex. Impressive brick undervaults; roof pierced by clock and gazebo. Development work carried out using original suppliers of materials wherever possible.

Trocadero   4 **E3**
Piccadilly Circus W1. Originally a dance hall, gutted and rebuilt by Robinson and Arun in 1985, the old Victorian façade hides a modern shopping, restaurant and leisure complex.

Vauxhall Cross   7 **E3**
85 Albert Embankment SE1. Terry Farrell, 1990-2. 10-storey glass construction built to house the headquarters of a government department. Rises in layers from the bank of the River Thames to form a group of three blocks linked by glazed courtyards and atria. 25 different make-ups of glass exist throughout the building.

Vickers' Tower   7 **E2**
Millbank SW1. Ronald Ward & Ptnrs, 1960-3. One of London's earliest glass-walled office skyscrapers, and still one of the most elegant.

Victoria Street South West   7 **C1**
redevelopment
Victoria St SW1. Elsom Pack & Roberts, 1975. Broken by a piazza giving for the first time a front view of Westminster Cathedral, this modern commercial development of the highest quality – a notable improvement on the rest of Victoria Street.

Museums and galleries

London's national museums and galleries contain some of the richest collections in the world; and are full of surprising treasures and oddities. They range from the vast British Museum to more recent and specialist additions, many of which incorporate interactive displays and exhibits. Access to special items or collections not on show is willingly given. In addition they offer a service of advice and scholarly reference unequalled anywhere in the world. Note that their reference libraries and print collections are further described under 'Reference libraries'.

The British Museum, the V & A and other national galleries give expert opinions on the age or identity of objects or paintings

– they will not however give you a valuation. Apart from the national art collections in the Tate Gallery, the National Gallery and the National Portrait Gallery, London is further enriched by other, once private, collections, now open to the public.

It has long been a tradition that national museums and galleries are free, but some have now found it necessary to introduce either voluntary contributions or a fixed admission fee. Special exhibitions usually have an entrance fee.

Alexander Fleming Laboratory
Museum   3 **E2**
St Mary's Hospital, Praed St W2. 0171-725 6528. Reconstruction of the 1920s

laboratory where penicillin was discovered. Guided tours by veterans of the antibiotic's introduction into medical practice, when it was hailed as a 'wonder drug'. Video gives the scientific background. *OPEN 10.00-13.00 Mon-Thur (& by appt 14.00-17.00), 10.00-17.00 Fri. CLOSED Sat, Sun & B.hols. Charge.*

Artillery Museum
The Rotunda, Repository Rd, Woolwich Common SE18. 0181-316 5402. The Rotunda was an architectural 'tent' once erected in Carlton House (1814). Notable collection of guns, muskets, ammunition and cannons. Usually *OPEN 13.00-16.00 Mon-Fri, 13.00-17.00 Sat & Sun (to 16.00 Nov-Mar). Please phone to check. Free.*

Bank of England Museum   5 E2
Threadneedle St EC2. 0171-601 5545. History of the 'Old Lady of Threadneedle Street' recreated through reconstructions of Soane's original designs, displays and an interactive video game. Also see the history of the banknote and real gold bars. Exhibits include Bank's first strongbox and the reproduction of the original Banking Hall. Audio cassette tour for visually-handicapped visitors. *Facilities for disabled visitors (phone in advance of visit to organise easier access). OPEN 10.00-17.00 Mon-Fri. Free.*

Barbican Art Gallery   2 E6
Barbican Centre EC2. Recorded information: 0171-588 9023. Large temporary exhibition gallery with a varied programme of international, contemporary and historical displays. *OPEN 10.00-18.45 Mon & Wed-Sat, 12.00-17.45 Tue, 12.00-18.45 Sun & B.hols. Charge.*

HMS *Belfast*   5 F4
Morgan's La, Tooley St SE1. 0171-407 6434. The last survivor of the Royal Navy's World War II war cruisers. Seven decks to explore bringing to life a sailor's experiences of war at sea. *OPEN 10.00-18.00 Mon-Sun (to 16.30 Nov-Mar). Charge.*

Bramah Tea & Coffee Museum   5 G5
The Clove Building, Maguire St SE1. 0171-378 0222. Charts the development of tea and coffee, from the 17th and 18thC coffee houses frequented by Pepys, Boswell and Dr Johnson, to the Boston Tea Party and the 19thC tea clipper races, up to the arrival of instant coffee and tea bags. Café where tea and coffee can be sampled; special Bramah house blends are available. *OPEN 10.00-18.00 Mon-Sun. Charge.*

British Museum   1 G6
Great Russell St WC1. 0171-636 1555. One of the largest and greatest museums in the world. The Egyptian sculpture gallery dramatically highlights colossi of pharaohs, sphinxes, sarcophagi, priests, chantresses, architectural elements and the Rosetta Stone. Upstairs mummies preside, striking a chill and thrill to the heart. Other rooms contain tomb paintings and papyri, including editions of the Book of the Dead, and domestic utensils which were used by the living.

Cycladic, Bronze Age and Archaic remains are part of an extensive Greek and Roman collection. The Elgin marbles, sculptures from the Parthenon in Athens, and Roman pavements, are impressively displayed and still generate a sense of awe. Personified breezes in the Nereid room convey a similar sense of movement and life. The Portland Vase and the bronze head of Augustus with staring glass eyes are remarkable among the Roman exhibits. The Wolfson galleries in the basement also house an immense collection of classical sculpture.

Be sure to see the colossal winged lion and bull with human heads in the Assyrian Transept, the sculptures from the throne-room of the palace at Nimrud and harps and lyres in the Babylonian Room. Europe 1500-1800 brings together European collections from the Renaissance to the Neo-classical period. Coins and Medals, Medieval and Later Antiquities, Oriental Antiquities, Korean Art, Mexican Antiquities, Amaravati Buddhist Sculptures, Japanese Antiquities, Prehistoric and Romano-British Antiquities, Prints and Drawings, are some other collections on view. All are outstanding. Building 1823-47 by Sir Robert Smirke; the domed reading room 1857 is by Sidney Smirke. New collection of prehistoric art from Mexico; exhibition on Sir Norman Foster's Millennium rebuilding project. Museum *OPEN 10.00-17.00 Mon-Sat, 14.30-18.00 Sun. Films Tue-Fri, lectures Tue-Sat, gallery talks. Free. Reading room OPEN to members only. Facilities for disabled visitors (phone 0171-637 7384 for details).*

BT Museum   5 C3
145 Queen Victoria St EC4. 0171-248 7444. History of the rise and development of telecommunication from the early 19thC to the fax machine. Collection of early telegraphs and just about every model of telephone produced in the UK. *OPEN 10.00-17.00 Mon-Fri. CLOSED B.hols. Free.*

Cabinet War Rooms   4 E5
Clive Steps, King Charles St SW1. 0171-930 6961. Fascinating reconstruction of the underground emergency accommo-

dation, comprising a suite of 21 rooms, used by Winston Churchill, his War Cabinet and the Chiefs of Staff of Britain's armed forces during World War II. *OPEN 10.00-18.00 Mon-Sun, from 09.30 in summer (last admittance 17.15). Charge (includes personal audio guide).*

Chelsea Royal Hospital   6 G3
Royal Hospital Rd SW3. 0171-730 0161. Small museum housed in a part of the hospital built in 1819 by Sir John Soane. Prints, drawings, manuscripts, uniforms, medals and other items related to the history of the hospital. *OPEN 10.00-12.00 & 14.00-16.00 Mon-Sat, 14.00-16.00 Sun. CLOSED Sun Oct-Mar & B.hols. Free.*

Church Farm House Museum
Greyhound Hill NW4. 0181-203 0130. A 17thC gabled farmhouse, whose stone-floored kitchen with its huge fireplace is equipped with Victorian cooking utensils. Bedrooms are used for small, changing exhibitions. *OPEN 10.00-17.00 Mon-Thur, 10.00-13.00 & 14.00-17.30 Sat, 14.00-17.30 Sun. CLOSED Fri. Free.*

Commonwealth Institute   3 B6
Kensington High St W8. 0171-603 4535. Centre for Commonwealth education and culture. Promotes the Commonwealth countries through a programme of exhibitions reflecting Commonwealth peoples and issues. Scenery, natural resources, way of life and industrial development of Commonwealth countries. Reference library of current Commonwealth literature. Art exhibitions, craft shop. *OPEN 10.00-17.00 Mon-Sat, 14.00-17.00 Sun. CLOSED B.hols. Charge.*

Courtauld Institute Galleries   4 G3
Somerset House, Strand WC2. 0171-873 2526. The Courtauld Collection of French Impressionists (including fine paintings by Cézanne, Van Gogh, Gauguin) and the Lee, Gambier-Parry and Fry, Hunter & Brouse Collections. The Princes Gate collection of Flemish and Italian Old Masters is on permanent exhibition. *OPEN 10.00-18.00 Mon-Sat, 14.00-18.00 Sun. Charge.*

Crafts Council Gallery   2 C3
44a Pentonville Rd, N1. 0171-278 7700. Six exhibitions a year of contemporary craft; also an information service on where to learn about or buy crafts; picture library which surveys the best of crafts in Britain. Shop. Café. *OPEN 11.00-18.00 Tue-Sat, 14.00-18.00 Sun. CLOSED Mon & B.hols. Free.*

Cricket Museum
Lord's Cricket Ground NW8. 0171-266 3825. Tours of the whole ground including museum run daily throughout the year. Collection includes the 'Ashes', Wisden Trophy and cricket memorabilia. Modern displays include a 'talking head' of W.G. Grace and videos of great performances. Donations. *OPEN 10.30-17.00 Mon-Sat; 13.00-17.00 Sun. Tours at 12.00 & 14.00 Mon-Sun (& 10.00 matchdays). No tours during Test & Cup matches. Charge.*

Cuming Museum
Newington District Library, Walworth Rd SE17. 0171-701 1342. The archaeology and history of Southwark from earliest times to the present. *OPEN 10.00-17.00 Tue. CLOSED Sun, Mon & B.hols. Free.*

Design Museum   5 G4
Butler's Wharf, 28 Shad Thames SE1. 0171-378 6055. A fascinating introduction to 20thC design, technology and consumer culture. Examines the role of design in everyday life through a changing programme of exhibitions and displays – which includes cars, furniture, domestic appliances, graphics and ceramics. Also has a library, bookshop and riverside café/bar. *OPEN 11.30-18.00 Mon-Fri, 12.00-18.00 Sat & Sun. Charge.*

Dulwich Picture Gallery
College Rd SE21. 0181-693 5254. English, Italian, Spanish, Dutch and French paintings exhibited in one of the oldest and most beautiful art galleries in England. Notable works by Rembrandt, Rubens, Canaletto and Gainsborough. Building 1811-14 by Sir John Soane. *OPEN 10.00-17.00 Tue-Fri, 11.00-17.00 Sat, 14.00-17.00 Sun. CLOSED Mon & B.hols. Small charge.*

Fenton House
Hampstead Gro NW3. 0171-435 3471. Built in 1693. The Benton Fletcher collection of early keyboard instruments and the Binning collection of porcelain and furniture. *OPEN Apr-Oct 11.00-17.30 Sat, Sun & B.hols, 14.00-17.30 Mon-Wed; Mar 14.00-17.00 Sat & Sun only. CLOSED Nov-Feb. Charge.*

Florence Nightingale Museum   4 G5
St Thomas' Hospital, 2 Lambeth Palace Rd SE1. 0171-620 0374. Mementoes of the 'Lady with the lamp' together with the recreation of a ward during the Crimean War. Films and lectures. *OPEN 10.00-16.00 Tue-Sun. CLOSED Mon. Charge.*

Geffrye Museum
Kingsland Rd E2. 0171-739 9893. Housed in former 18thC almshouses. Period rooms and furniture from 1600 to the 1950s. Knot garden inspired by parquetry on door of oak livery cupboard. *OPEN 10.00-17.00 Tue-Sat, 14.00-17.00 Sun. CLOSED Mon except B.hols. Free.*

Goldsmiths' Hall   5 D2
Foster La EC2. 0171-606 7010. Fine collection of antique plate. The largest collection of modern silver and jewellery in

the country. *Special public open days: phone for details.*

Guildhall Gallery   **5 D2**
Aldermanbury EC2. 0171-606 3030. Rebuilt gallery scheduled to open in 1997. Selections from the Guildhall's permanent collection may be viewed *by special arrangement only. Free.*

Gunnersbury Park Museum
Gunnersbury Park W3. 0181-992 1612. Items illustrating the local history of Ealing and Hounslow, including archaeology, costume, transport, domestic life, trades, crafts and industries. Housed in former Rothschild Regency country mansion in large park. *OPEN Mar-Sep 13.00-17.00 Mon-Fri, 14.00-18.00 Sat & Sun; Oct-Feb 13.00-16.00 Mon-Sun. Free.*

Hayward Gallery   **5 A4**
Belvedere Rd, South Bank Centre SE1. 0171-928 3144. Changing exhibitions of major works of art arranged by the Arts Council. Fine modern building and river setting. *OPEN 10.00-20.00 Tue & Wed, 10.00-18.00 Thur-Mon. Charge.*

Heinz Gallery   **4 B2**
Royal Institute of British Architects, 21 Portman Sq W1. 0171-580 5533. Regular exhibitions of architectural drawings. *OPEN 11.00-17.00 Mon-Fri, 10.00-13.00 Sat. CLOSED Aug. Free.*

Horniman Museum & Gardens
100 London Rd SE23. 0181-699 2339. Varied collections of ethnography, musical instruments and natural history. Started by Frederick J. Horniman who was a tea magnate and an instinctive collector. The Music Room has computer displays that allow visitors to explore an instrument's evolution, while sampling its sound through headphones. 'Living Waters' aquarium helps visitors discover the complex ecology of waterlife. Education centre and reference library. Gardens. *OPEN 10.30-17.30 Mon-Sat, 14.00-17.30 Sun. CLOSED B.hols. Free.*

Imperial War Museum   **5 B6**
Lambeth Rd SE1. 0171-416 5000. This popular national museum tells the story of wartime from Flanders to the Gulf War. Weapons, aircraft, submarines, sound and film exhibits, art galleries. The 'Blitz and Trench Experience', multi-sensory displays, and operation 'Jericho', where visitors can experience at first hand what it was like to fly with the RAF on their daring 1944 raid over France, are not to be missed. Education and research programmes. Guided tours *(by arrangement – phone 0171-416 5350).* Shop and café. *OPEN 10.00-18.00 Mon-Sun. Charge (free after 16.30).*

Institute of Contemporary   **4 E4**
Arts (ICA)
Nash House, The Mall SW1. 0171-930 0493. Three galleries in which changing exhibitions explore new themes and media in contemporary art. Also two cinemas, theatre, lunchtime and evening talks; bar, restaurant and bookshop. *OPEN 12.00-19.30 Mon-Sun, to 21.00 Fri. Charge.*

Iveagh Bequest, Kenwood
Kenwood House, Hampstead La NW3. 0181-348 1286. Fine house by Robert Adam. Paintings by Rembrandt, Vermeer, Reynolds and Gainsborough. Also sculpture and 18thC English furniture. Music and poetry recitals. *OPEN Apr-Sep 10.00-18.00 Mon-Sun; Oct-Mar 10.00-16.00 Mon-Sun. Free.*

Jewish Museum   **1 D2**
129-131 Albert St NW1. 0171-284 1997. Jewish festivals and history illustrated by ceremonial objects. Two audio-visual programmes. Shop. *OPEN 10.00-16.00 Sun-Thur. CLOSED Fri, Sat & Jewish hols. Charge.*

London Canal Museum
12-13 New Wharf Rd N1. 0171-713 0836. Housed in an 1850s ice house on Battlebridge Basin; blocks of ice imported from Norway were carried here on the Regent's Canal to vast ice wells, one of which has been partly excavated and is on show. Museum tells the story of the development of London's canals, from the early days as an important trade route, to today's more leisurely pursuits. Exhibitions, special events, shop. *OPEN 10.00-16.30 Tue-Sun & B.hol Mon. Charge.*

London Planetarium   **1 C5**
Marylebone Rd NW1. 0171-486 1121. A study of planets, stars and the universe. Interactive exhibitions and virtual reality shows at the new-look Planetarium. The latest computer technology is used for the shows, aided by the Digistar 2, the world's most advanced star projector. Shop. Shows *every 40 mins Mon-Sun; first show 12.20 (10.20 Sat & Sun), last show 17.00. Charge.*

London Transport Museum   **4 F3**
The Piazza, Covent Garden WC2. 0171-379 6344. Story of London's transport. Historic road and rail vehicles, working exhibits and audio-visual displays. Shop and café. *OPEN 10.00-18.00 (last admission 17.15) Mon-Sun. Charge.*

Madame Tussaud's   **1 C5**
Marylebone Rd NW1. 0171-935 6861. Among waxwork effigies of the famous

and notorious, meet the Royal Family, Pavarotti, Nelson Mandela and Cher. Murderers lurk in the Chamber of Horrors. Mingle with celebrities at 'The Garden Party'. Experience some of the greatest events that have shaped London's heritage at 'The Spirit of London' where you journey through 400 years of London's history in a replica of a black taxi cab. *OPEN 10.00-17.30 Mon-Fri (from 09.30 in summer), 09.30-17.30 Sat & Sun. Charge.*

Martinware Pottery Collection
Public Library, 9-11 Osterley Park Rd, Southall, Middx. 0181-574 3412. Collection of Martinware, including birds, face mugs and grotesques. *OPEN 09.00-19.45 Tue, Thur & Fri, 09.00-17.00 Wed & Sat. CLOSED B.hols. Free.*

Museum of Garden History   7 **F1**
St Mary-at-Lambeth, Lambeth Palace Rd SE1. 0171-261 1891. The church beside Lambeth Palace was rescued by the Tradescant Trust from demolition in the 1970s, and exhibits the discoveries and travels of the two John Tradescants, father and son, buried in the churchyard beside Captain Bligh of the *Bounty*. Successively gardeners to Charles I and Henrietta Maria, they introduced plants from abroad, some of which feature in the churchyard garden. Café. *OPEN mid Mar-mid Dec 10.30-16.00 Mon-Fri, 10.30-17.00 Sun. CLOSED Sat. Free.*

Museum of London   5 **D1**
150 London Wall EC2. 0171-600 3699. A three-dimensional history of the City and London area, with models, reconstructions and even the new Lord Mayor's Coach of 1756. The new Roman London gallery houses nearly 2000 original objects and the latest evidence from recent archaeological discoveries. Lectures, films, shop and restaurant. *OPEN 10.00-17.50 Tue-Sat, 12.00-17.50 Sun. CLOSED Mon. Charge (free after 16.30).*

Museum of Mankind   4 **D3**
6 Burlington Gdns W1. 0171-437 2224. Exciting collection of primitive artefacts and clothing. Changing exhibitions illustrate a variety of non-Western societies and cultures. Film shows *13.30, 15.00 Tue-Fri. Café. OPEN 10.00-17.00 Mon-Sat, 14.30-18.00 Sun. Free.*

Museum of the Moving   5 **A4**
Image (MOMI)
Under Waterloo Bridge, South Bank SE1. 0171-401 2636. Part of the South Bank complex, this bright, exciting museum charts the history of moving images from Chinese shadow puppets to film,

television, video, satellite and hologram technology. Forty main exhibit areas plus changing exhibitions. Plenty of opportunity for taking part. Lectures, films, Victorian magic lantern shows. *OPEN 10.00-18.00 Mon-Sun. Charge.*

Musical Museum
368 High St, Brentford, Middx. 0181-560 8108. The only musical museum in Europe that has ten reproducing pianos and three reproducing pipe organs all under one roof. In all around 200 instruments, some of which will be played during the 1½-hr tour. *OPEN 14.00-17.00 Sat & Sun, 14.00-16.00 Wed-Fri. Charge.* No small children. Parties *by arrangement.* Send sae for list of concerts.

National Army Museum   6 **F4**
Royal Hospital Rd SW3. 0171-730 0717. The story of the Army from 1400 to present day, its triumphs and disasters, its professional and social life all over the world. Uniforms, pictures, weapons and personal relics, plus a 400sq ft model of the Battle of Waterloo. *OPEN 10.00-17.30 Mon-Sun. Free.*

National Gallery   4 **E3**
Trafalgar Sq WC2. 0171-839 3321/747 2885. Houses the national collection of Western European painting, comprising over 2000 pictures dating from the 13thC to the early 20thC. Galleries are divided, by period, into four areas comprising paintings of various schools, hung to emphasise the links existing between painters of different nationalities. Rich in early Italian (Leonardo da Vinci, Raphael, Botticelli and Titian), Dutch and Flemish (Rembrandt, Rubens, Frans Hals, Van Dyck), Spanish 15-18thC (Velázquez and El Greco), British 18th and 19thC (Constable, Turner, Gainsborough and Reynolds), and the Impressionists (Monet, Cézanne and Van Gogh). A booklet, *20 Great Paintings*, on sale in the shop in several languages, leads the time-pressed to 20 masterpieces. Daily guided tours (except *Sun*) highlight selected pictures. Brasserie and café. Films and lectures. Building 1838 by W. Wilkins. Sainsbury Wing, R. Venturi 1991. *OPEN 10.00-18.00 Mon-Sat, 14.00-18.00 Sun. Free (charge for special exhibitions).*

National Maritime Museum
See under Greenwich in 'Historic London'.

National Portrait Gallery   4 **E3**
2 St Martin's Pl WC2. 0171-306 0055. Founded in 1856, an historic collection of contemporary portraits of famous British men and women, forming a fascinating

study of human personality. There are now over 9000 portraits in the primary collection, from Henry VIII to Churchill, Shakespeare to the Princess of Wales, and Lawrence of Arabia to Mick Jagger. The importance of the sitter is the main criterion for inclusion. The collection includes paintings, miniatures, sculptures, drawings, caricatures and photographs, and is arranged chronologically, from the medieval period to the present day. Post-war portraits, and photography and video galleries, now take up the first floor. The gallery has constantly changing displays and a programme of special temporary exhibitions; the annual competition for young portrait painters produces exciting developments in modern portraiture. Education centre, resource centre, library, bookshop. *OPEN 10.00-18.00 Mon-Sat, 12.00-18.00 Sun. CLOSED some B.hols. Free (charge for some special exhibitions)*.

National Postal Museum   **5 D2**
King Edward Bldg, King Edward St EC1. 0171-239 5420. Superb displays of stamps including the Phillips collection and the 'Berne' collection. Reference library. Tours by *prior arrangement*. *OPEN 09.30-16.30 Mon-Fri. CLOSED Sat, Sun & B.hols. Free*.

Natural History Museum   **6 D1**
& Geological Museum
Cromwell Rd SW7. 0171-938 9123. Made up of the Life Galleries and Earth Galleries where advanced and innovative methods of display involve, interest and entertain visitors of all ages. In the Life Galleries walk among huge skeletons and watch moving dinosaurs come to life. Exhibits on human biology, marine invertebrates and meteorites. Don't miss 'Creepy Crawlies', the world of anthropods revealed using audio-visual aids, or the lifesize model of a 90ft (27.5m) blue whale. In the Earth Galleries learn about the Earth's resources, Britain's fossils and minerals, and see brilliant gems on view. New garden sanctuary allows visitors to explore Britain's flora and fauna. Discovery Centre, shops, café, picnic area. *OPEN 10.00-17.50 Mon-Sat, 11.00-17.50 Sun. Charge (free after 16.30 Mon-Fri, after 17.00 Sat, Sun & B.hols, and for educational groups booking in advance)*.

North Woolwich Old Station
Museum
Pier Rd E16. 0171-474 7244. Housed in what was North Woolwich station are three exhibition galleries telling the story of the Great Eastern Railway in photographs, plans, models, documents and relics. Houses GER steam locomotive built in 1876 and a restored Victorian station booking office. *Phone for opening times. Free*.

Old Royal Observatory
See under Greenwich in 'Historic London'.

Percival David Foundation of   **1 F5**
Chinese Art
53 Gordon Sq WC1. 0171-387 3909. Chinese ceramics from Sung to Ch'ing dynasty. Reference library. *OPEN 10.30-17.00 Mon-Fri. CLOSED Sat, Sun & B.hols. Free*.

Photographers' Gallery   **4 E3**
5 & 8 Great Newport St WC2. 0171-831 1772. Frequent exhibitions, often with new British work. Print room, coffee bar, bookshop. *OPEN 11.00-18.00 Mon-Sat. CLOSED Sun. Free*.

Pollock's Toy Museum   **4 D1**
1 Scala St W1. 0171-636 3452. Three rickety floors packed with a magical mix of bygone toys. Look out for the oldest teddy in the world. Shop selling toy theatres. *OPEN 10.00-17.00 Mon-Sat (Under 18s free Sat). CLOSED Sun & B.hols. Charge*.

Public Record Office   **5 B2**
Chancery La WC2. 0181-876 3444. Permanent display of records on major events in the history of England. Houses the Domesday Book of 1086 and one of the four existing Magna Cartas. *OPEN 10.00-17.00 Mon-Fri. CLOSED Sat, Sun & B.hols. Free*.

Queen's Gallery   **4 C5**
Buckingham Palace, Buckingham Palace Rd SW1. 0171-839 1377. Pictures and works of art from all parts of the Royal collection. Exhibitions changed at intervals. *OPEN 09.30-16.30 Mon-Sun. CLOSED B.hols. Charge*.

Rock Circus   **4 E3**
London Pavilion, Piccadilly W1. 0171-734 7203. The skills and artistry of Madame Tussaud's combined with the latest audio techniques bring to life the great rock stars. See the Beatles, Buddy Holly, Stevie Wonder, Madonna. *OPEN Sep-May 11.00-21.00 Wed, Thur, Sun & Mon, 12.00-21.00 Tue, 11.00-22.00 Fri & Sat; Jun-Aug 10.00-22.00 Wed-Mon, 12.00-22.00 Tue. Charge*.

Royal Academy of Arts   **4 D3**
Burlington House, Piccadilly W1. 0171-439 7438. Presents Britain's major exhibitions of visual arts and holds a series of major special-loan exhibitions throughout the year. Probably most famous for its annual Summer Exhibition *May-Aug*, in which the work of living artists is dis-

played, and in most cases is for sale. Ten works from its permanent collection, including paintings by Constable and Reynolds, have been copied in relief 'thermoforms' for the blind and visually impaired. Restaurant. *OPEN 10.00-18.00 Mon-Sun. Charge.*

Royal Air Force Museum
Grahame Park Way NW9. 0181-205 2266. (10-min walk from Colindale station on the Northern Line.) The first national museum of aviation telling the fascinating story of flight through the display of over 65 historic aircraft. Situated on the site of a former wartime airfield, see the legendary Sopwith Camel, the mighty Vulcan, the Spitfire, Hurricane, Lancaster, Wellington, Flying Fortress plus the Panavia Tornado, which saw extensive action during the Gulf War. One hall commemorates the 50th anniversary of the Battle of Britain and uses the latest display techniques. Also a flight simulator which allows visitors to experience the thrill of flying in an RAF Tornado and a replica of the No.11 Group Operations Room at RAF Uxbridge. A *20-minute* video gives the complete story of this important period. Cinema, shop. The Bomber Command Hall is also incorporated into the museum. *OPEN 10.00-18.00 Mon-Sun. CLOSED B.hols. Charge.*

Royal Mews   4 C6
Buckingham Palace Rd SW1. 0171-839 1377. The Queen's horses are on view here plus the royal and state carriages including the gold coach and the glass coach. The gold state coach has been used for every coronation since George IV. It is 24ft (8m) long, weighs four tonnes and when in use is drawn by eight horses. The glass coach is used for royal weddings. *Open Jan-Mar 12.00-16.00 Wed; Apr-Sep 12.00-16.00 Tue-Thur; Oct-Dec 12.00-16.00 Wed; except on state occasions. Last admission 15.30. Charge.*

St Bride's Crypt Museum   5 C2
St Bride's Church, Fleet St EC4. 0171-353 1301. Interesting relics found during excavations. A unique continuity of remains from Roman London to the present day. *OPEN 08.00-17.00 Mon-Sun. Free.*

Science Museum   3 E6
Exhibition Rd SW7. 0171-938 8000. The history of science and its application to industry. A large collection of very fine engineering models, steam engines, early motor cars, aeroplanes and all aspects of applied physics and chemistry. Explore the history of printing, textiles, and many other industries through working models. Special features include space exploration, with the actual Apollo 10 space capsule. The Wellcome galleries examine the history of medicine with a reconstruction of a 1980s operating theatre. The 'Launch Pad' is a popular interactive hands-on gallery of large working models which demonstrate scientific principles and present challenging activities. *OPEN 10.00-18.00 Mon-Sun. CLOSED B.hols. Charge (free after 16.30). Free lectures & films – write for brochure.*

Serpentine Gallery   3 E4
Kensington Gardens W2. 0171-402 6075. Changing monthly exhibitions of contemporary art, sculpture, paintings, drawings and prints. *OPEN 10.00-18.00 Mon-Sun. Free.*

Shakespeare's Globe   5 D4
Exhibition
New Globe Walk, Bankside SE1. 0171-928 6406. Part of Sam Wanamaker's International Globe Centre, the central focus of which will be the rebuilt Globe Theatre (due to open June 1996). The exhibition tells the story of Elizabethan theatre-going, the history of the Globe and the rebuilding project. Tour of the building site, where authentic Tudor methods are being used. *OPEN 10.00-17.00 Mon-Sun. Charge.*

Sherlock Holmes Museum   1 B5
221b Baker St NW1. 0171-935 8866. In a Grade II listed building, a collection of Victorian memorabilia relating to Sherlock Holmes and his friend Dr Watson, the world-famous characters created by Sir Arthur Conan Doyle. Personal exhibits on display. *OPEN 10.00-18.00. Charge.*

Sir John Soane's Museum   4 G2
13 Lincoln's Inn Fields WC2. 0171-405 2107. Soane's personal collection of antiquities, paintings and drawings, including Hogarth's Election and the Rake's Progress, original Piranesi drawings and most of the architectural drawings of the Adam brothers. New exhibition *Soane: Connoisseur and Collector.* Building designed by Soane, 1810-13. *OPEN 10.00-17.00 Tue-Sat; also 18.00-21.00 1st Tue of month. Free.*

South London Gallery
65 Peckham Rd SE5. 0171-703 6120. Holds varied exhibitions each year with a policy to explore new developments in the visual arts. Founded in 1891, it was the first gallery to open on a Sun. *OPEN during exhibitions 11.00-17.00 Tue-Sun (11.00-20.00 Wed). CLOSED Mon & B.hols. Free.*

Tate Gallery   7 **E2**

Millbank SW1. 0171-887 8000. Recorded information: 0171-887 8008. Designed 1897 by Sidney H.J. Smith. Representative collections of British painting from the 16thC to the present day. Fine examples of Blake, Turner, Hogarth, the pre-Raphaelites, Ben Nicolson, Spencer and Francis Bacon; sculpture by Moore and Hepworth. Also a particularly rich collection of foreign paintings and sculpture from 1880 to the present day, including paintings by Picasso, Chagall, Mondrian, Pollock, Lichtenstein, Rothko, Degas, Marini and Giacometti. *Art Now* gallery dedicated to contemporary art. Sculpture tours for the visually handicapped (*by appointment*). Hi-tech "wand" offers 4-hour guided tours. The Clore Gallery was built in 1986 to house the Turner bequest. *OPEN 10.00-17.50 Mon-Sat, 14.00-17.50 Sun. Lectures and films at various times. Restaurant. Shop. Free (charge for some exhibitions).*

Theatre Museum   4 **F3**

Russell St WC2. 0171-836 7891. Branch of the V & A. Devoted to theatre, ballet, opera, circus and music hall. Costumes, playbills, scenery, props. Café. *OPEN 11.00-19.00 Tue-Sun. Charge.*

Tower Bridge Museum   5 **G4**

Tower Bridge SE1. 0171-403 3761. Exhibition focusing on the history, design and continuing use of the bridge. The huge old steam engines and boilers can also be seen, of one of the great masterpieces of Victorian engineering. Ornate Gothic architecture. Panoramic view. *OPEN Apr-Oct 10.00-18.30; Nov-Mar 10.00-17.15 daily. Last admission 1¼ hrs before closing.*

Tower Hill Pageant   5 **G3**

1 Tower Hill Ter EC3. 0171-709 0081. 'Dark ride' through the history of London in an automated car. From the Roman port to the modern docklands. Tableaux, sound and smell effects. Europe's largest holograms depict medieval life. Based on archaeological finds in the area, some of which are displayed in the museum of waterfront archaeology above. *OPEN Apr-Oct 09.30-17.30; Nov-Mar 09.30-16.30 daily. Charge.*

Tower of London, the Jewel   5 **G3**
House and Royal Armouries

Tower Hill EC3. 0171-709 0765. The Crown Jewels (heavily guarded). London's oldest museum with the largest collection of armour and arms in Britain: 10-20thC. *OPEN Mar-Oct 09.00-18.00 Mon-Sat, 10.00-18.00 Sun; Nov-Feb 09.00-17.00 Mon-Sat, 10.00-17.00 Sun. Charge.*

Victoria and Albert Museum   6 **D1**

Cromwell Rd SW7. 0171-938 8500. The V & A is Britain's National Museum of Art and Design and has some of the world's finest collections of furniture, ceramics and glass, metalwork and jewellery, textiles and dress from the Middle Ages to the 20thC, as well as paintings, prints and drawings, posters and photographs, and sculpture. It also has superb collections from China, Japan, India and the Middle East. More than 300 paintings hang the length of the restored Great Staircase in the Henry Cole wing. There is a full programme of courses, events and introductory tours. Restaurant (Jazz Brunch on *Sun*) and café. *OPEN 10.00-17.50 Tue-Sun, 12.00-17.50 Mon. Admission by voluntary donation.*

Wallace Collection   4 **B2**

Hertford House, Manchester Sq W1. 0171-935 0687. A private collection of outstanding works of art which was bequeathed to the nation by Lady Wallace in 1897. Splendid representation of the French 17th and 18thC artists, including paintings by Boucher, Watteau and Fragonard. Home to the 'Laughing Cavalier' by Frans Hals and also several Rembrandts, a Titian, some Rubens, and paintings by Canaletto and Guardi. Important collections of French furniture, Sèvres porcelain, Majolica, Limoges enamel and armour. *OPEN 10.00-17.00 Mon-Sat, 14.00-17.00 Sun. CLOSED some B.hols. Free.*

Westminster Abbey   4 **F6**
Museum

The Cloisters, Westminster Abbey SW1. 0171-222 5152. The Cloisters contain the famous wax effigies of British monarchs including Elizabeth I and Charles II, and Admiral Lord Nelson. Also plans, paintings, prints and documents. Forms part of a complex with the Chapter House and the Chamber of Pyx. *OPEN 10.30-16.00 Mon-Sun. Charge.*

Whitechapel Art Gallery

80 Whitechapel High St E1. 0171-522 7878. Frequent public exhibitions of great interest. The Whitechapel has successfully introduced new ideas on modern British art into London. *OPEN 11.00-17.00 Tue & Thur-Sun, 11.00-20.00 Wed. CLOSED Mon & B.hols. Free.*

Wimbledon Lawn Tennis Museum

Church Rd SW19. 0181-946 6131. Display of tennis through the ages including equipment, clothing, photographs and videos offering the viewer any pre-recorded tournament match. Also a library of tennis literature. *OPEN 10.30-17.00 Tue-Sat, 14.00-17.00 Sun. CLOSED Mon. Charge.*

Outdoor London

Parks and gardens

London is particularly rich in parks, gardens, commons, forests and heathland with over 80 parks within ten miles of the centre of London. They are all that remain of early London's natural surrounding countryside and range from the vast open spaces of Richmond Park to the manicured gardens of Regent's Park. Left by accident, gift, or longsighted social intention, they provide a welcome breathing space. The ten royal parks are still the property of the Crown and were originally the grounds of royal homes or palaces. All parks are free, but there may be charges for some facilities. (See under 'Children's London' for Playparks and One o'clock clubs.)

Garden Day Tours
62 Redington Rd NW3. 0171-431 2758. Guided tours of private London gardens, and visits to gardens and houses in the surrounding countryside. *Phone for details.*

Alexandra Park & Palace N22
0181-365 2121. Home to the Victorian Palace, at one time the BBC headquarters. Set in 196 acres (79.4ha) of parkland with a superb view of the London skyline, the Palace is now an exhibition, entertainments and leisure venue. Attractions include a boating lake, pitch & putt, ice rink, animal enclosure, children's playground, conservation area and arboretum. *OPEN 24 hrs.*

Battersea Park SW11   6 F5
0181-871 7530. An interesting riverside park of 200 acres (81ha) which was a favourite dueling spot in the early 19thC. Redesigned in the 1950s for the Festival of Britain. Boating lake, deer park and children's zoo. The London Peace Pagoda which stands close to the river was built by monks and nuns of the Japanese Buddhist order Nipponzan Myohoji and completed in 1985. Based on ancient Indian and Japanese designs, it stands at 110 ft (33.5m) and has a double roof. The park also contains the Pump House art gallery and a herb garden. All-weather sports surface. Floodlit football pitch. Easter Show. Park, playing fields, athletics track, tennis courts *OPEN dawn-dusk.*

Blackheath SE3
0181-305 1807 (for the area north of the A2, Shooters Hill). 0181-852 1762 (for the area to the south). 275 acres (111.4ha) of open grassland jointly administered by the boroughs of Lewisham and Greenwich and used for general recreation. Ideal for kite-flying and watching the sunset. Good views in all directions especially from Point Hill in the north-west. Play soccer and cricket, sail model boats on Prince of Wales pond. Bowling green and tennis courts. Migratory birds in winter, particularly seagulls. Occasional circuses, festivals and funfairs. Some of the advanced runners competing in the London Marathon, held *every spring,* start from here. *OPEN 24 hrs.*

Bostall Heath SE2
0181-311 1674. Woods and heath. Fine views of London and the Thames Estuary. Orienteering courses and cricket practice nets. Bowling green. *OPEN Apr-Sep 13.30-19.00 Mon-Sat, 11.00-19.00 Sun.* Heath *OPEN 24 hrs.*

Brockwell Park SE24
Dulwich Rd SE24. 0171-926 0105. Fine old English garden with an attractive chain of ornamental lakes, a walled garden and a yew arch. Tennis courts. *OPEN 09.00-dusk.*

Clissold Park N16
0181-800 1021. Originally a private estate, the mansion surrounded by gardens still survives. 54 acres (21.9ha) including a fishing lake, bowling green, playpark for children, croquet lawn, flower garden, rose garden and many chestnut trees which are splendid in spring. Also an aviary of tropical birds; fallow deer graze here. *OPEN 07.00-dusk.*

Crystal Palace Park SE20
0181-778 7148. Named after Paxton's 1851 Great Exhibition building which was moved here from Hyde Park and unfortunately burnt to the ground in 1936; the vast, impressive ruins still remain. Now a National Youth & Sports Centre with an Olympic swimming pool and fine modern sports stadium in an open park of 70 acres (28.4ha). Has boating lake with pedalos (in *summer*). Fishing lake; four islands in the lake are 'colonised' by 20 life-sized replicas of primeval animals. Playpark, farmyard, shire horse cart rides, ranger-guided walks, circular maze. *OPEN 08.00-$\frac{1}{2}$ hr before dusk.*

Danson Park
Bexleyheath, Kent. 0181-303 7777.

Pleasant 200-acre (81ha) park with large lake. 'Old English' garden and rock garden. Landscaped about 1760 by Capability Brown, Palladian mansion by Sir Robert Taylor, 1756. Wide variety of recreational facilities, including boating and windsurfing. *OPEN 07.30-sunset Mon-Fri, 09.00-sunset Sat & Sun*.

Dulwich Park SE21
0181-693 5737. Famous for its rhododendrons and azaleas. A favourite garden of Queen Mary, wife of George V. Boating lake and tennis courts. Good for kite-flying. Tree trail. 'Touch maps' for the blind. *OPEN 08.00-21.00 (to 16.30 winter).*

Eltham Park SE9
0181-850 2031. Split by a railway line into two sections, the south is recreational open space but the north is woodland: oaks, chestnuts, birches, bluebells, anemones. The ornamental pond complete with ducks commands a view right across to central London. *OPEN 24 hrs.*

Epping Forest, Essex
6000 acres (2430ha) of natural woodland, six miles long and two miles wide stretching from Chingford to Epping. It was 'dedicated to the delectation of the public forever' in 1878. Many hornbeam, oak, ash, maple, beech and birch trees; it also offers a superb variety of all kinds of natural life – so many grey squirrels that they have become a problem. High Beech is a popular spot and there are large areas to ramble through where you can get thoroughly lost, or even stumble upon the remains of two ancient British camps at least 2000 years old – Loughton Camp and Ambersbury Banks. *OPEN 24 hrs.*

Finsbury Park N4
0171-263 5001. 115 acres (46.6ha) opened in 1869. Many sporting activities – soccer, American and Gaelic football, cricket, fishing, bowling, tennis, boating. Also floodlit athletics track, two children's playgrounds, nursery and tea-room. Plane trees predominate. The oldest aqueduct in London runs through the park and there is a reservoir underground. *OPEN 06.30-½ hr after sunset.*

Greenwich Park SE10
0181-858 2608. A royal park of 200 acres (81ha) with pleasant avenues lined with chestnut trees, sloping down to the Thames. Impressive views of the river and two classical buildings: the Queen's House by Inigo Jones and the Royal Naval College (once a Tudor royal palace). Contains the National Maritime Museum and the Old Royal Observatory. 13 acres (5.3ha) of wooded deer park, a bird sanctuary and Bronze age tumuli. Children's boating lake; entertainment in *summer*. The London Marathon, held *every spring*, starts from here. Bandstand used in *summer*. *OPEN 07.00 (for traffic, 05.00 for pedestrians)-22.00 summer, 07.00-18.00 (or dusk) winter.*

Hainault Forest, Essex
0181-500 3106. Formerly part of the great forest of Essex, or Waltham Forest. Now a Country Park of 1100 acres (445.5ha) of extensive woodland, with a lake, two 18-hole golf courses, a playing field and facilities for angling, riding, cross-country running and orienteering. Country farm with rare species. *OPEN 24 hrs.*

Hampstead Heath NW3
0181-348 9930/0181-455 5183. Open, hilly 800 acres (324ha) of park and woods. Fine views of London. Foxes can sometimes be seen. Crowded on *Bank holidays* with visitors to the famous fair and the equally famous pubs – the Bull & Bush, Spaniard's Inn and Jack Straw's Castle. Includes Parliament Hill (*the* place for kite-flyers), Golders Hill (containing a fine English town garden) and Kenwood. Ponds, open-air concerts in *summer*, tennis courts. Olympic track, orienteering, cricket, football, rugby, rounders, horse-riding (for permit holders). Also swimming in Hampstead Ponds, a children's zoo and bandstand at Golders Hill, and much of interest to the ornithologist (over 100 species). *OPEN 24 hrs.* Kenwood and Golders Hill *OPEN dawn-dusk.*

Hampton Court & Bushy Park, Surrey
0181-781 9500. 2000 acres (810ha) of royal park bounded on two sides by the Thames. Hampton is the formal park of the great Tudor palace with ancient courts, superb flower gardens, gracious lawns, formal Dutch-style ponds and roses, the famous maze and the 'great vine' planted in 1768 during the reign of George III. Recently restored Privy Garden. Bushy Park is natural parkland with an artificial plantation, aquatic plants and ponds. Two herds of deer, red and fallow, run in the park. Both parks have many fine avenues including the mile-long Chestnut Avenue with 'Diana' fountain in Bushy Park. Hampton Court itself is described in *'Sightseeing'. OPEN 07.00-dusk.*

Holland Park W8   3 **A5**
0171-602 9483. Behind the bustle of Kensington High St. 55 acres (22.3ha) of calm and secluded lawns and gardens with peacocks. Once the private garden of Holland House (partially restored after bombing during the war). Dutch garden

dating from 1812 with fine bedding displays. Also iris and rose gardens, yucca lawn, Japanese garden and the Orangery, where craft fairs, art exhibitions and other events are held during *May-Sep*. On the north side is a remarkable woodland of 28 acres (11.3ha) containing 3000 species of rare British trees and plants. 66 species of birds. Open-air theatre offers dance, opera and classical music in *summer*. Restaurant, *OPEN to 24.00*, looks on onto Flower Garden which is illuminated at night. *OPEN 07.30-sunset summer; 7.30-dusk winter*.

Hyde Park W1   3 **F4**
0171-298 2100. A royal park since 1536, it was once part of the forest reserved by Henry VIII for hunting wild boar and bulls. Queen Elizabeth I held military reviews here (still held on special occasions). It was the haunt of highwaymen until 1750 and even today is patrolled at night by police. The Great Exhibition of 1851 was held opposite Prince of Wales Gate. Hyde Park now has 360 acres (137.7ha) of parkland, walks, Rotten Row for horse-riders, and the Serpentine – a fine lake for boating and swimming. The Serpentine Bridge is by George Rennie, 1826. The famous Speakers' Corner, a tribute to British democracy, is near Marble Arch – public executions were held at Tyburn gallows nearby until 1783. Baseball and soft-ball often played. Bandstand used in *summer*. Guided bat-watching tours run by The London Bat Group!. *OPEN 05.00-24.00*. The Lido *OPEN May-Sep & B.hols 10.00-18.00. Charge for swimming*.

Kensington Gardens W8   3 **D4**
0171-298 2117. A formal and elegant addition to Hyde Park; when the gardens were first opened to the public, soldiers, sailors and servants were not allowed in! 275 acres (111.4ha) of royal park containing William III's lovely Kensington Palace, Queen Anne's Orangery, the peaceful 'Sunken Garden' nearby, the Round Pond, perfect for sailing model boats, and, on the south, the magnificent Albert Memorial – the nation's monument to Queen Victoria's husband. *(Due to extensive restoration work, the memorial is currently covered - see page 28.)* The famous Broad Walk, originally flanked by ancient elms, is now replanted with fragrant limes and maples, and the nearby 'Flower Walk' is the home of wild birds, woodpeckers, flycatchers and tree-creepers. Queen Caroline produced both the Long Water (Peter Pan's statue is here) and the Serpentine by ordering the damming of the Westbourne river. A

stone balustrade separates the Long Water from formal ponds and fountains. Good children's playground with the Elfin Oak, carved with lots of birds and animals. *OPEN dawn-dusk*.

Lee Valley Park
(01992) 717711. A huge expanse stretching 23 miles from Ware in Hertfordshire to the East End, following the course of the River Lea. The park offers sailing, angling, windsurfing, swimming, football, badminton, golf, tennis, squash, horse-riding, bowls, cycling, ice-skating. Also an open farm, birdwatching and dragonfly sanctuary. Riverside chalets, camping and caravanning. *Telephone above number for further details*.

Lesnes Abbey Woods SE2
Commemorate the former 800-year-old abbey, now excavated. Woods and open ground with good views. 20 acres (8.1ha) of wild daffodils in the *spring*. Café. *OPEN 08.00-16.30 winter, 08.00-20.00 (or dusk) summer*.

Osterley Park
Isleworth, Middx. 0181-560 3918. Used to be the private estate of the Earl of Jersey, part of it is still farmland. An open park but some cedars and cork trees. Osterley Park House is a classic building designed by Robert Adam. *OPEN Apr-Oct 13.00-17.00 (last admission 16.30) Wed-Sun. CLOSED Mon & Tue. Charge. Park OPEN dawn to dusk. Free*.

Peckham Rye Park SE15
0181-693 3791. Open park with English, Japanese and water gardens. Sporting facilities include bowling, tennis and football. *OPEN 06.00-½ hr after sunset*.

Primrose Hill NW8   1 **B2**
0181-486 7905. A minor royal park of simple grassy hillside 206ft (61.7m) high giving a fine view over London. Children's play areas and a boating lake. Puppet shows in *summer. OPEN 24 hrs*.

Regent's Park NW1   1 **C4**
0171-486 7905. A royal park of 472 acres (191ha), it was originally part of Henry VIII's great hunting forest in the 16thC. The Prince Regent in 1811 planned to connect the park (and a new palace) via the newly built Regent Street to Carlton House. Although never fully completed, the design (1812-26) by John Nash is of great distinction. It forms two concentric circles – the Inner with gardens and Outer with Regency terraces and imposing gateways. Contains London Zoo, the Regent's Canal, a fine boating lake with 30 species of birds, a bandstand, fragrant flower gardens and the very fine Queen Mary's Rose Garden.

It is also home to the golden-domed London Mosque. Open-air theatre. Restaurant and cafeterias. Sports facilities include football, rounders, softball, cricket, hockey and rugby. There are also tennis courts and an athletics track. *OPEN 05.00 (or dawn-dusk.*

Richmond Park, Surrey

0181-948 3209. The largest and wildest of London's royal parks; 2358 acres (954.2ha) first enclosed as a hunting ground by Charles I in 1637. Retains all the qualities of a great English feudal estate – a natural open park of spinneys and plantations, bracken and ancient oaks (survivors of the great oak forests of the Middle Ages) and over 600 red and fallow deer. Badgers, weasels and the occasional fox can be seen. Pen Ponds are well stocked with fish. Fine views of the Thames valley from White Lodge (early 18thC and once a royal residence) and the restaurant of Pembroke Lodge. Golf, riding, polo (for spectators), rugby, football. *OPEN 07.00-½ hr before dusk (from 07.30 in winter).*

Royal Botanic Gardens, Kew

Kew Road, Richmond, Surrey. 0181-940 1171. Superb botanical gardens of 300 acres (121.5ha). Founded in 1759 by Princess Augusta. Delightful natural gardens and woods bounded by the river on one side, and stocked with thousands of flowers and trees. The lake, aquatic garden and pagoda were designed by Sir William Chambers in 1760. The magnificent curved glass Palm House and the Temperate House, 1844-8, are by Decimus Burton. Beneath the Palm House is a Marine Display which has examples of algae and coral reef. The Princess of Wales Conservatory houses orchids and cacti, and water lilies the size of mattresses. New Evolution House takes you on an expedition across thousands of millions of years. New lilac garden. Kew's scientific aspect was developed by its two directors Sir William and Sir Joseph Hooker and the many famous botanists who worked here. 17thC Queen's Garden with formal rosebed. Cafeteria and gift shop in the Orangery. *1-hr* tours available from the Victoria Gate Visitor Centre. Gardens *OPEN 09.30; closing times vary according to season. Charge.*

St James's Park   4 E5
& Green Park SW1   4 C5

0171-930 1793. St James's Park is the oldest royal park, acquired in 1532 by Henry VIII, laid out in imitation 'Versailles' style by Charles II and finally redesigned in the grand manner for George IV by John Nash in the 1820s. A most attractive park with fine promenades and walks, and a romantic Chinese-style lake, bridge, and weeping willows. The bird sanctuary on Duck Island has some magnificent pelicans and over 20 species of duck and goose. Good views of Buckingham Palace, the grand sweep of Carlton House Terrace, the domes and spires of Whitehall and, to the east, Westminster Abbey. The Mall and Constitution Hill are frequently part of ceremonial and royal occasions. Bandstand used in *summer. OPEN dawn-24.00.* Green Park is just that – a welcome green space in the heart of London with an abundance of lime, plane and hawthorn trees. *OPEN dawn-dusk.*

Shooters Hill SE18

0181-856 1015. Hundreds of acres of woods and open parkland containing Oxleas Woods, Jackwood and Eltham Parks. Castlewood has a folly erected 1784 to Sir William James for his exploits in India. *OPEN 24 hrs.*

Streatham Common SW16

0171-926 9331. The Rookery was formerly the garden of an 18thC mansion; rock garden, wild garden, a 'white' garden and splendid old cedars. Paddling pools. Play area. Café. Common *OPEN 07.00-22.00 in summer, 07.30-16.30 in winter.* Rookery and café *OPEN 09.00-dusk.*

Trent Park, Enfield

0181-449 8706. Formerly part of the royal hunting forest Enfield Chase. Now a country park of 413 acres (167.3ha) of woodland and grassland, with a water garden, two lakes, animal enclosure, a nature trail, horse rides and several new self-guided trails. Guided walks *throughout the year.* Picnic facilities and a trail for the blind. *OPEN 07.30-dusk.*

Victoria Embankment   4 F3
Gardens WC2

The joy of the lunchtime office worker on a fine summer day. Banked flowers, a band, shady trees, deckchairs and a crowded open-air café.

Victoria Park E9

0181-985 1957. With 218 acres (88.2ha) and a four-mile perimeter, this park was known as 'the lung of the East End'; it is also the oldest enclosed park, established in 1845 by Sir James Pennythorne (who also laid out Battersea Park). Several listed historical buildings survive; of note are two alcoves from the original London Bridge which were placed at the east end of the park in 1861, a splendid drinking fountain erected for Burdett Coutts, and two gate pillars at Bonner Bridge. The four gate lodges also date back to 1850. Of natural interest are planes, oaks, birches, hawthorns, cherries, honey locusts, gladitsia, a Kentucky coffee tree and a bitter orange. Also fallow deer and various fowl. A wide variety of sports facilities for football, tennis, cricket, bowling, hockey and softball; athletics track; fishing lake. Children's play areas. *OPEN 07.00-dusk.*

Waterlow Park N6
0171-272 2825. Presented by Sir Sidney Waterlow to the people of London in 1889. 26 acres (10.5ha). Contains Lauderdale House where Nell Gwynne lived. *OPEN 07.30-dusk.*

Wimbledon Common SW19
0181-788 7655. 1100 acres (445.5ha), including Putney Heath, comprising wild woodland, open heath and several ponds. Golf course, 16 miles of horse rides. Playing fields. Bronze age remains. Rare and British flora. Protected by act of 1871 as a 'wild area' for perpetuity. Said to be haunted by an 18thC highwayman who gallops across the Common by night. Famous old 19thC windmill with a museum inside. Museum *OPEN Apr-Oct 14.00-17.00 Sat, Sun & B.hols.* Tea room *OPEN 09.30-17.30.* Park *OPEN 24 hrs. Cars not admitted after dusk.*

Botanic gardens and arboreta

Many of the London parks have living botanical collections; Holland Park has a good arboretum, and others have bog gardens, rock gardens, and extensive rose gardens. Queen Mary's Rose Garden in Regent's Park is an outstanding example. Most of the 'great houses' have fine collections of plants, often specialising in one botanical aspect. Some of the specialist commercial nurseries are almost miniature botanical gardens; for instance Syon Park in Middlesex.

Avery Hill
Bexley Rd SE9. 0181-850 2666. A Kew in miniature. Good collection of tropical and temperate Asian and Australasian plants in glasshouses, including a selection of economic crops. *OPEN 10.00-16.00 Mon-Sun.* Park *OPEN 07.00-½ hr before dusk (or 21.00). Free.*

Bedgebury National Pinetum
Goudhurst, Kent. (01580) 212060. Situated in the lovely undulating country-side of the Weald of Kent. First planted in 1925, the forest consists of over 200 species of temperate zone cone-bearing trees laid out in genera. Of great use to foresters and botanists. *OPEN 10.00-dusk. Charge.*

Borde Hill Arboretum
Haywards Heath, W. Sussex. (01444) 450326. Created by Col Stephenson R. Clarke at the end of the 19thC. The garden and park now extend to nearly 400 acres (162ha). Comprehensive collections of native and exotic trees and shrubs from Eastern Asia. *OPEN Apr-Oct 10.00-18.00 Mon-Sun. Small charge.*

Cambridge University Botanic Garden
Bateman St, Cambridge. (01223) 336265. The first garden was established in 1761 and moved to its present 40-acre (16.2ha) site ¾ mile (1.2km) south of the city in 1846. Extensive collection of living plants; fine specimens of trees and shrubs; glasshouses, pinetum, ecological area, chronological bed, scented garden and geographically arranged alpine garden. *OPEN Mar-Sep 10.00-18.00 Mon-Sun; Feb & Oct 10.00-17.00 Mon-Sun; Nov-Jan 10.00-16.00 Mon-Sun.* Glasshouse *OPEN all year 10.00-12.30 & 14.00-16.00 Mon-Sun. Free (charge on weekends & B.hols Nov-Mar).*

Chelsea Physic Garden   6 F4
Royal Hospital Rd SW3. 0171-352 5646. Founded in 1673 by the Worshipful Society of Apothecaries to study the therapeutic qualities of plants. Still used for medical teaching purposes today. Glasshouses full of plant exotica, rockery, beds of plants associated with past gardeners. *OPEN Apr-Oct 14.00-17.00 Wed, 14.00-18.00 Sun; 12.00-17.00 Mon-Fri during Chelsea Show & Chelsea Festival weeks. Charge.*

Oxford Botanic Garden
Rose La, by Magdalen Bridge, Oxford. (01865) 276920. Oldest botanical garden in Britain founded in 1621 by Henry, Lord Danvers. About 3 acres (1.2ha) within high stone walls, another 3 acres (1.2ha) outside pleasantly situated by the river. Glasshouses, rock garden, some notable trees. Entrance arch by Inigo Jones. *OPEN 09.00-17.00 (to 16.30 winter) Mon-Sun. Free (charge Jul & Aug).*

Royal Botanic Gardens, Kew
Kew Rd, Richmond, Surrey. 0181-940 1171. One of the world's great botanical gardens. Famous for its natural collections, identification of rare plants, economic botany and scientific research. Nearly 300 acres (121.5ha) of pure

OPEN SPACES IN LONDON

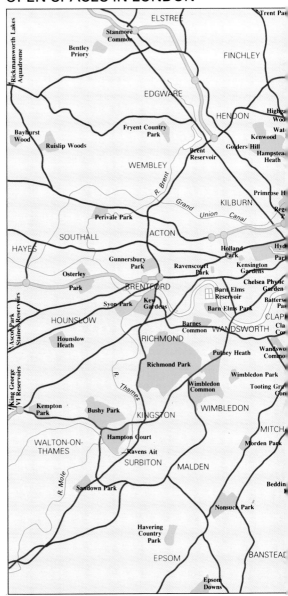

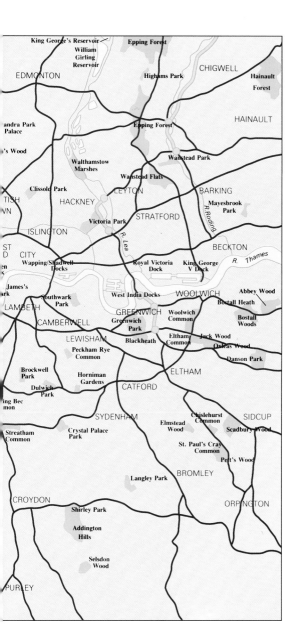

aesthetic pleasure. Arboretum, alpine, water and rhododendron gardens. Magnificent tropical orchid, palm, temperate and Australasian houses plus the Princess of Wales Conservatory with several different climatic zones under one roof. Herbarium contains Sir Joseph Hooker's famous *HMS Erebus* and Indian plant collections. Marine Display with examples of algae and coral reef. New Evolution House. Lilac garden. Library of rare books on botany and exploration. Gardens *OPEN 09.30; closing times vary according to season. Charge.*

Savill Garden, Windsor Great Park
(01753) 860222. Approach by Englefield Green. Created by Sir Eric Savill in 1930s. Outstanding woodland garden together with large collections of roses, herbaceous plants and alpines, in 35 acres (14.2ha). There is also a lake. *OPEN 10.00-dusk daily all year. Charge.*

Sheffield Park Garden
Nr Uckfield, E. Sussex. (01825) 790231. Gardens with five lakes and house by James Wyatt. Magnificent rhododendrons and azaleas in *May and Jun.* Brilliant *autumn* colours with maples and other shrubs. *OPEN Apr-mid Dec 11.00-dusk (or 18.00) Tue-Sun; Mar 11.00-16.00 Sat & Sun. CLOSED B.hol Mon. Charge.*

Syon Park
Brentford, Middx. 0181-560 0881. 55 acres (22.3ha) of gardens surrounding a 16thC mansion house designed by Robert Adam. The main gardens surround the lake, and around the lakeside are weeping willows and swamp cypresses. The Great Conservatory has an impressive central dome and elegant curving wings. Formal bedding areas and lawns. Garden centre. Butterfly House. *OPEN 10.00-18.00 (dusk in winter) Mon-Sun. Charge.*

Wakehurst Place
Ardingly, W. Sussex. (01444) 892701. A very lovely 500-acre (202.5ha) 'satellite' garden to the Royal Botanic Gardens at Kew; chosen because of its humid climate, clear air, lakes and running streams, and its variety of soils. The open woodland and high forest contain large numbers of rare trees, shrubs and plants from all over the world, particularly from Chile, SE Asia and New Zealand. Mansion open to the public. *OPEN 10.00-dusk Mon-Sun. Charge.*

Wisley Gardens
Wisley, Surrey. (01483) 224234. A fine 240-acre (97.2ha) horticultural garden originally created by C.F. Wilson as a wild and woodland garden, acquired by the Royal Horticultural Society in 1904. Famous for its trials and improvements of new varieties. Greenhouses and pinetum. Notable collections of old-fashioned and new roses, rhododendrons, camellias, heathers, rock garden plants and bulbs from the Near East. *OPEN Mar-Oct 10.00-19.00 Mon-Sat; Nov-Feb 10.00-sunset Mon-Sat. OPEN Sun 09.00-19.00 (to members of RHS only.) Charge.*

Zoos, aquaria and wildlife parks

All zoos ask visitors not to bring dogs.

Aquaria

Brighton Sea Life Centre
Marine Pde (opp Palace Pier), Brighton, E. Sussex. (01273) 604233. Oldest public aquarium in Britain containing 48 tanks with 70 different species of marine and freshwater fish. Main feature is the Shark Tunnel; watch the sharks and other fish swim above you. *OPEN 10.00-17.00 Mon-Sun. Charge.*

London Aquarium   **1 C3**
Regent's Park NW1. 0171-722 3333. Part of London Zoo. Marine and Tropical Halls. Excellently lit and displayed. A well-stocked aquarium of both sea and freshwater fish and amphibians from European and tropical waters. Particularly notable are the fine sea fish, the octopuses and sting-rays. *OPEN Apr-Oct 10.00-17.30 Mon-Sun; Nov-Mar 10.00-16.00 Mon-Sun. CLOSED Xmas Day. Charge (includes admittance to London Zoo).*

Underwater World
Holt Pound, Farnham, Surrey. (0420) 22140. A large, indoor aquarium full of amazing tropical fish. Next door is **Birdworld** where you will find a huge variety of birds from the tiny humming bird to the huge ostrich. Both *OPEN Apr-Aug 09.30-18.00 Mon-Sun; Sep 09.30-17.00 Mon-Sun; Oct-Mar 09.30-16.00 Mon-Sun. Charge.*

Zoos: London

London Zoo   **1 C3**
Regent's Park NW1. 0171-722 3333. Having survived threatened closure in recent years, a ten-year redevelopment plan is in place to turn this famous zoo into a centre for animal conservation and captive breeding. The zoo was originally laid out by Decimus Burton in 1827; since then many famous architects have

designed special animal houses. Reptile House, Moonlight World (where day and night are reversed so that rarely seen nocturnal animals are kept awake during the day), Penguin Pool, Invertebrate House. Animal feeding. Children's zoo. *OPEN Apr-Oct 10.00-17.30 Mon-Sun; Nov-Mar 10.00-16.00 Mon-Sun. CLOSED Xmas Day. Charge (includes admittance to London Aquarium).*

Zoos and wildlife parks: out of London

Chessington World of Adventures
Leatherhead Rd, Chessington, Surrey. (01372) 727227. A zoo of 65 acres (26.3ha) on the outskirts of London. A monorail travels high above the zoo animals. Also spectacular theme park – The Mystic East, Calamity Canyon, Circus World and Toytown. London 12 miles (A3). *OPEN Apr-Oct (all attractions) 10.00-17.00 Mon-Sun (last admission 15.00); Nov-Mar (zoo only) 10.00-16.00 Mon-Sun. CLOSED Xmas Day. Charge.*

Colchester Zoo
Standway Hall, Colchester, Essex. (01206) 330253. A good general collection, including an aquarium and reptile house. 40 acres (16.2ha). London 50 miles (A12). *OPEN 09.30-dusk Mon-Sun. Charge.*

Cotswold Wildlife Park
Bradwell Gro, nr Burford, Oxon. (01993) 823006. Set in 120 acres (48.6ha) of gardens and parkland. Tropical birds, rhinos, zebras and otters. Reptile house. Tropical marine aquarium. Adventure playground, farmyard. Narrow gauge railway (in *summer*). London 70 miles (M40). *OPEN 10.00-18.00 (or dusk) Mon-Sun. CLOSED Xmas Day. Charge.*

Hollanden Farm Park
Great Hollanden Farm, Mill Lane, Hildenborough, Kent. (01732) 833858. 50 rare breeds within a natural farming environment. Coffee shop, farm shop, gift shop. Group visits *by prior arrangement.* London 45 miles (A21). *OPEN Easter-Sep 10.30-17.00 Mon-Sun. Charge.*

Howletts Wild Animal Park
Bekesbourne, nr Canterbury, Kent. (01227) 721286. 55 acres (22.3ha) of zoo park including the largest collection of gorillas and tigers in the world. Leopards, African elephants, deer, monkeys. London 60 miles (A2). *OPEN Apr-Oct 10.00-17.00 Mon-Sun; Nov-Mar 10.00-dusk (or 16.00) Mon-Sun. Charge.*

Linton Zoo
Hadstock Rd, Linton, Cambs. (01223) 891308. A wonderful combination of beautiful gardens and wildlife from all over the world set in 16 acres of grassland. Wealth of rare and exotic creatures. London 55 miles (M11). *OPEN 10.00-dusk Mon-Sun. Charge.*

Longleat Safari Park
Warminster, Wilts. (01985) 844328. Visitors to the magnificent Renaissance house can choose to drive through the game park where the animals roam at will. You can stop your car and watch in safety but it is extremely foolhardy to get out. Also has gorilla island. No soft-topped cars allowed. London 90 miles (M4). *OPEN mid Mar-Oct 10.00-17.30 Mon-Sun. CLOSED Nov-Feb. Charge.*

Marwell Zoological Park
Colden Common, Nr Winchester, Hants. (01962) 777406. 100 acres (40.5 ha) of park with a two-mile road system. Specialise in breeding endangered wildlife species – big cats including Siberian tigers, rhinos, scimitar-horned oryx. Encounter Village, Tropical House, restaurant, adventure playground, special trains. London 70 miles (M3). *OPEN 10.00-18.00 (to 17.00 winter) Mon-Sun. CLOSED Xmas Day. Charge.*

Mole Hall Wildlife Park
Mole Hall, Widdington, nr Newport, Essex. (01799) 540400. In grounds of moated manor. 25 acres (10.1 ha) of grass. Animals include chimps, otters, llamas, wallabies and flamingoes. Butterfly House, pets corner, picnic and play areas, café and shop. London 35 miles (A11). *OPEN 10.30-18.00 (or dusk) Mon-Sun. Charge.*

Port Lympne Zoo Park
Port Lympne, Lympne, nr Hythe, Kent. (01303) 264647. 300 acres of spaciously laid out animal park, including 15 acres (6.1 ha) of splendid terraced gardens and Sir Philip Sassoon's historic house. Siberian and Indian tigers, black rhinos, Indian elephants, black panthers, antelope, deer, capucin monkeys, timber wolves. London 60 miles (M20). *OPEN Apr-Oct 10.00-17.00 Mon-Sun; Nov-Mar 10.00-dusk Mon-Sun. Charge.*

Whipsnade Wild Animal Park
Dunstable, Beds. (01582) 872171. A 600-acre (242.4ha) 'natural' zoo of woods and downland in the Chilterns. Over 2500 rare and exciting animals in large open-air enclosures. Some species roam freely throughout the park. You can travel within the park in your own car, by foot or

aboard the open-topped double-decker bus. There is a Discovery Centre where you can get closer to smaller members of the animal kingdom with hands-on displays, a miniature desert and wall-to-wall rainforest. Children's adventure playground. Steam railway. London 35 miles (M1). *OPEN Apr-Oct 10.00-18.00 Mon-Sat, 10.00-19.00 Sun; Nov-Mar 10.00-16.00 Mon-Sun. CLOSED Xmas Day. Charge.*

Woburn Safari Park
Woburn, Beds. (01525) 290407. Britain's largest drive-through wildlife park. The Safari Trail takes you past tigers, bears, wolves, rhinos and monkeys. Sealion and parrot shows. Leisure area with adventure playground, boating lake, train, computer centre, pets corner. London 40 miles (M1). *OPEN Mar-Oct 10.00-17.00 Mon-Sun; Nov-Feb 11.00-15.00 Sat & Sun. Charge.*

Children's London

Looking at London

London is full of fascinating things for children (and parents) to see and do – traditional ceremonies and events, historic sights and museums, festivals and fairs, shows and films, clubs, classes, junior sports and plenty of open spaces. It can also be tiring and expensive, so it's best to plan expeditions round a few places at a time; start with one of the famous sights – Changing of the Guard, St Paul's, the Tower, or a well-known museum – and combine it with a river trip, picnic in a park, a swim at one of London's many pools or a children's show. Take advantage of discounts on admission. Most attractions offer half-price tickets for children under 16. Phone Kidsline: 0171-222 8070 for information on events and entertainments 09.00-16.00 Mon-Fri during holidays, 16.00-18.00 Mon-Fri during term time. Under 5s travel free on buses and tubes, and under 14s pay a reduced flat fare until 22.00, as do 14 and 15 year olds with a Child Rate Photocard. It is also advisable to avoid travelling in the rush hour (08.00-09.30 & 16.30-18.30 Mon-Fri).

For more information on what London has to offer children see Nicholson's Children's London.

Sights

HMS Belfast   **5 F4**
Morgan's La, Tooley St SE1. 0171-407 6434. Last survivor of the Royal Navy's World War II cruisers moored near Tower Bridge. Explore bridge, seven decks, gun turrets, sick bay, galleys, engine rooms and punishment cells. Educational activi-

ties for children: film shows and lectures. Contact the schools' officer for further information. Cross gangplank from Symon's Wharf, or by ferry *(summer only)* from Tower Pier. *For opening hours see page 56. Charge.*

Buckingham Palace   **4 D5**
St James's Park SW1. The official London residence of the Queen; now open to the public *(see 'Historic London' on page 30)*. The royal flag flies from the roof if the Queen is at home. A popular time to visit is *11.30* for the Changing of the Guard *(every day in summer, alternate days in winter)*.

Cutty Sark & Gipsy Moth IV
King William Wlk SE10. 0181-858 3445. Explore the old, romantic Cutty Sark tea-clipper. Below deck there is a fascinating collection of photographs, ship's logs and figure-heads. *Gipsy Moth IV* nearby, is the small boat in which Sir Francis Chichester sailed single-handed around the world in 1966. *OPEN 10.00-18.00 Mon-Sat, 12.00-18.00 Sun (17.00 winter).* Gipsy Moth IV *CLOSED Nov-Easter. Charge.*

Houses of Parliament   **4 F5**
St Margaret St SW1. 0171-219 3000. Site of the old Palace of Westminster. Tours of medieval, hammer-beamed Westminster Hall available by contacting local member of parliament to obtain a permit. The appealing, small 14thC Jewel Tower with moat, opposite, is a further surviving fragment. Education sheets on application to the education office. *For opening hours see page 34. Charge.*

London Dungeon   **5 E4**
34 Tooley St SE1. 0171-403 0606. Gruesome and realistic exhibition displaying the darker side of British history –

murders, executions and tortures – in an eerie, vaulted cellar under London Bridge station. Children under 10 must be accompanied by an adult. *OPEN 10.00-17.30 Mon-Sun (to 16.30 Oct-Mar). Charge.*

London Planetarium **1 C5**
Marylebone Rd NW1. 0171-486 1121. Boggle your mind with stories of stars, space and the cosmos. Programmes through the day *Mon-Sun. Phone for times. Charge (combined ticket with Madame Tussaud's available). For further details see page 58.*

Madame Tussaud's **1 C5**
Marylebone Rd NW1. 0171-935 6861. Life-size wax figures of historic and contemporary, famous and notorious people. Royalty, pop stars, film stars, statesmen and astronauts. Journey through 400 years of London's history in a replica of a black taxi cab at 'The Spirit of London'. Chamber of Horrors genuinely gruesome, unsuitable for young children. *OPEN 10.00-17.30 Mon-Fri (from 09.30 in summer), 09.30-17.30 Sat & Sun. Charge (combined ticket with Planetarium available).*

Old Royal Observatory
Greenwich Park SE10. 0181-858 4422. Most of the pioneer work in the development of astronomy and nautical navigation was done here. Stand astride the Meridian Line. Interactive science stations. Sound and light show in a dome which houses the largest refracting telescope in the UK. See the 17thC Astronomer Royal's rooms and the restored Octagon room by Wren. Houses a collection of old clocks and telescopes. *For further details and opening hours see page 33. Charge.*

Royal Mews **4 C6**
Buckingham Palace Rd SW1. 0171-930 4832. The Queen's horses and coaches, ready for use on state occasions, including the huge gold Coronation coach (used for every coronation since George IV) and the glass State coach (used mainly for Royal weddings). *OPEN Apr-Sep 12.00-16.00 Tue-Thur; Oct-Mar 12.00-16.00 Wed only; except on state occasions. Charge.*

Russian Submarine
Long's Wharf, Thames Barrier, Unity Way SE18. 0181-855 7560. U-475 Foxtrot was in active service with the Russian Baltic Fleet up until April 1994. It was the Soviet Navy's largest conventional submarine, capable of performing underwater operations continuously for four days. Visitors can explore the engine rooms and control stations. *OPEN 10.00-18.00 (dusk in winter). Charge.*

St Katharine's Dock **5 G4**
St Katharine's Way, Tower Bridge E1. 0171-488 0555. Home to the Nore Lightship and magnificent Thames barges. Also a yacht haven, with shops and restaurants.

St Paul's Cathedral **5 D2**
Ludgate Hill EC4. 0171-248 2705. Exciting climb to the Dome, for a terrific view over the roof-tops and river. 259 steps take you to the Whispering Gallery, inside the Dome; 120 more up a narrow stone staircase lead to the broad Stone Gallery, at the base of the Dome; then the final, and most hair-raising climb, is to the Golden Gallery, at the top of the Dome. *For opening hours see page 46. Charge.*

Thames Flood Barrier
Unity Way, Eastmoor St SE18. 0181-854 1373. A shining, technological marvel, built as a bulwark against dangerously high tides. The Thames Barrier Visitor Centre has an exhibition, a film show on the history of the river and a video about the construction of the barrier. Shop. Café. *OPEN 10.00-17.00 Mon-Fri, 10.00-17.30 Sat, Sun & B. hols. Charge.*

Tower of London **5 G3**
Tower Hill EC3. 0171-709 0765. The best time to visit the Tower is definitely *Nov-Feb*, when it's not only cheaper to get in, but much less crowded. An amazing fortress, scene of the famous executions of Anne Boleyn and Sir Thomas More – you need plenty of time to explore all the different towers, the vast collection of armour and weapons, and the Crown Jewels in their specially designed display hall. Edward I's Medieval Palace has been restored, and costumed interpreters help recreate the atmosphere of Edward's court in the 1280s. No unaccompanied children under 10. *OPEN Mar-Oct 09.00-18.00 Mon-Sat, 10.00-18.00 Sun; Nov-Feb 09.00-17.00 Mon-Sat, 10.00-17.00 Sun. Charge.*

Trafalgar Square WC2 **4 E4**
Always popular with children who like to chase and feed the pigeons, climb the lions and watch the fountains. Parents will enjoy the bustling, colourful crowd which always congregates here. On the north wall, look for the Imperial Standards of Length (in yards, feet and inches). Carol singing round a giant Christmas tree every evening for ten days before Christmas. Traditional revelry on New Year's Eve.

Trocadero   4 **E3**

Coventry Street W1. Modern shopping, restaurant and leisure complex which houses, amongst other things, Funland (0171-734 3859), a games centre with kiddy rides, video games and virtuality simulation rides; and Quasar (0171-734 8151), a hi-tech version of hide and seek with laser beams. *Virtual reality theme park due to open in summer 1996.* OPEN 10.00-22.00 Mon-Thur & Sun; 10.00-24.00 Fri & Sat. Charge.

Westminster Abbey   4 **F6**

Broad Sanctuary SW1. 0171-222 7110. The Abbey is easiest to explore if you think of it in three sections: the Nave and Transept (with Poets' Corner and the tomb of the Unknown Soldier); Chapel and Shrine of Edward the Confessor (with the Coronation Chair); and Henry VII's Chapel, with a wonderful fan-vaulted roof and the tombs of many kings and queens. The Abbey Museum, in the East Cloister, has a collection of death masks and funeral effigies, including Nelson in his uniform and King Charles II in his garter robes. *For further details and opening hours see page 46. Charge.*

Westminster Cathedral   7 **C1**

Ashley Pl, off Victoria St SW1. 0171-834 7452. Striking Byzantine-style building in red and white brick. See view from the top of Campanile (273ft – 83.7m) over Westminster and the Thames. Lift usually OPEN Apr-Sep 06.45-20.00 Mon-Sun. Charge.

Trips & tours

See also 'London tours' in 'Sightseeing'.

Citisights of London

213 Brooke Rd E5. 0181-806 4325. Archaeologists and historians working in association with the Museum of London provide a series of walks and tours looking at the history and archaeology of London.

London from the top of a bus

Original London Sightseeing Tours (0181-877 1722) will take you round London in traditional double-decker buses, some of which are open-topped, or, armed with a (free) LRT Bus Map, you can devise your own 'tour' by taking one of the cross-town routes through the centre. For example, the no. 6 bus goes from Marble Arch to St Paul's Cathedral via Oxford St, Regent St, Piccadilly Circus, Trafalgar Sq, Strand, Fleet St and Ludgate Hill.

London Wall Walk   5 **D1**

Follow a sequence of tile panels tracing

1³/₄ miles (2.8km) of the City's Roman and medieval defensive wall – parts of which survive – between the Museum of London and Tower Hill. A map of Roman London on sale in the Museum of London incorporates the route.

River trips

See 'Sightseeing'.

On the Thames you can take a trip down-river to Greenwich, or to the docks at Tilbury to see the 'big ships', or upriver to Battersea, or further up towards Hampton Court. Or take a canal trip from Little Venice to Regent's Park Zoo in one of the original painted narrowboats.

Silver Jubilee Walkway

12 mile (19km) walkway created for the Queen's Silver Jubilee in 1977. Circles the centre of London, passing close to many famous and historic buildings. Start at Leicester Square (4 **E3**) and follow the discs set in the pavement. Leaflet obtainable from the London Tourist Board Information Centre, Victoria Station Forecourt SW1 (7 **B1**).

Ceremonies

Take advantage of the splendid pageantry which still survives by watching the Changing of the Queen's Guards (daily in summer) or pick one of the seasonal celebrations: Trooping the Colour – one of the most spectacular ceremonies in England which marks the Queen's official birthday in Jun, the Lord Mayor's Procession (Nov), or the Chinese New Year celebrations (Jan/Feb). See 'Sightseeing': 'Daily ceremonies and events' and 'Annual events'.

London at work

See what goes on behind the scenes – a chance to see how things work. Some places offer organised tours or group visits.

Airports

London Gatwick

West Sussex. (01293) 503843. Busy airport with all types of aircraft, including light planes. 800 ft (244 m) viewing gallery gives close view of aircraft movements. OPEN Apr-Oct 08.00-18.00 Mon-Sun; Nov-Mar 09.00-16.00 Mon-Sun. Charge.

London Heathrow

Middx. 0181-759 4321. Underground straight to Heathrow Central. From the viewing terrace watch the planes landing and taking off. Telescopes and refreshments. *OPEN 09.00-½ hr before dusk. Charge.*

Arts

Royal National Theatre   5 A4
South Bank SE1. 0171-928 2252. Gives you a glimpse of the hard work and effort which goes into making the magic of the stage. A chance to see the prop stores and workshops. *Young children must be accompanied. To arrange tours phone or write to the above address. Tours last approximately 1 hour and take place at 10.15. 12.30 & 17.30 Mon-Sat (maximum of 30 in group). Charge.*

Royal Opera House   4 F2
Covent Garden WC2. 0171-240 1200. Visit workshops, dressing rooms, rehearsal rooms and the incredible wardrobe. *Young children must be accompanied. Essential to pre-book. Groups must be a minimum of 16 and maximum of 25. To arrange tours phone or write to the Assistant House Manager at the above address. Charge.*

Business & finance

Bank of England   5 E2
Threadneedle St EC2. 0171-601 4444. Museum of the Bank of England with exhibits relating to its history together with a video explaining the work of the bank today (aimed at 13 plus). *For opening hours see page 29. Free.*

Fire stations

Be right on the spot when the siren goes. For permission to visit your local fire station (only for children of 12 years and above) write to the PR Dept, London Fire Brigade HQ, 8 Albert Embankment SE1.

Glass blowing

London Experimental Glass Workshop
7 The Leather Mkt, Weston St SE1. 0171-403 2800. One of the longest-established studios in Britain, famous worldwide for innovative use of swirling, brilliant colour. *No organised tours but visitors welcome 10.00-18.00 Mon-Fri and by appointment Sat & Sun.*

The Glasshouse   2 D2
21 St Albans Pl N1. 0171-359 8162. Watch glass being blown in the workshop from viewing gallery. Telephone to

arrange suitable time. *OPEN 10.00-17.30 Tue-Fri. Free.*

Law

Old Bailey   5 C2
Old Bailey EC4. 0171-248 3277. Trials in the Central Criminal Court can be watched from the public galleries. Worth going to see the wigs and robes worn by the judges and barristers. Minimum age 14. Under 16s must be accompanied by an adult. *OPEN 10.30-13.00 & 14.00-16.00 Mon-Fri. CLOSED B.hols. Free.*

Music

Boosey & Hawkes Musical Instrument Factory
Deansbrook Rd, Edgware, Middx. 0181-952 7711. Tour shows how a flat piece of brass is transformed into a shiny, tuneful instrument. Write well in advance. Minimum age 11. *Tours at 10.00 & 14.00 Wed. Charge (includes refreshments).*

Royal Philharmonic Orchestra   2 C5
16 Clerkenwell Grn EC1. 0171-608 2381. *For details about attending rehearsals, and about community and education projects, please contact the Music Circle on 0171-336 8540.*

Politics

Houses of Parliament   4 F5
St Margaret St W1. 0171-219 3000. To attend a debate in the House of Commons *apply to your local MP in writing, or queue at the St Stephen's entrance* (long queues in summer). *OPEN 09.30-10.00 Mon-Thur, 15.00-17.30 Fri (when House is sitting).* Tours of Westminster Hall and Palace of Westminster also *by application to your local MP. Free.*

Postal services

Several of the large central offices offer conducted tours. At each place you can see sorting, postal machinery and the Post Office underground railway. Minimum age 12. In each case, write in advance to the Postmaster Controller. Mark envelope 'Visits'.

Mount Pleasant   2 C5
Rosebery Av EC1. 0171-239 2191. Biggest sorting office in the country; underground railway. *Groups of 30 (children should be over nine). Visits Jan-Nov. Book ten days in advance. Free.*

National Postal Museum 5 D2
King Edward Bldg, King Edward St EC1.
0171-239 5420. Superb displays of
stamps. Tours by *prior arrangement.*
OPEN 09.30-16.30 Mon-Fri. Free.

Sport

Lord's Cricket Ground
St John's Wood Rd NW8. 0171-266
3825. A chance to learn some of the history of cricket in the MCC museum and to
look round the famous pavilion. *Minumum
age 7. Young children must be accompanied. Tours 12.00 & 14.00 Mon-Sun,
10.00 on a match day. No tours during
Test and Cup matches. Charge.*

Wembley Stadium
Empire Way, Wembley, Middx. 0181-902
8833. See behind the scenes and view
the famous turf on a guided tour. Visit the
dressing rooms, walk through the players'
tunnel and on to the pitch, then climb to
the Royal box to collect the cup! *Tours
summer 10.00-16.00 Mon-Sun. Charge.*

Wimbledon Lawn Tennis Museum
All England Club, Church Rd SW19.
0181-946 6131. The history of lawn
tennis with an excellent video showing
films of great matches. You are even
allowed to peek into the famous Centre
Court. *OPEN 10.30-17.00 Tue-Sat,
14.00-17.00 Sun. CLOSED Mon. Charge.*

Telephone services

BT Museum 5 C3
145 Queen Victoria St EC4. 0171-248
7444. Displays history of telecommunications, highlighting the best of present-day
design and offering a glimpse of the
future. *For opening hours see page 56.
Free.*

Museums for children

*For a full list see 'Museums and galleries'.
Many museums have educational events
or programmes, such as quizzes, trails,
lectures and film shows. Ask about
project sheets with activities based on the
displays. The following have special
features of particular interest to children.*

Baden-Powell House 6 C2
Queen's Gate SW7. 0171-584 7030.
Exhibition of the life of Baden-Powell,
founder of the scout movement. *OPEN
07.00-21.00 Mon-Sun. Free.*

**Bethnal Green Museum of
Childhood**
Cambridge Heath Rd E2. 0181-980
2415. An enchanting collection of historic
toys, dolls and dolls' houses and model
theatres, including an 18thC Venetian
marionette theatre. Special collection of
children's costumes. Regular *Sat* workshop provides facilities for drawing, puppetry and story-telling. Shop sells replicas
of old-fashioned games and toys. *OPEN
10.00-17.50 Mon-Thur & Sat, 14.30-
17.50 Sun. Free.*

Cabaret Mechanical Theatre 4 F3
Unit 33, Covent Gdn Market WC2. 0171-
379 7961. A unique collection of contemporary automata and mechanical
sculpture; over 100 hand-carved, hand-
painted moving models operated by
push-button. Great fun for inquisitive
children as the mechanics of the pieces
are all exposed. *OPEN 10.00-18.30 Mon-
Sat, from 11.00 Sun. Charge.*

Gunnersbury Park Museum
Gunnersbury Park W3. 0181-992 1612.
Set in a beautiful park, the Rothschild
Regency family mansion, now a museum
with collection of coaches, including
a travelling chariot, town chariot and
hansom cab. Costume gallery. Hands-
on exhibitions. Shop. *OPEN Apr-Oct
13.00-17.00 Mon-Fri, 13.00-18.00 Sat &
Sun; Nov-Mar 13.00-16.00 Mon-Sun.
Free.*

Horniman Museum
100 London Rd SE23. 0181-699 2339.
Collection includes arts, crafts and musical instruments from all over the world.
African masks, American Indian and
Eskimo art, stuffed animals, 'Living
Waters', a live aquaria and an observation
beehive. In the Music Room instruments
of all periods come alive at the touch of a
computer key. Refreshments. *OPEN
10.30-17.30 Mon-Sat, 14.00-17.30 Sun.
CLOSED B.hols. Free.* Children's Centre
provides crafts, drawing materials etc for
children over 8. Art and craft work is
based on observation and drawing of the
museum exhibits. *OPEN 10.30-12.30 &
13.30-15.30 Sat during termtime, Mon-
Sat during school hols. CLOSED B.hols.
Free. For further details see page 58.*

Kew Bridge Steam Museum
Green Dragon La, Brentford, Middx. 0181-
568 4757. Huge Victorian building housing
six gigantic beam engines, restored to
working order by volunteers. Under steam
at weekends. Also a working forge. New
gallery due to open in 1996: *Water for Life*

will explain the history of London's water supply. Tea-room open weekends. *OPEN 11.00-17.00 Mon-Sun inc B.hols. Charge (under 5s free).*

London Fire Brigade Museum   5 **D5**
94a Southwark Bridge Rd SE1. 0171-587 2894. Exhibits fire-fighting gear from the 17thC to the present. You can see the old uniforms and leather buckets that were once used. Not suitable for under 5s – climbing on the engines not allowed! *OPEN 09.30-16.00 Mon-Fri. Charge. By appointment only.*

London Toy & Model Museum   3 **D3**
21-23 Craven Hill W2. 0171-706 8000. Toys, dolls and trains including collection of pre-1914 toys, in a Victorian house. Model railway in the garden. *OPEN 10.00-17.30 Mon-Sun. Charge.*

London Transport Museum   4 **G3**
The Piazza, Covent Gdn WC2. 0171-379 6344. History of London's public transport told on video, with working exhibits and gleamingly-preserved historic vehicles of road and rail. 'Drive' a bus or tube or work the signals. Activity sheets available. *OPEN 10.00-18.00 (last admission 17.15) Mon-Sun. Charge.*

Museum of the Moving Image (MOMI)   5 **B4**
Under Waterloo Bridge, South Bank SE1. 0171-401 2636. Tells the history of moving images from Chinese puppet shows to hologram technology. Special series of exhibits at eye-level for those under 3ft, guided by *Sesame Street*'s Oscar the Grouch. Take part in film and television-making processes. Lectures and study rooms for groups. *OPEN 10.00-18.00 Mon-Sun. Charge.*

National Army Museum   6 **F3**
Royal Hospital Rd SW3. 0171-730 0717. Spacious museum tells the story of the British Army from 1400 to the present day. Uniforms, armour, weapon gallery, music and soldiers' songs on push-button machines. Junior Club during *summer hols. OPEN 10.00-17.30 Mon-Sun. Free.*

Pollock's Toy Museum   4 **D1**
1 Scala St W1. 0171-636 3452. Old toys, theatres and dolls crammed into two houses. Also toys for sale, including the colourful Victorian cut-out theatres for which Pollock's is famous. *For further details and opening hours see page 60. Charge (under 18s free Sat).*

Ragged School Museum
46-50 Copperfield Rd E3. 0181-980 6405. These late Victorian canal-side warehouses were converted for use as a Ragged School by Dr Barnardo. Visitors can now experience for themselves how Victorian children were taught, in a reconstructed classroom of the period. There are also displays on local history and life in the East End. *OPEN 10.00-17.00 Wed & Thur and 14.00-17.00 first Sun of the month. Free (voluntary donation).*

Royal Air Force Museum
Grahame Park Way NW9. 0181-205 2266. Plane-spotters will particularly enjoy this impressive collection of aircraft which are all exhibited in former hangars, including a man-lifting kite, airship, historic planes from World Wars I and II, and modern bombers and missiles. *OPEN 10.00-18.00 Mon-Sun. CLOSED B.hols. Charge.* Also comprises the Battle of Britain Hall and Bomber Command Hall. *OPEN same hours. Charge. For further details see page 61.*

Sherlock Holmes Museum   1 **B5**
221b Baker St NW1. 0171-935 8866. Said to be the actual house on which Conan Doyle modelled his imaginary 221b. The great detective's domestic world has been recreated based on detailed study of the stories. See Holmes' cluttered sitting room and bedroom, full of personal touches. In Dr Watson's room you can sit by the fire and read the stories and period magazines. *OPEN 09.30-18.00 Mon-Sun. Charge.*

Tower Hill Pageant   5 **G3**
1 Tower Hill Terrace EC3. 0171-709 0081. London's first 'darkride' museum where an automated car takes you on a journey through converted wine vaults near the Tower of London. The Pageant focuses on the riverside port area and depicts scenes from 2000 years of London's history. See Londoners fleeing in panic before the Great Fire of 1666 and get a bird's eye view of the city from a German bomber as it blitzed the docks in 1940. Europe's largest holograms depict medieval life. *OPEN Apr-Oct 09.30-17.30 Mon-Sun; Nov-Mar 09.30-16.30 Mon-Sun. Charge.*

Winston Churchill's Britain at War Theme Museum   5 **F4**
64-66 Tooley St SE1. 0171-403 3171. A hands-on theme museum where you can relive the drama of life in Britain during the Second World War. Journey to the London underground where many spent sleepless nights while the bombing raids went on overhead. Hear Hitler's declara-

tion of war and Churchill's promise that Britain would never be defeated. Huddle inside an Anderson shelter. Wait for the 'all-clear'. Experience the sights, sounds and smells of the Blitz. *OPEN Apr-Sep 10.00-17.30 Mon-Sun; Oct-Mar 10.00-16.30 Mon-Sun. Charge.*

London's countryside

London's parks and surrounding country-side are surprisingly rich in outdoor pursuits, and there is a great variety of wildlife to be found even in the heart of the metropolis. Some of the opportunities are listed here.

Aeroplanes

The airshow season runs from Apr-Oct, and gives children a chance to see planes at close quarters.

Shuttleworth Collection
Old Warden Aerodrome, nr Biggleswade, Beds. (01767) 627288. Famous collection of vintage aircraft. Film and introductory talk for pre-booked groups. *OPEN Apr-end Oct 10.00-17.00 Mon-Sun; Nov-Mar 10.00-16.00 Mon-Sun*. Special flying displays *first Sun of month May-Oct. Charge.*

Animal & bird enclosures in parks

These are local parks with small animal and bird enclosures. They are open dawn-dusk Mon-Sun, unless otherwise stated, and all are free. See also 'Zoos, aquaria and wildlife parks'.

Battersea Park SW11   **6 G5**
0181-871 7540. Zoo with small collection of animals. Reptile house, wide variety of primates, otter, meerkat and mongoose enclosures, flamingoes, ponies and donkeys, deer, wallabies, rheas. *OPEN Easter-Sep 10.00-17.00 Mon-Sun; Nov-Mar 11.00-15.00 Sat & Sun only. CLOSED 2 weeks in Feb.*

Clissold Park N16
0181-806 1826. Fallow deer, rabbits, guinea pigs, tropical birds including a mynah bird, a peacock and a collection of waterfowl.

Crystal Palace Park SE20
0181-778 7148. Farm with shire horses, cows, pigs, rabbits, chickens, donkeys, penguins, otters, goats, sheep and ponies. Shire horse cart rides round the park for children. *OPEN*

11.00-17.00 Mon-Sun. For further details see page 63.

Golders Hill Park NW11
0181-455 5183. Fallow deer, pygmy goats, wallabies and blackbuck. Birds include pheasants, cranes, flamingoes and rheas.

Hainault Forest, Essex
0181-500 3106. Ponies, donkeys, cows and pigs. Also collection of domestic and wild fowl, including peacocks and guinea fowl.

Holland Park W8   **3 A5**
0171-602 9483. Collection of birds, including peacocks, sparrow hawk, great spotted woodpecker and peafowl.

Maryon Wilson Park SE7
0181-854 0446. Ponies, goats, a donkey, fallow deer and Jacob sheep, as well as rabbits and chickens. Guided tours.

Plashet Park E6
0181-503 5994. A mini-zoo with a small collection of animals. Tropical aviary and butterfly house. *OPEN summer 09.00-17.00 Tue-Sun; winter 09.00-16.00 Tue-Sun. OPEN B.hol Mon.*

Sydenham Wells Park SE26
Wells Park Rd. 0181-695 6000. Aviary where they breed budgies; also ducks, colourful pheasants and geese. Rabbits in their warrens.

Syon Park, Brentford
London Butterfly House, Syon Park, Brentford, Middx. 0181-560 7272. A greenhouse full of tropical and temperate butterflies. Gallery featuring variety of insects and bizarre invertebrates. *OPEN Apr-Oct 10.00-17.00 Mon-Sun; Nov-Mar 10.00-15.30 Mon-Sun. Charge.*

Victoria Park E2
0181-985 1957. A small enclosure on the eastern side of the park with fallow deer and pygmy goats. A wide variety of wild birds can be seen on the other side of the park. Fishing permitted in western lake.

Birdwatching

See *'Natural history'* under *'Activities and Interests'*.

Cemeteries

Some children find cemeteries fascinating rather than morbid or frightening, and many of London's older cemeteries are wonderful places to explore, not only for their monumental stonework and strange epitaphs but also as the peaceful haunt of many small animals and birds. See 'Looking at history' in 'Historic London'.

Fairs

There are over 200 fairs a week held in England during the summer; the following is a selection of some in London.

Holiday Fairs
Alexandra Park, Blackheath, Hampstead Heath and Wormwood Scrubs (*Easter, spring & summer B.hols*).

Other Occasional Fairs
Clapham Common (*mid Apr*), Crystal Palace (*early May & Aug*), Tooting Bec Common (*early May*), Victoria Park (*early May*).

Farms

There are several farms in and around London which are open to visitors. In London itself, there are small city farms which welcome visits from families and school groups; it is advisable to phone in advance if you're going in a large group. Outside London you can visit large working farms which organise open days and farm trails.

College Farm
Fitzalan Rd N3. 0181-349 0690. Small children's farm with cows, goats, pigs, sheep and shire horses. Special events on *first Sun of month* – craft stalls, donkey rides, bouncy castle. *OPEN 10.00-18.00 Mon-Sun. Charge.*

Freightliners Farm
Entrance: Sheringham Rd N7. 0171-609 0467. Small, busy city farm with cows and calves, sheep, goats and kids, ducks, pigs, geese, bees and chickens. Lots of opportunities to get involved with the animals. Café and farmshop. *Phone for times of tours. Groups must phone in advance. OPEN 09.00-13.00 & 14.00-17.00 Tue-Sun. CLOSED Mon. Free (voluntary donation).*

Hackney City Farm
1a Goldsmith's Row, off Hackney Rd E2. 0171-729 6381. Sheep, rabbits, calves, guinea pigs, poultry, ducks and bees. Pottery, spinning and weaving classes. Ecological pond, beekeeping, butterfly tunnel. Loan scheme under which schools can borrow animals. *OPEN 10.00-16.30 Tue-Sun. CLOSED Mon (except B.hols). Free.*

Kentish Town City Farm
Grafton Rd NW5. 0171-916 5420. Horses, pigs, chickens, sheep, goats and rabbits. Feeding twice daily. *OPEN 09.00-17.00 Tue-Sun. OPEN B.hols. Free.*

Mudchute Farm
Pier St E14. 0171-515 5901. Large (32-acre – 13ha) city farm run by staff and volunteers who look after the beef cattle, ponies, sheep, goats, pigs, poultry, rabbits and bees. There is also a riding school and pony club, a nature study centre and café. The Mudchute is the venue for the annual Isle of Dogs Agricultural Show. *OPEN 09.00-17.00 Mon-Sun. Free.*

Stepping Stones Farm
Stepney Way E1. 0171-790 8204. 6-acre (2.4ha) urban farm in the East End. Activities vary with the seasons, but the livestock population usually includes pigs, goats, cows, sheep, ducks, geese, rabbits and donkeys. Wildlife pond. Picnic garden. Produce shop. *OPEN 09.30-18.00 (dusk in winter) Tue-Sun. CLOSED Mon (except B.hols). Free (voluntary donation).*

Surrey Docks Farm
Rotherhithe St SE16. 0171-231 1010. 2-acre (0.8ha) site with goats, pigs, donkeys, ducks, geese and hens plus small orchard, vegetable garden, duckpond, bee observation room, herb garden and riverside walk. Blacksmith demonstrates traditional skills. Farm shop sells fresh produce. *OPEN 10.00-13.00 & 14.00-17.00 Tue-Sun. CLOSED Mon & Fri in school hols. Free.*

Vauxhall City Farm
Tyers St SE11. 0171-582 4204. Tours to visit the pigs, goats, sheep and rabbits. Pony and donkey rides. *OPEN 10.30-17.00 Tue-Thur, Sat & Sun. Charge (for tours only).*

Fish & fishing

The river Thames is now cleaner than it has been for centuries, and supports a growing number of fish including salmon and trout. Many fish are to be found in London's ponds, lakes and canals. See 'Fishing' and 'Fishing: lakes and ponds' under 'Sport'.

London Anglers' Association
Izaak Walton House, 2a Hervey Park Rd E17. 0181-520 7477. Membership gives information about places to fish and a London Anglers' Licence for coarse fishing on the Grand Union/Regent's Canal and River Lea. *Annual charge.*

Kite-flying

Flying your own kite is a great pleasure but you can meet other kite-flyers, or see the experts in action, at the following places in London: Blackheath, Clapham Common, Dulwich Park, Hampstead Heath on the top of Parliament Hill Fields, Primrose Hill, Richmond Park and near the Round Pond in Kensington Gardens. There are regular stunt kite events at Blackheath and an Indoor Kite Festival at London Arena, Limeharbour, Docklands.

Model villages

Bekonscot
Warwick Rd, Beaconsfield, Bucks. (01494) 672919. A raised viewing platform offers a bird's eye view of the miniature land of shops, houses, cottages, pubs. Model (gauge 1) railway travels round the village. Picnic facilities and playground. *OPEN Feb-Oct 10.00-17.00 Mon-Sun. Charge.*

Nature reserves & nature trails

English Nature
Northminster House, Peterborough, Cambs. (01733) 340345. Will give regional office number who will supply a list of reserves and leaflets about individual reserves in England.
Camley Street Natural Park 1 G3
12 Camley St NW1. 0171-833 2311. A park which has been created in a former coal drop on the Grand Union Canal to provide a wildlife refuge and a place to enjoy nature in the city. Visitor centre, classroom. *OPEN 10.00-17.00 Mon-Fri, 11.00-17.00 Sat & Sun. CLOSED B.hols. Free (voluntary donation).*
East Ham Nature Reserve
Norman Rd E6. 0181-470 4525. A nature reserve in the heart of East London's largest churchyard. Follow the nature trail. See pheasants and butterflies. Special activities during *school hols. OPEN 09.00-17.00 (dusk in winter) Mon-Sun. Visitor Centre OPEN 14.00-17.00 Sat & Sun. Free.*
Horniman Gardens
London Rd SE23. 0181-669 8924. Three walks: Coach trail, Dutch Barn trail and Railway trail following the track of the old Crystal Palace high level railway line. *OPEN dawn-dusk Mon-Sun. Free.*

Steam & traction engines

*Once common, these early engines have now become collectors' pieces. Rallies are held periodically by clubs in various parts of the country. They are colourful and unusual, and the engines themselves are superb. Contact the **National Traction Engine Trust** for a list of rallies and clubs. The junior section is called the Steam Apprentice Club and is for enthusiasts under 21. For information write to Mrs Sylvia Dudley, 12 Hillway, Woburn Sands, Bucks. A useful book is* Traction Engines *by Harold Bonnett (Shire Publications). Apart from the Science Museum, the following collections are worth seeing:*
Kew Bridge Steam Museum
See *'Museums for children'* section.
National Motor Museum
Beaulieu, Hants. (01590) 612345. More than 250 vehicles and displays which illustrate the story of motoring, including the traction engine, 'Supreme'. *OPEN May-Sep 10.00-18.00 Mon-Sun; Oct-Apr 10.00-17.00 Mon-Sun. Charge.*
Thursford Museum
Thursford, Fakenham, Norfolk. (01328) 878477. A superb collection of various engines and machines including fairground and other organs, fairground rides and traction engines – all working. *OPEN Easter-Oct 13.00 (11.30 Jun, Jul & Aug)-17.00 Mon-Sun. Charge.*

Windmills

Once a prominent feature of south-east England, though most are now derelict. Discovering Windmills *by J. Vince (Shire Publications) is an inexpensive introduction and guide. Two remaining in London are:*
Brixton Windmill
Blenheim Gdns, Brixton Hill SW9. A reminder of Lambeth's rural past. The early 19thC tower mill was in use until 1934. *OPEN to school parties by appointment only.*
Wimbledon Windmill
Wimbledon Common SW19. Contact: Honorary Curator, 0181-947 2825, for information. A hollow post mill, built in 1817, now housing a museum with models and photographs explaining how windmills work. *OPEN Apr-Oct 14.00-17.00 Sat, Sun & B.hols. Small charge.*

Zoos

See under 'Zoos, aquaria and wildlife parks' in 'Outdoor London'.

Activities and interests

In London you can enjoy just about every hobby you can imagine, from arts, crafts and theatre to natural history, science and sport (see 'Sport'). Scouts, guides and youth clubs are also listed here under 'Youth organisations'.

Archaeology

The best way to get experience, and maybe join in a dig, is to join the junior section of an archaeological society – for local clubs, enquire at your nearest library or contact the organisations below:

**London and Middlesex   5 D1
Archaeological Society (LAMAS)**
Contact: Young LAMAS, c/o MOLAS, Number One London Wall EC2. 0181-505 1241. *Phone for details of activities.*

Young Archaeologists' Club
Bowes Morrell House, 111 Walmgate, York. (01904) 671417. For 9-16 year olds. The club is linked to British Archaeology and organises visits to sites, fieldwork and lectures (usually outside London). Magazine with news from around the world.

Arts & crafts

See also 'Community arts centres', and 'Museums for children' (several have painting and crafts workshops).

Camden Arts Centre
Arkwright Rd NW3. 0171-435 2643. *Sat & Sun morning and afternoon* sessions for 4-17 year-olds in painting and drawing, sculpture and ceramics. Courses *during school hols.* Local schools visit *during term time.*

Chelsea Pottery   7 B2
5 Ebury Mews SW1. 0171-259 0164. Good, well-established studio. Children's classes *10.00-13.00 & 14.00-17.00 Sat.* Minimum age 5. Annual membership. *Charge.*

Susan Meyer-Michael
99 North End Rd NW11. 0181-455 0817. Pottery and clay modelling. Small groups, family groups, or individuals. *Sessions by arrangement only. Charge.*

Astronomy

Greenwich Planetarium (Old Royal Observatory) and the London Planetarium show projections of the sky and stars (see 'Looking at London'). There is also an annual Astronomy Exhibition held in London each Feb. Phone 0171-915 0054 for details.

Hampstead Scientific Society
The Secretary, 22 Flask Wlk NW3. 0171-794 9341. Organises talks and outings, and also has its own observatory at Lower Ter NW3 (nr Whitestone Pond). *OPEN Sep-Apr 20.00-22.00 Fri & Sat, 11.00-13.00 Sun, weather permitting. Monthly meetings Sep-Jun. Annual junior subscription.*

Junior Astronomical Society
The Secretary, 36 Fairway, Keyworth, Notts. For interested beginners of any age. Meets four times a year in London. Quarterly magazine and bi-monthly newsletter sent to members. *Annual subscription.*

Boat clubs

Opportunities to learn canoeing, rowing and sailing. (You can hire rowing boats by the hour in some parks. See 'Parks and gardens' in 'Outdoor London').

The Sports Council
Greater London & SE Region, Crystal Palace National Sports Centre, Ledrington Rd SE19. 0181-778 8600. The information 'unit' can provide you with a list of canoeing and sailing centres in and around London.

Westminster Boating Base   7 D4
Dinorvic Wharf, 136 Grosvenor Rd, SW1. 0171-821 7389. Youth programme including canoeing and sailing.

Book clubs

Bookworm
W. Heffer & Sons, 20 Trinity St, Cambridge. (01223) 568568. Bookworm is for 0-12 year-olds. Run through schools or groups.

Puffin School Book Club   3 C6
c/o Penguin Books Ltd, 27 Wright's La W8. 0171-938 2200. Established book club for 0-13 year-olds. Encourages an interest in reading and books. There are three clubs: Fledgling (0-6 yrs), Flight (7-9 yrs) and Post (9-13 yrs).

Scholastic Publications
Westfield Rd, Southam, Leamington Spa, Warks. (01926) 887799. Promotes a variety of book clubs: Seesaw (0-6 yrs), Lucky (7-9 yrs), Chip (9-12 yrs) and Scene (12+ yrs). Monthly Club News. Children join through their schools.

Brass rubbing

You can learn how to make your own rubbings at brass rubbing centres, which provide replicas of many historic monumental brasses plus everything you need. The cost of rubbings is graded according to the sizes of the brasses. Once experienced, search out brasses in old churches all over the country, but ask for permission first.

All Hallows-by-the-Tower   **5 F3**
Byward St EC3. 0171-481 2928. At the west end of the church, an appealing assembly of about 30 brasses, although space allows for no more than 10 people to make rubbings at one time. Free instruction available. *OPEN 11.00-16.00 Mon-Fri, 11.00-17.00 Sat, 13.00-17.00 Sun. Book for groups. Charge.*

London Brass Rubbing Centre   **4 F3**
St-Martin-in-the-Fields WC2. 0171-437 6023. Replicas on display of 70 British and European brasses ranging from animal figures, children and wool merchants to a crusader knight which stands 7ft (2.1m) tall. Instruction available. *OPEN 10.00-18.00 Mon-Sat, 12.00-18.00 Sun. Charge.*

Community arts centres

These are centres which organise a great variety of activities for both children and adults. Usually a small charge.

Battersea Arts Centre
Lavender Hill SW11. 0171-223 6557. Children's day on *Sat*, with workshops, acting classes and puppetry, plus shows and films. Workshops *during school hols.*

Inter-Action Social   **5 B3**
Enterprise Trust
HMS President (1918), nr Blackfriars Bridge, Victoria Embankment EC4. 0171-583 2652. Facilities for computing, children's workshops and a hands-on technology centre.

Jackson's Lane Community Centre
269a Archway Rd N6. 0181-340 5226. *After-school* and *holiday* workshops for children including arts and crafts, dance and shadow puppets, plus an excellent programme of visiting theatre and dance groups, children's shows *Sat*. Also run a parent and toddlers group.

Riverside Studios
Crisp Rd W6. 0181-741 2255. Spacious arts centre which organises some children's educational visits and holiday activities. Children's entertainment at *weekends.*

Cricket

Many London parks have practice nets which can be booked through the park authorities.

English Schools Cricket Association
c/o Mr Lake, 38 Mill House, Woods Lane, Cottingham, North Humberside (01482) 844446. Governing body for cricket in schools.

MCC Indoor Cricket School
Lord's Cricket Ground, St John's Wood Rd NW8. 0171-286 3649. Coaching from 8 years upwards, beginners and advanced.

Cycling

British Cycling Federation
National Cycling Centre, Stuart St, Manchester. 0161-230 2301. A society for all sorts of cyclists: racers, commuters, tourists and general leisure riders. Comprehensive insurance, an annual handbook with advice and tips, a coaching service and information on racing.

Cycling Proficiency Tests
Most boroughs organise their own cycling proficiency lessons and tests for 9-13 year-olds. Certificates are issued to those who pass tests in the theory and practice of safe bicycling. Enquire at your local town hall for details or contact the Royal Society for the Prevention of Accidents (RSPA), Cannon House, The Priory, Queensway, Birmingham. 0121-200 2461.

Lee Valley Cycle Circuits
Temple Mills La E15. 0181-534 6085. Coaching to improve cycling ability, training ground for more experienced cyclists. Bikes for hire. BMX and mountain bike track. Minimum age 7. *OPEN Mar-Sep 08.00-20.00 Mon-Sun; Oct-Feb 08.00-13.30 Mon-Fri. Charge.*

Dancing

Dance Works   **4 B2**
16 Balderton St W1. 0171-629 6183. Classes on *Sat* for 5-10 year-olds in classical ballet. *Mon evening* classes in tap and jazz for 3-5 yrs, 5-9 yrs, 9-16 yrs. *Thur evening* classes in contemporary dance for 5-10 yrs. *Charge.*

Imperial Society of Teachers   **2 A4**
of Dancing
Imperial House, 22-26 Paul St EC2. 0171-377 1577. Teachers of ballet by the Cecchetti method and other types of dance. Send sae for a list of teachers and local dance schools.

Islington Dance Factory
Vergers Cottage, 2 Parkhurst Rd N7. 0171-607 0561. Community arts centre specialising in dance and music. Classes for 6-18 year-olds *after school* and on *Sat*: ballet for 6-11 yrs, dance theatre workshop for 8-12 yrs and 13+ yrs, contemporary elementary dance class for 12-18 yrs, boys' ballet classes, adult *evening* classes. *Charge*.

The Place   1 **F4**
17 Duke's Rd WC1. 0171-387 0031. The Young Place offers dance classes for ages 6-8, 8-10, 10-12 and 13-17 on *Sat mornings*. Also the home of the Richard Alston Dance Company. A Youth Dance Group offers extensive and exciting dance experience for 13-18 year-olds.

Royal Academy of Dancing   6 **D6**
36 Battersea Sq, SW11. 0171-223 0091. Classes in classical ballet for children aged 5-17, leading to RAD graded examinations. Entry to all classes is by audition only. Send sae for lists of teachers, addressed to the Registration & Membership Department.

Royal Ballet School
White Lodge, Richmond Park, Surrey. 0181-748 6335. This is the Lower School for children aged 11-16. Auditions are held to determine potential for classical ballet training. Accepted children receive a full-time general education in addition to being taught classical ballet.

Anna Scher Children's   2 **C2**
Theatre
70-72 Barnsbury Rd N1. 0171-278 2101. *After-school* classes for children from age 6 in improvisation, poetry, production, stage technique and theory of theatre. Lessons are imaginatively and thoroughly planned. Long waiting list for places. *Charge*.

Greenwich and Lewisham Young People's Theatre
Burrage Rd SE18. 0181-854 1316. Lively *evening* workshops *Mon-Fri during school terms* for 11-25 year-olds, ranging from drama to visual arts. Occasional performances by outside groups. *Charge*.

National Youth Theatre
Holloway Rd N7. 0171-281 3863. Ages 14-21. Auditions are held in *Feb & Mar* (closing date to apply for audition *end Dec*) to select the casts of plays to be rehearsed and performed during the summer hols. Only cost is your own food and accommodation during the *summer* and sometimes a few *weekends* in between.

Polka Children's Theatre
240 The Broadway SW19. 0181-543 4888. Workshops and courses for 3 year-olds upwards. Music, clowning and puppet-making may be on the agenda.

Questors Theatre
Mattock La W5. 0181-567 0011. Excellent amateur theatre club with drama playgroups on *Sat mornings* for 5-9 year-olds. Emphasis on imaginative play and role-playing activities. Junior Drama Workshops are held on *weekday evenings* and *Sun mornings*. Role-playing, improvisation and acting exercises. Groups graded according to age and experience. *Charge*.

Theatre Royal Stratford East
Gerry Raffles Sq E15. 0181-534 0310. Theatre workshop for 9-14 year-olds on *Sat mornings* and on *Mon evenings* for those aged 14 upwards. Drama, games, mime, maskwork. Usually lead to performances in the theatre. *Free*.

Upstream Children's Theatre
Ilderton School, Varcoe Rd, off Old Kent Rd SE16 (entrance in Ilderton Rd). 0171-232 2869. Educational drama and theatre workshops for 3-12 year-olds. Workshops include improvisation, story-telling, stage performance, puppetry, music.

Children's Film Unit
9 Hamilton House, Upper Richmond Rd, SW15. 0181-871 2006. Organises movie making for 8-16 year-olds. Camera skills, sound, make-up, continuity, script-writing. Sessions on *Sat* and full length movie made in the *summer hols*.

English Folk Song & Dance   1 **C2**
Society
Cecil Sharp House, 2 Regent's Park Rd NW1. 0171-485 2206. The Hobby Horse Club is the children's section. Members receive a badge, a birthday card, newsletters and a list of festivals where there will be children's events. There is a children's day of dance held *once a month*.

Football Association   3 **D3**
16 Lancaster Gate W2. 0171-262 4542.

Each county has a youth section that the Football Association will put you in touch with or you can contact the English Schools Association, 4a Eastgate St, Stafford, Staffs. (01785) 51142. Almost all sports centres (*see 'Sport, Health and Fitness'*) offer five-a-side football as one of their activities.

Go-karting

RAC Motor Sports Association
Motor Sports House, Riverside Park, Colnbrook, Slough, Berks. (01753) 681736. Organise go-karting for children from 8 years on. Supply information on fixture lists and regulations, as well as safety details.

Gymnastics

Most sports centres provide classes and coaching for all ages, including under-5s.
Amateur Gymnastics Association
The Secretary, Mrs J. Thatch, 4 Victoria Rd E4. 0181-529 1142. Organising body for the sport; will provide advice and a list of clubs.

Life-saving

Your local swimming baths should provide information about coaching and tests.
Royal Life-Saving Society
Mountbatten House, Studley, Warks. (01527) 853943. They will send you info-rmation on your local branch.

Music

There is a professional register of music teachers which should be available in the reference section of your library.
London College of Music
Thames Valley University, St Mary's Road, Ealing W5. 0181-231 2304. *Sat morning* junior music school for children over 5. Also individual lessons for any instrument.

National Youth Jazz Orchestra
Meets at the London Studio Centre, 42-50 York Way, Kings Cross on *Sat*. Two sessions – *10.30* and *14.30*. Musicians must be of a high standard. Details from 11 Victor Rd, Harrow, Middx. 0181-863 2717.

National Youth Orchestra of Great Britain
Causeway House, Lodge Causeway, Fishponds, Bristol BS16 3HD. Write for detailed information and application forms. Children aged 11-17 can apply for

audition to be trained, and once a member of the orchestra remain so until they are 19 (subject to annual re-audition).
Youth Music Centre
Contact: Jane Barnett on 0181-343 1940. Lively centre with music school, orchestras and classes on *Sat mornings during term time* for ages 4-16. All types of classical music. *Charge.*

Natural history & conservation

In urban areas, reservoirs have become an important habitat for birds.
Barn Elms Reservoirs SW13
Walthamstow Reservoirs N17
Walton Reservoirs, Surrey
Phone or write to: Thames Water, Customer Services Centre, PO Box 1850, Swindon, Wilts SN1 4TW. (01734) 591159 to obtain their free leaflet *'Reservoir Leisure Guide'*.
Lifewatch   1 **C3**
London Zoo, Regent's Park NW1. 0171-722 3333. For 4-15 year-olds. Membership (*charge*) gives free entry to London Zoo throughout the year, one free admission to Whipsnade Wild Animal Park, subscription to the London Zoo magazine three times a year, hol lectures, films and outings.
London Natural History Society
Contact: Mr Barrett, Secretary, 21 Green Way, Frinton-on-Sea, Essex CO13 9AL. (01255) 674678. Welcomes junior mem-bers to the regular outings and meetings in London and elsewhere. Birdwatching excursions *midweek* and most *week-ends*. Covers the area within a 20-mile (32km) radius of St Paul's Cathedral. Newsletter and bulletin every two months. *Charge.*
Young Ornithologists' Club
c/o The Royal Society for the Protection of Birds (RSPB), The Lodge, Sandy, Beds. (01767) 680551. Junior membership gives a badge, a bi-monthly magazine *(Bird Life)* and a chance to take part in outings to RSPB reserves and join in special projects. They also organise holiday courses. Family, school and group membership also available. *Charge.*

Poetry

Poetry Society   4 **F2**
22 Betterton St, Covent Garden WC2. 0171-240 4810. Occasional children's workshops and events including chil-dren's poetry competitions. Also runs the

Poets in Schools scheme whereby well-known poets visit schools. Enquiries to Education Officer.

Puppet Centre Trust
Battersea Arts Centre, Lavender Hill SW11. 0171-228 5335. National reference centre for everything to do with puppetry. Offers information and consultancy service, exhibition and shop. Bi-monthly magazine.

The Harbour Club
Watermeadow La SW6. 0171-371 7700. Tennis, swimming and basketball camps *mornings during the school hols.* Tennis coaching for all standards; Munchkin Club for 2-5 year-olds includes musical movement too. Parents must be members.

Girl Guides Association   **4 C6**
17-19 Buckingham Palace Rd SW1. 0171-834 6242. For girls aged 7-11 there are Brownie packs and at the age of 10 girls can become Guides. From 14-25 they become Rangers.

London Union of Youth Clubs
64 Camberwell Rd SE5. 0171-701 6366. To put you in touch with your local clubs. If you live in Greater London you should contact youth and community departments in local boroughs. The Union is for 7-25 year-olds but mainly deals with 12-21 year-olds.

National Association of Boys' Clubs
369 Kennington Lane SE11. 0171-793 0787. For girls too! Information about clubs, adventure courses and activity holidays.

Scout Association   **3 D5**
Baden-Powell House, 65 Queen's Gate SW7. 0171-584 7030. Headquarters of the movement. They will give you the address of your nearest group. Boys aged 6-8 become Beavers, at the age of 8-11 become Cubs and above that age Scouts. 16-21 year-olds can become Venture Scouts. Girls can now also join the Scout movement – *phone for details.*

Most parks offer facilities for children's play – swings, roundabouts, slides etc.

Conventional playgrounds
Provided by borough councils in most local parks. They usually have tarmac surfaces with swings, roundabouts, slides, seesaws, climbing frames, and iron rocking-horses. Some of this equipment is potentially dangerous for small children and newer, safer playgrounds have swings made of rubber tyres, rubber matting instead of concrete and built-up slides made of durable plastic. *OPEN 08.00-19.00 (or dusk) Mon-Sun.*

Handicapped Adventure Playground Association
Fulham Palace, Bishops Av SW6. 0171-736 4443. The Association runs five playgrounds for the handicapped in London and provides information about its services as well as play ideas for handicapped children. All the playgrounds are carefully planned and landscaped with children with special needs in mind. Also advisory service which gives help to those wishing to set up their own playground.

One o'clock clubs
Enclosed area in some parks for children under 5. Each club has a building for indoor play (painting, drawing, modelling etc) and an enclosure with climbing frames, swings and sandpit for outdoor play. There are playworkers to supervise activities but a parent or guardian is expected to stay on the premises. Informal and friendly. To find your nearest club, contact the local borough council. *OPEN 13.00-16.30 Mon-Fri. Free.*

Playparks
Intended for children of 5-15 years – the aim is towards free play with structures for climbing, swinging etc and playworkers to supervise. You'll find them in Alexandra Park, Battersea Park, Crystal Palace Park, Holland Park and on Hampstead Heath (Parliament Hill Fields). Contact the local borough council for information. *OPEN summer 11.30-20.00 Mon-Sun.*

The following are indoor play centres OPEN daily:

Fantasy Island Playcentre
Vale Farm, Watford Rd, Wembley. 0181-904 9044. Giant multi-level 'obstacle course' for 2-12 year-olds.

Kidstop
Edgware Rd NW9. 0181-201 3580. Multi-level play arena.

There are innumerable organisations which arrange holidays for unaccompanied children, and others which arrange family holidays.

Camp Beaumont   **3 F1**
Worthington House, 203-205 Old

Marylebone Rd NW1. 0171-724 2233. Residential and day camps around London – Brentwood, Mill Hill, Orpington, Windsor and Wimbledon – during the *summer*. An incredible range of activities to get involved in – water sports, ball sports, motor sports, stage and screen. Centres vary in the activities they offer so everyone is matched to a suitable centre. From the nursery day camps for the small ones to holidays for the independent teenager.

English Tourist Board
Ring (01432) 357335 to obtain a copy of their annual publication *Activity Holidays*, which is packed with information covering a huge range of holidays in England, from walking, riding, sailing, birdwatching and painting to underwater swimming, archery or fossil hunting. Also multi-activity holidays. There is a special section on holidays for unaccompanied children, and places welcoming families are indicated. Also useful is their Tourist Information Directory – visit the British Travel Centre, 12 Lower Regent St SW1 (4 **D3**) or write to Dept D, English Tourist Board, Thames Tower, Blacks Rd W6.

PGL Young Adventure
Alton Court, Penyard Lane, Ross-on-Wye, Herefordshire. (01989) 764211. Holidays for ages 3-18. Up to 40 activities including canoeing, pony trekking, sailing, camping, hobby holidays under expert guidance at 30 locations in Britain and abroad. Also family holidays. Brochures available.

Trent Park Equestrian Centre
Bramley Rd, Southgate N14. 0181-363 8630/9005. 'Own-a-Pony' weeks where everyone 'adopts' a pony and visits the stable every day for a week to look after and ride it. Also 4-day holidays looking after a pony and riding it twice a day. *Phone for details*.

YHA Adventure Holidays
Youth Hostel Association, Trevelyan House, St Stephen's Hill, St Albans, Herts. (01727) 855215. Adventure holidays for 11-15 year-olds (in groups of 10-12) with experienced instructors. Large range of special interest holidays as well as multi-activity holidays. Older YHA members can also arrange their own cycling or walking holidays and make use of the YHA hostels.

Exchanges

Amitié Internationale des Jeunes
36 Chaulden House Gdns, Hemel Hempstead, Herts. (01442) 250886. Exchanges between French and British

school-children, 11-18 year-olds. Escorts are provided on the journey between London and Paris.

Central Bureau for   4 **B2**
Educational Visits & Exchanges
10 Spring Gdns SW1. 0171-389 4004. They publish several excellent guides including *Volunteer Work*, *Working Holidays*, *A Year Between*, *Study Holidays* and *Home From Home* covering opportunities both at home and abroad. Send an sae (no personal callers).

Entertainment

Venues which provide children's shows, films and concerts. For information about current productions, see children's section of Time Out *or call (0891) 559 905 (also for ticket availability; calls cost 39p per minute cheap rate and 49p at other times).*
Many West End and provincial theatres stage pantomimes for children at Christmas: look in Time Out *in the autumn.*

Children's theatre

The following theatres put on children's shows regularly throughout the year. Phone for programme details. For drama workshops, see 'Activities and interests'.

Barbican   5 **D1**
Silk St EC2. 0171-638 4141. Annual festival for all the family in the *summer hols* with concerts, clowns, scavenger hunts and workshops. *Phone for details.*

Little Angel Marionette   2 **D2**
Theatre
14 Dagmar Pas, off Cross St N1. 0171-226 1787. London's only permanent puppet theatre, which presents an excellent variety of shows by the resident company and visiting puppeteers. Essential to book in advance. Regular performances at *15.00 Sat & Sun* for older children and adults. Special show for the very young (4-6 year-olds) *11.00 Sat & Sun*. Extra shows during *half-term and school hols.*

Polka Children's Theatre
240 The Broadway, Wimbledon SW19. 0181-543 4888. Extremely attractive theatre complex, exclusively for children. 300-seat theatre with plays, puppet shows and concerts; exhibitions of toys and puppets; children's workshop, adventure room, garden playground and café catering with children in mind. Age 3

upwards. Full facilities for handicapped children including a loop system for deaf children. *OPEN Tue-Sat.*

Puppet Theatre Barge
Bookings and details from 78 Middleton Rd E8. 0171-249 6876. A marionette theatre in a converted Thames barge, which has regular moorings at Little Venice *Nov-May*. Tours up the Thames to Oxford from *May-Sep* and is moored at different places on the river. Its position is listed in the London entertainment guides. Performances *Sat & Sun* and *daily during school holidays.*

Tricycle Theatre
269 Kilburn High Rd NW6. 0171-328 1000. Fun children's shows *every Sat 11.30 & 14.00*, plus productions by the Tricycle themselves, put on at *half terms*. Children under 7 yrs must be accompanied by a paying adult. *Term time and half term workshops.* Essential to book in advance. Wheelchair access and a loop system for deaf children.

Unicorn Theatre for Children   4 F3
Arts Theatre, Great Newport St WC2. 0171-836 3334. Well-established children's theatre which presents plays (often specially commissioned) and other entertainment for the 4-12s. Public performances 11.00 & *14.30 Sat & 14.30 Sun* (extra performances during *school hols)*. Performances for schools *Tue-Fri* during term time. Also a children's club, which organises workshop sessions.

Young Vic Theatre   5 B5
66 The Cut SE1. 0171-928 6363. A good choice of revivals and new experimental theatre, specially written children's plays and adaptations of Shakespeare, including five of their own productions per year. Aimed primarily at young audiences. A comprehensive education service and out-of-school workshops. Age approx 12 upwards.

Children's films

Remember there are age limits for certain films: U = suitable for all ages; PG = parental guidance advised and unsuitable for young children; 12 = suitable for 12 years and over; 15 = suitable for 15 years and over; 18 = suitable for 18 years and over.
Saturday morning cinema clubs show children's films at cheap prices. See children's section in Time Out.

Barbican   5 D1
Silk St EC2. 0171-638 4141. Children's cinema club on *Sat*; films for members *14.30*.

National Film Theatre   5 A4
South Bank SE1. 0171-928 3535. Junior matinees, usually *Sat & Sun afternoons.*

Children's concerts

Several organisations arrange children's concerts (mainly classical music) through the autumn and winter. Also look out for steel bands, brass bands and jazz bands at summer festivals and fairs in the parks. For details of pop concerts look in Melody Maker, New Musical Express *and* Time Out.

Arthur Davison Orchestral Concerts
Fairfield Hall, Croydon, Surrey. 0181-688 9291. Orchestral concerts for children – selection of short pieces, using a wide variety of instruments. A good way of introducing children to music. Season tickets available for seven concerts *Sep-May at 11.00 Sat. Charge.*

Ernest Read Concerts for   5 A4 Children
Royal Festival Hall, South Bank SE1. 0171-928 3191. Orchestral concerts for children over 7, arranged by the Ernest Read Music Association. Season tickets available for six concerts, *Oct-May*. Tickets issued from May. *Phone 0181-942 0777 for details. Charge.*

Morley College Family   5 B0 Concerts
61 Westminster Bridge Rd SE1. 0171-928 8501. Series of informal concerts designed to introduce children and their parents to a wide variety of music, from classical to pop, ethnic to electronic. Season tickets available for eight monthly concerts, *Oct-May 10.30-12.30 Sat.* Tickets issued in *Sep* or can be purchased at the door.

Music for Youth
4 Blade Mews, Deodar Road SW15. 0181-870 9624. *Every Nov* over 1200 talented young performers chosen from the National Festival of Music for Youth on the South Bank appear in three public concerts at the Royal Albert Hall.

Radio & TV shows

See 'Radio and TV shows' in 'Theatres, cinemas, music and comedy'.

Party entertainers

Frog Hollow   3 D6
15 Victoria Gro W8. (01672) 564222. Provides presents, toys and paper tableware. Hires out low tables and chairs and has a list of recommended entertainers.

OPEN 09.00-17.30 Mon-Sat (& 10.00-17.00 Sun Oct-Dec).

Len Belmont
48 Morland Estate E8. 0171-254 8300. Well-known and popular children's entertainer with ventriloquist, magic and balloon modelling acts. Guaranteed to get a party started.

'Prof' Alexander's Punch & Judy
59 Wilton Way E8. 0171-254 0416. Traditional show lasting ½ hr. Also does magic shows.

Children's restaurants

Fast food restaurants or sandwich bars are always a good idea and can be found all over London. In case you are looking for something more substantial, below are listed a selection of restaurants which welcome children.

Garfunkels   **4 C2**
265 Regent St W1. 0171-629 1870. Chain of family restaurants with vast American-style menu and separate menu for children. *OPEN 11.30-23.30 Mon-Sat, 12.00-23.30 Sun.*

Selfridges Food Garden Café   **4 B2**
Oxford St W1. 0171-629 1234. A useful one to remember if in Oxford Street. Burgers and pasta in half portions. *OPEN 09.30-18.45 Mon-Sat (to 20.00 Thur).*

Smollensky's Balloon   **4 D4**
1 Dover St W1. 0171-491 1199. Excellent international menu with special junior dishes. Entertainments on *Sat & Sun afternoons:* Punch & Judy, magicians, clowns and story-tellers. *OPEN 12.00-23.45 Mon-Sat, 12.00-22.30 Sun.*

Children's shopping

Books & comics

Foyles, Dillons, and Hatchards have good children's book departments. See 'Shopping'.

Children's Book Centre   **3 B6**
237 Kensington High St W8. 0171-937 7497. The largest children's bookshop in the country with some 30,000 titles. In the *school hols* there are story-telling sessions. *OPEN 09.30-18.30 Mon-Sat (to 18.00 Tue, to 19.00 Thur), 12.00-18.00 Sun.*

Comic Showcase   **4 F2**
76 Neal St WC2. 0171-240 3664. Lots of whizzy reading for the whole family. *OPEN 10.00-19.00 Thur-Sat, 10.00-18.00 Sun-Wed.*

Carnival & party novelties

Barnum's
67 Hammersmith Rd W14. 0171-602 1211. Masks, fairground novelties, balloons, flags. For hire and sale. *OPEN 09.00-17.30 Mon-Fri, 10.00-17.00 Sat.*

Escapade
150 Camden High St NW1. 0171-485 7384. Get all your party kit here. Stuffed full of costumes, jokes, tricks, masks, wigs and novelties. *OPEN 10.00-19.00 Mon-Fri, 10.00-18.00 Sat, 12.00-17.00 Sun.*

Magic, jokes & tricks

Davenports Magic Shop   **4 F4**
Charing Cross Underground Shopping Concourse WC2. 0171-836 0408. Jokes, tricks, puzzles, practical jokes – some at pocket money prices. Plus elaborate tricks for the professionals. *OPEN 10.15-17.30 Mon-Fri, 09.30-16.30 Sat.*

Models

See 'Models' under 'Shops and services.'

Posters

Poster Shop   **4 F3**
28 James St WC2. 0171-240 2526. A vast range of colourful posters. *OPEN 10.00-20.00 Mon-Sat, 11.00-18.00 Sun.*

Toys & games

Many department stores have very good toy departments, especially Harrods, Selfridges and Heal's. Most of the following specialist shops will send catalogues on request. Remember you can also borrow toys. Contact Play Matters, Association of Toy and Leisure Libraries, 68 Churchway NW1 (0171-387 9592) for details of your local toy library.

Benjamin Pollock's Toy Shop   **4 F3**
44 Covent Garden Mkt WC2. 0171-379 7866. In addition to toys and Victorian cut-out model theatres, sells antique dolls for children and collectors. Also specialises in christening presents. *OPEN 10.30-18.00 Mon-Sat.*

Dolls' Hospital
16 Dawes Rd SW6. 0171-385 2081. Casualty department for broken limbs, spare part surgery, antique restoration, etc. Also a few toys and dolls for sale.

Phone for opening times. CLOSED Wed & Thur.

Early Learning Centre   3 B6
225 Kensington High St W8. 0171-937 0419. Bright, educational toys for babies upwards. Play area for under 8s. Other branches. *OPEN 09.00-18.00 Mon-Sat.*

Hamleys   4 D3
188-196 Regent St W1. 0171-734 3161. Largest toyshop in London. Play areas. Has nearly everything. All ages. *OPEN 10.00-19.00 Mon-Fri (to 20.00 Thur), 09.30-19.00 Sat, 12.00-18.00 Sun.*

Just Games   4 D3
71 Brewer St W1. 0171-734 6124. All the old favourites such as Scrabble and Spillikins as well as some more unusual new ones. *OPEN 10.00-18.00 Mon-Sat (to 17.45 Mon, to 19.00 Thur).*

Kristin Baybars
7 Mansfield Rd NW3. 0171-267 0934. Tiny treasure chest which specialises in craftsman-made dolls' houses, miniatures and unusual small toys. *OPEN 11.15-18.00 Tue-Sat. CLOSED Mon.*

London Dolls House   4 F3
Company
29 The Market, Covent Garden WC2. 0171-240 8681. Ready-built antique and new dolls houses and kits, plus miniature furniture and other extras. Staff even offer a dolls house design service. *OPEN 10.00-19.00 Mon-Sat.*

Singing Tree
69 New King's Rd SW6. 0171-736 4527. Not just for children, this amazing shop stocks new and antique dolls' houses and everything to go in them. Collectors' items in miniature. Mail order service. *OPEN 10.00-17.30 Mon-Sat.*

Eric Snook's Toyshop   4 F3
32 The Market, Covent Garden WC2. 0171-379 7681. Smart toy shop selling Beatrix Potter characters and hand-made wooden toys. *OPEN 10.00-19.00 Mon-Sat, 11.00-18.00 Sun.*

Toys 'R' Us
Tilling Rd, Brent Cross NW2. 0181-209 0019. Huge toy warehouse selling games and toys for   children of all ages. *OPEN 09.00-22.00 Mon-Sat (to 21.00 Thur), 11.00-17.00 Sun.*

Virgin Games Centre   4 C2
14-16 Oxford St W1. 0171-631 1234. Renowned for its incredible fantasy games. Whole department devoted to war games. Complete Trivial Pursuit range and a whole floor of computer games. *OPEN 09.30-20.00 Mon-Sat, (to 22.00 Tue) 12.00-18.00 Sun.*

Children's clothes

For everyday wear the best buys are in the chain stores and department stores but you can also find stylish designer wear for even the youngest children.

C & A   4 B2
501-509 Oxford St W1. 0171-629 7272. (Main branch.) Good selection of inexpensive clothes, especially sports kit, for children up to 16. *OPEN 09.30-19.00 Mon-Sat (to 20.00 Thur).*

The Gap   4 D3
144-146 Regent St W1. 0171-287 5095. All-American denims, sweatshirts and cotton knits for 2-13 year-olds. Other branches. *OPEN 09.30-19.00 Mon-Sat (to 20.00 Thur), 12.00-18.00 Sun.*

Hennes   4 D2
Oxford Circus W1. 0171-493 4004. Huge selection of casual fun clothes for children (and adults). High fashion at budget prices. *OPEN 10.00-18.30 Mon-Fri (to 20.00 Thur), 09.30-18.00 Sat.*

Laura Ashley   4 D2
256 Regent St W1. 0171-437 9760. Pastoral prints on cotton lawn, corduroys and drills, smocks, shirts and Victorian party dresses. Sailor suits. Straw boaters with lots of flowers. *OPEN 10.00-18.30 Mon & Tue, to 19.00 Wed & Fri, to 20.00 Thur, 09.30-19.00 Sat, 12.00-18.00 Sun.*

Marks & Spencer   4 B2
458 Oxford St W1. 0171-437 7722. (Largest branch, first to get the new ranges.) Excellent value for children's clothes. *OPEN 09.00-19.00 Mon, Wed & Sat, 09.00-20.00 Thur & Fri, 12.00-18.00 Sun.*

Mothercare   4 B2
461 Oxford St W1. 0171-580 1688. (Main branch.) Good quality everyday clothes at reasonable prices. Co-ordinated tops and bottoms as well as accessories for babies and children up to 8. *OPEN 09.30-18.00 Mon & Tue, 09.30-19.00 Wed-Sat (to 20.00 Thur), 12.00-18.00 Sun.*

Next   3 C5
54-60 Kensington High St W8. 0171-938 4211. Special section full of trendy childrenswear: thick cotton tracksuits, tartan duffle coats and a small range of interesting shoes. *OPEN 10.00-18.30 Mon-Fri (to 20.00 Thur), 10.00-18.30 Sat.*

Pollyanna
811 Fulham Rd SW6. 0171-731 0673. Beautifully designed, practical but unusual clothes for boys and girls up to 8. *OPEN 09.30-17.30 Mon-Sat.*

Help for parents

Education & schools

Advisory Centre for Education (ACE)
Unit 1b, Aberdeen Studios, 22-24 Highbury Grove N5. 0171-354 8321. Provides free help and advice for parents, students and teachers. Ask for their list of publications. They also publish information sheets and an excellent magazine, *ACE Bulletin*, available by annual subscription. *Manned 14.00-17.00 Mon-Fri.*

Independent Schools   4 D6
Information Service (ISIS)
56 Buckingham Gate SW1. 0171-630 8793 (Head Office). Information about independent and private schools.

National Association for Gifted Children
Park Campus, Boughton Green Rd, Northampton. (01604) 792300. Advice of all kinds, and counselling, for parents and teachers of gifted children. Activities and counselling for the children. Newsletter *four times a year.*

Pre-school playgroups

London Pre-school   7 C1
Learning Alliance
314 Vauxhall Bridge Rd SW1. 0171-828 2417. For information about playgroups in inner and outer London.

Pre-school Playgroups   2 B4
Alliance
Head Office, 61 King's Cross Rd WC1. 0171-833 0991. For publications and advice on pre-school education.

Children in hospital

Action for Sick Children   1 G4
Argyle House, 29-31 Euston Rd NW1. 0171-833 2041. Help and advice for parents in preparing children for hospital.

Babysitters & childminders

Babysitters Unlimited
2 Napoleon Rd, Twickenham, Middx. 0181-892 8888. *Annual membership and fee at each booking. Hourly rates vary according to the time of day.* Covers central London.

Childminders   1 C6
9 Paddington St W1. 0171-935 3000/2049. Covers 20-mile radius from central London. *Annual membership and fee at each booking. Hourly rates.*

South of the River
128c Northcote Rd SW11. 0171-228 5086. South London only. *Annual membership.* Office *OPEN 09.30-17.00 Mon-Fri, 10.00-14.00 Sat.*

Universal Aunts
PO Box 304, Clapham SW4. 0171-738 8937. Office *OPEN 09.30-17.00 Mon-Fri.*

Theatres, cinemas, music and comedy

Ticket agencies and theatre information

Ticket agencies will book tickets for all occasions – but remember they charge a commission. Lists of current theatre, cinema, dance, music and comedy programmes can be found in the daily papers, Time Out, *and* What's On. *The charge for 0891 and 0839 telephone numbers is 39p per minute cheap rate and 49p per minute at other times.*

Albemarle of London 4 **B2**
74 Mortimer St W1. 0171-637 9041. A.Ax.Dc.V.

Artsline 1 **F3**
54 Chalton St NW1. 0171-388 2227. Free advice and information for disabled people on access to arts and entertainment.

Centre Point Tickets 4 **E2**
96 Charing Cross Rd WC2. 0171-434 1647. A.V.

Evening Standard Theatrecall & Entertainment Guide
0839 200 002. Preview reports and booking information.

Fenchurch Booking Agency 5 **C4**
94 Southwark St SE1. 0171-928 8585. A.V.

First Call
0171-240 1000. A.Ax.Dc.V.

Keith Prowse
0171-420 0000. A.Ax.Dc.V.

Society of London Theatre 4 **E3**
Half-Price Ticket Booth (SOLT)
Leicester Sq WC2. Unsold tickets at half-price on the day of performance from the pavilion on the south side of Leicester Square. *OPEN from 12.00 (for matinées) & 14.30-18.30 (for evening performances).* Maximum 4 tickets. No credit cards.

Theatreline
Information about West End productions and ticket availability provided by the Society of London Theatre. Musicals (0891 559 900), Plays (0891 559 901), Comedies (0891 559 902), Thrillers (0891 559 903).

Ticketmaster UK Ltd 4 **F3**
48 Leicester Sq WC2 (office only). 0171-344 4444. A.Ax.V.

Theatre

The tradition of live theatre in London has flourished for more than four centuries, since the first regular playhouse – aptly named the Theatre – went up in Shoreditch in 1576. A penny bought standing room in the circular roofless building; tuppence included a stool for 'quiet standing'. Marlowe's Tamburlaine electrified audiences with its new style of 'great and thundering speech'. During a performance of Dr Faustus the Theatre actually cracked. In 1597 bankruptcy (due to inflation) set in and the building's timber and materials were transported across the river to become the Globe, made famous by Shakespeare. In 1644 the Globe was pulled down; a working reconstruction of the theatre is now being built at Bankside, close to its original site, following the original designs of 1599. The Drury Lane, where Pepys caught cold from draughts in 1663, still stands on its original site despite fire, plague and World War II bombs. Covent Garden, built in 1732, and the Haymarket, 1721, are national monuments, while the reputation of London theatre has never been equalled due to the number and quality of theatre people and stage-names – from Garrick to Frohman, from Nell Gwynne to Bernhardt, from Sheridan to Shaw, from Chaplin to the Ballet Rambert. Government subsidies during and after World War II sustained the tradition which partly gave way in the 70s to sex, farce and formula: the West End's answer to inflation. Subsidised companies such as the National and the Royal Shakespeare continue to stage quality productions including new plays, revivals, Shakespeare and large-scale musicals. The Theatre of Comedy Company, formed in 1982, has also made a significant contribution to the nature of West End theatre with its nucleus of leading actors, actresses, writers and directors presenting limited seasons of high-quality comedies. Fringe theatre adds an alternative – and usually less expensive – source of vitality, providing opportunities for new talent and new ideas.

West End theatres

Adelphi   **4 F3**
Strand WC2. 0171-344 0055. Musicals including *Sunset Boulevard*.

Albery   **4 F3**
St Martin's La WC2. 0171-369 1730. Originally the New Theatre. Renamed 1973. Musicals, comedy and drama.

Aldwych   **4 G3**
Aldwych WC2. 0171-836 6404. Former London home of the Royal Shakespeare Company. Offers a varied programme of plays, comedies and musicals.

Ambassadors   **4 E2**
West St WC2. 0171-836 6111. Small theatre. Original home of *The Mousetrap*.

Apollo   **4 E3**
Shaftesbury Av W1. 0171-416 6070. Old tradition of musical comedy. Now presents musicals, comedy and drama.

Apollo Victoria   **7 C2**
17 Wilton Rd SW1. 0171-630 6262. Auditorium completely transformed to accommodate the hit rollerskating railway musical *Starlight Express*.

Barbican   **2 E6**
Barbican Centre, Silk St EC2. 0171-638 8891. Purpose-built for the Royal Shakespeare Company; main auditorium for large-scale productions in repertory and the Pit, a smaller studio theatre, for new works.

Cambridge   **4 F2**
Earlham St WC2. 0171-494 5054. Large theatre well suited to musical productions.

Comedy   **4 E3**
Panton St SW1. 0171-369 1731. Good intimate theatre showing unusual comedy and small-cast plays.

Criterion   **4 E3**
Piccadilly Circus W1. 0171-369 1747. Listed building housing the only underground auditorium in London.

Drury Lane (Theatre Royal)   **4 G2**
Catherine St WC2. 0171-494 5062. Operated under Royal charter by Thomas Killigrew in 1663 and has been burnt or pulled down and rebuilt four times. Nell Gwynne was an actress here and Orange Moll sold her oranges. Garrick, Mrs Siddons, Kean and others played here. General policy now is vast musicals like *Miss Saigon*.

Duchess   **4 G3**
Catherine St WC2. 0171-494 5075. Opened 1929. Plays, serious drama, light comedy and musicals.

Duke of York's   **4 F3**
St Martin's La WC2. 0171-836 5122. Built by 'Mad' (Violet) Melnotte in 1892.

Associated with names like Frohman, G. B. Shaw, Granville Barker, Chaplin and the Ballet Rambert. *Royal Court productions will be staged here during renovations.*

Fortune   **4 F2**
Russell St WC2. 0171-836 2238. Small compared with its neighbour, Drury Lane. Intimate revues (Peter Cook and Dudley Moore shot to fame here in *Beyond the Fringe*), musicals and modern drama.

Garrick   **4 F3**
Charing Cross Rd WC2. 0171-494 5085. Built 1897. Notable managers included Bourchier and Jack Buchanan. Varied bills.

Gielgud Theatre   **4 E3**
Shaftesbury Av W1. 0171-494 5065. Formerly the Globe Theatre, renamed in honour of Sir John Gielgud. A wide variety of successful plays and comedies.

Greenwich Theatre
Crooms Hill SE10. 0181-858 7755. Stages a season of eight plays annually including new works, revivals and classics, often with famous names in the cast.

Haymarket (Theatre Royal)   **4 E3**
Haymarket SW1. 0171-930 8800. Originally built in 1721 as the Little Theatre in the Hay, it became Royal 50 years later. The present theatre was built by Nash in 1821 and is sometimes enlivened by the ghost of Mr Buckstone, Queen Victoria's favourite actor-manager. He no doubt approves of the policy to present plays of quality.

Her Majesty's   **4 E4**
Haymarket SW1. 0171-494 5400. A fine Victorian baroque theatre founded by Beerbohm Tree. Successes include *West Side Story, Fiddler on the Roof, Amadeus* and, most recently, Lloyd Webber's *Phantom of the Opera*.

London Palladium   **4 D2**
8 Argyll St W1. 0171-494 5020. Second in size to the Coliseum; houses top variety shows, television specials and star-studded annual pantomimes.

Lyric   **4 E3**
Shaftesbury Av W1. 0171-494 5045. Oldest theatre in Shaftesbury Avenue (built 1888). Eleonora Duse, Sarah Bernhardt, Owen Nares and Tallulah Bankhead all had long runs here. Plays.

Lyric Hammersmith
King St W6. 0181-741 2311. Rebuilt and restored to original Victorian splendour inside modern shell. Also studio theatre. Wide-ranging productions.

Mermaid   **5 C3**
Puddle Dock, Blackfriars EC4. 0171-236 2211. Plays and musicals. Restaurant; two bars overlooking the Thames.

New London Theatre   4 F2
Drury La WC2. 0171-405 0072. Can convert from a 900-seat conventional theatre to an intimate theatre-in-the-round within minutes. Opened 1972 on the site of the old Winter Gardens. The hit musical *Cats* is well-established here.

Old Vic   5 B5
Waterloo Rd SE1. 0171-928 7616. Built 1818. For a long time the home of the National Theatre Company, then housed the Prospect Theatre Company. It now shows plays and musicals amid recreated Victorian decor.

Palace   4 E2
Shaftesbury Av W1. 0171-434 0909. Listed building. Originally intended by D'Oyly Carte to be the Royal English Opera House but eventually became the Palace Theatre of Varieties. Staged performances by Pavlova and Nijinski. Now owned by Sir Andrew Lloyd Webber whose musical *Jesus Christ Superstar* enjoyed a record run here; *Les Misérables* is its latest success story.

Phoenix   4 E2
Charing Cross Rd WC2. 0171-369 1733. A large theatre showing comedies, plays and musicals.

Piccadilly   4 E3
Denman St W1. 0171-369 1734. A pre-war theatre which showed the first season of 'Talkies' in Britain. A varied post-war history of light comedy, plays and musicals. Many Royal Shakespeare Company productions staged here. Transformed into a cabaret theatre 1983.

Playhouse   4 F4
Northumberland Av WC2. 0171-839 4401. Edwardian theatre used as a BBC studio and then closed in 1975. Restored to former glory and re-opened in 1987. Stages musicals, serious drama and comedies.

Prince Edward   4 E2
Old Compton St W1. 0171-734 8951. Started life as a cabaret spot called the London Casino in 1936 and has also been a cinema. Now a large theatre where musicals are staged; the hit show *Evita* ran for 2900 performances here.

Prince of Wales   4 E3
Coventry St W1. 0171-839 5987. Rebuilt 1937, this large, modern theatre has housed many musicals.

Queen's   4 E3
Shaftesbury Av W1. 0171-494 5040. Very successful between the wars. Still presents good drama and varied productions.

Royal Court   6 G2
Sloane Sq SW1. 0171-730 1745. Home of the English Stage Company which produces many major experimental plays. *Productions will transfer to Duke of York's during renovations, due to late 1996.*

Royal National Theatre   5 A4
South Bank SE1. Box office 0171-928 2252. Complex of three theatres: Olivier, Lyttelton and Cottesloe. Home of the Royal National Theatre Company. Stages a wide mixture of plays in repertory, including new works, revivals, Shakespeare and musicals. Also foyer entertainment, bookstall, and tours of the building including backstage and workshops. Restaurants, bars, exhibitions.

St Martin's   4 E2
West St WC2. 0171-836 1443. Intimate playhouse with unusual polished teak doors. *The Mousetrap* continues its record run here having transferred from the Ambassadors, its original home.

Savoy   4 G3
Strand WC2. 0171-836 8888. Entrance is in the forecourt of the Savoy hotel. The first London theatre to be fully electrically lit and fireproofed, it was, ironically, badly damaged by fire in 1990, but has been restored to its Art Deco splendour. Produces a variety of plays, comedies and musicals.

Shaftesbury   4 E3
Shaftesbury Av WC2. 0171-379 5399. Permanent base of the Theatre of Comedy Company.

Strand   4 F3
Aldwych WC2. 0171-930 8800. Large theatre presenting a mixture of straight plays, comedies and musicals.

Vaudeville   4 F3
Strand WC2. 0171-836 9987. Listed building which originally ran farce and burlesque (hence the name).

Victoria Palace   7 C1
Victoria St SW1. 0171-834 1317. Musicals, variety shows and plays. Once home of the *Crazy Gang* and the *Black and White Minstrel Show;* the musical *Buddy* is a recent success.

Whitehall   4 F4
14 Whitehall SW1. 0171-867 1119. Restored to its full Art Deco splendour. Now one of the Wyndham Theatres group staging varied productions.

Wyndham's   4 F3
Charing Cross Rd WC2. 0171-369 1736. Small, pretty and successful theatre founded by Sir Charles Wyndham, the famous actor-manager. Edgar Wallace was a manager here for a while. Plays, comedy and musicals.

Young Vic   **5 B5**
66 The Cut SE1. 0171-928 6363. Young people's repertoire theatre mainly showing the classics and established modern plays, but also some new plays and musicals.

Fringe, pub & experimental theatre

The best weekly listings are in Time Out. *Many fringe theatres are clubs. If membership (***M***) is necessary it can be bought before the performance.*

Almeida   **2 D1**
Almeida St N1. 0171-359 4404. Best known for international contemporary dance, theatre and music work. Good offbeat productions.

Arts Theatre   **4 F3**
6 Great Newport St WC2. 0171-836 2132. A 340-seat theatre showing plays for adults in the evening. Performances by the Unicorn Theatre for Children which has programmes at *13.30 Tue-Thur & 10.15 Wed & Fri* for schools, and for general public at *11.00 & 14.30 Sat, 14.30 Sun.*

Baron's Court Theatre
Baron's Ale House, 28A Comeragh Rd W14. 0171-602 0235. Exciting and innovative productions at this small theatre-in-the-round. (**M**)

Bloomsbury   **1 F5**
15 Gordon St WC1. 0171-388 8822. Owned by University College and used by the students 12 weeks a year. International plays, dance, cabaret and opera.

Bridewell   **5 B2**
Bride La, off Fleet St EC4. 0171-936 3456. Flexible 80-seat auditorium transformed from a derelict Victorian swimming pool. Resident and visiting companies.

Bridge Lane Theatre   **6 E6**
Bridge La SW11. 0171-228 8828. Professional companies offering new works or neglected classics. (**M**)

Bush Theatre
Bush Hotel, Shepherd's Bush Grn W12. 0181-743 3388. Première performances of British and international plays, some of which transfer to the West End. (**M**)

Café Theatre   **3 D1**
Bridge House, Delamere Ter W2. 0171-240 9582. Lively, friendly upstairs theatre restaurant. Flexible programme of plays or cabaret and late-night satirical review. All-inclusive price for complete evening or separate dinner and show. (**M**)

Cochrane Theatre   **2 A6**
Southampton Row WC1. 0171-242 7040. Visiting theatre companies.

Cockpit Theatre   **1 A5**
Gateforth St NW8. 0171-402 5081. Fringe theatre venue for professional companies with a modern theatre-in-the-round which is also adaptable to other forms of staging.

Donmar Warehouse   **4 F2**
41 Earlham St WC2. 0171-867 1150. Welcomes touring companies but also mounts its own productions. *Closure threatened at time of going to press.*

The Gate   **3 B3**
Prince Albert Pub, 11 Pembridge Rd W11. 0171-229 0706. British premières of foreign works and rare revivals.

Grace Theatre   **6 F6**
The Latchmere Pub, 503 Battersea Pk Rd SW11. 0171-223 3549. Quality productions of new work, contemporary drama classics, musicals. (**M**)

Hampstead Theatre
Swiss Cottage Centre, Avenue Rd NW3. 0171-722 9301. Dedicated to the presentation of new plays and the encouragement of new writers. Bar and snacks. (**M**)

King's Head Theatre Club   **2 D2**
115 Upper St N1. 0171-226 1916. Theatre at the back. One of London's leading fringe theatres with many West End transfers. Encourages new work but also performs revivals. Tickets available for performance only or for dinner and performance. (**M**)

Lilian Baylis   **2 C4**
Sadler's Wells Theatre, Rosebery Av EC1. 0171-713 6000. Small studio theatre staging contemporary dance, music, theatre and small scale touring drama.

Man in the Moon   **6 D4**
392 King's Rd SW3. 0171-351 2876. Successful fringe theatre that performs lots of new plays or revives old plays that haven't been performed for some time. (**M**)

Old Red Lion
418 St John's St N1. 0171-837 7816. Performances of a mixed bag of new plays and revivals. Pub has good food at all times.

Orange Tree
1 Clarence St, Richmond, Surrey. 0181-940 3633. Highly successful established fringe theatre which started life above an early Victorian pub. Now in a new theatre offering a full range of productions – classics, revivals, new work and musicals.

Questors

Mattocks La W5. 0181-567 5184. Plays by well-known writers plus some off-beat productions. (**M**)

Theatre Royal Stratford East

Gerry Raffles Sq E15. 0181-534 0310. Joan Littlewood's brainchild; has its own company which stages new plays and musicals. Bar and snack bar.

Theatre Upstairs   6 **G2**

Royal Court Theatre, Sloane Sq SW1. 0171-730 2554. New plays and playwrights in a small studio space above the main theatre.

Tom Allen Centre

Grove Crescent Rd E15. 0181-519 6818. Touring companies, workshop productions, youth theatre and world music in this community art centre.

Tricycle Theatre

269 Kilburn High Rd NW6. 0171-328 1000. Well-established fringe theatre where an excellent selection of new plays is performed. *Sat* children's shows. Youth theatre workshop, art gallery, restaurant and bar.

Tube Theatre

0171-586 6828. A comedian poses as a clumsy commuter on the tube. You follow and see the reaction! In its 24th year; the 'longest running show *under* the West End'. Group bookings only; minimum 12 people.

Vanbrugh   1 **F6**

Malet St WC1. 0171-580 7982. Theatre club presenting a complete range of classic and contemporary drama by RADA students. Three theatres. Members bar. (**M**)

The Little Angel   2 **D2**

14 Dagmar Pas, Cross St N1. 0171-226 1787. London's only permanent puppet theatre. Excellent shows *11.00 & 15.00 daily during school holidays (5s and over)*. Otherwise *15.00 Sat & Sun only*, and *11.00 Sat & Sun (3-5 year-olds)*.

Puppet Theatre Barge

Little Venice W9. 0171-249 6876. Marionette performances in a converted barge. Moored in London *Oct-May*, travels up the Thames as far as Oxford in *summer*. Shows at *15.00 Sat, Sun & B.hols; 15.00 Mon-Fri during school holidays*. Book in advance to avoid disappointment.

Holland Park Theatre   3 **A5**

Holland Park W8. 0171-602 7856. 700-seat open-air theatre (covered by canopy) which gives performances of dance and opera *Tue-Sat Jun-Aug*. Times vary so check with booking office.

Regent's Park Open-air   1 **C4**
Theatre

Inner Circle, Regent's Park NW1. 0171-486 2431. Lovely in good weather. Plays by Shakespeare and others. *End May-Sep 20.00 Mon-Sat*. Book in advance.

Wimbledon Open-air Theatre

Cannizaro Park, Westside, Wimbledon Common SW19. 0181-540 0362. Enchantingly set in a walled garden with seating for nearly 700. Plays and opera *Jul & Aug*.

English ballet lagged almost two centuries behind the Danes and Russians before the founding of the Royal Academy of Dancing in 1920. By 1930, Marie Rambert's Ballet Club had landed with some éclat on to the West End stage. That same year Ninette de Valois was assembling the Sadler's Wells company up in Islington. One night in 1934 an unknown dancer stepped out of the Sadler's corps to do her first solo at the Old Vic; in 1946 that same dancer and company opened at Covent Garden to mass hysteria. Margot Fonteyn in her 40 years as a ballerina became the embodiment of British ballet history. The première of Benjamin Britten's Peter Grimes, also in 1946, marked the birth of British opera. Very shortly thereafter a permanent British opera school and orchestra were established; regular and festival seasons came into being; a string of high achievers suddenly appeared. Such composers as Walton, Tippett, Searle, Bennet and Davies provided an exciting repertory that launched British opera onto a worldwide stage.
Information about productions and ticket availability can be obtained on 0891-559 904. (Calls cost 39p per minute cheap rate and 49p per minute at other times.)

London Coliseum   4 **F3**

St Martin's La WC2. 0171-632 8300. Largest London theatre, seating 2400. Houses the resident English National Opera *Aug-Jun*, and is host to visiting dance and ballet companies during summer months.

The Place   1 **F4**

17 Duke's Rd WC1. 0171-387 0031. The Place presents contemporary dance work

of an exciting and experimental nature. It is home of the Richard Alston Dance Company, Showbana Jeyasingh Dance Company, Random Dance Company, and others.

Royal Opera House, Covent Garden   4 F2
Royal Opera House, Bow St WC2. 0171-304 4000. Recorded information 0171-836 6903. The world-famous Royal Opera and Royal Ballet companies maintain an international reputation. Summer 'Proms' performances. *Plans to close for redevelopment in 1997.*

Sadler's Wells   2 C4
Rosebery Av EC1. 0171-713 6000. Once a spa (the original well discovered by Richard Sadler is under a trap-door at the back of the stalls). Birthplace of the English National Opera and the Royal Ballet Company. Host to leading national and international ballet, dance and opera companies.

Music

Jazz, folk & rock

Britain is world-famous for its contemporary music scene and London is the hub of the industry, attracting well-known bands and soloists. There is a vast number of different places to go to hear live bands from huge concert arenas to shady basement clubs. The major concert halls are listed below along with some of the more established and popular smaller venues. Consult Time Out, City Limits *or* New Musical Express *to find out who's playing when and where.*

Academy Brixton
211 Stockwell Rd SW9. 0171-924 9999. Huge venue with space for about 4000. Music events continue, but programming is being mixed to include dance, opera and theatre.

Africa Centre   4 F3
38 King St WC2. 0171-836 1973. Popular venue for African and London-based black bands.

Astoria   4 E2
157 Charing Cross Rd WC2. 0171-434 0403. Large auditorium for live music – anything from hard rock to reggae to classical. Restaurant and bars.

The Blue Note   2 G4
1 Hoxton Sq N1. 0171-729 8440. East London's new jazz venue in the former home of The Bass Clef.

Cecil Sharpe House   1 C2
2 Regent's Park Rd NW1. 0171-485

2206. Regular live folk bands perform in the huge dance hall. Traditional dancing.

Dingwalls Jazz Factory   1 D1
Camden Lock NW1. 0181-267 1577. A good selection of live bands in this club by the Regent's Canal. R&B, jazz.

Fairfield Hall
Croydon, Surrey. 0181-688 9291. A modern concert hall with a number of large bands or soloists.

The Forum
9-17 Highgate Rd NW5. 0171-284 1001. Formerly the Town & Country Club, this remains one of the best live music venues in London. Rock, folk, world and jazz.

The Grand
St John's Hill SW11. 0171-738 9000. Converted theatre offering indie, rock and reggae.

Hammersmith Apollo
Queen Caroline St W6. 0181-741 4868. Formerly the Hammersmith Odeon, this is west London's legendary live music venue. Plays host to a wide range of musical talents.

100 Club   4 D2
100 Oxford St W1. 0171-636 0933. Historically the home of trad jazz. Friendly and comfortable, it features live jazz groups (trad, modern and African) and the occasional new-wave band.

Jazz Café   1 D2
5 Parkway NW1. 0171-916 6060. All kinds of jazz at this popular Art Deco Camden venue. Restaurant and café.

Marquee   4 E2
105 Charing Cross Rd WC2. 0171-437 6603. One of the original London rock clubs; a popular and lively spot.

Mean Fiddler
24-28a Harlesden High St NW10. 0181-961 5490. Stages well-known indie rock bands plus folk and country & western.

Powerhaus   2 C3
1 Liverpool Rd N1. 0171-837 3218. Packed venue offering the best in new indie and rock.

Rock Garden   4 F3
6-7 The Piazza, Covent Gdn WC2. 0171-240 3961. Restaurant upstairs and on street level. Live concerts downstairs in a converted vegetable warehouse. Five bands a night with focus on new, up-and-coming bands.

Ronnie Scott's   4 E2
47 Frith St W1. 0171-439 0747. Reputedly the best jazz in London. On the stand a succession of big name jazz men and women. Can be typically hot and smoky on a busy night. Advisable to book.

Royal Albert Hall   **3 E5**
Kensington Gore SW7. 0171-589 8212.
Has a varied selection of artistes through-
out the year. New home of the Royal
Philharmonic Orchestra.

Shepherd's Bush Empire
Shepherd's Bush Grn W12. 0181-740
7474. Formerly the BBC's TV Theatre.
Now venue for a wide range of live music.

Venue, New Cross
21 Clifton Rise SE14. 0181-692 4077.
Former cinema and dance hall, now
stages up to three bands per night.

Wembley Arena
Empire Way, Wembley, Middx. 0181-900
1234. Enormous capacity auditorium for
major concerts.

Wembley Stadium
Empire Way, Wembley, Middx. 0181-900
1234. London's largest pop venue, used
for the real megastars. Open-air.

Barbican Hall   **5 C1**
Barbican Centre, Silk St EC2. 0171-638
8891. Base of the London Symphony
Orchestra. Three one-month seasons a
year.

Central Hall   **4 E5**
Storey's Gate SW1. 0171-222 8010. A
large hall offering organ recitals and
orchestral concerts. Listed building –
housed the first meeting of the
General Assembly of the United Nations
in 1946.

Conway Hall   **4 G1**
Red Lion Sq WC1. 0171-242 8032.
Seats 550. Two halls, one of which is
famous for *Sun eve* chamber music concerts *Oct-Apr.*

Royal Festival Hall   **5 A4**
South Bank SE1. 0171-928 8800. Built in
1951 for the Festival of Britain. Seats
3000. Orchestral and choral concerts.
Foyer bar and music.

RFH2 (Queen Elizabeth Hall)   **5 A4**
South Bank SE1. 0171-928 8800.
Orchestral and choral works, chamber
music and recitals. Also film shows.

RFH3 (Purcell Room)   **5 A4**
South Bank SE1. 0171-928 8800.
Smallest of the South Bank concert halls;
ideal for chamber music and solo concerts.

Royal Albert Hall   **3 E5**
Kensington Gore SW7. 0171-589 8212.
Victorian domed hall named after Prince
Albert, built 1871. Orchestral, choral,
pop concerts, sporting events and public
meetings. Famous for the 'Proms', a
series of concerts by a variety of orchestras, ensembles and individuals from

around the world. New home of the Royal
Philharmonic Orchestra.

St John Smith Square   **7 E1**
Smith Sq SW1. 0171-222 1061. Unique
18thC church used for solo recitals,
chamber, orchestral and choral works.
Seats approx 800. Restaurant. Art
exhibitions held in the crypt.

Wigmore Hall   **4 C2**
36 Wigmore St W1. 0171-935 2141.
Seats 550. Instrumental, song, chamber
music and chamber orchestral recitals.
Fine acoustics for chamber music and
solo recitals. Popular Coffee Concerts.
Intimate atmosphere.

*The following churches have above-
average choirs or organists.*
All Hallows-by-the-Tower, Byward St
EC3; All Saints, Margaret St W1; All
Souls, Langham Pl W1; Bloomsbury
Central, Shaftesbury Av WC2; Brompton
Oratory, Brompton Rd SW7; Central Hall,
Storey's Gate SW1; St Botolph Aldgate,
Aldgate High St EC3; St Bride, Fleet St
EC4; St Giles Cripplegate, Fore St EC2;
St James, Spanish Pl W1; St Lawrence
Jewry, Gresham St EC2; St Martin-in-the-
Fields, Trafalgar Sq WC2; St Mary the
Virgin, Bourne St SW1; St Michael-upon-
Cornhill, Cornhill EC3; St Paul's
Cathedral, Ludgate Hill EC4; Southwark
Cathedral, London Bridge SE1; West-
minster Abbey, Broad Sanctuary SW1;
Westminster Cathedral, Ashley Pl SW1.

*Mostly held in the City churches at
lunchtime Mon-Fri. Chamber music,
choral music, violin, piano and organ
recitals. Concerts are usually free though
donations are customary.*

All Hallows-by-the-Tower   **5 F3**
Byward St EC3. 0171-481 2928. Mainly
classical hi-fi recordings *13.00 Mon.*
Organ recitals *13.15 Thur.* Free.

Bishopsgate Institute   **5 F2**
230 Bishopsgate EC2. 0171-247
6844. Classical and chamber music.
*13.05 Tue Jan-end Apr & Sep-end
Dec.* Charge.

St Anne & St Agnes (Lutheran)   **5 D2**
Gresham St EC2. 0171-373 5566.
Chamber ensembles *13.10 Mon (except
B.hols)* and *13.10 Fri (not every Fri).*
Services with voices and instruments
13.10 Wed. Free.

St Bride   **5 B2**
Fleet St EC4. 0171-353 1301. Organ

recitals *13.15 Wed*. Song, piano or chamber recitals *Tue & Fri 13.15. Free.*

St John's   **7 E1**
Smith Sq SW1. 0171-222 1061. Solo recitals and chamber music in unique 18thC church. *13.00 Mon (for BBC Radio broadcast Oct-Jul) & 13.00 alt Thur in the main hall Sep-Jul.* Concerts most eves *(phone for details).* Restaurant and Footstool Gallery. OPEN 11.30-14.45 Mon-Fri & during eve concerts. *Charge.*

St Lawrence Jewry   **5 D2**
Gresham St EC2. 0171-600 9478. Concert pianist recitals *13.00 Mon (except B.hols).* Organ recitals *13.00 Tue.* Music *every lunchtime in Aug. Free.*

St Martin-in-the-Fields   **4 F3**
Trafalgar Sq WC2. 0171-839 8362. Wide variety of classical music. *13.05 Mon-Wed & Fri. Free.* Evening concerts *Thur, Fri & Sat. Charge.*

St Mary-le-Bow   **5 D2**
Cheapside EC2. 0171-248 5139. Live classical music concerts. *13.05 Thur. Free.*

St Michael-upon-Cornhill   **5 E2**
Cornhill EC3. 0171-626 8841. Organ recitals *13.00 Mon. Free.*

St Olave   **5 F3**
Hart St EC3. 0171-488 4318. Lunchtime recitals of chamber music *13.05 Wed & Thur. Free.*

St Paul's Cathedral   **5 D2**
St Paul's Churchyard EC4. 0171-248 2705. Organ recitals *13.15 Fri (except Aug, Oct, Easter & Xmas). Free.*

Southwark Cathedral   **5 E4**
Borough High St, London Bridge SE1. 0171-407 3708. Organ recitals *13.10 Mon.* Live music recitals *13.10 Tue. Free.*

Open-air music

There is a surprising variety of summertime outdoor music in London from lunchtime brass bands in squares and gardens to evening concerts and opera in vast parks. Many are free, and any charge is usually nominal. For current programmes, see Time Out *and* What's On *in London.*

Alexandra Park
Wood Green N22. 0181-883 7173. Very enthusiastic community music programme. International music and dancing *Jun-Aug 15.00-17.00 Sun.* Mixed perfor-

mances *school summer hols 14.00-15.00 Thur. Free.*

City venues
Information from City Information Centre, St Paul's Churchyard EC4. 0171-606 3030. There are often lunchtime musical events in the summer but dates and times vary so it is advisable to collect a copy of the Diary of Events, issued monthly, for exact details.

Broadgate   **5 F1**
EC2. Lunchtime jazz. *Free.*

Finsbury Circus Gardens   **5 E1**
Moorgate EC2. Lunchtime band concerts. *Free.*

Paternoster Square   **5 C2**
EC4. Mostly military bands. Eat lunch at an open-air café and listen to the music. *Free.*

St Paul's Steps   **5 C2**
St Paul's Cathedral, Ludgate Hill EC4. Delightful setting. Military bands. *Free.*

Crystal Palace Bowl
Crystal Palace Park SE26. 0181-778 9496. Summer season only of concerts in the lakeland bowl. *Phone for details. Charge.*

Greenwich Park
SE10. 0181-858 2608. Brass bands. *Jun-end Aug 15.00 & 18.00-21.30 Sun & B.hols. Free.*

Holland Park   **3 A5**
W8. 0171-602 7856. Varied programme in the Court Theatre *Jun-Aug at 19.30 Tue-Sat. Charge.*

Hyde Park   **4 B4**
W2. 0171-298 2100. Military and brass bands. *End May-end Aug 15.00-16.30 & 18.00-19.30 Sun & B.hols. Free.*

Kenwood
Hampstead La NW3. Contact English Heritage 0171-973 3427 for details. Lakeside symphony concerts by leading orchestras, opera, jazz and brass in fine park. *Jun-end Aug 19.30 Sat.*

Lincoln's Inn Fields   **4 G2**
WC2. Military bands entertain *some summer lunchtimes. Free.*

Marble Hill House
Richmond Rd, Twickenham, Middx. Contact 0171-973 3427 for details. Orchestral concerts, brass bands or jazz, sometimes accompanied by fireworks. *Early Jul-early Aug 19.30 Sun. Charge.*

Regent's Park   **1 C4**
NW1. 0171-486 7905. Military and brass bands. *End May-end Aug 12.30-14.00 & 17.30-19.00 Mon-Sat, 15.00-16.30 & 18.00-19.30 Sun & B.hols. (Not every day, check first) Free.*

St James's Park 4 E5
SW1. 0171-930 1793. Military and concert bands. *End May-end Aug 12.30-14.00 & 17.30-19.00 Mon-Sat, 15.00-16.30 & 18.00-21.00 Sun & B.hols. Free.*

Tower Place 5 F3
EC3. Military bands play in a modern pedestrian square with fine views of the Tower and the Thames. *Some summer lunchtimes. Free.*

Victoria Embankment Gardens 4 F4
Nr Embankment Tube Station WC2. Riverside setting for military bands, massed bands and light orchestras. *Some summer lunchtimes. Free.*

Arts centres

Put on shows – theatre, music, dance – and usually have workshop facilities and classes in a variety of arts skills.

Africa Centre 4 F3
38 King St WC2. 0171-836 1973. Courses in African languages, dance and politics. Library, art gallery, exhibition space, bookshop. Hall for film shows, plays, dance or music performances by travelling companies. Restaurant and bar.

Tom Allen Centre
Grove Crescent Rd E15. 0181-519 6818. East End community arts centre with cinema, theatre, exhibition space and workshops. Bar.

Barbican 2 E6
Barbican Centre, Silk St EC2. 0171-638 8891. A concert hall, two theatres, three cinemas, a public library, an art gallery and sculpture court. Foyer entertainment. Restaurants. Gift shops.

BAC (formerly Battersea Arts Centre)
Old Town Hall, Lavender Hill SW11. 0171-223 2223. A lively, informal community arts centre with theatre, cabaret space, gallery, café and bookshop. Fringe and alternative theatre productions.

Drill Hall Theatre 4 E1
16 Chenies St WC1. 0171-631 1353. Extensive off-West End programme of cabaret and opera. Dance workshops; photography courses and darkrooms available. Huge range of classes and courses. Productions particularly reflect gay and lesbian culture. Bar and restaurant. *Women-only bar Mon.*

Institute of Contemporary Arts (ICA) 4 E4
Nash House, The Mall SW1. 0171-930 3647. A good range of arts entertainment. Three galleries, theatre, two cinemas, seminar-room for lectures and talks, video reference library, arts bookshop, bar and restaurant. Membership available on daily and annual basis.

Oval House
54 Kennington Oval SE11. 0171-735 2786. Two theatres for fringe and experimental work. Workshops and classes in theatre, dance, music and drama. Holiday projects for children. Coffee bar and restaurant.

Riverside Studios
Crisp Rd W6. 0181-741 2251. Theatre, dance, films, visual arts, comedy and all kinds of music. Classes in contemporary dance. Workshops, lectures, discussions. Gallery with varied exhibitions. Bar and restaurant serving excellent food.

South Bank 5 A4
South Bank SE1. Recorded information: 0171-633 0932. Consists of the Royal National Theatre (0171-928 2252), the Royal Festival Hall (0171-928 3002), the RFH2 (Queen Elizabeth Hall) (0171-928 3002), the RFH3 (Purcell Room) (0171-928 3002), the Hayward Gallery (0171-928 3144), the National Film Theatre (0171-928 3232) and the Museum of the Moving Image (0171-401 2636). *See separate entries in relevant sections.*

Watermans Arts Centre
40 High St, Brentford, Middx. 0181-568 1176. Broad range of arts activities and entertainment. Theatre, cinema and exhibition gallery. Studio where youth drama classes are held. Bar and self-service restaurant overlooking the river.

Comedy and cabaret

London's live cabaret circuit provides some of the capital's cheapest, liveliest grass-roots entertainment. At 'new comedy' clubs anything goes – from mime and dance to slapstick and satire. Improvisation nights – unscripted comedy from regular performers – are popular. The clubs are to be found in the back rooms of pubs, at fringe theatres or in purpose-built cabaret clubs. The major venues are listed below, but the circuit is ever-changing, with new places opening and one-nighters changing venue. Check Time Out *for details.*

Aztec Comedy Club
The Borderland, 47-49 Westow St SE19. 0181-771 0885. Lively comedy club above a Mexican restaurant. Food served at your table.

Banana Cabaret
The Bedford, Bedford Hill SW12. 0181-

673 8904. Great venue, rated highly on the cabaret circuit. Top comedians.

BAC (Battersea Arts Centre)
Old Town Hall, Lavender Hill SW11. 0171-223 2223. Adaptable theatre accommodates a lively mix of dance, cabaret and mime. Licensed café.

Canal Cafe Theatre   3 D1
The Bridge House, Delamere Terrace W2. 0171-289 6054. Different cabaret shows. Newsrevue is a favourite, a topical comedy based on current affairs with sketches and songs. Bar and restaurant.

Cartoon at Clapham
The Plough Inn, 196-198 Clapham High St SW4. 0171-738 8763. Strong line-ups at this large, comfortable pub venue.

Comedy Café   2 G4
66 Rivington St EC2. 0171-739 5706. Open spot for new acts; also established comics. Bar. Food available.

Comedy Store   4 E3
1 Oxenden St WC2. (01426) 914433. The London comedy venue where a lively array of comedians line up for a *2-3-hour* show. The audience is encouraged to join in at the end. Improvisation from the famous Comedy Store Players. Food and drink available. 18s and over.

Cosmic Comedy Club
177 Fulham Palace Rd W6. 0171-381 2006. Established comedy venue. *Mon-Sat at 19.30*. New acts *Tue;* stand up *Fri & Sat*. Good food.

Downstairs at The King's Head
2 Crouch End Hill N8. 0181-340 1028. A fine selection of acts in this club below a popular Crouch End pub. Monthly try-out nights.

East Dulwich Cabaret
The East Dulwich Tavern, 1 Lordship Lane SE22. 0181-299 4138. Pub venue with quality comedy line-ups.

Jongleurs Battersea
The Cornet, 49 Lavender Gardens SW11. 0171-924 2766. Very popular venue offering comedy, visual acts, music and dance. Show package offers buffet, two comedians, two speciality acts and disco. Essential to book.

Jongleurs Camden Lock   1 D1
211-216 Chalk Farm Rd NW1. 0171-924 2766. Newer Jongleurs venue where the show has the same formula of comedy and audience baiting as its Battersea counterpart. Seats 500. Show package (see above). Restaurant. Spacious bar. Essential to book.

Meccano Club   2 D2
The Market Tavern, 2 Essex Rd N1. 0181-800 2236. Good comedy, often from big names, in this pub basement venue. Improvisation a speciality. Food available.

Oranje Boom Boom   4 E3
De Hems Dutch Coffee Bar, Macclesfield St W1. 0181-694 1710. Stand-up comedy and variety from established and new acts. Licensed bar.

Red Rose Club
Plimsoll Arms, 52 St Thomas's Rd N4. 0181-675 3819. One of north London's premier cabaret venues, featuring varied and consistently high-quality acts at low prices. Food available.

Up the Creek
302 Creek Rd SE10. 0181-858 4581. Regular comedy, music and magic. Late bar. Food available upstairs.

Cinemas

Cinema came to Britain before World War I and became so popular that moralists feared for the future of church attendance and novel reading. Picture palaces sprung up everywhere in the '20s. The ornate, gilded buildings with huge chandeliers, elaborate ceilings and luxurious carpets certainly lived up to their name at first but were gradually reclassified by the audience as 'flea pits' and 'dumps'. With the advent of television after World War II it seemed there would be no need for cinemas and many did close down or become bingo halls. However, in the '70s the cinema was saved from economic collapse by the development of complexes whereby one large cinema encompassed at least two smaller ones, each showing a different new release. These cinemas have even survived videos. There has been increasing interest in foreign, experimental and classical films and these audiences are catered for by specialist organisations like the National Film Theatre and the Institute of Contemporary Arts, but also by cinemas which present 'alternative', rather than 'blockbuster/commercial' films. For current programmes see the Evening Standard, Time Out or What's On & Where to Go in London. Alternatively telephone the cinemas, many of which have 24-hr answering services giving details of programmes. See local papers for suburban programmes. All cinemas show general new release films unless otherwise indicated. (M) = membership.

Astral   4 E3
3-7 Brewer St W1. 0171-734 6387. Censored sex films.

Barbican   2 **E6**
Barbican Centre, Silk St EC2. 0171-638 8891. Cinema 1 shows general current releases, 2 repertory and 3 is usually used for conferences.

Camden Plaza   1 **D2**
211 Camden High St NW1. 0171-485 2443. *Closed. Future uncertain.*

Chelsea Cinema   6 **E3**
King's Rd SW3. 0171-351 3742. Quality films, often foreign. Spacious seating.

Clapham Picture House
Venn St SW4. 0171-498 3323. Mixed programme of new releases and 'arthouse' films.

Coronet Notting Hill   3 **B4**
Notting Hill Gate W11. 0171-727 6705.

Curzon Mayfair   4 **C4**
Curzon St W1. 0171-369 1720. Specially selected new films in very plush surroundings.

Curzon Phoenix   4 **E2**
Phoenix Theatre, Charing Cross Rd WC2. 0171-369 1721. Under same management as Curzon Mayfair and showing a similar selection of films.

Curzon West End   4 **E3**
93 Shaftesbury Av W1. 0171-369 1722. Formerly the Columbia; now under the same management as the Curzon Mayfair and showing a similar selection of films.

Electric   3 **A2**
191 Portobello Rd W11. 0171-792 2020. Everything from mainstream American to obscure imports.

Empire   4 **E3**
Leicester Sq WC2. 0171-437 1234. Three screens. Bookable first releases in cavernous 'movie palace'. Adjustable seats, perfect vision, Dolby stereo.

Everyman
Holly Bush Vale NW3. 0171-435 1525. Weekly classic revivals.

Gate Cinema   3 **B4**
Notting Hill Gate W11. 0171-727 4043. Quality art films. *Late shows Fri & Sat.*

Institute of Contemporary Arts (ICA)   4 **E4**
Nash House, The Mall SW1. 0171-930 3647. Two cinemas with bookable seats. Films by contemporary directors. Also seasons of foreign and unusual theme films. Day, associate or full (**M**) on-the-spot.

Lumière   4 **F3**
42 St Martin's La WC2. 0171-836 0691. Foreign and quality films.

Metro   4 **E3**
11 Rupert St W1. 0171-437 0757. Independent cinema showing foreign and quality films.

MGM Baker Street   1 **B6**
Station Approach, Marylebone Rd NW1. 0171-935 9772. Two modern cinemas.

MGM Chelsea   6 **D4**
279 King's Rd SW3. 0171-352 5096. Four screens.

MGM Fulham Road   6 **C3**
Fulham Rd SW10. 0171-370 2636. Five screens.

MGM Hampstead
Pond St NW3. 0171-794 4000. Three screens.

MGM Haymarket   4 **E3**
Haymarket SW1. 0171-839 1527. Three screens showing long-running British and American releases and new releases.

MGM Panton Street   4 **E3**
Panton St SW1. 0171-930 0631. Four small cinemas under one roof showing long-running and very new releases.

MGM Piccadilly   4 **E3**
215-217 Piccadilly W1. 0171-437 3561. Two screens. Four screens.

MGM Shaftesbury Avenue   4 **E2**
135 Shaftesbury Av W1. 0171-836 6279. Two screens.

MGM Swiss Centre   4 **E3**
Swiss Centre, Leicester Sq WC2. 0171-439 4470. Four screens.

MGM Tottenham Court Road   1 **F6**
Tottenham Court Rd W1. 0171-636 6148. Three screens.

MGM Trocadero   4 **E3**
Piccadilly Circus W1. 0171-434 0031. Seven screens. *Late shows Fri & Sat.*

Minema   4 **B5**
45 Knightsbridge SW1. 0171-369 1723. Intimate cinema showing modern classics.

National Film Theatre   5 **A4**
South Bank SE1. 0171-928 3232. Shows rare foreign films, revivals of classics and seasons of notable directors' works. London Film Festival *Nov*. (**M**)

Odeon Haymarket   4 **E3**
Haymarket SW1. (0426) 915353.

Odeon Kensington   3 **B6**
Kensington High St W8. (0426) 914666. Six screens. *Late shows Fri & Sat.*

Odeon Leicester Square   4 **E3**
Leicester Sq WC2. (0426) 915683. *Late shows Fri & Sat.*

Odeon Marble Arch   3 **G2**
10 Edgeware Rd W2. (0426) 914501. *Late shows Fri & Sat.*

Odeon Mezzanine   4 **E3**
Leicester Sq WC2. (0426) 915683. Five screens.

Odeon Swiss Cottage
Finchley Rd NW3. (0426) 914098. Four screens.

Odeon West End **4 E3**
Leicester Sq WC2. (0426) 915574. Two screens. Preserved exterior with completely modernised interior. Built by Jack Buchanan – licensed bar named after him. New releases.

Phoenix
52 High Rd N2. 0181-444 6789. European, American and Asian films.

Plaza **4 E3**
Lower Regent St W1. 0171-437 1234. Four screens.

Prince Charles **4 E3**
Leicester Pl, Leicester Sq WC2. 0171-437 8181. Small cinema showing films between first run and video release.

Renoir **2 A5**
Brunswick Sq WC1. 0171-837 8402. Quality and foreign films.

Rio
107 Kingsland High St E8. 0171-254 6677. Everything from European films to cult American pictures. *Late show Sat.*

Riverside Studios
Crisp Rd W6. 0181-741 2255. Mixed programme. Often have themes to coincide with studio theatre productions.

Screen on Baker Street **1 B5**
96 Baker St W1. 0171-935 2772.

Screen on the Green **2 D2**
Islington Grn, 83 Upper St N1. 0171-226 3520. *Late shows Fri & Sat.*

Screen on the Hill
203 Haverstock Hill NW3. 0171-435 3366. Quality films. *Late shows Fri & Sat.*

UCI **3 C2**
Whiteleys, Queensway W2. 0171-792 3303. Huge 8-screen complex showing latest releases.

Warner Acton
Royale Leisure Park, Kendall Av W3. 0181-896 0099. Nine screens and the most advanced sound and projection equipment.

Warner West End **4 E3**
Leicester Sq WC2. 0171-437 4347. Nine screens.

Radio and TV shows

Free tickets obtainable. Write enclosing stamped addressed envelope and preference of programme.

BBC Radio & Television
Ticket Unit, Broadcasting House W1. 0171-765 5243.

Capital Radio **1 E5**
Euston Tower, Euston Rd NW1.

Carlton Television
0171-240 4000. Programmes are made by various companies, but the Duty Office will refer you to the relevant contact.

Channel 4
Ring the Duty Office on 0171-306 8333 for referral to the relevant contacts.

ITV
Ticket Unit, London Television Centre SE1.

London Weekend Television **5 B4**
Kent House, Upper Ground SE1.

Poetry

The societies and venues listed below are well established. There are many other poetry readings and discussions on offer every week but as the venues change, new groups are formed and others fade, it is advisable to check the weekly listings in Time Out.

Apples & Snakes
Contact: 0171-639 9656. Performance poetry in cabaret style. *Fortnightly* spot at Battersea Arts Centre *Fri at 20.30.* Other venues listed in press.

City Lit **4 F2**
Stukeley St WC2. 0171-242 9872. Day and evening classes on the writing and appreciation of verse, contemporary poetry, verse speaking and poetry workshops.

Institute of Contemporary Arts (ICA) **4 E4**
The Mall SW1. 0171-930 3647. Occasional lectures and readings by distinguished poets, followed by discussion.

Pentameters
Three Horseshoes Pub, Heath St NW3. 0171-435 6757. Arranges readings by distinguished poets at regular intervals.

Poetry Library **1 G2**
Royal Festival Hall, South Bank Centre SE1. 0171-921 0943. Information on poetry competitions, workshops, day and evening classes and readings. Lists of poetry groups, magazines and bookshops are also available. Constantly expanding audio and video collection and special children's poetry information service. *OPEN 11.00-20.00 Mon-Sun.*

Poetry Round **6 B2**
Periquito Hotel, 33-44 Barkston Sq SW5. 0171-373 7851. Weekly poetry forum. *20.00 Mon.*

Poetry Society **4 F2**
22 Betterton St WC2. 0171-240 4810. Produces a quarterly journal *Poetry Review* in which both new and established poets can appear. Holds readings and discussions.

THEATRES

Adelphi 0171 344 0055
Albery 0171 369 1730
Aldwych 0171 416 6003
Ambassadors 0171 836 1171
Apollo 0171 494 5070
Apollo Victoria 0171 416 6070
Arts 0171 836 2132
Cambridge 0171 494 5054
Comedy 0171 369 1731
Criterion 0171 369 1747
Dominion 0171 580 8845
Donmar Warehouse
0171 867 1150
Duchess 0171 494 5075
Duke of York's 0171 836 5122
Fortune 0171 836 2238
Garrick 0171 494 5085
Gielgud 0171 494 5065
Her Majesty's 0171 494 5400
London Coliseum
0171 632 8300
London Palladium
0171 494 5020
Lyric 0171 494 5045
Mermaid 0171 236 2211
New London 0171 405 0072
Old Vic 0171 928 7616
Palace 0171 434 0909

Phoenix 0171 369 1733
Piccadilly 0171 369 1734
Players 0171 839 1134
Playhouse 0171 839 4401
Prince Edward 0171 734 8951
Prince of Wales
0171 839 5987
Queen's 0171 494 5041
Royal Court 0171 730 1745
Royal Festival Hall
0171 928 8800
Royal National 0171 928 2252
Royal Opera House
0171 304 4000
Royalty 0171 494 5090
St Martin's 0171 836 1443
Savoy 0171 836 8888
Shaftesbury 0171 379 5399
Strand 0171 930 8800
Theatre Royal, Drury Lane
0171 494 5062
Theatre Royal, Haymarket
0171 930 8800
Vaudeville 0171 836 9987
Victoria Palace 0171 834 1317
Whitehall 0171 369 1735
Wigmore Hall 0171 935 2141
Wyndham's 0171 369 1736
Young Vic 0171 928 6363

CINEMAS

Curzon Mayfair 0171 369 1720
Curzon Phoenix 0171 369 1721
Curzon West End 0171 369 1722
Empire 0171 437 1234
Lumiere 0171 836 0691
MGM Baker St 0171 935 9772
MGM Haymarket 0171 839 1527
MGM Panton St 0171 930 0631
MGM Piccadilly 0171 437 3561
MGM Shaftesbury Avenue
0171 836 6279
MGM Swiss Centre 0171 439 4470
MGM Tottenham Court Rd
0171 636 6148
MGM Trocadero 0171 434 0031

Minema 0171 369 1723
National Film Theatre
0171 928 3232
Odeon Haymarket
01426 915353
Odeon Leicester Sq 01426 915683
Odeon Marble Arch 01426 914501
Odeon Mezzanine
(Odeon Leicester Sq)
01426 915683
Odeon West End 01426 915574
Plaza 0171 437 1234
Prince Charles 0171 437 8181
Renoir 0171 837 8402
Warner West End 0171 437 4347

© Nicholson

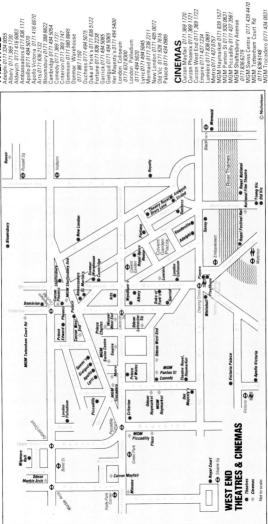

WEST END
THEATRES & CINEMAS

◆ Theatres
● Cinemas

Not to scale

Nightlife

*After the theatres, cinemas, pubs and wine bars have locked their doors, life goes on in London. Whether you're after soulful tunes, Seventies disco classics or hard-core rave sounds, there is a club, or club night, to suit. If it's a more exclusive clientele and relaxed ambience you're after, members-only clubs (**M**) provide good food, good wine and lavish entertainment. And if you're starving in the small hours, a number of cafés and restaurants are only too happy to fill that gap.*

As in any major city, London's nightlife on the whole tends to be expensive, but it needn't break the bank. To save money find out about night buses for your journey home (see night bus map) or join the hardened clubbers in one of the all-night cafés and get the first tube home! For more detailed information see Nicholson's London Nightlife Guide.

£ = low priced **££** *= medium priced* **£££** *= high priced.*

Nightclubs

The following is a selection of clubs to suit every age and taste. One-nighter clubs are inspired by the latest dance music and the DJ is the main attraction. However, trends change continually so it is worth checking Time Out *for a roundup of club nights.*

Strict dress codes are generally a thing of the past, but check with the club beforehand if you're unsure of their door policy. Entry fees are around £8 during the week; expect to pay upwards of £10 at weekends.

Annabel's   4 **C3**
44 Berkeley Sq W1. 0171-629 2350. Legendary haunt of the rich and famous. Exclusive, expensive and very difficult to join. (**M**) – long waiting list. Temporary membership (3 weeks) available. Entrance with registered members only. *OPEN to 03.00 Mon-Sat.*

Astoria   4 **E2**
157 Charing Cross Rd WC2. 0171-434 0403. Semi-converted theatre hosting various one-nighters. Also a live music venue. *OPEN to 03.00 (to 08.00 Sat).*

Borderline   4 **E2**
Orange Yd, Manette St, off Charing Cross Rd W1. 0171-734 2095. Live bands and one-nighters. *OPEN to 03.00 Mon-Sat, to 23.30 Sun.*

Camden Palace   1 **E3**
1a Camden High St NW1. 0171-387 0428. Spacious and lively disco which attracts the young and trendy. Different one-nighters. *OPEN to 02.30 Tue-Thur, to 04.30 Fri, to 03.30 Sat.*

Club UK
Buckhold Rd SW18. 0181-877 0110. Three dancefloors. House and garage. Chill-out room swathed in purple drapes. *OPEN to 06.00 Fri & Sat.*

The Dome
178 Junction Rd N19. 0171-272 8153. Large venue, popular with students. Various one-nighters. *OPEN to 24.00 Mon-Wed, to 01.00 Thur, to 02.00 Fri & Sat.*

Electric Ballroom   1 **D2**
184 Camden High St NW1. 0171-485 9006. Established venue with two clubs offering anything from glamour punk to House dance. R&B, jazz and swing upstairs. *OPEN Fri & Sat to 02.00.*

Equinox   4 **E3**
Leicester Sq WC2. 0171-437 1446. Huge, luxurious venue offering mainstream chart and dance music. Student nights *Tue & Wed. OPEN to 03.00 Mon-Thur, to 04.00 Fri & Sat.*

Gardening Club 2   4 **C4**
196 Piccadilly W1. 0171-734 3416. Atmospheric club with a good range of one-nighters. *OPEN Sun-Thur to 03.30, to 06.00 Fri & Sat*

Hippodrome   4 **E3**
Cranbourn St WC2. 0171-437 4311. One of London's landmarks, but not a club many Londoners frequent. A black cave of brass and chrome illuminated by an amazing light system. Popular with young European tourists. *OPEN to 03.00 Mon-Thur, to 03.30 Fri & Sat.*

Legends   4 **D3**
29 Old Burlington St W1. 0171-437 9933. Sleek with lot of chrome and contrasting colours. Attracts a smart crowd. *OPEN Thur to 03.00, to 06.00 Fri, to 05.00 Sat.*

Limelight   4 **E3**
136 Shaftesbury Av W1. 0171-434 0572.

Uniquely housed in a converted church, this club is a maze of wood-panelled passages and stairs leading to three levels. One-nighters range from rock to dance and reggae. *OPEN to 03.00 Mon-Sat.*

Maximus 4 **E3**
14 Leicester Sq WC2. 0171-734 4111. Mainstream disco with alcoved seating and a packed dancefloor. *OPEN Tue-Thur to 03.00, to 06.00 Fri & Sat.*

Ministry of Sound 5 **D6**
103 Gaunt St SE1. 0171-378 6528. Huge New York-style venue offering the biggest sound system in Britain, big-name DJs, laser shows and a cinema. *OPEN Thur & Fri to 07.00, to 10.00 Sat/Sun.*

Le Palais
242 Shepherd's Bush Rd W6. 0181-748 2812. Mainstream disco with lasers, video wall, fast-food, bar and theme party nights. Regularly hosts live acts. *OPEN to 03.00 Fri, to 03.30 Sat.*

Samantha's 4 **D3**
3 New Burlington St W1. 0171-734 6249. Long-established, ever-popular split-level disco with two dance floors, four bars, cocktail bar and games room. *OPEN to 03.30 Mon-Sat.*

Stringfellows 4 **F3**
16-19 Upper St Martin's La WC2. 0171-240 5534. Celebrity spot. Mirrored walls create endless reflections of pulsating coloured lights in disco below. (**M**) or entrance fee. A la carte restaurant. *OPEN to 03.30 Mon-Sat.*

Subterania 3 **A1**
12 Acklam Rd W10. 0181-960 4590. A trendy and friendly venue under the Westway flyover. Stylish interior. Regularly features live bands. *OPEN to 01.30 Mon-Thur, to 02.30 Fri & Sat.*

Tokyo Joe's 4 **D3**
85 Piccadilly W1. 0171-409 1832. Fashionable and exclusive basement nightclub. Two bars and a restaurant serving Italian food. Attracts a prestigious clientele. (**M**). *OPEN to 03.30 Mon-Sat.*

Wag Club 4 **E3**
35-37 Wardour St W1. 0171-437 5534. Once the trendiest club in town, the Wag still attracts an exuberant, young clientele. Always busy at weekends. *OPEN to 03.00 Tue-Thur, to 06.00 Fri & Sat.*

Members-only clubs

To join an exclusive clientele in a relaxed and well-tended setting, choose one of London's traditional members-only clubs

or casinos. They cater, in most cases, for expense account businessmen and employ hostesses whose job it is to boost the sales of drinks.

Membership: For most of these clubs you have to be a member, although short-term membership is usually available for visitors. You can only enter a gaming house as a member or a guest of a member. By law, when you join a gaming club, you will not be admitted until you have filled in a declaration of your intent to gamble and 48 hours have elapsed from the time you signed this declaration. Membership charges vary considerably. In some clubs visitors from overseas get reduced rates or free membership. A few clubs may insist on a potential member being proposed by an existing member.

These clubs generally close at 04.00, except on Sat when they close at 03.00. The number (**48**) after the club's title means that the 48 hours rule applies. (**M**) means that membership is usually necessary for entry.

The Clubman's Club 4 **D3**
5 Albemarle St W1. For an annual sub-scription fee, you can obtain free membership or benefits at several hundred clubs all over Britain and worldwide. Also discounts for car hire and hotels.

Clubs

Director's Lodge 4 **B2**
13 Mason's Yard, Duke St SW1. 0171-839 6109. Wine, dine and dance to a resident band and guest singer. Hostesses. Restaurant serves Thai food. (**M**). *OPEN to 03.00 Mon-Fri.* A.Ax. Dc.V. **£££**

New Georgian Club 4 **D3**
4 Mill St W1. 0171-493 0561. Club with cabaret. Lounge bar and hostesses. Gourmet restaurant. (**M**). *OPEN to 03.00 Mon-Fri.* A.Ax.Dc.V. **£££**

Pinstripe 4 **D3**
21 Beak St W1. 0171-437 5143. Victorian decor. Restaurant and bar. (**M**) or entrance fee. *OPEN to 24.00 Mon-Fri.* A.Ax.Dc.V. **££**

Casinos

Charlie Chester Casino (48) 4 **E3**
12 Archer St W1. 0171-734 0255. Modern nightclub and casino. Smart American-style restaurant. (**M**). *OPEN to 04.00.* No credit cards. **£**

Clermont Club (48) 4 **C3**
44 Berkeley Sq W1. 0171-493 5587. An opulent 18thC town house. A la carte

restaurant. (**M**). *OPEN to 04.00.* A.Ax.Dc.V. **£££**

Golden Horseshoe (48) 3 C3
79-81 Queensway W2. 0171-221 8788. Casino on two floors with a bar and small restaurant. (**M**). *OPEN to 04.00.* A.Ax.Dc.V. **££**

Dinner and entertainment

Restaurants where music, dancing and cabaret complement the cuisine. Booking is advisable.

Anemos 4 D1
32 Charlotte St W1. 0171-636 2289. Greek party restaurant. Plenty of plate-smashing and Greek dancing. *OPEN to 01.00 Mon-Sat.* A.Ax.Dc.V. **££**

Barbarellas Restaurant 6 B5
428 Fulham Rd SW6. 0171-385 9434. Stylish and sophisticated Anglo-Italian restaurant where you can dance until the early hours. *OPEN to 03.00 Mon-Sat.* A.Ax.Dc.V. **££**

Beefeater by the Tower 5 G4
of London
Ivory House, St Katharine's Way E1. 0171-224 9000. Five-course medieval banquets are served nightly with jugglers and magicians performing between courses. Henry VIII in full costume proposes the toasts. Unlimited wine and beer. *OPEN to 23.30 Mon-Sat.* A.Ax.Dc.V. **£££+**

Brick Lane Music Hall 5 G1
152 Brick La E1. 0171-377 8787. Music hall entertainment for the 1990s in the Old Bull and Bush style. Traditional three-course English dinner. *OPEN Wed-Sat.* Meal served *19.30*; show starts at *21.00.* A.Dc.V. **£££**

Claridges 4 C3
Brook St W1. 0171-629 8860. French cuisine, sedate '30s atmosphere. Ballroom to Latin American dancing to Claridges Dance Orchestra. *OPEN Fri & Sat to 22.45, dancing to 01.00.* A.Ax.Dc.V. **£££+**

The Cockney 4 C2
161 Tottenham Court Rd W1. 0171-224 9000. True London hospitality. Pearly Kings and Queens, Buskers and four-course meal. Music hall revue and cabaret while you eat. Late-night dancing. *OPEN to 23.30.* A.Ax.Dc.V. **£££+**

Costa Dorada 4 E2
47-55 Hanway St W1. 0171-631 5117. Spanish cuisine with flamenco dancers and cabaret nightly. *OPEN to 03.00 Mon-Sat.* A.Dc.V. **£££**

Flanagan's 4 B1
100 Baker St W1. 0171-935 0287. Completely phoney but enjoyable Victorian dining rooms. Cockney songs and elegantly costumed waiters and serving girls. Steak 'n' kidney pudding and enormous plates of fish and chips. *OPEN to 22.30.* A.Ax.Dc.V. **££**

Gracelands Palace
881-883 Old Kent Rd SE15. 0171-639 3961. Elvis impersonation by Paul Chan. Karaoke. Shows *Fri & Sat or by request. OPEN to 24.00 Mon-Sun.* A.Ax.Dc.V. **££**

L'Hirondelle 4 D3
99-101 Regent St W1 (entrance in Swallow St). 0171-734 7482. Theatre restaurant with two floor-shows nightly and a cabaret. International à la carte menu. *OPEN to 02.00 Mon-Sat.* Floor shows *23.00 & 01.00.* A.Ax.Dc.V. **£££+**

Kerzenstüberl 4 B2
9 St Christopher's Pl, off Wigmore St W1. 0171-486 3196. Dinner dancing. Plenty of 'gute Stimmung' here to warm the heart; an informal, hearty atmosphere and loads of goodwill backed up by excellent Austrian cooking. Accordion music nightly. *OPEN to 23.00.* A.Ax.Dc.V. **££**

London Entertains
0171-224 9000. Organises special evenings at three venues, with 3-5 course meal, a show and, usually, unlimited drinking. A.Ax.Dc.V. **£££+**

Royal Roof Restaurant 3 B6
Royal Garden Hotel, 2-24 Kensington High St W8. 0171-937 8000. Anglo-French restaurant with dinner dancing on *Sat eve. OPEN to 22.30, to 23.00 Sat.* A.Ax.Dc.V. **£££+**

Savoy (River Restaurant) 4 G3
Savoy Hotel, Strand WC2. 0171-836 4343. Elegant and formal with resident quartet. Worldwide and well-deserved reputation for classic cooking and service. *OPEN to 23.30 Mon-Sat,* band plays until *24.00, to 00.30 Fri, to 01.00 Sat.* A.Ax. Dc.V. **£££+**

School Dinners Cabaret Club 4 B2
1 Robert Adam St W1. 0171-486 2724. Traditional English cuisine served by St Trinian style waitresses and muscle-bound schoolboy waiters. Comedy, party games, karaoke and dancing. *OPEN to 01.00 Mon-Sat.* A.Ax.Dc.V. **£££**

Southamptons 124 4 F1
and All That Jazz
124 Southampton Row WC1. 0171-405 1466. A massive refurbishment of the old Entrecote restaurant brings great jazz and an excellent and varied menu. *OPEN to 01.30 Mon-Sat, to 24.00 Sun.* A.Ax.V. **££**

Talk of London 4 **F2**
Drury La cnr Parker St WC2. 0171-224 9000. Modern purpose-built theatre restaurant with tiered seating. 'International' menu. Features some of London's most popular cabaret acts. *OPEN to 23.00 Mon-Sun.* A.Ax.Dc. V. **£££+**

Terrazza Est 5 **B2**
109 Fleet St EC4. 0171-353 2680. Known as Spaghetti Opera – Italian cuisine and opera singing by Royal Opera House and English National Opera performers. *OPEN to 23.00 Mon-Fri.* A.Ax.Dc.V. **£££+**

Gay nightlife

London boasts an eclectic mix of gay bars and clubs but the scene changes fast and often, so keep an eye on the weekly gay listings in *Time Out*.
A reliable source of information on all gay clubs and meeting places is the Lesbian and Gay Switchboard: 0171-837 7324 (24-hr service).
See also 'Gay pubs' in 'Eating and drinking'.

The Bell 2 **B3**
259 Pentonville Rd N1. 0171-837 5617. Large, comfy pub next to the Scala cinema, with varied one-nighters. Very popular with a young, lively and varied clientele. *OPEN to 01.00 Mon, to 02.00 Tue-Thur, to 03.00 Sat, to 24.00 Sun.*

The Fridge
Town Hall Pde, Brixton Hill SW2. 0171-326 5100. Venus Rising, Europe's biggest lesbian night, *first Wed of every month to 03.00;* Love Muscle – commercial house and dance music *Sat to 06.00.*

G.A.Y. 4 **E2**
157 Charing Cross Rd WC2. 0171-734 6963. Enormous barn-like disco with lasers and video screens. *OPEN Mon, Thur & Sat to 05.00.*

Heaven 4 **F4**
The Arches, Villiers St WC2. 0171-930 2020. Vast dancefloor, great sound system, three bars and a stage for cabaret performance. Amazing light show. *OPEN Tue, Wed, Fri & Sat to 04.00.*

Turnmills 2 **C5**
63b Clerkenwell Rd EC2. 0171-250 3409. Jazz Goes Pop – straight night *Sat to 02.00;* Trade – all-night party *Sat 03.00-13.00 Sun;* ff – techno and dance music *Sun to 05.00.*

Sex, sleaze and strip clubs

Soho, once the red-light area of London, now flashes its neon only at unsuspecting tourists. The number of establishments permitted to show naked flesh is severely limited and hostess bars are not even licensed, so don't be tempted by billboards promising live bed shows, hostess bars and peep shows.
A relatively new arrival on the West End scene are strip shows for women in the form of male dance troupes such as The Chippendales, who will strip down to the tiniest G-string. Such shows are good for a laugh and are always packed. Check the theatre listings in Time Out *or the* Evening Standard *for details.*

Capricorn Club 4 **D1**
32 Goodge St W1. 0171-580 2878. Hostesses, dancing and erotic cabaret. *OPEN to 24.00 Mon-Fri.*

Carnival Revue Club 4 **E2**
12 Old Compton St W1. 0171-437 8337. Continuous performances *12.00-23.00 Mon-Sat.*

Raymond Revuebar 4 **D3**
Walkers Ct, off Brewer St W1. 0171-734 1593. Considered the most 'respectable' of its kind. Performances at *20.00 & 22.00 Mon-Sat.*

Sunset Strip 4 **E2**
30 Dean St W1. 0171-437 7229. Continuous strip shows *12.30-22.30 Mon-Sat.*

All-night bars and cafés

Some hotel coffee shops stay OPEN 24 hrs *and serve light meals to non-residents.*

Bar Italia 4 **E2**
22 Frith St W1. 0171-437 4520. Authentic Italian café serving pizza, panettone and parma ham sandwiches. *OPEN 24 hrs Mon-Sun.* No credit cards. **£**

Harry's Bar 4 **D3**
19 Kingly St W1. 0171-434 0309. Do people go to Harry's because they have stayed out late, or do they stay out late because they are going to Harry's? Excellent late-night cooked breakfasts at this nightclubbers' institution. *OPEN to 06.00.* A.V. **£**

Istanbul Iskembecisi
4 Stoke Newington Rd N16. 0171-254 7291. Shish kebabs and moussaka are among the Turkish dishes served in this relaxed all-night restaurant. *OPEN to 05.00.* No credit cards. **£**

Lido   **4 E3**
41 Gerrard St W1. 0171-437 4431. Wonderful Chinese restaurant open till dawn. Busy and friendly. *OPEN to 04.00.* A.A.x.Dc.V. **£**

Ridley Hot Bagel Bakery
13-15 Ridley Rd E8. 0171-923 0666.

Delicious fresh, hot bagels with fillings such as chopped liver, cream cheese and smoked salmon. *OPEN 24 hrs.* No credit cards. **£**

Up All Night   **6 C4**
325 Fulham Rd SW10. 0171-352 1996. Steaks, burgers and spaghetti. *OPEN to 06.00.* A.Ax.V. **££**

Yung's   **4 E3**
23 Wardour St W1. 0171-437 4986. Small, comfortable Chinese restaurant. Excellent fish dishes. *OPEN to 04.30.* A.Ax.Dc.V. **££**

Eating and drinking

Restaurants

These have been chosen primarily for authentic food and good cooking. They cover a selection from classic cuisine in elegant surroundings to a late-night supper in Chinatown. For more detailed information on where and what to eat see Nicholson's London Restaurant Guide.
Restaurant Services, 0181-888 8080 offers free up-to-the-minute information and advice on London's restaurants from 09.00-20.00 Mon-Sat. They will also make reservations.
Average prices for a full meal for one including VAT but without wine:

£	*£10.00 and under*
££	*£10.00-£20.00*
£££	*£20.00-£30.00*
£££+	*£30.00 and over*
Reserve	*– advisable to reserve*
OPEN	*Last orders to . . .*
A	*Access (incorporating Mastercard, Eurocard)*
Ax	*American Express*
Dc	*Diners Club*
V	*Visa (incorporating Barclaycard)*
B	*breakfast*
L	*lunch*
D	*dinner*

Service charge: *many restaurants now add service on to the bill, usually at 12½%, but do not always say so – if in doubt ask. However they do usually say if service is not included. 12½% is normally the minimum; give up to 15% for above-average service.*
Cover charge: *not to be confused with*

the service charge. This is for napkins, bread and water, and is normally added to the bill. Most restaurants, however, have now dispensed with this charge.

African & Caribbean

African and Caribbean cooking is influenced by Indian, Chinese and European cuisines. Great use is made of fruit, vegetables, rice and coconut, and a wide range of exotic ingredients and fiery pepper sauces liven up meat and fish stews. Food tends to be spicy and filling.

Afric-Carib
1 Stroud Green Rd N4. 0171-263 5464. Restaurant and takeaway specialising in spicy Nigerian dishes. Chicken, beef or fish with plantains and yams. Palm wine and African music. Relaxed, informal atmosphere. *LD OPEN to 24.00.* A.V. **£**

The Calabash   **4 F3**
38 King St WC2. 0171-836 1976. African cuisine in the basement of the Africa Centre in Covent Garden. Masks, head-dresses and African textiles adorn the walls and a tasty selection of regional dishes is available. Beef with green bananas and coconut cream, couscous, chicken and groundnut stew, vegetarian dishes. African wine and beer available. Friendly service. *LD OPEN to 22.30. CLOSED L Sat & LD Sun.* A.Ax.Dc.V. **££**

Cuba   **3 B6**
11-13 Kensington High St W8. 0171-938 4137. This restaurant/bar is a relaxed and friendly place to discover

Cuban cuisine. Cuban coffee and rum. Nightclub. *LD Reserve. OPEN to 02.00, to 23.30 Sun. CLOSED L Sun.* **££**

Eutens 4 **F2**
4-5 Neal's Yard, off Neal St WC2. 0171-379 6877. A large, bright restaurant offering Black British cuisine. Chilli prawns with pimento sauce, pan-fried sea bream, chicken in coconut and coriander are some of the tempting dishes. *LD OPEN to 23.30. CLOSED D Sat & LD Sun.* A.Ax.Dc.V. **££**

American

American restaurants now offer not only traditional burgers and pecan pie but increasingly popular Cajun and southern dishes.

Chicago Rib Shack 3 **G5**
1 Raphael St SW7. 0171-581 5595. Wood-smoked barbecued meats with salads and trimmings. Cheesecake, mud pie and ice-cream to follow. Free valet parking service *after 18.30. LD OPEN to 23.45, to 22.45 Sun.* A.Ax.V. **££**

Christopher's 4 **F3**
18 Wellington St WC2. 0171-240 4222. The curving staircase and domed ceiling provide a dramatic entrance to this elegant American restaurant. An east-coast steak and lobster house serving up New York strip steak or Maine lobster (both imported from the US), grills of beef, lamb and chicken, Caesar salad. Vegetarian dishes. *LD OPEN to 23.45. CLOSED L Sat & D Sun.* A.Ax.Dc.V. **£££**

Ed's Easy Diner 4 **E2**
12 Moor St W1. 0171-439 1955. '50s and '60s diner with counter-top juke-boxes and stools. Burgers, cheese fries, malts, milkshakes and US beers. Other branches. *LD OPEN to 24.00 Mon-Thur & Sun, to 01.00 Fri & Sat* A.V. **£**

Fatboy's Diner 4 **F3**
21-22 Maiden Lane WC2. 0171-240 1902. A 1940s American dining carriage which served for many years before being transported across the Atlantic. Lively and noisy offering huge, tasty burgers, hot dogs, ice-cream floats. *LD OPEN to 24.00, to 22.30 Sun.* No credit cards. **££**

Hard Rock Café 4 **C5**
150 Old Park La W1. 0171-629 0382. Ever-popular hamburger joint identifiable by the long queues outside. Vast room on two levels with a shorts bar. Good quality food and non-stop rock. Huge collection of American memorabilia. *LD OPEN to 00.15, to 00.45 Fri & Sat.* A.Ax.Dc.V. **££**

Joe Allen 4 **G3**
13 Exeter St WC2. 0171-836 0651. In a converted Covent Garden warehouse, the London 'Joe Allen' follows the pattern of the New York and Paris restaurants. First-rate cocktail bar for diners. Steaks, burgers, delicious spinach salad, spare ribs and chilli, followed by cheesecake or brownies. *LD Reserve. OPEN to 01.00, to 24.00 Sun.* No credit cards. **££**

Old Orleans 4 **G3**
29 Wellington St WC2. 0171-497 2433. Huge portions of Deep South food. Seafood gumbo, blackened snapper, vast burgers, chocolate fudge brownies. Cocktail bar. Other branches. *LD OPEN to 23.00.* A.Ax.Dc.V. **££**

Planet Hollywood 4 **E3**
13 Coventry St W1. 0171-287 1000. The biggest restaurant in Europe, packed with movie memorabilia, and a three-dimensional diorama of its celebrity backers, Arnold Schwarzenegger, Sylvester Stallone and Bruce Willis. Burgers, ribs, swordfish, pizzas and pasta, plus Mexican dishes and a wide range of desserts. Bar area. Memorabilia shop next door in Trocadero Centre *(OPEN to 24.00). LD (no reservations). OPEN to 01.00.* A.Ax.Dc.V. **££**

Rock Island Diner 4 **E3**
London Pavilion, Piccadilly Circus W1. 0171-287 5500. '50s and '60s diner. Party atmosphere with dancing waiters and waitresses and its own radio station. Burgers, ribs, chilli, salads. *LD OPEN to 23.30, to 22.30 Sun.* A.Ax.Dc.V. **£**

Thank God It's Friday's 4 **F3**
(TGI Friday's)
6 Bedford St WC2. 0171-379 0585. Large, loud and lively. Burgers are the mainstay, but there's also chicken chimichanga and blackened Cajun chicken. Over 600 cocktails! Other branches. *LD OPEN to 23.30, to 23.00 Sun.* A.Ax.V. **££**

Central European

Covering the cuisines of Austria, Germany and Switzerland. Lots of meat-based dishes, but also cheeses and vegetables. Sausages, red cabbage and sauerkraut characterise German cooking. Dumplings are widely used in Austria. Fondue is a well-known Swiss speciality which involves dipping bread into melted cheese or meat into hot oil. Hearty and filling food.

Kerzernstüberl 4 **B2**
9 St Christopher's Pl W1. 0171-486

3196. Authentic Austrian food, accordion music, dancing and singing. Leberknödel soup, Bauernschmaus, Viennese goulash. Sachertorte to follow. *LD Reserve. OPEN to 22.45. Licensed to 01.00. CLOSED L Sat & LD Sun.* A.Ax.Dc.V. **££**

St Moritz   **4 E3**
161 Wardour St W1. 0171-734 3324. Two floors rigged out like a ski hut in the famous resort. Cheese and beef fondues are the house speciality. Also assiette de grison (mountain-air dried and cured beef), veal in cream and mushroom sauce. Nightclub downstairs. *LD Reserve. OPEN to 23.30. CLOSED L Sat.* A.Ax.Dc.V. **££**

Chinese

*Contrary to popular belief, Chinese cuisine offers a huge variety of styles and ingredients. Most of the Chinese restaurants in this country are Cantonese. Dishes are savoury and cooked simply and quickly in order to bring out the   natural flavour of the food. Blends of meat and seafood and stir-fried vegetables are   traditional. Steamed dim sum (lunch-time snacks) are a great way to experiment with unfamiliar flavours; they are normally served until 18.00. Pekingese food from the north is considered the highest form of Chinese cuisine. Drier and more highly seasoned than Cantonese, it shows Muslim and Mongolian influences. Great dishes are Peking duck and Mongolian hot-pot. Szechuan cooking from western China is characterised by strong flavours. Double-cooked pork and tea-smoked duck are specialities. Gerrard Street in Soho (**4 E3**) is the heart of London's Chinatown.*

Chuen Cheng Ku   **4 E3**
17 Wardour St W1. 0171-437 1398. Authentic Cantonese restaurant, popular with Chinese customers. Delicious fish dishes, dim sum and excellent value lunches. *LD Reserve D. OPEN to 23.45.* A.Ax.Dc.V. **££**

Dumpling Inn   **4 E3**
15a Gerrard St W1. 0171-437 2567.

Small, lively restaurant with genuine Pekingese cooking. Very crowded. Prawns in chilli sauce, beef and dumplings in oyster sauce. *LD OPEN to 23.45.* A.Ax.V. **££**

Fung Shing   **4 E3**
15 Lisle St WC2. 0171-437 1539. A broad cross-section of Cantonese dishes on offer. Huge choice of seafood dishes. Hotpots (chicken with clam sauce) are a speciality. Vegetarian dishes. Excellent service. *LD Reserve D. OPEN to 23.30.* A.Ax.Dc.V. **££**

Gallery Rendezvous   **4 D3**
53-55 Beak St W1. 0171-734 0445. Delicious Pekingese food, many specialities. Snow prawn balls, shark fin soup, Peking duck. Banqueting suite where you can dine in splendour. *LD Reserve. OPEN to 22.45.* A.Ax.Dc.V. **££**

Good Earth   **6 E1**
233 Brompton Rd SW3. 0171-584 3658. Predominantly Cantonese cuisine with a large selection of meat-free dishes such as flaked yellow fish in hot piquant sauce. An ample menu for meat-eaters too. *LD Reserve. OPEN to 22.45, to 22.15 Sun.* A.Ax.Dc.V. **££**

Good Friends
139-141 Salmon La E14. 0171-987 5498. Cantonese restaurant in the original Chinatown of Limehouse, where London's first wave of Chinese immigrants arrived as seamen in the late 18thC. Excellent reputation. *LD Reserve. OPEN to 23.00, to 23.30 Sat & Sun.* A.Ax.Dc.V. **££**

Harbour City   **4 E3**
46 Gerrard St W1. 0171-439 7859. Authentic Cantonese and Pekingese food. Renowned for its dim sum, available during the day. Wide range from duck's tongue to crab and coriander dumpling in soup. In the evening try Cantonese braise beef hot-pot or the chef's specials. *LD OPEN to 23.30 Mon-Sun.* A.Ax. Dc.V. *L* **£** *D* **££**

Ken Lo's Memories of China   **7 A2**
67-69 Ebury St SW1. 0171-730 7734. Ken Lo's cookery books have popularised Chinese cuisine. The windows of his restaurants are etched with Tang dynasty horses and the menu features many delicious regional specialities:

these include Cantonese sea bass, Szechuan crispy beef. Cantonese seafood with black bean sauce. Other branches. *LD OPEN to 23.00, to 22.00 Sun. CLOSED B.hols.* A.Ax.Dc.V. **£££+**

Mr Chow   3 **F5**
151 Knightsbridge SW1. 0171-589 7347. Pekingese food in surroundings of old-style opulence. Peking duck, sole in wine and Mr Chow's noodles. *LD Reserve. OPEN to 23.45.* A.Ax.Dc.V. **£££**

Mr Kai of Mayfair   4 **B4**
65 South Audley St W1. 0171-493 8988. Modern, stylish restaurant with simple decor and creative cuisine. Sizzling lamb, chilli prawns in fresh pineapple, crispy Peking duck. *LD Reserve. OPEN to 23.15, to 22.15 Sun.* A.Ax.Dc.V. **£££**

Oriental   4 **B4**
Dorchester Hotel, 55 Park Lane W1. 0171-629 8888. Exquisite Cantonese cuisine in sumptuous surroundings. Set menus or try one of the chef's specials. Correct dress essential. *LD Reserve. OPEN to 23.00. CLOSED L Sat & LD Sun.* A.Ax.Dc.V. **£££+**

Poons   4 **E3**
4 Leicester St WC2. 0171-437 1528. Wind-dried meats are a speciality at this family-run Cantonese restaurant. Other branches. *LD Reserve. OPEN to 23.30.* A.Ax.Dc.V. **££**

West Zender   4 **F3**
4a Upper St Martin's Lane WC2. 0171-497 0376. Stylishly designed, you walk over a thick, glass gangplank to enter this restaurant, one of the Zen chain. Modern oriental menu with a huge choice of noodle dishes. *LD Reserve. OPEN to 23.30, to 23.00 Sun.* A.Ax.Dc.V. **££**

East European

Covering the cuisines of Hungary, Russia and Poland. Hungarian food is distinguished by unusual but extremely tasty dishes. Paprika is a popular ingredient and freshwater fish, such as carp and pike, are widely used. If you like fish, try one of the Russian restau-rants listed below. They also serve such delights as borscht (cold beetroot soup) and blinis (savoury or sweet pan-cakes). Polish food is hearty and filling. Meat dumplings and boiled beef will almost certainly be on the menu; and you can accompany your meal with native Polish vodkas.

Borshtch 'n' Tears   3 **G6**
46 Beauchamp Pl SW3. 0171-589 5003. Crowded, informal, lively Russian restaurant. Try the borscht, beef Stroganoff, chicken Dragomiroff, golubtsy (stuffed cabbage leaves) or blinis. Russian music. *LD OPEN to 01.00, to 00.30 Sun.* Ax. **££**

Daquise   6 **D2**
20 Thurloe St SW7. 0171-589 6117. Very popular with Polish émigrés, Daquise serves simple, well-prepared dishes. Borscht, stuffed cabbage, sausages and shashlik. Also open for morning coffee and afternoon tea, with some of the most delicious pastries in London. *LD OPEN to 23.00.* No credit cards. **££**

Gay Hussar   4 **E2**
2 Greek St W1. 0171-437 0973. Intimate, cosy, much-loved Hungarian restaurant. Cold wild cherry soup, pike with beetroot sauce, roast saddle of carp, goulash. To follow, sweet cheese pancakes and poppy seed strüdel. Hungarian wines. *LD Reserve. OPEN to 22.45. CLOSED Sun.* A.Ax.Dc.V. **££**

Kaspia   4 **C3**
18 Bruton Place W1. 0171-493 2612. In plush surroundings behind a caviar shop, this restaurant only serves fish and caviar. Three set-price menus, the Sanka, Troika and Trois Caviars, or spe-cialities of smoked salmon, blinis and quail's eggs. Russian and Polish vodkas and champagnes. *LD Reserve. OPEN to 23.30. CLOSED LD Sun.* A.Ax.Dc.V. **£££+**

Nikita's   6 **B4**
65 Ifield Rd SW10. 0171-352 6326. A cavernous basement restaurant serving imaginative Russian dishes. Try the scallops zubrovka (with ginger and saffron) or the borscht served hot with sour cream. Wide selection of vodkas. *D Reserve. OPEN to 23.30. CLOSED Sun.* A.Ax.V. **£££**

English

It is the quality of the ingredients in English restaurants that makes for good food – fresh meat and vegetables, salmon and game. Many restaurants now serve dishes using traditional ingredients but with a modern outlook. For traditional roasts, carveries offer set-price meals and customers are served generous portions from enormous succulent joints of beef, lamb or pork (starter and dessert is usually included in the price). Many pubs also serve good lunches based on traditional English cooking. See 'Pubs' section.

Beeton's
58 Hill Rise, Richmond, Surrey. 0181-940 9561. A weekly-changing menu which may include tomato and basil soup, nut roast with mango chutney, lamb with peanut and curry sauce. Unlicensed. *LD Reserve. OPEN to 22.00. CLOSED D Sun & Mon.* No credit cards. *L* **£** *D* **££**

Betjeman Carving Restaurant
Charing Cross Hotel, Strand WC2. 0171-839 7282. Carvery. *LD OPEN to 22.00.* A.Ax.Dc.V. **££**

Bowlers Restaurant   **5 F1**
Great Eastern Hotel, Liverpool St EC2. 0171-283 4363. Carvery. *LD OPEN to 22.00, to 21.30 Sat & Sun.* A.Ax.Dc.V. **££**

The English House   **6 F2**
3 Milner St SW3. 0171-584 3002. Charming dining room in the style of an English country house. Classic English cooking. Menu changes every two months. *LD Reserve. OPEN to 23.15 (to 22.00 Sun).* A.Ax.Dc.V. **£££+**

George & Vulture   **5 E2**
3 Castle Ct, off Cornhill EC3. 0171-626 9710. Built in 1170 and restored after the Great Fire, this hostelry was one of Dickens' haunts. Traditional English fare like Dover sole, roast beef, liver and bacon, sherry trifle. *L OPEN to 14.45. CLOSED Sat & Sun.* A.Ax.Dc.V. **££**

The Greenhouse   **4 C4**
27a Hays Mews W1. 0171-499 3331. White walls with lush green plants create a conservatory effect. Simple English cooking enlivened by French and Italian flavours. Wonderful choice of traditional puddings including bread and butter pudding and baked rice pudding. *LD Reserve. OPEN to 23.00. CLOSED L Sat.* A.Ax.Dc.V. **£££**

Maggie Jones   **3 C5**
6 Old Court Pl, off Kensington Church St

W8. 0171-937 6462. Cosy and pleasant with its wooden settles and country atmosphere. Hearty portions of traditional English cooking. *LD Reserve. OPEN to 23.30.* A.Ax.Dc.V. **£££**

Porters   **4 F3**
17 Henrietta St WC2. 0171-836 6466. Well-established theme restaurant specialising in pies – lamb and apricot, turkey and chestnut. Good old bread and butter pudding, rhubarb crumble or Stilton to follow. Traditional Sunday lunch. *LD OPEN to 23.30, to 22.30 Sun.* A.Ax.Dc.V. **££**

Printer's Pie   **5 B2**
60 Fleet St EC4. 0171-353 8861. Pretty, old house. Competently prepared simple English dishes; grills, pies and steak 'n' kidney pudding. Traditional sweets. *LD Reserve L. OPEN to 21.30. CLOSED Sat & Sun.* A.Ax.Dc.V. **££**

Quality Chop House   **2 D6**
94 Farringdon Rd EC1. 0171-837 5093. A lovingly preserved 'working-class caff' where labourers came to eat for over a hundred years. Now serves traditional English fare plus some European dishes. Always busy and lively. *LD Reserve. OPEN to 23.30. CLOSED L Sat.* No credit cards. **££**

Rules   **4 F3**
35 Maiden La, Strand WC2. 0171-836 5314. Rich in associations; Dickens, Thackeray, Edward VII and Lillie Langtry all dined here. Genuine Edwardian eating house with very good traditional English food like jugged hare, steak 'n' kidney pie or pudding, venison and grouse. Seasonal menu. *LD Reserve. OPEN to 24.00.* A.Ax.Dc.V. **£££**

Shepherd's   **7 D1**
Marsham Ct, Marsham St SW1. 0171-834 9552. Richly panelled and dignified, close to the Houses of Parliament. Attractively presented traditional English dishes. Fine wine list. *LD Reserve L. OPEN to 23.30. CLOSED D Sun.* A.Ax.Dc.V. **£££**

Simpson's-in-the-Strand   **4 F3**
100 Strand WC2. 0171-836 9112. A famous restaurant with an Edwardian club atmosphere. Large carvings from enormous joints of beef and lamb are excellent. Correct dress essential. *LD Reserve. OPEN to 23.00. CLOSED Sun.* A.Ax.Dc.V. **£££**

Strand Palace Hotel   **4 F3**
Strand WC2. 0171-836 8080. Carvery.

LD OPEN to 22.00 (to 21.00 Sun). A.Ax.Dc.V. **££**

Throgmorton Restaurants   5 E2
27a Throgmorton St EC2. 0171-588 5165. Huge establishment comprising three underground restaurants; the Long and Short Rooms and the Oak Room. Generous portions of roast beef, fried fish, and steak 'n' kidney pie. *L Reserve. OPEN to 15.00. CLOSED Sat & Sun.* A.Ax.Dc.V. **££**

Tiddy Dols   4 C4
55 Shepherd Market W1. 0171-499 2357. Occupying eight, quaint 18thC houses in Shepherd Market. Dishes include roast fillet of beef, roast highland pheasant, beef Wellington and the original gingerbread Tiddy Dol Players entertain. *D Reserve. OPEN to 23.30.* A.Ax.Dc.V. **£££**

Tower Thistle Hotel   5 G4
St Katharine's Way E1. 0171-481 2575. Carvery. *LD OPEN to 23.30 Fri, to 24.00 Sat.* A.Ax.Dc.V. **££**

Wiltons   4 D4
55 Jermyn St SW1. 0171-629 9955. Fine food and unyielding tradition. Baby lobsters, crabs, salmon, halibut, sole and turbot. Chops, grills, marvellous game. Stilton to follow. Fine wine list, good port. *LD Reserve. OPEN to 22.30. CLOSED L Sat & LD Sun.* A.Ax.Dc.V. **£££+**

Fish

As well as those restaurants that specialise in elaborately cooked fish dishes, London has a large number of fish and chip 'take away' shops, mostly to be found in residential areas, but too numerous to list here. Fish and chips is a national dish which you can take away soused with vinegar, salt and pepper. Eaten hot it can be delicious and good value.

Bentley's   4 D3
11-15 Swallow St W1. 0171-734 4756. Famous seafood restaurant and oyster bar offering a wide variety of excellent fish dishes, plus oysters, prawns and crab. *LD Reserve. OPEN to 22.30. CLOSED Sun.* A.Ax.Dc.V. **£££**

Bibendum Oyster Bar   6 E2
Michelin House, 81 Fulham Rd SW3. 0171-589 1480. Friendly atmosphere in this elegant oyster bar. Plateau de fruits de mer, langoustines, four varieties of oyster. Queueing often neces-

sary. *LD Reserve. OPEN to 22.15, to 22.00 Sun.* A.V. **££**

Café Fish   4 E3
39 Panton St SW1. 0171-930 3999. Blackboard menus list wide selection of fish which you can have shallow or deep fried, charcoal grilled or steamed. Cover charge includes fish pâté and French bread. Good cheeseboard and wine list. Pianist every night. Downstairs wine bar. *LD Reserve. OPEN to 23.30. CLOSED LD Sun.* Wine bar *OPEN to 23.00.* A.Ax.Dc.V. **££**

Lobster Pot
3 Kennington Lane SE11. 0171-582 5556. French restaurant full of nautical knick-knacks. Changing menu; rock salmon served with crayfish, poached lobster. *LD OPEN to 23.30. CLOSED LD Sun & Mon.* A.Ax.Dc.V. **£££**

Lucullus   3 F5
48 Knightsbridge SW1. 0171-245 6622. Superb array of fresh fish at the entrance. Speciality is salmon stuffed with broccoli mousse wrapped in filo pastry with champagne sauce. Seafood platter. Also lamb, steaks, chicken. Piano bar. *LD Reserve. OPEN to 23.30.* A.Ax.Dc.V. **£££**

Manzi's   4 E3
1-2 Leicester St WC2. 0171-734 0224. London's oldest seafood restaurant. On two floors; upstairs is more sedate, with a fuller menu, whereas downstairs is lively and bustling. Wide range of fish and shellfish as well as simpler dishes such as poached salmon or grilled turbot. *LD Reserve. OPEN to 23.30. CLOSED L Sun* (upstairs *CLOSED LD Sun).* A.Ax.Dc.V. **£££**

Poissonnerie de l'Avenue   6 E2
82 Sloane Av SW3. 0171-589 2457. Beautifully cooked fresh dishes; fish comes from the restaurant's own fish shop next door. Coquilles St Jacques au vin blanc, moules, sole, turbot, oysters, Dublin Bay prawns. *LD Reserve. OPEN to 23.30. CLOSED Sun.* A.Ax.Dc.V. **£££**

Sheekey's   4 F3
28-32 St Martin's Ct, off St Martin's La WC2. 0171-240 2565. Established since 1896, it is noted for its shellfish and seafood. Fresh salmon, steamed turbot with lobster sauce, stewed eels. Crowded and theatrical. *LD Reserve. OPEN to 23.15. CLOSED L Sat & LD Sun.* A.Ax.Dc.V. **£££**

Sweetings   6 D2
39 Queen Victoria St EC4. 0171-248

3062. Tiny 150-year-old City eatery. Fish parlour, with excellent service. Sit at the bar and eat herrings with mustard, whitebait, excellent fish pie. Quieter restaurant at the back. Queuing often necessary as they don't take bookings. *L OPEN to 15.00. CLOSED Sat & Sun.* No credit cards. **££**

Wheeler's
Chain of restaurants dating back over 100 years to the fish shop in Old Compton St which today is one of the many branches. Welcoming atmosphere with sophistication. Scallops, lobster Normande, sole Egyptian and shellfish. A.Ax.Dc.V. **£££**
Some branches are listed below:

Alcove   **3 B6**
17 Kensington High St W8. 0171-937 1443. *LD Reserve. OPEN to 22.15.*

Wheeler's Old Compton Street   **4 E2**
19 Old Compton St W1. 0171-437 2706. *LD Reserve. OPEN to 23.15, to 22.30 Sun.*

French

The following all serve French cuisine; some specialise in simple French provincial dishes, others in highly sophisticated haute cuisine. It should also be noted that French cuisine is amongst the most expensive in the world.

Ark   **3 C4**
122 Palace Gdns Ter W8. 0171-229 4024. Cosy and friendly atmosphere with good provincial French food. Champignons de campagne, fruits de mer, chicken pilaf. *LD Reserve. OPEN to 23.00. CLOSED L Sat & LD Sun.* A.Ax. V. **££**

Auberge de Provence   **4 D6**
St James's Court Hotel, 41 Buckingham Gate SW1. 0171-821 1899. Rustic hotel dining room. Mediterranean herbs and flavourings add zest to the provençal inspired cooking. Steamed sea bass with tomato, basil and olive oil, noisettes of lamb with basil and creamed aubergines. Provençal wines. Vegetarian dishes. *LD Reserve. OPEN to 23.00. CLOSED L Sat & LD Sun.* A.Ax.Dc.V. **£££+**

Café des Amis du Vin   **4 F2**
11 Hanover Place, off Long Acre WC2. 0171-379 3444. Popular, lively spot with a wine bar in the basement, café on the ground floor and restaurant on the first floor. Intimate atmosphere in which to enjoy regional French cuisine. *L Reserve. OPEN to 23.30. CLOSED Sun.* A.Ax.Dc.V. **£££**

Café Royal Grill Room   **4 D3**
68 Regent St W1. 0171-437 9090. Plush rococo setting. Classic French cooking with some international touches. Menu changes daily. Share a roasted Bresse chicken or rack of lamb. Good wine list. *OPEN to 23.00. LD Reserve. CLOSED L Sat and LD Sun.* A.Ax.Dc.V. **£££+**

Claridge's Restaurant   **4 C3**
Brook St W1. 0171-629 8860. Distinguished French cooking in luxurious surroundings. The atmosphere is typical of the sedate thirties. Polished service. Large and notable wine list. *LD Reserve. OPEN to 22.45.* A.Ax.Dc.V. **£££+**

Connaught Restaurant   **4 B3**
Carlos Pl, off Mount St W1. 0171-499 7070. Known as one of the grandest hotel dining rooms in the world. Old-fashioned panelling, mirrors and chandeliers are the setting for the famous Connaught terrine, oeuf de cailles Maintenon, langoustines and excellent game. Impeccable food, fine wines and a formal atmosphere – jacket and tie must be worn. *LD Reserve. OPEN to 22.15.* A.Ax.V. **£££+**

L'Epicure   **4 E2**
28 Frith St W1. 0171-437 2829. Something of a Soho institution. First-class cuisine with excellent flambéd dishes. Châteaubriand, crêpes de volaille, crêpes Suzette to follow. *LD OPEN to 23.15. CLOSED L Sat & LD Sun.* A.Ax.Dc.V. **£££**

L'Escargot   **4 E2**
48 Greek St W1. 0171-437 6828. A secluded dining room upstairs and a brasserie on the ground floor. First-class cuisine from a frequently changing menu. Excellent wine list and efficient service. *LD Reserve. OPEN to 23.30. CLOSED L Sat & LD Sun.* A.Ax.Dc.V. Restaurant **£££** Brasserie **££**

L'Etoile   **4 D1**
30 Charlotte St W1. 0171-636 7189. One of the oldest French restaurants in London. Old-fashioned service and atmosphere with traditional dishes on the menu; rognons, ris de veau and tripes à la mode de Caen. *LD Reserve. OPEN to 23.00. CLOSED L Sat & LD Sun.* A.Ax.Dc.V. **£££**

Le Gavroche   **4 B3**
43 Upper Brook St W1. 0171-408 0881. One of the best restaurants in London,

renowned for its luxurious atmosphere and imaginative *haute cuisine*. Cooking and service faultless. *LD Reserve. OPEN to 23.00. CLOSED Sat & Sun*. A.Ax. Dc.V. **£££**

Au Jardin des Gourmets   4 **E2**
5 Greek St W1. 0171-437 1816. Famous for its climate-controlled cellar which harbours old and rare clarets. Ambitious menu in elegant surroundings; modern and traditional dishes. *LD Reserve. OPEN to 23.15. CLOSED L Sat & LD Sun*. A.Ax.Dc.V. **£££**

Mon Plaisir   4 **F2**
21 Monmouth St WC2. 0171-836 7243. Small, typically French restaurant. Friendly atmosphere and helpful service. Short, unpretentious menu: cassoulet, suprême de volaille au bleu bresse, coq au vin. Other branches. *LD Reserve. OPEN to 23.15. CLOSED L Sat & LD Sun*. A.Ax.Dc.V. **££-£££**

Nico at Ninety   4 **B3**
90 Park Lane W1. 0171-409 1290. Nico Ladenis is one of London's most well-known and inventive chefs, formerly of Chez Nico and Simply Nico. Classic French dishes in sumptuous surroundings. *LD Reserve. OPEN to 23.00. CLOSED Sat & Sun*. A.Ax.Dc.V. *L* **£££** *D* **£££+**

Pierre Victoire
136 Upper Richmond Rd SW15. 0181-789 7043. Informal and friendly, with a conservatory and roof garden. Roast monkfish tail with red wine, cinnamon and roasted garlic, Dover sole with black butter sauce. Delicious desserts. Occasional pianist. Jazz on *Wed eve*. Other branches. *LD Reserve. OPEN to 23.00. CLOSED D Sun*. A.V. *L* **£** *D* **££**

La Poule au Pot   7 **A2**
231 Ebury St SW1. 0171-730 7763. Cheerful and crowded. Rustically furnished with brick walls and copper knick-knacks. Robust, provincial cooking. Set lunch menu. *LD Reserve. OPEN to 23.15, to 22.30 Sun. CLOSED L Sat & L Sun*. A.Ax.Dc.V. **£££+**

Au Provençal
295 Railton Rd SE24. 0171-274 9163. Fine French provincial cooking in a popular local restaurant. Moules marinières, wild duck, chicken with tarragon. Vegetarian dishes on the menu. *D Reserve. OPEN to 22.30*. A.V. **££**

St Quentin   6 **E1**
243 Brompton Rd SW3. 0171-589 8005.

Lively Knightsbridge restaurant in the style of a Parisian brasserie. Classic French cooking; foie gras, beef tournedos. Cheeses and pâtisseries supplied by a nearby gourmet shop. *LD OPEN to 23.30, to 23.00 Sun*. A.Ax.Dc.V. **£££**

La Tante Claire   6 **F4**
68 Royal Hospital Rd SW3. 0171-352 6045. Highly regarded and beautiful restaurant offering innovative, perfectly executed French cuisine. Pig's trotters stuffed with sweetbreads are chef Pierre Koffman's speciality. *LD OPEN to 23.00. CLOSED LD Sat & Sun*. A.Ax.Dc.V. **£££+**

Thierry's   6 **D4**
342 King's Rd SW3. 0171-352 3365. Authentic cooking. Robust dishes like rack of lamb, confit de canard, cassoulet, moules, soufflé au fromage. *LD Reserve D. OPEN to 23.00, to 22.30 Sun*. A.Ax.Dc.V. **£££**

Villandry Dining Room   4 **B1**
89 Marylebone High St W1. 0171-224 3799. Excellent food on the daily changing menu at this popular lunchtime dining room. Dishes are simply prepared and made with the freshest ingredients; French ham with potatoes lyonnaise, red pepper and pesto tart, cassoulet. *L Reserve. OPEN to 15.00. CLOSED Sun*. A.Ax.Dc.V. **££**

There is more to Greek and Cypriot food than moussaka and kebabs; the use of fresh ingredients and interesting herbs and spices produce sizzling meat dishes and meze offers a multi-course meal with a selection of samplers from the menu. A new style of cooking – ocakbasi – has become popular in London's Turkish restaurants. Similar to a barbecue, meat is grilled over charcoal in a narrow pit, in front of which you can sit.

Café Grec   4 **D1**
18 Charlotte St W1. 0171-436 7411. Authentic cuisine; the owner and chef are both from the Greek mainland. Unusual dishes: recipes from Ancient Greece may be ordered two days in advance. Vegetarian dishes. Excellent service. *LD Reserve. OPEN to 23.00. CLOSED L Sat & L Sun*. A.Ax.Dc.V. **££**

Cypriana   4 **D1**
11 Rathbone St W1. 0171-636 1057. Traditional Cypriot food in airy surroundings. Specialities are kleftiko, afelia,

stifado, dolmades. *LD OPEN to 23.00.
CLOSED L Sat & LD Sun.* A.Ax.Dc.V. **££**

Istanbul Iskenbecisi

9 Stoke Newington Rd N16. 0171-254
7291. Attractive surroundings in this late-
night Turkish restaurant. The menu is for
the strong-stomached – boiled brain, roast
head of sheep and lamb's tongue. You
can of course choose a more conventional
shish kebab or goulash. *LD Reserve D.
OPEN to 05.00.* No credit cards. **£**

Mangal

10 Arcola St E8. 0171-275 8981. Tiny,
busy establishment run by one of the best
Turkish chefs in London. Specialise in
ockbasi. Also serves Lahmacun (a
Turkish pizza covered with spicy minced
lamb). Unlicensed. *LD Reserve. OPEN to
24.00.* No credit cards. Other branch at 4
Stoke Newington Rd N16, 0171-254
7888. **£**

Mega Kalamaras   **3 C3**

76-78 Inverness Mews, off Inverness Pl
W2. 0171-727 9122. Also smaller and
less expensive **Micro Kalamaras** 66
Inverness Mews W2. 0171-727 5082.
True taverna atmosphere. Superb Greek
dishes ranging from dolmades to baklava.
Micro is unlicensed. *D Reserve. Micro
OPEN to 23.00, Mega to 24.00. CLOSED
Sun.* A.Ax.Dc.V. **££**

Psistaria   **4 D6**

82 Wilton Rd SW1. 0171-821 7504.
Psistaria means grill, and grilled meat and
fish are the specialities in this Cypriot
restaurant. Attractive and spacious with
friendly service. Occasional live entertainment. *LD Reserve. OPEN to 23.30, to 23.00 Sat.
CLOSED LD Sun.* A.Ax.Dc.V. **££**

White Tower   **4 E1**

1 Percy St W1. 0171-636 8141. Old-
fashioned, refined atmosphere. First-class
cuisine with Middle Eastern influences. *LD
Reserve. OPEN to 22.30. CLOSED L Sat
& LD Sun.* A.Ax.Dc.V. **£££**

Indian

*Although most of London's Indian restau-
rants are run by Bangladeshis, you will
find various influences in the cooking.
Hindu cooking uses fish and vegetables in
rich liquid juices; Muslims use more meat
and the food is drier. Moghul influences
bring ingredients from the Middle East
and also tandoori food (fish and meat
marinated in yoghurt and spices and
cooked in a clay oven). As a general rule,*
*north Indian food comprises spicy curries
eaten with rice and breads, while food
from the south is predominantly vegetarian. In all Indian cooking classic spices
and flavourings are used generously.*

Bombay Brasserie   **6 C2**

Courtfield Close, Courtfield Rd SW7.
0171-370 4040. Fashionable, colonial-
style venue, with plants, fans and wicker
chairs. Dishes from several regions
including Bombay thali, Goan fish curry.
Cobra coffee flambé to finish. Excellent
lunchtime buffet. *LD Reserve D. OPEN to
24.00.* A.Dc.V. **£££**

Chutney Mary   **6 C5**

535 King's Rd SW10. 0171-351 3113.
London's first Anglo-Indian restaurant
where chefs from different regions recreate dishes from colonial days. Curried
mango soup, lamb patties with chutney.
Bombay bangers. *LD Reserve. OPEN to
23.15, to 22.00 Sun.* A.Ax.Dc.V. **£££**

Gopal's of Soho   **4 E2**

12 Bateman St W1. 0171-434 1621.
Up-market restaurant with pleasant
surroundings and high-quality cooking.
Pungent Goan lamb with vinegar, fish
curry, good breads and south Indian
nariyal pilau rice. *OPEN to 23.30, to
23.00 Sun.* A.Ax.V. **££**

Khan's   **3 C2**

13-15 Westbourne Gro W2. 0171-727
5420. The vast dining hall with oriental
arches and palm tree pillars was
formerly a Lyons tea house. Cheap,
cheerful and noisy with excellent north
Indian cuisine. Kofti dilruba – spiced
curried meatballs – is one of the
specialities. *LD Reserve D. OPEN to
24.00.* A.Ax.Dc.V. **£**

Lahore Kebab House

2 Umberston St E1. 0171-481 9737.
Unlicensed 'caff' widely known for its
authentic food and huge portions. Curried
quails, tikka, tandoori and kebabs. Freshly
baked breads, hot rice pudding.
Vegetarian dishes. *LD OPEN to 24.00.*
No credit cards. **£**

Last Days of the Raj   **4 F2**

22 Drury La WC2. 0171-836 1628.
Bengali specialities in crowded theatre-
land restaurant. Meat thali, lamb
tandoori, hot and sour chicken. *LD
Reserve. OPEN to 23.30. CLOSED L
Sun.* A.Ax.Dc.V. **££**

Mumtaz   **1 A4**

4-10 Park Rd NW1. 0171-723 0549.
One of the most lavishly decorated

Indian eateries in London. Good tandoori dishes and wide vegetarian selection. *LD OPEN to 23.15, to 22.30 Sun.* A.Ax.V. **£££**

Ragam 1 **E6**

57 Cleveland St W1. 0171-636 9098. Popular, friendly restaurant serving dishes from southern India. The kalan is a Keralan dish made from buttermilk, coconut and sweet mangoes. Avial is made from mixed vegetables cooked with yoghurt and curry leaves; both are delicious. *LD Reserve. OPEN to 23.30, to 24.00 Fri.* A.Ax.Dc.V. **£**

Ravi Shankar 1 **E5**

133-135 Drummond St NW1. 0171-388 6458. Inexpensive southern Indian restaurant serving authentic vegetarian dishes. Excellent Mysore masala dosai, thali and tasty snacks. *LD OPEN to 22.45.* A.V. **£**

The Red Fort 4 **E2**

77 Dean St W1. 0171-437 2115. A trendsetter in Bangladeshi fish dishes and now one of the most acclaimed Indian restaurants in the world. Luxurious surroundings and excellent cooking. Try quails in mild spice or chicken karahi. Have a cocktail in the elegant bar while waiting for your table. *LD Reserve. OPEN to 23.30.* A.Ax.Dc.V. **££**

Salloos 4 **B5**

62 Kinnerton St SW1. 0171-235 4444. Luxurious Pakistani restaurant tucked away in a mews in Knightsbridge. Tandoori dishes are marinated for 24 hours and are always cooked to order. Some excellent 'special' recipes; try the chicken taimuri, pieces of chicken marinated, cooked in various sauces and deep-fried in batter. *LD OPEN to 23.15. CLOSED Sun.* A.Ax.Dc.V. **£££**

Star of India 6 **C3**

154 Old Brompton Rd SW5. 0171-373 2901. Unusual Renaissance setting for excellent Indian food. Prawn biryani, whole stuffed tandoori chicken, kebabs. *LD OPEN to 24.00, to 23.30 Sun.* A.Ax.Dc.V. **££**

Veeraswamy's 4 **D3**

99-101 Regent St (entrance in Swallow St) W1. 0171-734 1401. Authentic food in London's oldest Indian restaurant. Moglai, Delhi, Madras, Ceylon and Vindaloo curries. Lunch buffet. *LD Reserve. OPEN to 23.30. CLOSED Sun.* A.Ax.Dc.V. **££**

Inexpensive eating

There are lots of inexpensive restaurants and diners in London where you can eat a three-course meal for around £10. Those listed here do not include the cafés serving 'sausage, egg and chips', nor the international 'fast food' chains which can be found on nearly every high street. This list prizes all styles of cooking and features restaurants where you will find a good atmosphere and which offer good value for money.

Barocco 4 **E2**

13 Moor St W1. 0171-437 2324. Unlicensed café serving mainly Italian dishes, but some British choices too. Dish of the day and excellent trifle for dessert. *LD OPEN to 22.45. CLOSED Sun.* No credit cards.

Boggi's 2 **C5**

34 Topham St EC1. 0171-837 8392. This cheerful restaurant has a daily variety of specials such as fettuccini with cream and mushrooms and spaghetti bolognese. Choice of desserts. Unlicensed. *L OPEN to 15.00. CLOSED Sat & Sun.* No credit cards.

Café in the Crypt 4 **F3**

Crypt of St Martin-in-the-Fields, Duncannon St WC2. 0171-839 4342. Friendly restaurant serving wholesome food to tourists and office workers. Beef bake, spinach and cheese pancakes, cappuccino. Licensed. *LD OPEN to 20.30.* A.V.

Centrale 4 **E2**

16 Moor St W1. 0171-437 5513. Consistently good Italian cooking at this West End restaurant. Vegetarian dishes. Unlicensed. *LD OPEN to 21.45.* No credit cards.

Charlotte Restaurant

221 West End Lane NW6. 0171-794 6476. Intimate restaurant serving breakfast, lunch and dinner. Predominantly French menu; cabillaud aux poivres (cod in pepper sauce) comes with légumes vertes au beurre or pommes lyonnaise. Licensed. *BLD OPEN to 23.30. CLOSED Sun.* No credit cards.

Chelsea Kitchen 6 **E3**

98 King's Rd SW3. 0171-589 1330. The daily menu offers healthy portions of moussaka, goulash or spaghetti; followed by home-made puddings. Licensed. *LD OPEN to 23.45, to 23.00 Sun.* No credit cards.

Costa's Grill   3 B4
14 Hillgate St W8. 0171-229 3794.
Good, friendly Greek restaurant specialising in charcoal grills. Eat outside in the summer. Costa's Fish Restaurant next door. *LD OPEN to 22.30. CLOSED Sun.* Fish shop also *CLOSED Mon.* No credit cards.

Diana's Diner   4 F2
39 Endell St WC2. 0171-240 0272. Good, traditional British and Italian cuisine; two choices from the menu are braised liver with mash, or onions and spaghetti napoli. Unlicensed. *LD OPEN to 20.00, to 17.00 Sun.* No credit cards.

Diwana Bhel Poori House   1 E5
121 Drummond St NW1. 0171-387 5556. Good value vegetarian Indian food. Try the thali, a set meal which includes a variety of delicacies, or bhel poori which are small snacks sold from street stalls in Bombay. *LD OPEN to 23.30.* A.Ax.Dc.V.

Gaby's Continental Bar   4 E2
30 Charing Cross Rd WC2. 0171-836 4233. Busy Middle Eastern café serving salt beef, pastrami, felafels, houmous and baklava in generous portions. Licensed. *LD OPEN to 23.15, to 03.00 Fri & Sat, to 21.15 Sun.* No credit cards.

Geales   3 B4
2-4 Farmer St W8. 0171-727 7969. Large selection of excellent fish and chips; cod's roe, clams, sole. Varied wine list. *LD OPEN to 23.00. CLOSED Sun & Mon.* A.V.

Jimmy's   4 E2
23 Frith St W1. 0171-437 9521. Greek-Cypriot basement restaurant, especially popular with students. Huge helpings at very reasonable prices. Beef stew, moussaka, lamb tava, plus fresh salads, baklava, kataifi. *LD OPEN to 23.00. CLOSED Sun.* No credit cards.

Mustoe Bistro   1 B1
73 Regent's Park Rd NW1. 0171-586 0901. Small, intimate bistro popular with locals. Aubergine and yoghurt, eggs madras, garlic or pepper steak. Vegetarian dishes. Good desserts. *D Reserve. OPEN to 23.15, to 22.45 Sun.*

Pollo   4 E3
20 Old Compton St W1. 0171-734 5917. Very busy ground floor and basement restaurant. Huge varied menu – pasta, chicken, steaks, burgers. *LD OPEN to 24.00.* No credit cards.

Spaghetti House   4 E3
24 Cranbourn St WC2. 0171-836 8168.

There are several branches of this restaurant. Genuine Italian spaghetti houses, friendly and busy. Minestrone, pasta, veal, steak and chicken dishes. Delicious pastries or ice-cream to follow. *LD OPEN to 23.00. CLOSED L Sun.* A.Ax.Dc.V.

Standard   3 C2
23 Westbourne Gro W2. 0171-727 4818. Large, popular Indian restaurant serving over 80 specialities including tandoori and vegetarian dishes. Also fish masala. *LD Reserve. OPEN to 24.00.* A.Ax.V.

Star Café   4 E2
22b Great Chapel St W1. 0171-437 8778. Relaxed and friendly restaurant on two floors. Excellent menu featuring unusual dishes such as cauliflower, asparagus and aubergine gratin and poached salmon hollandaise. Licensed. *BL OPEN to 17.00 Mon-Fri. CLOSED Sat & Sun.* No credit cards.

Stockpot   4 E3
40 Panton St SW1. 0171-839 5142. Crowded, noisy and excellent value. Home-made soups, casseroles and puds at popular prices. *BLD OPEN to 23.15, to 21.45 Sun.* No credit cards.
Also at: 6 Basil St SW3 (**3 G5**). 0171-589 8627. *LD OPEN to 23.00, to 22.30 Sun.*

Vecchio Alpino   1 C6
42 Marylebone High St W1. 0171-935 4640. Alpine-style restaurant. Busy at all times. Quick service. Generous portions of pasta, fish and chicken dishes. *LD OPEN to 23.00. CLOSED Sun.* A.Ax.Dc.V.

Wong Kei   4 E3
41-43 Wardour St W1. 0171-437 6833. Cheap and cheerful Cantonese restaurant on four floors. Always busy and bustling. *LD OPEN to 23.30.* No credit cards or cheques.

International

These restaurants master a number of different cooking styles and offer an array of authentic tastes from all corners of the globe. Some pick from the best dishes of the world, blending styles and flavours to create distinctive new ones.

Bateaux London   5 A3
Departs from Temple Pier, Victoria Embankment WC2. 0171-925 2215. The luxury restaurant cruiser 'Symphony' combines fine dining in a luxurious setting with magnificent views of London from the river. The international menu is freshly

prepared on board by the ship's own chef. Music and dancing on *dinner* cruises.· *LD (Reserve)*. Lunch cruises depart *12.45*, dinner cruises *20.00*. A.V. *L* **£££** *D* **£££+** *Phone for details and reservations*.

Belgo Noord   **1 D1**
72 Chalk Farm Rd NW1. 0171-267 0718. Stylish Belgian restaurant. Moules au gratin, wild boar sausages with stoemp. Beer list offers 50 varieties. *LD OPEN to 23.00, to 22.00 Sun*. A.Ax.V. **££** Also Belgo Centraal, 50 Earlham St WC2 (**4 E2**). 0171-813 2233.

The Canteen   **6 C6**
Unit 4G Harbour Yard, Chelsea Harbour SW10. 0171-351 7330. Owned by Michael Caine. Magnificent views of the marina. Varied menu includes sea-bass, lobster, rump of lamb, with bisquit glacé or lemon tart to follow. *LD Reserve. OPEN to 24.00, to 22.30 Sun*. A.V. **£££**

dell 'Ugo   **4 E2**
56 Frith St W1. 0171-734 8300. Soho restaurant on three floors. On street level is a café serving salads with Mediterranean produce. Upstairs the restaurant is dominated by one wall of abstract painting. Menu includes squid with lentils, a choice of one-pot dishes and delicious puddings. *LD Reserve. OPEN to 00.15. CLOSED Sun*. A.Ax.Dc.V. **££**

Hornimans
124 Kirkdale SE26. 0181-291 2901. Named after the wealthy tea merchant and situated close to the museum he founded. Old-fashioned pastel decor, more adventurous set-price menus. Quail with crisp spinach and walnut dressing, followed by grilled swordfish. Children welcome. Vegetarian menu. *LD (Reserve Sat & Sun) OPEN to 23.00, to 22.30 Sun*. A.Ax.V. *L* **£** *D* **££**

Pomegranates   **7 C4**
94 Grosvenor Rd SW1. 0171-828 6560. Highly original and adventurous restaurant with truly international menu. Welsh, Turkish, Malaysian, Greek, French, Italian and Chinese dishes all prepared from first-class ingredients. Multi-national wine list too. *LD Reserve D. OPEN to 23.15. CLOSED L Sat & LD Sun*. A.Ax.Dc.V. *L* **££** *D* **£££**

Quaglino's   **4 D4**
16 Bury St SW1. 0171-930 6767. Sir Terence Conran's large and glamorous brasserie seating 400. A sweeping stair-

case descends from the entrance foyer (where a shop sells foodstuffs offered on the menu) to a bar and antipasti bar. From there a marble staircase descends to the main restaurant. Varied menu; crustacea, plateau de fruits de mer, black pudding, roast duck with coriander and ginger. Live music (jazz trio) and dancing to *02.00 Fri & Sat*. *LD Reserve*. OPEN to *24.00, to 01.00 Fri & Sat, to 23.00 Sun*. A.Ax.Dc.V. **£££**

South Bank Brasserie   **5 B4**
Gabriel's Wharf, Upper Ground SE1. 0171-620 0596. Restaurant on two floors overlooking the River Thames. A huge choice of dishes from China, South East Asia, eastern Europe and the Middle East. Also unusual vegetarian dishes. *LD OPEN to 23.00*. A.Ax.Dc.V. **££**

Italian

There are plenty of places to eat Italian food in London, from old-fashioned ristorantes and trattorias to the new style of restaurants where chefs draw on Italian ingredients to produce their own inter-pretations of traditional dishes.

L'Accento   **3 C2**
16 Garway Rd W2. 0171-243 2201. Excellent food at this busy restaurant. Tagliatelle with walnut sauce, ravioli filled with pumpkin purée, gnocchi with saffron and courgettes. All-Italian wine list. *LD OPEN to 23.30, to 22.30 Sun*. A.V. **££**

Bertorelli Cafe Italien   **4 D1**
19 Charlotte St W1. 0171-636 4174. Brasserie, wine bar and more formal dining rooom in which to sample classic Italian dishes. Tables on a raised platform outside during *summer*. Vegetarian dishes. Italian wines. *LD OPEN to 23.00*. Restaurant *CLOSED LD Sun*. A.Ax.Dc.V. Wine bar **£** Brasserie **££** Restaurant **£££**

Biagi's   **4 A2**
39 Upper Berkeley St W1. 0171-723 0394. Intimate trattoria decorated with fishing nets. Good varied Italian dishes. Scalloppine alla crema, entrecôte alla piz-zaiola, saltimbocca. *LD Reserve. OPEN to 23.00*. A.Ax.Dc.V. **££**

Cibo
3 Russell Gdns W14. 0171-371 6271. Modern, elegant dining room serving regional dishes. Menu changes weekly and may include gnocchi in duck sauce, baked sea bass with herbs or grilled scal-lop kebab in basil and lemon sauce. *LD*

OPEN to 23.00. CLOSED L Sat & D Sun. A.Ax.Dc.V. **£££**

La Famiglia   **6 C4**
5 Langton St SW10. 0171-351 0761. Lively and very popular. High standard of cooking – pasta and fagioli, sea bream with fennel, tiramisu. Tables in the garden during summer. *LD OPEN to 23.45, to 22.30 Sun.* A.Ax.Dc.V. **£££**

L'Incontro   **7 A3**
87 Pimlico Rd SW1. 0171-730 6327. Sumptuous, comfortable restaurant with a wealthy clientele enjoying Venetian cooking. Salt cod with olive oil, cuttlefish in ink with polenta. Excellent Italian wines. *LD Reserve. OPEN to 23.30, to 22.30 Sun. CLOSED L Sat & Sun.* A.Ax.Dc.V. *L* **££** *D* **£££+**

Leoni's Quo Vadis   **4 E2**
26-29 Dean St W1. 0171-437 4809. Pretty pastel dining room in one of Soho's oldest buildings where Karl Marx lived while he was writing *Das Kapital*. The specialities are rich, traditional Italian dishes. Excellent courteous service. *LD Reserve. OPEN to 23.00, to 22.30 Sun. CLOSED L Sat & Sun.* A.Ax.Dc.V. **££**

Luigi's
15 Tavistock St WC2. 0171-240 1795. Something of an institution now. Luigi's is crowded and popular with after-theatre diners. Photographs of entertainment personalities decorate the walls. Good, authentic food: cannelloni, mussels grilled with garlic and breadcrumbs, veal and chicken dishes. Extensive wine list. *LD Reserve. OPEN to 23.30. CLOSED Sun.* A.Dc.V. **£££**

Opera Terrace   **4 F3**
45 East Terrace, Covent Garden WC2. 0171-379 0666. This informal trattoria has been taken over by the Chez Gerard group. Large outdoor terrace overlooking Covent Garden piazza. Serves new-wave Italian cuisine; fresh pasta dishes, chargrilled chicken and fish. Live music. *LD OPEN to 23.00, to 22.30 Sun.* A.Ax.Dc.V. **££**

Orso   **4 G3**
27 Wellington St WC2. 0171-240 5269. Trendy restaurant serving modern Italian food. Daily-changing menu may include grilled scallops with red and yellow peppers, venison with polenta and small pizzas with various toppings. *LD Reserve. OPEN to 24.00.* No credit cards. **£££**

Osteria Antica Bologna
23 Northcote Rd SW11. 0171-978 4771. Lively restaurant serving up innovative regional dishes. You can have your starters as an Italian version of meze (a selection of dishes at once). *LD Reserve. OPEN to 23.30, to 22.30 Sun.* A.Ax.V. **££**

Portofino   **2 D2**
39 Camden Pas N1. 0171-226 0884. Small, popular. Good friendly service and excellent cooking. Generous portions. Fresh fish in season. *LD OPEN to 23.30. CLOSED Sun & B.hols.* A.Ax.Dc.V. **££**

Riva
169 Church Rd SW13. 0181-748 0434. Dishes inspired by ingredients and cooking methods of northern Italy. Grilled polenta topped with stewed eel and olives, snails cooked with nuts and wild fennel. Pavement seating in *summer*. Impressive selection of Italian wines. *LD Reserve. OPEN to 22.45.* A.V. **£££**

River Café
Thames Wharf Studios, Rainville Rd W6. 0171-381 8824. Light and airy restaurant serving modern Italian food. Only the freshest possible ingredients are used and the menu changes daily. Superb dishes include chicken stuffed with parsley and garlic, and chargrilled peppers with anchovies. *LD Reserve. OPEN to 21.30. CLOSED D Sun.* A.V. **£££**

San Lorenzo   **3 G6**
22 Beauchamp Pl SW3. 0171-584 1074. One of London's best known Italian restaurants offering a different menu every day. Fashionable clientele who enjoy excellent pasta and bollito misto. Unusual veal and chicken dishes. *LD Reserve. OPEN to 23.30. CLOSED Sun.* **£££+**

Sol e luna   **4 F2**
Thomas Neal Centre, 22 Shorts Gdns WC2. 0171-379 3336. One of the new style of Italian restaurants, serving innovative pastas and salads, and pizzas baked in a wood-fire stove. Welcoming and friendly. *LD OPEN to 24.00, to 22.30 Sun.* A.Ax.Dc.V. **££**

Terrazza Est   **5 B2**
109 Fleet St EC4. 0171-353 2680. Lively atmosphere in this basement restaurant where opera singing begins around *19.30 Mon-Fri.* Set à la carte menu, salads and pasta dishes are the mainstay. Good desserts. *LD Reserve. OPEN to 23.00. CLOSED Sat & Sun.* A.Ax.Dc.V. **£££+**

Japanese

In Japanese cooking only the freshest ingredients are used as a high proportion of food is eaten raw. Ingredients are cooked separately to preserve flavours and are cut to emphasise the natural shape and texture of the food. Plain rice, noodles and miso soup form the basis of any meal; noodle bars are the latest trend. Etiquette is important; however restaurant staff will usually be happy to explain the 'rules'.

Benihana
100 Avenue Rd NW3. 0171-586 7118. Lively restaurant where diners are seated round a rectangular grill, facing the chef, as he prepares, with much twirling and flashing of blades, grilled vegetables, seafood, chicken and beef. 12-course Kaiseki meal available. *LD Reserve. OPEN to 23.45, to 22.45 Sun. CLOSED L Mon.* Also at 77 King's Rd SW3 and at Piccadilly W1. A.Ax.Dc.V. *L* **££** *D* **£££**

Masako   4 **B2**
6-8 St Christopher's Pl W1. 0171-935 1579. Authentic Japanese restaurant with private dining rooms attended by charming waitresses in kimonos. Completely oriental atmosphere. Try the set sukiyaki or tempura meals. *LD OPEN to 22.00. CLOSED Sun.* A.Ax.Dc.V. **£££+**

Miyama   4 **C4**
38 Clarges St W1. 0171-499 2443. Extensive menu at this friendly Japanese restaurant. Teppan-yaki counter. *LD OPEN to 22.30.* A.Ax.Dc.V. *L* **££** *D* **£££+**

Ninjin   1 **D5**
244 Great Portland St W1. 0171-388 4657. This restaurant below a Japanese supermarket is inexpensive, comfortable and friendly. Comprehensive menu and generous portions. Good selection of Kushiyaki (meat skewers). *LD Reserve. OPEN to 22.30. CLOSED LD Sun.* A.Ax.Dc.V. *L* **££** *D* **£££**

Suntory   4 **D4**
72 St James's St SW1. 0171-409 0201. Elegant with traditional touches. Try teppan-yaki, sushi or sashimi, all exquisitely prepared. Private tatami rooms. *LD Reserve. OPEN to 22.00. CLOSED LD Sun.* A.Ax.Dc.V. **£££+**

Wagamama   4 **F1**
4 Streatham St WC1. 0171-323 9223. A basement noodle bar with simple decor. Emphasis on the menu is on health and balance. Huge bowls of ramen noodle soup and fried rice or noodles topped with vegetables, chicken or seafood. Super-efficient waiters and waitresses send your order direct to the kitchen via hand-held computer pads. Be prepared to queue to get in. Non-smoking. *LD (no reservations). OPEN to 23.00, to 22.00 Sun.* No credit cards. **£**

Jewish

Orthodox Jews are allowed to eat only fish with scales and cloven-hoofed animals which chew the cud, and may not mix dairy products with meat. Menus usually show an East European and Middle Eastern influence although American/Jewish cuisine, served in New-York style delis, is becoming more popular.

Bloom's   5 **G2**
90 Whitechapel High St E1. 0171-247 6001. Bustling Kosher restaurant. Large helpings of lockshen soup and meat balls, salt beef, stuffed kishka. *LD OPEN to 21.30. CLOSED D Fri & LD Sat.* Also at 130 Golders Green Rd NW11. 0181-455 1338. *LD OPEN to 23.00, to 04.00 Sat. CLOSED D Fri & L Sat.* A.Ax.Dc.V. **££**

Harry Morgan's
31 St John's Wood High St NW8. 0171-722 1869. All-Jewish menu care of Mrs Morgan. Very reasonable prices. Gefilte fisch, latkes (sweet, fried, crisp potato pancakes), blintzes, Hungarian goulash, black cherry cheesecake. *LD OPEN to 22.00. CLOSED D Fri.* No credit cards. **££**

Widow Applebaum's   4 **C2**
46 South Molton St W1. 0171-629 4649. American-Jewish deli offering 101 dishes. Mirrors and photos of New York in the jazz age. Wooden bench seating with tables outside in *summer*. Matzo balls, hot salt beef and pastrami, apfelstrüdel and ice-cream sodas. *LD OPEN to 22.00.* A.Ax.Dc.V. **££**

Korean

Bulgogi is the Korean speciality – meat marinated in a spicy sauce and barbecued at the table. Seafood and fish also feature strongly. Kim chee (preserved cabbage dish) accompanies everything; other common ingredients are garlic, ginger and soy sauce. Desserts are simple, but fruit-cutting is a dazzling Korean art.

Arirang 4 **D2**
31-32 Poland St W1. 0171-437 9662.
This was the first Korean restaurant in
London. Waitresses in national dress
steer you through the large menu which
includes yuk kwe (beef strips with sugar,
pears and spices), ojingo pokum (hot,
sweet squid), and tangsaoyuk (sweet and
sour meatballs). *LD Reserve. OPEN to
22.30. CLOSED Sun.* A.Ax.Dc.V. **£££**

Jin 4 **E2**
16 Bateman St W1. 0171-734 0908.
Authentic restaurant with smart white and
gold frontage and a glamourous interior.
Specialise in set meals which are barbecued at the table. Formal but friendly service. *LD OPEN to 23.00. CLOSED Sun.*
A.Ax.Dc.V. **££**

Malaysian, Indonesian & Singaporean

*Coconut, peanut and coriander are
some of the characteristic flavours in this
cuisine. For hotter tastes try sambals (fiery
pickles served as condiments). Malaysian
specialities include satay – a spicy peanut
dip. Singapore boasts mild and creamy
curries; Indonesia is famous for rijstafel (a
collection of small dishes served with
rice).*

Bintang
93 Kentish Town Rd NW1. 0171-284
1640. Tiny restaurant with bamboo walls,
Malaysian artefacts and crisp white linen.
Specialise in seafood. Set menus. Tiger
beer available. Friendly service. *LD OPEN
to 24.00.* A.V. **££**

Melati 4 **E3**
21 Great Windmill St W1. 0171-437
2745. Very popular. Rice and noodle
dishes, meat and seafood specialities.
Fried rice with shredded chicken and
shrimps, fish cutlets in coconut sauce. *LD
Reserve. OPEN to 23.30, to 00.30 Fri &
Sat.* A.Ax.Dc.V. **££**

Nusa Dua 4 **E2**
11-12 Dean St W1. 0171-437 3559.
Cheerfully decorated restaurant. Crispy
prawns in hot dip, grilled fish with ginger
and garlic, coconut pancake roll. Very
good value set menu. *LD OPEN to 23.30.
CLOSED L Sat & LD Sun.* A.Ax.Dc.V. **££**

Rasa Sayang 4 **E2**
10 Frith St W1. 0171-734 8720.
Unpretentious restaurant serving authentic Singaporean and Malaysian food.
Try the beef satay, prawns, orange

chicken. *LD Reserve D. OPEN to
23.30, to 00.45 Sat, to 22.00 Sun.
CLOSED L Sat.* Also at 38 Queensway
W2. 0171-229 8417. *OPEN to 23.15,
to 22.45 Sun.* A.Ax.Dc.V. **££**

Singapore Garden
83 Fairfax Rd NW6. 0171-328 5314.
Friendly atmosphere in this homely
restaurant decked out with plants and
flowers. Seafood is a speciality, as are
the traditional ironpot dishes with
chicken, lamb or beef. *LD Reserve.
OPEN to 22.00, to 22.30 Fri & Sat.*
A.Ax.Dc.V. **££**

Mexican & Tex-Mex

*Mexican dishes are largely variations of
tortillas (thin corn or flour pancakes),
minced or shredded meats, frijoles (red
beans cooked until soft and mushy) and
chilli. Ceviche (raw fish marinated in lime
juice), chicken mole (in a spicy chilli and
bitter chocolate sauce) and tamales
(pancakes of meat slow-baked in corn
husks) are also popular dishes. Rice,
avocados and tomatoes are common
accompaniments.*

Café Pacifico 4 **F2**
5 Langley St WC2. 0171-379 7728.
Crowded cantina in a converted warehouse. No booking at night, but have a
Mexican cocktail while you wait. Young
clientele. Guacamole, nachos, tacos,
enchiladas, quesadillas, tostados, chi-
laquiles. Fresh pineapple or helados to
follow. *LD Reserve L. OPEN to 23.45, to
22.45 Sun.* A.Ax.V. **££**

Chiquito 4 **E3**
20 Leicester Sq WC2. 0171-839 6925.
Large, bright restaurant decorated with
artefacts and colourful wall-hangings.
Fresh ingredients and mild spices are
used to prepare north Mexican cuisine;
chicken Monterez, enchiladas,
chimichangas. Mexican fried ice-cream.
Margaritas, Mexican beer. *Lunchtime
buffet. LD OPEN to 23.45, to 22.45 Sun.*
A.Ax.Dc.V. **££**

La Cucaracha 4 **E2**
12-13 Greek St W1. 0171-734 2253.
London's first Mexican restaurant, in
the cellars of a converted monastery.
Hacienda-style decoration with sunny
covered terrace at the back. Ceviche,
tacos, burritos, avocado Mexicana
(baked and stuffed with crabmeat),
enchiladas. Spicy and delicious.

LD OPEN to 00.30 Mon-Sat, to 23.30 Sun. Disco on Thur, Fri & Sat. A.Ax.Dc.V. **££**

Down Mexico Way   4 **D3**
25 Swallow St W1. 0171-437 9895. Elaborately decorated with hand-painted tiles and a grand fireplace. An interesting menu including nachos, ceviche, jalapeno muffins, mesquite smoked dishes and marvellous Mexican soup. Late bar to *03.00 Mon-Sat* (with DJ *Thur-Sat*). *LD OPEN to 24.00, to 22.30 Sun.* A.Ax.Dc.V. **££**

Los Locos   4 **F3**
24 Russell St WC2. 0171-379 0220. Mexican bar and restaurant with lots of Tex-Mex specials. Nachos, tacos, carnitas, steaks, alligator, enchiladas, grilled shrimps, fajitas – cooked over mesquite wood. Limited wine list, Mexican beer and cocktails. Disco *from 23.30 every night. D OPEN to 21.30. Disco to 03.00.* A.Ax.Dc.V. **££**

Middle Eastern

Charcoal grilling is a popular method of cooking throughout the area, and dishes are often spicy. Yoghurt is a common ingredient. Ginger, almonds, nutmeg, coriander and cinnamon are also widely used.

Al Hamra   4 **C4**
31-33 Shepherd Market W1. 0171-493 1954. Elegant Lebanese restaurant. The meze is excellent and features several dishes not commonly available. Also a variety of charcoal-grilled meats and sweet, sugary desserts to follow. Lebanese wine or arak. *LD OPEN to 23.15.* A.Ax.Dc.V. **£££**

Fakhreldine   4 **C4**
85 Piccadilly W1. 0171-493 3424. This huge and elaborately decorated restaurant overlooks Green Park. Extensive list of meze dishes, felafel and pitta, kibbeh, charcoal grills. *LD OPEN to 01.00.* A.Ax.Dc.V. **£££**

Hafez   3 **B2**
5 Hereford Rd W2. 0171-221 3167. A small Iranian restaurant full of character. Traditional flat breads are baked in the huge mosaic oven at the front. Chelo kebabs are Hafez's speciality. Vegetarian dishes. **Hafez II** is at 559 Finchley Rd NW3. 0171-431 4546. *LD OPEN to 01.30.* No credit cards at Hafez. A.Ax.Dc.V. at Hafez II. **£**

La Reash Cous-Cous House   4 **E2**
23 Greek St W1. 0171-439 1063. Not all couscous, despite the name; a variety of other dishes popular throughout the Middle East. Try chicken tagine which is served piping hot in a traditional Moroccan cooking pot. Vegetarian dishes. *LD OPEN to 24.00.* A.Ax.V. **££**

Modern European

These restaurants combine the techniques of French and English cooking whilst incorporating ideas and ingredients from around the world. Attractive and fairly expensive, they are pleasant and relaxing places in which to eat.

Alastair Little   4 **E2**
49 Frith St W1. 0171-734 5183. Fashionable restaurant with an imaginative, frequently-changing menu. Asparagus hollandaise, salmon fishcakes, rhubarb and pistachio trifle to follow. *LD Reserve. OPEN to 23.30. CLOSED L Sat & LD Sun.* A.Ax.V. **£££+**

Atlantic Bar & Grill   4 **D3**
20 Glasshouse St W1. 0171-734 4888. Glamorous and fashionable. Sweep down the wave of stairs to the cavernous art nouveau style dining room, where you can choose from a menu of light dishes,mixed platters and main dishes. *D open to 23.30, to 22.30 Sun. Bar open to 03.00, to 23.30 Sun.* A.Ax.Dc.V. **£££**

Bibendum   6 **E2**
Michelin House, 81 Fulham Rd SW3. 0171-581 5817. Lofty dining room in the unusual 1910 Michelin building. Long menu of elegant and inventive French and English dishes is renowned. *LD Reserve. OPEN to 23.00, to 22.15 Sun.* A.V. **£££+**

Fulham Road   6 **E2**
257-259 Fulham Rd SW3. 0171-351 7823. Another Stephen Bull venture which has already gained a Michelin star. Has a reputation for offal-based dishes. *LD OPEN to 23.00, to 22.00 Sun.* A.Ax.V. **£££**

Langan's Bistro   1 **D6**
26 Devonshire St W1. 0171-935 4531. Peter Langan's first restaurant, decorated with original Hockneys and Proctors, and inverted parasols. Gratin of Arbroath smokies, avocado and tomato salad with hazelnut sauce, poached salmon trout with dill sauce, breast of chicken with tarragon sauce. Mrs Langan's chocolate mousse is an unmissable dessert. *LD*

Reserve. OPEN to 23.30. CLOSED L Sat & LD Sun. A.Ax.V. **£££**

Langan's Brasserie   **4 C4**
Stratton St W1. 0171-493 6437. Buzzing atmosphere and stylish surroundings. Changing menu may include oyster mushrooms, soufflé with anchovies, black pudding. Live music *every night. LD Reserve. OPEN to 23.45, to 24.00 Sat. CLOSED L Sat & LD Sun.* A.Ax.Dc.V. **£££**

Museum Street Café   **4 F1**
47 Museum St WC1. 0171-405 3211. Charming decor and piles of freshlybaked bread. Excellent weekly-changing set menu may include tomato and salmon soup, beef sirloin au poivre with spinach gratin, baked red mullet with wild rice. Non-smoking. *LD Reserve. OPEN to 21.30. CLOSED Sat & Sun.* A.Ax.V. **££**

The People's Palace
Royal Festival Hall, South Bank SE1. 0171-928 9999. Opened in 1995, this glass-fronted restaurant on the third floor of the Royal Festival Hall is overseen by Gary Rhodes of The Greenhouse *(see page 112)*. From the set menu: homemade corned beef followed by mushroom risotto, or grilled sea bream with caper and parsley butter. Wonderful river views. *LD OPEN to 23.00.* A.Ax.Dc.V. **£££**

One Nine Two   **3 A3**
192 Kensington Park Rd W11. 0171-229 0482. Trendy wine bar and restaurant. Daily menu may include fish soup, grilled quail, calves' liver, cheesecake, chocolate truffle cake. Carefully selected wine list. *LD OPEN to 23.30, to 23.00 Sun.* A.Ax.Dc.V. **££**

Savoy Grill   **4 G3**
The Savoy Hotel, Strand WC2. 0171-836 4343. World-famous, well-deserved reputation for classic English and French cooking. Delightful panelled room, soft lighting and a very fine wine list. *LD Reserve. OPEN to 23.15. CLOSED L Sat & LD Sun.* A.Ax.Dc.V. **£££+**

Stephen Bull   **4 A2**
5 Blandford St W1. 0171-486 9696. Black and white decor and artful lighting. Innovative menu changes frequently. Good fish dishes, twice-cooked goat's cheese soufflé, langoustines with noodles, ginger and soy, pear and pista-

chio tart. *LD Reserve. OPEN to 22.30. CLOSED LD Sat & Sun.* A.V. **£££**

Open-air

More and more London restaurants are providing outdoor seating areas. The following places have pavement or terrace seating or tables in a garden, enclosed courtyard or conservatory.

Anemos   **4 D1**
32 Charlotte St W1. 0171-636 2289. Friendly, crowded and noisy. Eat outside at the pavement tables in *summer*. Humous, excellent kebabs, moussaka. *LD Reserve D. OPEN to 01.00. CLOSED Sun.* A.Ax.Dc.V. **££**

Au Bon Accueil   **6 E2**
19-21 Elystan St SW3. 0171-589 3718. Tables set out on the pavement in *summer*. Comfortable French restaurant with good unpretentious cooking – seafood crêpes, venison casserole, jugged hare, pheasant in red wine. *LD Reserve. OPEN to 23.30. CLOSED L Sat & LD Sun.* A.Ax.Dc.V. **££**

Barbican, Waterside Café   **2 E6**
Level 5, Barbican Centre EC2. 0171-638 4141. Self-service café by the man-made lake of the arts centre. Snacks or full meals. *LD OPEN to 20.00.* A.Ax.Dc.V. **£**

Dan's   **6 E3**
119 Sydney St SW3. 0171-352 2718. Bright, airy room with hanging plants and seating for 40 in the garden. Modern European cuisine – warm spinach mousse with basil, rack of lamb with honey and mustard, chocolate truffle cake to follow. *LD OPEN to 22.30. CLOSED L Sat & LD Sun.* A.AxV. **£££**

La Famiglia   **6 C4**
7 Langton St SW10. 0171-351 0761. Attractive, with pretty rear garden seating 100. Southern Italian cooking. Fourteen types of pasta. Italian wine. *LD OPEN to 24.00.* A.Ax.Dc.V. **££**

Glaisters   **6 C4**
4 Hollywood Rd SW10. 0171-352 0352. Also at 8-10 Northcote Rd SW11. 0171-924 6699. Pretty walled garden at the back. Wide-ranging menu; anything from burgers to Dover sole. *LD OPEN to 23.30, to 22.30 Sun.* A.Ax.V. **££**

San Lorenzo Fuoriporta
Worple Rd Mews SW19. 0181-946 8463. Cheerful, lively trattoria with tables in the garden during *summer*. Traditional menu

– scalloppine di vitello alla San Lorenzo, petti di pollo, good fresh vegetables and home-made pasta. *LD Reserve. OPEN to 23.00, to 22.30 Sun.* A.Ax.Dc.V. **£££**

Scandinavian

Fish, salads, fruit, cheese and wholegrain bread make this type of cooking extremely healthy. The traditional smorgasbord is a good way to sample lots of dishes at once.

Anna's Place
90 Mildmay Pk N1. 0171-249 9379. Intimate restaurant offering excellent home-made Swedish cooking and hospitable service. For starters, camembert with parsley, then gravadlax, beef or herring, duck breast with cabbage. *LD Reserve. OPEN to 22.45. CLOSED Sun & Mon.* No credit cards. **££**

Copenhagen Pâtisserie
196 Haverstock Hill NW3. 0171-435 7711. A variety of open sandwiches, cakes and pastries. Pavement seating. *BLD OPEN to 21.00, to 19.30 in winter.* A.V. **£**

Garbo's   4 A1
42 Crawford St W1. 0171-262 6582. Pleasant restaurant serving Scandinavian home cooking. Try the herring salad Baltic, cabbage stuffed with minced pork, beef and rice or the smoked eel. Lunchtime smørgasbord. Imported Swedish beer and schnapps. *LD Reserve. OPEN to 23.30. CLOSED L Sat & LD Sun.* A.Ax.V. **££**

Spanish & Portuguese

Although Spanish cuisine varies from region to region, fish and seafood are the common ingredients, often cooked in garlic and olive oil. Tapas bars, serving simple snacks, are still popular in London. Stews, soups and simple fish dishes form the basis of Portuguese cooking.

Albero & Grana   6 E2
89 Sloane Av SW3. 0171-225 1048. Striking decor and original approach to traditional and modern Spanish cuisine. Lasagne of black pudding with green pepper sauce, grilled entrecote of beef, rice pudding brulée. Tapas bar at front of restaurant. *D OPEN to 24.00 Mon-Sat, to 22.30 Sun.* A.Ax.V. **££-£££**

Bar Gansa   1 D2
2 Inverness St NW1. 0171-267 8909. One of the best tapas bars in London with a lively crowd and occasional live music. *LD OPEN to 23.30, to 22.30 Sun.* A.V. **£**

Caravela   3 F5
39 Beauchamp Pl SW3. 0171-581 2366. Small, intimate, Portuguese restaurant. King prawns piri piri, fresh grilled sardines. Delicious orange roll dessert. Wine list exclusively Portuguese. Fado singer *Fri or Sat eve. LD Reserve. OPEN to 00.45, to 23.30 Sun.* A.Ax.Dc.V. **£££**

Casa Santana
44 Golborne Rd W10. 0181-968 8764. Lively, jolly Portuguese tapas bar with a rustic feel. Hearty servings of traditional stews and fish dishes. *LD OPEN to 22.30.* No credit cards. **££**

Galicia   3 A2
323 Portobello Rd W10. 0181-969 3539. Crowded restaurant where tapas are served at the bar. The Spanish chef prepares authentic dishes which include marinated anchovies and pulpo a la Gallega (octopus served on a wooden plate with rock salt and pimentos). Good selection of Galician wines. *LD OPEN to 23.30. CLOSED Mon.* A.Ax.Dc.V. **££**

El Rincón Latino
148 Clapham Manor St SW4. 0171-622 0599. Very popular restaurant run by two half-Spanish, half-Colombian sisters. Authentic Spanish and Latin American food. Excellent wine list. Spanish breakfast of chocolate con churros is served *11.00-14.00 Sat. LD Reserve. OPEN to 24.00. CLOSED Sun.* A.Ax.Dc.V. **££**

Triñanes
298 Kentish Town Rd NW5. 0171-482 3616. Serves tapas divided into vegetable, meat and seafood varieties. Small selection of more substantial dishes. Live music and flamenco dancing *Fri & Sat eve. LD OPEN to 02.00, to 01.00 Sun.* No credit cards. **££**

Thai & Vietnamese

Thai cuisine encompasses many different flavours and styles of cooking, and uses interesting mixtures of meat, seafood and vegetables. Dishes tend to be spicy with either sweet and sour or hot chilli sauces, and are always beautifully presented.

Vietnamese cuisine is a combination of Chinese and French cooking. Root ginger, coriander, coconut milk, chilli and lemon grass are common ingredients.

Bahn Thai   4 **E2**

21a Frith St W1. 0171-437 8504. High-quality authentic Thai food makes this a very popular restaurant where the dishes are chilli-rated for spiciness! Thai specialities like crispy frog's legs and Thai blue swimming crab. *LD OPEN to 23.15, to 22.30 Sun.* A.Ax.Dc.V. **££**

Blue Elephant   6 **A5**

4-6 Fulham Bdwy SW6. 0171-385 6595. One of London's best Thai restaurants. The surroundings resemble a tropical jungle and the food is beautifully presented, Royal Thai style, by unobtrusive waiters and waitresses in Thai costume. Excellent *Sun* brunch buffet. *LD OPEN to 00.30, to 22.30 Sun. CLOSED L Sat.* A.Ax.Dc.V. **£££**

Bonjour Vietnam   6 **A5**

593-599 Fulham Rd SW6. 0171-385 7603. One of the Zen chain of restaurants. A huge 30ft fish tank is part of the relaxed, welcoming atmosphere. Sample traditional and new-wave Vietnamese dishes such as Saigon spicy chicken with chilli or steamed scallops. *LD OPEN to 23.15, to 23.00 Sun.* A.Ax.Dc.V. **££**

Chiang Mai   4 **E2**

48 Frith St W1. 0171-437 7444. Light, airy restaurant serving authentic Thai cuisine. Chilli-hot grated papaya salad, pad Thai noodles, khao soi (chicken curry soup with noodles). Set menus. *LD Reserve. OPEN to 23.00.* A.Ax.V. **££**

Pho   4 **E3**

2 Lisle St W1. 0171-437 8265. A very popular, thriving café-style restaurant serving freshly-cooked food. Try the Vietnamese soup (Pho) which is a wonderful blend of flavours and textures. *LD OPEN to 23.30.* No credit cards. **£**

Sri Siam   4 **E3**

16 Old Compton St W1. 0171-434 3544. Also at 85 London Wall EC2 (**5 E1**). Popular Thai restaurant, attracting a fashionable crowd. The food is excellent; beautifully cooked and presented. The soups and stir-fry dishes are particularly popular. Set lunch menu. *LD (Reserve D) OPEN to 23.15, to 22.30 Sun. CLOSED L Sun.* A.Ax.Dc.V. **££**

Vegetarian & wholefood

Vegetarian restaurants are very popular in London and some of the best are listed below. See also the 'Indian' and 'Inexpensive' sections. For further information contact the Vegetarian Society: 0161-928 0793. It publishes the International Vegetarian Travel Guide, *which includes a directory of vegetarian restaurants, shops, guest houses and hotels throughout the UK and the world.*

Café Santé   4 **F3**

17 Garrick St WC2. 0171-240 7811. New-style vegetarian café with sleek black tables and chairs. Interesting salads, hot dishes which change daily, plus a few non-vegetarian meals. Unlicensed. *LD OPEN to 02.00, to 04.00 Fri & Sat, to 24.00 Sun.* No credit cards. **£**

Cranks   4 **D2**

37 Marshall St W1. 0171-437 9431. The original healthfood restaurant. Innovative vegetarian dishes. Try the vegan tofu-topped lentil quiche or the nut burger with couscous, beans and almonds. Other branches. *LD Reserve D. OPEN to 20.00. CLOSED Sun.* A.V. **££**

Food For Thought   4 **F2**

31 Neal St WC2. 0171-836 0239. Daily-changing menu always features a soup, a salad, stir-fried vegetables and a few hot dishes. Good choice of puddings too. Always busy. Unlicensed. Non-smoking. *BLD OPEN to 20.00, to 16.00 Sun.* No credit cards. **£**

The Gate

51 Queen Caroline St W6. 0181-748 6932. Tucked behind the Hammersmith Apollo above a Christian Community Centre, this is an airy, spacious restaurant. Innovative dishes like pea and mint soup and shiitake mushroom and spinach lasagne. Organic wines and beers. *LD OPEN to 22.45. CLOSED Sun.* A.Ax.Dc.V. **££**

Leith's   3 **A3**

92 Kensington Park Rd W11. 0171-229 4481. Up-market restaurant with an excellent vegetarian menu. Hot and cold starters such as artichoke pie and asparagus mousse. Beautifully presented main courses and hand-made sweets.

D Reserve. LD OPEN to 23.30. CLOSED L Sat & LD Sun. A.Ax.Dc.V. **£££**

Mandeer 4 **E2**
21 Hanway Pl W1. 0171-323 0660. Highly- acclaimed pioneering Indian vegetarian and wholefood restaurant. Specialities include aubergine bhajis, thali Mandeer or puffed lotus savoury. Generous set menu available. Very reasonable self-service lunchtime buffet. Licensed. *LD OPEN to 21.45. CLOSED Sun.* A.Ax.Dc.V. **£**

Mildred's 4 **E2**
58 Greek St W1. 0171-494 1634. Trendy glass-fronted café with an excellent vegetarian and vegan menu. Organic produce is used wherever possible. Also fish and seafood dishes. The vegetable stir-fry with satay sauce is popular. Organic wines and beers. Herbal teas. *LD OPEN to 22.45. CLOSED Sun.* No credit cards. **£**

Neal's Yard Dining Rooms 4 **F2**
Aka World Food Cafe
14 Neal's Yard WC2. 0171-379 0298. A light, airy vegetarian restaurant where you can either sit at the bar or at large shared tables. International dishes include Egyptian pitta, Indian thali, Turkish meze and Indonesian sambal. Unlicensed. Non-smoking. *LD OPEN to 20.00 (to 17.00 Mon, to 18.00 Sat). CLOSED Sun.* No credit cards. **£**

The Place Below 5 **D2**
St Mary-le-Bow, Cheapside EC2. 0171-329 0789. Situated in the crypt of St Mary-le-Bow, this is an excellent café which offers a short menu of lunch dishes and a gourmet vegetarian menu on *Thur & Fri evenings*. Roquefort terrine, aubergine and fennel casserole, fresh exotic fruit. Home-made olive and garlic bread, home-made lemonade. Unlicensed. Non-smoking. *CLOSED Sat & Sun.* No credit cards. *L* **£** *D* **££**

Vijay
49 Willesden La NW6. 0171-328 1087. Traditional south Indian vegetarian food served here as well as tasty meat curries for any non-vegetarian friends. Try their masala dosai, sambar or vegetables cooked in yoghurt and coconut. Genuine Indian sweets – almond cakes and kulfi. *LD Reserve. OPEN to 22.45, to 23.45 Fri & Sat.* A.Ax.Dc.V. **£**

Breakfast and brunch

'Hot bread' and pastries can be obtained as early as 06.00 from bakeries. Continental-style cafés, brasseries and pâtisseries serve fresh croissants and coffee and more substantial brunches. For a traditional English breakfast try the cafés around markets and main-line stations or splash out at one of the traditional hotels. Times are given for breakfast or brunch only. Price symbols for this section only are: **£** *under £5;* **££** *£5–£10;* **£££** *over £10.*

Cafés, brasseries and pâtisseries

La Brasserie 6 **E2**
272 Brompton Rd SW3. 0171-584 1668. French-style café serving continental breakfast. *OPEN all day from 08.00.* A.Ax.Dc.V. **£££**

Fleur de Lys 6 **C1**
13a Gloucester Rd SW7. 0171-589 4045. Pâtisserie where everything is baked on the premises. *OPEN from 08.00 Mon-Sat.* No credit cards. **£**

Frocks
95 Lauriston Rd E9. 0181-986 3161. Popular for traditional Sunday brunch. Salmon scrambled eggs, eggy bread, sausage cakes and bubble & squeak feature in set menu. *Served all day Sat & Sun.* A.Ax.Dc.V. **££**

Hotels

Serve breakfast to non-residents from around 07.00 (08.00 Sun).

Brown's Hotel 4 **C3**
Dover St W1. 0171-493 6020. English or Continental. *OPEN from 07.15, from 08.00 Sun.* A.Ax.Dc.V. **£££**

Cadogan 6 **F1**
75 Sloane St SW1. 0171-235 7141. English or Continental. *OPEN from 07.30.* A.Ax.Dc.V. **£££**

Claridge's 4 **C3**
Brook St W1. 0171-629 8860. English, à la carte or Continental. A.V. **££-£££**

Hyde Park Hotel 4 **B5**
66 Knightsbridge SW7. 0171-235 2000. English, Continental or à la carte. *OPEN from 07.00, from 08.00 Sun.* A.Ax.Dc.V. **£££**

Ritz 4 **D4**
Piccadilly W1. 0171-493 8181. English, à la carte or Continental. *OPEN from*

07.00, from 08.00 Sat & Sun.
A.Ax.Dc.V. **£££**

Savoy   **4 G3**
Strand WC2. 0171-836 4343. English,
Continental or fitness breakfast. *OPEN
from 07.00, from 08.00 Sun* A.Ax.Dc.V.
£££

Afternoon tea

*Afternoon tea is a British institution, at one
time very fashionable. Most large department stores such as Fortnum & Mason,
Selfridges and Harrods serve afternoon
tea in their restaurants but if you want to
avoid the hustle and bustle of busy shopping areas, the following pâtisseries and
hotels are your best bet.*

Tea & cakes

The Gallery Tearoom
103 Lavender Hill SW11. 0171-350 2564.
Camp surroundings coupled with over-
the-top interpretations of traditional afternoon tea. Strong on savouries. Served
11.00-19.00 Mon-Sun.

The Muffin Man   **6 B1**
12 Wright's La W8. 0171-937 6652. A
range of set teas: Devon, 'Muffin Man',
traditional. Served *all day Mon-Sat.*

Pâtisserie Valerie   **4 E2**
44 Old Compton St W1. 0171-437 3466.
Soho pâtisserie with tea, coffee and hot
chocolate. Excellent cream cakes and
sandwiches. Served *all day Mon-Sun.*
Other branches, including:

Pâtisserie Valerie   **1 C6**
105 Marylebone High St W1. 0171-935
6240. Traditional tea shop with its own
bakery and delicious pâtisserie. Afternoon
tea served *15.00-19.00 Mon-Fri.*

Tea in hotels

*Excellent service and a comfortable sense
of welcome. Expect to pay between £10-
£15 for a full tea.*

Brown's   **4 D3**
Dover St W1. 0171-493 6020. Very
English, country house setting. Sand-
wiches, cakes, tarts. Served *15.00-18.00.*

Claridge's   **4 C3**
Brook St W1. 0171-629 8860. A touch of
class in the comfortable reading room,
where liveried footmen serve sandwiches
and assorted pastries. *Reserve. Served
15.00-17.30.*

Dorchester   **4 B4**
Park La W1. 0171-629 8888. Dainty

sandwiches, cakes and pastries in
opulent surroundings. *Served 15.00-
17.45.*

Ritz   **4 D4**
Piccadilly W1. 0171-493 8181. A good
comfortable hotel. Tea in the Palm Court,
with dainty sandwiches, pastries and
cream cakes. *Reserve. Served at 15.15 &
16.30.*

Thé dansant

Waldorf Hotel   **4 G3**
Aldwych WC2. 0171-836 2400. Opulent
Palm Court tea lounge with comfort and
good service. Edwardian elegance.
London's most famous tea dance with
full set tea *Sat & Sun 15.30-18.00
(Reserve).*

Ice-cream

Baskin-Robbins
Delicious American ice-cream, 31
flavours. *OPEN 11.00-23.00.*
Empire Cinema, Leicester Sq WC2. **4 E3**
0171-734 8222.
Plaza Cinema, Lower Regent St W1. **4 E3**
0171-930 0144.

Haagen-Dazs
16 flavours of American ice-cream.
83 Gloucester Rd SW7. 0171-373 **6 C2**
9988. *OPEN 10.00-23.00.*
Leicester Sq WC2. 0171-287 9577. **4 E3**
OPEN 10.00-24.00, to 01.00 Fri-Sun.
The Piazza WC2. 0171-240 0436. **4 F3**
OPEN 10.00-23.00.
88 Queensway W2. 0171-229 **3 C3**
0668. *OPEN 10.00-23.00.*

Marine Ices   **1 C1**
8 Haverstock Hill NW3. 0171-485 3132.
Huge choice of Italian ice-cream and
water ices. Also restaurant. *OPEN 10.30-
23.00 (to 19.00 Sun).*

Pubs

*The British pub is an institution which has
evolved from the Saxon alehouse, the
medieval tavern and inn, to the Victorian
'public house'. For centuries London was
one of the great brewing capitals; in the
11thC the Domesday Book recorded
that the monks of St Paul's Cathedral
brewed 67,000 gallons of ale annually. In
the 12thC children drank beer as a
preventative to typhoid. In 1437 a
Brewers' Company was set up and many
breweries were established alongside the
Thames. In the 16thC workmen's wives*

blended malt, yeast, water and sugar at home. By the end of the 17thC there was a switch from unhopped, heavy and sweet ale to lighter and more bitter hopped beer. By 1733 there were almost 100 gin shops (drinking houses) in St Giles next to tuppenny brothels. A publican's placard in Southwark promised: 'Drunk for 1d. Dead drunk for 2d. Clean straw for nothing'. The rise of gin palaces resulted from the Beerhouse Act of 1830 which permitted the unlicensed sale of beer. Throngs of gin palace patrons spurred the brewers into improving their premises and it was out of these gin mills, taverns and inns that London's 7000 pubs evolved.

The British pub has always been a great meeting place and a venue for games (such as darts and dominoes) and entertainment (Shakespeare presented his plays in taverns, and Music Hall was born in Victorian pubs). Today London's thriving fringe theatre and music scene is largely based in pubs.

The variety of London's pubs is enormous: historic pubs in the City, modern pubs of unusual design and decor, riverside pubs, theatre pubs.

Traditional pub hours are 11.00-15.00 & 17.30-23.00 Mon-Sat, 12.00-14.30 & 19.00-22.30 Sun. *However, new laws have relaxed these hours and pubs are officially allowed to open* 11.00-23.00 Mon-Sun. *Not all pubs take advantage of these opening hours so it is advisable to check in advance. Many pubs in the City are closed on* Sat & Sun *and also close early at around 21.00.*

🍺*sign in this chapter means open* 11.00-23.00 Mon-Sat, *and open traditional hours on* Sun *(*12.00-14.30 & 19.00-22.30*) as a minimum.*

B *means bar food (snacks or full meals). Some pubs have a separate restaurant:* **L** *restaurant lunch;* **D** *restaurant dinner.*

Nicholson's London Pub Guide *gives more detailed information on where to drink in the capital.*

Argyll Arms   4 **D2**
18 Argyll St W1. 0171-734 6117. Traditional Victorian pub which has retained all its original features. The old manager's pulpit-like office still stands in the middle of the main bar. *CLOSED Sun.* **B**

🍺**Barley Mow**   5 **C1**
50 Long La EC1. 0171-606 6591. Built on the site of a monastery, this 400-year-old inn specialises in real ale and

bitter. Stylish Edwardian interior, exposed beams.

🍺**Blackfriar**   5 **C3**
174 Queen Victoria St EC4. 0171-236 5650. Triangular building near Blackfriars station. Stunning art nouveau temple of marble and bronze; lunchtime hot and cold bar food. *CLOSED Sat & Sun.* **B**

🍺**Buckingham Arms**   4 **D6**
62 Petty France SW1. 0171-222 3386. This attractive mid-Victorian pub is a popular gathering place for business people. **B**

🍺**Bunch of Grapes**   6 **E1**
207 Brompton Rd SW3. 0171-589 4944. Victorian pub with finely engraved snob-screens separating the bars and impressively carved wooden pillars. Traditional ales. **B**

🍺**Captain's Cabin**   4 **E3**
4-7 Norris St, Haymarket SW1. 0171-930 4767. A cosy nautical pub well situated for a pre-theatre drink. **B**

🍺**Cartoonist**   5 **B2**
76 Shoe La EC4. 0171-353 2828. In the heart of the old newspaper world, this Victorian pub is wallpapered with cartoons. Its outside sign is changed every year, the design being chosen from those submitted by cartoonists. Headquarters of the International Cartoonist Club. *CLOSED Sat & Sun.* **B**

🍺**Chelsea Potter**   6 **E3**
119 King's Rd SW3. 0171-352 9479. Trendy meeting place for the locals with an alternative juke box in the bar. **B**

🍺**Cheshire Cheese**   5 **B3**
5 Little Essex St WC2. 0171-836 2347. Intimate Jacobean pub with original oak beams and three bars. *CLOSED Sat & Sun.* **B**

🍺**Cheshire Cheese, Ye Olde**   5 **B2**
145 Fleet St EC4. 0171-353 6170. Rebuilt after the Great Fire with low-ceilinged interiors, oak tables, sawdust on the floor. Although new bars have been added, most of this pub hasn't changed much since Dr Johnson used to drop in. Snacks and good traditional English cooking. **B L D** *(Reserve)*

🍺**Cittie of Yorke**   5 **A1**
22-23 High Holborn WC1. 0171-242 7670. A huge pub in the Victorian grand manner with cosy cubicles where lawyers used to have confidential chats with their clients. Cellar bar. *CLOSED Sun.* **B**

🍺**Cock Tavern, Ye Olde** 5 **B2**
22 Fleet St EC4. 0171-353 8570. Lawyers have replaced the journalists who used to frequent this tavern, which boasts literary and Dickensian

associations and mementoes. Nell Gwynne, Pepys and Garrick once drank here. Carvery restaurant which also serves fish, puddings, pies and vegetarian dishes. *CLOSED Sat & Sun.* **B L** *(Reserve)*

✪ Crown & Two Chairmen   **4 E2**
31 Dean St W1. 0171-437 8192. Earned its name nearly 200 years ago by playing host to royalty who arrived by sedan chair – a crown carried by two chairmen. Real ale, hot and cold bar food. Rub shoulders with writers and people from the film world. **B**

✪ Dirty Dick's   **5 F1**
202-204 Bishopsgate EC2. 0171-283 5888. The original pub named after Nat Bentley, well-known 18thC miser of the ballad. Remnants of mummified cats and mouse skeletons are preserved behind glass. *CLOSED Sat, & Sun eve.* **B L** *(Reserve)*

✪ Dover Castle   **1 D6**
43 Weymouth Mews W1. 0171-580 4412. Mews pub patronised by BBC staff. Good food served in a separate eating room. *CLOSED Sun.* **B**

✪ Duke of Cumberland
235 New King's Rd SW6. 0171-736 2777. Edwardian elegance prevails. Popular with the young and trendy. Summertime drinking on Parson's Green. Real ale. **B**

✪ Duke of Wellington   **7 A2**
63 Eaton Ter SW1. 0171-730 3103. Traditional pub – pictures of the Iron Duke abound as do brass and copperware. Used by shoppers and workers as well as Chelsea locals. Good snacks. **B**

✪ Eagle   **2 E4**
2 Shepherdess Wlk N1. 0171-253 4715. Victorian music hall pub immortalised in the song *Pop goes the Weasel*. People used to spend their money here after 'popping the weasel', ie after pawning their possessions. Barbecues in *summer. CLOSED Sat & Sun.* **B**

✪ Edgar Wallace   **5 B3**
40 Essex St WC2. 0171-353 3120. On an original Elizabethan site but now with the famous writer as the theme of the pub. Dr Johnson and his circle used to meet here regularly once a week. Small upstairs restaurant. *CLOSED Sat L & Sun eve.* **B L**

✪ Flask
77 Highgate West Hill N6. 0181-340 3969. Dating back to 1663, this tavern is named after the flasks which people used to buy here to fill with water at the Hampstead wells. Highwayman Dick Turpin once hid in the cellars and William Hogarth and Karl Marx both drank

here. Crowded forecourt for outdoor drinking. **B L** *(Reserve)*

✪ Fox & Grapes
Camp Rd, Wimbledon Common SW19. 0181-946 5599. Julius Caesar camped near here. Mock Tudor pub rambling right on to the common. Good lunches, though limited menu on *Sun.* **B L D**

✪ French House   **4 E2**
49 Dean St W1. 0171-437 2799. Centre for the Free French during the war. De Gaulle drank here as did Brendan Behan and Dylan Thomas. Good wines. **B L D**

✪ George   **5 B2**
213 Strand WC2. 0171-353 9238. Fine old timbered inn built in 1723. Stands opposite the Royal Courts of Justice. Upstairs carvery. *CLOSED Sat eve & Sun.* **B L** *(Reserve)*

✪ George Inn   **5 E4**
77 Borough High St SE1. 0171-407 2056. Unique galleried coaching inn rebuilt in 1676 after the Great Fire of Southwark. Featured in Dickens' *Little Dorrit.* Courtyard entertainment in *summer.* Wine bar with good selection of wines, pâtés and cheeses. Restaurant. **B L D** *(Reserve)*

✪ Globe   **4 F2**
37 Bow St WC2. 0171-836 0219. Nearest pub to the Royal Opera House, frequented by members of the orchestra. Used in Hitchcock's *Frenzy.* **B**

✪ Golden Lion   **4 D4**
25 King St SW1. 0171-930 7227. Traditional Victorian pub with Oscar Wilde and Lillie Langtry associations. *CLOSED Sat eve & Sun.* **B L**

✪ Green Man
Putney Heath SW15. 0181-788 8096. 15thC ale house overlooking the Heath. Associated with duels and highwaymen. Barbecues in *summer.* **B**

Grenadier   **4 B5**
18 Wilton Row SW1. 0171-235 3074. Once an officers' mess for the Duke of Wellington's soldiers. Full of military bric-à-brac. **B L D** *(Reserve)*

✪ The Guinea   **4 C3**
30 Bruton Pl W1. 0171-409 1728. Pleasant old pub hidden away in a narrow, cobbled Mayfair mews. Originally known as the One Pound One, probably because of the cattle pound that once stood nearby. Became The Guinea in the reign of Charles II when the gold coin of the same name was first minted. Good but pricey English dining room. *CLOSED Sun.* **B L D** *(Reserve)*

Holly Bush
22 Holly Mount, Heath St NW3. 0171-435 2892. Unspoiled, pleasant pub in

picturesque setting. Olde-worlde with gas lighting and open fires in winter. *Sun* lunches. **B**

Island Queen   2 D3
87 Noel Rd N1. 0171-226 5507. Is without doubt the most outlandish decor of any pub in London; giant papier-mâché caricatures of politicians and famous figures are suspended from the ceiling! **B L D**

☞ King of Bohemia
10 Hampstead High St NW3. 0171-435 6513. Bow-fronted Georgian pub – a fashionable local. **B**

☞ King's Head & Eight Bells   6 E4
50 Cheyne Wlk SW3. 0171-352 1820. 18thC decor with pots, jugs and prints of old Chelsea. Quite a few famous regulars. **B**

Lamb   2 B5
94 Lamb's Conduit St WC1. 0171-405 0713. A busy Bloomsbury local with some intriguing music hall photographs and Hogarth prints. Original snob-screens. Non-smoking area. **B L**

☞ Lamb & Flag   4 F3
33 Rose St WC2. 0171-497 9504. A 300-year-old pub, originally called 'The Bucket of Blood' because of the bare fist fights in the upstairs room (Dryden apparently got the 'once-over' here). **B**

☞ Marquess of Anglesey   4 F2
39 Bow St WC2. 0171-240 3216. A pub with a chequered history. It was changed from an inn to a coffee house in the 18thC, converted back to a pub in the 19thC, extended in 1858, demolished in 1941 and rebuilt in 1953. **B L D**

☞ The Mayflower
117 Rotherhithe St SE16. 0171-237 4088. This famous Tudor riverside inn was originally called *The Shippe,* but changed its name when *The Mayflower,* which carried the Pilgrim Fathers from this part of the Thames, reached America. **B L D** *(Reserve)*

☞ Mitre, Ye Olde   5 B1
1 Ely Ct EC1. 0171-405 4751. Built in 1546 by the Bishop of Ely for his servants. Associations with Elizabeth I and Dr Johnson. *CLOSED Sat & Sun.* **B**

Museum Tavern   4 F1
49 Great Russell St WC1. 0171-242 8987. Opposite the British Museum, this tavern attracts students and sightseers. Karl Marx wrote and drank here. **B**

☞ Nag's Head   4 F3
10 James St WC2. 0171-836 4678. Famous and lively Edwardian pub with a strong theatrical flavour. **B**

☞ Old Bull & Bush
North End Rd NW3. 0181-455 3685. The pub made famous by the Florrie Forde song. The 17thC building was once the country home of the painter William Hogarth. **B**

☞ Old Butler's Head   5 E2
Mason's Av, Coleman St EC2. 0171-606 3504. Pleasant, renovated 17thC inn with English cooking. *CLOSED Sat & Sun.* **L**

☞ Printer's Devil   5 B2
98 Fetter La EC4. 0171-242 2239. A printers' and journalists' pub taking its title from the traditional nickname for a printer's apprentice. Notable collection of early prints and etchings illustrate the history of printing. Pizza restaurant upstairs. *CLOSED Sat eve & Sun.* **B**

☞ Red Lion   1 D4
2 Duke of York St SW1. 0171-930 2030. Plenty of Victoriana in this friendly pub. Beautifully preserved mirrors and rich mahogany panelling. **B**

☞ Red Lion   4 C4
1 Waverton St W1. 0171-499 1307. Lovely 17thC Mayfair inn with forecourt. Frequented by models, actors and young businessmen. English restaurant. **B L D** *(Reserve)*

☞ Roebuck
130 Richmond Hill, Richmond. 0181-948 2329. Large ground floor with wood beams and prints of old Richmond. Terrific Thames views. **B**

☞ Rose & Crown   4 C5
2 Old Park La W1. 0171-499 1980. 200-year-old country-style pub now surrounded by Park Lane houses. Said to be haunted by those hanged at Tyburn gallows (now Marble Arch) who sometimes incarcerated overnight in the cellars here. **B**

☞ Running Footman   4 C4
5 Charles St W1. 0171-499 2988. Pub which once had the longest name in London, 'I am the Only Running Footman'. Popular with croupiers from the clubs nearby. **B L D**

☞ Salisbury   4 F3
90 St Martin's La WC2. 0171-836 5863. Glittering Edwardian pub in the heart of theatreland. Cut-glass mirrors, illuminated gilt statuettes and sumptuous red velvet seats. A meeting place for theatre people. **B**

☞ Seven Stars   5 A2
53 Carey St WC2. 0171-242 8521. Behind the Law Courts. This early 17thC pub is one of the smallest in London. *CLOSED Sat & Sun.* **B**

☞ Sherlock Holmes   4 F4
10 Northumberland St WC2. 0171-930 2644. Upstairs is a perfect replica of Holmes' study at 221b Baker St. The

whole pub is saturated with relics of the legendary fictitious detective. **B L D** (Reserve)

◗ Spaniards Inn
Spaniards Rd NW3. 0181-455 3276. Famous 16thC inn, once the residence of the Spanish Ambassador to the court of James I. The poets Shelley, Keats and Byron drank here, as did Charles Dickens. Pretty garden. **B**

Spotted Dog, The Old
212 Upton La E7. 0181-472 1794. 17thC inn used by City merchants during the Great Plague. Dick Turpin connections. Oak beams, plaster whitewash, prints. **B L D**

◗ Still & Star   **5 G2**
1 Little Somerset St, Aldgate E1. 0171-488 3761. The only pub of this name in England, possibly derived from the distillation equipment (still) and the symbol of an early licensee's association (star). Set in 'blood alley' where Jack the Ripper struck. CLOSED Sat & Sun. **B**

◗ Watling, Ye Olde   **5 D2**
29 Watling St EC4. 0171-248 6235. Oak-beamed tavern rebuilt by Wren after the Great Fire of 1666. Stands on one of the oldest roads in London. Upstairs bistro. CLOSED Sat & Sun. **B L**

◗ Williamson's Tavern   **5 D2**
1-3 Groveland Ct, Bow La EC4. 0171-248 6280. Inviting City tavern built after the Great Fire. This was the original residence of the Lord Mayor of London before Mansion House was built. CLOSED Sat & Sun. **B**

◗ Wrestlers
98 North Rd N6. 0181-340 4297. L-shaped bar with leaded glass windows, named after the wrestling that was once a regular event here. **B**

Outdoor drinking

Duke of Clarence   **3 A4**
203 Holland Park Av W11. 0171-603 5431. Medieval-style interior with typically Victorian bar. Beautiful flagged courtyard with conservatory bar. Barbecues in summer. **B**

◗ Jack Straw's Castle
North End Way NW3. 0171-435 8885. Marvellous views over Hampstead Heath. Courtyard with tables and chairs. **B L D** (Reserve)

◗ Scarsdale Arms   **3 A6**
23a Edwardes Sq W8. 0171-937 1811. Pretty terrace surrounded by plane trees at the front. Good bar food and real ales. **B**

◗ Spaniard's Inn
Spaniard's Rd NW3. 0181-455 3276.

Once the residence of the Spanish Ambassador to the Court of James I, then a pub run by two Spanish brothers who took it over in 1620. Shelley, Keats, Byron and Dickens drank here; a scene of The Pickwick Papers was set in the large garden, which has its own bar. **B**

◗ Swan Tavern   **3 E3**
55 Bayswater Rd W2. 0171-262 5204. Popular beer garden opposite Hyde Park. Illuminated from dusk. **B**

◗ Waterside Inn   **1 G2**
82 York Way N1. 0171-837 7118. Red-brick pub with olde-worlde feel inside and seating along the Regent's Canal outside. **B**

◗ Windmill Inn, Ye Olde
Clapham Common South Side SW4. 0181-673 4578. Popular and lively Victorian pub with two patios. **B L D**

◗ Windsor Castle   **3 B4**
114 Campden Hill Rd W8. 0171-727 8491. Built in 1835 when you could see Windsor Castle from here. Large walled garden with bar and snack bar. **B L D**

Real ale specialists

◗ Bricklayer's Arms   **2 G5**
63 Charlotte Rd EC2. 0171-739 5245. More than 50 real ales on hand pumps. At lunchtime a City pub and in the evening a traditional East End boozer. CLOSED Sat eve & Sun. **B**

Goose & Firkin   **5 C6**
47 Borough Rd SE1. 0171-403 3590. The first of the Firkin chain of pubs which were opened to revive the ancient craft of brewing on the premises. Friendly, casual with good bar food. **B**

◗ Hole in the Wall   **5 B4**
5 Mepham St SE1. 0171-928 6196. Built into the arches by Waterloo Station. Twelve real ales. **B**

Three Kings
171 North End Rd W14. 0171-603 6071. Once the Nashville Rooms, known for its visiting bands, and now a huge temple of real ale with 18 handpumps, at least 9 real ales, lagers and ciders.

Riverside pubs

◗ Anchor   **5 D3**
1 Bankside/34 Park St SE1. 0171-407 1577. 18thC replacement of original destroyed by Great Fire of 1666. Exposed beams, large open fireplace and general Olde-English decor. **B L D** (Reserve)

Angel
101 Bermondsey Wall East SE16. 0171-237 3608. 15thC Thames-side pub on

piles, with extensive views over the river and the Pool of London. English cooking. **B L D**

Black Lion
2 South Black Lion La W6. 0181-748 7056. Lovely 400-year-old riverside pub with a prize-winning paved garden. **B**

Blue Anchor
13 Lower Mall W6. 0181-748 5774. Right on the river by Hammersmith Bridge where you can watch the rowers from the nearby clubs. **B**

Bull's Head
Strand on the Green W4. 0181-994 0647. 350-year-old Chiswick waterfront tavern with old-world atmosphere. Cromwellian links. **B**

City Barge
27 Strand on the Green W4. 0181-994 2148. 16thC inn on Chiswick waterfront. Views over Oliver's Island, where Cromwell hid from the Cavalier army. **B L**

Cutty Sark
Ballast Quay, Lassell St SE10. 0181-858 3146. There has been a pub on this site for over 400 years. Quiet Georgian pub with wooden interior. Overlooks river and wharves near *Cutty Sark* in dry-dock. *OPEN all day in summer.* **B L D**

☞ Dickens Inn   **5 G3**
St Katharine's Way E1. 0171-488 1226. Pub in Dickensian style. Fine views of diverse crafts in St Katharine's Dock. Food on three levels. **B L D**

☞ Dove
19 Upper Mall W6. 0181-748 5405. 18thC pub with a terrace overlooking the river. James Thomson wrote *Rule Britannia* here. **B**

Grapes
76 Narrow St E14. 0171-987 4396. Traditional atmospheric pub with balcony overlooking river. **B L D** *(Reserve)* in fish restaurant upstairs.

☞ London Apprentice
62 Church St, Old Isleworth, Middx. 0181-560 1915. Famous 16thC Thames-side pub with fine Elizabethan and Georgian interiors. Prints of Hogarth's 'Apprentices'. **B L D** *(Reserve)*

☞ Mayflower
117 Rotherhithe St SE16. 0171-237 4088. Tudor inn connected historically with the Pilgrim Fathers. The only pub in England licensed to sell British and American stamps. Drink on the jetty in good weather. **B** *(Reserve)*

Prospect of Whitby
57 Wapping Wall E1. 0171-481 1095. Historic dockland tavern with many famous and infamous associations. Decorated with nautical souvenirs and

fine pewter. Excellent English menu in upstairs restaurant. Food bar overlooking the river. Beer garden. **B L D**

Ship
10 Thames Bank SW14. 0181-876 1439. 16thC pub with terrace at the Mortlake end of the Oxford and Cambridge boat race course. **B L**

☞ Ship
41 Jew's Row SW18. 0181-870 9667. Just beside Wandsworth Bridge, this pub is at its best in *summer* when you can sit out on the patio overlooking the river. **B**

☞ PS Tattershall Castle   **4 F4**
Victoria Embankment WC2. 0171-839 6548. Several bars on board London's only paddle-steamer pub. Outside drinking on deck. Restored engine room on view. **B D**

☞ Town of Ramsgate
62 Wapping High St E1. 0171-488 2685. 15thC tavern with a grisly past; the riverside garden was once the hanging dock for petty criminals. **B**

Trafalgar Tavern
Park Row SE10. 0181-858 2437. Smart Thames-side inn close to Wren's imposing Royal Naval College. Good food in the restaurant. **L D**

White Swan
Riverside, Twickenham, Middx. 0181-892 2166. Attractive black-and-white balconied pub overlooking the river. Excellent lunchtime food. *OPEN all day in summer.* **B**

Music pubs

These vary enormously, from pubs with a pianist who plays old-time favourites to those with professional facilities and large audience capacity for rock and jazz bands. The pubs listed below are all established live music venues, but it's best to check in advance what is happening each night. Most pubs with a separate music room ask for gate money; you should expect to pay around £5.

Bull & Gate
389 Kentish Town Rd NW5. 0171-485 5358. Indie and rock *every night.* **B**

Bull's Head
373 Lonsdale Rd SW13. 0181-876 5241. Modern jazz by top English and international musicians *every night*, plus *Sun L.* **B L D** *(Reserve)*

Dublin Castle   **1 D2**
94 Parkway NW1. 0171-485 1773. Music *every night.* Anything from rockabilly to R & B. **B**

Half Moon
93 Lower Richmond Rd SW15. 0181-780 9383. Music *every night* including rock, folk and jazz bands. **B**

King's Head   **2 D2**
115 Upper St N1. 0171-226 0364. Live music *every night* after the stage performance. Folk, rock or jazz. **D**

Minogues   **2 C2**
80 Liverpool Rd N1. 0171-354 4440. Live music *every night*, generally traditional Irish, but also blues *Tue & Sun*.

Ruskin Arms
386 High St North E12. 0181-472 0377. Visiting bands play heavy rock *Thur-Sun*. Boxing gym upstairs.

Station Tavern
41 Bramley Rd W10. 0171-727 4053. Blues played *Mon-Sat eve & Sun L*.

Swan   **6 A5**
1 Fulham Bdwy SW6. 0171-385 1840. Mixed bands and R & B *every night*. Late opening. **B**

Tufnell Park Tavern
162 Tufnell Park Rd N7. 0171-272 2078. 1930s decor provides a suitable backdrop for live jazz *Thur-Sun eve*. **B**

Water Rats   **2 A4**
328 Grays Inn Rd WC1. 0171-837 7269. Influential venue. Indie hopefuls, ex-punk bands, major label bands. Full of A&R men.

The Windmill
Clapham Common South Side SW4. 0181-673 4578. Lively Victorian pub which stages opera nights on *Mon & Fri*.

Gay pubs & bars

Gay and drag pubs have been combined because while not all gay pubs offer drag acts, all pubs with drag acts attract an at least partially gay clientele. For further information contact the Lesbian & Gay Switchboard 0171-837 7324 (24 hrs). See also 'Gay nightlife'.

☞ Black Cap
171 Camden High St NW1. 0171-485 1742. Two bars. Second offers drag shows *six nights a week*. Late opening.

The Edge   **1 E2**
11 Soho Sq W1. 0171-439 1313. Smart gay/straight bar on two levels. *Late opening*. **B**

King's Arms   **4 D2**
23 Poland St W1. 0171-734 5907. Busy, friendly gay men's pub in central position.

Market Tavern   **7 E4**
Market Towers, 1 Nine Elms La SW8. 0171-622 5655. Atmospheric and friendly pub with separate, quieter bar. Men only night *Wed*. Late opening.

Royal Oak
62 Glenthorne Rd W6. 0181-748 2781. Large, busy pub with entertainment *Mon & Sat eve & Sun L*. Theme night on *Tue*. **B**

Royal Vauxhall Tavern   **7 F3**
372 Kennington La SE11. 0171-582 0833. First London pub to put on drag shows *every evening*. Late opening. **B**

Theatre pubs

*You normally need to become a member (**M**) of the theatre club; if so, membership can be bought before the performance, and the cost is usually nominal.*

Bush Theatre
See 'Fringe, pub & experimental theatre'.

DOC Theatre Club
Duke of Cambridge, 64 Lawford Rd NW5. 0171-485 4303. Stages classical and modern plays with an emphasis on European theatre. **M** *Closed at time of publication.*

Etcetera Theatre
Oxford Arms, 265 Camden High St NW1. 0171-482 4857. General fringe shows with new work from visiting companies. Also in-house productions. **M**

The Finborough
Finborough Arms, Finborough Rd SW10. 0171-373 3842. Innovative 'new writing' theatre where the policy is to produce new work only. **M**

The Gate
See 'Fringe, pub & experimental theatre'.

Grace Theatre   **6 F6**
See 'Fringe, pub & experimental theatre'.

Hen & Chickens
109 St Paul's Rd N1. 0171-704 2001. Regular *Mon eve* cabaret spots. Productions by visiting theatre companies the rest of the week.

King's Head   **2 D2**
See 'Fringe, pub & experimental theatre'.

Man in the Moon   **6 D4**
See 'Fringe, pub & experimental theatre'.

Orange Tree
See 'Fringe, pub & experimental theatre'.

Pentameters
Three Horseshoes Pub, 28 Heath St NW3. 0171-431 7206. Classics, new work and occasional poetry readings. **M**

Wine bars

Cheaper and more informal than restaurants and an alternative to the pub, wine bars are excellent meeting places. Wine is served by the glass or bottle and a selection of cheeses, pâtés and salads is usually available. Below we list a selection of well-established wine bars, many of which have their own restaurants.

Assume that the bars listed here are open traditional pub hours except where there is the ☙ sign which means open all day 11.00-23.00 Mon-Sat, 12.00-14.30 & 19.00-22.30 Sun. Very few wine bars open all day on Sun.

B *bar food* **L** *restaurant lunch* **D** *restaurant dinner*

Andrew Edmunds 4 **D3**
46 Lexington St W1. 0171-437 5708. Small but charming wine bar/restaurant which serves excellent wines and imaginative food. Daily specials. **B L D**

☙ **Archduke** 5 **A4**
Concert Hall Approach SE1. 0171-928 9370. Underneath the railway arches. Good range of wines, live jazz *Tue-Sat*. Upstairs restaurant. *CLOSED Sun*. **B D**

L'Artiste Musclé 4 **C4**
1 Shepherd Market W1. 0171-493 6150. Cheerful French wine bar with seating outside in *summer*. Fine selection of cheeses. **B**

Balls Bros
One of the oldest wine bar chains in London, especially useful for City workers. Most branches *OPEN to around 21.00. CLOSED Sat & Sun*. Food availability varies. Not all branches are listed.
6 Cheapside EC2. 0171-248 2708. 5 **D2**
Hay's Galleria, Tooley St SE1. 5 **F4**
0171-407 4301.
The Hopsellers, 24 Southwark St 5 **D4**
SE1. 0171-403 6851.
Moor House, London Wall EC2. 5 **E1**
0171-628 3944.
St Mary-at-Hill EC3. 0171-626 5 **F3**
0321.
42 Threadneedle St EC2. 0171-628 5 **E2**
3850.

☙ **Le Beaujolais** 4 **E3**
25 Litchfield St WC2. 0171-836 2955. Lively, mixed clientele in this popular, yet intimate wine bar. Good French wines and authentic French cooking. *CLOSED L Sat & LD Sun*. **B**

☙ **Bill Bentley's** 3 **F6**
31 Beauchamp Pl SW3. 0171-588 5080. Dark, cosy bar in the old-fashioned tradition with an excellent fish restaurant upstairs. The wine, mostly good quality French, is reasonably priced and complemented well by the delicious snacks from the oyster bar. Other branches. *OPEN to 23.00. CLOSED Sun*. **B L**

☙ **Brahms & Liszt** 4 **F3**
19 Russell St WC2. 0171-240 3661. Lively, crowded Covent Garden wine bar. Music is loud, food varied, with the emphasis on cheeses and salads. Some hot dishes. *OPEN to 01.00*. **B**

Cork & Bottle 4 **E3**
44-46 Cranbourn St WC2. 0171-734 7807. A spacious basement with an unusual variety of top-class bargain wines. The walls are covered with prints and posters about wines and champagnes. **B**

Davy's Wine Bars
Dusty barrels, old prints and sawdust-covered floors create the Victorian image of these houses, the names of which date back to the wine trade of 100 years ago. The chain offers a good selection of wines and good food. *Phone to check opening times*. The City bars *CLOSE at 20.00 or 20.30*. Most branches are *CLOSED Sat & Sun*. The following list is a selection:

Boot & Flogger 5 **D4**
10-20 Redcross Way SE1. 0171-407 1184.

Bung Hole 5 **A1**
57 High Holborn WC1. 0171-242 4318.

City Boot 5 **E1**
7 Moorfields High Wlk EC2. 0171-628 2360.

☙ **Crusting Pipe** 4 **F3**
27 The Market, Covent Garden WC2. 0171-836 1415.

Davy's Wine Vaults
165 Greenwich High Rd SE10. 0181-858 7204.

Tappit Hen 4 **F3**
5 William IV St WC2. 0171-836 9839.

Dover Street Wine Bar 4 **D4**
8-9 Dover St W1. 0171-629 9813. Basement wine bar. Live jazz, funk or soul bands *six nights a week*. *OPEN to 03.00. CLOSED Sun*. **L D**

☙ **Ebury Wine Bar** 7 **A2**
139 Ebury St SW1. 0171-730 5447. Wine bar/restaurant serving a range of food and around 70 different wines. **B**

⚲ **Gordon's Wine Bar**   **4 F4**
47 Villiers St WC2. 0171-930 1408. 300-year-old wine cellar where the ancient stone walls and ceilings drip with water! Excellent selection of wines, ports and sherries. *CLOSED Sat & Sun.* **B**

⚲ **Shampers**   **4 D3**
4 Kingly St W1. 0171-437 1692. Always a congenial atmosphere here. 160 different varieties of wine and 20 different champagnes. Brasserie downstairs. Taped jazz. *CLOSED LD Sun.* **B D**

Soho Soho   **4 E2**
11-13 Frith St W1. 0171-494 3491. Spacious, colourful French wine bar, café and brasserie. French food. *OPEN to 01.00.* **B L D**

El Vino   **5 B2**
47 Fleet St EC4. 0171-353 6786. Something of an institution. Thoroughly masculine atmosphere. Women were not allowed to buy drinks at the bar until 1982. Jacket and tie required. *OPEN to 20.00. CLOSED Sat & Sun.* **B L** (Reserve)

Brasseries & cafés

Continental-style brasseries and cafés offer informal, stylish surroundings where you will find good food (from snacks to full meals) and alcoholic drinks (which you can consume without having to eat).
Most of the bars listed below are open all day.

La Brasserie   **6 E2**
272 Brompton Rd SW3. 0171-584 1668. The most authentic French-style brasserie in London. Sophisticated but unpretentious. *OPEN to 24.00, to 23.30 Sun.*

Brasserie du Coin   **2 B5**
54 Lamb's Conduit St WC1. 0171-405 1717. Typical French brasserie with wooden floors and candlelit tables. Wine list is mostly French with some Portuguese and Italian choices. *OPEN to 22.30, to 23.00 Sat. CLOSED Sun.*

Café des Amis du Vin   **4 F2**
11 Hanover Pl, Long Acre WC2. 0171-379 3444. Sandwiched between a wine bar in the basement and an elegant restaurant upstairs. The walls are adorned with photographs from the nearby Royal Opera House. *OPEN to 23.30. CLOSED Sun.*

Café Bohème   **4 E2**
13 Old Compton St W1. 0171-734 0623.

Perennially popular French-style brasserie/bar in the heart of Soho. *OPEN to 03.00 Mon-Wed, OPEN 24hrs Thur-Sat, to 23.00 Sun.*

Café Flo
A growing chain of chic Parisian-style cafés. Reasonably-priced à la carte menus plus well-prepared set menus. *OPEN to 23.30, to 23.00 Sun.*
676 Fulham Rd SW6. 0171-371 9673.
205 Haverstock Hill NW3. 0171-435 6744.
127-129 Kensington Church St W8. **3 B4** 0171-727 8142.
51 St Martin's La WC2. 0171-836   **4 F3** 8289.
334 Upper St N1. 0171-226   **2 D2** 7916.

Café Pelican   **4 F3**
45 St Martin's La WC2. 0171-379 0309. Renowned for impeccable service. Relaxed atmosphere, piano jazz in the background. *OPEN to 00.30, to 22.30 Sun.*

Café Rouge
Successful chain which has taken over many of the Dome branches. Friendly, lively atmosphere and standard brasserie fare.
38-39 Hampstead High St NW3. 0171-435 3404.
309 King's Rd SW3. 0171-352 2226. **6 D4**
98-100 Shepherd's Bush Rd W6. 0171-602 7732.
85 Strand on the Green W4. 0181-995 6575.
34 Wellington St WC2. 0171-836   **4 G3** 0998.

Camden Brasserie   **1 D2**
216 Camden High St NW1. 0171-482 2114. Relaxed ambience. Open fire in winter. Serves quality Mediterranean food. *OPEN to 23.30, to 22.30 Sun.*

Covent Garden Brasserie   **4 F3**
1 Covent Garden Piazza WC2. 0171-240 6654. This Parisian-style brasserie provides a refuge from the hustle and bustle of the piazza. Snacks and substantial French and Italian dishes. French, Chilean and Californian wines.

Soho Brasserie   **4 E2**
23-25 Old Compton St W1. 0171-439 9301. Arty French interior and a smart clientele. Outside tables in *summer*. Modern European menu.

Tuttons Brasserie   **4 F2**
11-12 Russell St WC2. 0171-836 4141. Right on the edge of Covent Garden piazza, this is a large, airy brasserie with a relaxed atmosphere. International menu. *OPEN to 23.30, to 24.00 Fri & Sat.*

Shops and services

London has an amazing array of shops from the world-renowned department stores to smaller specialist outlets, selling anything from up-to-the-minute fashions to antiques and unusual crafts.

Consumer protection

Always keep the receipt for goods you buy and, if you're not satisfied, take them back to the shop and ask to speak to the manager. If the fault is entirely theirs you don't have to accept a credit note: ask for cash.

The *Trade Descriptions Act* protects the consumer against fraudulent claims made for goods, and the *Sale of Goods Act* against merchandise not up to standard – contact the Trading Standards Officer at your local Town Hall, your local Consumer Advice Centre or the Citizens Advice Bureau.

Opening times

Generally shops *open 09.00/10.00-17.30/18.00 Mon-Sat and are closed on Sun and B.hols*. West End shops stay *open late on Thur to 19.30/20.00, and until the same time on Wed* in Knightsbridge, King's Rd and Sloane Sq. A lot of Bond Street shops *do not open on Sat*. In cases where a shop's hours differ from the standard times above, the opening hours appear in italic at the end of the entry.

Shopping areas

The West End   4 **D2**
The capital's biggest shopping area consisting of three main streets. **Oxford Street** (4 **C2**) is over a mile long and has nearly all the major department stores including Selfridges, London's largest Marks & Spencer and an overwhelming assortment of individual fashion shops. It gets very crowded here, especially on *Sat* and at *lunchtime*. **Regent Street** (4 **D3**) is less hectic and offers luxurious items at Liberty, plus several china, glass and clothing stores. **Carnaby St** (4 **D3**) is still worth a visit. World-renowned in the 1960s, it has retained its busy and lively atmosphere, with frequent pavement shows and interesting clothes and

souvenir shops. Some of the high street chains have now also moved in. For real luxury try **New Bond Street** (4 **C3**) where you'll find shoes, jewellery, pictures, prints and designer clothes. Two pedestrianised streets just off Oxford St are well worth exploring – **St Christopher's Place** (4 **B2**) and **South Molton St** (4 **C2**). Both are packed with stylish small shops and attractive eating places.

Brent Cross
This vast shopping complex at the head of the M1 on the North Circular is north London's 'West End'. Ample free parking so the ideal way to avoid central London traffic and still visit branches of the main central London stores. Also has smaller, more individual, shops. *OPEN 10.00-20.00 Mon-Fri, 09.00-18.00 Sat.*

Camden   1 **D1**
Trendy and popular canalside area lined with shops and a huge, sprawling market. Very busy on a *Sat afternoon*. Shops deal in period clothes, alternative books, imported records, pine furniture and artefacts.

Charing Cross Road   4 **E2**
& Bloomsbury   4 **F1**
This is the area for books – new, second-hand, antique, specialist or bestsellers. Also prints and maps.

Covent Garden   4 **F3**
Once the site of the famous fruit and vegetable market, this is now a fashionable pedestrianised piazza. The arcades are lined with small specialist fashion and gift shops, plus plenty of places to eat and drink. There are also open-air craft stalls, an antiques market and an occasional craft market. Leading off the piazza in every direction, the streets reveal an interesting variety of shops and restaurants with the latest in fashion, hi-tech household equipment and exotic foods.

Hampstead
A quaint and pleasant place to browse. As well as the usual chain stores there are a number of exclusive clothes shops and narrow streets with arcades of antique and art dealers. Also plenty of wine bars, cafés and brasseries.

Hay's Galleria   5 **F4**
Tooley St SE1. Shopping and leisure complex near London Bridge. Lots of the main chain stores, plus coffee houses and wine bars.

Kensington High Street 3 C5
Less hectic than Oxford Street, though a similar range of shops, plus Barkers of Kensington – its own department store. Delve into the roads leading off for more individual fashion shops.

King's Road/Chelsea 6 F3
Still as much a place to be seen as to see; this area comes alive on *Sat*. One of the centres for up-to-the-minute fashion, it is particularly good for shoes and men's clothing.

Knightsbridge 4 A5
A fashionable area for the rich and famous, dominated by Harvey Nichols and Harrods, which can supply almost any demand if you are willing to pay the price. Exclusive furniture, jewellery and clothes can also be found in Beauchamp Place.

Piccadilly/Trocadero/ 4 E3
London Pavilion
Quality and tradition at Fortnum & Mason, Hatchard's, Simpson and Lillywhites; also the historic Burlington Arcade. The Trocadero and the London Pavilion cater for the more up-to-date market, providing one-stop shopping, refreshment and entertainment, while Tower Records now dominates Piccadilly Circus from the old Swan & Edgar building.

Portobello Road 3 A2
Most famous for its huge market where you can alternate from the expensive antique dealer to the rag-and-bone merchant. A variety of household goods and second-hand clothes. Also unusual art deco and craft shops in the surrounding streets. Excellent delis.

Soho 4 E2
Sex shops and porno cinemas are now giving way to excellent specialist food shops, oriental supermarkets, designer clothes shops, restaurants and wine bars. Berwick Street Market and Chinatown are definitely worth a visit.

Tottenham Court Road 4 E1
Stretching north from the end of Oxford Street, this area is buzzing with shops selling electronic equipment (stereos, videos, cameras and computers). Furniture and modern design also feature at Heal's and Habitat, with many smaller shops also selling sofas, sofa-beds and futons.

Whiteleys 3 C3
Queensway W2. One of the first department stores, now transformed into a lively, smart, cosmopolitan complex of shops, cafés, restaurants, bars and an eight-screen cinema.

Department stores

There are several large stores in London where you can buy practically anything. Others are slightly more specialised, but still offer a wide choice of goods. Most have coffee shops and restaurants serving good, reasonably-priced lunches and teas; many also have hairdressing salons.

Army & Navy 7 C1
101-105 Victoria St SW1. 0171-834 1234. Excellent food hall and wine department. Clothes, cosmetics, household goods, toys, books, china and glass. Hairdressing salon, coffee shop, restaurant.

Barkers of Kensington 3 C5
63 Kensington High St W8. 0171-937 5432. Good general store selling fashionable clothes, household and electrical goods. Hairdressing/beauty salon.

British Home Stores (BHS) 4 C2
252 Oxford St W1. 0171-629 2011. Inexpensive high street chain for clothes and household goods. Extensive home lighting department.

Debenhams 4 C2
334-338 Oxford St W1. 0171-580 3000. Fashion clothes at reasonable prices. Good departments for kitchenware, lingerie, hosiery, cosmetics.

D.H. Evans 4 C2
318 Oxford St W1. 0171-629 8800. Straightforward store with an excellent fashion and lingerie department. Unusual sizes well catered for in the dress department. Perfumery, furniture and household goods. Olympus Sports in the basement.

Dickins & Jones 4 D2
224 Regent St W1. 0171-734 7070. Fashionable store selling high-quality clothing, accessories and haberdashery. Excellent dress fabrics. China and glass. Coffee shop.

Fenwick 4 C3
63 New Bond St W1. 0171-629 9161. Good fashions and accessories. Imaginative gifts and stationery. Books. Also large store at Brent Cross Shopping Centre NW4. 0181-202 8200.

Fortnum & Mason 4 D4
181 Piccadilly W1. 0171-734 8040. World-famous. Luxury goods and exotic foods. Superb hampers for all occasions. Designer collection clothes.

Harrods 3 G6
Knightsbridge SW1. 0171-730 1234. The world's most famous department store. Superb men's, ladies' and children's fashions and accessories. Perfumery, gifts, china and glass, pets, toys, books, furniture, fabrics. Edwardian marble food halls. Hairdressing/beauty salon, gentle-

men's barber. Restaurants, tea and coffee shops. Also a wide range of services.

Harvey Nichols 4 **A5**
109-125 Knightsbridge SW1. 0171-235 5000. Stylish clothes from top British, Continental and American designers. Home furnishing and household goods. Restaurant. *OPEN 10.00-19.00 Mon-Fri (to 20.00 Wed), to 18.00 Sat.*

John Lewis 4 **C2**
278-306 Oxford St W1. 0171-629 7711. One of the largest dress fabric departments in Europe. Furniture, furnishings, china and glass, fashions. Good haberdashery and craft materials. Bureau de change, export bureau and interpreters. Branch at Brent Cross Shopping Centre NW4. 0181-202 6535.

Liberty 4 **D2**
210-220 Regent St W1. 0171-734 1234. Fashionable and famous, especially for its distinctive fabrics and unusual luxury goods. Fashion jewellery, wide range of glass and china, oriental rugs, prints and gifts. Designer collection clothes.

Littlewoods 4 **B2**
508-520 Oxford St W1. 0171-629 7847. Inexpensive high street chain for clothing and household goods.

Marks & Spencer 4 **B2**
458 Oxford St W1. 0171-437 7722. Quality clothes and accessories for men, women and children. Wide range of foods, home furnishings, cosmetics. Bureau de change. Numerous other branches. *OPEN 09.00-19.00 Mon-Wed & Sat, to 20.00 Thur & Fri, 12.00-18.00 Sun.*

Peter Jones 6 **F2**
Sloane Sq SW1. 0171-730 3434. Quality clothing, accessories and household goods. Also modern and antique furniture, glass and china. Large furnishing fabric department. Excellent linens: wide range of plain coloured sheets and towels in all sizes. Fashion clothes, hairdressing salon. Interpreters available. Restaurant, coffee shop.

Selfridges 4 **B2**
400 Oxford St W1. 0171-629 1234. Limitless household department. Furniture, men's and women's fashions, toys, food hall, sports clothing and equipment. Bank, information desk, garage with parking facilities for 700 cars.

Clothes: general

The following shops cater for men and women, unless otherwise stated. See 'Men's clothes' and 'Women's clothes' for specialist shops.

Clothes stores

For a good selection of quality clothing try the following well-known stores. Nearly all London's department stores have extensive collections of clothes and accessories.

Aquascutum 4 **D3**
100 Regent St W1. 0171-734 6090. Fine quality British raincoats, suits, knitwear and accessories for men and women.

Austin Reed 4 **D3**
103 Regent St W1. 0171-734 6789. English and Continental suits and accessories for men. Accent on quality. Valet service and barber. Options department for ladies, selling executive and designer wear suits and classic dresses.

Burberrys 4 **E3**
18 Haymarket SW1. 0171-930 3343. Classic raincoats for men and women cut in English style. Hats, scarves, knitwear, suits and accessories. Other branches.

C & A 4 **A2**
501-519 Oxford St W1. 0171-629 7272. Vast selection of reasonably-priced fashions and classics for all the family. Skirts, dresses, coats, knitwear, suits and leathers. Avanti collection for young men. Sportsworld department includes large seasonal collection of ski-wear. Full fashion range for 14-25 year-olds in the Clock House. Other branches.

Jaeger 4 **D3**
200-206 Regent St W1. 0171-200 4000. Four floors of well-cut English clothes. Suits, coats, knitwear and casual wear for men. Dresses, suits and separates for women in colour co-ordinated departments. Cashmere, camel and knitted garments. Original accessories, jewellery.

Moss Bros 4 **F3**
88 Regent St W1. 0171-494 0666. Famous for classic menswear. Women's designer clothes, jewellery and accessories. Other branches.

Simpson 4 **D3**
203 Piccadilly W1. 0171-734 2002. High-quality clothing for men and women. Suits, knitwear, dresses, separates. Daks country clothes, Squadron sportswear, luggage and accessories. Wine bar, restaurant, gentlemen's barber.

Fashion shops

Many of the following have several branches. Only the main ones are listed below.

Benetton 4 **C2**
255-259 Regent St W1. 0171-355 4881. Large range of colourful Italian knitwear and separates.

Boy 4 **D3**
49 Carnaby St W1. 0171-494 1355.

Slightly off-beat and trendy fashions for men, women and children.

French Connection   **4 D2**
10 Argyll St W1. 0171-287 2046. Colourful, fashionable styles. Other branches.

The Gap   **4 D2**
208 Regent St W1. 0171-287 3851. American-style casual wear for men, women and children. Co-ordinated colours.

Hennes   **4 B2**
481 Oxford St W1. 0171-493 8557. Also at 261-267 Regent St W1 (4 **D3**). 0171-493 4004. High fashion clothes for men, women and children.

Jigsaw   **4 F3**
21 Long Acre WC2. 0171-240 3855. Casual, sporty styles in natural fibres. Limited number of co-ordinating colours available but stock changes frequently. Accessories, lingerie and shoes.

Naf-Naf   **6 F2**
13-15 King's Rd SW3. 0171-730 8752. Casual and very popular French clothing. Tracksuits, sweatshirts, romper suits, bomber jackets in bright colours with Naf-Naf slogan on everything.

Next   **4 D3**
160 Regent St W1. 0171-434 2515. Colour co-ordinated fashion separates. Suits and casual wear. Shoes, accessories and cosmetics.

River Island   **3 C5**
124 Kensington High St W8. 0171-937 0224. Popular young styles for men and women at very reasonable prices.

Top Shop & Top Man   **4 D2**
Oxford Circus W1. 0171-636 7700. Large shop for variety of inexpensive fashions in styles to suit most tastes.

Way In   **3 G6**
Harrods, Knightsbridge SW1. 0171-730 1234. Fashionable clothes department within the famous store.

Designer wear

The following shops have been chosen for the quality and individuality of their goods. Prices vary – the South Molton Street and Knightsbridge areas tend to be expensive.

Arte   **4 C2**
12 South Molton St W1. 0171-408 0870. Bold and unusual fashions for the daring dresser. Other branches.

Browns   **4 C2**
23-27 South Molton St W1. 0171-491 7833. The very best of British and international designer clothing exclusive to the shop.

Feathers   **3 G6**
40 Hans Cres SW1. 0171-589 0356. Well-chosen collection of Continental clothes and accessories for women. Good knits, shoes, bags and belts.

Giorgio Armani   **3 G6**
37-42 Sloane St SW1. 0171-235 6232. Beautiful designs by Armani for men and women. Chic and expensive.

Hyper Hyper   **3 C5**
26-40 Kensington High St W8. 0171-938 4343. A fashion forum on two floors featuring the work of exciting young designers in individual units. A large variety of avant garde clothing for men and women. Also shoes and accessories for all occasions.

Issy Miyake   **6 E2**
270 Brompton Rd SW3. 0171-581 3760. Everything from tailored skirts to ethnic-looking scarves are carefully designed. Stocks a classic line for men as well as Issy Woman for the younger woman.

Joseph Tricot   **3 G6**
26 Sloane St SW3. 0171-235 5470. Joseph's fashions converted into wool. Some suede and leather garments.

Karl Lagerfeld   **4 D3**
173 New Bond St W1. 0171-493 6277. Excellent quality clothes for women. Soft fabrics and bold colours at bold prices. Also jewellery.

Katharine Hamnett   **3 G6**
20 Sloane St SW1. 0171-823 1002. Strong on unfussy casual wear for men and women. All her latest themes are stocked here.

Kelsey   **2 B5**
58 Lamb's Conduit St WC1. 0171-404 1616. Quality men's suit tailoring with flair. Also morning coats. Competitive prices.

Kenzo Paris   **3 G6**
15 Sloane St SW1. 0171-235 4021. Unusual clothes for women in colours that change every season.

Malcolm Levene   **4 B1**
13-15 Chiltern St W1. 0171-487 4383. Men's classic fashion and contemporary chic. Hand-made shoes, designer suits. Exclusive UK stockists of Kiehls – a range of skin and hair products.

Piero de Monzi   **6 D2**
68-70 Fulham Rd SW3. 0171-581 4247. Sporty but expensive clothes from Italy for men and women. Excellent knitwear.

Polo Ralph Lauren   4 **C3**
143 New Bond St W1. 0171-491 4967. Expensive American designer collection, ready-to-wear classic range and casual wear for men and women. Accessories.

Prada   4 **A5**
44 Sloane St SW1. 0171-235 0008. Beautifully cut and finished Italian designer wear and accessories.

St Laurent 'Rive Gauche'   4 **C3**
137 New Bond St W1. 0171-493 1800. Exclusive own-label Paris clothes for men and women.

Valentino   4 **C3**
160 New Bond St W1. 0171-493 2698. A shop for the woman who loves to dress well and has the money to indulge her tastes. The grand evening dresses take some beating.

Vincci   4 **D4**
60-67 Jermyn St SW1. 0171-629 0407. Range of shops which provide top Italian designs in unusual fabrics. Formal and casual menswear.

Wardrobe   4 **C3**
42 Conduit St W1. 0171-494 1131. Also at 3 Grosvenor St W1 (4 **C3**). 0171-629 7044. Good quality fashion for all ages. Consultancy service for working women with advice on clothes, make-up and hair.

World's End   6 **D4**
430 King's Rd SW3. 0171-352 6551. Designer Vivienne Westwood's eccentric shop. Unpredictable and often humorous fashions.

Shoe shops

There are many good shoe shop chains in addition to more expensive individual shops. This is a selection of both:

Atticus   3 **B4**
Vicarage House, 58-60 Kensington Church St W8. 0171-937 4600. Italian leather shoes. Stylish and practical mules, slingbacks and pumps.

Bally   4 **D3**
30 Old Bond St W1. 0171-493 2250. Good quality shoes for men and women.

Bertie   4 **B2**
409 Oxford St W1. 0171-629 5833. Imaginative styles and unconventional colours.

Charles Jourdan   3 **G5**
39-43 Brompton Rd SW3. 0171-581 3333. Beautiful shoes imported from France for men and women.

Church's   4 **D3**
58-59 Burlington Arc W1. 0171-493 8307. The famous high-quality classic men's and women's shoes. Wide range of fittings.

Clark's   4 **E2**
15 Oxford St W1. 0171-437 2593. Stock quality shoes in wide fittings as well as fashion shoes and children's footwear. Other branches.

Deliss   6 **F1**
41 Beauchamp Pl SW3. 0171-584 3321. Exclusive designs in all kinds of shoes and boots, made-to-measure from fabrics and leather. Bags and accessories.

Derber   3 **C5**
80 Kensington High St W8. 0171-937 1578. Popular and stylish shoes and boots for women. High fashion range for men.

Dolcis   4 **D2**
181 Oxford St W1. 0171-437 6401. Popular chain with many branches.

Dr Martens Department Store   4 **F3**
1-4 King St WC2. 0171-497 1460. 150 hardy boot and shoe styles by the makers of 'bovver boots', plus a menswear collection inspired by the 'great British worker' and branded fashion accessories.

Ferragamo   4 **D3**
24 Old Bond St W1. 0171-629 5007. Italian shoemakers. Smart, comfortable shoes.

Freed   4 **F3**
94 St Martin's La WC2. 0171-240 0432. Specialists in theatrical and ballet shoes. Also make excellent boots to order. Contact 0181-985 6121.

Gamba Shoes   4 **F3**
3 Garrick St WC2. 0171-437 0704. Ballet shoes, character shoes, pumps in satin and leather. Dyeing service for their own satin shoes – can match almost any colour.

Gucci   3 **G6**
17-18 Sloane St SW1. 0171-235 6707. Pricey, but well-made and distinctive styles.

Hobbs   4 **C2**
47 South Molton St W1. 0171-629 0750. Classic and fashion shoes for women in a good range of colours.

John Lobb   4 **D4**
9 St James's St SW1. 0171-930 3664. Top-quality, hand-made, made-to-measure shoes.

Kurt Geiger   4 **C2**
95 New Bond St W1. 0171-499 2707. Exclusive women's shoes and handbags.

Also at Harrods, Dickins & Jones and other big stores.

Lilley & Skinner   **4 B2**
360 Oxford St W1. 0171-560 2000. One of many branches for fashion shoes at reasonable prices.

Maxwell's   **4 B3**
29 South Audley St W1. 0171-495 8511. Hand-made bespoke boots and shoes of the highest quality.

Natural Shoe Store   **4 F2**
21 Neal St WC2. 0171-836 5254. Ultra-comfortable, foot-shaped shoes for men, women and children. De-Ja shoes created from recycled waste.

Pied à Terre   **4 C2**
19 South Molton St W1. 0171-493 3637. Unusual styles for men and women, including exotic suede slippers. Also do a cheaper range called Basics.

Pinet   **4 C3**
47-48 New Bond St W1. 0171-629 2174. Shoes in all kinds of skins exclusive to the shop.

Ravel   **4 C2**
248 Oxford St W1. 0171-499 1949. Fashion shoe chain with many branches.

Russell & Bromley   **4 C3**
24-25 New Bond St W1. 0171-629 6903. Fine hand-made shoes from Spain, France and Italy. Other branches.

Sacha   **6 E3**
67 King's Rd SW3. 0171-730 7183. Modern shoes in up-to-date styles.

Saxone   **4 B2**
502-504 Oxford St W1. 0171-629 2138. Fashion shoe shop with many branches.

Trickers   **4 D4**
67 Jermyn St SW1. 0171-930 6395. Quality hand-made shoes for women and ready-made shoes for men at reasonable prices.

Leather, suede & sheepskin clothes

Leather Rat   **4 C2**
37 South Molton St W1. 0171-499 2284. Stocked with a wide variety of styles.

Loewe   **4 C3**
130 New Bond St W1. 0171-493 3914. Quality hand-made Spanish leather and suede coats, dresses and suits for men and women.

Natural Leather   **4 F2**
33 Monmouth St WC2. 0171-240 7748. A safe bet if you want to buy a straight-forward, good quality designer leather jacket. *OPEN 11.00-19.00 Mon-Sat.*

Rivaaz   **6 E3**
113 King's Rd SW3. 0171-352 2480. Leather, suede and sheepskin fashions.

OPEN 10.00-19.00 Mon-Sat, 12.00-18.00 Sun.

Second-hand clothes

Markets are your best bet for period clothes – especially Portobello Rd, Kensington Market and Camden Lock. See also 'Charity shops'.

Acupuncture   **4 E3**
3 Tisbury Ct W1. 0171-439 3703. Cult fashion and a second-hand designer rail.

Angels & Bermans   **4 E2**
119-123 Shaftesbury Av WC2. 0171-836 5678. Military full dress uniform, 1800 onwards, for professional use. Hire only.

Annie's   **2 D2**
10 Camden Pas N1. 0171-359 0796. Original clothes and accessories of the '20s, '30s and '40s, plus large selection of antique lace dresses, blouses, etc.

Antiquarius Antique Market   **6 E3**
131-141 King's Rd SW3. 0171-351 5353. Victorian nighties, '20s flapper dresses and crepe dresses, '30s velvet evening dresses and more recent items. Quite expensive.

Cornucopia   **7 C2**
12 Upper Tachbrook St SW1. 0171-828 5752. Good range of second-hand clothes, shoes, jewellery and accessories, dating from 1910 into the 1960s, at reasonable prices. Specialise in glamorous evening wear.

Flip   **4 F3**
125 Long Acre WC2. 0171-836 7044. Also at 8 Southampton St WC2 (4 **F3**). 0171-379 5230. Large selection of second-hand American clothing.

The Frock Exchange   **6 B5**
450 Fulham Rd SW6. 0171-381 2937. Nearly new clothes and accessories.

Gallery of Antique Costume & Textiles
2 Church St, Lisson Gro NW8. 0171-723 9981. Selection of period clothes spanning three centuries. Some reproductions. Also large stock of decorative textiles including wall hangings and quilts. Film and theatre suppliers.

Lawrence Corner   **1 E4**
62-64 Hampstead Rd NW1. 0171-813 1010. Uniforms and Army/Navy surplus from World War II onwards. To hire or buy.

Pandora Dress Agency   **3 F6**
16-22 Cheval Pl SW7. 0171-589 5289. Very good used model garments bought and sold on commission.

Men's clothes

Bespoke tailors

Savile Row is renowned for expensive but long-lasting hand-tailored clothes in the finest cloths.

Anderson & Sheppard   4 **D3**
30 Savile Row W1. 0171-734 1420.

Blades   4 **D3**
8 Burlington Gdns, Savile Row W1. 0171-734 8911.

Buckleigh   6 **G3**
83 Lower Sloane St SW1. 0171-730 0770. Men's formal wear, bespoke and ready-made.

Douglas Hayward   4 **B3**
95 Mount St W1. 0171-499 5574.

Gieves & Hawkes   4 **D3**
1 Savile Row W1. 0171-434 2001. Classic but fashionable bespoke and ready-made clothes.

Henry Poole   4 **D3**
15 Savile Row W1. 0171-734 5985.

Huntsman & Sons   4 **D3**
11 Savile Row W1. 0171-734 7441. King of Savile Row from before 1800.

Kilgour, French & Stanbury   4 **D3**
8 Savile Row W1. 0171-734 6905.

Nutters of Savile Row   4 **D3**
19 Clifford St W1. 0171-437 6850. Exclusive but adventurous men's tailor.

Tom Gilbey   4 **D3**
2 New Burlington Pl W1. 0171-734 4877. An appointment is necessary at this design house where any type of suit can be made to measure. Women are also catered for. Tom Gilbey's Waistcoat Gallery has a large selection of bespoke and ready-to-wear waistcoats. Designer hire service available.

Fashion shops

Burtons   4 **D3**
114-120 Regent St W1. 0171-734 1951. Suits and accessories at reasonable prices.

Dunn & Co   4 **D3**
90 Regent St W1. 0171-494 2010. Classic suits and tweed jackets with a modern influence.

Hackett
65b New King's Rd SW6. 0171-371 7964. Well known for classic English style but stock ranges from formal to sportswear. Other branches.

Herbie Frogg   4 **C3**
38 New Bond St W1. 0171-499 2029. Stylish, classic suits by Hugo Boss. High fashion casual wear by Jino Cchietti.

Hornes   4 **E2**
4 Oxford St W1. 0171-636 7633. Casual wear, suits and shoes with the emphasis on co-ordination.

Jones   4 **F3**
13 Floral St WC2. 0171-240 8312. Exciting designer wear at average prices. Jeans, leather jackets, shirts, shoes.

Les 2 Zebras   4 **F3**
38 Tavistock St WC2. 0171-836 2855. Specialise in very chic, casual clothes for men by French, Italian and English designers. Knitwear, accessories, shoes and leather goods.

Tie Rack   3 **C5**
Kensington Arcade, Kensington High St W8. 0171-937 5168. Chain of shops selling ties in a range of different fabrics.

Woodhouse   4 **E2**
99-101 Oxford St W1. 0171-437 2809. Extensive range of fashionable clothes.

Shirts

These firms make top-quality shirts to measure:

Coles Ltd   6 **F2**
131 Sloane St SW1. 0171-730 7564.

Harvie & Hudson   4 **D4**
77 & 97 Jermyn St SW1. 0171-930 3949.

Hilditch & Key   4 **D4**
73 Jermyn St SW1. 0171-930 5336.

Turnbull & Asser   4 **D4**
71-72 Jermyn St SW1. 0171-930 0502. Also at 23 Bury St SW1 (4 **D4**). Ready-made and bespoke English cottons and silks.

Knitwear

The Scotch House   3 **G5**
2 Brompton Rd SW1. 0171-581 2151. Also at 84 Regent St W1 (4 **D3**). 0171-734 0203. A wide selection of tartans, Fair Isle, Shetland and Pringle knitwear.
S. Fisher of Burlington Arcade   4 **D3**
22-23 & 32-33 Burlington Arcade W1. 0171-493 4180. Very popular with overseas visitors for cashmere, lambswool and classic knitwear.

Sportswear

Lillywhites and Simpson have very extensive stocks of sports and casual wear.
See also 'Sports equipment' under 'Specialist shops and services'.

J.C. Cording   4 **D3**
19 Piccadilly W1. 0171-734 0830. Weatherproof and country clothing plus typical English fashion. Famous for old-

fashioned, classic-look cords and trousers. Exclusive luggage.

R.M. Williams   **4 C3**
2-4 Maddox St W1. 0171-629 6222. Authentic Australian clothing for men and women. Range of moleskin trousers and skirts. Also jackets, shoes and accessories.

Swaine, Adeney, Brigg   **4 D3**
10 Old Bond St W1. 0171-409 7277. Wide selection of English country and shooting clothes. Saddlery.

Military & naval dress

Moss Bros   **4 D3**
88 Regent St W1. 0171-494 0666. Make uniforms for officers in any of the services. War medals and ribbons. Ceremonial accoutrements can be hired.

Unusual sizes

Cooper's All Size   **3 F2**
72 & 74 Edgware Rd W2. 0171-402 8635. Ready-to-wear clothes for the tall and small. Chest sizes 34-60in (86-152cm). Alterations service.

High & Mighty   **4 A5**
81-83 Knightsbridge SW1. 0171-589 7454. Everything ready-to-wear for the big or tall man. Chest sizes 44-58in (112-147cm) up to 6ft 11in (2.06m) in height. Shoes up to size 15.

Magnus
63 Southend Rd NW3. 0171-435 1792. Outsize shoes for men in sizes 11-15 and women in sizes 8-11.

Clothes hire

Moss Bros   **4 D3**
88 Regent St W1. 0171-494 0666. Men's ceremonial and formal wear. Arrange to hire a week in advance.

Young's Dress Hire   **4 C2**
19-20 Hanover St W1. 0171-493 9153. Formal wear with a difference. A full range of morning suits, dinner suits, lounge suits, daywear and white tuxedos.

Women's clothes

Classic styles

Belville-Sassoon   **6 F2**
18 Culford Gdns SW3. 0171-581 3500. Extravagant and elegant dresses for day, cocktail and evening wear.

Caroline Charles   **6 E1**
56-57 Beauchamp Pl SW3. 0171-589 5850. Pretty feminine clothes exclusively designed. All ages.

Galicia   **4 F3**
24 Wellington St WC2. 0171-836 2961. Classic and fashion clothes. Separates, dresses, suits, coats and rainwear.

Panache   **6 F1**
24 Beauchamp Pl SW3. 0171-584 9807. A selection of the best designs from top international ready-to-wear collections. Printed silks, jersey, and French and Italian knits. Day and evening wear.

Peal & Co   **4 D3**
37 Burlington Arc W1. 0171-493 5378. Fashionable and classic knitwear and separates. Also cater for men.

The White House   **4 C3**
51-52 New Bond St W1. 0171-629 3521. Famous for their beautiful linen but also specialise in lovely clothes for women and children from little-known French, Italian and Swiss designers. Also exquisite lingerie.

Fashion shops

Up-to-date fashion without the expensive price tags of more exclusive designs. Many have more than one branch but main branches only are listed below.

Boules   **4 F3**
22-23 James St WC2. 0171-379 7848. Own-label fashions and accessories at affordable prices. *OPEN 10.30-19.30 Mon-Fri, 10.30-19.00 Sat, 12.00-18.00 Sun.*

Country Casuals   **4 D2**
Dickins & Jones, 226 Regent St W1. 0171-434 3633. Colour co-ordinated separates in classic and high fashion ranges. Matching accessories.

Dorothy Perkins   **4 C2**
379 Oxford St W1. 0171-495 0181. Women's fashions, dresses, co-ordinates, separates, shoes by Faith. Smart and casual wear.

Esprit   **3 G5**
1 Sloane St SW1. 0171-245 9139. Casual clothes for women. Attractive styles and colours.

Hobbs   **4 C2**
47 South Molton St W1. 0171-629 0750. Classic, easy-to-wear separates. Well made suits and co-ordinates.

Laura Ashley   **4 D2**
256-258 Regent St W1. 0171-437 9760. Distinctive cotton print dresses and separates in romantic styles. Nighties, evening and wedding dresses. Also corduroy and

woollens for winter. Accessories include boots, shoes, hats and jewellery.

Miss Selfridge   4 **B2**
400 Oxford W1. 0171-629 1234. Enormous selection of fashionable clothes. Excellent sweaters and shirts. Tights, jewellery, cosmetics and a good shoe shop.

Monsoon   4 **F3**
23 Covent Garden Mkt WC2. 0171-836 9140. Up-market Indian cottons, silks and velvets. Good for party clothes. Visit the Monsoon accessories shop 'Accessorize' next door for co-ordinating belts, hats, jewellery and shoes.

Richards   4 **C2**
263-265 Oxford St W1. 0171-499 5223. Large selection of dresses, separates, coats and leisurewear.

Stefanel   4 **C2**
15 South Molton St W1. 0171-629 7164. Italian knitwear and separates in bright fashion colours.

Wallis   4 **D2**
215 Oxford St W1. 0171-437 0076. Large range of dresses and well-cut quality fashions. Specialise in colour coordinates.

Warehouse   4 **D2**
19-21 Argyll St W1. 0171-437 7101. Young fashion from young designers at reasonable prices.

Knitwear

Jaeger   4 **D3**
204 Regent St W1. 0171-200 4000. Fashion and classic knitwear.

Patricia Roberts   4 **B5**
60 Kinnerton St SW1. 0171-235 4742. Beautiful and imaginative designer knitwear. An extensive collection of mohairs, Shetlands, cashmeres and cotton boucles in bright primary colours.

The Scotch House   3 **G5**
2 Brompton Rd SW3. 0171-581 2151. Enormous range of Scottish knitwear – Shetland, cashmere and lambswool.

Westaway & Westaway   4 **F1**
62-65 Great Russell St WC1. 0171-405 4479. Specialists in woollens and cashmere.

Lingerie, hosiery & nightwear

Marks & Spencer, Littlewoods and Fenwick carry good, inexpensive lingerie and nightwear, while Harvey Nichols, Harrods and Fortnum & Mason are excellent for more elegant styles.

Bradleys   4 **A5**
57 Knightsbridge SW1. 0171-235 2902. Speciality shop for fine lingerie, nightwear and beachwear.

Courtenay   4 **C3**
22 Brook St W1. 0171-629 0542. Pretty lingerie in silk, cotton, lace; also evening wear and accessories.

Fogal   3 **G5**
51 Brompton Rd SW3. 0171-225 0472. Tights, stockings and socks made from silk, cashmere and other exotic fabrics in all sizes, colours and patterns.

Janet Reger   6 **E1**
2 Beauchamp Pl SW3. 0171-584 9368. Glamorous, expensive nightwear and lingerie. Collectors' item catalogue also available.

Knickerbox   4 **C2**
469 Oxford St W1. 0171-355 1347. High street chain selling various styles of underwear for men and women.

Night Owls   6 **D3**
78 Fulham Rd SW3. 0171-584 2451. Unique little shop selling exquisite nightwear.

Rigby & Peller   6 **F1**
2 Hans Rd SW3. 0171-589 9293. Exclusive corsetières. Made-to-measure underwear and high-class Continental beachwear.

Sock Shop   4 **E2**
89 Oxford St W1. 0171-437 1030. High street chain of small shops stocked with all colours and styles of socks, tights and stockings. *OPEN 09.00-19.00 Mon-Sat, to 20.00 Thur.*

Maternity clothes

It is worth looking in the chain stores because they often stock their own range of maternity clothes.

Balloon   6 **E2**
77b Walton St SW3. 0171-584 3668. Elegant, expensive maternity wear.

Great Expectations   6 **D3**
78 Fulham Rd SW3. 0171-584 2451. Stylish, youthful and trendy maternity clothes.

Mothercare   4 **B2**
461 Oxford St W1. 0171-580 1688. (Main branch.) Good quality maternity and baby clothes and equipment at practical prices.

Unusual sizes

Base   4 **F2**
55 Monmouth St WC2. 0171-240 8914. Half the clothes here are designed by

Yugoslav Rushka Murganovic and the rest come from Europe or America. Bold designs and firm colours.

Buy & Large   **6 G2**
4 Holbein Pl, Sloane Sq SW1. 0171-730 6534. Full selection of clothes in fittings from 16-24. Good for evening wear.

Crispins   **1 C6**
28-30 Chiltern St W1. 0171-486 8924. Court shoes, boots, sandals and espadrilles in large sizes (8-11); plus narrow fittings in sizes 4-11.

Evans   **4 A2**
538-540 Oxford St W1. 0171-499 5372. General selection of clothes for the larger woman from size 14.

Lilley & Skinner   **4 B2**
360 Oxford St W1. 0171-560 2000. Special department for large and small size fashion shoes at reasonable prices.

Long Tall Sally   **1 C6**
21 Chiltern St W1. 0171-487 3370. Specialise in elegant clothes for tall women, sizes 12-20. Lingerie, separates, specially-designed evening wear.

Mary Fair   **1 B6**
61 Crawford St W1. 0171-262 9763. Individually-designed clothes in small sizes.

Bridalwear

Most large department stores have good bridalwear departments. There are also large specialist shops with extensive collections and fitters on hand to advise. Smaller, even more specialised shops deal in exclusive styles, sometimes using antique fabrics.

Berkertex Brides   **4 C2**
81 New Bond St W1. 0171-629 9301. Biggest bridal store in the country. Lots of satins, taffetas and lace. Good stock of formal registry office wedding dresses.

Catherine Buckley   **3 A3**
302 Westbourne Gro W11. 0171-229 8786. Designer of exclusive, elaborate wedding gowns often made in antique textiles to Edwardian styles. New and antique lace used with embroidery and beading.

David Fielden
0171-376 8148. Glamorous wedding dresses and evening wear made to order using an exotic array of materials. *By appt only.*

Laura Ashley   **4 B2**
449-451 Oxford St W1. 0171-355 1363. Tradition, nostalgia and femininity are Laura Ashley's trademarks in wedding dresses. Natural fabrics and reasonably priced.

Liberty   **4 D2**
210-220 Regent St W1. 0171-734 1234. Liberty has 12 designers working on its wedding dresses. Sample stock from which stock sizes made up, although made-to-measure service available for some designers.

Pronuptia de Paris   **4 C2**
19-20 Hanover St W1. 0171-493 9152. Large collection of bridalwear which changes every season. Full fitting service by specialists.

Dress hire

Contemporary Wardrobe   **2 A5**
The Horse Hospital, Colonnade, Herbrand St WC1. 0171-713 7370. Full-length gowns and cocktail dresses. Silk, taffeta, chiffon. Jewellery and gloves for hire. Make dresses to order.

One Night Stand   **7 A3**
44 Pimlico Rd SW1. 0171-730 8708. Ballgowns, cocktail and dinner wear. Over 400 garments in stock with new styles each season.

Twentieth Century Frox
614 Fulham Rd SW6. 0171-731 3242. Ballgowns and cocktail dresses.

Children's clothes

See 'Children's shopping' section in 'Children's London'.

Accessories

General

Accessorize   **4 F3**
Unit 22, Covent Garden Mkt WC2. 0171-240 2107. A large selection of earrings, costume jewellery, bags, belts, shoes and watches. *OPEN 10.00-20.00 Mon-Sat, 11.00-19.00 Sun.*

American Retro   **4 E3**
35 Old Compton St W1. 0171-734 3477. Sells original '50s American garb and natty accessories.

Brats   **6 D4**
281 King's Rd SW3. 0171-351 7674. An up-market accessory shop; all good designs and value for money.

Gallery   **4 D4**
1 Duke of York St, off Jermyn St SW1. 0171-930 5974. High quality accessories for men – blazer buttons and crests for various schools, universities and regiments. Shirts, ties, cuff links, braces.

Gucci   4 **D3**
33 Old Bond St W1. 0171-629 2716. Classic, matching accessories all emblazoned with the recognisable Gucci 'G's.

Hermes   4 **C3**
155 New Bond St W1. 0171-499 8856. Expensive, chic quality bags, scarves, jewellery and perfumes.

Mary Quant   4 **D3**
21 Carnaby St W1. 0171-494 3277. Bursting with novel accessories, including fancy tights, make-up and undies. Stock changes regularly.

Next Accessories   3 **C5**
54-58 Kensington High St W8. 0171-938 4211. Accessories in sophisticated colours and styles. 'Essentials' are a range of useful, well-designed objects which make great gifts – torches, diaries, luggage etc.

Filofaxes

Faxcessory   4 **F4**
15 Villier St WC2. 0171-321 0074. Filofaxes, inserts, briefcases.

Filofax Centre   4 **D3**
21 Conduit St W1. 0171-499 0457. Filofaxes to fit every pocket and an amazing range of inserts.

Just Facts   4 **D2**
43 Broadwick St W1. 0171-734 5034. Stocks the entire Filofax range.

Handbags & luggage

Most fashion and shoe shops carry a good range of handbags. For a selection of luggage, try the large department stores.

Alba Handbags   1 **B6**
189 Baker St NW1. 0171-935 3410. Good modern bags; exciting shapes and colours.

Mulberry   3 **B2**
11-12 Gees Court, St Christopher's Pl W1. 0171-493 2546. Full range of Scotch grain and leather luggage, fashion handbags and briefcases.

Salisburys   4 **A2**
530 Oxford St W1. 0171-355 1391. High street chain selling wide range of inexpensive bags, handbags and luggage.

Le Sport Sac   4 **C2**
3 South Molton St W1. 0171-499 2549. Wide range of bags including 'le sport sac' of New York, and Enny of Italy.

Hats

Bates   4 **E3**
21a Jermyn St SW1. 0171-734 2722. Edwardian-fronted men's hat shop, also favoured by the ladies.

David Shilling   3 **F1**
5 Homer St W1. 0171-262 2363. Famous and exclusive hat creations, as immortalised by Mr Shilling's mother at Ascot. Chic and elegant hats for everyday wear.

The Hat Shop   4 **F2**
58 Neal St WC2. 0171-836 6718. A wide variety of hats for men and women, ranging from classic panamas and boaters to designer specials.

Heady Heights
Delivery service. (09732) 96142. Designer hat hire – ideal for special occasions. Individualised service and fittings.

Herald & Hart Hatters
131 St Philip St SW8. 0171-627 2414. Amazing selection of straw hats and pins to keep them on.

Herbert Johnson   4 **C3**
30 New Bond St W1. 0171-408 1174. A fine range of hats. Famous for panamas. Everything from crash helmets to yachting caps.

James Lock   4 **D4**
6 St James's St SW1. 0171-930 5849. Hats for every occasion. Felt hats, tweed hats and caps. Famous for bowlers. Also top-quality riding and polo hats.

Specialist shops and services

London is an international centre of art, fashion, antiques and collectors' items. Many shops have specialised in certain goods and have become world-famous names. The list below represents only a selection of some of the best shops in each category. Some shops close on Sat afternoon and stay open late on Wed or Thur evenings.

'Which?' Magazine   1 **D5**
Consumers' Association, 2 Marylebone Rd NW1. 0171-486 5544. The best subscription periodical for unbiased testing of everyday products and services. Available at libraries for reference.

Animals

Animal Fair   3 **B6**
17 Abingdon Rd W8. 0171-937 0011. Animals for sale and services such as

boarding (for small animals) and grooming. Agency for kennels in the country.

Battersea Dogs Home   7 B5
4 Battersea Park Rd SW8. 0171-622 3626. Dogs and cats, some with pedigrees, all available for adoption.

Christopher Dog Consultants
30 Crooked Billet, Wimbledon Common SW19. 0181-947 3065. Long-established dog agency. Specialise in Yorkshire Terriers and Shihtzu but will direct you to the breeder of any dog. Also clipping and shampooing, and help with exporting.

Friends of Animals League
Foal Farm, Jail La, Biggin Hill, Kent. (01959) 572386. Mainly dogs, cats, and other domestic animals, rescued and available for adoption by carefully vetted homes.

National Canine Defence League   2 D4
17 Wakley St EC1. 0171-837 0006. Re-houses abandoned dogs and provides information on canine problems and care.

Antiques

There are hundreds of antique shops in London selling 18th and 19thC furniture, china and objets d'art. Good hunting grounds are the King's Rd, Portobello Rd, Camden Passage in Islington, Kensington Church St, Fulham Rd and Camden Town.

Antique fairs

Chelsea Antiques Fair   6 E3
Chelsea Old Town Hall, King's Rd SW3. 0171-937 5464. Held from *Mar-Sep*, this well-established fair offers a wide range of antiques and works of art.

PBFA Book Fairs (Provincial   2 A5
Booksellers Fairs Association)
Hotel Russell, Russell Sq WC1. (01763) 248400. Around 30,000 antiquarian and second-hand books on sale monthly *from 2nd Sun of the month 14.00-19.00 Sun & 10.30-19.00 Mon.* Extended fair *mid Jun, also Fri & Sat.*

Antique shops

Bluett & Sons   4 C3
60 Brook St W1. 0171-629 4018. Mainly Chinese, and some south-east Asian, ceramics and works of art.

Gallery of Antique Costume and Textiles
2 Church St NW8. 0171-723 9981. One of Europe's largest suppliers of antique costumes and textiles. Pillows of London is part of the Gallery.

Jeremy   6 F1
29 Lowndes St SW1. 0171-823 2923. English and French furniture and objets d'art.

Jonathan Harris   3 B5
54 Kensington Church St W8. 0171-937 3133. Fine quality and unusual European and Oriental furniture and works of art.

Mayorcas   4 D4
38 Jermyn St SW1. 0171-629 4195. Well-known dealers in antique textiles – costumes, embroidery, vestments, tapestry.

Myriad
131A Portland Rd W11. 0171-229 1709. Painted and decorative furniture and general antiques.

Pelham Galleries   4 B3
24-25 Mount St W1. 0171-629 0905. Specialists in English and Continental furniture, works of art, musical instruments and tapestries.

Radio Days   5 A5
87 Lower Marsh SE1. 0171-928 0800. Twenties and thirties artefacts and fifties kitsh. Good for theatre props.

Spink & Son   4 D4
5-7 King St SW1. 0171-930 7888. English paintings and watercolours. Silver, jewellery, paperweights, Oriental, Asian and Islamic art, textiles, medals and coins.

Antique markets

Covered antique markets can be found in Camden Passage, Portobello Rd, King's Rd and as follows:

Alfie's Antique Market
13-25 Church St NW8. 0171-723 6066. Five floors of antique stalls selling just about everything, also some repairs done. Coffee bar.

Antiquarius   6 E3
137 King's Rd SW3. 0171-352 7989. All aspects of fine, applied and decorative arts. Also worth visiting for the antique clothing.

Bermondsey and New   5 F5
Caledonian Market
Between Tower Bridge Rd and Bermondsey St SE1. One of the most famous antiques markets in southern England. Around 350 stalls outside plus 150 indoors. Mostly aimed at collectors and dealers, although the large variety and specialist goods make for fascinating

browsing. Snack bars and cafés. *OPEN 05.00-13.00 Fri only.*

Chelsea Antique Market   6 **E4**
245-253 King's Rd SW3. 0171-352 5581. A large, busy market covering all collectors' items.

Furniture Cave   6 **C5**
533 King's Rd SW10. 0171-352 4229. Several companies under one roof selling a wide range of non-contemporary furniture. Also have a large architectural and sculpture range.

Grays Market   4 **C3**
1-7 Davies Mews W1. 0171-629 7034. Two giant covered markets selling a huge selection of antiques.

Antiquities

Charles Ede   4 **C3**
20 Brook St W1. 0171-493 4944. Roman, Greek, Egyptian and Near Eastern antiquities. *OPEN Tue-Fri 12.30-16.30, or by appt.*

Aquaria

Aquapets
17 Leeland Rd W13. 0181-567 2748. Excellent general stock of fish, tanks and equipment.

Queensborough Fisheries
111 Goldhawk Rd W12. 0181-743 2730. Excellent selection of various tropical and pond fishes. Also equipment, tanks and water plants. *CLOSED Thur.*

Tachbrook Tropicals   7 **C2**
244 Vauxhall Bridge Rd SW1. 0171-834 5179. Importers and growers of over 200 species of tropical water plants for the aquarium. Also import fish. Accessories. Maintenance and servicing of aquaria.

Arts & crafts supplies

Alec Tiranti   1 **E5**
27 Warren St W1. 0171-636 8565. Large range of tools and material for wood and stone carving. Also plaster, resins, fibreglass and cold-pouring rubbers.

J. Blundell & Sons   4 **D2**
199 Wardour St W1. 0171-437 4746. Jewellery 'findings' and supplies. *OPEN 09.30-16.30 Mon-Fri.*

Candle Makers Supplies
28 Blythe Rd W14. 0171-602 4031. Sell everything for making your own candles as well as equipment for batik and silkpainting. Also wax dye-craft and resin casting. Candle-making, batik and silkpainting classes *some Sat.* Vast range of candles.

Cornelissen   4 **F1**
105 Great Russell St WC1. 0171-636 1045. Fine art, restoration and printmaking materials.

Daler Rowney Ltd   4 **E1**
12 Percy St W1. 0171-636 8241. Large and varied stock of general artists' paints and materials.

Green & Stone   6 **E4**
259 King's Rd SW3. 0171-352 0837. Established over 60 years ago. Modern equipment and a collection of Victorian materials such as easels, pens and 19thC watercolour paper.

The Handweaver's Studio & Gallery
29 Haroldstone Rd E17. 0181-521 2281. Fleece, yarns, dyes and other equipment for weaving and spinning. Books. Also tuition. *OPEN 10.00-17.00 Tue-Sat.*

Langford & Hill   4 **D3**
38-40 Warwick St W1. 0171-437 9945. The place in London to find a selection of the latest American and German commercial art materials, films, coloured papers, special inks, drawn curves, etc. Expert advice.

T.N. Lawrence   2 **C5**
119 Clerkenwell Rd EC1. 0171-242 3534. Everything for the engraver, etcher and print-maker.

Paperchase   4 **E1**
213 Tottenham Court Rd W1. 0171-580 8496. Exciting collection of papers and card. All types of artists' papers, book papers, Japanese papers, foils and display papers.

Reeves Dryad   3 **B5**
178 Kensington High St W8. 0171-937 5370. Think of a craft and they'll sell you the materials for it.

Russell & Chapple   4 **F2**
23 Monmouth St WC2. 0171-836 7521. Supply artists' fabrics.

Thorpe Modelmakers   5 **B1**
88 & 98 Gray's Inn Rd WC1. 0171-405 1016. Balsa wood, trees, cars and people for modelmaking.

Winsor & Newton   4 **E2**
51-52 Rathbone Pl W1. 0171-636 4231. Good general selection of artists' materials, papers and paints.

Astronomy

See also under 'Activities and interests' in the children's section.

Broadhurst, Clarkson & Fuller   2 **C5**
63 Farringdon Rd EC1. 0171-405 2156. Have been making telescopes for 200 years. All the most advanced equipment on sale.

Auctioneers: general

W. & F.C. Bonham & Sons 3 **F6**
Montpelier Galleries, Montpelier St SW7. 0171-584 9161. Paintings, furniture, carpets, porcelain, jewellery and silver.

Christie's 4 **D4**
8 King St, SW1. 0171-839 9060. Internationally famous. Comprehensive fine art auctioneers since 1766.

Christie's South Kensington 6 **D2**
85 Old Brompton Rd SW7. 0171-581 7631. All sorts of antique and antiquarian objects, including pictures, jewellery, silver, glass, ceramics, furniture and books.

Croydon Auction Rooms
144-150 London Rd, West Croydon, Surrey. 0181-688 1123. Miscellaneous sales *on Sat (fortnightly).*

Lots Road Galleries 6 **C5**
71 Lots Rd SW10. 0171-351 7771. General assorted sales *14.00 & 18.00 every Mon.* View *Mon before auction 10.00-16.00 Fri, Sat & Sun.*

Phillips 4 **C2**
101 New Bond St W1. 0171-629 6602. Fine arts auctioneers and valuers.

Phillips Marylebone Auction 3 **C3**
Rooms
10 Salem Rd W2. 0171-229 9090. General sale *10.00 Mon.* Viewing *17.15-19.30 Thur, 09.00-17.00 Fri, 09.00-12.30 Sat, 14.00-17.00 Sun.* Paintings sale *12.00 1st Tue of month.*

Sotheby's 4 **C3**
34-35 New Bond St W1. 0171-493 8080. Internationally famous for antiques and works of art. Paintings, ceramics, glass, furniture, silver, jewellery, books, manuscripts, photographic material and collectors' items.

Auctions: stamps & coins

Glendining 4 **C2**
101 New Bond St W1. 0171-493 2445. Coins, military and naval medals. *About 20 sales a year.*

Stanley Gibbons 4 **F3**
399 Strand WC2. 0171-836 8444. Stamps, postal history, albums and catalogues. *Sixteen auctions a year.*

Barbers

See also 'Hairdressers: men'.

Austin Reed 4 **C2**
103-113 Regent St W1. 0171-734 6789. Largely unchanged since 1930.

The Barber Shop at Harrods 3 **G6**
Knightsbridge SW1. 0171-589 1564.

Daniel Rouah 1 **B5**
7a Station Approach, Baker St Station NW1. 0171-487 3198.

George Trumper 4 **D4**
20 Jermyn St SW1. 0171-734 6553.

Bathrooms

Bathroom Discount Centre
297 Munster Rd SW6. 0171-381 4222. Suites by Ideal, Twyfords and Armitage Shanks, all at a discount.

Czech & Speake 4 **D4**
39c Jermyn St SW1. 0171-439 0216. Brass taps and shower fittings (some thermostatic) moulded from Edwardian originals. Also sell accessories and toiletries.

Sitting Pretty
131 Dawes Rd SW6. 0171-381 0049. Lavatory seats in mahogany or obeche (the latter can be stained to any colour). Also unfinished mahogany seats for the DIY enthusiast and reproduction, period suites.

Beauty specialists

Alternative & Orthodox 1 **C5**
Medicine Clinic
56 Harley House, Marylebone Rd NW1. 0171-486 8087. Treatments include aromatherapy, reflexology, facials, scarring treatments and stress alleviation. Own range of natural products designed to treat specific skin problems and types.

The Body Shop 3 **B6**
137 Kensington High St W8. 0171-376 0771. Sell a large range of preparations based on fruit, flowers, spices and woods, formulated by herbalists. Non-animal derived products. Other branches.

Cosmetics à la Carte 6 **G1**
19b Motcomb St SW1. 0171-235 0596. 'Beauty workshop' with advice and a chance to experiment.

Helena Harnik 4 **A2**
19 Upper Berkeley St W1. 0171-724 1518. Specialise in electrolysis and the treatment of problem skins.

Joan Price's Face Place 6 **F2**
33 Cadogan St SW3. 0171-589 9062.

Make-up lessons using many different products from various ranges. Also body and facial massages, pedicure and manicure, waxing, lash tinting, electrolysis, cathiodermie.

Konrad Treatment Room 4 **F3**
40 Tavistock St WC2. 0171-240 3696. Men-only treatment centre in the basement of this fashionable men's hairdressers. Hand-and-nail treatment, skin facials, massage.

Yves Rocher 4 **B2**
7 Gees Ct W1. 0171-409 2975. Shop packed with their famous beauty products – everything from shampoo to perfume. The emphasis is on natural beauty.

Bedroom shops

And So To Bed. . .
638-640 King's Rd SW6. 0171-731 3593. Specialists in antique, modern and designer beds. Brass headboards and wood and brass bedsteads. Complete range of bedlinen.

West London Bedding
313-321 North End Rd SW6. 0171-385 2000. Huge warehouse with brass, pine, sofa beds, divans. Very good value.

Books: new

Most department stores have book departments, the better ones being Harrods, Selfridges and Liberty. The following bookshops are recommended:

Barbican Business Book 5 **E1**
Centre
9 Moorfields EC2. 0171-628 7479. Wide range of business and finance books.

Books etc 4 **E2**
120 Charing Cross Rd WC2. 0171-379 6838. Well-organised general bookstore. Other branches.

Cinema Bookshop 4 **E2**
13-14 Great Russell St WC1. 0171-637 0206. Books relating to the cinema, including out-of-print titles and magazines.

Compendium 1 **D2**
234 Camden High St NW1. 0171-485 8944. Contemporary bookshop specialising in political and feminist literature. US fiction. Also the occult, mysticism, psychology and fringe subjects.

Countryside Bookshop 4 **D1**
39 Goodge St W1. 0171-636 3156. Collection of books, maps and field guides about the British countryside.

Dillons 1 **F5**
82 Gower St WC1. 0171-636 1577. Large academic and general stock including science and language. Some antiquarian and second-hand books. Other branches.

The Economists' Bookshop 5 **A2**
Clare Market, Portugal St WC2. 0171-405 5531. Specialists in social science and business books. Second-hand dept.

European Bookshop 4 **D3**
5 Warwick St, off Regent St W1. 0171-734 5259. Mainly French books but also Spanish, German and Italian, plus European periodicals.

Forbidden Planet 4 **E2**
71 New Oxford St WC1. 0171-836 4179. Specialists in science fiction, fantasy and horror. Large stock of comics and posters.

Foyles 4 **E2**
119-125 Charing Cross Rd WC2. 0171-437 5660. The biggest – has practically every English book in print.

French's Theatre Bookshop 1 **E5**
52 Fitzroy St W1. 0171-387 9373. Books on the theatre and play scripts.

Gay's the Word 2 **A5**
66 Marchmont St WC1. 0171-278 7654. Gay and feminist bookshop. New and second-hand. *OPEN 11.00-18.00 Mon-Sat, 14.00-18.00 Sun.*

Grant & Cutler 4 **D2**
55-57 Great Marlborough St W1. 0171-734 2012. New and second-hand books in German, French, Spanish, Portuguese and Italian.

Green Ink Bookshop
8 Archway Mall N19. 0171-263 4748. Books about Ireland and by Irish authors. Strong on history and politics. Irish newspapers, videos and cassettes.

Hatchards 4 **D3**
187 Piccadilly W1. 0171-439 9921. Something of an institution. Comprehensive selection of general books. Knowledgeable staff. Search facility.

HMSO Bookshop 5 **A1**
49 High Holborn WC1. 0171-873 0011. HMSO publications on every subject from cooking to parliament. No fiction.

Motor Books 4 **F3**
33-36 St Martin's Ct WC2. 0171-836 5376. Specialists in books on cars and aviation. Also military and railway books. Worldwide mail order service.

Pan Bookshop 6 **D3**
158-162 Fulham Rd SW10. 0171-373 4997. Wide selection of paperbacks and

most new hardbacks. *OPEN long hours: 10.00-22.00 Mon-Sat, 12.00-21.30 Sun.*

Silver Moon   4 **E3**
64-68 Charing Cross Rd WC2. 0171-836 7906. Good selection of feminist literature.

W.H. Smith
General books. Branches throughout London and at railway stations.

Sportspages   4 **E2**
94-96 Charing Cross Rd WC2. 0171-240 9604. Sports bookshop covering all aspects of sport and fitness. Also stocks magazines and videos.

Stanfords   4 **F3**
12-14 Long Acre WC2. 0171-836 1321. World's largest map and travel bookshop. Also wall maps of the world, globes and ancient plans of towns. Branch in Campus Travel, Victoria SW1.

The Talking Bookshop   4 **B2**
11 Wigmore St W1. 0171-491 4117. The first talking bookshop with all books on cassette or CD. All the classics and several new works. Mail order service with catalogue available.

Travel Bookshop
13 Blenheim Cres W11. 0171-229 5260. Books for every type of travel experience.

Travis & Emery   4 **F3**
17 Cecil Ct WC2. 0171-240 2129. New and second-hand music books. Theatrical and musical prints. Catalogues issued.

Waterstone's   3 **B6**
193 Kensington High St W8. 0171-937 8432. Good general bookshop. Other branches.

Watkins Books Ltd   4 **F3**
19-21 Cecil Ct WC2. 0171-836 2182. Mysticism, the occult, religions and astrology.

Wholefood   4 **B1**
24 Paddington St W1. 0171-935 3924. Books on nutrition and health, diets, natural childbirth, ecology and agriculture.

A. Zwemmer   4 **E2**
80 Charing Cross Rd WC2. 0171-379 7886. Also at 24 Litchfield St WC2 (4 **E3**). 0171-836 4710. Comprehensive stock of international books on art, architecture, design, fashion, film and photography.

Books: rare & antiquarian

The book collector is fortunate in having over 250 bookshops in London, many specialising in particular subjects. Charing Cross Rd, Cecil Ct and around the British Museum are good areas for browsing.

Bell Book & Radmall   4 **F3**
4 Cecil Ct WC2. 0171-240 2161. Modern first editions of English and American literature. Plus detective, science and fantasy fiction.

Bernard Quaritch   4 **D3**
5-8 Lower John St, Golden Sq W1. 0171-734 2983. Illuminated manuscripts, early printed books, English literature pre-1900, natural history, science and travel.

Dance Books   4 **F3**
9 Cecil Ct WC2. 0171-836 2314. All aspects of dancing and human movement. Also posters, photos, records and video cassettes.

David Drummond   4 **F3**
11 Cecil Ct WC2. 0171-836 1142. Rare and out-of-print books on the performing arts, and ephemera including circus, music hall and theatrical souvenirs. Also early children's books and Victorian valentines. *Unusual hours: 11.00-14.30 & 15.30-17.45 Mon-Fri, 11.00-14.15 first Sat in month (other Sats by appt only).*

G. Heywood Hill   4 **C4**
10 Curzon St W1. 0171-629 0647. Books with fine colour plates. Also an extensive collection of 19th and early 20thC children's books and general second-hand books. New books stocked as well.

Maggs Bros   4 **C3**
50 Berkeley Sq W1. 0171-493 7160. Collection of rare and fine books, illuminated manuscripts, autographed letters.

Marlborough Rare Books   4 **C3**
144-146 New Bond St W1. 0171-493 6993. Illustrated books, bibliography and architecture.

Otto Haas
49 Belsize Park Gdns NW3. 0171-722 1488. One of the best stocks of music, musical literature and autographs in the world. *By appt only.*

Pickering & Chatto   4 **E4**
17 Pall Mall SW1. 0171-930 2515. Rare and antiquarian books. English literature, science, medicine, economics. Literary manuscripts.

Sotherans   4 **D3**
2-5 Sackville St W1. 0171-439 6151. Established in London 1815. Antiquarian books, prints, periodicals and some modern books. Also binding and restoration. Separate Print Gallery at 80 Pimlico Rd SW1 (7 **A3**). 0171-730 8756.

Sangorski & Sutcliffe   **5 F5**
Zaehnsdorf
175r (entrance at 159) Bermondsey St
SE1. 0171-407 1244. Two companies at
the same address. Hand binding in all
styles and materials, design service.
Repair and restore leather bindings.

*Try the markets – Camden Lock for art
deco styles.*
Button Queen   **4 B2**
19 Marylebone La W1. 0171-935 1505.
Specialise in antique, old and modern
buttons, buckles, etc.
Taylors Buttons   **4 D3**
1 Silver Pl W1. 0171-437 1016. Largest
variety of buttons in London.

See under 'Photographic equipment'.

See under 'Sports equipment'.

Bernardout & Bernardout   **6 D2**
7 Thurloe Pl SW7. 0171-584 7658.
Oriental rugs and carpets, tapestries and
needlework. Some French and English
stock. Expert cleaners and repairers.
David Black Oriental Carpets
96 Portland Rd W11. 0171-727 2566.
Specialists in antique tribal rugs, carpets,
kilims, embroideries, Indian dhurries and
rare textiles. Valuations, restoration,
cleaning. Also new carpets and kilims.
Publish 7 volumes on antique carpets and
sell books by other publishers on antique
carpets. *OPEN 10.00-18.00 Mon-Fri &
11.00-17.30 Sat, or by appt.*
C. John   **4 B4**
70 South Audley St W1. 0171-493 5288.
Oriental and Persian carpets.
Kilim Warehouse
28a Pickets St SW12. 0181-675 3122.
A vast selection of antique, decorative
and new kilims from all parts of the
world. Cleaning and restoration
service.
Mayorcas   **4 D4**
38 Jermyn St SW1. 0171-629 4195.
Outstanding stock of European carpets,
textiles and tapestries.

Samad's   **4 B5**
33a Knightsbridge SW1. 0171-584 6902.
Variety of oriental carpets and rugs.

Anglo-Persian Carpet Co   **6 D2**
6 South Kensington Station Arc SW7.
0171-589 5457. Oriental carpets and
tapestries.
David Black Oriental Carpets
96 Portland Rd W11. 0171-727 2566.
Cleaning and repair service for oriental
and other antique carpets.

*The principal areas for antique ceramic
shops are Kensington Church St and
Knightsbridge – remember to look in the
back streets.*
Alistair Sampson Antiques   **4 B3**
120 Mount St W1. 0171-409 1799. Early
English pottery. Also 17th and 18thC oak
furniture, English brass, needlework,
primitive pictures and treen.
Haslam and Whiteway   **3 B4**
105 Kensington Church St W8. 0171-229
1145. Late 19thC Arts and Craft
Movement pieces.

China Repairers
64 Charles La NW8. 0171-722 8407.
Specialise in repairing antique and
modern china and glass.

*Charitable organisations such as Oxfam,
Notting Hill Housing Trust and Sue
Ryder Foundation run shops (numerous
branches – check in telephone directory
for your nearest one) selling second-hand
clothes, books and bric-à-brac in good
condition. Some also sell ethnic handi-
crafts. School and church halls often hold
beneficiary jumble sales where both
donations and buyers are welcome.*

Chinacraft   **4 C2**
198 Regent St W1. 0171-437 2332.
Fine English china, crystal and
figurines. Over 15 branches, most in
central London.
Craftsmen Potters Shop   **4 D2**
William Blake House, 7 Marshall St W1.
0171-437 7605. Only members of the

Craftsmen Potters Association can sell work here. This demands a high standard.

General Trading Company   **6 F2**
144 Sloane St SW1. 0171-730 0411. Some of the best designs in contemporary English and Continental glass and china. Large stock.

Gered   **4 D4**
173-174 Piccadilly W1. 0171-629 2614. Large showroom displaying and selling Spode, Royal Crown Derby, Royal Doulton and Wedgwood.

Lalique Ltd   **4 C3**
162 New Bond St W1. 0171-499 8228. Elegant displays of Lalique crystal, Limoges porcelain and Christofle silver.

Lawleys   **4 D3**
154 Regent St W1. 0171-734 3184. Popular chain selling Wedgwood, Royal Doulton, Waterford crystal and other top names.

Reject China Shop   **6 E1**
33-35 Beauchamp Pl SW3. 0171-581 0737. Also at 134 Regent St W1 (4 **D3**). 0171-434 2502. Reject china at low prices – the flaws tend to be hardly noticeable.

Rosenthal China Shop   **4 D3**
137 Regent St W1. 0171-734 3076. Specialise in Rosenthal china, glass and porcelain.

Villa Mimosa   **4 F3**
9 Central Av, Covent Garden Mkt WC2. 0171-836 0289. Ceramics from Italy – lamp-bases, tableware, chandeliers.

Villeroy & Boch
Have concessions in major department stores, eg Harrods, Dickins & Jones. Telephone 0181-871 0011 for details.

Chocolates & confectionery

Fortnum & Mason, Harrods and Selfridges all have excellent confectionery departments selling hand-made English and Continental chocolates.

Bendicks   **4 G3**
7 Aldwych WC2. 0171-836 1846. Famous for their bittermints, but also stock a wide range of chocolates.

Charbonnel et Walker   **4 D3**
28 Old Bond St W1. 0171-491 0939. Hand-made, mainly soft-centred chocolates. Exotic, extravagant presentation boxes in silk or satin, but they will fill anything with your chocolates!

Dugans Chocolates
149a Upper St N1. 0171-354 4666. Specialises in novelties from around the world, including over 60 types of chocolate. Also teas and coffees; celebration cakes made to order.

Prestat   **4 D4**
14 Princes Arc, Piccadilly SW1. 0171-629 4838. Delicious hand-made chocolates and fresh cream truffles. Seasonal novelties.

Rococo   **6 D4**
321 King's Rd SW3. 0171-352 5857. Traditional chocolatier. Over 50 types of loose hand-made chocolates. Delicious fresh cream truffles. Will design anything in chocolate.

Thornton's   **4 F3**
2 Covent Garden Mkt WC2. 0171-836 2173. Continental chocolates, toffee and seasonal novelties.

Clocks & watches

The Art of Swatch   **3 F6**
11 Brompton Arc SW3. 0171-589 1200. Stockists of all current Swatches, plus collectors' items from around the world.

Aubrey Brocklehurst   **6 C2**
124 Cromwell Rd SW7. 0171-373 0319. Specialise in longcase and bracket clocks; also barometers. Clock and furniture restorations.

Camerer Cuss   **4 D4**
17 Ryder St W1. 0171-930 1941. Antique watches and clocks.

Garrard & Co   **4 D3**
112 Regent St W1. 0171-734 7020. Pieces by the great English clockmakers of the past and an extensive range of French period carriage clocks. Top quality buys.

Pearl Cross   **4 F3**
35 St Martin's Ct WC2. 0171-836 2814. Antique jewellery, silver and presentation gold watches from 1880 onwards. Also antique pocket and wrist watches.

Peter K. Weiss   **5 A1**
18 Silver Vaults, Chancery La WC2. 0171-242 8100. Antique clocks and watches.

Ronald A. Lee   **4 C3**
1-9 Bruton Pl W1. 0171-629 5600. 17th and 18thC clocks of very high quality. Also furniture and fine art.

Clock restoration

See also under 'Clocks & watches'.

Clock Clinic
85 Lower Richmond Rd SW15. 0181-788 1407.

J. Walker   **4 C2**
1st Floor, 64 South Molton St W1. 0171-

629 3487. Antique and modern clock repairs.

Coffee & tea

Algerian Coffee Stores   4 **E3**
52 Old Compton St W1. 0171-437 2480. Established in 1887, the shop sells 30 different blends of coffee and over 100 leaf, flavoured and herb teas. Also coffee-making equipment.

Drury Tea & Coffee Co   4 **F2**
37 Drury La WC2. 0171-836 2607. Also at 3 New Row WC2 (4 **F3**). 0171-836 1960. Long-established company offering 32 different types of coffee and 35-40 types of tea. Also coffee-making equipment and good quality biscuits and preserves.

Ferns   4 **E2**
27 Rathbone Pl W1. 0171-636 2237. Old-established firm selling 14 blended coffees and a good selection of leaf, flavoured and herb teas. All own-label.

H.R. Higgins (Coffee man)   4 **B2**
79 Duke St W1. 0171-629 3913. Over 40 different types of coffee including original and blended, light, medium and dark roasts. Also over 20 teas.

The Tea House   4 **F2**
15a Neal St WC2. 0171-240 7539. More than 50 own-label leaf teas and tisanes in this striking red and black shop devoted to tea and 'teaphernalia'. Vast selection of teapots including unusual and novelty; caddies, preserves, biscuits.

Coins & medals

See also 'Auctions: stamps & coins'.
A.H. Baldwin   4 **F3**
11 Adelphi Ter WC2. 0171-930 6879. Good general selection. Ancient, medieval and modern; commemorative and military.

Dolphin Coins
2c Englands La NW3. 0171-722 4116. Hammered coins in gold and silver. Rare colonial coins. Foreign coins, banknotes and medals.

B.A. Seaby   4 **C3**
7 Davies St W1. 0171-495 2590. One of the largest coin shops in the world and publishers of standard coin catalogues for British, Roman and Greek coins.

Spink   4 **D4**
5-7 King St SW1. 0171-930 7888. They stock or can acquire any coin wanted by a collector. Also mint commemorative medals.

Computers

*Lots of high street chain stores now sell computers but their selection of software can be limited. The heart and soul of London's computer world is Tottenham Court Rd (4 **E1**) where dozens of shops sell computers, printers and electronic gear.*
See also 'Electronics shops'.
Centre Point Software   4 **E2**
20-21 St Giles High St WC2. 0171-836 0599. Huge selection of computer software, including all top computer games.

Copper & brass

Jack Casimar
23 Pembridge Rd W11. 0171-727 8643. Large stock of antique brass, copper and pewter.

Knobs & Knockers   6 **B5**
385 King's Rd SW10. 0171-352 5693. A huge selection of brass furniture and fittings.

Crafts: national

Africa
African Escape   3 **A2**
127 Portobello Rd W11. 0171-221 6650. African objects collected by the proprietors on travels across the continent.
Kikapu   4 **F3**
The Africa Centre, 38 King St WC2. 0171-240 6098. Baskets, jewellery, clothes.

Australia   5 **A3**
Australian Gift Shop, Western Australia House, 113-116 Strand WC2. 0171-836 2292. Aboriginal crafts and Australian-made gifts and souvenirs; books and food products including Vegemite.

Bangladesh   2 **D2**
Aarong, Wells House, 80-82 Upper St N1. 0171-354 3344. Run by the Bangladesh Rural Advancement Committee. Crafts made by Bangladeshi artisans.

Britain
Craft Council Gallery Shop   2 **C3**
44a Pentonville Rd N1. 0171-278 7700. High-quality British crafts. Glass, ceramics, jewellery, textiles, basketry.

Denmark   4 **C3**
Royal Copenhagen Porcelain and Georg Jensen Silver, 15 New Bond St W1. 0171-499 6541. Also Holmegaard glass.

Ireland 4 D4
The Irish Shop, 11 Duke St W1. 0171-224 3189. Waterford tweed, Donegal tweed, Irish linen, Belleek china, Arran sweaters, Celtic jewellery. Also at 14 King St WC2 (4 **F3**). 0171-379 3625.

Italy
Villa Mamosa 4 **F3**
9 Covent Gdn Mkt WC2. 0171-836 0289. Italian porcelain.

Japan
Asahi, 110 Golborne Rd W10. 0181-960 7299. Authentic Japanese kimonos and fans. Also at 44a Kensington Church St W8. 0171-795 6299.

Latin America 6 G6
Dorado, 280 Battersea Park Rd SW11. 0171-924 3985. Central and South American typical products. From Andean pipe music to genuine Panama hats.

Morocco 4 F3
The Kasbah, 8 Southampton St WC2. 0171-379 5230. Hand-made Berber jewellery, clothing, lanterns, antique kilims. Also Moroccan catering and interior design services.

New Zealand 4 E4
Kiwifruits New Zealand Shop, 6 Royal Opera Arc, Pall Mall SW1. 0171-930 4587. Gifts, crafts and books.

Peru
Inca, 45 Elizabeth St SW1. 0171-730 7941. Colourful, hand-made Peruvian clothes, sweaters, accessories and gifts.

Scotland 4 A5
The Scotch House, 2 Brompton Rd SW1. 0171-581 2151. Also 84 and 191 Regent St W1 (4 **D3**). Excellent tartans, kilts, rugs, foods and Fair Isle, Arran and Shetland woollens.

Spain 7 A2
Casa Pupo, 56 Pimlico Rd SW1. 0171-730 7111. Spanish, Italian and Portuguese furniture.

Switzerland 4 E3
Swiss Centre, Leicester Sq WC2. 0171-734 3130. Cuckoo clocks, army knives, cheese raclettes, dolls, chocolates.

Cycles

Edwardes
221-225 Camberwell Rd SE5. 0171-703 3676. Wide range of cycles for children and adults. Cycling accessories, second-hand bikes and repair service.

F.W. Evans Cycles
77-79 The Cut SE1. 0171-928 4785. One of the largest stockists of bikes and accessories. Also build touring bikes.

Freewheel
275 West End La NW6. 0171-435 3725. All kinds of bikes plus clothing and accessories.

W.F. Holdsworth
132 Lower Richmond Rd SW15. 0181-788 1060. A wide range of bikes and accessories.

Stuart Cycles
1 Ascot Pde, Clapham Park Rd SW4. 0171-622 4818. Hand-built and production bikes. Full range of services.

Cycle hire

See under 'Transport in London'.

Discount shopping

Cheap buys and bargains can often be found by looking in the local newspapers, at newsagents' notice-boards or in Time Out, Exchange & Mart *and the* Evening Standard. *Charity shops, jumble sales and markets are also useful for the low-budget shopper.*

Domestic help

Also refer to the classified adverts in The Lady *magazine, 40 Bedford St WC2* (4 **F3**). *0171-379 4717.*

Babysitters Unlimited
0181-892 8888. Can provide cleaners and babysitters.

Childminders 1 C6
9 Paddington St W1. 0171-935 4386. Babysitters (mostly trained nurses) supplied to the home and to hotels in central London and most suburban areas.

Curzon Cleaning Services
Long Lodge, 267-269 Kingston Rd SW19. 0181-643 7405. For all kinds of household, window and specialist cleaning. Not daily cleaning.

Lumley Employment 7 C3
85 Charlwood St SW1. 0171-630 0545. If you want a Cordon Bleu cook for a special occasion, this is the place to come. Catering services agency.

The Nanny Service 1 C6
9 Paddington St W1. 0171-935 3515. Temporary, permanent and non-maternity nannies. Residential and non-residential available for positions in London and the Home Counties.

Thames Cleaning Company
16 Hatherley Rd, Sidcup, Kent. 0181-300 5888. Clean carpets, dry-clean curtains,

polish hard floors and clean windows and venetian blinds. A full cleaning service.

Universal Aunts
PO Box 304, Clapham SW4. 0171-738 8937. A well-known agency that will provide all kinds of domestic help, including house-keepers, cooks, nannies, drivers, shopping, caretaking, secretarial work, gardening, babysitting, and a special 'meet and greet' service at all stations and airports. Office *OPEN 09.30-17.00.*

Dry-cleaning & laundry

There are many reliable dry-cleaners and launderers in London. Sketchley Cleaners is one of the largest chains, with branches on most high streets. For specialist treatment go to:

Dry Cleaning Information Bureau (DIB)
c/o 7 Churchill Ct, 58 Station Rd, Nth Harrow, Middx. Operates the *24-hr DIB Hotline: 0181-863 8658,* offering free advice on just about any cleaning problem or disaster.

Elegant Cleaners   3 **F2**
30-31 Kendal St W2. 0171-402 6108. Specialists in silk, evening gowns, suede, leather and fur.

Jeeves   6 **F1**
8-10 Pont St SW1. 0171-235 1101. A personal service. Everything is handfinished and the prices are reasonable. They collect and deliver in central London and have a postal service. Also carry out repairs and various other services.

Lewis & Wayne Ltd   6 **E2**
13-15 Elystan St SW3. 0171-589 5730. For garment cleaning and hand-finishing of evening gowns and bridalwear. Taking down and rehanging of curtains, on-site carpet cleaning. All types of hand-finished laundry.

Liliman & Cox   4 **C3**
34 Bruton Pl W1. 0171-629 4555. High quality cleaning of special garments such as beaded and embroidered dresses.

Suede Services
2a Hoop La NW11. 0181-455 0052. Specialise in cleaning, restoring, remodelling and repairing all skin garments, including pigskin.

Textile Services Association
7 Churchill Ct, 58 Station Rd, Nth Harrow, Middx. 0181-863 7755. A national trade body with about 350 parent company members who are themselves responsible for approx 2000 dry-cleaners and 500 laundries, all of whom display an LTSA code of practice sign. The associa-

tion also operates a consumer complaints service.

Electrical

Electrical Contractors'   3 **C3**
Association
32-34 Palace Ct W2. 0171-229 1266. 450 member firms in London area. High standard of work guaranteed.

Electronics shops

The area around Tottenham Court Rd and St Giles Circus is packed with shops selling electronic, video, radio and tape recording equipment at competitive prices. Edgware Rd also has a good selection. See also 'Computers'.

Henry's   3 **E1**
404 Edgware Rd W2. 0171-723 1008. Electronic and radio components, amplifiers. Specialise in test equipment. Prompt mail order service and personal computing.

Sonic Foto Centre   4 **E1**
256 Tottenham Court Rd W1. 0171-580 5826. Extensive selection of audio and video equipment.

Tandy   4 **E1**
224 Tottenham Ct Rd W1. 0171-436 8837. Chain selling a range of audio and video equipment. Many branches.

Estate Agents

National Association of Estate Agents
Arbon House, 21 Jury St, Warwick, Warks. (01926) 496800. Can give you the names of estate agents in a particular area.

Fancy dress hire

Angels & Bermans   4 **E2**
119 Shaftesbury Av WC2. 0171-836 5678. Vast range of costumes for men and women.

Panto Box
26 North St SW4. 0171-627 1772. All types of animal costumes and masks. Also costume jewellery for sale or hire.

Fish

See under 'Aquaria'.

Fishing tackle

See under 'Sports equipment'.

Flowers

See also under 'Gardening'.

The Flower Gallery   **7 A2**
114 Ebury St SW1. 0171-730 2375.
Fresh and dried flowers delivered daily.
Herbs also available.

Interflora
Interflora House, Sleaford, Lincs (Head
Office). (01529) 304545. Will deliver
flowers locally, nationwide or worldwide.
Linked to 136 countries. Telephone order
service for credit card holders
(A.Ax.Dc.V.). *Check in telephone directory
for your nearest Interflora florist.*

Jane Packer Floral Design   **4 B2**
56 James St W1. 0171-935 2673.
Bouquets, baskets, fresh and dried
flowers. Delivery service.

Joan Palmer   **4 E6**
31 Palmer St SW1. 0171-222 4364.
Bouquets, baskets, fresh flowers. Same-
day delivery in London area.

Moyses Stevens Floral Arts   **4 C3**
6 Bruton St W1. 0171-493 8171. Fresh
and dried flowers. Delivery service. Also at
157-158 Sloane St SW1 (**6 F2**). 0171-
259 9303.

Wild at Heart Flowers   **3 A3**
Westbourne Gro Lavatories W11. 0171-
727 3095. Former public convenience
transformed into a florist specialising in
unusual plants and flowers. Functions
catered for, delivery service.

Food: health shops

Cranks   **4 D2**
8 Marshall St W1. 0171-437 2915.
Appetising health foods, dried fruits and
grains. Restaurant next door.

The Grain Shop   **3 A2**
269a Portobello Rd W11. 0171-229
5571. Vegetarian, including macrobiotic,
food. Complete range of chemical-
free herbs, vegetables and grains.
Wholefood take-aways cooked on the
premises.

Health Foods
767 Fulham Rd SW6. 0171-736 8848.
Specialise in honeys and homoeopathic
and back remedies. Also a wide selection of vitamins, minerals and health
foods.

Holland & Barrett   **4 C2**
Unit C12/C13, West One Shopping
Centre, Oxford St W1. 0171-493 7988.
Complete range of wholefoods and cook-
ing herbs. Cosmetics made with natural
ingredients, natural vitamin supplements.
Wide range of take-aways.

**Neal's Yard Wholefood
Warehouse**   **4 F2**
21-23 Short's Gdns WC2. 0171-836
5151. Huge variety of health foods, nuts,
dried fruit.

Wholefood   **4 B1**
24 Paddington St W1. 0171-935 3924.
Organically-grown products, free-range
eggs, groceries and even wines.
Vitamins, nutrition books.

Food: exotic

*Soho is an area full of small Continental
and Chinese shops crammed with exotic
foods, wines and spices.*

T. Adamou
124-126 Chiswick High Rd W4. 0181-
994 0752. Established for 30 years, sells
a wide range of foods from Greece and
the Middle East.

Bims African Foodstore
104 Rye La SE15. 0171-732 1564.
Exotic foodstuffs arrive daily from Africa.
Plus a selection of cooking pots.

Carluccio's   **4 F2**
28a Neal St WC2. 0171-240 1487. Next
door to Antonio Carluccio's Neal Street
Restaurant. Extensive stock of wild mushrooms. Ready-cooked Italian delicacies.
Own-label delicacies available nationwide.

Fortnum & Mason   **4 D4**
181 Piccadilly W1. 0171-734 8040.
Exotic and unusual tinned and bottled
foods from all over the world. Famous for
hampers.

Fratelli Camisa   **4 E3**
1a Berwick St W1. 0171-437 7120.
Good Continental delicatessen. Wines,
fresh pasta and seasonal delicacies.

Harrods   **4 A6**
Knightsbridge SW1. 0171-730 1234.
International selection of top-quality fresh,
tinned and bottled foods.

International Cheese Centre   **1 E6**
21 Goodge St W1. 0171-631 4191. Over
400 cheeses. Wines and fresh sandwiches.

Lina Stores   **4 E3**
18 Brewer St W1. 0171-437 6482.
Amazing selection of Italian foods.
Excellent fresh pasta, bread and olives.

Maison Sagne   **1 C6**
105 Marylebone High St W1. 0171-935
6240. Croissants, superb sausage rolls,
pastries. Excellent gateaux and special
occasion cakes made to order.

La Marée   **6 E2**
76 Sloane Av SW3. 0171-589 8067.

French fishmonger renowned for its fruits de mer, plus cooked sea bass and salmon for dinner parties.

Neal's Yard Dairy   4 **F2**
17 Short's Gdns WC2. 0171-379 7646. Up to 30 cheeses from Ireland and Britain in stock at any one time.

Ninjin Food Store   1 **D5**
244 Great Portland St W1. 0171-388 2511. Japanese food specialists. Fresh meat and fish too.

Pak Continental Food Stores
191 Shepherds Bush Mkt W12. 0181-743 5389. Specialise in African and West Indian food.

Pâtisserie Valerie   4 **E3**
44 Old Compton St W1. 0171-437 3466. Excellent cakes and pâtisseries.

Paxton & Whitfield   4 **D4**
93 Jermyn St SW1. 0171-930 0259. Famous for superb English and Continental cheeses, traditional hams, teas, home-made pies and pâtés.

Products from Spain   4 **D1**
89 Charlotte St W1. 0171-580 2905. Importers of a vast range of Spanish foods – retail and wholesale.

Randall & Aubin   4 **E3**
16 Brewer St W1. 0171-437 3507/8. Pâtés, cheeses of all sorts, assorted cooked and fresh meats and game.

Yaohan Plaza
399 Edgware Rd NW9. 0181-200 0009. Japanese superstore sells amazing seafood such as scarlet salmon roe and octopus tentacles.

Foreign newspapers & periodicals

Many of the Soho and Queensway newsagents deal in foreign papers. European magazines are usually available at the larger newsagents and at the station and airport branches of W.H. Smith and John Menzies. The following shops stock a good selection of both:

Capital Newsagents   4 **E3**
48 Old Compton St W1. 0171-437 2479.

Fourboy's
6 Pembridge Rd W11. 0171-229 8020.

Harrods   4 **A6**
Knightsbridge SW1. 0171-730 1234.

News International   4 **E3**
50 Charing Cross Rd WC2. 0171-836 6313.

Selfridges   4 **B2**
400 Oxford St W1. 0171-629 1234.

Furnishing: fabrics & wallpapers

The big stores, particularly Peter Jones, John Lewis, Heal's and Liberty, have a large range of furnishing fabrics and wallpapers.

Cole & Son (Wallpapers)   4 **D1**
142-144 Offord Rd W1. 0171-607 4288. Exclusive and unusual French and Continental prints. Fine modern and traditional English hand-blocked designs. Complementary fabrics.

Colefax & Fowler   4 **C3**
39 Brook St W1. 0171-493 2231. Exclusive screen-printed wallpapers and co-ordinating chintzes based on 18th and 19thC country house designs.

Designers Guild   6 **D4**
271 & 277 King's Rd SW3. 0171-351 5775. Beautiful fabrics, wall-coverings, furniture and accessories.

Elizabeth Eaton   7 **A2**
85 Bourne St SW1. 0171-730 2262. Pretty American and French wallpapers. Fabrics, upholstery and furniture too.

Lewis & Wood   7 **A3**
48a Pimlico Rd SW1. 0171-730 5064. Affordable, quality fabrics inspired by English and French provincial styles.

Osborne & Little   6 **D4**
304-308 King's Rd SW3. 0171-352 1456. Wallpapers and fabrics. Exclusive designs.

Sanderson
No longer a retail outlet but their wide selection of floral and co-ordinated furnishing fabrics and wallpapers are available at John Lewis, D.H. Evans and Selfridges.

G. Thornfield   2 **B5**
321 Gray's Inn Rd WC1. 0171-837 2771. Large selection of well-known brands of wallpaper at discounted prices.

Watts & Co   7 **D1**
7 Tufton St SW1. 0171-222 7169. Unique and elegant patterns made up in the colour of your choice from original Victorian wallpaper blocks. They have about 32 designs and an unlimited range of colours.

Furniture: antique

See under 'Antique shops'.

Furniture: modern

The big stores such as D.H. Evans, Harrods, John Lewis and Selfridges have good selections. Marks & Spencer and Next sell their own ranges of stylish and co-ordinated furniture and accessories.

Futon Company 1 **E5**
169 Tottenham Court Rd W1. 0171-636 9984. Sell the traditional Japanese mattresses and a range of furniture with elements of Japanese design.

Habitat 4 **E1**
196 Tottenham Court Rd W1. 0171-631 3880. Popular international furniture at reasonable prices; colourful household goods.

Heal's 4 **E1**
196 Tottenham Court Rd W1. 0171-636 1666. Big selection of the best British and Continental designs.

Ikea
Brent Park, 255 North Circular Rd NW10. 0181-208 5600. Vast range of inexpensive and functional furniture. DIY and ready-made. Very good value. Restaurant. Good facilities for children.

Maples 1 **E5**
145 Tottenham Court Rd W1. 0171-387 7000. 50,000sq ft of furniture; all types and styles, including reproduction, futuristic and office furniture. Huge range of soft furnishings. Curtain-making service from Maples' own range of fabrics. English and Oriental carpets and rugs. Contract and design service.

Sofas & Sofa-Beds 4 **E1**
219 Tottenham Court Rd W1. 0171-636 6001. Wide range of sofas, in many different fabrics, which convert into double beds.

SPACE 3 **A2**
12 Dolland St SE11. 0171-820 0288. Unusual contemporary furniture sold at warehouse prices. Also fabrics and hand-woven rugs.

Wesley-Barrell 4 **D2**
60 Berners St W1. 0171-580 6979. Sell own-make settees, sofa-beds, beds and chairs, but also stock other makes of dining-room furniture.

Zarach Design 7 **B2**
13 Eccleston St SW1. 0171-730 3339. Ultra-modern furniture and fittings in chrome, leather, etc. More an interior design service but will order from catalogue.

Clifford Tracy
6/40 Durnford St N15. 0181-800 4774. Antique furniture restorers and cabinet makers. Excellent personal service.

W.R. Harvey & Co (Antiques) 1 **C1**
67-70 Chalk Farm Rd NW1. 0171-485

1504. Specialist restorers of fine antique furniture.

Phoenix Antique Furniture 5 **C5**
Restoration Ltd
96 Webber St SE1. 0171-928 3624. Cabinet work, polishing, upholstery; pieces made to commission.

Innovations
19 Paradise Rd, Richmond, Surrey. 0181-948 3792. New products on the market; anything from electric scissors to Italian water sandals. Mail order service available.

Most picture galleries are grouped in and around Bond St, South Kensington and St James's. Camden Lock is an interesting area for contemporary pictures and pottery, as are the open-air exhibitions by London's major parks.
This is a selection of specialist galleries often showing exhibitions of individuals' work. See the daily papers, Time Out *and the art press for current listings.*

Agnew 4 **D4**
43 Old Bond St W1. 0171-629 6176. Outstanding selection of old masters.

Annely Juda Fine Art 4 **C2**
23 Dering St W1. 0171-629 7578. Russian constructivism and contemporary paintings, drawings and sculpture.

Browse & Derby 4 **D3**
19 Cork St W1. 0171-734 7984. 19th and 20thC French and English paintings, drawings and sculpture.

Contemporary Applied Arts 4 **E1**
2 Percy St W1. 0171-436 2344. Comprehensive display of work by craftsmen in many materials, including many British pieces.

Crane Kalman 6 **E1**
178 Brompton Rd SW3. 0171-584 7566. 20thC British and European paintings and sculpture.

Curwen Gallery 4 **E1**
4 Windmill St, off Charlotte St W1. 0171-636 1459. Originals and prints by young British artists; also original prints by Henry Moore and Barbara Hepworth.

Editions Alecto 4 **D4**
Sackville House, 40 Piccadilly W1. 0171-937 6611. Contemporary and historical original prints including the official facsimile of the *Domesday Book.*

Editions Graphiques 4 **D3**
3 Clifford St W1. 0171-734 3944. 19th

and 20thC prints, graphics and paintings from 1880. Art nouveau and art deco objects.

Gimpel Fils   4 **C3**
30 Davies St W1. 0171-493 2488. Contemporary British, American and European art.

Grosvenor Prints   4 **F2**
28-32 Shelton St WC2. 0171-836 1979. A huge selection of antique prints and engravings.

Malcolm Innes Gallery   4 **D4**
7 Bury St SW1. 0171-839 8083. Paintings, watercolours and prints of the 19th and 20thC, specialising in Scottish and sporting subjects.

Marlborough Fine Art   4 **D3**
6 Albemarle St W1. 0171-629 5161. 19th and 20thC 'master' paintings, contemporary art and sculpture.

Marlborough Graphics   4 **D3**
6 Albemarle St W1. 0171-629 5161. Large selection of graphics: Kokoschka, Moore, Richards, Sutherland, Nolan, Kitaj, Pasmoore. Also contemporary graphics and photography.

Mayor Gallery   4 **D3**
22a Cork St W1. 0171-734 3558. Contemporary paintings, drawings and sculpture.

Redfern Gallery   4 **D3**
20 Cork St W1. 0171-734 1732. 20thC paintings, drawings, sculpture and graphics.

Tyron & Moorland Gallery   4 **D3**
23 Cork St W1. 0171-734 6961. Sporting and natural history pictures and paintings.

Waddington   4 **D3**
5, 11, 12 & 34 Cork St W1. 0171-437 8611. 20thC painting, works on paper, sculpture and graphics.

Zella 9   6 **C4**
2 Park Wlk SW10. 0171-351 0588. Limited edition contemporary prints and watercolours.

Games Workshop
1 Dalling Rd W6. 0181-741 3445. Science fiction and military board games. Role-playing games and lead miniatures.

Just Games   4 **D3**
71 Brewer St W1. 0171-437 0761. Up-to-date selection of board and card games and executive toys. More traditional games too.

Virgin Games Centre   4 **C2**
14-16 Oxford St W1. 0171-631 1234. Renowned for its incredible fantasy games. Department dedicated to war games. Stock the complete Trivial Pursuit range.

See also under 'Flowers'.

Camden Garden Centre   1 **E1**
2 Barker Drive, St Pancras Way NW1. 0171-485 8468. Garden and indoor plants. Terracotta pots and troughs.

Chelsea Gardener   6 **E3**
125-147 Sydney St SW3. 0171-352 5656. Trees, shrubs, roses, house plants. Garden furniture.

Clifton Nurseries
5a Clifton Villas W9. 0171-289 6851. A very comprehensive range of gardening plants; specialists in town gardens and window boxes. Landscaping service.

**All Seasons Gardening
and Landscaping**
125 Endlesham Rd SW11. 0171-228 7261. Young and enthusiastic firm tackling garden design. They'll take on any size job down to window boxes and just tidying up a scruffy corner.

New Covent Garden Market
Nine Elms Lane, Vauxhall SW8. 0171-720 2211. Cheapest way to buy plants in London – but you must buy by the box. Flower market *OPEN Mon-Fri until 11.00.*

Rassells   6 **A1**
80 Earl's Court Rd W8. 0171-937 0481. Ffor the greenfingered; terracotta pots and fibreglass tubs, trelliswork, hanging baskets, window boxes, house plants and herbs, perennials, bulbs and bedding plants. Fresh cut flowers.

Suttons Seeds   4 **G3**
33 Catherine St WC2. 0171-836 0619. The showplace of the famous seed company, offering a very wide selection. Also bulbs and garden supplies. Mail order and export service.

Syon Park Garden Centre
Syon Park, Brentford, Middx. 0181-568 0134. Housed in the old riding school are all the implements needed for gardening, plus a large selection of garden plants.

Thompson & Morgan
Poplar Rd, Ipswich, Suffolk. (01473) 688588. Seeds usually ordered by mail – this is one of the very best for quality. Particularly good for vegetables and unusual varieties.

John Lewis and Peter Jones both have good garden furniture departments, but they only stock the full range from Mar-Sep. See also under 'Gardening'.

Chelsea Gardener   6 **E3**
125-147 Sydney St SW3. 0171-352 5656. Full range of garden furniture.

Crowther of Syon Lodge
Syon Lodge, London Rd, Busch Corner, Isleworth, Middx. 0181-560 7978. Vast selection of period and period-style garden ornaments. Furniture and chimneypieces.

Julian Chichester Designs
Unit 12, 33 Parsons Green La SW6. 0171-371 9055. Fine English 18th and 19thC-style garden furniture.

Mallet at Bourdon House   4 C3
2 Davies St W1. 0171-629 2444. Garden statuary and furniture. Antique dealers.

Gemmology

Gemmological Association   5 B1
1st Floor, 27 Greville St EC1. 0171-404 3334. Supply crystal specimens and ornamental materials for students. Gem-testing equipment. Also run courses.

R. Holt & Company   2 C6
98 Hatton Gdn EC1. 0171-405 0197. Semi-precious and precious stones, cut and uncut. Facilities provided for testing stones. Some jewellery. Bead-stringing and stone-cutting on the premises.

Genealogy & heraldry

To help you trace your predecessors and make up the 'family' coat of arms try:

College of Arms   5 C3
Queen Victoria St EC4. 0171-248 2762. Will undertake research and help identify coats of arms. House official records of all coats of arms ever granted in England.

The Heraldry Society   4 F1
44-45 Museum St WC1. 0171-430 2172. Membership open to all. Small library. Sell heraldic books.

Society of Genealogists   2 E5
14 Charterhouse Bldgs, off Goswell Rd EC1. 0171-251 8799. Help to trace your ancestors. Library if you want to do your own research.

Geology

Gregory, Bottley & Lloyd   6 A4
13 Seagrave Rd SW6. 0171-381 5522. Fascinating stock of minerals, fossils, meteorites. Geology equipment.

Gifts

Covent Garden General Store   4 F2
111 Long Acre WC2. 0171-240 2058. Two floors with sections representing var-

ious companies. A huge range of tasteful gifts including pottery, comestibles, caneware and ornaments.

Crabtree & Evelyn   3 C5
6 Kensington Church St W8. 0171-937 9335. Unusual range of comestibles, toiletries and soaps, all delightfully packaged. Books and cards. Mail order service.

The Gift Centre   4 F1
140 Southampton Row WC1. 0171-837 4084. Wide selection of gift ideas.

Graham & Green
4 & 7 Elgin Cres W11. 0171-727 4594. Cushions covered in Victorian and Edwardian lace. Basketware specialists.

Halcyon Days   4 C3
14 Brook St W1. 0171-629 8811. Beautiful enamelware, little boxes for all occasions, thimbles, pin-cushions and needlecases. Some small antique items and antique enamel boxes. Catalogue.

The Museum Store   3 F6
50 Beauchamp Pl SW3. 0171-581 9255. Crafts from the gift shops of museums all over the world. Also at 37 The Market WC2 (0171-240 5760) and Perrins Ct NW3 (0171-431 7156).

Neal Street East   4 F2
5 Neal St WC2. 0171-240 0135. Interesting and enterprising gifts with a definite Chinese flavour: books, prints, clothes, ceramics, baskets, toys.

Past Times   3 F6
146 Brompton Rd SW3. 0171-581 7616. Reproduction jewellery, crafts and cards from 4000 years of British history. Also curiosities and books.

Glass: antique

Most antique dealers have good 18th-19thC glass as part of their stock in trade. See also under 'Antique shops' and 'Antique markets'.

Glass: modern

See under 'China, glass & porcelain'.

Guns: antique

Peter Dale   4 E4
11-12 Royal Opera Arc, Pall Mall SW1. 0171-930 3695. Antique weapons and armour for the collector.

Guns: modern

Boss 4 **E4**
13 Dover St W1. 0171-493 0711.
Manufacturers of top-quality sporting shot
guns. A long waiting list for purchasers.
Holland & Holland 4 **C3**
33 Bruton St W1. 0171-499 4411. The
top London gunsmiths.
James Purdey & Sons 4 **B3**
57 South Audley St W1. 0171-499 1801.
Fine gunsmiths.
John Rigby & Co (Gunmakers) 5 **C5**
66 Great Suffolk St SE1. 0171-734 7611.
Manufacturers and dealers in high-quality
hand-made modern sporting guns and
rifles.

Hairdressers: men

Gavin Hodge at Sweenys 6 **F1**
48 Beauchamp Pl SW3. 0171-589
3066/7. Fashionable barber in an elegant
club atmosphere. Women's hairdressing
too.
Stanley Alwin 4 **E3**
110 Shaftesbury Av W1. 0171-437 8933.
Some of the leading London hairdressers
come here to get their own hair cut.
Trumper 4 **C4**
9 Curzon St W1. 0171-499 1850. A very
famous establishment. Superb shopfront
and interior. The ultimate barber-shop
experience.

Hairdressers: women & unisex

*Nearly all the big department stores have
hairdressing salons which will cater for
men and women.*
Antenna 3 **B4**
27a Kensington Church St W8. 0171-938
1866. Synonymous with hair extensions.
Also cutting, colouring and perming.
Hair by Alan D 4 **C3**
215 Regent St W1. 0171-734 3381.
Fashionable styles, beauty treatments.
Many branches.
Hebe 4 **F3**
38 William IV St WC2. 0171-836 1132.
Full range of perms, colours and highlight-
ing products. Other branches.
Michaeljohn 4 **D3**
25 Albemarle St W1. 0171-629 6969.
Modern and fashionable.
Molton Brown 4 **C2**
58 South Molton St W1. 0171-629 1872.
Creative cutting; specialise in hand-drying

techniques. Hair products, accessories
and cosmetics.
Sissors 6 **F3**
69a King's Rd SW3. 0171-351 0911.
High-fashion styles for men and
women.
Steiner 4 **C3**
66 Grosvenor St W1. 0171-493 1144.
A world-famous salon linked with high-
quality hair-care products.
Toni & Guy 4 **C3**
10-12 Davies St W1. 0171-629 8348.
Ultra-modern and stylish salon.
Hairdressing to a high standard by well-
trained stylists.
Trevor Sorbie 4 **F3**
10 Russell St WC2. 0171-379 6901.
Innovative and excellent cutting, colouring
and perming.
Vidal Sassoon 4 **A5**
54 Knightsbridge SW1. 0171-235 7791.
Also at 60 South Molton St W1 (4 **C2**).
0171-491 8848. And 130 Sloane St SW3
(6 **F2**). 0171-730 7288. Famous avant-
garde styles.

Handbag & luggage repairs

Jeeves 6 **F1**
8 Pont St SW1. 0171-235 1101.
Handbag, luggage and shoe repairs and
renovations.

Herbalists

G. Baldwin & Co
171-173 Walworth Rd SE17. 0171-703
5550. Locally renowned, long-established
shop with huge range and helpful advice.
Sells health foods too.
Culpeper 4 **C3**
21 Bruton St W1. 0171-629 4559. Also at
8 Covent Garden Mkt WC2 (4 **F3**). 0171-
379 6698. Also specialists in pure
cosmetics, pot pourri and pomanders.
Neal's Yard Apothecary 4 **F2**
& Therapy Rooms
15 Neal's Yd WC2. 0171-379 7222.
Herbal remedies. Bach flower remedies
and natural cosmetics, books and leaflets.

Household & kitchen equipment

*Habitat, Heal's and Selfridges have excel-
lent household and kitchen departments.*
Casa Pupo 7 **A3**
56-60 Pimlico Rd SW1. 0171-730 7111.
Spanish ceramics, glassware, rugs,

ornaments and bedcovers at fairly reasonable prices.

David Mellor 6 **G2**
4 Sloane Sq SW1. 0171-730 4259. All sorts of kitchen equipment, some pottery, basketware.

Divertimenti 4 **B2**
45-47 Wigmore St W1. 0171-935 0689. Wide selection of cookware and tableware.

Elizabeth David 4 **F3**
3 North Row, Covent Gdn Mkt WC2. 0171-836 9167. Complete range of kitchen pots, pans, knives and pastry cooks' equipment from France and elsewhere.

General Trading Company 6 **F2**
144 Sloane St SW1. 0171-730 0411. A miscellany of antiques, china, glass and soft furnishings – all in elegant 'private house' setting.

The Reject Shop 4 **E1**
209 Tottenham Court Rd W1. 0171-580 2895. Also at 245 Brompton Rd SW3 (6 **E1**). 0171-584 7611. And Store B, Whiteleys of Bayswater, 141-165 Queensway W2 (3 **C2**). 0171-229 4449. Big selection of home accessories and furniture, lighting, cookware. Low prices.

William Page 4 **E2**
121 Shaftesbury Av WC2. 0171-379 6334. Excellent functional 'down-to-earth' pots, pans and cutlery as used by the local restaurant trade.

Icons

Maria Andipa's Icon Gallery 6 **E2**
162 Walton St SW3. 0171-589 2371. Byzantine, Greek, Russian and Ethiopian icons. Also ethnic jewellery.

Ironwork

G. & S. Allgood 1 **E5**
297 Euston Rd NW1. 0171-387 9951. Well-designed architectural ironmongery.

J.D. Beardmore 4 **E1**
3-4 Percy St W1. 0171-637 7041. Very large selection of good reproduction and architectural ironmongery and cabinet fittings.

Comyn Ching 2 **E5**
110 Golden La EC1. 0171-253 8414. An enormous range of ironmongery designs still produced from old patterns. Architectural and builders' ironmongers.

Jewellery & silver: antique

Many antique shops deal in silver and jewellery, particularly those in the Burlington Arcade. Also try the antique markets for a variety of choice and price.

Ann Bloom 4 **D3**
10a New Bond St W1. 0171-491 1213. Exclusive collection of fine period jewellery and period silver photograph frames.

Armour-Winston 4 **D3**
43 Burlington Arc W1. 0171-493 8937. Fine jewels and clocks.

Asprey 4 **D3**
165 New Bond St W1. 0171-493 6767. Unusual antique and modern jewellery. Also an excellent range of luxury gifts.

Beau Gems 5 **E2**
26 Royal Exchange EC3. 0171-623 7634. Stock mainly Victorian and art deco pieces, although they also have pieces from other periods. Another branch at 418 Strand WC2 (4 **F3**). 0171-836 7356.

Bentley 4 **D3**
8 New Bond St W1. 0171-629 0651. Long-established. Superb jewels and antique silver. Also Fabergé pieces. Buy as well as sell.

Bond Street Silver Galleries 4 **C3**
111-112 New Bond St W1. 0171-493 6180. 15 showrooms of antique, modern and second-hand jewellery and silver.

Collingwood 4 **D3**
171 New Bond St W1. 0171-734 2656. Long-established jewellers to the Queen – antique and modern gold and silverware.

Garrard 4 **D3**
112 Regent St W1. 0171-734 7020. Jewellers to the Queen. Fine antique and modern silver.

Green's Antique Galleries 3 **B4**
117 Kensington Church St W8. 0171-229 9618. Victorian jewellery and rings. Also silver.

The London Silver Vaults 4 **B2**
Chancery House, 53-64 Chancery La WC2. 0171-242 3844. Underground vaults like an Aladdin's cave crammed with antique and modern silver and plate.

Paul Longmire 4 **D4**
12 Bury St SW1. 0171-930 8720. Suppliers of jewellery to the Queen and Queen Mother. Vast selection of cuff links; seal engraved rings. Extensive display space as this shop has the largest windows of any privately-owned jewellers in the West End.

Philip Antrobus 4 **D3**
11 New Bond St W1. 0171-493 4557. Fine gold and gem-set jewellery ranging from antique to modern.

S.J. Phillips 4 **C3**
139 New Bond St W1. 0171-629 6261. Fine jewels, silver and objets d'art from England and the Continent.

Shrubsole 4 **F1**
43 Museum St WC1. 0171-405 2712. Fine antique English silver and old Sheffield plate for the discerning collector.

Tessiers 4 **D3**
26 New Bond St W1. 0171-629 0458.
Fine old firm of silversmiths. Antique jewels. Valuations and repairs of modern and antique jewellery.

London is rich in fine specialist jewellery shops. Many are world famous. Good areas to shop are: Bond St, the Burlington Arcade, Knightsbridge.

Argenta 6 **D3**
82 Fulham Rd SW3. 0171-584 1841.
Stunning modern silverware from Scandinavia and modern English designs. Their silversmith will make up individual pieces.

Butler & Wilson 6 **E2**
189 Fulham Rd SW3. 0171-352 3045.
Selection from art deco and Celtic pieces to modern jewellery.

Cartier 4 **D3**
175 New Bond St W1. 0171-493 6962. Top-class internationally famous jewellers.

Ciro Pearls 4 **D3**
9 New Bond St W1. 0171-491 7219.
Specialists in cultured and imitation pearl jewellery of all kinds. Also large selection of superior costume jewellery.

Cobra & Bellamy 6 **F2**
149 Sloane St SW1. 0171-730 2823.
Specialise in art deco silver and costume jewellery from the 1920s to 1950s.

Electrum Gallery 4 **C2**
21 South Molton St W1. 0171-629 6325.
Exhibit and sell contemporary designer jewellery to suit all the latest tastes.

Georg Jensen Silver 4 **D3**
15 New Bond St W1. 0171-499 6541.
Modern Danish jewellery and silver.

Jewel House Shop 5 **G3**
Tower of London EC3. 0171-488 5680. Glamourous costume jewellery inspired by the precious stones and design details of the Crown Jewels, which are on show nearby. Mail order service available.

Ken Lane 6 **E1**
58 Beauchamp Pl SW3. 0171-584 1985.
Wide range of exciting and daring costume jewellery.

Kutchinsky 6 **F1**
73 Brompton Rd SW3. 0171-584 9311.
Fine jewels, and top-quality Swiss watches.

Mappin & Webb 4 **D3**
170 Regent St W1. 0171-734 3801.
High-quality jewellery and silver.

National Association of 2 **G5**
Goldsmiths
St Luke's House, 78a Luke St EC2. 0171-613 4445. Can supply a list of jewellers who carry out repair and restoration work.

Garrard 4 **D3**
112 Regent St W1. 0171-734 7020.
Registered valuer.
Mappin & Webb 4 **D3**
170 Regent St W1. 0171-734 3801.
Registered valuer.

Selfridges, Harrods, many branches of Woolworths and other big stores have a while-you-wait service; as do many small local ironmongers, shoe repairers and some of the larger tube stations.

High as a Kite
153 Stoke Newington Church St N16. 0171-275 8799. Single line, box and stunt kites. Also frisbees, boomerangs and juggling equipment.
Kite Store 4 **F2**
48 Neal St WC2. 0171-836 1666. Kites of every imaginable design, including models you can assemble yourself. Also frisbees and boomerangs. Mail order service.

Most of the big department stores stock a range of knitting yarns and patterns. Harrods, John Lewis and Dickins & Jones are particularly good.

Colourway 3 **B2**
112a Westbourne Gro W2 (entrance in Chepstow Rd). 0171-229 1432. Yarns are mainly by Rowan and Annabel Fox. Also have tapestry kits, designer sweaters and books.

Patricia Roberts 4 **B5**
60 Kinnerton St SW1. 0171-235 4742.
Pure yarns in a vast range of seasonally changing colours. Patricia Roberts original patterns or buy the ready-knitted jumpers.

Left-handed

Anything Left-handed 4 **D3**
57 Brewer St W1. 0171-437 3910.
Potato peelers, pen nibs, scissors – every
gadget is designed for the left-handed.
Mail order service and catalogue. Mail
order hotline: 0181-770 3722.

Lighting

*Good lighting departments at Heal's,
Harrods, Habitat, John Lewis, Selfridges
and BHS.*

Christopher Wray's Lighting 6 **B6**
Emporium
600 King's Rd SW6. 0171-736 8434.
Over 2000 genuine, restored oil and gas
lamps. Also a lamp workshop to service,
restore, repair or convert to electricity any
oil or gas lamp.

London Lighting 6 **E2**
135 Fulham Rd SW3. 0171-589 3612.
Excellent, pricey collection of modern light
fittings.

Mr Light 6 **D3**
275 Fulham Rd SW10. 0171-352 7525.
Large range of indoor and outdoor lights
including desk lamps, corner lamps
and spotlights. Designs very modern or
traditional.

Thorn EMI 4 **C2**
4 Tenterden St, Hanover Sq W1. 0171-
355 4848. Customer advisory service on
lighting and all things electrical.

Linen

Givans Irish Linen Stores 6 **E3**
207 King's Rd SW3. 0171-352 6352.
Top-quality linen from this well-stocked
shop with an air of old-fashioned gentility.
CLOSED Sat.

Irish Linen 4 **D3**
35 Burlington Arc W1. 0171-493 8949.
Expensive, beautifully-made table cloths,
napkins, pillowcases, etc.

Linen Cupboard 4 **C2**
21 Great Castle St W1. 0171-629 4062.
Cut-price household linen and baby linen.
Stock all the famous makes.

The White House 4 **C3**
51 New Bond St W1. 0171-629 3521.
Stock the most luxurious and expensive
linen in London. Exquisite hand-
embroidery and hand-made lace edges.
Also silk and satin lingerie and regal
childrenswear.

Locksmiths

Barry Bros 3 **E2**
121-123 Praed St W2. 0171-262 9009.
Wide range of fire and crime prevention
equipment. Operate an emergency
service *08.00-24.00 Mon-Sun.*

Magazines & comics

Comic Showcase 4 **F2**
76 Neal St WC2. 0171-240 3664. New
and second-hand comics, cartoon strips,
calendars and original comic art work.

The Vintage Magazine Shop 4 **D3**
39-43 Brewer St W1. 0171-439 8525.
Vintage magazines from the 1900s, '30s,
'40s and '50s, sheet music, theatre
programmes, children's annuals. Also
movie shop with film star mags and
posters. American comic shop, and vintage pop and rock ephemera shop.

Maps: antique

The Map House 6 **E1**
54 Beauchamp Pl SW3. 0171-589 4325.
Antique maps, engravings, prints, atlases
and globes.

Maps: modern

Geographia Map Shop 5 **C2**
58 Ludgate Hill EC4. 0171-248 3554.
Stocks an extensive range of maps of all
parts of the world, including Ordnance
Survey maps, atlases, and globes. Good
choice of guide books as well.

National Map Centre 4 **E6**
22-24 Caxton St SW1. 0171-222
2466/4945. Stockists of Ordnance
Survey and other maps.

Stanfords 4 **F3**
12-14 Long Acre WC2. 0171-836 1321.
Maps of GB and the rest of the world;
Ordnance Survey maps, globes. Will
obtain any map, to any scale, of any part
of the world – but it may take time. Also
guide books and foreign geology section.

Media

BBC World 4 **G3**
Bush House, Strand WC2. 0171-257
2576. Information centre and shop –
geared mainly to the World Service, but
also deals with home radio and TV.
London showroom for BBC English
courses. Large range of technical

manuals and media books. Sell BBC publications, records, cassettes and videos. *CLOSED Sat & Sun.*

See also under 'Antiques', 'Guns: antique' and 'Models'.

Armoury of St James　　　4 **D4**
17 Piccadilly Arc SW1. 0171-493 5082. Armed services war medals.

Beatties of London　　　4 **F2**
202 High Holborn WC1. 0171-405 6285. Model trains, cars, kits, boats, games, radio-controlled toys, diecast aircraft, jigsaws, tools, electronic games.

Hamleys　　　4 **D3**
188-196 Regent St W1. 0171-734 3161. Good stocks of remote-controlled toys and train sets. Impressive working train system on show from time to time.

Hobby Stores　　　1 **D2**
39 Parkway NW1. 0171-485 1818. Wide range of kits and accessories. Mostly remote-controlled. Expert staff.

Julip Model Horses　　　6 **E1**
18 Beauchamp Pl SW3. 0171-589 0867. Every breed of horse and pony available, together with tack and other equipment.

Parker Gallery　　　7 **A3**
28 Pimlico Rd SW1. 0171-730 6768. Many kinds of ship models. Specialise in military, naval and topographical prints, oils and watercolours.

Tradition　　　4 **B4**
33 Curzon St W1. 0171-493 7452. The best selection of old and new model soldiers in London. Make their own. Militaria and military books.

Gambier Reeks
148-150 Penwith Rd SW18. 0181-870 3338. The full range of Yamaha motorbikes plus spare parts and accessories can be found here. Also good selection of second-hand bikes and an efficient workshop for repairs.

Motorcycle City
30-32 Clapham High St SW4. 0171-720 6072. Kawasaki and Honda specialists. Also range of second-hand motorbikes and accessories. Large workshop for repairs and services.

Automobile Association (AA)
30-31 Haymarket SW1. 0171-839 4355. Join the AA at any of the 30 centres in Greater London (check the telephone directory for the nearest). Provide various breakdown and recovery services, as well as legal advice, route details and discounts on various services and publications.

Royal Automobile Club (RAC)
RAC House, Bartlett St, South Croydon. 0181-686 0088. Membership offers a recovery breakdown service and access to insurance schemes and publications at a reduced rate.

Jack Donovan　　　3 **A2**
93 Portobello Rd W11. 0171-727 1485. Musical boxes. *OPEN Sat only.*

Talking Machine
30 Watford Way NW4. 0181-202 3473. Deal in early gramophones, phonographs, Victorian sewing machines, primitive typewriters, classic jukeboxes, early radio and TV equipment and old records.

Andy's Guitar Centre　　　4 **E2**
27 Denmark St WC2. 0171-916 5080. New and second-hand electric guitars and basses. Semi-acoustic and classical. Workshop where guitars are made and repaired. Many major pop groups among their customers.

J. & A. Beare　　　4 **D2**
7 Broadwick St W1. 0171-437 1449. Fine old violins, violas and cellos. Also restorers.

Bill Lewington　　　4 **E2**
144 Shaftesbury Av WC2. 0171-240 0584. New and second-hand wind and brass instruments.

Bluthner　　　4 **C3**
8 Berkeley Sq W1. 0171-753 0533. Pianos.

Boosey & Hawkes　　　4 **C2**
295 Regent St W1. 0171-580 2060. Manufacture whole range of brass and woodwind instruments. Sell instrumental accessories, music and books but no instruments from here. Music publishers.

Early Music Shop at   **1 B1**
the Folk Shop
2 Regents Park Rd NW1. 0171-284
0534. Reproduction instruments mainly
from the Renaissance and Baroque
periods.

T.W. Howarth   **4 B1**
31 Chiltern St W1. 0171-935 2407.
Manufacturers of oboes d'amore and
cor anglais. Woodwind specialists.
Music, accessories, woodwind repairs.

Ivor Mairants Musicentre   **4 E2**
56 Rathbone Pl W1. 0171-636 1481.
Specialise in guitars, of which they have a
huge range, and other fretted instruments
such as mandolins, banjos and ukuleles.
1001 accessories.

N.P. Mander
St Peter's Organ Works, St Peter's Clo,
Warner Pl E2. 0171-739 4747. Antique
organs supplied all over the world.
Restorations carried out and new
organs built for churches, cathedrals
and home use.

Morley Piano & Harpsichord
Workshops
34 Engate St SE13. 0181-318 5838.
Antique, reproduction, second-hand
and modern pianos, and early keyboard instruments. Domestic long-
term piano rental. Also tune, repair,
recondition and restore any keyboard
instrument.

Paxman   **5 C4**
Unit B4, Linton House, 164-180 Union St
SE1. 0171-620 2077. One of the most
famous horn makers in the world. They
sell all types, both new and second-hand.
Sheet music and repairs.

Professional Percussion   **1 D1**
205 Kentish Town Rd NW5. 0171-485
0822. Vast selection of drums,
drum kits and other percussion instruments. Accessories and second-hand
equipment too.

Ray Man Eastern Musical   **4 F2**
Instruments
29 Monmouth St WC2. 0171-240 1776.
Eastern and Indian instruments. Also a
selection of Chinese, African, Egyptian,
Japanese, Balinese and Indian records.
Lessons on Chinese instruments. Health
music. Hiring service too.

Roka   **4 E2**
5 Denmark St WC2. 0171-240 2610.
Repairs carried out on acoustic and electric guitars, amplifiers. Comprehensive
stock of spares , new and second-hand
guitars.

Salvi Harps at Holywell   **5 C4**
Music Ltd
58 Hopton St SE1. 0171-928 8451.
Italian firm which makes and sells harps
and everything to go with them.

Schott   **4 D2**
48 Great Marlborough St W1. 0171-437
1246. Music publishers and sellers of
educational and classical sheet music.
Sell recorders.

Steinway & Sons   **4 B2**
Steinway Hall, 44 Marylebone La,
Wigmore St W1. 0171-487 3391. Wide
variety of Steinway pianos.

Musical instrument restorations

Fiddles & Sticks   **3 A2**
13 All Saints Rd W11. 0171-221 4040.
Stringed instruments restored and
repaired.

Impact Percussion   **5 F5**
120-122 Bermondsey St SE1. 0171-403
5900. Percussion hire, retail and repair.

Munson & Harbour
Masterpiece Works, Hampshire St NW5.
0171-267 1610. Harp repairers.

Music: printed, antique

Otto Haas
49 Belsize Park Gdns NW3. 0171-722
1488. Rare collectors' items – manuscripts and printed music from the Middle
Ages to the 20thC. *By appt only.*

Travis & Emery   **4 E3**
17 Cecil Ct, Charing Cross Rd WC2.
0171-240 2129. Printed music from the
1700s. Also books on music.

Music: printed, modern

Chappell of Bond Street   **4 C3**
50 New Bond St W1. 0171-491 2777.
Established 1811. Publishers with a
worldwide reputation. Sheet music. Also
sell a variety of instruments.

Cramer Music   **4 F3**
23 Garrick St WC2. 0171-240 1612. Mail
order number for classical, educational
and popular music.

Novello   **4 E2**
8/9 Frith St W1. 0171-483 2161.
Famous publishers of educational,
church, vocal, instrumental and
orchestral music.

Needlework & embroidery

*Harrods, Selfridges, John Lewis and
Peter Jones have excellent needlework
departments.*

Ellis & Farrier   **4 D3**
20 Beak St W1. 0171-629 9964. Sell all

kinds of beads mostly for the embroidery trade; sequins, bugle beads; pearl drops, shaped stones; all colours and sizes. Will dye beads especially to customers' requirements.

Royal School of Needlework
Appt 12a, Hampton Ct Pal, East Molesey, Surrey. 0181-943 1432. Cleaning and restoration of all embroideries and textiles. New commissions also undertaken. Classes in all aspects of embroidery and related textile crafts.

New Age & astrology

Astrology Shop   4 **F2**
78 Neal St WC2. 0171-497 1001. Personal horoscopes, forecasts and children's birth charts.

Mysteries   4 **F2**
9-11 Monmouth St WC2. 0171-240 3688. Major supplier of mystical, magical and New Age books and cassettes. Psychic readings.

Mystic Maze   1 **E5**
126-130 Drummond St NW1. 0171-813 1212. Psychic readings, crystal healing, palmistry, tarot readings. New Age clothing, cassettes, jewellery.

Party services

Oscar's Den
127-129 Abbey Rd NW6. 0171-328 6683. Supplies all manner of entertainments and party novelties on any scale. From private fun-fairs to whacky inflatables.

Party Planners   3 **A2**
56 Ladbroke Gro W11. 0171-229 9666. Run by the Queen's cousin. Organise all types of parties from dinners to balls. Also conferences, overseas groups and weddings.

Searcy Tansley & Co
124 Bolingbroke Rd SW11. 0171-585 0505. High-class catering for cocktail parties, dances, etc.

The National Association of Toastmasters
29 Tolmers Gdns, Cuffley, Potters Bar, Herts. (01707) 873324. Professional toastmasters to officiate at any type of function can be supplied at short notice.

Wren Press   6 **C5**
26 Chelsea Wharf, 15 Lots Rd SW10. 0171-589 0777. For printing of party invitations, wedding lists and stationery.

Pens

Pencraft   4 **G2**
91 Kingsway WC2. 0171-405 3639. Very wide range of ballpoints and fountain pens.

Penfriend   4 **G3**
Bush House Arc, Bush House, Strand WC2. 0171-836 9809. Large selection.

W.H. Smith   4 **G2**
7-11 Kingsway WC2. 0171-836 5951. Repairs and sales of Parker pens.

Perfume

Stores and chemists usually stock a large range of the most popular perfumes. For something more unusual try the shops listed below. Large shops like Selfridges, Harrods and Dickins & Jones stock 'The Perfumer's Workshop' range which enables you to blend your own.

Chanel   4 **D3**
26 Old Bond St W1. 0171-493 5040. The whole perfume and cosmetics range.

Floris   4 **D4**
89 Jermyn St SW1. 0171-930 2885. Perfumers to the Court of St James since George IV, specialising in English flower perfumes, matching toiletries and preparations for men.

Penhaligon's   4 **C3**
20b Brook St W1. 0171-493 0002. Traditional toilet waters and hand-made fragrances. Also deal in old English silver scent bottles. Other branches.

Pest control

Your local council offers a free service for the disposal of vermin and insects, or try:

Rentokil   7 **D6**
2/3 Wendle Crt, 131-137 Wandsworth Rd SW8. 0171-498 5188. Give free surveys for pest control. They do the remedial work as well as clearing them out.

Photographic equipment

Dixons   4 **E2**
88 Oxford St W1. 0171-636 8511. Photographic as well as audio-visual equipment. Over 90 branches in London, all with excellent stocks.

Fox Talbot   4 **F3**
443 Strand WC2. 0171-379 6522. Large selection of top names.

Jessops   4 **E2**
67-69 New Oxford St WC1. 0171-240 6077. Wide range of photographic and dark-room equipment at competitive prices.

Keith Johnson & Pelling   1 **E5**
93-103 Drummond St NW1. 0171-380 1144. Large stocks of professional photographic and audio-visual equipment. Rental and repair service.

Leeds Photovisual   1 **G5**
20-26 Brunswick Centre, Bernard St WC1. 0171-833 1661. Cameras, films and all accessories. Hire service also available.

R.G. Lewis   4 **F2**
217 High Holborn WC1. 0171-242 2916. Developing, enlargements and photographic equipment.

Morgans   4 **E1**
179 Tottenham Court Rd W1. 0171-636 1138. Extensive selection of good second-hand cameras and photographic equipment.

Wallace Heaton   4 **C3**
64 New Bond St W1. 0171-629 7511. High-quality new photographic, cine and projection equipment.

Photography services

Atlas Photography
6 Blundell St N7. 0171-607 6767. All aspects of photographic services. Can enlarge, provide exhibition display prints, print T-shirts, supply film.

Joe's Basement   4 **E2**
113 Wardour St W1. 0171-434 9313. A professional photographic laboratory which is open *24 hrs*. Colour transparency film back in *2 hrs*, black and white in *6 hrs*; colour print film in *24 hrs*.

Picture framing & restoring

Association of British Picture Restorers
Station Av, Kew, Surrey. 0181-948 5644. Will recommend one of their highly skilled Fellows in your area for restoration of art on canvas or metal.
The **Institute of Paper Conservation** (01886 832323) offers a similar service with art on paper.

Border Line Arts   4 **F2**
5 Dryden St WC2. 0171-829 8413. *48-hr* framing service. Also do picture and frame restorations.

Bourlet Frames   3 **F2**
32 Connaught Sq W2. 0171-724 4837. Large range of styles and some handmade frames. Watercolour and oil restoration also undertaken.

F.A. Pollak   2 **C5**
Unit 3, 70 Rosebery Av EC1. 0171-837 6161. High-quality bespoke framing service.

J. & L. Tanous   6 **B6**
115 Harwood Rd SW6. 0171-736 6497. Modern and antique framing of quality. Fine art picture frame makers; gilders, restorers.

Plants

See under 'Flowers' and 'Gardening'.

Postcards

Memories
18 Bell La NW4. 0181-202 9080. Large collection of turn-of-the-century to pre-war postcards.

Pleasures of Past Times   4 **E3**
11 Cecil Ct WC2. 0171-836 1142. Extremely large classified collection of early postcards, greetings cards, early children's books and theatre ephemera.

Posters & reproductions

Art galleries sell reproductions of their more popular paintings, and museum shops normally have a good selection of posters.

Dillons Arts Shop   4 **F3**
8 Long Acre WC2. 0171-836 1359. Sell a wide range of posters on the performing and visual arts.

Medici Gallery   4 **C3**
7 Grafton St W1. 0171-629 5675. Reproductions, limited editions, graphics and greetings cards. Exhibitions *all year round*.

Paperchase   1 **F6**
213 Tottenham Court Rd W1. 0171-580 8496. Modern posters. Also prints and art books.

The Poster Shop   4 **F3**
28 James St WC2. 0171-240 2526. Posters from all over the world covering every subject. Huge selection. Framed posters too. Other branches.

Press cutting agencies

International Press Cutting Bureau
224-236 Walworth Rd SE17. 0171-708 2113. Monitoring service for worldwide press.

Romeike & Curtice
Hale House, 290-296 Green Lanes N13. 0181-882 0155. Extensive cuttings from newspapers, magazines, trade journals,

as well as advert checking and a foreign department.

Records, cassettes, CDs & videos

Caruso & Co 4 **D1**
10 Charlotte Pl W1. 0171-636 6622. English and foreign, vocal and operatic, and a large selection of Argentinian tango and classical records. Also nostalgia, 78s and second-hand records.

Cassettes Plus 4 **E2**
12 Earlham St WC2. 0171-836 8514. Specialist cassette shop offering London's largest selection – 10,000 titles. Also compact discs.

Cheapo Cheapo Records 4 **E3**
53 Rupert St W1. 0171-437 8272. Jazz, rock, classical, folk and blues. All second-hand stock.

HMV 4 **D2**
150 Oxford St W1. 0171-631 3423. Comprehensive stock of all types of music in a very large store.

James Asman 4 **F3**
23a New Row WC2. 0171-240 1380. Long-established jazz, blues and nostalgia records specialist run by jazz critic James Asman. Lots of imports and second-hand bargains. Collections bought.

Minus Zero 3 **A2**
2 Blenheim Cres W11. 0171-229 5424. New wave, punk, American and British sixties psychedelia, and rare and re-issued records.

Music Discount Centre 4 **F3**
437 Strand WC2. 0171-240 2157. Huge selection of classical cassettes and compact discs ranging from the very specialist to the more popular. Inexpensive. Other branches.

Music & Video Exchange 3 **B4**
38 Notting Hill Gate W11. 0171-243 8573. Exchange or select from thousands of second-hand records, cassettes, compact discs and videos. Rare deletions. Also at 229 Camden High St NW1 (1 **D2**). 0171-267 1898. And 90 Goldhawk Rd W12. 0181-749 2930.

Ray's Jazz Shop 4 **F2**
180 Shaftesbury Av WC2. 0171-240 3969. Jazz, blues, world and folk, on record, cassette and compact disc.

Tower Records 4 **D3**
1 Piccadilly W1. 0171-439 2500. Housed in the old Swan & Edgar building, this is said to be the 'greatest record store in the known world'. Full range of sounds and large selection of compact discs, videos and US imports.

Virgin Megastore 4 **E2**
14-16 Oxford St W1. 0171-631 1234. The largest entertainment store in the world. Progressive and popular music, blues, jazz, classical – almost everything at below the recommended price. Three-sided listening stands. Other branches.

Sex supermarkets

Ann Summers 4 **D3**
26 Brewer St W1. 0171-437 4016. The original sex supermarket, with all types of contraceptives, gadgets, and sex aids. Helpful staff; demonstrations.

Lovecraft 4 **E3**
46 Cranbourn St WC2. 0171-437 2105. 'Amusement arcade' sex supermarket. Wide selection of products.

Shells

Eaton's Shell Shop 4 **F2**
30 Neal St WC2. 0171-379 6254. Very varied shop offering as its main line an awe-inspiring selection of shells, minerals, crystals and fossils, costing anything from a few pence to hundreds of pounds. Popular with collectors, and theatre and cinema prop hunters. Also shell and semi-precious stone jewellery. Natural woven matting, bamboo poles, cane roller blinds made-to-measure and chair cane.

Shoe repairs

Most of the large tube and mainline stations have heel bars for quick repairs.

Jeeves Snob Shop 6 **F1**
8-10 Pont St SW1. 0171-235 1101. Superlative repairs and shoe services. Sports footwear, handbag and luggage repairs. Collect and deliver within London postal area. Other branches.

Shoe shine

Traditional Victorian Shoeshine Company
(01793) 772554. Re-introducing the art of the London Shoeblack. All methods of shoe care; cleaning of leather, suede and synthetic footwear by red-jacketed shoeshine boys and girls. Sites at Burlington Arcade W1 (4 **D3**), Charing Cross WC2 (4 **F4**) and the May Fair Hotel, Stratton St W1 (4 **C4**). Other sites around central London.

Silver

See under 'Jewellery & silver'.

Souvenirs

It's no problem finding souvenir shops in London. Try around Oxford St, Carnaby St and Leicester Sq. More sophisticated gifts can be found at a number of museums, and Covent Garden is an oasis for up-market and quirky gift ideas.
See also 'Gifts'.

Sponges

Maitlands **4 D4**
175 Piccadilly W1. 0171-493 1975. Marvellous selection of natural sponges in all sizes. Also hairbrushes, shaving brushes and perfumes.

Sports: general

Intersport **4 E1**
22 Tottenham Court Rd W1. 0171-631 1410. Complete range of Adidas, Reebok and Nike sports clothing, footwear and equipment, plus other brands.
Lillywhites **4 E3**
Lower Regent St SW1. 0171-930 3181. Excellent general stock of top English and Continental equipment for most sports.
Olympus Sports **4 C2**
301 Oxford St W1. 0171-409 2619. Wide range of tennis, squash and badminton equipment, swimwear, ski-wear; large training shoe department. Also hand luggage and sports bags.
Sports Exchange **3 B3**
14 Pembridge Rd W11. 0171-792 8100. Nearly new sporting equipment, clothing and accessories for a wide range of activities. Staffed by amateur enthusiasts who can give information and advice. List of sports clubs available.
Sportspages **4 E2**
94-96 Charing Cross Rd WC2. 0171-240 9604. Sports bookshop covering all aspects of sport and fitness. Also stocks magazines and videos.

Sports equipment: archery

Quicks Archery Specialists
Hampton Court Rd, Kingston, Surrey. 0181-977 5790.

Sports equipment: boating & yachting

Arthur Beale **4 F2**
194 Shaftesbury Av WC2. 0171-836 9034. Excellent small yacht chandler. Nautical clothing and books.
Force 4 **7 C1**
30 Bressenden Pl SW1. 0171-828 3900. Full range of boating equipment, hardware and clothing. Dinghies and small inflatables in stock. Nautical gifts, books and charts.
London Yacht Centre **5 F1**
13 Artillery La E1. 0171-247 0521. Very large stock of boating equipment with the advantage of being near Liverpool Street station – gateway to the east coast yachting resorts.

Sports equipment: boxing

Lonsdale **4 D3**
21 Beak St W1. 0171-437 1526. Punch bags, mouth guards, clothing. Also boxing videos and books.

Sports equipment: camping & mountaineering

In addition to those listed below, Simpson and Lillywhites also have small camping sections.
Blacks Camping & Leisure **4 E2**
53 Rathbone Pl W1. 0171-636 6645. Probably the most versatile camping shop in London. Supply the best British and Continental equipment and clothing; have equipped many mountaineering expeditions. Specialists in climbing and mountaineering.
Camping Centre
44-48 Birchington Rd NW6. 0171-328 2166. Possibly the largest exhibition of tents in the country – also trailer tents. Backpacking and outdoor clothing.
Camping & Outdoor Centre **7 B1**
27 Buckingham Palace Rd SW1. 0171-834 6007. Everything you could need to camp, climb or walk.
Survival Shop **1 F4**
Euston Station. 0171-388 8353. Everything you need to survive in the wilds. Swiss army knives, Mag-Lite torches, polythene map cases, first-aid kits, compasses, back packs, tents, boots and hats.
YHA Adventure Shops **4 F3**
14 Southampton St WC2. 0171-836 8541. Large stocks of climbing,

skiing and camping clothes and equipment.

Sports equipment: fencing

Leon Paul Equipment   1 **F1**
Units 1 & 2 Cedar Way, Camley St NW1. 0171-388 8132. World-famous fencing equipment, designed and tested to Olympic standards.

Sports equipment: fishing

Don's of Edmonton
239 Fore St N18. 0181-807 5396. Knowledgeable proprietor. Good stock. Specialise in game fishing, salmon, trout, salt water and big game tackle.

C. Farlow   4 **E4**
5 Pall Mall SW1. 0171-839 2423. Modern approach to anglers' needs. Specialists in trout and salmon fishing tackle. Large country clothing section. Staff are all anglers. Established 1840.

House of Hardy   4 **E4**
61 Pall Mall SW1. 0171-839 5515. Finest hand-made rods in the world and general fishing tackle.

Sports equipment: football

Soccer Scene   4 **D2**
30-31 Great Marlborough St W1. 0171-439 0778. Vast selection of team shirts including all the UK teams, top Continental clubs and national squads. Also footballs and all clothes and accessories.

Sports equipment: golf

Golf City   5 **C2**
13 New Bridge St EC4. 0171-353 9872. Clubs, trolleys, balls, shoes, clothes and accessories. Half sets of clubs available for the beginner.

Sports equipment: gym & fitness

Body Active   4 **F4**
Charing Cross Concourse, Charing Cross underground station WC2. 0171-240 1363. Gym equipment and clothing, body-building foodstuffs, videos and books.

Sports equipment: martial arts

Shaolin Way   4 **E3**
10 Little Newport St WC2. 0171-734 6391. Judo suits, karate outfits, videos and books.

Sports equipment: riding & saddlery

Bernard Weatherill   4 **D3**
8 Savile Row W1. 0171-734 6905. Excellent sporting tailors. Specialists in breeches.

Giddens of London   4 **D3**
15d Clifford St W1. 0171-734 2788. Top-quality riding clothes. Manufacture their own saddles and equestrian accessories.

Swaine, Adeney, Brigg   4 **D3**
10 Old Bond St W1. 0171-409 7277. Complete range of equestrian equipment and clothing.

Sports equipment: running

Run and Become, Become and Run   4 **E6**
42 Palmer St SW1. 0171-222 1314. Specialist running shop. Vast range of running shoes and shoes for many other sports. Plus comprehensive stock of running clothes and accessories. Help and advice from running experts.

Sports equipment: shooting

See under 'Guns: modern'.

Sports equipment: skating

Roadrunner   3 **A2**
253 Portobello Rd W11. 0171-792 0584. Specialise in 'in-line' skates. Sales, rental and skating lessons.

Skate Attack
95 Highgate Rd NW5. 0171-267 6961. Roller skates, ice skates and skateboards.

Sports equipment: skiing

Lillywhites, Simpson, C & A and Harrods have good ski clothes and equipment.

Blacks   3 **B6**
215 Kensington High St W8. 0171-938 1911. All ski equipment and clothing.

Ellis Brigham   4 **F3**
30-32 Southampton St WC2. 0171-240 9577. Large specialist ski shop with a full range of ski-wear and equipment. Also hire of ski equipment and ski repair workshop. Mountaineering equipment and sportswear.

Snow & Rock   3 **B6**
188 Kensington High St W8. 0171-937

0872. Clothes and equipment for skiing and mountaineering.

Sports equipment: sub aqua

Aquamarine
93 Elgar St SE16. 0171-231 1166. Sells and hires wet and dry suits and diving equipment. Also books and videos.

Collins & Chambers
197-199 Mare St E8. 0181-985 0752. Seibe-Gorman, Farallon, Aquastar and Pirelli concessionaires. Wide range of quality gear. 10% discount to BSAC members.

Sports equipment: tennis

The Racquet Shop
22 Norland Rd W11. 0171-603 0013. Repair of racquets for badminton, squash and tennis. Regripping and restringing service. Accessories. No racquets for sale.

Sports equipment: watersports

Windsurfer's World
146 Chiswick High Rd W4. 0181-994 6769. Boards, sails, board accessories, harnesses. Wetsuits and steamers. Windsurfer hire.

Stained glass

Goddard & Gibb Studios
41-49 Kingsland Rd E2. 0171-739 6563. Make and repair stained glass for all kinds of windows, door panels and Tiffany lampshades.

Stamps

See also 'Auctions: stamps & coins'.

Leo Baresch   4 **F3**
110 St Martin's La WC2. 0171-240 1963. Deal in all world collections, covers and stamps.

Stanley Gibbons International 4 **F3**
399 Strand WC2. 0171-836 8444. World-famous for stamps and catalogues. New issues to classics.

Stationery shops

W.H. Smith has branches at the main stations and throughout the suburbs, and most of the big stores have good selections.

Frank Smythson   4 **C3**
44 New Bond St W1. 0171-629 8558.

The absolute tops in posh diaries, stationery and leather goods.

Paperchase   1 **F6**
213 Tottenham Court Rd W1. 0171-580 8496. Exciting collection of paper products including stationery, cards, gifts and wrapping paper.

Papyrus   6 **D3**
48 Fulham Rd SW3. 0171-584 8022. High-class, stylish stationery and desk accessories.

Rymans   4 **D2**
6-10 Great Portland St W1. 0171-637 2668. Stationery, office equipment, business machines, furniture and many other useful things. Branches throughout London.

Tea

See under 'Coffee & tea'.

Theatrical supplies

See also 'Fancy dress hire'.

MBA Costumes   1 **D5**
52-56 Osnaburgh St NW1. 0171-388 4994. Manufacturers of theatrical costumes.

Stagesets
Unit L, Delta Wharf, Tunnel Av SE10. 0181-853 2370. Hire or sales of scenery, furniture, backcloths.

Theme shops

Belgian Trading   6 **D3**
97 Fulham Rd SW3. 0171-581 2002. Tintin merchandise from Captain Haddock's socks to Blue Lotus china.

The Disney Store   4 **D3**
140 Regent St W1. 0171-287 6558. Huge range of Disney products; videos, books, toys, stationery, clothing, jewellery, homeware.

Sherlock Holmes   1 **B5**
Memorabilia Company
230 Baker St NW1. 0171-486 1426. Sherlock Holmes related objects – mugs, T-shirts, posters, postcards, antique books and period magazines.

Tintin Shop   4 **F3**
34 Floral St WC2. 0171-836 1131. Packed with all Hergé's books about the young hero, plus T-shirts, postcards and other novelties.

Warner Bros Studio Store   4 **C2**
178-182 Regent St W1. 0171-434 3334. Toys and merchandise from all the animations and some live action films. Animation gallery where you can buy original cartoon footage. Interactive paint

station where children can work on animated scenes.

Tobacconists: pipes, cigars, tobacco & snuff

Astleys 4 **D4**
16 Piccadilly Arc SW1. 0171-499 9950. Established since 1862. Specialise in briar and meerschaum pipes.

Dunhill 4 **D4**
30 Duke St SW1. 0171-499 9566. Exclusive masculine luxury goods including pipes, lighters, cigars, writing instruments and leather goods.

Inderwick 4 **D3**
45 Carnaby St W1. 0171-734 6574. Established in the 18thC. Made pipes for Edward VII. Tobaccos blended for individual tastes.

J.J. Fox 4 **D4**
(Fox & Lewis Ltd)
19 St James's St SW1. 0171-930 3787. The best Havana cigars, as well as Turkish and Virginia cigarettes. Own mixtures. One of the biggest cigar merchants in Europe.

G. Smith & Sons 4 **E3**
74 Charing Cross Rd WC2. 0171-836 7422. Colourful blue and gold 19thC shopfront. Inside has old Victorian tobacco adverts. Distinguished snuff and snuff boxes. Full range of Havana and Continental cigars. Finest selection in UK of Turkish and Egyptian cigarettes.

Toys

See under 'Children's shopping'.

Umbrellas & walking sticks

Burberrys 4 **E3**
18 Haymarket SW1. 0171-930 3343. Also at 165 Regent St W1 (4 **D3**). 0171-734 4060.

James Smith 4 **F2**
53 New Oxford St WC1. 0171-836 4731. Famous store (established in 1830) for umbrellas, shooting sticks, walking sticks.

Swaine, Adeney, Brigg 4 **D3**
10 Old Bond St W1. 0171-409 7277. World-famous hand-made Brigg umbrellas and luxury leather goods.

Umbrella repairs

Carter's Umbrellas 5 **E2**
30 Royal Exchange Bldgs, Threadneedle St EC2. 0171-626 7724. Sales, repairs and refurbishment of umbrellas.

T. Fox & Co 5 **E1**
118 London Wall EC2. 0171-606 4720. Manufacturer, sales and repairs. Will undertake repairs of British-framed umbrellas.

Veterinary clinics

Beaumont Animals Hospital 1 **F2**
Royal Veterinary College, Royal College St NW1. 0171-387 8134. Clinic for domestic animals.

Blue Cross Animals Hospital 7 **B2**
1 Hugh St SW1. 0171-834 5556. Clinic for domestic animals. *24-hr emergency service.*

Wine

Most chain store wine merchants in London belong to big organisations who buy in bulk and offer competitive prices. Also listed are some completely independent shops specialising in individual service and small excellent parcels of wine. Harrods has a good wine department which buys selectively and independently.

Berry Bros & Rudd 4 **D4**
3 St James's St SW1. 0171-396 9600. Charming old wine merchant's shop. First-class list. Independent merchant.

Christie's 4 **D4**
8 King St SW1. 0171-839 9060. Wine auctions usually held on *Thur*.

Justerini & Brooks 4 **D4**
61 St James's St SW1. 0171-493 8721. Wine and spirit merchants. Will advise on laying down a cellar.

Oddbins 5 **C2**
41a Farringdon St EC4. 0171-236 7721. Wide range of drinkable wines from throughout the world as well as bargains in more illustrious wines. Other branches.

Soho Wine Market 4 **E2**
3 Greek St W1. 0171-437 9311. Cut-price wines and spirits – some excellent bargains.

Sotheby's 4 **C3**
34-35 New Bond St W1. 0171-493 8080. Auctions of fine and rare wines, spirits and vintage port.

Uncorked
15 Exchange Arc, Broadgate EC2. 0171-638 5998. Exclusively for conoisseurs. Art gallery ambience, prices start at £14.95. Advises on building up a wine cellar.

La Vigneronne 6 **D2**
105 Old Brompton Rd SW7. 0171-589 6113. Rare vintages of claret, burgundy

and Madeira. Also specialise in Alsace wines and wines from the South of France.

The Winery   **1 C6**
4 Clifden Rd W9. 0171-286 6475. Large selection of over 500 ports, sherries, wines and champagnes, including 20 own-label varieties bottled in the country of origin. Wine club offering good discounts to members.

Wine by the case

You have to buy in bulk from the following – a minimum of 12 bottles – but the wines tend to be correspondingly cheaper and a wide choice is offered.

Bibendum   **1 C1**
113 Regent's Park Rd NW1. 0171-722 5577. Large selection of fine vintage clarets and ports. Also good general stock at wide range of prices, and wine accessories. *OPEN 10.00-18.30 Mon-Sat (to 20.00 Fri).*

Majestic Wine Warehouse   6 E5
Unit 2, Albion Wharf, Hester Rd SW11. 0171-223 2983. Vast selection of wines at varying prices. Good value. Hire of glasses. *OPEN 10.00-20.00 Mon-Sun.* Other branches.

Wine clubs

Berry Bros, Justerini & Brooks and some others (see under 'Wine') will lay down wine and help customers invest in good wines.

The Wine Society
Gunnels Wood Rd, Stevenage, Herts. (01438) 740222. A wine-selling co-operative owned by its members, who receive regularly-updated lists. The range offered is wide and reliable.

Wine-making & brewing supplies

Larger branches of Boots sell wine- and beer-making supplies.

The Beer Shop   **2 G4**
8 Pitfield St N1. 0171-739 3701. Will supply all equipment and ingredients for wine and beer-making.

Markets

There are hundreds of markets in London ranging from open-air craft markets to Sunday morning street markets selling clothes and general household goods. You can also visit the wholesale markets; officially they sell only in bulk but they are interesting to look around. Food stalls and street entertainers are to be found around many of the markets, and cockney-type artists can be very entertaining.

Remember that on wet days and Mon *markets tend to be fairly dead. Opening times given here are a guide only. Markets often close early, depending on the state of business. EC = early closing. Also see 'Markets' under 'Antiques'.*

If you want to set up a market stall, contact the National Market Traders Federation on (01226) 749021. The Markets Year Book lists nationwide sites and is available from The World Fair, 2 Daltry St, Oldham, Lancs. (0161) 624 3687. For local information, ring the relevant borough markets office.

Berwick Street W1   **4 E2**
Busy and boisterous general market in the heart of Soho: the fruit and vegetables are good, and prices reasonable. Also meat, cheeses, fresh fish and household goods. *OPEN 09.00-18.00 Mon-Sat.*

Bethnal Green Road E1
General high street market. *OPEN 08.30-17.00 Mon-Sat.*

Billingsgate (wholesale)
North Quay, West India Dock Rd E14. Europe's principal inland fish market moved from the City to Docklands in 1982. Plenty of activity but can be a very wet and smelly experience! *OPEN 05.30-12.00 Tue-Sat, 05.30-10.00 Sun (shellfish only).*

Borough Market (wholesale)   5 E4
8 Southwark St SE1. Wholesale fruit and vegetables under the railway arches of London Bridge. *OPEN 02.00-09.00 Mon-Sat.*

Brick Lane E1   **5 G1**
An exciting place to go to on a *Sun morning* when Brick La and the surrounding streets – Cheshire St, Sclater St, Cygnet St and Bacon St – come alive with stalls, stallholders and potential customers jostling for space. Famous for second-hand furniture but come here for almost anything.

Brixton

Radiating from Atlantic Rd SW9. Large general market with a distinct West Indian flavour; exuberant atmosphere heightened by the loud reggae music reverberating around the railway arches. *OPEN 08.00-18.00 Mon-Sat, EC Wed.*

Broadway Market

London Fields E8. Plants and flowers. *OPEN 09.00-17.00 Sat during spring and summer.*

Camden Lock   **1 D1**

Where Chalk Farm Rd crosses Regent's Canal NW1. Amongst the cobbled courtyards and warehouses of the lock is a huge expanse of market selling everything from designer clothes and pine furniture to antique clothing, junk and bric-à-brac. Also a number of interesting food stalls. Refreshments. *OPEN 10.00-18.00 Mon-Sat, 09.30-17.30 Sun.*

Camden Passage   **2 D3**

Islington High St N1. A paved walk lined with shops and stalls; selling a mixture of antiques and attractive, but expensive, bric-à-brac. Also second-hand records and books, old clothes, prints and furniture. *OPEN 09.00-18.00 Mon-Sat. Market stall days (Wed & Sat) OPEN 06.45-16.00.*

Camden Town   **1 D2**

Inverness St NW1. Fruit, vegetables and junk stalls. *OPEN 09.00-13.00 Mon-Sat.*

Chapel Market   **2 C3**

White Conduit St, off Liverpool Rd N1. General market selling cheap fruit and vegetables and tat; also pet stall. *OPEN Tue-Sun, EC Thur & Sun.*

Chelsea Antiques Market   **6 E4**

245-253 King's Rd SW3. 0171-352 9695. Large, bustling market spreading back from the King's Rd. Mostly general stock, but some specialists. *OPEN 10.00-18.00 Mon-Sat.*

Columbia Road E2

Flowers and plants. *OPEN 08.00-13.00 Sun only.*

Covent Garden WC2   **4 F3**

Apple Market *OPEN Mon-Sun;* handmade British crafts *Tue-Sat,* antiques and collectables on *Mon,* arts and crafts on *Sun.*

The Cut   **5 B5**

Lower Marsh Rd, off Waterloo Rd SE1. Fruit, vegetables and all sorts of household items. Best times *12.00-14.00 Mon-Sat.*

East Street SE17

General items in the week, but mainly fruit, vegetables, plants and flowers *Sun. OPEN 07.00-14.00 Tue-Sun.*

Farringdon Road EC1   **2 C5**

Old and rare books, manuscripts and newspapers. *OPEN Mon-Fri.*

Gabriel's Wharf   **5 B4**

56 Upper Ground SE1. The South Bank's answer to Covent Garden – a collection of craft workshops including jewellery, fabric and leather designers, plus a restaurant bar and a garden centre. At *weekends* there is a market which also sells flowers, vegetables, designer gimmicks and clothes, to the accompaniment of live street entertainment. Market *OPEN 09.30-18.00 Sat & Sun.* Workshops *OPEN 11.00-17.00 Tue-Sun.*

Greener Market   **3 A2**

Portobello Green W11. Organic produce and environmentally responsible goods. *OPEN 12.00-20.00 Thur.*

Greenwich Market

College Approach, Stockwell St, and corner of Greenwich High Rd and Royal Hill SE10. Second-hand clothes, books and jewellery, antique furniture and collectables, arts and crafts.

High Street, Walthamstow E17

Over a mile of stalls and shops selling literally everything. Crowded and noisy. *OPEN Tue, Thur, Fri & Sat.*

Jubilee Market   **4 F3**

Jubilee Hall, Covent Garden WC2. Smallish market beside the paved shopping and market complex. Antiques *05.00-17.00 Mon,* general *09.00-17.00 Tue-Fri,* crafts *10.00-17.00 Sat & Sun.*

Kensington Market   **3 C5**

Kensington High St W8. A maze of off-beat clothes mingled with jewellery, antiques and records. Stall-holders prepared to buy, sell and barter. *OPEN 10.00-18.00 Mon-Sat.*

Kingsland Waste E8

For the DIY enthusiast – hardware, tools and timber. *OPEN 07.00-17.00 Sat.*

Kingston Markets

Kingston-on-Thames, Surrey. General market on *Mon* on Cattle Market Car Park, Fairfields Rd. *OPEN 08.00-14.00.* Ancient and Apple Market, Market Pl is mainly fruit, vegetables and fish but has some general stalls. *OPEN 08.00-17.30 Mon-Sat, EC Wed (to 14.00).*

Lambeth Walk SE11   **7 F2**
General market. Vegetables and fruit, clothing, electrical goods, materials. *OPEN 10.00-18.00 Mon-Sat, EC Thur (to 13.30).*

Leadenhall Market   **5 F2**
Gracechurch St EC3. General retail market: vegetables, poultry, plants, fish and endless other items. The late Victorian glass and ironwork of the building is superb. *OPEN 07.00-17.00 Mon-Fri.*

Leather Lane EC1   **2 C6**
Vast range of goods, but few leather stalls nowadays. Lively patter. Close to London's diamond trade in Hatton Garden. *OPEN 11.00-15.00 Mon-Fri.*

London Silver Vaults   **5 A1**
Chancery La WC2. Underground vaults like an Aladdin's cave crammed with antique and modern silverware. *OPEN 09.00-17.30 Mon-Fri, 09.00-12.30 Sat.*

Merton Abbey Mills
Off Merantun Way SW19. Crafts, antiques and hand-made goods. *OPEN 10.00-17.00 Sat & Sun.* Permanent craft shops open throughout the week.

New Covent Garden   **7 D5**
(wholesale)
Nine Elms SW8. London's foremost wholesale fruit, vegetable and flower market which has been in its present location since the end of 1974. Some of the old charm and vitality has been lost in the move from the age-old site in the centre of London, but it is still extremely lively and well worth a visit if you can get up in time. *OPEN 04.00-11.00 Mon-Fri, 09.00-09.00 Sat.*

North End Road SW6
Variety of stalls. Plants and flowers in *summer. OPEN 09.00-18.00 Mon-Sat, EC Thur.*

Northcote Road SW11
Busy market, selling mainly fruit and vegetables, near Clapham Junction. *OPEN 09.00-14.00 Mon-Sat.*

Petticoat Lane   **5 G2**
Petticoat Lane as such does not exist but is the name given to the market which radiates from Middlesex St E1 on *Sun mornings*. Some of the streets – Goulston St (good for fashion), Toynbee St and Wentworth St – are open during the week too. The other streets involved are Bell La, Strype St, Cobb St, Leyden St, New Goulston St and Old Castle St. Petticoat Lane is London's biggest market with 850 stalls. Well known for selling clothes, the choice extends from designer fashion to tack. The range of other goods on sale is very wide – china, electrics, linens, toys. *OPEN 09.00-14.00 Sun.*

Portobello Road W11   **3 A2**
Well-known and much-frequented market extending into Golborne Rd and Westbourne Grove. Fruit, vegetables and new goods sold *09.00-18.00 Mon-Wed, EC Thur (to 13.00).* Second-hand junk and bric-à-brac sold *08.00-17.00 Fri* and on *Sat 08.00-sunset* the famous antiques market is held, (now too established for many bargains to exist). The arcades off Portobello Rd open on *Sat only.*

Ridley Road E8
Famous East End market with Jewish and West Indian influences. *OPEN Tue-Sat, EC Thur.*

Roman Road E3
Traditional East End market, more than 160 years old. Large, busy, with lots of discount fashion stalls. Also fruit and vegetables. *OPEN 08.00-14.00 Tue & Thur, 08.00-17.00 Sat.*

Shepherd's Bush W12
Large, general open-air market alongside the railway arcade. Food stalls have a strong West Indian bias. Pets, household goods and the usual market tat. *OPEN 09.30-17.00 Mon-Sat, EC Thur.*

Smithfield   **5 C1**
Charterhouse St EC1. World's largest meat market; some interesting architecture and storage techniques but not for the squeamish. *OPEN 05.00-12.00 Mon-Fri.*

Spitalfields, New (wholesale)
23 Sherrin Rd E10. London's premier horticultural market, moved from the City to this modern market complex.

Spitalfields, Old   **5 G1**
Commercial St E1. Original home of the wholesale market. Now houses an organic market on *Fri-Sun*, where visiting farmers from around the country sell their produce. Also crafts and plants. *OPEN 10.00-17.00 Sun.*

Trafalgar Rd SE10
General street trading in Colom Rd, Tyler St and Earlswood St. *OPEN 09.00-17.00 Mon-Sat, EC Thur.*

Wembley
Stadium Way NW10. Mainly clothes stalls but good range of household goods, from china to three-piece suites. *OPEN 09.00-15.00 Sun.*

Wentworth Street E1   **5 G2**
Part of Petticoat Lane market on Sun. Fruit, vegetables and bric-à-brac. *OPEN 08.30-14.00 Sun-Fri.*

Whitechapel Market
Whitechapel Rd E1. Famous East End high street market. Huge array of stalls. *OPEN 08.30-17.00 Mon-Sat.*

Woolwich
Beresford Sq SE18. Variety of goods sold in this well-known south London market and in the adjacent covered market in Plumstead Rd. *OPEN 09.00-17.00 Mon-Sat, EC Thur.*

SHOPPING IN LONDON

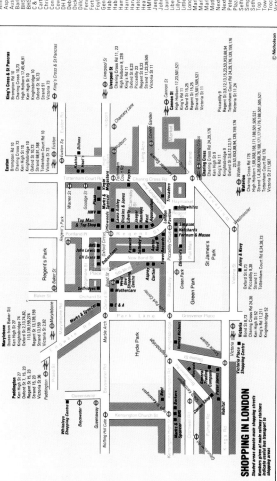

Shaded areas denote main shopping streets
Numbers given at main railway stations
indicate buses to main
shopping areas

© Nicholson

Oxford Street

Great Portland Street			**Hills Place**

Left	No.	No.	Right
Restaurant **Burger King**	214	221	**Miss Selfridge** *Fashion F*
Fashion F **Anne Brooks** (Petite Fashion)	216	225	**Benetton** *Fashion FM*
Fashion F **Evans**	218	227	**Crest of London** *Souvenirs*
		229	**Strings Sale Depot** *Fashion FM*
		231	**Jeans West** *Fashion FM*
		233	**The Byrite Company** *Fashion M*
		235	Thomas Cook *Bureau de change*

Argyll Street

STORE **TOP SHOP & TOP MAN**	214-216	241	Exchange International *Bureau de change*
		266	**Shellys** *Shoes FM*

Oxford Circus ⊖ **Regent Street**

Fashion F **Hennes**	238	251	South African Airways
		257	**Sock Shop**
John Prince's Street		261	**For Eyes** *Opticians*
		263	**Richards** *Fashion F*
Fashion M **Mister Byrite**	244	267	**J. D. Sports** *Sportswear*
Shoes FM **Bally**	246	271	**La Baguette Parisienne** *Take-away food*
Shoes FM **Ravel**	248	273	**Scottish Woollens** *Fashion, knitwear*
Jewellers **H. Samuel**	250	275	Salvation Army Hall
STORE **BHS**	252	277	**Ernest Jones** *Jewellers*
Shoes FM **Clarks**	260	283	**River Island** *Fashion FM*
Fashion F **Jane Norman**	262	285	**Boots** *Chemist*
Fashion F **Monsoon**	264	287	**Cecil Gee** *Fashion M*
Fashion F **Ann Harvey**	266	289	**The Deep Pan Pizza Co** *Restaurant*
Natural beauty products **The Body Shop**	268	291	*Bureau de change*
Greetings cards **Clinton**	270	291	**Mr Howard** *Fashion M*
Fashion F **Wallis**	272	291	**Shirts, Ties & Sock Shop** *Fashion FM*
		291b	**McDonald's** *Restaurant*

Holles Street			**Harewood Place**

STORE **JOHN LEWIS**	273-306	293	**Accessorize** *Accessories*
		295	**Tie Rack** *Fashion FM*
		297	**Saxone** *Shoes FM*
		299	**Babers** *Shoes M*
		299	Noel Nursing *agency*
		301	**Olympus Sports** *Sports goods and sportswear*
Old Cavendish Street		303	**Tesco Metro** *Foodstore*
		309	**Swatch** *Watches*
STORE **D.H. EVANS**	318	315	Acme *Employment agency*
		315	**The Gap** *Fashion FM, childrenswear*

Chapel Place			**Dering Street**

Shoes FM **K Shoes**	324	321	**Stefanel** *Fashion FM*
Sock Shop	326	321	Berlitz School of Languages
Fashion FM **Naf Naf**	328	321	**Next** *Fashion M*
Smokers' materials **Bond's**	328	325	**Next** *Fashion F*
Bank of Scotland	332		

Vere Street			**New Bond Street**

STORE **DEBENHAMS**	344-348	333	**Dolcis** *Shoes FM*
		335	**Splash** *Souvenirs*
		337	**Bonjour Paris** *Take-away food*
		339	*Bureau de change*
		347	**Café Zeynah** *Take-away food*
		341	**Wendy's** *Restaurant*

Marylebone Lane			**Woodstock Street**

Ties, shirts **Off The Cuff**	350	351	**Le Croissant** *Take-away food*
Telephones **British Telecom shop**	350	353	**Thorntons** *Chocolates*
TSB Bank	350	353	Brook Street *Employment agency*
		355	**House of Cashmere** *Fashion FM*
Marylebone Lane		357	**Selection** *Fashion FM*

Souvenirs **Crest of London**	354		**Sedley Place**
Fashion FM **Tie Rack**	356		
Accessories **Sunglass Hut**	357	359	**Churchill** *Gifts*
National Westminster Bank	358	361	**Oakland** *Fashion M*
		363	**HMV Shop** *Records, CDs & cassettes*
		369	**La Brioche Dorée** *Take-away food*
		369a	Foreign Exchange Corporation
		⊖	Bond Street
		373	**Leslie Davis** *Jewellers*

Stratford Place			**Davies Street (South Molton Street)**

Shoes FM **Lilley & Skinner**	360	379	**Burtons/Dorothy Perkins** *Fashion FM*
Fashion F **Kookai**	362	379	WEST ONE SHOPPING CENTRE
Fashion M **Woodhouse**	364	383	**Faith** *Shoes F*
Jewellers **H. Samuel**	366	385	**Boots** *Chemist*
		393	**Jeans West** *Fashion FM*
St Christopher's Place		395	**The Gap** *Fashion FM*

Shoes FM **Bally**	368		
Fashion M **Suits You**	370		
Natural beauty products **The Body Shop**	372		

James Street			**Gilbert Street**

STORE **C&A**	376	399	**Pizzaland** *Restaurant*
		399	Lloyds Bank

Bird Street			**Binney Street**

Shoes FM **Instep Sports**	386	407	**Eisenegger** *Fashion M*
Fashion F **Jane Norman**	388	409	**Bertie** *Shoes FM*
Shoes FM **Barratts**	388	409	**Bruce Jeremy** *Fashion M*
		411	Kelly Temporary services *Employment agency*
		413	**Mappin & Webb** *Jewellers*

Left	No.		No.	Right
Duke Street				*Duke Street*
			415	**Ciro Citterio** *Fashion M*
			419	**Principles** *Fashion FM*
				Lumley Street
			425	**Review** *Fashion M*
			427	**Samuel Maynard** *China & gifts*
			429	**Burger King** *Restaurant*
STORE **SELFRIDGES**	400			*Balderton Street*
			431	Midland Bank
			435	**Sock Shop**
			439	**Boots** *Chemist*
			443	British Nursing Association
			443	**Churchill** *Gifts*
			445	**London House** *Fashion FM*
			447	**Grip** *Fashion M*
			449	**Jean Jeanie** *Fashion FM*
			451	**Laura Ashley** *Fashion F*
Orchard Street				*North Audley Street*
STORE **MARKS & SPENCER**	458		455	**American Burger** *Restaurant*
National Westminster Bank	466		461	**Mothercare** *Baby store*
Shoes FM **Bally**	468		467	**House of Scotland** *Fashion FM*
Jewellers **H. Samuel**	472		469	**Knickerbox** *Underwear*
Shoes FM **Clarks**	476		471	**House of Cashmere** *Cashmeres*
Fashion F **Etam**	484		473	**Jacadi** *Childrenswear*
Chemist **Boots**	488		473	**Adams** *Childrenswear*
Shoes FM **Russell & Bromley**	494		479	**Aberdeen Steak House** *Restaurant*
Travel goods **Baggage Company**	498		481	**Hennes** *Fashion F*
Watches of Switzerland	500		483	**Oakland** *Fashion M*
Shoes FM **Saxone**	502		485	**The Highlands** *Fashion FM*
			487	Alfred Marks *Employment agency*
			487	**Tie Rack** *Fashion FM*
			489	**Bay Trading Co** *Fashion M*
			491	**Ryman** *Stationery*
			493	**Dixons** *Cameras & electronics*
STORE **LITTLEWOODS**	506			*Park Street*
Fashion FM **Benetton**	522		505	**C&A** *STORE*
Novelty goods **Cascade**	524		523	**Pizza Hut** *Restaurant*
Fashion F **Next**	526		527	**Virgin Records** *Records, CDs & cassettes*
Travel goods **Salisburys**	530		537	**Cerex** *Souvenirs*
Fashion F **Wallis**	532			
Fashion F **Evans**	538			
Old Quebec Street				*Park Lane*
Restaurant **Kentucky Fried Chicken**	542			
Bureau de change **Chequepoint**	548			
Marble Arch	⊖			
Bureau de change **Berkeley Credit**	550			
Cumberland Hotel	552			
China & glass **Chinacraft**	556			
Great Cumberland Place				*Marble Arch*

Bond Street – new and old

Left	No.		No.	Right
Oxford Street				*Oxford Street*
Shoes FM **Dolcis**	87		325	**Next** *Fashion F*
Fashion F **Warehouse**	89		81	**Berkertex Brides** *Bridalwear*
Fashion M **Blazer**	90			
Fashion M **Cecil Gee**	92			
Fashion FM **Pringle of Scotland**	92			
Restaurant **Mirinae**	94			
Shoes FM **Grant**	94			
Blenheim Street				
Shoes F **Carvela**	95			*Dering Street*
Royal Bank of Scotland	97		75	**Cerruti 1881** *Fashion M*
Linens **Frette**	98		74	**Alexander Juran** *Oriental carpets*
Employment agency **Manpower**	98		74	**Paul Kaye** *Portrait photographer*
Fashion F **Betty Barclay**	99		73	**Louis Feraud** *Fashion F*
Shoes FM **Lanzoni**	100		72	**Timberland** *Fashion M*
Auctioneers **Phillips**	101		70	**Susan Woolf** *Fashion F*
Jewellers **Watches of Bond Street**	102		70	**Kabaret** *Bar*
Leather goods **Henry's**	103		69	**Please Mum** *Childrenswear*
Shoes F **Ivory**	104		68	**Robina** *Fashion F*
Fashion F **Laurel**	105		66	**Escada** *Fashion F*
Fashion F **Cerruti**	105-6		65	**Guy Laroche** *Fashion F*
Fashion F **Alexon**	107		64	**Dixons** *Cameras & electronics*
Fashion F **Lanvin**	108			
Sylvia Lewis Beauty Clinic	108			
Hairdressing salon **Stephen Way Hair**	109			
Shoes FM **Russell & Bromley**	109			

South Molton Street

Oxford Street

Pub Hog in the Pound Tavern	28
Employment agency Select Appointments	28
Designer fashion FM Browns	23
Teas & Coffees Whittards	22
Bond Street Secretarial Bureau	22
Japanese jewellery Electrum	21
Fashion jewellery Butler & Wilson	20
Shoes FM Pied à Terre	19
Fashion F Genny	18
Employment agency Reed	17
Fashion M Joseph	16
Fashion FM Stefanel	15
Fashion F French for Less	14
Shoes FM Rider	13
Designer fashion F Arte	12
Restaurant Grand Café	11
Fashion F Pied à Terre	9
Hats The Hat Shop	8
Fashion FM Sisley	6
Designer jewellery André Bogaert	5
Designer jewellery Agatha	4
Handbags & luggage City Bag Store	3
Fashion M Daniel James	2
Shoes FM Podium	1
Restaurant Wheelers	1
Fashion F Ronit Zilkha	34

Oxford Street

35	Foto Inn Developing & printing
36	Bertie Shoes FM
37	Leather Rat Leather fashion FM
39	Gigli Fashion FM
40	The Red Rock Café
41	The Tube Shoes & fashion F
42	Alma Fashion M
43	Saga Japanese restaurant
45	Hexagone Fashion F
45	ROC Recruitment Secretarial agency
45	Karen Millen Fashion F
46	Widow Applebaum's Jewish restaurant
47	Hobbs Fashion & shoes F
48	Grosvenor Gallery
48	Cable & Co Fashion M
49	Skindeep Leather fashions FM
50	Browns Labels for Less Fashion FM
51	Vertice Italian fashion FM
52	Anvers Fashion FM
53	Geno Ventti Hairdressing salon
54	Fabrice Karel Fashion F
54	Reed Accountancy Employment agency
55	Oliver Fashion M
56	Bang & Olufson TV & hi-fi

Globe Yard

57	Adolfo Dominguez Hairdressing salon
57	Molton Brown Hairdressing salon
59	Shane English School
60	Office Shoes FM
60	Vidal Sassoon Hairdressing salon
64	South Molton Drug Stores
65	Post Office
66	Kenneth Jay Lane Jewellers
67	Monsoon Fashion F
68	Celia Loe Fashion F

Regent Street

Great Castle Street

Fashion FM Original Levi's Store	269
Restaurant Garfunkel's	265
Fashion F Hennes	260
214-216	TOP SHOP & TOP MAN STORE

Oxford Street

South African Airways	259
Fashion FM Benetton	257
Clearance store Warehouse Clearance	251-9
266	Shellys Shoes FM
264	Ratners Jewellers
260	Bally Shoes FM
256	Laura Ashley Fashion F
254	Thorntons Chocolates
254	Off the Cuff Shirts M
246	National Westminster Bank

Princes Street

Chocolates Godiva	247
Fashion FM House of Scotland	241
Beauty products & comestibles Crabtree & Evelyn	239
Cameras & film City Photo	239
Underwear Damart Thermawear	235
Fashion FM London House	231
Opticians Dollond & Aitchison	229

Little Argyll Street

244	DICKINS & JONES STORE

Hanover Street

Building society Woolwich	227
Irish airline Aer Lingus	223

Maddox Street

Jewellers Pravins	221
Telecom Electronics	219
British cloth Tops	217
Hairdressing salon Alan d	215
Cyprus Government Tourist Office	213
Fashion FM, childrenswear Scottish Wear	207-9
Moroccan National Tourist Office	205
China & glass Villeroy & Boch	203

Great Marlborough Street

214-222	LIBERTY STORE
212	Barclays Bank
208	The Gap Fashion FM

Conduit Street

The Pen Shop	199
Fashion FM Racing Green	193-7
Jewellery & accessories Carré Blanc	189
Jewellers Peter Trevor	189
Textiles Court	187
Israeli airline El Al	185

Foubert's Place

200	Jaeger Fashion FM
198	House of Chinacraft China & glass
188	Hamleys Toys
184	The London House Fabrics & woollens
170	Mappin & Webb Jewellers
160	Next Fashion FM
158	Waterford/Wedgwood China & glass
156	British Airways Travellers Shop

New Burlington Place

Noble Furs	183
Fashion FM R.M.Williams	181
Royal Jordanian airline Alia	177
Cashmeres House of Cashmere	175
Bureau de change	173
Saudi Arabian Airlines	171
Fashion FM Regents	169

New Burlington Street		**Beak Street**

Left	No.	No.	Right
Japanese National Tourist Organisation	167	154	**Lawleys** *English china & glass*
Fashion FM **Burberrys**	157	152	**Bally** *Shoes FM*
Gifts **Past Times**	155	146	**Vivella** *Shoes FM*
The English Teddy Bear Company	153	144	**Gap Kids** *Childrenswear*
		140	**The Disney Store** *Gifts*
New Burlington Mews		138	**The Cashmere Gallery** *Cashmeres*
		134	**Reject China Shop** *China*
Fashion M **Cougar**	151	132	Lloyds Bank
Fabrics **The Woollens Centre**	149		

Heddon Street		

Singapore Airlines	145	
Fashion FM **Oxfords**	143	
Knitwear & fashions FM **Scottish Woollens**	141	
China **Rosenthal**	139	
China **Wilson & Gill**	137	
Jewellers **Thomas**	135	
Midland Bank	133	

Heddon Street			**Regent Place**

Fashion FM **The Highlands**	129	130	**Boodle & Dunthorpe** *Jewellers*
Fashion FM **Cyril**	129	126	**Ryman** *Stationers*
Fashion M **Hunters**	125	124	**Watches of Switzerland**
New Gallery Centre	123	122	**Tie Rack** *Fashion FM*
Fashion M **Sacci**	121a	114	**Burton/Dorothy Perkins** *Fashion FM*
Fabrics **Fine Textiles**	121	112	**Garrard** *Gold & silversmiths*
Pens **Pencraft**	119		
Bureau de change A.M.B.	117		
TSB Bank	115		

Vigo Street			**Glasshouse Street**

Fashion M **Austin Reed**	103	100	**Aquascutum** *Fashion FM*
Shoes FM **Clarks**	101	90	**Dunn & Co** *Fashion M*
The London Textile Co	99	88	**Moss Bros** *Fashion M*
Restaurant **The Veeraswamy**	99	86	**The Scotch House** *Fashion FM*
		82	**K Shoes** *Shoes FM*

Swallow Street			**Quadrant Arcade**

Building society Bristol & West	95	80	**British Designer Knitwear Group** *Fashion FM*
Ties, shirts M **Off The Cuff**	93	76	**Alexandra** *Workwear*
Fashion M **Buzzz**	91	74a	**Angus Steak House** *Restaurant*
Handbags & luggage **Salisbury**	87		
Bureau de change & ticket agency Eurochange	83		**Air Street**
China & glass **Chinacraft**	71	70	**Café Royal** *Restaurant & bars*
Opticians **Paris-Miki**	69	62	**House of Cashmeres** *Cashmeres*
		60	**Estridge** *Cashmeres*
Air Street		56	**Stereo Regent Street** *Hi-fi*
		52	Barclays Bank
Sock Shop	61		
Fashion M **Lacoste**	59		
Fashion F **Jigsaw**	57		
Fashion FM **Tie Rack**	55		
Records, CDs & cassettes **Tower Records**	49		

Piccadilly Circus

Kings Road

Sloane Square		**Sloane Square**

STORE **PETER JONES**			Sloane Square
		9	Post Office
		11	**The Coffee Shop**
		11	**HoHo** *Chinese restaurant*
		13	**Naf Naf** *Fashion FM*
		15	**Osh Kosh B'gosh** *Childrenswear*
		17	**Roberto's** *Nightclub*
		21	Ladbrokes *Bookmakers*
		23	**Forbuoys** *Newsagents & tobacconists*
		25	**Lazer** *Fashion M*
		27	Eurochange *Bureau de change*
		31	**Astuces** *Fashion F*
			Duke of York's Headquarters

Cadogan Gardens		

Childrenswear & accessories **Trotters**	34	
Children's playthings **Early Learning Centre**	36	
Fashion F **Hampstead Bazaar**	38	
Fashion F **Sidney Smith**	36	
London School of Bridge	38	
Fashion M **Cecil Gee**	44	
Wine Bar **Blushes**	52	
Natural beauty products **The Body Shop**	54	
Fashion FM **Jeans West**	54	
Restaurant **Pizza Hut**	56	
Chemist **Boots**	58	
Shoes FM **Russell & Bromley**	64	
Sock Shop	68	

Blacklands Terrace		

Fashion FM, childrenswear, home furnishings **Next**	72	

Lincoln Street

Boulangerie/pâtisserie **Guys & Dolls**	74		
Fashion F **Oasis**	76		
Restaurant **Pizzaland**	80		
Fashion F **Esprit**	82		
Shoes FM **Hobbs**	84		
Fashion F **Jeffrey Rogers**	86		
Fashion FM **Stefanel**	88		
Shoes FM **Cable & Co**	90		
Shoes FM **Bally**	92		
Fashion F **Benetton**	94		
Fashion F **Warehouse**	96		
Restaurant **The Chelsea Kitchen**	98		
Shoes FM **Office London**	100		
Fashion F **Stirling Cooper**	102		
Fashion F **Longpoint Bay**	104		
Fashion FM **Petroleum**	106		

Cheltenham Terrace

33	National Westminster Bank
33a	**Blazer** Fashion M
33b	**Dune** Shoes FM
33c	**Chipie** Fashion M
33d	**Monsoon** Fashion F
33e	**Martins of Chelsea** TV & hi-fi
33f	**David Clulow** Opticians
33g	**Pied à Terre** Shoes FM
33h	**Our Price** Records, CDs & cassettes

Anderson Street

Walpole Street

35	**Safeway** Supermarket

Building Society Chelsea	112
Fashion M **Reiss**	114

Tryon Street

Royal Avenue

Fashion FM **The Leather Warehouse**	118
Shoes FM **Bertie**	118
Fashion F **Laura Ashley**	120
Fashion FM & childrenswear **Gap**	122
SHOPPING MALL KINGS WALK	124
Fashion F **Kookai**	124a
Fashion M **Woodhouse**	
Shoes FM **Shellys**	124b
Fashion F **Jigsaw**	124c
Fashion F **Et Vous**	126
Shoes FM **Ravel**	128
Bureau de change **Chequepoint**	130
Fashion F **Moa**	132

49	**McDonald's** Restaurant
51	**Miso** Designer clearance store
53	**Pineapple** Designer clearance store
55	**Oddbins** Wine merchants
57	**Helen Storey** Fashion F
59	**Karen Millen** Fashion F

Bywater Street

Wellington Street

Beauty products & comestibles **Crabtree & Evelyn**	134
Fashion FM **Legacy**	136
Building Society Abbey National	138
Ice-cream **Haagen-Dazs**	138a

61	**Dentics** Dentist
63	**Renegade** Shoes FM
65	**Sonico Jeans** Fashion FM
67a	**Harvest** Leather fashion M
69	**Designerwear Clearance Sale** Designer clearance sto

Markham Square

Smith Street

Fashion FM **French Connection**	140
Greetings cards **Post Impressions**	146

Markham Street

69a	**Sissors** Hairdressing salon
71	**Morgan** Fashion F
73	**Bruce Jeremy** Fashion F
75	**In Wear** Fashion F
77	**Benihana** Restaurant
79	**New Man** Fashion M
85	**MARKS & SPENCER** STORE
95	**The Pier** Household goods & furnishings
97	**Cotton Club** Fashion F
99	**Woodhouse** Fashion M
	Car Park
105	**Ware on Earth** Household goods
107	**Liaison** Nightclub
109a	**R. Soles** Leather boots
109	**The Poster Shop**
113	**Rivaaz** Leatherwear FM
115	**Kodo** Fashion F

Chemist **Boots**	150
Restaurant **The Pheasantry**	152

Stationery **Ryman**	152
Books **Dillons**	152

Jubilee Place

Radnor Walk

Lloyds Bank	164
Fashion FM **Chelsea Leather**	168
Film processing **Snappy Snaps**	170
Restaurant **Choy's**	172
Shoes FM **Blue Velvet**	174
Opticians **Chelsea Eye Centre**	176

119	**Chelsea Potter** Pub
121	**The Common Market** Fashion FM
123	**Victoria Wine** Wine merchants
123a	**Awards** Fashion FM

Burnsall Street

Shawfield Street

Fashion F **Blu di Blu**	178
Shoes FM **R. Soles**	178a
Fashion FM **Forest Ranger**	182
New age gifts **Paradise Farm**	182a
Teas & coffees **Whittard**	184
Fashion FM **Soldier Blue**	184a

125	**Wax Lyrical** Candles
127	**Picasso** Restaurant
129	**Juke Box** Fashion M
131	**Gore Booker** Interior goods
135	**Antiquarius** Antiques, fashion FM
137	**Basia Zarsycka** Bridalwear, shoes, jewellery
139	**Quincy** Fashion M
141	**Edwina Ronay** Fashion F

Flood Street

Dry cleaners **Sketchley**	186	145	**Jaeger** *Fashion FM*	
Leather fashion FM **Sloane's Leathers**	186a	147	**Quarzo** *Fashion FM*	
Clearance store **The Designer Outlet**	188a	150	**Omcar** *Fashion FM*	
Natural goods **Natural Fact**	192	151	**Shoe Repairs & Things** *Shoe repair*	
Candles **Angelic**	196	153	**Boy** *Fashion M*	
Supermarket **Waitrose**	198	155	**Original Levi's Store** *Fashion FM*	
Pub **The Trafalgar**	200	155a	Chelsea Methodist Church	
Chelsea Cinema	206	157	**Hittite** *Fashion F*	
Furnishings **Habitat**	206	159	**Skindeep** *Leather fashion FM*	
		161	**The Boot Store** *Shoes M*	

Chelsea Manor Street   *Chelsea Manor Street*

National Westminster Bank	224		TOWN HALL	
Post Office	232		Citizen's Advice Bureau	
Household goods **Reject Shop**	234	181	**Chenil Galleries** *Antiques*	
		183	**The Garage** *Designer fashion FM*	
Sydney Street		185	**David Clulow** *Opticians*	
		187	**Photo-Optix** *Cameras*	
		191	**Philp** *Fashion FM*	
		193	**Steinberg & Tolkien** *Antique clothing & jewellery*	
COUNCIL OFFICES	250	195	**Henry J Bean's Bar & Grill** *Bar*	
		199	**Prime Time** *Videos*	
Dovehouse Street		201	**Amagansett** *Fashion M*	
		203	**Chelsea Audio-Visual Centre**	
		205	**Pucci Pizza** *Italian restaurant*	
CHELSEA FIRE STATION		207	**Givans** *Linen*	
		209	**Oddbins** *Wine merchants*	

Manresa Road   *Oakley Street*

KING'S COLLEGE LONDON   *Glebe Place*

219	**David Pettifer** *Antiques*		
221	**My Old Dutch** *Restaurant*		
237	**Chelsea Food Fayre**		

Bramerton Street

Carlyle Square		241	**Designers Sale Studio** *Fashion F*	
		243	**Ironworks** *Ironware*	
		245	**Nottinghill Housing Trust** *Charity shop*	
		245a	**Chelsea Antique Market**	
		247	**Joanna Booth** *Antiques*	
		249	**Made in Italy** *Restaurant*	
		251	**S. Borris** *Delicatessen*	
		253	**Chelsea Antique Market**	
		255	**Isaac. T. Lloyd** *Chemist*	
		257	**Newsagents**	
		259	**Green & Stone** *Artists' materials*	
		263	**Ellessential** *Hairdressing salon*	
		265	**Holme Place** *Launderers & drycleaners*	
		271	**Designers Guild** *Furnishings*	
		271b	**The Stockpot** *Restaurant*	
Estate agents De Groot Collis	296	275	**David Tron** *Antiques*	
Pub **Cadogan Arms**	298	277	**Designers Guild** *Fabric & wallpapers*	

Church Street   *Old Church Street*

National Westminster Bank	300	279	MGM Cinema	
Interior designers **Osborne & Little**	304	279	**Mr Light** *Lighting*	
Antiques **Godson & Coles**	310	279	**Europa Foods** *Supermarket*	
Restaurant **Le Gourmet**	312	279c	**Delcor** *Interiors*	
Artists' materials **Chelsea Art Stores**	314	281	**Brats** *Gifts & cards*	
Restaurant **The Argyll**	316	283	**Wilde One's** *Ethnic fashion & gifts*	
Maps & prints **Old Church Galleries**	320	285	**Shoefax** *Shoes FM*	
Furniture **Shaker**	322	287	**Raffles** *Club*	
Furniture **Sofa Workshop**	324	289	**Sasha Hetherington** *Evening wear F*	
Carpets **Bernadout**	328	289a	**The Jam** *Restaurant*	
Restaurant **Lo Spuntino**	330	289	**Joanna's Tent** *Fashion FM & childrenswear*	
Restaurant **Big Easy**	334			
Antiques **Monro Heywood**	336			
Furniture **William Yeoward**	336		*Paultons Square*	
Restaurant **Travellers**	338			
Restaurant **Thierry's**	342	303	**Solino Leather** *Leatherwear FM*	
Antiques **Tony Bunzl**	344	305	**Bamboo Kitchen** *Chinese take-away*	
Barclays Bank	348	307	**Chrysalis** *Persian & Eastern rugs*	
		309	**Million Dollar Sports** *Sportswear*	
The Vale		313	**Kaffee Opera** *Coffee shop*	
		317	**Gregor Schumi** *Hairdressing salon*	
		319	**J. & F. E. Simpson** *Jewellers*	
Fashion M **The Bad Apple**	350	321	**Rococo** *Chocolates*	
Fashion M **Nigel Hall**	350	323	**Dept.** *Shoes & fashion M*	
Designer fashion FM **The Bluebird Garage**	350			
Wellworth Food & Wines	350b			
Fashion M **Daniel James**	352		*Beaufort Street*	
National Westminster Bank	352a			

Money and business services

Money

Currency

The unit of currency is the pound sterling (£) divided into 100 pence (p). There are coins for 1p, 2p, 5p, 10p, 20p, 50p and £1, with notes for £5, £10, £20 and £50.

Exchange facilities

There is no exchange control in Britain, so you can carry any amount of money through customs, in or out of the country. The best rate of exchange is always to be found in a bank. Bureaux de change will exchange most currencies and will cash cheques, but charge more to do so. They can be found at airports, main-line train stations, central tube stations and in the larger department stores. Bureaux de change stay open outside banking hours. The larger hotels sometimes have facilities for changing major currencies, and will accept travellers' cheques in payment of bills. Most restaurants will also accept travellers' cheques as long as they are accompanied by a valid form of identification.

Chequepoint Bureau de Change
13 Davies St W1. 0171-409 1122.　**4 C3**
222 Earl's Court Rd SW5.　**6 B2**
0171-373 9515.
Marble Arch, 548 Oxford St W1.　**4 A2**
0171-723 2646.

Eurochange Bureaux Ltd
95 Buckingham Palace Rd SW1.　**7 B1**
0171-834 3330.
Leicester Sq Tube Stn, 45 Charing　**4 E3**
Cross Rd WC2. 0171-439 2827.
Paddington Tube Stn, 179 Praed　**3 E2**
St W2. 0171-258 0442.
Tottenham Court Rd Tube Stn W1.　**4 E2**
0171-734 0279.

Thomas Cook Ltd
123 High Holborn WC1. 0171-831　**4 G1**
4408.
104 Kensington High St W8.　**3 C5**
0171-376 2588.
Selfridges, 400 Oxford St W1.　**4 B2**
0171-629 9188.
39 Tottenham Court Rd W1.　**4 E1**
0171-636 2320.
100 Victoria St SW1. 0171-828 8985.**7 C1**

Banks

Banks are traditionally open 09.30-15.30 Mon-Fri although some branches are open until 16.30 or later. They are closed B.hols and often close early on the day before a B.hol. Some selected branches open on Sat. Longer banking hours at Heathrow and Gatwick Airports: 24-hr opening all year; and at Luton Airport: OPEN 06.00-23.00 in summer.
England's main high street banks are Barclays, Lloyds, Midland, National Westminster and the TSB (Trustee Savings Bank). Their head offices are listed below together with several other British banks and international departments.

Bank of Ireland　**5 D3**
36 Queen St EC4. 0171-236 0707.
Bank of Scotland　**5 E2**
38 Threadneedle St EC2. 0171-601 6666.
Barclays Bank plc　**5 E2**
54 Lombard St EC3. 0171-626 1567.
Coutts & Co　**5 E3**
International Dept, 27 Bush La, Cannon St EC4. 0171-623 3434.
Lloyds Bank plc　**5 E2**
71 Lombard St EC3. 0171-626 1500.
Lloyds Bank International Ltd　**5 E3**
11-15 Monument St EC3. 0171-775 2000.
Midland Bank plc　**5 E2**
Poultry EC2. 0171-260 8000.
National Westminster Bank plc　**5 E2**
41 Lothbury EC2. 0171-726 1000.
Royal Bank of Scotland　**5 E2**
67 Lombard St EC3. 0171-623 4356.
TSB　**5 E2**
60 Lombard St EC3. 0171-929 1755.

Credit cards

The major credit cards – Access, American Express, Diners Club, Visa – are accepted in most places as a form of payment. Carte Blanche is less popular.
Access and Visa
To report lost or stolen cards contact the emergency number of the issuing bank *(24-hr emergency service):*
Barclays　(01604) 230230
Lloyds　(01702) 364364
Midland　0181-450 3122
National Westminster (0113) 2778899
Royal Bank of Scotland (01702) 362988

TSB (01273) 204471
Visa cards issued abroad: (01604) 230230
American Express 4 **E3**
6 Haymarket SW1. 0171-930 4411.
OPEN 09.00-17.30 Mon-Fri, 09.00-16.00 Sat (09.00-18.00 Sat for foreign exchange only). Customer service handles any enquiry or billing problem. Acts as travel agent, sells and cashes personal cheques on an emergency basis if customer has an American Express card. If card is lost the company can issue an emergency replacement card. To report lost or stolen cards call (01273) 696933 for a *24-hr emergency service.*

Barclaycard
Barclaycard Centre Dept G, Northampton, Northants. (01604) 230230. To report lost or stolen cards during office hours contact any Barclays bank or ring the above number *(24-hr service)* and write a confirming letter within seven days.

Diners Club
Diners Club House, Kingsmead, Farnborough, Hants. (01252) 516261. *24-hr service* for reporting lost cards and the telephone call should, within seven days, be followed by a confirming letter.

Eurocard
See under 'Access and Visa' above.

Eurocheque card
In case of loss contact issuing branch or telephone this emergency number: (0113) 2778899. Confirm the loss in writing within seven days.

Mastercard
To report lost or stolen cards contact (01702) 362988 *(24-hrs).*

Taxes

Most goods and services purchased in the UK are subject to VAT (value added tax) at the standard rate of 17½ %. Luxury items – tobacco, perfume, alcoholic beverages and motor vehicles – are subject to higher rates. Overseas visitors can reclaim the VAT paid on high value items by obtaining a VAT 407 form from the retailer. On returning home the goods must be certified by the customs officer. Evidence of this plus the form must then be returned to the retailer, who will send the refund to the visitor's country of origin. However, this procedure can be lengthy. A good alternative is to shop in stores showing the London Tax Free Shopping sign. This system entails filling in a voucher, presenting it to customs with the goods and returning it to the London Tax Free Shopping organisation who will then immediately refund your money in the currency of your country of residence.

Tipping

Should be an expression of pleasure for service rendered and never a duty; it is still possible not to tip at all if the circumstances justify this. These guidelines give some idea of the average tip:

Restaurants Many now add on a service charge, usually 12½%, but do not always say so – if in any doubt ask them. They usually say if it is *not* included. 12½% is the minimum; give up to 15% for above-average service.

Taxis 10-15%.
Women's hairdressers 15% to the hairdresser, 5% to the shampooer.
Men's hairdressers 15%.
Cloakroom attendants 10p per article when collected.
Washroom services 10p if individual attention is given.
Commissionaires For getting a taxi; up to 50p depending on the effort expended.
Pubs & bars Never at the bar, but buy the barman a drink if you wish. For waiter service in the lounge, from 10p per drink.
Hotels Almost all add it to your bill, usually 10%. Give extra to individuals for special service, from 50p.
Porters 50p-£1 per case depending on how far it is carried.

Business services

London offers a number of back-up services to make life easier for the travelling business man or woman. There are organisations which hire out offices or conference rooms by the hour, day or month along with complete secretarial and communication services. They will provide you with a London address while you are overseas and a message service whereby someone will handle telephone calls and forward your telexes. Other agencies deal with secretarial and staffing services only. It is worth enquiring about the amenities available at your hotel, as most of the major ones help their business guests by providing communication facilities.

Angela Pike Associates 4 **D3**
Meridian Hotel, Piccadilly W1. 0171-434 4425. *24-hr* secretarial business bureau. *7 days a week.*

Business Centre Heathrow
Queen's Bldg, Heathrow Airport. 0181-759 2434. For high-flyers between flights. Private office accommodation, work

cubicles and services including the use of personal computers. Video conference facilities.

Business Space   **4 D3**
211 Piccadilly W1. 0171-439 8985. Luxury offices and conference rooms for hire with all the necessary services.

Extel Financial   **2 F5**
Fitzroy House, 13-17 Epworth St EC2. 0171-251 3335. Deals with all kinds of queries and problems. Also publishes financial data on more than 7000 British and foreign businesses. *Charge.*

Conference services

Conference Associates &   **4 C2**
Services Ltd
4 Cavendish Sq W1. 0171-499 0900. Professional conference organisers who arrange everything from the budgeting to the hosting of any size meeting or conference.

Video/Audio Conferencing
British Telecom organises national and international video conferencing. Phone the Conference Booking Centre on 0171-606 0541 for details.

Conference centres

Alexandra Palace & Park
Wood Green N22. 0181-365 2121.
Barbican Arts and Conference   **2 E6**
Centre
Barbican EC2. 0171-638 4141.
Cabot Hall
Cabot Place West, Canary Wharf E14. 0171-418 2783/0171-344 4444.
Earl's Court Exhibition Centre   **6 A3**
Warwick Rd SW5. 0171-385 1200.
Olympia Exhibitions
Hammersmith Rd W14. 0171-603 3344.
Queen Elizabeth II Conference   **4 E5**
Centre
Broad Sanctuary SW1. 0171-222 5000.
Wembley Conference Centre
Wembley Complex, Empire Way, Wembley, Middx. 0181-902 8833.

Courier services: international

The following all offer door-to-door collection and delivery services around the world.

Datapost
Head Office: 33 Grosvenor Pl SW1. (0800) 884422. Freephone Datapost for a speedy door-to-door collection and delivery service.

DHL
0181-890 9000.

Intelpost
Royal Mail, Mount Pleasant, Farringdon Rd EC1. 0171-239 2495. Public facsimile system enabling copies of documents to be transmitted to 29 countries in four continents.

TNT Skypack
0181-561 2345.

UPS
0800 456789..

Courier services: nationwide

See Yellow Pages *for extensive listings of local and national messengers.*

Employment agencies

There are many different agencies all over London (see Yellow Pages *for listings). The ones given below are the main offices of some of the largest firms, which have branches in most commercial districts.*

Alfred Marks Group
16 Maddox St W1. 0171-491 4645. **4 C3**
Brook Street
353 Oxford St W1. 0171-493 8531. **4 C2**
131 Cannon St EC4. 0171-623 3966. **5 E3**
Kelly Temporary Services
82-83 Strand WC2. 0171-836 3856. **4 F3**
Office Angels
25 Oxford St W1. 0171-434 9545.   **4 E2**
71-75 Buckingham Palace Rd SW1. **7 B1**
0171-630 0844.
Reed Employment
5 High Holborn WC1. 0171-405   **5 A1**
6525.

Storage

Berkley Safe Deposit Co   **4 C3**
13-15 Davies St W1. 0171-409 1122. Rental of strong boxes.
Metro Store
81-89 Carnwath Rd SW6. 0171-736 5433. Rents out warehouse space by the week.

Translation

Conference Interpreters Group
10 Barley Mow Pass W4. 0181-995 0801. Internationally-recognised interpreters in most widely-spoken languages.
Interlingua/TTI
Rothschild House, Whitgift Centre, Croydon, Surrey. 0171-240 5361. Rapid translations done in over 70 languages. Also interpreters for meetings and conferences. Typesetting, printing and executive language tuition done in-house. *OPEN 09.00-17.30 Mon-Fri.*

Transport

For taxis and car hire see 'Transport in London' section.

Air London

(01293) 549555. Can organise any plane from executive jets to air ambulances, from air taxis to 747s.

Business information

These are the major organisations available to help the business man or woman with trade enquiries and export and import information. Do not overlook the assistance you can get from your bank, your own trade association, or the trade sections of embassies and chambers of commerce who do much to promote trade between countries.

Association of British   **7 D1**
Chambers of Commerce
9 Tufton St SW1. 0171-222 1555.

British Exporters Association   **4 E5**
16 Dartmouth St SW1. 0171-222 5419.

Central Office of Information   **5 B6**
Hercules Rd SE1. 0171-928 2345.

Chamber of Commerce   **5 D3**
35 Queen St EC4. 0171-248 4444.

Companies House   **2 F5**
55-71 City Rd EC1. 0171-253 9393. Searches undertaken for information on any company registered under the Companies Act for £1 fee.

Confederation of British   **4 E2**
Industry (CBI)
Centrepoint, 103 New Oxford St WC1. 0171-379 7400.

Department of Trade and   **7 C1**
Industry
1 Victoria St SW1. 0171-215 5000. The Enquiry Service will put you through to the appropriate officer of the DTI's Export Services for information and advice on exporting. Market assessments; Export Intelligence Service (subscribers are informed of export opportunities in their area of business as they arise); appoinment of overseas agents; reports on standing of overseas traders; foreign tariff and import regulations; assistance for companies at overseas trade fairs and exhibitions; service for foreign business visitors wishing to buy British goods.

Institute of Export   **2 G5**
Export House, 64 Clifton St EC2. 0171-247 9812.

Institute of Practitioners in **4 B6**
Advertising
44 Belgrave Sq SW1. 0171-235 7020.

Travel and holiday information

Passports

Applications for, and renewals of, full 10-year passports can be handled by your bank or travel agency for a small charge. Personal applications only to the Passport Office and a birth certificate must be produced. British Visitors passports, valid for one year, can be obtained from main post offices. These are for holiday-makers only and are valid in Canada and many European countries, usually those that don't require visas. They are issued on production of a medical card, birth certificate or expired but uncancelled passport.

Passport Office   **4 D6**
Clive House, Petty France SW1. 0171-279 3434. *OPEN 09.00-16.00 Mon-Fri. OPEN Sat for emergencies only (phone 0171-279 4000 for appt).*

Home Office   **4 E5**
50 Queen Anne's Gate SW1. 0171-273 3000.

Immigration Office
Lunar House, 40 Wellesley Rd, Croydon, Surrey. 0181-686 0688. Deals with questions concerning the granting of British visas to foreigners and entry under the

Commonwealth Immigration Act. Subject to approval, visas are then supplied by the Foreign Office.

Passport photographs

These can be done by any photographer, who will know the size and other requirements. Basically you should submit two identical black and white (certain colour photos are also acceptable), full face photographs of yourself without a hat. The size should be no more than 2in by 1½in (50mm by 38mm). The paper should be ordinary photographic paper, unglazed and unmounted. It is possible to have the photos taken in one of the street or station photograph machines (those that have the words 'Passport' or 'Passport approved' marked on them).

Inoculations and vaccinations

These can be carried out by your own doctor under the National Health Service free – though the doctor may make a charge for signing the certificate. The certificate should then be taken for stamping to the Health Department of the local authority in which the vaccinator practises. International certificates are required for cholera and yellow fever. Details of international requirements are given in 'Health Advice for Travellers' available at all post offices.

British Airways Immunisation Clinic 4 D3
156 Regent St W1. 0171-439 9584. All inoculations including yellow fever. *OPEN 09.30-17.00 Mon-Fri, 10.00-16.00 Sat.* Also at Heathrow Airport 0181-562 5825. *OPEN 09.00-12.30 & 14.00-16.30 Mon-Fri (appt only);* 101-102 Cheapside EC2 (5 **D2**). 0171-606 2977. *OPEN 09.00-13.00 & 14.00-16.30 (appt only).* British Airways Victoria Station SW1 (7 **B2**). 0171-233 6661. *OPEN 08.15-11.30 & 12.30-15.45 Mon-Fri (appt only). Charge.*

Unilever House 5 C3
Blackfriars EC4. 0171-822 6017. *Appt only. OPEN 15.15-16.00 Mon-Fri* for all main inoculations required for travelling. *Charge.*

Vaccinating Centre 3 G2
53 Great Cumberland Pl W1. 0171-262 6456. A centre for vaccinations and inoculations. *OPEN Mon-Fri 09.00-16.45. No appt necessary. Charge.*

Money: currency exchange

For full details on currency and exchange facilities see 'Money' section of 'Money and business services'.

Embassies & High Commissions

Embassies have consulates in the same building unless a separate address is given. All these offices deal with emigration. A full list of embassies and high commissions is in the London Diplomatic List, *available from the HMSO Bookshop, 49 High Holborn WC1 (5 **A1**).*

Australia 4 G3
Australia House, Strand WC2. 0171-379 4334.

Austria 4 B6
18 Belgrave Mews West SW1. 0171-235 3731.

Bahamas 4 C4
10 Chesterfield St W1. 0171-408 4488.

Bangladesh 3 D6
28 Queen's Gate SW7. 0171-584 0081.

Barbados 4 E2
1 Great Russell St WC1. 0171-631 4975.

Belgium 4 B6
103 Eaton Sq SW1. 0171-235 5422.

Brazil 4 A3
32 Green St W1. 0171-499 0877.
Consulate: 6 St Alban's St SW1. 4 E3
0171-930 9055.

Bulgaria 3 D6
186-188 Queen's Gate SW7. 0171-584 9400.

Canada 4 C3
MacDonald House, 1 Grosvenor Sq W1. 0171-258 6600.

Chile 1 D6
12 Devonshire St W1. 0171-580 6392.
Consulate: 0171-580 1023.

China 1 D6
49 Portland Pl W1. 0171-636 5726.

Cuba 4 F2
167 High Holborn WC1. 0171-240 2488.

Cyprus 4 B3
93 Park St W1. 0171-499 8272.

Czech Republic 3 C4
26 Kensington Palace Gdns W8. 0171-727 4918.

Denmark 5 G6
55 Sloane St SW1. 0171-235 1255.

Egypt 4 B4
26 South Audley St W1. 0171-499 2401.

Finland 4 B6
38 Chesham Pl SW1. 0171-235 9531.

France   4 **A5**
58 Knightsbridge SW1. 0171-201 1000.
Consulate: 21 Cromwell Rd SW7.   6 **D2**
0171-838 2000.

Germany   4 **B6**
23 Belgrave Sq SW1. 0171-235 5033.

Ghana
104 Highgate Hill N6. 0181-342 8686.

Greece   3 **A4**
1a Holland Park W11. 0171-221 6467.

Guyana   3 **C3**
3 Palace Ct, Bayswater Rd W2. 0171-
229 7684.

Hong Kong Government Office 4 **C3**
6 Grafton St W1. 0171-499 9821.

Hungary   4 **B6**
35 Eaton Pl SW1. 0171-235 4048.
Consulate: 35b Eaton Pl SW1.   7 **A1**
0171-235 2664.

Iceland   4 **C5**
1 Eaton Ter SW1. 0171-730 5131.

India   4 **G3**
India House, Aldwych WC2. 0171-836
8484.

Iran   3 **E5**
16 Prince's Gate SW7. 0171-223 3000.
Consulate: 50 Kensington Court   3 **C5**
W8. 0171-937 5225

Iraq   3 **D6**
21-22 Queen's Gate SW7. 0171-584
7141.

Ireland   4 **C5**
17 Grosvenor Pl SW1. 0171-235 2171.
Passport office: 0171-245 9033.

Israel   3 **C5**
2 Palace Grn W8. 0171-957 9500.

Italy   4 **C3**
14 Three Kings Yd W1. 0171-312 2200.
Passport office: 38 Eaton Pl SW1. 4 **B6**
0171-235 9371.

Jamaica   3 **D6**
2 Prince Consort Rd SW7. 0171-823 9911.

Japan   4 **C4**
101 Piccadilly W1. 0171-465 6500.

Jordan   3 **B5**
6 Upper Phillimore Gdns W8. 0171-937
3685.

Kenya   1 **D6**
45 Portland Pl W1. 0171-636 2371.

Kuwait   6 **C1**
46 Queen's Gate SW7. 0171-589 4533.

Lebanon   3 **C4**
15 Palace Gdns Mews W8. 0171-229
7265.

Luxembourg   4 **B5**
27 Wilton Cres SW1. 0171-235 6961.

Malaysia   4 **B5**
45 Belgrave Sq SW1. 0171-235 8033.

Malta   4 **C4**
36-38 Piccadilly W1. 0171-292 4800.

Mexico   4 **B5**
8 Halkin St SW1. 0171-235 6393.

Morocco   6 **C1**
49 Queen's Gate Gdns SW7. 0171-581
5001.

Nepal   3 **C4**
12a Kensington Palace Gdns W8. 0171-
229 1594.

Netherlands   6 **C1**
38 Hyde Park Gate SW7. 0171-584 5040.

New Zealand   1 **E4**
New Zealand House, 80 Haymarket
SW1. 0171-930 8422.

Nigeria   4 **F4**
Nigeria House, 9 Northumberland Av
WC2. 0171-839 1244.

Norway   4 **B6**
25 Belgrave Sq SW1. 0171-235 7151.

Pakistan   3 **G6**
36 Lowndes Sq SW1. 0171-235 2044.

Peru   3 **G6**
52 Sloane St SW1. 0171-235 1917.
Consulate: 0171-235 6867.

The Philippines   3 **C4**
9a Palace Grn W8. 0171-937 3646.

Poland   1 **D6**
47 Portland Pl W1. 0171-580 4324.
Consulate: 73 New Cavendish St   1 **D6**
W1. 0171-580 0476.

Portugal   4 **B6**
11 Belgrave Sq SW1. 0171-235 5331.
Consulate: 62 Brompton Rd SW3. 3 **F6**
0171-581 8724.

Romania   3 **C5**
4 Palace Grn, Kensington Palace Grn
W8. 0171-937 9666.

Russian Federation   3 **C4**
13 Kensington Palace Gdns W8. 0171-
229 3628.

Saudi Arabia   4 **C4**
30 Charles St W1. 0171-917 3000.

Sierra Leone   1 **D6**
33 Portland Pl W1. 0171-636 6483.

Singapore   4 **B5**
9 Wilton Cres SW1. 0171-235 5465.

Slovakia (Republic of)   3 **C4**
25 Kensington Palace Gdns W8. 0171-
243 0803.

Slovenia (Republic of)
Heather Lodge, Kingston Hill, Kingston-
upon-Thames, Surrey. 0171-495 7775.

South Africa   4 **F4**
South Africa House, Trafalgar Sq WC2.
0171-930 4488.

Spain   4 **B6**
24 Belgrave Sq SW1. 0171-235 5555.

Sri Lanka   3 **F3**
13 Hyde Park Gdns W2. 0171-262 1841.

Sweden   4 **A1**
11 Montagu Pl W1. 0171-724 2101.

Switzerland   4 **A1**
16 Montagu Pl W1. 0171-723 0701.

Tanzania   4 **C4**
43 Hertford St W1. 0171-499 8951.

Thailand   6 **C1**
30 Queen's Gate SW7. 0171-589 0173.
Trinidad & Tobago   4 **B6**
42 Belgrave Sq SW1. 0171-245 9351.
Tunisia   3 **E5**
29 Prince's Gate SW7. 0171-584 8117.
Turkey   4 **B6**
43 Belgrave Sq SW1. 0171-393 0202.
Consulate: Rutland Gdns SW7.   3 **F5**
0171-589 0949.
USA   4 **B3**
24 Grosvenor Sq W1. 0171-499 9000.
Venezuela   6 **D2**
1 Cromwell Rd SW7. 0171-584 4206.
Consulate: 56 Grafton Way W1.   1 **E5**
0171-387 6727 (Visas Dept).
Vietnam   3 **C6**
12 Victoria Rd, Kensington W8. 0171-937
1912.
Yugoslavia (Federal Republic of) 6 **B2**
5 Lexham Gdns W8. 0171-370 6105.
Zambia   3 **D5**
2 Palace Gate W8. 0171-589 6655.
Zimbabwe   4 **F3**
429 Strand WC2. 0171-836 7755.

Tourist offices

Australia
Australian Tourist Commission, 10-18
Putney Hill SW15. 0181-780 1424.
Austria   4 **C3**
Austrian National Tourist Office, 30 St
George St W1. 0171-629 0461.
Bahamas   4 **C4**
Bahama Island Tourist Office, 10
Chesterfield St W1. 0171-629 5238.
Barbados   4 **E1**
Barbados Tourist Board, 263 Tottenham
Court Rd W1. 0171-636 0090.
Belgium   4 **C2**
Belgian National Tourist Office, 29 Princes
St W1. 0171-629 1988.
Bermuda   6 **E5**
Bermuda Dept of Tourism, 1 Battersea
Church Rd SW11. 0171-734 8813.
Britain   4 **E4**
British Tourist Authority Information
Centre, 12 Lower Regent St SW1.
Personal callers only.
Canada   4 **E4**
Canadian Government Travel Bureau,
Canada House, Trafalgar Sq SW1. 0171-
930 8540.
Czech Republic/Slovakia   5 **D4**
Cedok Independent Travel, 49 Southwark
St SE1. 0171-378 6009.
Denmark   4 **A5**
The Danish Tourist Board, 55 Sloane St
SW1. 0171-734 2637.

Egypt   4 **D4**
Egyptian Tourist Centre, Egypt House,
170 Piccadilly W1. 0171-493 5282.
Finland   4 **E3**
Finnish Tourist Board, 30-35 Pall Mall
SW1. 0171-839 4048.
France   4 **D4**
French Government Tourist Office, 178
Piccadilly W1. 0891 244123.
Germany   4 **C4**
German National Tourist Office,
Nightingale House, 65 Curzon St W1.
0171-495 3990.
Gibraltar   4 **G3**
Gibraltar National Tourist Office, 179
Strand WC2. 0171-836 0777.
Greece   4 **D3**
The National Tourist Organisation of
Greece, 4 Conduit St W1. 0171-734
5997.
Holland   4 **D6**
The Netherlands National Tourist Office,
25-28 Buckingham Gate SW1. (0891)
200277.
Hong Kong   4 **E4**
Hong Kong Tourist Association, 125 Pall
Mall SW1. 0171-930 4775.
Hungary   4 **D3**
Hungarian Travel Centre, 6 Conduit St
W1. 0171-493 0263.
Iceland   1 **E5**
Iceland Tourist Information Bureau, 172
Tottenham Court Rd W1. 0171-388
5599.
Ireland   4 **C3**
Irish Tourist Office, Ireland House, 150
New Bond St W1. 0171-493 3201.
Israel   4 **D2**
Israel Government Tourist Office, 18 Great
Marlborough St W1. 0171-434 3651.
Italy   4 **C2**
Italian State Tourist Dept (ENIT), 1 Princes
St W1. 0171-355 1438.
Jamaica   3 **E6**
Jamaica Tourist Board, 1-2 Prince
Consort Rd SW7. 0171-224 0505.
Japan   4 **D3**
Japan National Tourist Organisation, 20
Savile Row W1. 0171-734 9638.
Jersey   4 **C3**
Jersey Tourist Information Office, 38
Dover St W1. 0171-493 5278.
Kenya   4 **C3**
Kenya Tourist Office, 25 Brooks Mews
W1. 0171-355 3144.
Lebanon   4 **D4**
Lebanese Tourist Office, 90 Piccadilly
W1. 0171-409 2031.
Luxembourg   4 **D3**
Luxembourg National Tourist Office,
Kingsland House, 122 Regent St W1.
0171-434 2800.

Malta 4 **C4**
Malta Government Tourist Office, 36-38 Piccadilly W1. 0171-292 4800.

Mexico 4 **E4**
Mexico Tourist Board, 60 Trafalgar Sq WC2. 0171-734 1058.

Morocco 4 **D2**
Moroccan National Tourist Office, 205 Regent St W1. 0171-437 0073.

New Zealand 4 **E4**
New Zealand Government Tourist Bureau, New Zealand House, 80 Haymarket SW1. 0171-930 8422.

Northern Ireland 4 **C4**
Northern Ireland Tourist Board, 11 Berkeley St W1. 0171-355 3040.

Norway 4 **E3**
Norwegian Tourist Board, Prince Charles House, Lower Regent St W1. 0171-839 6255.

Poland 4 **D2**
Polish Travel Office, 82 Mortimer St W1. 0171-580 8028.

Portugal 4 **D3**
Portuguese Tourist Office, 25 Sackville St W1. 0171-494 1441.

Russia (Commonwealth of Independent States)
Intourist, Intourist House, 219 Marsh Wall, Isle of Dogs E14. 0171-538 8600.

Scotland 4 **E4**
Scottish Tourist Board, 19 Cockspur St SW1. 0171-930 8661.

Slovenia
Slovenian Tourist Office, 2 Canfield Pl NW6. 0171-372 3767.

South Africa
South African Tourism Board, 5 Alt Grove SW19. 0181-944 6646.

Spain 4 **D4**
Spanish National Tourist Office, 57 St James's St SW1. 0171-499 0901.

Sweden 4 **C2**
Swedish National Tourist Office, 73 Welbeck St W1. (0891) 200280.

Switzerland 4 **E3**
Swiss National Tourist Office, Swiss Centre, Coventry St W1. 0171-734 1921.

Thailand 4 **D3**
Thailand Tourist Office, 49 Albemarle St W1. 0171-499 7679.

Tunisia 4 **B2**
Tunisian National Tourist Office, 77a Wigmore St W1. 0171-224 5561.

Turkey
Turkish Tourism and Information Office, 170-173 Piccadilly W1. 0171-734 8681.

USA 4 **B3**
United States Travel and Tourism Administration, 24 Grosvenor Sq W1. 0171-495 4466. Telephone enquiries only.

Vietnam
Vietnam Tourist Office, 93 Chiswick High Rd W4. 0181-961 0117.

Wales 4 **E4**
Wales Tourist Board, 12 Lower Regent St SW1. Personal callers only.

Zimbabwe 4 **F4**
Zimbabwe Tourist Office, 429 Strand WC2. 0171-836 7755.

Travel agents and tour operators

Travel agents, who retail package holidays and travel tickets, can be found all over London. Most belong to the Association of British Travel Agents (ABTA); if they do they can only sell the holidays of tour operators who also belong to ABTA. Buying from ABTA agents is a good idea since any complaints can be addressed to the Association if the agent and operator do not give satisfaction. All-inclusive tours sold by ABTA tour operators are covered by a bond to safeguard holiday-makers' money. Agents and operators advertise in newspapers and magazines, and operators' brochures are available at travel agents. You can often book directly with the operator. Agents also sell insurance and travellers' cheques.

Association of British Travel 4 **D1**
Agents
55 Newman St W1. 0171-637 2444.

London Tourist Board 7 **B1**
Information Centre
Victoria Station Forecourt SW1. Personal callers only. Information on travel and holidays in Britain.

Thomas Cook 4 **C4**
45 Berkeley St W1. 0171-499 4000. The biggest travel agency and also a tour operator. Sell their own travellers' cheques.

Airports

London City Airport
King George V Dock, Connaught Rd E16. 0171-474 5555.

London Gatwick Airport
West Sussex. (01293) 535353.

London Heathrow Airport
Bath Rd, Heathrow, Middx. 0181-759 4321.

London Stansted Airport
Stansted, Essex. (01279) 680500.

Luton Airport
Luton, Beds. (01582) 405100.

Southend Airport
Southend-on-Sea, Essex. (01702) 340201.

Westland Heliport
Lombard Rd SW11. 0171-228 0181.

Air services

Check-in facilities for most major airlines are at the airports. For information contact airline booking offices. See telephone directories for details.
British Airways　　　　　　　　**7 B2**
Central London Air Terminal, Victoria Station SW1. 0171-834 9411. *OPEN 06.00-20.00 Mon-Sun.*

Airport bus services

London Transport
A1 Heathrow, Cromwell Rd, Knightsbridge, Victoria.
A2 Heathrow, Paddington, Marble Arch, Baker St, Euston, Russell Sq.
Flightline
747 Gatwick, Heathrow, Luton, Stansted.
757 Luton, Victoria.
777 Gatwick, Victoria.

Airport river services

See 'Transport in London'.

Cheap air tickets

Considerable savings can be made on full price air tickets – any travel agent can give details of arrangements which vary according to destination. ABC (Advance Booking Charter) and APEX (Advance Purchase Excursion) return tickets are available to many worldwide destinations including N. America and Australia; tickets for these must be bought 21 or 30 days in advance and neither outward nor return dates can be altered. The classified ads in Time Out are a source of other less official cheap flights. If you are a student, special rates are available – check with the student travel office (see 'Student London').

Airlines

Most of the world's airlines operate services to London and many have booking offices here (listed in the telephone directory). Travel agents will also make bookings.

British Airways Sales Shops
0181-897 4000. British Airways sell tickets and make bookings for any airline that belongs to IATA (International Air Transport Association). If you book by phone *(24 hrs)*, you can have your ticket sent by mail or collect and pay for it at one of the Sales Shops.
101-102 Cheapside EC2.　　　　　**5 D2**
OPEN 09.00-17.30 Mon-Fri (from 09.30 Wed).
156 Regent St W1.　　　　　　　**4 D3**
OPEN 09.30-18.00 Mon-Fri, 10.00-16.00 Sat.
Victoria BR Station SW1.　　　　**7 B2**
OPEN 06.00-20.00 Mon-Fri.
200 Buckingham Palace Rd SW1　**7 B2**
OPEN 09.00-17.15 Mon-Fri (business travel only).

Specialist air and helicopter charter

All the big airlines also operate charter flights for all purposes, subject to availability.
Air Amiga Ltd
Stapleford Aerodrome, Stapleford Tawney, Essex. (01708) 688361. One Bell Jet Ranger, three twin Squirrels, one Long Ranger. Can supply many sizes of aircraft.
Air London International
Mack House, Aviation Ct, Gatwick Rd, Crawley, W. Sussex. 0171-378 6935. Helicopter and aircraft charter. Will supply almost any size of aircraft.
Alan Mann Helicopters
Fairoaks Airport, Chobham, Surrey. (01276) 856177. Operate a fleet of four 4-seater Jet Ranger helicopters, two twin Squirrels, one single squirrel and one Bell 47 for training.
Cabair
Elstree Aerodrome, Elstree, Herts. 0181-953 4411. Piper, Drummond-Kougar, Jet Ranger and Navajo air-taxi operators and helicopter charter.
Instone Air Transport　　　　　**5 E4**
Bridge House, 4 Borough High St SE1. 0171-407 4411. Freight specialists, air brokers and aviation consultants.
Lynton Aviation
Denham Airfield, Uxbridge, Middx. (01203) 304231. Fleet of helicopters and jets for all types of charter.

Accommodation

Hotel booking agents

Accommodation Service of   7 **C1**
the London Tourist Board
London Tourist Board Information Centre, Victoria Station Forecourt SW1. (0839) 123435. Bookings on arrival. *OPEN 08.00-19.00 Mon-Sun, reduced hours in winter.* Credit card hotline: 0171-824 8844 *(09.30-17.30 Mon-Fri).*

Expotel Hotel Reservations
Kingsgate House, Kingsgate Pl NW6. 0171-328 1790. Worldwide hotel and conference booking service. *OPEN 08.30-18.30 Mon-Fri, 13.00-16.00 Sat. Free.*

Hotel Booking Service   4 **D3**
4 New Burlington Place W1. 0171-437 5052. Excellent and knowledgeable service to business firms and general public. All types of hotel reservations in London, UK and worldwide. *OPEN 09.30-17.30 Mon-Fri. Free.*

Hotel Finders
20 Bell La NW4. 0181-202 7000. All kinds of hotels. *OPEN 09.00-17.30 Mon-Fri, 09.00-13.00 Sat. Free.*

Hotelpacc Group Services Ltd   4 **B5**
40-46 Headfort Pl SW1. 0171-235 9696. Hotel accommodation for groups (10 people or more) in London, UK and worldwide. Facilities for coach and tour operators and conference organisers. *OPEN 09.30-18.00 Mon-Fri. Free.*

Hotel Reservations Centre   4 **C6**
10 Buckingham Palace Rd SW1. 0171-828 2425. *OPEN 09.00-18.00 Mon-Fri* for bookings all over Britain. Also at Victoria Station, Platforms 7 & 8 (7 **B1**). 0171-828 1849. *Free.*

Thomas Cook   7 **B1**
All kinds of hotels in London, Britain and worldwide. Sales desk at Victoria Station, Platform 9/10. 0171-828 4646. *OPEN 07.00-23.00 Mon-Sun.* Also desks at the following stations: South Kensington, Earls Court, Euston, Charing Cross, King's Cross and Paddington. Also at Gatwick Airport. *Charge.*

Note

It is compulsory for hotels to display their prices. Visitors should make sure exactly what is included in the price, ie breakfast, VAT, service, etc. Many hotels have facilities for conferences, banquets, receptions etc, but in each entry we refer to this as conference facilities. Capacity, where given in numbers, is approximate at the upper end of the scale – check first. Small conference facilities means capacity for 20 people or less. Large conference facilities means the capacity is flexible according to the requirements; air cond = air conditioning, conf cap = conference capacity, P = parking, s pool = swimming pool.

Hotels: top price

Over £120 per night, single room with bath or shower. Prices should be checked because they may vary considerably within the category and breakfast, VAT and service may not be included in the charge.

Athenaeum   4 **C4**
116 Piccadilly W1. 0171-499 3464. Comfortable and friendly traditional hotel with modern facilities. 156 rooms all with bath and TV. Four conf rooms. Air cond. No-smoking rooms. Health spa. Also fully serviced apartments. A.Ax.Dc.V.

The Beaufort   6 **E1**
33 Beaufort Gdns SW3. 0171-584 5252. Beautifully decorated small Victorian hotel. 28 rooms. Air cond. Health club membership. Video. A.Ax.Dc.V.

Belgravia Sheraton   6 **G1**
20 Chesham Pl SW1. 0171-235 6040. Small luxury hotel, personal service. 90 rooms. Health club. Air cond. Conf cap 20. A.Ax.Dc.V.

Berkeley   4 **B5**
Wilton Pl SW1. 0171-235 6000. Modern building. Interior stylish and elegant. French restaurant. 160 rooms. TV. S pool. Air cond. P. Conf cap 200. A.Ax.Dc.V.

Britannia   4 **B3**
Grosvenor Sq W1. 0171-629 9400. International hotel in listed building. Three restaurants. 318 rooms. Satellite/cable TV. 24-hour business centre. Fitness centre. Conference capacity 100. Air cond. A.Ax.Dc.V.

Brown's   4 **C3**
Albemarle St W1. 0171-493 6020. Traditional English country house atmosphere. Courteous service. 116 rooms all

with TV and bath. Air Cond. 7 conf rooms. A.Ax.Dc.V.

Cadogan 4 **A6**
75 Sloane St SW1. 0171-235 7141. Comfortable and friendly. Restaurant. 69 rooms all with TV and bath. Small conf facilities. A.Ax.Dc.V.

Chelsea Hotel 4 **A6**
17 Sloane St SW1. 0171-235 4377. Modern hotel. 'First Floor' restaurant. King-size beds. 224 rooms all with satellite TV and bath. Conf cap 100. Air cond. A.Ax.Dc.V.

Claridge's 4 **C3**
Brook St W1. 0171-629 8860. Traditional luxury and lavish atmosphere. Haute cuisine in the restaurant and good smørgasbørd in the Causerie. 189 rooms. Secretarial service. A.Ax.Dc.V.

Connaught 4 **C3**
Carlos Pl W1. 0171-499 7070. Dignified and distinguished. Excellent service. Restaurant with unrivalled reputation. 90 rooms all with bath and TV. Book well in advance. A.Ax.Dc.V.

Conrad 6 **C6**
Chelsea Harbour SW10. 0171-823 3000. Modern luxury hotel with wonderful harbour views. 160 rooms all with TV and bath. Restaurant and bar. Fitness centre. S pool. Air cond. P. Conf facilities. A.Ax.Dc.V.

Dorchester 4 **B4**
Park La W1. 0171-629 8888. Luxury with courteous, efficient service. Dinner dances in the Terrace Restaurant. Grill room and Cantonese restaurant. Good food. 244 rooms. 52 suites. P (limited). Conf cap 500. A.Ax.Dc.V.

Dukes 4 **D4**
35 St James's Pl SW1. 0171-491 4840. Unique situation on secluded gas-lit courtyard. 62 rooms including 26 suites all with bath and TV. Banqueting and conference facilities for 100. Air-conditioned. A.Ax.Dc.V.

Four Seasons 4 **B4**
Hamilton Pl, Park La W1. 0171-499 0888. Luxurious modern hotel, with every comfort. Two haute cuisine restaurants. Views over Hyde Park. 227 rooms. Fitness centre. P. Air cond. Conf facilities. Secretarial services. A.Ax.Dc.V.

Grosvenor House 4 **B3**
Park La W1. 0171-499 6363. Unobtrusive luxury and service. 453 rooms, 70 suites, 151 apartments. Air cond. S pool, saunas, gymnasium, health club and beauty salon. Banqueting and conf cap 1500. Bookshop, boutique, garage and restaurants. A.Ax.Dc.V.

Hilton (Park Lane) 4 **B4**
22 Park La W1. 0171-493 8000. Modern luxurious hotel overlooking Hyde Park. Good restaurant with views and dancing. 452 rooms. Air cond. P. Steam room, fitness centre and beauty salon. Conf cap 1000. A.Ax.Dc.V.

Hilton (Regent's Park) 4 **N4**
18 Lodge Rd, St John's Wood NW8. 0171-722 7722. Modern hotel overlooking Lord's Cricket Ground. Minski's Restaurant and Japanese Restaurant. 377 rooms. P. Air cond. Conf facilities. A.Ax.Dc.V.

Holiday Inn King's Cross 2 **B4**
1 King's Cross Rd WC1. 0171-833 3900. 405 rooms all with bath and TV. No-smoking rooms. Conf cap for up to 200. Health and leisure club with sauna, solarium, fitness centre, beauty therapy room. S pool. Air cond. A.Ax.Dc.V.

Holiday Inn Mayfair 4 **C4**
3 Berkeley St W1. 0171-493 8282. Modern hotel with elegant interior. 186 rooms. Conf cap 50. A.Ax.Dc.V.

Howard 5 **A3**
Temple Pl WC2. 0171-836 3555. Modern luxury with traditional design. 135 rooms. Air cond. P. Conf cap 200. A.Ax.Dc.V.

Hyatt-Carlton Tower 6 **F1**
Cadogan Pl SW1. 0171-235 1234. International standards of luxury and service in this sophisticated hotel. Good food in the Chelsea Room and the Rib Room. 224 rooms. Air cond. Health club. P. Conf facilities. A.Ax.Dc.V.

Hyde Park 4 **A5**
66 Knightsbridge SW1. 0171-235 2000. Traditional standards of luxury and comfort. Restaurant. 186 rooms. Fitness centre. Air cond. A.Ax.Dc.V.

Inter-Continental 4 **B5**
1 Hamilton Pl W1. 0171-409 3131. Good modern hotel. Central location. 460 rooms. Two restaurants. Air cond. Sauna, health club. P. Conf facilities. A.Ax.Dc.V.

Marriott (Marble Arch) 4 **A2**
134 George St W1. 0171-723 1277. Newly renovated hotel with fitness centre and sauna. Air cond. P. 240 rooms. Conf cap 150. A.Ax.Dc.V.

May Fair Inter-Continental London 4 **C4**
Stratton St W1. 0171-629 7777. Traditional hotel with modern amenities. Air cond. S pool. Theatre. 287 rooms. Conf cap 300. A.Ax.Dc.V.

Meridien Hotel 4 **D3**
21 Piccadilly W1. 0171-734 8000. Deluxe hotel with own health club attached. Three restaurants. 263 rooms. Air cond. Conf facilities. A.Ax.Dc.V.

Ritz   4 **D4**
Piccadilly W1. 0171-493 8181. Grandeur and elegance. Period rooms. Unobtrusive efficient service. Beautiful restaurant. 24-hr currency exchange. Babysitting. 129 rooms. Air cond. A.Ax.Dc.V.

Royal Garden   3 **C5**
2-24 Kensington High St W8. 0171-937 8000. Comfortably modern, pleasantly run. Two restaurants. Good food. 403 rooms. Valet and secretarial services. Conf cap 500. A.Ax.Dc.V.

Royal Lancaster   3 **E3**
Lancaster Ter W2. 0171-262 6737. A tall modern block geared to business people and conferences. Magnificent views over Kensington Gardens and Hyde Park. Choice of restaurants: La Rosette specialises in seasonal French dishes, The Park Restaurant offers British cuisine, Pavement Cafe (international brasserie), Nipa Thai (Thai food). 418 rooms. Air cond. P. Valet, secretarial and interpreting services. Conf cap 1000. A.Ax.Dc.V.

Savoy   4 **G3**
Strand WC2. 0171-836 4343. World-famous in reputation and clientele. Edwardian in atmosphere and service, yet still faultlessly up-to-date, having recently undergone major refurbishment. Fitness centre. S pool. Air cond. 202 rooms. 24-hr currency exchange. Car hire. A.Ax.Dc.V.

Scandic Crown, Nelson Dock
265 Rotherhithe St SE16. 0171-231 1001. Luxury hotel overlooking the River Thames. 390 rooms with bath and satellite TV. Restaurant. Fitness and leisure club with sauna, solarium and gymnasium. S pool. P. Conf facilities. Hotel riverboat to Canary Wharf. A.Ax.Dc.V.

Selfridge   4 **B2**
Orchard St W1. 0171-408 2080. Traditional comfort plus modern facilities. All bedrooms have air cond, bath, TV, radio. Two restaurants. 298 rooms. Conf facilities. A.Ax.Dc.V.

Sheraton Park Tower   4 **A5**
101 Knightsbridge SW1. 0171-235 0172. Modern hotel with beautiful glass-encased restaurant. P. 295 rooms including 19 suites. Air cond. Secretarial service. Conf cap 250. A.Ax.Dc.V.

Stafford   4 **D4**
16-18 St James's Pl SW1. 0171-493 0111. Elegant and comfortable. Good restaurant. Private dining rooms. 74 rooms (12 converted to carriage house rooms). Small conf facilities. A.Ax.Dc.V.

Westbury   4 **C3**
New Bond St W1. 0171-629 7755.

Modern with American standards of luxury and efficiency. Restaurant. 244 rooms. Conf cap 100. A.Ax.Dc.V.

Hotels: medium price

£60-£120 per night, single room with bath or shower. Continental breakfast and inclusive of VAT and service charge. Prices should be checked as they may vary considerably within the category.

Basil Street Hotel   4 **A5**
Basil St SW3. 0171-581 3311. Victorian decor, country house atmosphere. Women's Club. 95 rooms. Small conf facilities. A.Ax.Dc.V.

Blakes   4 **C3**
33 Roland Gdns SW7. 0171-370 6701. Informal atmosphere. Showbiz clientele. Each room individually and luxuriously decorated. 50 rooms including 16 suites. Air cond. A.Ax.Dc.V.

Bloomsbury Crest   1 **G5**
Coram St WC1. 0171-837 1200. Modern tourist hotel. Coffee shop and restaurant. Conf facilities. 284 rooms. P. A.Ax.Dc.V.

Bonnington   4 **F1**
92 Southampton Row WC1. 0171-242 2828. Modernised well-established hotel. Restaurant. 215 rooms. Conf facilities. A.Ax.Dc.V.

Charing Cross   4 **F4**
Strand WC2. 0171-839 7282. Spacious hotel. Victorian, but modernised and comfortable. Cocktail bar and carvery. 218 rooms. Conf facilities. A.Ax.Dc.V.

Cumberland   4 **A2**
Great Cumberland Pl, Marble Arch W1. 0171-262 1234. Large, busy hotel. Valeting service. Coffee shop and 3 restaurants. 900 rooms. Conf cap 500. A.Ax.Dc.V.

De Vere Park   3 **D5**
1 De Vere Gdns, 60 Hyde Park Gate W8. 0171-584 0051. Victorian, spacious and modernised. Thai restaurant. 92 rooms. A.Ax.Dc.V.

Drury Lane Moathouse   4 **F2**
Drury La WC2. 0171-208 9988. Ultra-modern hotel in the heart of theatreland. Maudie's Restaurant is good. 163 rooms. Air cond. P. Conf cap 30. A.Ax.Dc.V.

Durrants   4 **B2**
George St W1. 0171-935 8131. Elegant family-owned hotel. 96 rooms including 3 suites. Restaurant. Conf facilities. A.Ax.V.

Forte Crest   1 **D6**
Regent's Park
Carburton St W1. 0171-388 2300. Modern hotel. Restaurant. 317 rooms all with bath. P. Conf facilities. A.Ax.Dc.V.

Forum Hotel   **6 C2**
97 Cromwell Rd SW7. 0171-370 5757. Modern hotel. Shops. 910 rooms with bath. 3 restaurants, coffee shop, fitness room. P. Conf facilities. A.Ax.Dc.V.

Gloucester   **6 C2**
Harrington Gdns SW7. 0171-373 6030. Modern large hotel. Air cond. 549 rooms. Conf cap 500. A.Ax.Dc.V.

Great Northern   **1 G3**
King's Cross N1. 0171-837 5454. Spacious, comfortable old-style hotel. Modern decor. Coffee house. 90 rooms. Conf facilities. A.Ax.Dc.V.

Great Western Royal   **3 E2**
Praed St W2. 0171-723 8064. Traditional, spacious and modernised. Efficient service. Restaurant. 238 rooms. Conf facilities for up to 400. A.Ax.Dc.V.

Grosvenor   **7 B1**
101 Buckingham Palace Rd SW1. 0171-834 9494. The building is a fine example of French Renaissance-style architecture in Britain. 366 rooms with bath. Conf cap 200. A.Ax.Dc.V.

Hilton (Kensington)
179-199 Holland Park Av W11. 0171-603 3355. Modern, well-furnished building with sandstone finish and smoked glass windows. Shops. Entertainment. 606 rooms with bath. Air cond. P. Conf cap 300. A.Ax.Dc.V.

Hotel Russell   **1 G5**
Russell Sq WC1. 0171-837 6470. Victorian splendour. Shop. 328 rooms all with bath and TV. Two restaurants. 24-hr currency exchange. Conf facilities. Special weekend rates throughout the year. A.Ax.Dc.V.

Jurys Kensington   **3 D6**
109-113 Queensgate SW7. 0171-589 6300. Irish owned hotel refurbished to a high standard of comfort. 171 rooms, all with private bath. 24-hr room service. Restaurant. A.Ax.Dc.V.

Kensington Close   **3 C6**
Wright's La W8. 0171-937 8170. Good-value hotel with plenty of facilities. Two restaurants. S pool, saunas, sun-beds, gym and squash. Garden. 530 rooms. Conf facilities. A.Ax.Dc.V.

Kensington Palace   **3 D5**
De Vere Gdns W8. 0171-937 8121. Restful and modernised traditional hotel. Kensington Restaurant. 298 rooms. Large conf facilities. A.Ax.Dc.V.

London Embassy Hotel   **3 C3**
150 Bayswater Rd W2. 0171-229 1212. Modern hotel overlooking Kensington Gardens. Restaurant and cocktail bar. 193 rooms all with TV. P. Conf facilities. A.Ax.Dc.V.

Holiday Inn Garden Court   **4 C2**
Welbeck St W1. 0171-935 4442. Well-appointed, friendly and modern. 143 rooms. A.Ax.Dc.V.

London International Olympia
380 Kensington High St W14. 0171-603 3333. Large, modern hotel, next to Olympia and near the motorail terminal. Brasserie/restaurant. 405 rooms with bath. P (charge). Conf facilities. A.Ax.Dc.V.

Marriott (Regent's Park)   **1 A1**
128 King Henry's Rd NW3. 0171-722 7711. Modern building outside the centre but within easy access. S pool, sauna, gym, air cond, in-house movies. P. 303 rooms. Executive floor with own check-in facilities. Conf cap 400. A.Ax.Dc.V.

Mountbatten   **4 F2**
Monmouth St WC2. 0171-836 4300. Theatreland hotel with luxurious marble interior. Valet service. Restaurant, cocktail and wine bars. 127 rooms including 7 suites. Conf facilities. A.Ax.Dc.V.

Norfolk   **6 D2**
Harrington Rd SW7. 0171-344 9955. Elegantly modernised Victorian hotel close to the Natural History Museum and the Victoria & Albert Museum. 96 rooms all with spa baths. 25 air-conditioned executive rooms. Gym. Brasserie, winery, tavern. Conf cap 60. A.Ax.Dc.V.

Park Court   **3 D3**
75 Lancaster Gate W2. 0171-402 4272. Full range of services for guests with children. 390 rooms with bath. Conf facilities. A.Ax.Dc.V.

Regency Hotel   **6 D2**
100 Queen's Gate SW7. 0171-370 4595. Traditional, elegant and courteous. 210 rooms. Bar. International restaurant. Conf cap 200. Health spa. TV. A.Ax.Dc.V.

Regent Palace Hotel   **4 D3**
12 Sherwood St W1. 0171-734 7000. At the heart of the West End. Carvery, bars. 891 rooms. A.Ax.Dc.V.

Rembrandt   **6 D2**
11 Thurloe Pl SW7. 0171-589 8100. Modernised, well run. Restaurant with carvery. Conservatory. Romanesque health club. 200 rooms. Conf cap 200. A.Ax.Dc.V.

Royal Court   **6 G2**
Sloane Sq SW1. 0171-730 9191. Attractive, luxurious, country house style hotel. 102 rooms all with bath or shower. 'No. 12 Nomads Feast' international restaurant. Wine bar and tavern. A.Ax.Dc.V.

Royal Horseguards   **4 F4**
2 Whitehall Ct SW1. 0171-839 3400.

Victorian building facing across the Thames to the Festival Hall. Traditionally furnished and comfortable. 376 rooms all with bath and TV. Restaurant. Conf facilities. A.Ax.Dc.V.

Royal Trafalgar   **4 E3**
Whitcomb St WC2. 0171-930 4477. Hotel behind the National Gallery. Restaurant. Has its own pub 'The Battle of Trafalgar'. 108 rooms. Special weekend rates. A.Ax.Dc.V.

Sherlock Holmes   **1 B6**
108 Baker St W1. 0171-486 6161. Spacious modern hotel with its name as a theme. 126 rooms with bath. Restaurant. Conf facilities. A.Ax.Dc.V.

Strand Palace   **4 G3**
372 Strand WC2. 0171-836 8080. Large, international style hotel on the Strand. 783 rooms. Three restaurants. 24-hr currency exchange. Babysitting. Conf facilities. A.Ax.Dc.V.

Swallow International   **6 B2**
147 Cromwell Rd SW5. 0171-370 4200. Modern hotel with restaurant and the Fountain Brasserie. 417 rooms. P. Conf facilities for 200. Pool, sauna and gym. A.Ax.Dc.V.

Tara (Copthorne)   **3 C6**
Scarsdale Pl, Wright's La W8. 0171-937 7211. Modern hotel. Four restaurants. 825 rooms with bath. P. Conf facilities. Ten rooms with disabled facilities. A.Ax.Dc.V.

Tower Thistle   **5 G4**
St Katharine's Way E1. 0171-481 2575. Large and comfortable modern hotel next to Tower Bridge and the Tower of London. Three restaurants, one overlooking the river. Discotheque. 803 rooms. Air cond. P. Conf facilities. A.Ax.Dc.V.

Waldorf   **4 G3**
Aldwych WC2. 0171-836 2400. Edwardian-style elegance. Suitable for the business executive. Modernised and central. Brasserie, restaurant, wine bar, tea dances in the 'Palm Court' *Sat-Sun*. 292 rooms. Conf facilities. A.Ax.Dc.V.

White House   **1 D5**
Albany St NW1. 0171-387 1200. Former apartment hotel now offering full service. Overlooks Regent's Park. First class public rooms. Restaurant with good reputation. Wine bar. Coffee shop. 577 rooms. Conf facilities. A.Ax.Dc.V.

White's   **3 D3**
90-92 Lancaster Gate W2. 0171-262 2711. Charming, balustraded exterior, unobtrusive and modernised. Overlooks Hyde Park. Restaurant. 55 rooms. Air cond. P. Conf facilities. A.Ax.Dc.V.

Hotels: modest price

£30-£60 per night, single room. The following hotels offer particularly good accommodation for this price range, and all have several in-room facilities (TV, direct-dial telephone, tea & coffee-making facilities, etc). Some rooms may be more expensive; breakfast, VAT and service are not always included.
For cheaper accommodation, see p202-3 and 'hostels' in 'Student London'.

Academy   **1 E5**
17-21 Gower St WC1. 0171-631 4115. Smart and civilised, excellent service. 33 rooms, most with private bath. Restaurant and cocktail bar. Patio garden. A.Ax.Dc.V.

Aster House   **6 D2**
3 Sumner Pl SW7. 0171-581 5888. English country house style, family-run. 12 rooms with bath or shower. Conservatory, garden. A.Ax.Dc.V.

Blandford Hotel   **4 B1**
80 Chiltern St W1. 0171-486 3103. Small comfortable hotel. Good value. 33 rooms all with bath and TV. P. A.Ax.Dc.V.

Hart House   **4 B2**
51 Gloucester Pl, Portman Sq W1. 0171-935 2288. Small, family-run tourist hotel. 16 rooms, 13 with private bath. A.Ax.Dc.V.

Hotel 167   **6 B3**
167 Old Brompton Rd SW5. 0171-373 0672. Small hotel with bold modern decor. 19 rooms, all with private bath. A.Ax.Dc.V.

Ibis Hotel   **1 E4**
3 Cardington St NW1. 0171-388 7777. Part of a French-run chain. Good value, quality hotel. 300 rooms all with bath and TV. Restaurant and bar. Conf cap 130. P. A.Ax.Dc.V.

La Reserve   **6 B5**
422-428 Fulham Rd SW6. 0171-385 8561. Designer decor and sophistication. 41 rooms, all with private bath. Bar and restaurant. P. A.Ax.Dc.V.

Hotels near Heathrow Airport

All these are air conditioned and provide free transport to and from the airport. Prices vary considerably. £70-£120 per night, single room with bath or shower. Breakfast is often extra. Inclusive of VAT and service charge.

Ariel
Bath Rd, Hayes, Middx. 0181-759 2552. Circular in design. Restaurant *OPEN all*

day. 186 rooms with bath and TV. Conf facilities. A.Ax.Dc.V.

Arlington
Shepiston La, Hayes, Middx. 0181-573 6162. Transit hotel for the airport. Restaurant. 80 rooms. Bar. Special week-end rates. A.Ax.Dc.V.

Edwardian International
140 Bath Rd, Hayes, Middx. 0181-759 6311. Luxurious hotel. Two restaurants. Health club. S pool. Business centre. 460 rooms all with bath and TV. P. Conf facilities. A.Ax.Dc.V.

Excelsior
Bath Rd, West Drayton, Middx. 0181-759 6611. Fully soundproofed. Indoor pool. Three restaurants. *24-hr* service. 839 rooms. Health and fitness centre. Conf facilities. A.Ax.Dc.V.

Heathrow Park Hotel
Bath Rd, Longford, Middx. 0181-759 2400. New hotel built as near as possible to the airport and geared to cater for transit visitors. Restaurant. Bar. Coffee shop. 306 rooms. Conf cap 600. A.Ax.Dc.V.

Holiday Inn Heathrow
Stockley Rd, West Drayton, Middx. (01895) 445555. Modern hotel with 9-hole golf course, pool, sauna, gym. Two restaurants. All rooms have bath, TV, telephone, radio, in-house movies. 380 rooms. Conf facilities. A.Ax.Dc.V.

Master Robert
366 Great West Rd, Hounslow, Middx. 0181-570 6261. 3 miles from Heathrow, 10 miles from central London. 100 rooms with bath and TV. Conf facilities. Restaurant and cocktail bar. A.Ax.Dc.V.

Forte Crest
Sipson Rd, West Drayton, Middx. 0181-759 2323. All rooms have bath, TV, telephone, mini bars, babysitting service. 572 rooms. Three restaurants. 33 conference rooms. A.Ax.Dc.V.

Ramada Hotel
Bath Rd, Hounslow, Middx. 0181-897 6363. Pleasant modern exterior. Leisure centre, restaurant, bar. 635 rooms with bath, TV, mini bar, air cond. Conf facilities. A.Ax.Dc.V.

Sheraton Heathrow
Colnbrook by-pass, West Drayton, Middx. 0181-759 2424. Recently refurbished, with a well-designed interior. Restaurant, bar, shops. Free transport links with central London three times a day. Also transportation to Heathrow airport terminals. 431 rooms, all with TV and soundproofing. Conf facilities. A.Ax.Dc.V.

Sheraton Skyline
Bath Rd, Hayes, Middx. 0181-759 2535. Luxurious hotel. Quadrangular in design.

Gourmet restaurant. S pool, fitness centre, babysitting service. 353 sound-proofed rooms. 5 suites. A.Ax.Dc.V.

Hotels near Gatwick Airport

All these provide free transport to and from the airport. £70-£120 per night, single room with bath or shower. Breakfast is often extra. Inclusive of VAT and service charge.

Chequers Thistle Hotel
Brighton Rd, Horley, Surrey. (01293) 786992. Country house style hotel. Restaurant, snack bar. 78 rooms. Conf facilities. A.Ax.Dc.V.

Holiday Inn
Langley Dri, Crawley, W. Sussex. (01293) 529991. Modern, efficient airport hotel recently refurbished. Two restaurants, bar. 207 rooms. Fitness centre. S pool. Conf cap 230. A.Ax.Dc.V.

George Hotel
High St, Crawley, W. Sussex. (01293) 524215. 15thC building retaining original features yet providing modern, well-equipped bedrooms in the rear extension. Restaurant. 86 rooms. Conf facilities. A.Ax.Dc.V.

Post House
Povey Cross Rd, Horley, Surrey. (01293) 771621. New, spacious hotel. Heated outdoor s pool. Restaurant. 210 rooms. P. Conf facilities. A.Ax.Dc.V.

Bed and breakfast/ guest houses

Staying at a bed and breakfast is a good way to encounter English family life. They are good value; breakfasts are traditional English, and your host can give you tips on sightseeing. Many are situated in streets around main line stations, but also scan notice boards outside newsagents and look in local papers or make a reservation through Bed-and-Breakfast (GB), PO Box 66, 94 Bell St, Henley-on-Thames, Oxon. (01491) 578803. There are also hundreds of small guest houses, many of which are to be found in Victoria, Earl's Court, Bayswater and Bloomsbury. It is much easier to find a room in winter than in summer. Beware of hotel touts who operate at the main stations, particularly Victoria; the accommodation they offer is usually inadequate and expensive.

Self-catering

Self-catering apartments are an ideal alternative to hotels if you are staying in London for a longer period. An apartment gives you flexibility and privacy and the use of a kitchen means you save on restaurant bills. You can choose between holiday lets (short-term accommodation in a rented flat) and serviced apartments which offer a higher level of facilities (eg maid, reception, security). The best way of finding such accommodation is through an agency:

Holiday Flat Services Ltd
140 Cromwell Rd SW7. 0171-935 2412. Serviced apartments and privately-owned holiday lets. Short or long-term let. All standards from economy to deluxe.

London Tourist Flats
17 St Mary's Rd SW19. 0181-947 0573. Studios, one-bedroom and two-bedroom self-contained apartments in the Wimbledon area. Minimum two-week let.

Number One Apartments   6 **C2**
1 Harrington Gdns SW7. 0171-370 4044. Studio, one-bedroom and two-bedroom serviced apartments in Kensington. Daily maid service, porterage, 24-hr reception and security. Short or long-term let.

Another option is a self-catering holiday resort:

Lawrence Wharf
273-301 Rotherhithe St SE16. 0171-815 0815. London's first self-catering holiday resort situated in Docklands overlooking the Thames. 139 luxury one, two and three-bedroom apartments. Short or long-term let. Guests can share the facilities of the Scandic Crown International Hotel at a small charge.

Camping sites

Certainly the cheapest accommodation in London, camping can provide a pleasant alternative for the visitor. Book in advance in summer.

Abbey Wood Caravan Club
Federation Rd, Abbey Wood SE2. 0181-310 2233. Electric hook-ups available for caravans. Pitch your own tent *(Easter-October). OPEN all year.*

Crystal Palace Caravan Club
Crystal Palace Pde SE19. 0181-778 7155. Pitch your own tent. *OPEN all year.*

Lee Valley Leisure Complex
Picketts Lock Centre, Picketts Lock La N9. 0181-345 6666. Pitch your own tent. *OPEN all year.*

Tent City Acton
Old Oak Common Lane W3. 0181-743 5708. Shared accommodation in large tents or pitches for your own tent. Free facilities and entertainments. Profits to charity. *OPEN Jun-mid Sep.*

Tent City Hackney
Millfields Rd E5. 0181-985 7656. Pitch your own tent. Comprehensive facilities: free kitchen, entertainment, baggage storage, barbeques. Can accommodate up to 450 people. *OPEN Jun-Aug.*

Property Rental

Publications like the Evening Standard, the Times, Loot and Time Out are good sources for advertisements for flats and houses to rent, as are local newsagents' windows and local papers.

Flats and Flat-sharing

Agencies will help you find a flat or a bed-sit, a place in a ready established flat, or else find you a kindred spirit to search with. They do try to match up carefully according to age, interests, background, etc and may charge a fee for their services.

Capital Radio   1 **E5**
Euston Tower, Euston Rd NW1. 0171-608 6080. Flatshare list available from the foyer at *16.00 every Fri.*

Flatmates   6 **E2**
313 Brompton Rd SW3. 0171-589 5491.

Jenny Jones   4 **C2**
40 South Molton St W1. 0171-493 4801.

London Accommodation Bureau   3 **C3**
102 Queensway W2. 0171-727 5062.

Luxury Rentals

The following agencies specialise in good quality luxury properties and company lets.

Benham & Reeves Residential Letting Office
51-53 Heath St NW3. 0171-435 9681. Furnished and unfurnished flats and houses.

Chestertons Residential   3 **B5**
Off Hornton St, Kensington High St W8. 0171-937 7260. And in Mayfair, Hyde Park, Notting Hill Gate, Chelsea, Pimlico.

Claridges
1109 Finchley Rd NW11. 0181-455 0007. Furnished and unfurnished properties. Visitors and company lets.

Cluttons   **7 A2**
7 Lower Sloane St SW1. 0171-824 8822. Mostly unfurnished properties.

Marsh & Parsons   **3 B4**
9 Kensington Church St W8. 0171-937 0577. This is their Head Office. There are several other branches in West London.

Mainly deal in the sale of property but sometimes in rented property as well. Normally operate very much on a local basis and they advertise in the local papers which is a good source for assessing the market in any particular area.

Sport, health and fitness

Sports centres

Britannia Leisure Centre   **2 G2**
40 Hyde Rd N1. 0171-729 4485. Large indoor centre. Squash, badminton, weight-training, table tennis, basketball, volleyball, martial arts, swimming pool with wave machine and slide, sauna, sunbed, spa bath. Also tennis courts, and five-a-side courts, all floodlit. Tuition in most activities, over-50s classes, clubs for children and adults. Facilities for the disabled. *No membership requirement.*

Brixton Recreation Centre
27 Brixton Station Rd SW9. 0171-926 9780. Indoor sports centre. Squash, badminton, weight-training, swimming pool, bowls, sauna, solarium. Classes plus social and cultural activities. *No membership requirement. Reduced rates 14.00-16.00.*

Chelsea Sports Centre   **6 E3**
Chelsea Manor St SW3. 0171-352 6985. Facilities for swimming, sub aqua, badminton, table tennis, yoga, volleyball, weight-training, aerobics, roller-skating. Gymnasium, aerobics studio, solarium. Sports injuries clinic. *No membership requirement.*

Crystal Palace National Sports Centre
Crystal Palace SE19. 0181-778 0131. Opened in 1964, this is the largest multi-sports centre in the country. Superb facilities for over 50 different sports include a floodlit stadium (seating 16,000 spectators), Olympic-size swimming and diving pools, a large indoor sports hall and a dry-ski slope. National and international events are frequently staged, including swimming, water polo, athletics and basketball events. Courses in many sports including skiing, squash and swimming. *Modest annual membership fee.*

Elephant & Castle Leisure   **5 C6**
Centre
22 Elephant & Castle SE1. 0171-582 5505. Facilities for badminton, basketball, cricket, five-a-side football, netball, squash, volleyball and martial arts. Swimming pool and gymnasium. *No membership requirement.*

Finsbury Leisure Centre   **2 E4**
Norman St EC1. 0171-253 4490. Indoor centre with facilities for netball, badminton, squash, weight-training, basketball, martial arts, roller-skating. Outdoor facilities for football, netball and tennis. Also swimming pool, Turkish bath, sunbeds and sauna. *No membership requirement.*

Jubilee Hall Recreation Centre   **4 F3**
The Piazza, Covent Garden WC2. 0171-836 4835. Indoor centre offering aerobics, badminton, basketball, dance, football, martial arts, weight-training, weight-lifting. Sauna, solarium and jacuzzi for women only. Sports injury clinic with staff trained in acupuncture and reflexology. Wholefood café and clothes shop. *No membership requirement.*

Jubilee Sports Centre
Caird St, Queens Park W10. 0181-960 9629. Indoor facilities for most sports including martial arts, squash, badminton, basketball, swimming and tennis. Crèche. *No membership requirement.*

Latchmere Sports Centre
Burns Rd, Battersea SW11. 0181-871 7470. Indoor centre with sports hall,

projectile room, multi-gym, meeting rooms and crèche. Also leisure pool and aerobics studio. *No membership requirement.*

Lee Valley Leisure Centre
Picketts Lock La N9. 0181-345 6666. Indoor facilities for soccer, gymnastics, badminton, basketball, hockey, netball, volleyball, martial arts, roller-skating, shooting, bowls and swimming. Outdoor facilities: soccer, hockey, tennis and golf. Tuition available in most sports. Aerobics studio. *No membership requirement.*

Michael Sobell Sports Centre
Hornsey Rd N7. 0171-609 2166. Large indoor centre adaptable to most sports. Classes in badminton, basketball, climbing, cricket, gymnastics, martial arts, netball, five-a-side football, short tennis, squash, table tennis, volleyball, weight-lifting and yoga. Health suite. There is also an ice rink, a sauna and a soft play area. *Modest annual membership fee.*

Queen Mother Sports Centre *7* **C2**
223 Vauxhall Bridge Rd SW1. 0171-798 2125. Large indoor centre with multi-gym, sauna, steam room, solarium and swimming pool. Facilities for badminton, weight-training, squash, martial arts, aerobics, yoga, gymnastics and short tennis for children. Tuition available for most activities. *No membership requirement (except day membership for squash and weight-training).*

Swiss Cottage Sports Centre
Winchester Rd NW3. 0171-413 6490. Indoor facilities for badminton, basketball, volleyball, gymnastics, weight-training, keep fit, martial arts, squash and swimming. Outdoors: football and tennis. Sunbed and massage. *No membership requirement*

Tottenham Sports Centre
703 High Rd N17. 0181-801 6401. Facilities for archery, shooting, bowling, gymnastics, children's football, martial arts, table tennis, badminton, aerobics, yoga. *No membership requirement.*

YMCA: Central *4* **E2**
112 Great Russell St WC1. 0171-637 8131. Indoor only. Badminton, basketball, gymnastics, keep fit, aerobics, sub aqua, swimming, table tennis, volleyball and yoga. Also weight-training, short tennis and sunroom. *Membership necessary. Day membership available.*

Sports venues

Lord's Cricket Ground
St John's Wood Rd NW8. 0171-289

1611. Famous cricket ground built in 1814. Home of Middlesex County Cricket Club. Stages county and international test matches *Apr-Sep.*

The Oval *7* **F4**
Kennington SE11. 0171-582 6660. Originally a market garden, this has been a cricket ground since 1845. Surrey County Cricket club and the English international team play here *May-Sep.*

Twickenham
Whitton Rd, Twickenham, Middx. 0181-892 8161. Venue for rugby internationals, home internationals and finals of club, county and divisional competitions. Matches mainly *Jan-Mar.*

Wembley Stadium
Wembley Way, Middx. 0181-900 1234. Vast, impressive venue for various major sporting events including international football and hockey matches, American football, the Rugby League Challenge Cup Final and the FA Cup Final .

Wembley Arena, which also stages sporting events, is part of the same complex.

Wimbledon
All England Lawn Tennis Club, Church Rd SW19. Recorded information: 0181-946 2244. Venue for the famous tennis championships which take place *last week Jun-first week Jul.* Advance seats for Centre Court and No 1 Court are allocated by public ballot. To enter, write *Sep-Dec* for an application form.

Ticket agents: sport

Tickets are available for most events but sometimes they must be bought months in advance. Apply to the box office of the venue concerned or try:

First Call *4* **F2**
73-75 Endell St WC2. 0171-420 1000. Tickets for major sports events in the capital.

Sport

London has facilities for nearly all types of sport and has a formidable number of clubs, sports grounds and associations. This list gives the main authorities, places and events not only for the spectator but also for those who want to take part. There are numerous facilities for inexpensive tuition and training; the Sports Council runs hundreds of courses all over London. For sports equipment see the 'Specialist shops & services' section.

Greater London & SE Region Sports Council
PO Box 480, Ledrington Rd SE19. 0181-778 8600. Answers individual enquiries about sport in the London and SE areas. Information on grants and loans, facilities and events.

Sports Council   1 **F5**
Information Centre, 16 Upper Woburn Pl WC1. 0171-388 1277. Answers all kinds of enquiries about sport and physical recreation nationally and internationally. Also produces a calendar of events.

Sportsline
0171-222 8000. Gives details of clubs and events in the London area.

American Football

American Football
American football is now immensely popular in Britain. As well as national league division games, American league sides have exhibition games at Wembley Stadium. If you want to play or watch the great gridiron game, contact the:

British American Football Association
22A Market Pl, Still Lane, Boston, Lincs. (01205) 363522.

Archery

There are about 20 archery clubs in London, each of which has some facilities for shooting. The County of London outdoor championships are held in Aug. *Indoor championships in* Feb. *Numerous inter-county matches throughout the year.*

County of London Archery Association
Hon Sec, Mr Miller, Flat 9/N, Peabody Av, Sutherland St SW1. 0171-821 1735. For information on the sport in London.

Grand National Archery Society
National Agricultural Centre, 7th St, Stoneleigh, Kenilworth, Warks. (01203) 696631. Will supply information about national and international archery.

Southern Counties Archery Society
Hon Gen Sec, Mr A.L. Francis, 5 Fordington Rd, Winchester, Hants. (01962) 854932. For information about archery in all the southern counties and London.

Athletics

The major events are held at Crystal Palace.

British Athletics Federation
225A Bristol Rd, Edgbaston, Birmingham, West Midlands. 0121-440 5000. For all information on athletics.

Badminton

All England championships at Birmingham in Mar; *also many other tournaments throughout the country during the year. All England junior championships held at Watford, Herts.*

Badminton Association of England
National Badminton Centre, Bradwell Rd, Loughton Lodge, Milton Keynes, Bucks. (01908) 568822. Gives information on local clubs, promotes all national and international events in England, and supplies a diary of events and handbook.

Baseball

There are National League and Southern Baseball League clubs at Sutton, Croydon, Hendon, Purfleet and Wokingham.

Basketball

Championship play-offs take place at Wembley, which also hosts the occasional visit by the internationally-renowned Harlem Globetrotters.

English Basketball Association
48 Bradford Rd, Stanningley, Leeds. (0113) 2361166. Will supply a club list.

Billiards & snooker

Over 300 clubs in London and a variety of leagues and competitions.

Centre Point Snooker Club   4 **E2**
Centre Point, New Oxford St WC1. 0171-240 6886. *Open to 06.00.*

New World Snooker Clubs
A chain of London snooker clubs which will remain *open up to 24 hrs* if there are people still playing. Check the phone book for your nearest club.

Wandsworth Billiards & Snooker Centre
63 Wandsworth High St, Wandsworth SW18. 0181-874 1252. *Open 24 hrs.*

Bowls

National championships held at Beach House Park, Worthing, W. Sussex in Aug. *Public greens in Battersea Park, Finsbury Park, and many other London parks.*

English Bowling Association
The Secretary, Lyndhurst Rd, Worthing,

W. Sussex. (01903) 820222. For information.

Boxing

ABA championships held in May. Bouts take place at Wembley and the Royal Albert Hall. For detailed listings, consult Boxing News.

British Boxing Board of   **5 D5**
Control
52a Borough High St SE1. 0171-403 5879. Controls and administers professional boxing.

London Amateur Boxing Association
58 Comber Grove SE5. 0171-252 7008. Supplies a list of London clubs.

Canoeing

Various suitable rivers such as the Thames, Kennet, Wey, Medway, Rother and Stour – all within easy reach of London.

British Canoe Union
Adbolton La, West Bridgeford, Nottingham, Notts. (0115) 9821100. For information and advice.

Chess

4 Nations Chess League
PO Box 175, Croyden, Surrey. For information about local competition squads.

Clay pigeon shooting

Clay Pigeon Shooting Association
107 Epping New Rd, Buckhurst Hill, Essex. 0181-505 6221. For a list of clubs. Organises home and overseas championships.

Cricket

Many amateur clubs throughout London and first-class cricket at Lord's and the Oval (see 'Sports venues'). The season is Apr-Sep.

National Cricket Association
Lord's Cricket Ground, St John's Wood Rd NW8. 0171-289 6098. Gives information on amateur clubs and coaching facilities.

Croquet

Croquet Association
Mr B.C. Macmillan, The Secretary, Hurlingham Club, Ranelagh Gdns SW6.

0171-736 3148. For information and advice.

Cycling

The spectacularly fast 6-day indoor event is held at Wembley Arena.

British Cycling Federation
National Cycling Centre, 1 Stuart St, Manchester. 0161-230 2301. Information on road, track and circuit racing.

Lee Valley Cycle Circuits
Temple Mills La E15. 0181-534 6085. An enclosed road circuit with facilities for recreational riding, racing, training and coaching. BMX track. Camp site. Mountain bike course.

Drag racing

Events take place infrequently at various airfields around London.

British Drag Racing Association
29 Westdrive, Caldicott, Cambs. (01954) 210028. Arranges meetings at Santa Pod and Avon Park.

Santa Pod Raceway
Airfield Rd, Hinwick, Northants. (01234) 782828. Meetings are held regularly at England's only permanent drag racing venue, Santa Pod Raceway, Podington, Nr. Wellingborough, Northants.

Fencing

Amateur Fencing Association
1 Baron's Gate, 33 Rothschild Rd W4. 0181-742 3032. For information and lists of events and clubs.

Fishing

To fish anywhere in the Thames area it is necessary to hold a Thames Water Authority Rod Licence. An additional permit is needed to fish in royal parks. The season is 16 Jun-14 Mar.

London Anglers' Association
Izaak Walton Hse, 2A Hervey Park Rd E17. 0181-520 7477. Gives information on clubs and offers associate membership.

National Rivers Authority (NRA)
For information on obtaining a fishing licence in your area.
For Anglian region (Norfolk, Suffolk and Essex): Kingfisher House, Goldhay Way, Orton Goldhay, Peterborough. (01733) 371811.
For South East region: Guildborne House, Chatsworth Rd, Worthing, W Sussex. (01903) 820692.

Fishing: lakes & ponds

To fish in lakes or ponds you must hold a permit or day ticket from the local borough council, unless marked free. Reductions for under-16s and OAPs. To fish anywhere in the Thames area you must hold a Thames Water Authority Rod Licence.

Battersea Park   **6 F5**
Roach, bream, flat-fish and very large carp. *Free.*

Chestnut Abbey Cross Pit, Herts
Good pike, perch, roach, tench. Crowded in summer.

Chingford Connaught Waters
All species. Crowded in summer. *Free.*

Clapham Common Eagle Pond
Good carp, some roach, pike, bream. *Free.*

Crystal Palace Boating Lake
Good carp, pike, roach, tench, gudgeon and perch.

Epping, Copped Hall Estate Pond
Carp, tench, perch, gudgeon, some rainbow trout. *Summer only.*

Finsbury Park
Carp, perch, tench and roach.

Hampton Court Ponds
Tench, pike, roach, perch. Beautiful water but often crowded.

Hampstead Heath Ponds
Good tench, roach, bream, pike. *Free.*

Hollow Ponds
Whipps Cross E17. Tench, pike, eels (but get there very early in the morning). *Free.*

Hyde Park Serpentine   **3 F4**
Good roach, perch.

Northmet Pit, near Cheshunt, Herts
Good summer tench and winter pike, also perch, roach, rudd.

Osterley Park, Middx
Tench, perch, roach.

Richmond Park Pen Ponds
Good roach and perch.

Rickmansworth Lakes, Herts
Good roach, perch, tench, bream, pike.

Seven Islands, Mitcham Common, Surrey
Pike, perch, bream. *Free.*

South Weald Park, Essex
Good tench, crucian carp, roach, rudd, pike, perch.

Tooting Common Pond
Roach, perch, carp.

Victoria Park Lake E9
Good eels, pike, perch, bream, gudgeon.

Wandsworth Common Pond
Carp, roach, tench, pike.

Windsor Great Park
Obelisk Pond, Johnson's Pond and Virginia Water. Carp, tench, pike, roach, rudd, bream and perch. Permits from Crown Estate Office, Great Park, Windsor, Berks (enclose sae). (01753) 860222.

Fishing: reservoirs

A number of Thames Water reservoirs are well stocked. Season 16 Jun-14 Mar for coarse fishing, 15 Mar or 1 Apr-30 Nov for trout. Thames Water licence needed. Day tickets from gate, but written applications only for seasons (two types – midweek and weekend) to:

North London Division
New River Head, Rosebery Av, London EC1, for **Barn Elms** – trout.

Eastern Division
The Grange, Crossbrook St, Waltham Cross, Herts, for **Walthamstow** – coarse, trout.

Fishing: rivers & canals

Grand Union Canal
Denham, Bucks. From Black Jack's Lock (No. 85) to Denham Lock (No. 87).

Lee Relief Channel Fishery
Waltham Abbey to Fishers Green. All species and the occasional trout. Day permits.

River Lee
Walthamstow to Hertford. Best fishing above Enfield Lock at Waltham Abbey, Cheshunt, Broxbourne, Rye House and St Margarets.

River Thames
Fishing starts above Kew. Probably England's best coarse fishing river. All species. Various stretches.

Flying

Aircraft Owners & Pilots   **7 B2**
Association
50a Cambridge St SW1. 0171-834 5631. For information, help and advice on all aspects of light aviation.

Football (soccer)

This is by far the most popular British sport from both the player's and spectator's point of view. The English Football League has 92 clubs divided into 4 divisions; the London clubs are listed here. Then there are the Southern and Isthmian League clubs, many of them in London and well worth watching. Finally there are hundreds of amateur clubs which encourage new players of all standards. Football League matches are played every Sat and most B.hols at 15.00, occasional midweek matches at 19.30. The season lasts from Aug to May. Occasional international matches at Wembley Stadium, domestic and European knock-out competitions at club grounds. The FA and League Cup Finals are held at Wembley (see 'Sports venues'), but it's impossible to get in unless you have a ticket in advance.

London Football Association
Aldworth Gro SE13. 0181-690 9626. For information on leagues and clubs.

Arsenal FC
Highbury Stadium, Avenell Rd N5. 0171-354 5404. Recorded ticket information 0171-359 0131.

Charlton Athletic FC
Selhurst Park SE25. 0181-859 8888. Offices at: The Training Ground, Sparrows Lane, New Elton SE9.

Chelsea FC   6 **B5**
Stamford Bridge, Fulham Rd SW6. 0171-385 5545.

Crystal Palace FC
Selhurst Park SE25. 0181-771 8841.

Fulham FC
Craven Cottage, Stevenage Rd SW6. 0171-736 6561.

Leyton Orient FC
Brisbane Rd E10. 0181-539 2223.

Millwall FC
The New Den, Senegal Fields SE16. 0171-232 1222.

Queen's Park Rangers FC
South Africa Rd W12. 0181-743 0262.

Tottenham Hotspur FC
White Hart Lane Ground, 748 High Rd N17. 0181-808 8080.

West Ham United FC
Boleyn Ground, Green St E13. 0181-472 2740.

Wimbledon FC
Selhurst Park SE25. 0181-7718841.

British Gliding Association
Kimberley House, Vaughan Way, Leicester, Leics. (0116) 2531051. For information and help, club list and details of training courses.

London Gliding Club
Tring Rd, Dunstable, Beds. (01582) 663419. The home of British gliding. Contact the secretary for a familiarisation flight on a temporary membership basis so that you can see what it's about before committing yourself.

Playscape
The Old Bus Garage, Triangle Pl, Nelson's Row SW4. 0171-978 1148. And at Hester Rd SW11. 0171-228 8006.

The Daily Telegraph Golf Course Guide, published by HarperCollins, gives details and maps of all the courses in the British Isles. Also the Golfers' Handbook can be obtained from most libraries.

Golf club membership tends to be expensive and you need to have a handicap. An alternative is The Golf Club of Great Britain, which provides a handicapping facility for non-club members, stages tournaments and maintains a list of private clubs where its members can play. Contact at 3 Sage Yard, Off Douglas Rd, Surbiton, Surrey. 0181-390 3113. Playing Card members can play at 700 private courses without a handicap, enter tournaments and receive coaching. Contact at 3-5 Northfields Prospect, Putney Bridge Rd SW18. 0181-877 9988.

Municipal courses, where it is not necessary to be a member, can be found at:

Addington Court
Featherbed La, Addington, Croydon, Surrey. 0181-657 0281. Two 18-hole courses, a 9-hole course and a pitch and putt course of 18 holes.

Beckenham Place Park
Beckenham Hill Rd, Beckenham, Kent. 0181-650 2292. 18 holes.

Coulsdon Manor
Coulsdon Rd, Coulsdon, Surrey. 0181-660 6083. 18 holes.

Hainault Forest
Romford Rd, Chigwell, Essex. 0181-500 2470. Two 18-hole courses, a putting green and practice field.

Lee Valley LeisureCentre
Picketts Lock La N9. 0181-803 3611. 18-hole course.

Royal Epping Forest
Forest Approach, Station Rd, Chingford, Essex. 18 holes.

The following are golf clubs in and near London for which membership is necessary, although many will extend guest facilities to members of comparable clubs from overseas. A handicap certificate is often needed if not a member.

Hampstead GC
Winnington Rd N2. 0181-455 0203. 9 holes. Bar lunches served.

Highgate GC
Denewood Rd N6. 0181-340 1906.
London's most central 18-hole course.
Lunches served.

North Middlesex GC
Friern Barnet La, Whetstone N20. 0181-445 1604. 18 holes. Bar lunches except *Mon*. Full lunch *Sun* only.

Richmond GC
Sudbrook Park, Petersham, Richmond, Surrey. 0181-940 4351. 18 holes. Lunches served. *No visitors at weekends.*

Royal Mid-Surrey GC
Old Deer Park, Richmond, Surrey. 0181-940 1894. 36 holes. Men's 6337 yds (5791m); ladies' 5544 yds (5067m). Lunches served.

Sandown Golf Centre
Sandown Park, More La, Esher, Surrey. (01372) 463340. Two 9-hole courses; one 9-hole pitch and putt course.

Sunningdale GC
Ridgemount Rd, Sunningdale, Berks. (01344) 21681. 36 holes. Two courses. Lunches served except *Mon. Visitors welcome Mon-Thur; require letter of introduction and handicap certificate.*

Wentworth GC
Wentworth Dri, Virginia Water, Surrey. (01344) 842201. Three 18-hole and one 9-hole course. *Visitors by arrangement Mon-Fri.* Lunches served.

Greyhound racing

It is advisable to check times in the Evening Standard.

Catford Stadium
Catford Bridge SE6. 0181-690 2261. *19.30 Mon, Thur & Sat.*

Hackney Stadium
Waterden Rd E15. 0181-986 3511. *19.45 Mon, Wed, Fri, 13.00 Tue, 11.00 Sat.*

Walthamstow Stadium
Chingford Rd E4. 0181-531 4255. *18.30 Tue, Thur & Sat.*

Wembley Stadium
Empire Way, Wembley, Middx. 0181-902 8833. *19.30 Mon, Wed & Fri.*

Wimbledon Stadium
Plough La SW17. 0181-946 5361. *19.30 Tue, Wed, Fri & Sat.*

Gymnastics

Competitions at the Royal Albert Hall and Crystal Palace. See 'Children's London: Activities and interests'.

Hang-gliding

British Hang-Gliding Association
Cramfield Airfields, Cramfield, Milton Keynes, Bucks. Write for information.

Hockey

Men's internationals held at Willesden Sports Centre, women's at Wembley.

All England Women's Hockey Association
51 High St, Shrewsbury, Shropshire. (01743) 233572.

Hockey Association
Norfolk House, 102 Saxongate West, Milton Keynes. (01908) 241100.

Horse racing

Courses in and near London: Ascot, Berks (famous for its Royal meeting in Jun*); Epsom, Surrey (stages the world-famous Derby in* Jun *and also the Oaks); Kempton Park, Sunbury-on-Thames, Middx; Lingfield Park, Surrey; Sandown Park, Esher, Surrey (famous for the Whitbread Gold Cup); and Windsor, Berks. Flat racing season* Mar-Nov. *Steeplechasing* Aug-Jun. *Point to point racing (amateur) season* Mar-Apr.

Jockey Club (incorporating the National Hunt Committee)   **4 B2**
42 Portman Sq W1. 0171-486 4921. Governing body, responsible for rules, meetings, training and promotion of horse racing.

Racecourse Association
Winkfield Rd, Ascot, Berks. (01344) 25912. Can supply information on all aspects of racing.

Ice hockey

British Ice Hockey Association
The Secretary, 517 Christchurch Rd, Boscombe, Bournemouth, Dorset. (01202) 303946. For information on clubs and events.

Lacrosse

The main events are held Feb-Apr, *including the Clubs and Colleges Tournament and a home international in London.*

All England Women's Lacrosse Association
4 Western Court, Bromley St, Digbeth, Birmingham. 0121-773 4422. For lists of clubs and fixtures. For details of coaching courses telephone the British Lacrosse Coaching Foundation (01270) 878171.

English Lacrosse Union
The Secretary, Mr R. Balls, Lynton, 70 High Rd, Rayleigh, Essex. (01268) 770758. Men only. Gives details of events and coaching courses.

Martial arts

Amateur Karate Association 1 **G4**
120 Cromer St WC1. 0171-837 4406.
British Judo Council
1a Horn La W3. 0181-992 9454. Supplies free explanatory leaflet and details of clubs.
Judokan Club
Latymer Ct, Hammersmith Rd W6. 0181-748 6787. Classes in judo and karate.
London Judo Society 7 **E6**
89 Lansdowne Way SW8. 0171-622 0529. Judo and karate club.

Motorcycle racing

Road racing at Brands Hatch.
Auto-Cycle Union
ACU House, Wood St, Rugby, Warks. (01788) 540519. Governs all motorcycle competitions. Also trials and grass track. Publishes a handbook of forthcoming road racing and scrambling events.

Motor racing

Several clubs in the London area.
British Automobile Racing Club
Thruxton Racing Circuit, nr Andover, Hants. (01264) 772696. For details of club, championships and general information.
British Racing & Sports Car Club
Brands Hatch Circuit, Fawkham, nr Dartford, Kent. (01474) 874445. Stages meetings at Brand's Hatch and seven other car circuits. Also organises major international events in this country.
RAC Motor Sports Association
Motor Sports House, Riverside Park, Colnbrook, Slough, Berks. (01753) 681736. Controls competitions. Supplies list of championship events.

Mountaineering

British Mountaineering Council
177-179 Burton Rd, West Didsbury, Manchester. 0161-445 4747. Supplies a list of clubs and information on where to find mountain huts etc to members only.

Netball

Played lunchtimes in Lincoln's Inn Fields WC2.
All England Netball Association
Netball House, 9 Paynes Park, Hitchin, Herts. (01462) 442344. For information and advice.

Orienteering

This sport can be enjoyed by people of all ages and involves competitive navigation on foot with map and compass. Events take place most Sundays.
British Orienteering Federation
Riversdale, Dale Rd North, Darley Dale, Matlock, Derbyshire. (01629) 734042.

Parachuting

British Parachute Association
5 Wharf Way, Glen Parva, Leicester, Leics. (0116) 2785271. For information, a list of clubs and help.

Parascending & paragliding

Parascending involves being towed into the air behind a four-wheel drive vehicle. Paragliding is flying with different shaped chutes off hills. These increasingly popular sports are easier and cheaper than hang-gliding. There are now at least 140 parascending or paragliding clubs in Britain.
British Hang-gliding and Paragliding Association
Old Schoolroom, Loughborough Rd, Leicester. (0116) 2611322. Responsible for training instructors. Information on local clubs.
Green Dragons Paragliding Club
Warren Barn Farm, Wodingham, Surrey. (01883) 652666.

Polo

Played Apr-Sep at Smiths Lawn, Windsor, Berks. Matches most weekends, B.hols & during Ascot week; Sun at Ham House, Richmond; Tue, Thur & Sat at Richmond Park (nr Roehampton Gate); Wed, Fri, Sat, Sun & B.hols at Cowdray Park, Midhurst, W. Sussex, also Thur during the British Open Championships (beginning Jul) and during Goodwood week; Wed, Sat & Sun at Woolmers Park, Hereford. Play starts middle or late afternoon.

Ascot Park Polo Club
Ascot Park, Sunningdale. (01344) 21312.
Offers lessons for beginners, including
those who haven't ridden before.

*Real tennis is the original form of tennis
and Henry VIII's court at Hampton
Court still exists. Nowadays it's rather
obscure, as is rackets which is a form
of squash but with a much larger
court.*

Tennis & Rackets Association
c/o Queen's Club, Palliser Rd W14. 0171-
385 3421. Actively promotes both sports.

Queen's Club
Palliser Rd W14. 0171-385 3421. Stages
matches in both sports. Real tennis
events *Sep-Apr*.

**Association of British Riding
Schools**
Old Brewery Yard, Penzance,
Cornwall. (01736) 69440. Deals with
general equestrian matters ranging
from insurance and legal matters to
helping those interested in a career
with horses. Publishes a handbook listing approved riding schools.

Hyde Park Riding Stables 3 **E3**
63 Bathurst Mews W2. 0171-723 2813.
Open *all year round* for riding in Hyde
Park. Caters for riders of all abilities, from
5yrs upwards. Lessons and jumping
tuition available.

Wimbledon Village Stables
24b High St SW19. 0181-946 8579.
Stylish stables. Experienced riders as
well as beginners welcome. Show
jumping, dressage and gymkhanas
held regularly. Film shows, lectures and
demonstrations.

*The most famous event is the Oxford and
Cambridge boat race from Putney to
Mortlake in Mar or Apr. The Head of the
River event on the Thames is held in Mar
and is one of the largest of its kind in
the world. Important regattas are held
at Chiswick, Hammersmith, Henley-on-
Thames, Kingston, Putney, Richmond,
Twickenham and Walton.*

Amateur Rowing Association
6 Lower Mall W6. 0181-748 3632.
Publishes the British Rowing Almanac
annually, which gives a list of clubs and
coming events. Also a monthly club
magazine.

*Twickenham is the home of rugby union
(see 'Sports venues') and some international matches are staged there.
Besides this there are a number of top-
class clubs in the London area which
provide excellent spectator sport and a
plethora of lesser clubs which encourage
new members of all standards.*

Rugby Football Union
Rugby Rd, Twickenham, Middx. 0181-
892 8161. Controlling body of the sport
and headquarters of rugby. The important
matches, including internationals, are
played there.

International Yacht Racing 5 **B4**
Union
27 Broadwall SE1. 0171-928 6611.
Publishes an annual international fixture
list and booklet on racing rules.

Royal Ocean Racing Club 4 **D4**
20 St James's Pl SW1. 0171-493 2248.
To become eligible to join you must have
a total of 400 miles off-shore racing.

Royal Yachting Association
Romsey Rd, Eastleigh, Hants. (01703)
627400. National authority providing
information on all forms of yachting,
sailing and powered boating.

*The most important competitions held
at Bisley Camp are: The Services
Meeting, beginning of Jul; NRA Small-
bore Meeting later in Jul; NSRA British
Small-bore Meeting later in Jul; NSRA
British Small-bore Rifle Championship
in Aug.*

**Holland & Holland Shooting
Grounds**
Ducks Hill Rd, Northwood, Middx.
(01923) 825 349. Clay pigeon training
ground. Instruction for beginners.

National Rifle Association
Bisley Camp, Brookwood, Woking,
Surrey. (01483) 797777. Full-bore. Will
recommend a suitable club (by letter
only), but these are rare in London.

**National Small-bore Rifle
Association**
Lord Roberts House, Bisley Camp,
Brookwood, Woking, Surrey. (01483)
476969. Small-bore and air weapons.
Will recommend a suitable club on receipt
of sae.

Showjumping

The two major events are: the Royal International Horse Show at Wembley in Jul and the Horse of the Year Show at Wembley in Oct. There are also notable events staged at Windsor, Richmond and Clapham Common. See also 'Riding'.
British Show Jumping Association
British Equestrian Centre, Stoneleigh, Kenilworth, Warks. (01203) 696516.

Skating

National Skating Association   2 **E5**
of Great Britain
15-27 Gee St EC1. 0171-253 3824. For information and advice on ice and roller-skating.
Broadgate Ice   5 **F1**
Eldon St EC2. 0171-588 6565. Open-air ice rink. Broomball, a Canadian version of ice hockey, is played here. *OPEN Oct-Apr 12.00-14.30 & 15.30-18.00 Mon-Fri (19.00-22.30 on Fri only), 11.00-13.30, 14.00-16.00 & 19.00-22.30 Sat & Sun.*
Queen's Ice Skating Club   5 **C3**
17 Queensway W2. 0171-229 0172. Fee for skate hire. Tuition available. *OPEN 10.00-16.30 & 19.30-22.00 Mon-Fri, 10.00-17.00 Sat & Sun.*
Roller City London
Stonehill Business Park, North Circular Rd, Edmonton N18. 0181-807 5511. London's only purpose-built roller rink. *OPEN 15.00-24.00 Mon-Fri (from 10.00 during school hols), 10.00-24.00 Sat, 10.00-22.00 Sun.* Skate hire available.
Streatham Ice Rink
386 Streatham High Rd SW16. 0181-769 7771. Admission and skate-hire charge. *OPEN 10.00-16.00 Mon-Fri, 11.00-16.45 Sat & Sun. Evening sessions usually 19.30-22.30. Phone to check.*

Skiing

British Ski Federation
258 Main St, East Calder, West Lothian, Scotland. (01506) 884343.
Ski Club of Great Britain   7 **A1**
118 Eaton Sq SW1. 0171-245 1033. National club for recreational skiing. Equipment advice for members.

Artificial ski centres provide practice and can be great fun. Most centres run courses for beginners and hire out all the necessary equipment.
Crystal Palace National Sports Centre
Ledrington Rd SE19. 0181-778 0131.

Hillingdon Ski Centre
Park Rd, Uxbridge, Middx. (01895) 255183.
Mountaintop Ski Centre
Beckton Alps, Alpine Way E6. 0171-511 0351.

Squash

A number of sports centres have public squash courts – prior booking essential.
Squash Rackets Association
Westpoint, 33-34 Warple Way W3. 0181-746 1616. Publishes the *SRA Annual* which gives a list of clubs and courts. Also *Squash & Fitness* quarterly.

Stock car racing

Events mostly staged Sat eve Mar-Sep.
Spedeworth International
Wimbledon Stadium, Plough La SW17. 0181-946 5361.
Wisbech Stadium, Cromwell Rd, Wisbech, Cambs. (01945) 584736.

Sub aqua

British Sub Aqua Club
Telfords Quay, Ellesmere Port, South Wirral, Cheshire. 0151-357 1951. For information on branches where training courses are run. To join you will have to pass a swimming test and produce a certificate of fitness signed by your doctor. BSAC training is recognised worldwide as being of the highest order. Holborn branch and London branch are well-equipped, active groups who train throughout the year and dive regularly. *See also 'Sports equipment: sub aqua' under 'Shops and services'.*

Swimming

Magnificent Olympic-standard pool at the Crystal Palace National Sports Centre. High-standard competitions. Excellent tuition and facilities for members.
Amateur Swimming Association
Harold Fern House, Derby Sq, Loughborough, Leics. (01509) 230431. The authority governing national swimming events.
Public baths (indoor)
Chelsea Manor St SW3. 0171-352   6 **E3**
6985.
Marshall St W1. 0171-439 4678.   4 **D2**
Norman St EC1. 0171-253 4011.   2 **E4**
Oasis, 32 Endell St WC2. 0171-831 4 **F2**
1804. Also an outdoor pool *May-Oct.*

Queen Mother Sports Centre, 223   **7 C2**
Vauxhall Bridge Rd SW1. 0171-798 2125.
225 Queensway W2. 0171-798 3689. 3 **C2**
Seymour Pl W1. 0171-723 8019.   **4 A1**
Public baths (outdoor)
Finchley Open Air Pool, High Rd N12.
0181-883 6232.
Swimming in the parks (outdoors)
Hampstead Pond NW3. 0171-435 2366.
OPEN May-Sep 10.00-16.30. Free.
Highgate Ponds N6. 0181-340 4044.
Men only. *OPEN Apr-Sep 07.30-20.30
Mon-Sun; Oct-Mar 07.00-15.00 Mon-
Sun. Free.*
Kenwood Pond N6. 0181-340 5303.
Women only. *OPEN 08.00-dusk all year
round. Free.*
Parliament Hill Lido NW5. 0171-485
3873.   *OPEN 10.00-18.00 May-Sep;
07.00-09.30 Oct-Apr. Free before 09.00.*
Serpentine Lido Hyde Park W2.   3 **F4**
0171-724 3104. *OPEN 10.00-18.00.*
Tooting Bec Lido SW16. 0181-871 7198.
*OPEN 06.30-19.30 Easter-Oct, 07.00-
17.00 Oct-Easter (members only).*

Table tennis

English Table Tennis Association
Queensbury House, Havelock Rd,
Hastings, E. Sussex. (01424) 722525.

Tennis

*There are public courts in most London
parks. There are also plenty of clubs to
join and indoor centres for which membership is usually necessary. The major event,
of course, is Wimbledon fortnight which
begins at the end of Jun (see 'Sports
venues'). There are also various other
tournaments held in London; those which
take place immediately before Wimbledon,
such as the one at Queen's Club, usually
include several top professionals.*
Lawn Tennis Association
Palliser Rd W14. 0171-385 2366. The
governing body of lawn tennis in Britain.
Will supply a list of clubs.
London Tennis Network   6 **D6**
195 Battersea Church Rd SW11. Partner-
finding service. Can also help members
locate a court or find a coach.
Queen's Club
Palliser Rd W14. 0171-385 3421. For
membership enquiries.

Ten pin bowling

*Bowling alleys often stay open late; phone
for opening times.*
British Ten Pin Bowling Association
Postal address: 114 Balfour Rd, Ilford,

Essex. 0181-478 1745. No bowling centre, but provides list of bowling centres
and other information and advice.
Airport Bowl
Bath Rd, Harlington, Middx. 0181-759
1396.
Bexleyheath Superbowl
Albion Rd, Bexleyheath, Kent. 0181-303
3325.
Dagenham Superbowl
New Rd, Dagenham, Essex. 0181-592
0347. 24 lanes.
Lewisham Bowl
11-29 Belmont Hill SE13. 0181-318
9691. 24 lanes, automatic scoring, fast
food and bar.
Streatham Mega Bowl
142 Streatham Hill SW2. 0181-678 6007.
Trocadero Lazer Bowl   4 **E3**
13 Coventry St W1. 0171-287 8913. Also
Bowlingo, a more compact version
with skiddy black lanes and fluorescent
lighting.

Volleyball

National League season runs Oct-Mar.
English Volleyball Association
27 South Rd, West Bridgford,
Nottingham, Notts. (0115) 9816324.
Supplies a list of clubs and fixtures.

Water polo

Occasional games at Crystal Palace.
Amateur Swimming Association
Harold Fern House, Derby Sq,
Loughborough, Leics. (01509) 230431 for
details.

Water skiing

*Several clubs to join and championships
to watch. The season is May-Sep.*
British Water Ski Federation
390 City Rd EC1. 0171-833 2855. For
information and club lists. Residential
summer courses.
Princes Water Ski Club
Clockhouse La, Bedfont, Middx. (01784)
256153. Four slalom courses, two jumps.
All equipment provided.

Weight-lifting

*National championships held at Crystal
Palace.*
**British Amateur Weight-Lifters
Association**
Grovenor House, 131 Hurst St, Oxford,
Oxon. (01865) 200339. Comprises 12
regional associations which organise

meetings, clubs, championships. Will supply information on clubs and events.

Greater London Amateur Weight-Lifters Association
The Secretary, Mr J. Jackson, 66 Ivy Rd NW6. 0181-452 0113.

Windsurfing

Docklands Sailing Centre
Kingbridge, Millwall Dock E14. 0171-537 2626. Purpose-built centre with 35 acres (14.5ha) of water in the dock.

Peter Chilvers Windsurfing
Gate 5, Royal Victorian Dock E16. 0171-474 2500. 83 acres (34.5ha) of enclosed water at the end of Victoria Dock. Roped-off area for beginners.

Windsurfing Information Centre
Royal Yachting Association, Romsey Rd, Eastleigh, Hants. (01703) 629962. Contact for full details of recognised windsurfing centres, classes, equipment hire, events and venues.

Wrestling

Main professional bouts at the Royal Albert Hall.

British Amateur Wrestling Association & English Olympic Wrestling Association
Wrestling Academy, 41 Great Clowes St, Salford. 0161-832 9209. Write for information.

Health and fitness

With the increasing awareness of the importance of health and fitness, clubs and dance centres have sprung up all over London, offering the opportunity to take classes in aerobics, dance or yoga; or simply to relax in the sauna or spa bath. Beauty treatments are often available in these centres along with bar and restaurant facilities. Some clubs require membership, some an entrance fee which varies depending on which equipment is used. A selection of clubs and dance centres is listed below. Local newspapers and newsagents' windows carry announcements of classes in your area. Local council education authorities also offer tuition.

Dance centres

Keep Fit Association   **7 C2**
Francis House, Francis St SW1. 0171-233 8898. Answers all kinds of enquiries about keep fit and dance.

Dance Attic
368 North End Rd SW6. 0171-610 2055. Gym and dance studio. Classes held in ballet, jazz, contemporary, tap, belly-dancing, flamenco, lambada. Also fitness and aerobics. *Membership required.*

Danceworks   **4 B2**
16 Balderton St W1. 0171-629 6183. Wide range of classes. Ballet, tap, various jazz forms, salsa, belly-dancing, gypsy flamenco. Also aerobics boxercise, sauna, sunbeds. Café. *Daily membership available.*

Pineapple Dance Studio   **4 F2**
7 Langley St WC2. 0171-836 4004. Qualified teachers for every type of dance imaginable from belly to break. Also gymnasium for weight-training, hydro fitness, body control studios, café-bar, resident osteopath and masseur. *Membership required.*

Health clubs & fitness centres

Dave Prowse Star Gym   **5 D5**
12 Marshalsea Rd SE1. 0171-407 5650. Two gymnasiums, sauna, solarium and showers. Dance and aerobics classes. *Membership.*

Earl's Court Gym   **6 B3**
254 Earl's Court Rd SW5. 0171-370 1402. Weights, aerobics, solarium, sauna. Cardio-vascular machines. *No membership requirement.*

Elements   **7 D2**
40 Vauxhall Bridge Rd SW1. 0171-834 2289. Gymnasium, sunbeds, beauty treatments, massage, dance studio. Sauna and steam room. *Membership.*

The Fitness Centre   **5 D4**
Crown House, 56-58 Southwark St SE1. 0171-403 6078. Gymnasium, sauna, steam. Dance and aerobics classes. Beauty salon. Health bar. *No membership requirement.*

Hogarth Club
1a Airedale Av W4. 0181-995 4600. American-style club with nautilus gym, spa bath, sauna, swimming pool, squash and tennis courts. Dance and exercise classes. Bar and restaurant. Creche. *Daily membership available.*

Holmes Place Health Club   **6 C4**
188a Fulham Rd SW10. 0171-352 9452. Swimming pool, three gymnasiums, steam room, sauna, sunbeds. Exercise classes. *Membership.*

Holmes Place Barbican Health Club   **2 E6**
97 Aldersgate St EC1. 0171-374 0091. Top class facilities for fitness training: exercise machines, aerobics floor, 25m

pool, running track, sauna, solarium, spa bath, whirlpool. Restaurant and bar. *Membership.*

Metropolitan Club   **4 D2**
27-28 Kingly St W1. 0171-734 5002. Gymnasium with videos to relieve the tedium of exercising. Swimming pool with whirlpool attached, steam room, sauna and sunbeds. Dance studio with full range of work-outs. *Membership.*

The Sanctuary   **4 F3**
12 Floral St WC2. 0171-240 9635. Exotic setting for sauna, solarium, steam room, swimming pool, spa bath. For the real sybarite. Women only. *Daily membership available.*

Westside Fitness & Leisure   **3 B6**
Centre
201-207 Kensington High St W8. 0171-937 5386. Weight-training, step classes, aerobics, yoga, stretch classes for all levels. *No membership required.*

Saunas

Telephone for appointment as times vary considerably. See also under 'Health clubs and fitness centres' and 'Turkish baths'.

Oasis   **4 F2**
Endell St WC2. 0171-836 9555. Swimming pools, paddling pool, sauna, warm baths and showers. Heated outdoor pool and sunbathing facilities in summer. *No membership required.*

Swiss Cottage Sauna
2 New College Parade, Finchley Rd NW3. 0171-586 4422. Unisex. *OPEN 24 hrs. No membership required.*

Turkish baths

Ladywell Baths
Lewisham High St SE13. 0181-690 2123. Excellent and inexpensive. Also indoor pool and public baths.

Porchester Centre   **3 C2**
Porchester Rd W2. 0171-792 2919. Three dry heat rooms, steam room, cold plunge, massage, exercise room. Also two swimming pools.

Rainbow Centre
41 East St, Epsom, Surrey. (01372) 749606. Turkish bath plus other facilities including sauna, sunbeds, swimming pool, conditioning gym and indoor bowls. Creche and play area.

Mind, body and spirit

Life in a hi-tech society has brought about a return to ancient and natural forms of
therapy. This, combined with the idea of prevention rather than cure, has made alternative medicine a regular practice for many people. Some treatments are available under the National Health Service, but most are private. Health food shops and health magazines (also Time Out) often advertise practitioners and teachers, some of whom are registered, some not. The Institute for Complementary Medicine Year Book is a comprehensive guide to all aspects of alternative medicine which is updated each year and available in most bookshops. Below are listed some of the bodies which will give advice about the various therapies and supply a list of registered practitioners.*

General

Community Health Foundation   **2 G4**
188 Old St EC1. 0171-251 4076. Health education centre offering a wide range of courses including shiatsu massage and holistic massage, stretch yoga, tai chi, body work and dance. Also wholefood cookery .

Institute of Complementary   **4 C1**
Medicine
21 Portland Pl W1. 0171-237 5165. Provides detailed information on all aspects of alternative medicine.

The Isis Centre for Holistic Health
5 Clonmell Rd N17. 0181-808 6401. Individual and group sessions of a medical and counselling nature. Treatments in homoeopathy, osteopathy, psychotherapy, acupuncture and massage. Regular classes in 'technologies for creating'.

Neal's Yard Therapy Rooms   **4 F2**
2 Neal's Yard WC2. 0171-379 7662. Individual consultations *(by appt only)* for acupuncture, Alexander technique, autogenic training, aromatherapy, bach flower remedies, biodynamic therapy, chiropractic, colour therapy, counselling, cranial osteopathy, healing, herbalism, homoeopathy, hypnotherapy, iridology, applied kinesiology, massage, naturopathy, nutrition and diet, osteopathy, polarity therapy, psychotherapy, reflexology, shiatsu, touch for health.

Acupuncture

Chinese method of treating ailments by pricking the skin or tissue with needles.
British Acupuncture   **7 B3**
Association
34 Alderney St SW1. 0171-834 1012. *OPEN 09.00-17.00 Mon-Fri. Appt only.*

Alexander technique

The re-education of the body in order to achieve the posture that nature intended and to carry out bodily activities with maximum ease and a minimum of energy and tension.

Society of Teachers of the   6 **C4**
Alexander Technique
20 London House, 266 Fulham Rd SW10. 0171-351 0828. Will supply a list of qualified teachers (send sae).

Chiropractic

The correction of spinal displacements by manipulation of the spine to ensure the flow of nervous energy from the spine to all parts of the body is unimpaired.

British Chiropractic   7 **D1**
Association
29 Whitely St, Reading, Berks. (01734) 757557. Will provide information and addresses of recognised practitioners.

Homoeopathy

Natural medicine based on the principle of treating like with like – ie a substance which would produce symptoms of sickness in a healthy person will cure a sick person showing those same symptoms.

British Homoeopathic   4 **C1**
Association
27a Devonshire St W1. 0171-935 2163. Provides a list of medical doctors trained in homoeopathy (send sae).

Royal London Homoeopathic   2 **A5**
Hospital
Great Ormond St WC1. 0171-837 8833. N H S treatment by registered homoeopaths (*appt only*). *OPEN 09.00-17.00 Mon-Fri.*

Society of Homoeopaths
2 Artizan Rd, Northampton. (01604) 21400. Maintains a register of professional homoeopaths who practise according to the Society's registration standards and code of ethics. Send sae for a copy.

Hypnotherapy

The Hypnotherapy Centre   4 **A2**
1 Wythburn Pl W1. 0171-262 8852.

Provides information and a list of registered practitioners of cure by hypnosis.

Osteopathy

Manipulation of the joints to correct structural imbalance as the body cannot function effectively unless structurally sound.

British Osteopathic   1 **B5**
Association
8 Boston Pl NW1. 0171-262 5250. Clinic *OPEN 10.00-16.00 Tue-Fri by appt.* Also provides a list of registered osteopaths.

British School of Osteopathy   4 **E4**
1-4 Suffolk St, Pall Mall SW1. 0171-930 4601. *OPEN 09.00-17.00 Mon-Fri by appt.* Specialist sports injury clinic *OPEN 09.00-17.00 Wed.*

Reflexology

Massage treatment which stimulates nerve centres in the feet.

British School of Reflexology
Holistic Healing Centre, 92 Sheering Rd, Old Harlow, Essex. (01279) 429060. Information and addresses of practitioners. Training school.

International Institute of Reflexology
15 Hartfield Close, Tonbridge, Kent. (01732) 350629. Provides information and addresses of practitioners. Seminars.

Yoga & meditation

Iyengar Yoga Institute
223a Randolph Av W9. 0171-624 3080. Classes for all levels from beginners and remedial to teacher training.

London Buddhist Centre
51 Roman Rd E2. 0181-981 1225. Specialises in meditation. Holds classes in yoga, Alexander technique and tai-chi.

Sivananda Yoga Centre
51 Felsham Rd SW15. 0181-780 0160. Courses and beginners' classes available in meditation and yoga. Yoga for pregnancy and pre-pregnancy. Courses on vegetarian cookery. Fasting clinic. Indian music. Also arranges retreats.

Students' London

Reference libraries

There are over 400 specialist libraries in London. The following are the most important and have been classified in sections to help both the enquiring visitor and the serious research worker. The British Museum Library can usually solve problems of research because of its vast collections. It is, however, busy and understaffed, so try other libraries first. Public libraries, maintained by each borough, offer access to magazines, newspapers and reference books. Some have large reference departments specialising in certain subjects.

General

British Library   4 **F1**
Great Russell St WC1. 0171-636 1544. This is the national copyright library which holds one copy of every printed book published in the UK. It is also a wide-ranging reference library with an incomparable collection of books, periodicals and manuscripts in English and foreign languages, but should only be used as a library of last resort. Admission to the Bloomsbury Reading Rooms is restricted to academics and professional researchers, who have to obtain a pass from the Reader Admissions office. Adults over 21 only. Reading Rooms *OPEN 09.00-17.00 Mon, Fri & Sat, 09.00-21.00 Tue-Thur. CLOSED Sun & B.hols.* Exhibition galleries *OPEN 10.00-17.00 Mon-Sat, 14.30-18.00 Sun. Free.*

British Library Newspaper Library
Colindale Av NW9. 0171-323 7355. National collection of newspapers from the UK and overseas countries. London newspapers prior to 1801 held at British Museum main building. Adults over 18 only. *OPEN 10.00-16.45 Mon-Sat. Free.*

Government Departments
Extensive collections. Available by appointment only. Official publications, history and information associated with the department. The following few (of many) have particularly large collections: Treasury; Home Office; Foreign and Commonwealth Office; Army Dept; Navy Dept; Dept of Environment.

London Library   4 **D4**
14 St James's Sq SW1. 0171-930 7705. Writers' and scholars' library with many distinguished authors among its members. Permanent collection of standard and authoritative works dating from the 16thC including a unique stock of foreign language books. One million volumes. Substantial annual membership fee enables readers to take out 10 books at a time. *OPEN 09.30-17.30 Mon-Sat (to 19.30 Thur). Members only.*

Art & architecture

British Architectural Library   4 **A2**
Drawings Collection
Heinz Gallery, 21 Portman Sq W1. 0171-580 5533. The most extensive collection of architectural drawings in the world, including practically all the surviving drawings of Palladio. May be consulted on specific research projects *by appt only*. Exhibition of new architects throughout the year. *OPEN 11.00-17.00 Tue-Thur, 10.00-13.00 Sat. CLOSED Aug.*

British Architectural Library   1 **D6**
66 Portland Pl W1. 0171-580 5533. 120,000 volumes; 60,000 photographs. Architecture and related arts, from 15thC to the present day. *OPEN 13.30-17.00 Mon, 10.00-20.00 Tue, 10.00-17.00 Wed, Thur & Fri, 10.00-13.30 Sat. CLOSED Aug. Free.*

British Museum   4 **F1**
Great Russell St WC1. 0171-636 1555. Very extensive collection of original drawings, etchings and engravings in Dept of Prints and Drawings. *OPEN 10.00-13.00 & 14.15-16.00 Mon-Fri, 10.00-12.30 Sat. Pass required – apply to Prints Dept.*

Courtauld Institute of Art   4 **G3**
Somerset House, Strand WC2. 0171-872 0220. The Witt Library houses a collection of over a million photographs, reproductions of paintings and drawings. *OPEN 10.00-18.00 Mon-Fri. Free.*

National Art Library, Victoria   6 **D1**
& Albert Museum
Cromwell Rd SW7. 0171-589 6371. A million volumes on fine and applied arts of all countries and periods. Sculpture, ceramics, silver, furniture, musical instruments, English costume. Prints and drawings department has exten-

sive collections dealing with art, architecture, pure and applied design and graphics. *OPEN 10.00-17.00 Tue-Sat. CLOSED Mon, Sun & B.hols. Free. Lectures.*

Royal Academy of Arts   4 D3
Burlington House, Piccadilly W1. 0171-439 7438. Fine arts. 15,000 volumes, original drawings, mainly 18th-19thC. *OPEN 10.00-18.00 Mon-Sun.*

Royal Society of Arts   4 F3
8 John Adam St WC2. 0171-930 5115. 15,000 books on industrial art and design. May be used for reference by accredited researchers, *by prior appt. OPEN 10.00-13.00 Mon-Thur (& 14.00-17.00 Wed only). By appt only. Charge.*

St Bride Printing Library   5 C2
St Bride Institute, Bride La EC4. 0171-353 4660. A public reference library of paper, typography, bookbinding and printing. *OPEN 09.30-17.30 Mon-Fri. CLOSED B.hols. Free.*

Sir John Soane's Museum   4 G2
Library
13 Lincoln's Inn Fields WC2. 0171-405 2107. Art and architecture, 15th-19thC architectural drawings, including many of the drawings from the office of Robert and James Adam and those from Soane's own office. Changing exhibitions. *OPEN 10.00-17.00 Tue-Sat. CLOSED Mon. OPEN 18.00-21.00 first Tue of month. By appt only for groups. Free.*

Westminster Reference   4 E3
Library
Art and Design Department, St Martin's St WC2. 0171-798 2038. English and European books. Painting, drawing, architecture, design, furniture, pottery, costume and sculpture. Periodicals. Also the Preston Blake Library, which contains approx 600 volumes on William Blake. *OPEN 10.00-19.00 Mon-Fri, 10.00-17.00 Sat. Free.*

Ecclesiastic

Dr Williams' Library   1 F5
14 Gordon Sq WC1. 0171-387 3727. Modern and 17th-18thC books on theology, Byzantine history, Dissenting history. 112,000 volumes. *OPEN 10.00-17.00 Mon-Fri (to 18.30 Tue & Thur). CLOSED B.hols. Free.*

Jews' College
44a Albert Rd NW4. 0181-203 6427. Hebraica and Judaica. 80,000 books and manuscripts. *OPEN 09.00-18.00 (to 17.00 in vacations) Mon-Thur, 09.00-13.00 Fri, 09.30-12.30 Sun (term-time). CLOSED B.hols & Jewish hols. Free.*

Lambeth Palace   5 A6
Lambeth Palace Rd SE1. 0171-928 6222. The archives of Archbishops of Canterbury from medieval times. 150,000 books, 3500 manuscripts, records, much larger number of archives. *OPEN 10.00-17.00 Mon-Fri to public on production of a letter of introduction. Free.*

Sion College   5 C3
Victoria Embankment EC4 (entrance in John Carpenter St). 0171-353 7983. Theological books from 17thC to present day. 100,000 volumes. *OPEN 10.00-17.00 Mon-Fri. Check times. Appt preferred. Free.*

Westminster Abbey Library   4 F6
& Muniment Room
The Cloisters, Westminster Abbey SW1. 0171-222 5152. 16th-18thC theology and history of Westminster Abbey. Archives from before the Norman Conquest. 14,000 volumes. *Appt preferred. OPEN 10.00-13.00 & 14.00-16.45 Mon-Fri. Free.*

Film, sound, photo

British Film Institute   4 E1
21 Stephen St W1. 0171-255 1444. An extensive collection of over 200,000 films, five million original stills, 19,000 books and scripts. *OPEN 10.30-17.30 Mon & Fri, 10.30-20.00 Tue & Thur, 13.00-20.00 Wed. Charge.*

Hulton Picture Library   3 A1
Unique House, 21-31 Woodfield Rd W9. 0171-266 2662. Seventeen million photographs and prints on every conceivable subject. Available for reproduction. Reuters archive. *OPEN 09.00-18.00 Mon-Fri. Appt only. Charge to reproduce photograph or print.*

National Sound Archive   3 E6
29 Exhibition Rd SW7. 0171-589 6603. National archive of sound recordings. 180,000 discs, tapes and cylinders. Also a library, with documentation on all aspects of sound recording. 150 current periodicals. Record catalogues and release sheets. *Reference only.* Listening service *(appt only)* and library. *OPEN 10.00-17.00 (to 21.00 Thur) Mon-Fri. Free.*

Geography

British Library Map Library   4 F1
Great Russell St WC1. 0171-636 1544. Holds over two and a half million printed maps and 20,000 manuscripts. *OPEN 10.00-16.30 Mon-Sat. Identification necessary. Free.*

Royal Geographical Society   **3 E5**
1 Kensington Gore SW7. 0171-589 5466. Geography in all aspects. 150,000 books, 850,000 maps together with several thousand atlases. Public Map Room. *OPEN 10.00-17.00 Mon-Fri. CLOSED B.hols & part Jun & Jul. Free.*

History & archaeology

Guildhall Library   **5 D2**
Aldermanbury EC2. 0171-606 3030. A reference library which also provides the official repository for deposited archives relating to the City of London. 230,000 volumes and printed items of London topography and history. *OPEN 09.30-17.00 Mon-Sat (Prints and Map dept closed Sat). CLOSED B.hols. Free.*

Institute of Archaeology   **1 F5**
University of London, 31-34 Gordon Sq WC1. 0171-387 7050. Archaeology, particularly Europe, Western Asia, Latin America. World prehistory, conservation and human environment. 1000 current periodicals, 48,000 monographs and 27,000 journals. *OPEN term time only 10.00-20.00 Mon-Fri, 10.00-16.30 Sat. Free.*

Institute of Classical Studies   **1 F5**
University of London, 31-34 Gordon Sq WC1. 0171-387 7697. Includes the Hellenic and Roman Societies Library. 85,000 volumes. Classical Antiquity. Open to members of Roman or Hellenic societies. *OPEN 09.30-18.00 Mon-Fri (to 20.00 Tue & Thur during term time), 10.00-16.30 Sat. CLOSED Sat in Aug. Free.*

Institute of Historical Research   **1 F6**
University of London, Senate House, Malet St WC1. 0171-636 0272. 120,000 volumes. Concentrates on principal sources for British and foreign medieval and modern history. Holds regular research seminars. *OPEN 09.00-20.45 Mon-Fri, 09.00-16.45 Sat. Members only.*

Library of the Museum in Docklands Project
Unit 14 Poplar Business Park, 10 Prestons Rd E14. 0171-515 1162. Houses Port of London Authority archive and has a large and unique collection of material on the London Docks including 20,000 photographs, prints and engravings. *OPEN 10.00-17.00 Tues, Wed &-Fri by appt. CLOSED Sat & B.hols. Free.*

Museum of London Library   **5 D1**
London Wall EC2. 0171-600 3699. London history and topography. *OPEN 09.30-17.30 Tue-Fri by appt only. Free.*

National Maritime Museum Library
Romney Rd SE10. 0181-858 4422. Large collection of prints and drawings. 50,000 books, maps, charts. Portraits. *Open to anyone for genuine research. Identification necessary. For longer projects ticket issued. OPEN 10.00-17.00 Mon-Sat. Free. Appt required on Sat.*

Society of Antiquaries   **4 D3**
Burlington House, Piccadilly W1. 0171-734 0193. Archaeological and antiquarian research. 130,000 volumes. *OPEN 10.00-17.00 Mon-Fri by appt only. Free.*

Law & public records

British Library Official Publications & Social Sciences Service   **4 F1**
Great Russell St WC1. 0171-636 1544. Official British publications and political and educational journals. *Reader's pass required. OPEN 09.30-16.45 Mon-Fri. CLOSED B.hols.*

Inns of Court
The principal law libraries (Inner Temple, Middle Temple, Lincoln's Inn and Gray's Inn). *OPEN by special permission only.*

Institute of Advanced Legal Studies   **1 G6**
University of London, 17 Russell Sq WC1. 0171-637 1731. Centre for legal studies. 105,000 volumes. *OPEN 10.00-20.00 Mon-Thur, 10.00-17.30 Fri, 10.00-17.15 Sat. Free to academic researchers. Charge to commercial organisations.*

Public Record Office   **5 B2**
Chancery La WC2. 0181-876 3444. Government archives and records of the Courts from 11thC to 1800. Records from 1800 to present day stored in Ruskin Av, Kew. *For access to either need reader's pass. OPEN 09.30-17.00 Mon-Fri. CLOSED B.hols.* Census rooms at Chancery Lane *OPEN 09.30-17.00 Sat.*

Literature

British Library   **4 F1**
Great Russell St WC1. 0171-636 1544. The most comprehensive literary collection of printed books and manuscripts in London. Adults over 21 only. *Reader's pass required. OPEN 09.00-17.00 Mon, Fri & Sat, 09.00-21.00 Tue-Thur. Free.*

Poetry Library   **4 G4**
Royal Festival Hall, South Bank Centre SE1. 0171-921 0664. Collection of poetry for loan and reference plus information on poetry events. *OPEN 11.00-20.00 Mon-Sun. Identification required to join library.*

British Library Science   4 **G2**
Reference & Information Service
Aldwych Reading Room, 9 Kean St WC2. 0171-412 7288 ex7288. Historical medical books. All current British clinical publications and foreign periodicals. OPEN 09.30-17.30 Mon-Fri. Free.

British Medical Association   1 **F5**
Library
Tavistock Sq WC1. 0171-387 4499. Over 80,000 books and 2000 modern medical periodicals. British and foreign. OPEN 09.00-18.00 Mon-Fri. BMA members free. Charge to non-members.

Medical Research Council
The Ridgeway NW7. 0181-959 3666. All bio-medical sciences. 20,000 volumes and 300 periodicals. OPEN 09.00-17.15 Mon-Fri to members only, or by application to director or librarian.

Pharmaceutical Society   7 **F2**
1 Lambeth High St SE1. 0171-735 9141. Pharmaceutical subjects. Historical collections of pharmacopoeias, herbals and botanical works. 60,000 volumes. Letter of authenticity required. OPEN 09.00-17.00 Mon-Fri for bona fide students of pharmacy and allied subjects.

Royal College of Physicians   1 **D5**
11 St Andrews Pl NW1. 0171-935 1174. History and biography of medicine. Medical portraits. 50,000 volumes and pamphlets. OPEN 09.30-17.30 Mon-Fri for serious researchers.

Royal College of Surgeons   4 **G2**
Lincoln's Inn Fields WC2. 0171-405 3474. Medical and surgical books and journals including large historical collections on anatomy and surgery. 160,000 volumes. OPEN 09.00-18.00 Mon-Fri. Letter of introduction from a Fellow or another library necessary.

Wellcome Institute for the   1 **F5**
History of Medicine
183 Euston Rd NW1. 0171-611 8888. History of medicine and allied sciences. Original texts. 400,000 volumes. OPEN 09.45-17.00 Mon-Fri (to 19.00 Tue & Thur), 09.45-13.00 Sat. Identification required.

Westminster Public Library   1 **B6**
(Health Information)
Marylebone Rd NW1. 0171-798 1039. Includes nursing, dentistry, psychiatry, speech and music therapy. Plus general health information for patients. Textbooks and periodicals. OPEN 09.30-19.00 Mon-Fri, 09.30-17.00 Sat. Free.

BBC Music Library   4 **C1**
156 Great Portland St W1. 0171-580 4468. All forms of printed music. OPEN 09.30-17.30 Mon-Fri to non-BBC employees by appt with the librarian only. Charge.

British Library Music Library
Great Russell St WC1. 0171-636 1544. Printed music and books about music. Reader's pass required. OPEN 09.30-16.45 Mon-Fri. Manuscripts room OPEN 10.00-16.45 Mon-Sat.

Central Music Library   7 **B2**
160 Buckingham Palace Rd SW1. 0171-798 2192. (Westminster City Libraries.) Books on music, music scores and parts, music periodicals. OPEN 13.00-19.00 Mon-Fri, 10.00-17.00 Sat. Free.

Theatre Museum Library   4 **F3**
1e Tavistock St WC2. 0171-836 7891. Individual play texts available for study in the study rooms by appointment only between 10.30-16.30 Tue-Fri.

British Library Science   4 **G2**
Reference & Information Service
Aldwych Reading Room, 9 Kean St WC2. 0171-412 7288 ex7288. Periodicals, books and pamphlets on the life sciences and technologies, medicine, earth sciences, astronomy and pure mathematics. OPEN 09.30-17.30 Mon-Fri. Free.

Geological Society   4 **D3**
Burlington House, Piccadilly W1. 0171-734 2356. 300,000 volumes and papers. 39,000 maps. OPEN 10.00-17.30 Mon-Fri to Fellows only (or to bona fide researchers introduced by a Fellow).

Linnean Society   4 **D3**
Burlington House, Piccadilly W1. 0171-434 4479. Reference library. Botany, biology and zoology. Historical, biological manuscripts. 100,000 books. OPEN 10.00-17.00 Mon-Fri by appt only. Letter of introduction required.

Natural History Museum   6 **D1**
Cromwell Rd SW7. 0171-938 9191. Research library. Botany, zoology, entomology, palaeontology, mineralogy and anthropology. Large collection of manuscripts, drawings and prints. 760,000 volumes. Bona fide researchers only. Appointment preferred. Identification necessary. OPEN 10.00-16.30 Mon-Fri. Free.

Royal Botanic Gardens, Kew
Kew Rd, Richmond, Surrey. 0181-940 1171. Botany and travel. Prints and drawings. Extensive and historical record of millions of dried specimens of plants from all over the world. 100,000 volumes.

OPEN Mon-Fri to bona fide researchers only. Appt and opening times by written application to the director.

Royal Horticultural Society   **7 D2**
Lindley Library, Vincent Sq SW1. 0171-834 4333. Over 50,000 volumes of horticultural and botanical books. Collection of original 17th-20th century plant drawings. Large number of periodicals. *OPEN 09.30-17.30 Mon-Fri. Appt preferred.*

Zoological Society   **1 C3**
Regent's Park NW1. 0171-722 3333. 150,000 volumes on zoology and related subjects, original zoological drawings and prints. Photographic library. *OPEN 09.30-17.30 Mon-Fri to members, associate members and non-members once they have purchased a ticket.*

Politics, economics & social sciences

British Library Humanities   **4 F1**
& Social Sciences
Great Russell St WC1. 0171-636 1544. Extensive collection of historical and current works. *Reader's pass required. OPEN 09.00-16.45 Mon, Fri & Sat, 09.00-20.45 Tue-Thur. CLOSED B.hols.*

British Library of Political   **4 G2**
& Economic Science
London School of Economics, 10 Portugal St WC2. 0171-405 7686. Social science. 790,000 bound volumes, including pamphlets, periodicals and manuscripts. *OPEN to research scholars by special permit: Oct-Jun 09.00-21.20 Mon-Fri, 10.00-17.00 Sat; Jul-Sep 09.00-19.00 Mon-Fri, to 21.20 Tue. CLOSED B.hols.*

City Business Library   **5 D2**
1 Brewers Hall Gdn EC2. 0171-638 8215. Public reference library. Major source of British and overseas directory material, company reports and financial information. Also newspapers, periodicals, timetables, statistical handbooks and series on commodities and overseas markets. *OPEN 09.30-17.00 Mon-Fri. Free.*

House of Lords Record Office   **4 F6**
House of Lords SW1. 0171-219 3074. Law and parliamentary history. 100,000 volumes, and manuscripts. *OPEN 09.30-17.00 Mon-Fri, to persons undertaking research of volumes not available elsewhere. Appt necessary. Free.*

Institute of Bankers' Library   **5 E2**
10 Lombard St EC3. 0171-623 3531. Comprehensive library on banking and allied subjects. 30,000 volumes. *OPEN 09.00-17.00 Mon-Fri (to 18.00 Thur). Charge for non-members.*

Institute for the Study of   **5 C5**
Drug Dependence (ISDD)
Waterbridge House, 32-36 Loman St SE1. 0171-928 1211. Reference library and information service covering all aspects of the non-medical use of drugs. Over 50,000 journals, articles and books; extensive press cuttings. *OPEN 09.30-17.30 Mon-Fri. Appointment preferred. Free.*

Marx Memorial Library
37a Clerkenwell Grn EC1. 0171-253 1485. Extensive collection of political, social and philosophical literature. Lenin used an office in the building between 1901 and 1902. *OPEN to the public 13.00-18.00 Mon & Fri, 13.00-20.00 Tue-Thur. Large groups by appt only. Membership required. Small charge.*

Science

British Library Science   **5 B1**
Reference & Information Service
Holborn Division, 25 Southampton Bldgs, Chancery La WC2. 0171-323 7496. Formerly known as the Patent Office, it contains periodicals, books, patents, trade marks, literature and reports on inventive sciences, engineering, industrial technologies and commerce. Main library *OPEN 09.30-21.00 Mon-Fri, 10.00-13.00 Sat (for opening times of annexes check with main library). CLOSED B.hols. Free.*

Aldwych Branch   **5 A2**
9 Kean St WC2. 0171-636 1544 ex7288. Has all the rest of the British Library's scientific literature, with emphasis on life sciences and technologies, medicine, biotechnology, earth sciences, astronomy and pure mathematics. *OPEN 09.30-17.30 Mon-Fri. CLOSED B.hols. Free.*

Institution of Civil Engineers   **4 E5**
Great George St SW1. 0171-222 7722. All branches of engineering; 19thC engineering history. Film library. 100,000 books and pamphlets. *OPEN 09.15-17.30 Mon-Fri to its members and members of the Institution of Mechanical Engineering. Non-members on application to the librarian (charge).*

Royal Aeronautical Society   **4 B4**
4 Hamilton Pl W1. 0171-499 3515. One of the finest collections in the world of historical and modern aeronautical books, prints and photographs. *OPEN 10.00-17.00 Mon-Fri. Charge for non-members.*

Royal Astronomical Society   **4 D3**
Burlington House, Piccadilly W1. 0171-734 4582. 27,000 volumes. Astronomy and geophysics. *OPEN 10.00-17.00 Mon-Fri to Fellows. Non-Fellows should contact the librarian in writing. Identification necessary.*

Royal Institution of Great Britain   4 **D3**
21 Albemarle St W1. 0171-409 2992. General science and history of science since 1799. Many complete scientific periodicals. Biography. Portraits. 50,000 volumes. *OPEN to non-members by appt 10.00-17.30 Mon-Fri.*

Royal Society of Chemistry   4 **D3**
Burlington House, Piccadilly W1. 0171-437 8656. Early works, periodicals. 100,000 volumes. *OPEN 09.30-17.30 Mon-Fri. Letter of introduction necessary for non-members. No appt necessary.*

Science Museum   3 **E6**
Imperial College Rd SW7. 0171-938 8111. A national reference library of pure and applied science, specialising in the history of science, technology and medicine. More than 450,000 volumes. *OPEN 09.30-21.00 Mon-Fri, 09.30-17.30 Sat. Free.*

Cultural institutes

Will provide comprehensive information on their country. Most organise language tuition, exhibitions and film shows. Some also run summer courses and exchanges.

Austrian Institute   3 **F5**
28 Rutland Gate SW7. 0171-584 8653.

Commonwealth Institute   3 **B6**
Kensington High St W8. 0171-603 4535.

Goethe Institut   6 **D1**
50 Prince's Gate SW7. 0171-411 3400.

Greek Institute
34 Bush Hill Rd N21. 0181-360 7968.

Hispanic & Luso Brazilian Council   4 **B6**
2 Belgrave Sq SW1. 0171-235 2303.

Institut Français du Royaume-Uni   6 **D2**
17 Queensberry Pl SW7. 0171-589 6211.

Italian Cultural Institute   4 **B6**
39 Belgrave Sq SW1. 0171-235 1461.

Polish Institute   4 **C1**
73 New Cavendish St W1. 0171-636 6032.

Society for Co-operation in Russian and Soviet Studies
320 Brixton Rd SW9. 0171-274 2282.

Spanish Institute   7 **A1**
102 Eaton Sq SW1. 0171-935 1518.

Swedish Cultural Dept   1 **B6**
11 Montagu Pl W1. 0171-724 2101.

Language tuition

A cosmopolitan city such as London offers a wide variety of facilities for learning almost any language, in colleges, cultural centres and private schools, where you can choose between group or individual tuition. Prices and standards vary enormously. There is no centrally-maintained register of private language schools, although most can be found in the Yellow Pages. *The* Adult Education Institute *publishes* Floodlight *with details of all sorts of courses run in the capital (available from newsagents). Private tutors may be found by contacting embassies or cultural institutes, by looking in the local newspaper or putting an advert in the paper yourself. You can also enquire at local colleges to see if staff or foreign students could assist. For information about facilities, methods and tuition contact:*

Centre for Information on Language Teaching (CILT)   4 **F3**
20 Bedfordbury WC2. 0171-379 5101.

English as a foreign language

Association of Recognised English Language Schools   5 **C5**
2 Pontypool Pl, Valentine Pl SE1. 0171-242 3136. Gives information and advice on the many English language schools within the association in the Greater London area. Such schools are recognised by the British Council as being of a high standard.

Cambridge School of English   1 **G5**
8 Herbrand St WC1. 0171-734 4203. Classes at all levels for students of 15+. Literature and film-study courses. Preparation for London Chamber of Commerce exam.

Canning School   3 **B6**
4 Abingdon Rd W8. 0171-938 2111. Intensive business-orientated training courses for managers from international, European and Far Eastern companies. Small groups and one-to-one. Specialised courses in negotiation, presentation and cross-cultural skills.

International House   4 **C4**
106 Piccadilly W1. 0171-491 2598. General and executive courses for all levels. Also teacher training courses. Language laboratory and social club.

Sels College   4 **F2**
64-65 Long Acre WC2. 0171-240 2581. Intensive courses throughout the year. All levels from beginners to Cambridge Proficiency. Small groups. Accommodation arranged.

Other languages

The schools and colleges listed below offer tuition in practically any language.

All Languages Ltd 2 **G4**
Nelson House, 362 Old St EC1. 0171-739 6641.
Butler School of Languages 7 **C1**
170 Victoria St SW1. 0171-834 0606.
Conrad Executive Language Training 4 **F3**
15 King St WC2. 0171-240 0855.
Language Studies International 4 **B2**
Woodstock House, 10-12 James St W1. 0171-499 9621.

Secretarial training

London Business College 4 **C2**
PO Box 2998, NW8. 0171-586 0084. Correspondence courses in secretarial skills, office practice and word processing. Also refresher courses.
Pitman Training Group 4 **F1**
154 Southampton Row WC1. 0171-837 4481. Courses of varying length and intensity including typing, shorthand, secretarial administration, business communication, audio-typing, word processing. Special courses for overseas students.
Sight & Sound 4 **E2**
118-120 Charing Cross Rd WC2. 0171-379 4753. Full- or part-time, day or evening courses in copy-typing, audio, shorthand, word processing, book-keeping, computing, data processing, PAYE.

Student information

Nowhere is it more exciting to be a student than in London. Cheap theatre and entertainment abound (see 'Theatres, cinemas, music and comedy') and there are many restaurants offering unusual and inexpensive food (see 'Eating and drinking'). London has some of the best-stocked reference libraries in the world (see the section 'Reference libraries'). For advice on problems or emergencies, see 'Social services' and 'Emergency & late-night help'.

Grants, charitable trusts & sponsorships

Advisory Centre for Education
22 Highbury Grove N5. 0171-354 8321. Publishes *ACE Bulletin* which reports on all aspects of the state sector of education.

Association of Commonwealth Universities 1 **F5**
36 Gordon Sq WC1. 0171-387 8572. Publishes four directories providing information on sources of funding for university students and staff wishing to study in other countries, primarily within the Commonwealth. Information service on general aspects of UK and Commonwealth universities. Phone for appt.
British Council
10 Spring Gdns SW1. 0171-930 8466. Offers grants to help foreign postgraduates to study, train or make professional contacts in Britain and to enable British specialists to teach, advise or establish joint projects abroad.
Charities Aid Foundation 4 **F1**
114-118 Southampton Row WC1. 0171-400 2300. Information service. Publishes *Directory of Grant-making Trusts*.
Charity Commission 4 **E3**
St Alban's House, 6th Floor, 57-60 Haymarket SW1. 0171-210 4477. Keeps a fully-comprehensive register of all registered charities in England and Wales.
National Council for Voluntary Organisations 4 **E1**
8 All Saints St N1. 0171-713 6161. Their *Voluntary Agencies Directory* lists 2000 voluntary organisations, and details of membership, staffing, recruitment of volunteers and funding for research.
National Union of Students
461 Holloway Rd N7. 0171-272 8900. Maintains an educational grants advisory service to student unions. Non-union members must write in for information. Also publishes *Grants Information Sheet* – a breakdown of what constitutes eligibility for grants.

Useful organisations

British Council 4 **E4**
10 Spring Gdns SW1. 0171-930 8466. Promotes Britain abroad – cultural, educational and technical cooperation between Britain and other countries.
British Youth Council 1 **F4**
57 Chalton St NW1. 0171-387 7559. Made up of representatives from national youth organisations and local youth councils. Aims to represent the views of young people and to look at ways of giving them a voice in society at local, national and international levels.
National Union of Students
461 Holloway Rd N7. 0171-272 8900. At least 2 million students are members. Represents students' rights. Organises and advises on social, cultural and educational events. Research staff deal with welfare problems. Trains student

union officers. Produces publications including *The Welfare Manual*.

Social clubs & societies

British Federation of   6 **G6**
Women Graduates
4 Mandeville Courtyard, 142 Battersea Park Rd SW11. 0171-498 8037. Open to women graduates of all nations. Club facilities.

International Students' House   1 **D5**
229 Great Portland St W1. 0171-631 3223. Open to all full-time students, professional trainees, foreign language assistants, au pairs (over 17) and student nurses. Excellent social and recreational facilities – most sports catered for. Coach visits to places of interest. Also a hostel.

London Union of Youth Clubs
64 Camberwell Rd SE5. 0171-701 6366. Will provide details of local youth clubs with social, recreational and community facilities.

Victoria League   3 **B2**
55 Leinster Sq W2. 0171-229 3961. Hospitality in British homes arranged for Commonwealth students and nurses. Programme of social activities. London hostel.

Student travel

There are lots of cheap ways for students to get around.

The Young Person's Railcard
For anyone under 24 yrs or in full-time education. Entitles holders to a discount on British Rail fares. Available from British Rail stations. *Charge.*

The Young Person's Coach Card
For 16-23 year-olds. Entitles holders to 33% discount when travelling on National Express coaches. Available from travel agents and coach stations. *Charge.*

The Inter-Rail Card
For anyone under 26 planning a trip to Europe. Entitles holder to unlimited train travel in 21 countries for one month. Contact any major British Rail station. *Charge.*

STA Travel   6 **D2**
74 Old Brompton Rd SW7. Also at 117 Euston Rd NW1 (1 **F4**). Telesales: 0171-937 9962. Wide range of low-cost fares worldwide. Special rates for students. *OPEN 09.30-19.00 Mon-Thur, 10.00-18.00 Fri, 10.00-16.00 Sat.*

Student accommodation

Reasonably-priced accommodation is notoriously difficult to find in London. College accommodation services only deal with their own students – but don't rely on them. Initially it may well be necessary to settle for a temporary solution like one of the hostels listed below. Foreign students can try the welfare office of their London embassy. Flat shares or flats to rent are advertised in the Evening Standard, Time Out, Loot and local papers.

British Council   4 **E4**
Accommodation Unit
10 Spring Gdns SW1. 0171-930 8466. Advice for overseas students on finding accommodation. *OPEN 09.00-16.00 Mon-Fri.*

King's Campus Vacation   6 **C5**
Bureau
552 King's Rd SW10. 0171-351 6011. Can arrange accommodation for visitors and foreign students during the vacation period in various halls of residence. Single and twin rooms.

London Tourist Board   7 **B1**
Information Centre, Victoria Station Forecourt SW1. Advice line: (0839) 123435. Bookings in hostels, guest houses and hotels. Information on youth accommodation, self-catering and camping. *OPEN 09.00-18.00 Mon-Fri, 09.00-17.00 Sat.* Also at Heathrow Airport.

University of London   1 **F6**
Accommodation Office
Union Building, Malet St WC1. 0171-636 2818. They find accommodation for London University students only, but will supply anybody with a list of halls of residence, many of which are open to all students during vacations, particularly *Jul-Sep.*

Women's Link   5 **C1**
1A Snowhill Ct EC4. 0171-248 1200. Accommodation advisory service. Publish a useful booklet *Hostels in London*.

Hostels

There is a large selection of hostel accommodation in London. Rooms are spartan but very clean, and usually shared. Mainly bed and breakfast and mixed unless otherwise shown. Mostly for young people. Prices vary depending on how long you stay. Weekly rates tend to be better value than daily rates. It is cheaper to share a room or a dormitory than to have a single room. For bed and breakfast for a day you should expect to pay £8.00-£20.00.

b = bed only, bb = bed and breakfast
fb = full board, sc = self-catering

Carr-Saunders Hall **1 E5**
18-24 Fitzroy St W1. 0171-580 6338. Accommodaton (halls) only available during *Easter* vacation and *summer* vacation *(Jul-Sep)*. TV lounge. Mostly single rooms, some twin. 150 beds. *bb*. Also have 200 beds in flats. *sc*.

Central University of Iowa Hostel **4 F1**
7 Bedford Pl WC1. 0171-580 1121. TV lounge. Twin and dormitory accommodation *(May-Aug)*. 33 beds. Two weeks maximum stay. *bb*.

Centre Français **3 B3**
61-69 Chepstow Pl W2. 0171-221 8134. Single, double and multi-bedded rooms for young people. 166 beds. Restaurant, TV room, launderette, library and conference room. *bb*.

International Students' House **1 D5**
229 Great Portland St W1. 0171-631 3223. Single, double or twin rooms and dormitory in *summer*. TV lounge, games room, squash court. 294 beds. *bb & sc*.

London Friendship Centre
3 Creswick Rd W3. 0181-992 0221. Dormitory accommodation, single, twin and family rooms. 53 beds. Games room, library, TV lounge, garden. Advance booking necessary. Short-stay hostel. *bb*.

O'Callaghans **6 B3**
205a Earl's Court Rd SW5. 0171-370 3000. TV lounge. Accommodation in shared and twin rooms. *bb*.

Passfield Hall **1 F5**
1 Endsleigh Pl WC1. 0171-387 7743. Accommodation only available during *vacations (Mar-Apr & Jul-Sep)*. TV lounge, games room. Single, twin and triple accommodation. 198 beds. *bb*.

Rosebery Avenue Hall
90 Rosebery Av EC1. 0171-278 3251. Accommodation only available during *vacations (Mar-Apr & Jul-Sep)*. TV lounge and bar. Single rooms; some double and twin. 195 beds. *bb*.

Sass House **3 E3**
11 Craven Ter W2. 0171-262 2325. Single, double and twin. 36 beds. *bb*.

Women's Link **4 F1**
Helen Graham House, 57 Great Russell St WC1. 0171-248 1200. 300 beds. Single and double rooms. Long-term accommodation only (six months +). *sc*.

YWCA: London Regional Office **4 E2**
16-22 Great Russell St. 0171-580 4827. Provides current information on all 18 London hostels. *Applications must be made to individual hostels, numbers are listed in telephone book.*

Youth Hostel Association (YHA)
Headquarters at 8 St Stephen's Hill, St Albans, Herts. (01727) 855215. Hostels are for members only. Join at any hostel. To reserve accommodation ring 0171-248 6547. Youth hostels offer dormitory accommodation. Maximum stay three nights. *bb*. Cost reduction for under 18s. *CLOSE at 23.30.* London hostels are at:
38 Bolton Gdns SW5. 0171-373 **6 B3**
7083.
36 Carter La EC4. 0171-236 4965. **5 C2**
84 Highgate West Hill N6. 0181-340 1831.
Holland House, Holland Wlk W8. **3 A5**
0171-937 0748.
Island Yard, Salter Rd SE16. 0171-232 2114.
14 Noel St W1. 0171-734 1618. **4 D2**
4 Wellgarth Rd NW11. 0181-458 9054.

Social services

London boasts an enormous range of helping organisations. To help you find your way through the maze of official and voluntary services, this section signposts the main referral agencies who will either be able to offer direct help or can put you in touch with the appropriate organisation. Information or help is given willingly and most of it is free.

General

Church Army
Church Army HQ, Independence Rd SE3. 0181-318 1226. Offers help to anyone in need: homes, hostels, holidays, youth services, prison welfare and social work.

Citizens Advice Bureaux (CAB)
Head Office: 0171-251 2000. Look in telephone directory for local branch. General advisory service plus help on any matter.

Family Welfare Association
501-505 Kingsland Rd E8. 0171-254

6251. Counselling service to individuals, groups and families on all problems, from financial to marital. Trained caseworkers. *OPEN 09.00-13.00 & 14.00-17.00 Mon-Fri.*

Help Advisory Centre   3 **A2**
57 Portobello Rd W11. 0171-221 7914. Help on assertiveness and communication skills, workshops on emotional and personal problems, women's groups, psychotherapy groups. Can also refer to specialists. *OPEN 11.00-18.30 Mon-Fri.*

Help Line
Capital Radio wavebands: 95.8 MHz, 1548 kHz. 0171-388 7575. Runs many telephone services for listeners: Help Line *09.30-17.30* for information and advice; flat sharing; job finders; community projects, etc.

International Social Service of Great Britain
Cranmer House, 39 Brixton Rd SW9. 0171-735 8941. Help with personal and family problems extending across national frontiers. Can help with repatriation of immigrants with settled status.

Just Ask   5 **F2**
46 Bishopsgate EC2. 0171-628 3380. Trained counsellors to help people with personal problems. *24-hr answerphone service.*

Piccadilly Advice Centre   4 **F2**
100 Shaftesbury Av W1. 0171-434 3773. Free information, advice and referral service on housing and jobs for the young, single, homeless and unemployed. *OPEN 14.00-18.00 & 19.00-21.00 Mon-Wed, Sat & Sun, 14.00-18.00 only Fri. CLOSED Thur.*

Salvation Army   5 **D3**
101 Queen Victoria St EC4. 0171-236 5222. Help on any problem. *24-hr telephone service.*

Samaritans   4 **D2**
46 Marshall St W1. 0171-734 2800. 14 branches throughout London. Advice and encouragement if you are despairing or suicidal. Walk-in service *09.00-21.00. 24-hr telephone service.*

Women's Royal Voluntary Service
234-244 Stockwell Rd SW9. 0171-416 0146. A nationwide service for all kinds of local community welfare work. Trained members help in both local and national emergencies.

Addresses from the local Town Hall, Citizens Advice Bureau or local post office.

Department of Social Security (DSS)
The term 'Social Security' covers all the schemes which provide direct financial assistance in time of need. It includes both National Insurance contributory schemes, eg sickness and unemployment benefit, and a range of non-contributory schemes. A great number of free explanatory leaflets on benefits are available from any local office of the DSS. To obtain more information, or if in difficulty, it's worth consulting some of the books listed under 'Publications' or contacting a local welfare rights group.

Environmental Health Departments
Will investigate 'nuisances' (noise, dampness, smells); food control and hygiene (inspection of premises and consumer complaints); defective housing; responsible for prevention of spread of infection.

Housing Departments
Let and maintain council housing. Deal with problems connected with rents, rates, welfare, maintenance, transfers, homelessness.

Social Services Departments
Have a wide range of duties and responsibilities laid on them by central government concerning the welfare of children, the elderly, and the mentally or physically handicapped. Social workers offer assistance with personal, practical and emotional problems.

These should be available in most large bookshops like Dillons and Foyles and also from public libraries.

Annual Charities Digest
Family Welfare Association, 501-505 Kingsland Rd E8. 0171-254 6251. Basically for professionals. Lists major charities, what they use their funds for, and those eligible to apply for help.

Consumer's Guide to the British Social Services
Phyllis Willmot. Penguin.

Guide to the Social Services
Family Welfare Association, 501-505 Kingsland Rd E8. 0171-254 6251. Published annually.

Women's Rights: A Practical Guide
Anna Coote and Tess Gill. Penguin.

Either see your doctor for help through the NHS or contact one of the following non-profit-making organisations. They may be able to help you to get an NHS abortion even if you have been turned down; otherwise they will arrange a private abortion as cheaply as possible. Where indicated contraception is also available. Charge for services unless otherwise stated.

British Pregnancy Advisory Service   7 C2
7 Belgrave Rd SW1. 0171-828 2484. Pregnancy tests and abortion service. Service for infertility, vasectomy and artificial insemination. *OPEN 09.00-17.00 Mon-Fri.*

Brook Advisory Centre   1 F6
Central Clinic, 233 Tottenham Court Rd W1. 0171-323 1522. Phone 0171-580 2991 for an appointment. Services for young people up to 25. Small annual donation covers pregnancy testing and contraception. Counselling and abortion help. Also offer counselling for sexual problems. *OPEN 09.30-19.30 Mon-Fri.*

Help Advisory Centre   3 A2
57 Portobello Rd W11. 0171-221 7914. Free pregnancy testing and abortion advice. *OPEN 11.00-18.30 Mon-Fri.*

Life   4 C2
83 Margaret St W1. 0171-436 1524. Anti-abortionist organisation. Free pregnancy testing and counselling for women. *OPEN 10.30-16.30 Mon-Fri (& 18.00-20.00 Tue-Thur).*

Pregnancy Advisory Service   4 D1
11-13 Charlotte St W1. 0171-637 8962. London's oldest-established pregnancy advisory service. Abortion advice, pregnancy testing, including test which can confirm pregnancy within 14 days of conception. 'Morning after' contraception effective within 72 hours of unprotected sex. Comprehensive abortion service. Sterilisation for women. No appointment necessary for pregnancy testing. Other services *by appt only. OPEN 09.30-17.30 Mon-Wed & Fri, 09.30-12.30 Thur & Sat.*

The Well Woman Centre   1 E5
Marie Stopes House, 108 Whitfield St W1. 0171-388 0662/4843. Pregnancy tests, counselling and abortion services. Contraception and sterilisation for men and women. Counselling help for psychosexual problems. Also offer a range of women's health care services including medical check-ups, cancer screening and help with pre-menstrual and menopausal problems. *OPEN 09.00-20.00 Mon-Wed, to 17.00 Thur & Fri, 09.30-17.00 Sat.*
For advice on the legal position only:

Abortion Law Reform Association/A Woman's Right to Choose campaign   4 D1
27-35 Mortimer St W1. 0171-637 7264. Two pressure groups which thwart efforts to restrict abortion and work to make abortion more freely available. Advice only; they cannot help you obtain an abortion.

Demand is always greater than supply as far fewer babies are now placed for adoption. There are, however, many older, handicapped or black children who need parents. Either apply through the Social Services department of the local authority or direct to an adoption agency. Many organisations cater only for a particular religious denomination so it is as well to get information about all the agencies and their requirements before applying (lists obtainable from the British Agencies for Adoption and Fostering).

British Agencies for Adoption and Fostering   5 C4
200 Union St SE1. 0171-593 2000. Not an adoption agency but a national federation of adoption agencies through which efforts are made to place children with special needs. Publish a list of agencies and other literature and information on adoption and fostering including a photo list of children awaiting adoption. Train social workers and have medical and legal groups.

Independent Adoption Service
121-123 Camberwell Rd SE5. 0171-703 1088. Find families for children of all ages and from all communities.

Parents for Children   2 F1
41 Southgate Rd N1. 0171-359 7530. A home-finding agency for older and handicapped children. Offer information and advice to people considering this type of parenthood. Long-term support to family after a child is placed.

Parent to Parent Information on Adoption Services (PPIAS)
Lower Boddington, nr Daventry, Northants. (01327) 260295. An informal self-help organisation, largely of adoptive parents, who offer advice and support on all aspects of adoption. *Annual subscription.*

For information on AIDS (Acquired Immune Deficiency Syndrome) the following centres offer advice and counselling, and have facilities for examination and testing. The National AIDS Helpline *is a 24-hr telephone advice service: 0800 567123.*

Ambrose King Centre
London Hospital (Whitechapel), White-

chapel Rd E1. 0171-377 7307. Free testing for HIV virus and other sexually transmitted diseases. (New patients are asked to come early; it may be necessary to wait, though everyone is seen on the day they attend.) *No appt or doctor's note necessary. OPEN 09.30-17.30 Mon-Fri (to 14.30 Thur).*

Body Positive   6 **A3**
51b Philbeach Gdns SW5. 0171-835 1045/6. A self-help group for people affected by HIV. *OPEN 11.00-17.00 Mon-Fri & Sun (to 21.00 Mon & Fri).* Helpline: 0171-373 9124 *(19.00-22.00 Mon-Fri).*

Health Information Service (HIS)
Freephone 0800 665544 for automatic transfer to your regional advice centre, which can provide information about all medical conditions, including AIDS. Can also refer you to local help organisations.

Terrence Higgins Trust   2 **B5**
52-54 Gray's Inn Rd WC1. 0171-242 1010. This is the main organisation dealing with AIDS. Telephone the AIDS Helpline for information *12.00-22.00 Mon-Sun,* or write enclosing sae. Legal line: 0171-405 2381. Operates *19.00-22.00 Wed.*

Alcoholism is now widely recognised as an illness. Help and treatment can be claimed under the NHS either through your doctor or through hospitals. Other useful centres are:

Accept
724 Fulham Rd SW6. 0171-371 7477. Independent organisation providing a counselling service and treatment centre; for problem and dependent drinkers, their families and friends. Also help for people with tranquilliser problems.

Al-Anon   5 **E6**
61 Great Dover St SE1. 0171-403 0888. Information and help for families and friends of problem drinkers. *24-hr telephone service.*

Alateen   5 **E6**
61 Great Dover St SE1. 0171-403 0888. Information and help for teenagers with parents or relatives who have drinking problems. *24-hr telephone service.*

Alcoholics Anonymous   6 **C3**
11 Redcliffe Gdns SW10. 0171-352 3001. (Head Office: PO Box 1, Stonebow House, Stonebow, York. (01904) 644026/7/8/9.) Give help to people wishing to recover from alcoholism or in need of the support and companionship of fellow sufferers. Meetings. Telephone

service *10.00-22.00. 24-hr answering service.*

Greater London Alcohol   2 **D5**
Advisory Service
30-31 Great Sutton St EC1. 0171-253 6221. For people with drinking problems and their families. Telephone advice and information for Greater London *09.00-17.00 Mon-Fri;* counselling service for the City and Hackney.

Turning Point
New Loom House, 101 Back Church La E1. 0171-702 2300. Runs rehabilitation hostels and advice centres for people with alcohol- and drug-related problems.

Dial **999** *for an emergency, otherwise:*
St John Ambulance Brigade   3 **G1**
Edwina Mountbatten House, 63 York St W1. 0171-258 3456. Will arrange a private ambulance and collection of ambulance cases from airports, docks or rail terminals. Need at least *48 hrs* notice. *Charge.*

See also 'Veterinary clinics' under 'Shops & services'.
Royal Society for the Prevention of Cruelty to Animals (RSPCA)
HQ, The Causeway, Horsham, W. Sussex. (01403) 264181. Telephone for information on animal clinics and hospitals. All complaints of cruelty to animals investigated in strict confidence. Rescue service for animals in distress.

Cruse Bereavement Care
126 Sheen Rd, Richmond, Surrey. 0181-940 4818. Counselling for the bereaved.

Social Services departments, either through their own specialist workers or in conjunction with voluntary organisations, provide a wide range of services for blind people. Ask to see a social worker who will be able to tell you how to get any special help you may need and what financial assistance, training and aids are available.
Royal National Institute for   4 **C1**
the Blind (RNIB)
224 Great Portland St W1. 0171-388 1266. Provide active help and advice on practically any problem concerning blind

people. Also publish a directory of all agencies for blind people.

Cancer prevention

Cancer can often be treated successfully if detected early enough. Women should have a regular cervical smear test; see your GP or local family planning clinic. They will also carry out breast examinations but it is advisable for women over 25 to learn to give themselves a monthly breast examination. The Women's National Cancer Control Campaign publishes an excellent leaflet on this.

The Well Woman Centre   **1 E5**
Marie Stopes House, 108 Whitfield St W1. 0171-388 0662/2585. Examination and screening for breast cancer and cervical smear tests. *Charge.*

Women's Nationwide Cancer   **2 G4**
Control Campaign
Suna House, 128-130 Curtain Rd EC2. 0171-729 4688. Education and information service. Publish a list of clinics offering check-ups. Send sae for leaflet on breast self-examination and cervical cancer. Mobile screening service available. Helpline: 0171-729 2229.

Cancer relief

Cancer Relief   **6 E3**
MacMillan Fund
Anchor House, 15-19 Britten St SW3. 0171-351 7811. Financial assistance, homes, nursing teams, for needy cancer patients and their families. Any request, however unusual, is considered.

Marie Curie Cancer Care   **4 B6**
28 Belgrave Sq SW1. 0171-235 3325. Homes, nursing and welfare services for the seriously ill.

Children

Social Services departments have a duty to promote the welfare of children in their area. They can do this by offering advice, practical assistance and, in certain circumstances, financial help to prevent family breakdown. They, or the NSPCC, will also investigate allegations of neglect or ill-treatment of children. If you suspect that a child is being seriously ill-treated and you feel prompt action is called for, you can call in the police. If a child shows signs of having psychological or emotional difficulties you can get advice and help from your local child guidance clinic. Your GP or the child's school can put you in touch. Children who need someone to talk to can call Childline on (0800) 1111.

Will offer confidential support and advice. OPEN 24 hrs Mon-Sun.

Child Poverty Action Group   **2 F4**
(CPAG)
4th Flr, 1-5 Bath St EC1. 0171-253 3406. Excellent information service on welfare rights. Help with tribunals. Useful publications (available only to advisers and representatives of claimants). Information line: 0171-253 6569. *OPEN 14.00-16.00 Mon-Thur.*

Invalid Children's Aid   **2 E5**
Nationwide
Barbican Citygate, 1-3 Dufferin St EC1. 0171-374 4422. Educate children and young people with special needs. Also special schools for asthmatic and language disordered children.

National Association for
Gifted Children
Park Campus, Boughton Green Rd, Northants. (01604) 792300. Advice of all kinds for parents and teachers of gifted children. Activities for the children. Newsletter for members.

National Autistic Society
276 Willesden La NW2. 0181-451 1114. Provide information and support to children with autism, their parents and carers. Special schools. Publications.

National Society for the   **2 G4**
Prevention of Cruelty to Children
(NSPCC)
42 Curtain Rd EC2. 0171-825 2500. Supports children who have been abused and protects those who could be at risk. Investigates reports of neglect or ill-treatment of children. Has set up Child Protection Line, manned by qualified and experienced personnel, to listen and advise on physical and sexual abuse and neglect. (0800) 800500. *OPEN 24 hrs.*

Royal Society for Mentally   **2 E5**
Handicapped Children and Adults
123 Golden La EC1. 0171-454 0454. Support for people with learning difficulties. Care centres, day nurseries, leisure clubs, speech therapy, training schemes.

Shaftesbury Society
16 Kingston Rd SW19. 0181-542 5550. Hostel accommodation for young people with learning or physical difficulties.

Contraception

Contraception is now freely available under the NHS whether you are married or single. You can consult your GP or visit your local family planning clinic. For other organisations offering contraception services see under 'Pregnancy & abortion'.

Brook Advisory Centre   **1 F6**
Central Clinic, 233 Tottenham Court Rd

W1. 0171-323 1522. Eleven clinics in the London area offer sympathetic advice and contraception to young people. *Free to students, unemployed people, and those under 18; otherwise a small annual donation.*

Family Planning Association   **4 D1**
27-35 Mortimer St W1. 0171-636 7866. Supplies a list of clinics and leaflets on aspects of sex education. Bookshop and mail order. Phone-in service for information and advice.

International Planned   **1 C4**
Parenthood Federation
Inner Circle, Regent's Park NW1. 0171-486 0741. Reading materials on family planning in several languages.

Pregnancy Advisory Service   **4 D1**
11-13 Charlotte St W1. 0171-637 8962. Registered charity providing pregnancy testing, 'morning after' birth control, sterilisation, abortion advice.

Dating agencies

There are many commercial organisations in London which offer introductions to suitably matched people who are looking for a partner. Some are less than scrupulous in their attempts to match clients' requirements and/or make exorbitant charges, so enquire about terms and conditions before handing over any money.

Dateline International   **3 B6**
23 Abingdon Rd W8. 0171-938 1011. Computer dating service with a complete cross-section of many thousands on file.

The Marriage Bureau   **4 B2**
(Katherine Allen)
18 Thayer St W1. 0171-935 3115. Established bureau. Famous for creating successful partnerships.

Deaf people

Visit your Social Services department for advice on benefits and services available. They, or the Citizens Advice Bureau, will be able to put you in touch with local and national voluntary organisations.

British Association of the
Hard of Hearing
7-11 Armstrong Rd W3. 0181-743 1110. A self-help organisation with 180 clubs for those with acquired hearing loss, total or partial. Social clubs, lip-reading groups, advice on hearing aids.

National Deaf Children's   **2 E5**
Society
15 Dufferin St EC1. 0171-250 0123. Information and guidance for parents and those concerned with deaf children. Literature available. Regional branches. Run a Technology Information Centre in Birmingham, which has a lending scheme for equipment. 0121-454 5151.

Royal Association in Aid of Deaf
People
27 Old Oak Rd W3. 0181-743 6187. Concerned with the spiritual, social and general welfare of deaf and blind/deaf people in London, Essex, Surrey and Kent. Trained staff to act as interpreters and counsellors. Special social clubs.

Royal National Institute for   **2 F5**
Deaf People
19-23 Featherstone St EC1. Information, education, training, hostels, homes for the deaf. Hearing aids tested free. Extensive library. Research laboratories.

Diabetics

The British Diabetic   **4 C1**
Association
10 Queen Anne St W1. 0171-323 1531. Aim to educate the diabetic to come to terms with his or her condition and lead an active life. Literature and advisory services available. Also sponsor diabetic research.

Disabled people

Much more attention has been given to the needs of disabled people in recent years largely due to the efforts of pressure groups working on their behalf. The DSS publishes a mini-guide to services for disabled people (leaflet HB1), available free from local Social Security offices and Social Services departments.

Artsline   **1 E3**
54 Charlton St NW1. 0171-388 2227. Telephone or postal service offering information and advice to disabled people on all aspects of the arts and entertainment in London: theatres, cinemas, concert halls, colleges, bookshops, museums and galleries. From access and facilities to opportunities for taking up creative interests. *OPEN 09.30-17.30 Mon-Fri.*

Disabled Drivers Association
Ashwellthorpe, Norwich, Norfolk. (01508) 489449. An association 'of the disabled, for the disabled, by the disabled' concentrating on all problems of mobility. Information and advice, help with holidays and travel arrangements (home and abroad), local groups. *OPEN 10.00-16.00 Mon-Fri.*

Disabled Living Foundation
380-384 Harrow Rd W9. 0171-289 6111.
Information service. Enquiries by phone or
letter (with sae), personal calls *by appt.*
Advice on equipment and facilities for
independent living. Permanent display of
aids and equipment.

Disablement Income Group
Unit 5, Archway Business Centre, 19-23
Wedmore St N19. 0171-263 3981.
Advice and information service. Issues
publications. Other branches.

**Royal Association for   4 D1
Disability and Rehabilitation
(RADAR)**
25 Mortimer St W1. 0171-250 3222.
Information and advice on education,
welfare, mobility, training and employment
of disabled people. Help with housing,
travel and holiday queries. Publications
include *Access for Disabled* guides.

Sexual Problems of the Disabled
286 Camden Rd N7. 0171-607 8851.
Give advice and information on sexual
matters to disabled people and those
working with them. Free advisory leaflets.

Discharged prisoners

*These organisations try to welcome the
discharged prisoner back into society.
You can also go to your local court and
ask for the Probation Officer who should
give you advice and help.*

Apex Charitable Trust
1-4 Brixton Hill Pl SW2. 0181-671 7633.
Operate a range of centres offering
employment services for ex-offenders and
youngsters at risk.

**National Association for the Care
and Resettlement of Offenders**
169 Clapham Rd SW9. 0171-582 6500.
Run projects to test out new ideas and
educate the public about the care of
offenders and prevention of crime.
Service voluntary organisations providing
facilities for offenders in the community.

Discrimination

*If you feel strongly about civil rights,
issues of sexual or racial discrimination or
inequality, the following organisations may
be able to help in individual cases, or may
welcome your support. They campaign to
promote awareness on these issues and
to improve or implement legislation.*

**Commission for Racial   4 C6
Equality**
Elliot House, 10-12 Allington St SW1.
0171-828 7022. Investigate complaints
of inequalities or discrimination on

racial grounds. Bring cases to court if
necessary.

**National Council for Civil   5 E5
Liberties (NCCL)**
21 Tabard St SE1. 0171-403 3888.
Campaigning organisation for the
protection of civil liberties. All advice by
letter only.

Drug dependence

The Misuse of Drugs Act 1971 *made it
illegal to possess cannabis, LSD, cocaine,
amphetamines, opium, morphine or
heroin. The police can search suspects
and their property and, with a warrant,
their premises. Your GP, or one of the
voluntary organisations below which
specialise in counselling people with drug
problems, can advise you about treatment. See also 'Drug dependence units'
in the 'Hospitals' section.*

**City Roads (Crisis   2 D3
Intervention)**
354-358 City Rd EC1. 0171-278 8671.
Provide immediate short-term help (up
to three weeks) for people in a state of
crisis through drug abuse. Offer medical
and social work support. Links with other
agencies to offer long-term rehabilitation.
OPEN 24 hrs, 7 days a week.

Community Drug Project
146 Camberwell Rd SE5. 0171-703
0559. Advice and counselling for people
with drug-related problems, principally
aimed at users of heroin, cocaine, stimu-
lants or other drugs. Needle exchange
service. *OPEN 10.00-17.00 Mon-Fri.
Drop-in service (no appt necessary)
14.00-17.00 Mon-Fri (& 10.30-12.00
Thur).*

The Hungerford Drug Project   4 E2
32a Wardour St W1. 0171-437 3523.
Counselling information, advice and referral service for people experiencing problems with their drug use.

Phoenix House
1 Eliot Bank SE23. 0181-699 1515.
Long-term residential rehabilitation for
drug addicts and alcoholics who need
extensive support. Therapeutic community staffed by ex-addicts and social
workers. Phone them for an interview if
you think you need such treatment.

Release   2 E5
388 Old St EC1. 0171-729 9904.
Specialise in giving legal advice to those
arrested for drug offences. Drugs
counselling and referrals for illegal and
prescribed drugs. General advice and
information on drugs, legal and practical
help.

Turning Point
101 Back Church La E1. 0171-702 2300. Counselling service and residential centres for the after-care of addicts who have undergone treatment.

Dyslexia

Many children and adults are handicapped by dyslexia (word-blindness).

The British Dyslexia Association
98 London Rd, Reading, Berks. (01734) 668271. Information and advice service. Branches throughout the country.

The Dyslexia Institute
133 Gresham Rd, Staines, Middx. (01784) 463935. Professional assessment and specialist teaching. Advisory service for parents and teachers. Train teachers and carry out research. Fifteen regional centres.

Eating disorders

Overeaters Anonymous
Box 19, Stretford, Manchester. Self-supporting organisation that follows a 12-step programme of recovery and offers advice to anyone suffering from overeating, anorexia or bulimia. Phone 0181-868 4109 for information on meetings in London and south east England.

The elderly

Most people prefer to stay in their own homes and retain their independence as far as possible in old age, and Social Services departments provide a range of services to help them do just this, sometimes with the help of local voluntary organisations. Home-helps can be arranged to cope with housework and shopping for those no longer able to manage alone, and the 'meals on wheels' service supplies cooked lunches to the elderly, infirm or housebound. Anyone on a pension who needs extra heating because of illness or restricted mobility should be eligible for financial help from the DSS. Services and facilities for the elderly vary from district to district but a call at the Social Services department, Citizens Advice Bureau or local 'Age Concern' branch should help you find out.

Abbeyfield Society
53 Victoria St, St Albans, Herts. (01727) 857536. Family-sized houses where 7-9 people live together with resident housekeeper responsible for main meals. Own

bed-sitting room, own furniture. Also 'extra care' houses of 20-30 people requiring personal care.

Age Concern
Astral House, 1268 London Rd SW16. 0181-679 8000. The focal point of all voluntary welfare organisations for the old. Excellent information service.

British Red Cross   **4 B5**
9 Grosvenor Cres SW1. 0171-235 5454. Provide regular visitors who act as friends and helpers. Loan medical equipment for nursing in the home. Organise holidays for handicapped people.

Carers National   **3 E2**
Association
29 Chilworth Mews W2. 0171-490 8898. Pressure group which aims to improve legislation for those who care for elderly relatives at home. Advice on financial matters and information about short-stay nursing homes.

Counsel & Care   **1 E1**
Twyman House, 16 Bonny St NW1. 0171-485 1566. Comprehensive advisory service for the elderly and those concerned with their welfare. Advice about suitable homes and how to apply. Useful fact sheets on care of the elderly. Give financial help when needed. *OPEN 10.30-16.00 Mon-Fri.*

Country Houses Association   **4 G2**
41 Kingsway WC2. 0171-836 1624. Charitable association for preservation of historic country houses providing accommodation for retired and semi-retired people.

Pre-retirement Association
26 Frederick Sanger Rd, Surrey Research Park, Guildford, Surrey. (01483) 301170. Give advice and information to help people face retirement successfully.

Epilepsy

British Epilepsy Association
Head office: 40 Hanover Sq, Leeds, W. Yorks. (0113) 2439393. Advisory service covering welfare, training, education, employment and social adjustment.

Gambling

Gambling can be as compulsive as drug addiction and may cause distress to both the addict and his or her family.

Gamblers Anonymous   **6 D5**
PO Box 88 SW10. 0171-384 3040. An organisation with several meeting places in the London area. Constructive help and advice to compulsive gamblers.

Haemophilia

Haemophilia Society   **5 B6**
123 Westminster Bridge Rd SE1. 0171-928 2020. A society for sufferers from haemophilia and those interested in their welfare. Advice and assistance given.

Homelessness

Local authorities must give housing advice to anyone with a housing problem; enquire at your local housing department. Finding somewhere to live is particularly difficult for young single people coming to London and many of the following organisations offer advice and short-term accommodation. It is important to know your rights if you are a tenant and to get proper advice if you have difficulties.

Alone in London Service   **2 B4**
188 King's Cross Rd N1. 0171-278 4224/5. An advice and counselling service for young, homeless people under the age of 21. *OPEN 09.00-13.00 Mon-Wed & Fri.* Advice line *OPEN 14.00-16.00 Mon, Tue & Fri, 12.00-19.00 Thur.*

Homeless Network   **4 D6**
12 Caxton St SW1. 0171-799 2404. Co-ordinating body for voluntary organisations providing a direct service to single homeless people in London. Day centres with washing facilities and social activities. Short- and medium-stay hostels.

London Hostels Association   **7 B2**
54 Eccleston Sq SW1. 0171-834 1545. Hostels for men and women in the London area. Minimum stay one month. Advance reservations for groups. Enquiries to Accommodation Section: 0171-828 3263.

Off the Streets   **4 E2**
Office: 54 Dean St W1. 0171-434 2861. *OPEN 09.00-17.30.* Night Shelter: Centrepoint shelter, 25 Berwick St W1 (**4 D2**). 0171-287 9134. *OPEN 20.00-08.00 every night of the year.* Provides basic accommodation, food and advice for up to 24 young people (male aged 16-19, female aged 16-21) who are new to and at risk in central London. Admission by interview.

Tent City
Old Oak Common La W3. 0181-743 5708. (East Acton tube.) Very inexpensive short-term tourist accommodation. Deposit required from UK residents; passport from foreign visitors. *OPEN Jun-Sep.*

YMCA
640 Forest Rd E17. 0181-520 5599. Head Office which will send lists of hostels catering for both sexes in the UK and abroad. Enquiries and bookings should be made direct to the particular hostel.

YWCA of Great Britain
Clarendon House, 52 Cornmarket St, Oxford, Oxon. (01865) 726110. Clubs and hostels for young people and women of all ages, classes and creeds. Temporary accommodation and permanent bed-sitting rooms and flats.

Homosexuality

Lesbian & Gay Switchboard
0171-837 7324. *24-hr telephone service* giving information on accommodation, activities and entertainments for lesbians and gay men. Legal and medical referrals and counselling service. Will put you in touch with local groups.

Lesbian Line
0171-251 6911. Phone service only. Advice for women. *14.00-22.00 Mon & Fri, 19.00-22.00 Tue-Thur.*

London Friend   **2 B3**
86 Caledonian Rd N1. 0171-837 3337. Telephone helpline for lesbians and gays *every eve 19.30-22.00.* Also face-to-face counselling, social support groups, coffee, tea and snacks. *Phone for details.* Women's number 0171-837 2782.

Legal aid & advice

There is a legal aid scheme whereby your legal costs can be subsidised on a means-tested basis. To find out about this and to get legal advice, go to your local Citizens Advice Bureau (see under 'General'); to any solicitor displaying the Legal Aid sign; or to your neighbourhood Law Centre.

Amnesty International   **2 C5**
British Section, 99-119 Rosebery Av EC1. 0171-814 6200. Support concerning immigration, deportation and other cases. About 40 groups in the London area.

Central London Law Centre   **2 E2**
47 Charing Cross Rd WC2. 0171-437 5854/5764. *OPEN 15.00-19.00 Tue* (Employment), *15.00-19.00 Wed* (Housing), *15.00-19.00 Thur* (Immigration). *OPEN at other times by appt.*

Legal Aid Board   **5 A1**
29-37 Red Lion St WC1. 0171-813 5300. Advice on legal aid system.

Mary Ward Legal Centre   **2 A6**
42 Queen Sq WC1. 0171-831 7079. Legal advice. *Appt only. OPEN 09.30-17.30 Mon-Fri.* Run on a green form legal aid basis. Also has a financial advice service, debt counselling and tax advice.

Release   2 **E5**
388 Old St EC1. 0171-729 9904. Emergency: 0171-603 8654. Specialise in drugs law. Deal with criminal legal emergencies. General legal advice and information on handling the police, the courts, prisons, lawyers and the legal aid system.

South Islington Law Centre   2 **D2**
131-132 Upper St N1. 0171-354 0133. *OPEN (by appt) 10.00-13.00 Mon* (Housing), *15.30-17.30 Wed* (Housing), *16.00-17.30 Wed* (Employment); *OPEN (walk-in) 16.00-17.30 Tue* (Immigration), *10.00-12.00 Fri* (Immigration).

Southwark Law Centre
Hanover Park Hse, Hanover Park SE16. 0171-732 2008. *OPEN (by appt) 14.00-16.00 Tue & Wed; walk-in service 17.00-19.00 Thur.* Telephone advice *14.00-17.00 Mon-Thur.*

Marriage guidance

Catholic Marriage Advisory   3 **C5**
Council
23 Kensington Sq W8. 0171-243 1898. Help for those, of all denominations, with marital problems. Meetings arranged for parents, teachers, school pupils and engaged couples. Natural family planning. *Appt only. Phone for details.*

Institute of Marital Studies
Tavistock Centre, 120 Belsize La NW3. 0171-435 7111. Professional help with marital problems. *OPEN by appt 09.30-17.30 Mon-Fri.*

London Marriage Guidance   4 **C1**
76a New Cavendish St W1. 0171-580 1087. Confidential counselling and education service for those with difficulties in their personal relationships. *Appt only. Phone for details.*

Mental health

If you have a severe emotional problem, the best person to see is your doctor who may recommend psychiatric help. Social workers are also able to give advice and assistance to the mentally ill and their families and can tell you about local facilities and support groups.

Brent Adolescent Centre
Johnston House, 51 Winchester Av NW6. 0171-328 0918. Confidential walk-in service for young people from 15-21 years old with personal and emotional problems. Trained psychotherapists. *OPEN 16.30-19.00 Mon, 12.00-14.30 Thur.*

MIND (National Association   4 **C1**
for Mental Health)
Granta House, 15-19 Broadway E15

0181-519 2122. Advisory service on all aspects of mental health.

Samaritans   4 **D2**
46 Marshall St W1. 0171-734 2800. A voluntary organisation to help people who have thoughts of suicide or despair. *24-hr telephone service.* Also walk-in service *09.00-21.00.* Totally confidential. Many London branches; see telephone directory.

Westminster Pastoral   3 **C5**
Foundation
23 Kensington Sq W8. 0171-937 6956. A large counselling centre, offering individual, group, or family and marital counselling for those with emotional difficulties. Also has an extensive training programme with both short and full-time courses for counsellors.

Missing persons

It is advisable to inform the police, although they can do little unless there is suspicion of foul play.

The Salvation Army Family   1 **G4**
Tracing Service
105-109 Judd St WC1. 0171-383 2772. Enquiries for close relatives are accepted. Also carry out searches abroad. No adoption, business, wills, divorces, friends or under-17s.

Nursing

The NHS can provide a district nurse. Apply to your local health authority. For private nurses look in telephone directory, at the advertisements in a nursing magazine, or contact one of the following:

British Nursing Association   4 **B2**
443 Oxford St W1. 0171-629 9030. Nursing agency supplying all types of nurses.

Langham Nurses Association   3 **C2**
85 Maitland Ct, Gloucester Ter W2. 0171-723 1444. Private, qualified nurses available (resident or non-resident).

One-parent families

Gingerbread   2 **C5**
16-17 Clerkenwell Close EC1. 0171-336 8183. Network of self-help groups for one-parent families. Advice on housing, the law, social security, baby-sitting, etc. Over 300 local groups.

National Council for One-Parent
Families
255 Kentish Town Rd NW5. 0171-267 1361. Will help and advise single parents and single pregnant women with any problem. Confidential.

Parents

Parents Anonymous, London
0171-263 8918. Confidential telephone listening service *(18.00-06.00)* for parents under stress who fear they may physically or emotionally abuse their children. Can also help with any emotional crisis in the family. One of many OPUS (Organisations for Parents under Stress) groups.

Pregnancy tests

A pregnancy test can always be done by your doctor – or consult your local family planning clinic. Magazines, newspapers and some chemists carry advertisements for private firms carrying out pregnancy tests, at a fee. You can also buy do-it-yourself kits at most chemists. See also 'Pregnancy & abortion' and 'Contraception'.

Rape

London Rape Crisis Centre
0171-837 1600. A free and confidential service run by women for women who have been raped or sexually assaulted and need support, information or any other help.
Survivors
0171-833 3737. National organisation for men who have been raped or sexually assaulted.

Service & ex-servicemen

Royal British Legion   **4 E4**
48 Pall Mall SW1. 0171-930 8131. Give assistance and financial aid to service and ex-servicemen and women, and their dependents. Apply to local branch.
Soldiers', Sailors' &   **5 G5**
Airmen's Families Association
19 Queen Elizabeth St SE1. 0171-403 8783. Financial advice and other aid for the families of service and ex-servicemen.

Singles clubs

Breakaway
57 Garrick Close W5. 0181-991 2169. A social club for professional people organising social, sporting and cultural activities in London and the home counties. *Annual or 3-month fee.*
London Village
24 Upper Park Rd NW3. 0171-586 7455. Membership organisation created by people aged 20-45 for their own age group. All kinds of social activities arranged. *Charge.*

Smoking

Action on Smoking & Health   **4 A1**
(ASH)
109 Gloucester Pl W1. 0171-935 3519. Advice on smoking-related problems and addresses of withdrawal clinics in London area.
Smokers' Clinic
Maudsley Hospital, Denmark Hill SE5. 0171-703 6333. Help and advice for anyone wishing to give up smoking. Telephone first.

Venereal diseases

See list under 'Hospitals'. All treatment is free, anonymous if desired and completely confidential. You do not need an appointment or letter from your own doctor.

Women's issues

There are many issues which specifically concern women; for example, equal pay, sex discrimination, combining work with child-rearing. Several organisations now exist to monitor legislation, promote research and provide practical help and advice. See also 'Abortion Law Reform Association' in the 'Pregnancy & abortion' section and 'NCCL' under 'Discrimination'. The feminist movement has been growing for years and many groups covering the whole feminist/political/radical spectrum exist in London. For further information consult the London Women's Handbook *available in libraries and women's centres.*
Equal Opportunities Commission
Overseas House, Quay St, Manchester. (0161) 833 9244. Advice on all queries and complaints regarding the Equal Pay and Sex Discrimination Acts.
Feminist Library   **5 B6**
5 Westminster Bridge Rd SE1. 0171-928 7789. Library and information service on issues affecting women. Collects and collates information on research which has been or is being undertaken. *OPEN 11.00-20.00 Tues, 14.00-17.00 Sat.*
London Women's Aid   **2 F5**
52-54 Featherstone St EC1. 0171-251 6537. Help for battered women. Co-ordinates local women's aid centres. *24-hr telephone service* to put battered women in touch with their nearest women's refuge and to offer advice and support.
National Alliance of Women's Organisations
279-281 Whitechapel Rd E1. 0171-247 7052. An umbrella organisation comprising over 220 women's organisations and

aiming to provide a national and European voice for women in the nineties. Advice on fundraising and setting up groups. Resource centre *OPEN 10.00-17.00 Mon-Thur by appt.*

Rights of Women 2 **F5**
52-54 Featherstone St EC1. 0171-251 6577. Free legal advice for women by women in the legal profession. Enquiries by letter only or telephone to speak to a qualified solicitor *19.00-21.00 Tue-Thur.*

Women's National 4 **E5**
Commission
Caxton House, Tothill St SW1. 0171-273 5486. Publishes a list of established women's organisations in London and the UK.

Voluntary social work

Many organisations rely heavily on volunteers to carry out much needed work in the community. If you can offer skills such as teaching, driving, typing, decorating and maintenance or sewing, so much the better, but many opportunities exist for people who can offer time, patience, good humour and commitment for tasks such as visiting the elderly or helping in clubs and hospitals.

Camden Volunteer Bureau 2 **B4**
Instrument House, 207-215 King's Cross Rd WC1. 0171-837 3443. Guides people into the type of voluntary work that they are most suited to. Work in Camden only for over 250 organisations.

Community Service 2 **B3**
Volunteers
237 Pentonville Rd N1. 0171-278 6601. Produce various publications full of unusual suggestions for helping in the community. Minimum of four months full-time work. Board, lodging and pocket money.

London Voluntary Service 1 **F4**
Council
356 Holloway Rd N7. 0171-700 8107. Co-ordinate and support the work of the voluntary sector groups in London. Contact them for the address of your local Volunteer Bureau.

Samaritans 4 **D2**
46 Marshall St W1. 0171-439 2224. Volunteers required to help on *24-hr telephone service* befriending the suicidal and despairing. Work in one of 14 branches. Information given about selection procedures, training etc.

Women's Royal Voluntary Service
234-244 Stockwell Rd SW9. 0171-416 0146. Men and women volunteers welcome for all community work.

Police stations

These are the most important police stations within a 3-mile radius of Piccadilly Circus.

City of London

Headquarters & all 5 **E2**
departments
26 Old Jewry EC2. 0171-601 2222.
Bishopsgate 5 **F2**
182 Bishopsgate EC2. 0171-601 2222.
Snow Hill 5 **C1**
5 Snow Hill EC1. 0171-601 2222.
Wood Street 5 **D2**
37 Wood St EC2. 0171-601 2222.

Metropolitan

Battersea
112-118 Battersea Bridge Rd SW11. 0171-350 1122.
Charing Cross 4 **F3**
Agar St WC2. 0171-240 1212.
Chelsea 6 **E2**
2 Lucan Pl SW3. 0171-589 1212.
Hyde Park 3 **F4**
North of Serpentine W2. 0171-289 2076.
Kensington 3 **B6**
72-74 Earl's Court Rd W8. 0171-376 1212.
King's Cross 2 **C3**
2 Tolpuddle St N1. 0171-704 1212.
New Scotland Yard 4 **E6**
Broadway SW1. 0171-230 1212.
Southwark 5 **D5**
323 Borough High St SE1. 0171-407 4759.
Victoria 7 **B2**
202-206 Buckingham Palace Rd SW1. 0171-730 1212.
West End Central 4 **D3**
27 Savile Row W1. 0171-437 1212.

Hospitals

General hospitals

The following hospitals all have 24-hr *Accident & Emergency departments:*
Charing Cross Hospital
Fulham Palace Rd W6. 0181-846 1234.
Chelsea & Westminster Hospital
369 Fulham Rd SW10. 0181-746 8000.

Guy's Hospital   **5 E4**
St Thomas St SE1. 0171-955 5000.
London Hospital (Whitechapel)
Whitechapel Rd E1. 0171-377 7000.
Queen Mary's University Hospital
Roehampton La SW15. 0181-789 6611.
Royal Free Hospital
Pond St NW3. 0171-794 0500.
St George's Hospital
Blackshaw Rd SW17. 0181-672 1255.
St Thomas' Hospital   **5 A6**
Lambeth Palace Rd SE1. 0171-928 9292.
University College Hospital   **1 F5**
Gower St WC1. 0171-387 9300.
Whittington Hospital
Highgate Hill N19. 0171-272 3070.

Children's hospitals

Belgrave Unit
King's College Hospital, Denmark Hill
SE5. 0171-274 6222. *24-hr casualty.*
Children's Hospital Sydenham
321 Sydenham Rd SE26. 0181-693
3000. *24-hr casualty.*
The Hospital for Sick   **2 A5**
Children
Great Ormond St WC1. 0171-405 9200.
Queen Elizabeth Hospital for Sick
Children
Hackney Rd E2. 0171-739 8422. *24-hr
casualty.*
St Mary's Children's   **3 E2**
Hospital
South Wharf Rd W2. 0171-725 6163. *24-
hr casualty.*
Westminster Children's   **7 C2**
Hospital
(Westminster Hospital Teaching Group)
Udall St SW1. 0181-746 8000. *24-hr
casualty.*

Dental hospitals

Dental Emergency Care Service
0171-400 0400/0181-677 6363. *OPEN
24 hrs.* Private or NHS.
Eastman Dental Hospital   **2 B4**
256 Gray's Inn Rd WC1. 0171-837 3646.
London Hospital Dental Institute
New Rd E1. 0171-377 7000.

Drug dependence units

*The following hospitals have special
clinics to deal with drug abuse and
dependency. Each drug unit can accept
patients only from its local catchment
area. They prefer people to have a letter
of referral from a GP but will see them
without if necessary. A few units have in-*
*patient facilities but any unit will offer help
and guidance for further treatment if
required. Emergency cases should go to
their nearest casualty department. The
Maudsley Hospital operates a 24-hr
general emergency clinic.*
Hackney Hospital
Drug Dependency Unit, 230 Homerton
High St E9. 0181-919 8629. *OPEN
10.00-11.00 Mon, Wed & Fri.* At other
times *by appt only.*
London Hospital (St Clements)
2a Bow Rd E3. 0171-377 7000. *OPEN
09.30-17.30 Mon-Fri.*
Maudsley Hospital
Denmark Hill SE5. 0171-703 6333.
Queen Mary's University Hospital
Roehampton La SW15. 0181-789 6611.
*OPEN 14.00-17.00 Mon, 10.00-12.00
Wed.*
St George's Hospital (Tooting)
Blackshaw Rd SW17. 0181-672 1255.
*OPEN 09.00-17.00 Mon-Fri (to 20.00
Wed).* CLOSED *Tue morning.* Walk-in
service and appt then made.
St Mary's Hospital   **3 E2**
Praed St W2. 0171-725 6666. Drug
Dependency Centre: 0171-725 6486.
University College Hospital   **1 E4**
Drug Dependence Unit, National
Temperance Hospital, 122 Hampstead
Rd NW1. 0171-387 9541. *OPEN 09.00-
19.00 Tue, 09.00-13.00 Fri.*
West Middlesex Hospital
Twickenham Rd, Isleworth, Middx.
0181-560 2121. *OPEN 14.00-20.00
Mon, 10.00-18.00 Tue-Thur, 10.00-
13.00 Fri.*

Ear, nose and throat hospitals

Royal National Throat, Nose   **2 B4**
and Ear Hospital
330 Gray's Inn Rd WC1. 0171-837 8855.

Eye hospitals

Moorfields Eye Hospital   **2 F4**
City Rd EC1. 0171-253 3411. *OPEN 24
hrs Mon-Sun.*

Foot hospitals

London Foot Hospital   **1 E5**
33 Fitzroy Sq W1. 0171-636 0602.
.

Heart and chest hospitals

London Chest Hospital
Bonner Rd E2. 0181-980 4433.

National Heart and Chest   6 **E3**
Hospital (Brompton Hospital)
Fulham Rd SW3. 0171-352 8121.

Royal London Homoeopathic   2 **A5**
Hospital
Great Ormond St WC1. 0171-837 3091.

Newham General Hospital
Forest La E7. 0171-476 4000.
Queen Charlotte's Maternity
Hospital
339 Goldhawk Rd W6. 0181-748 4666.
Whipps Cross Hospital
Whipps Cross Rd E11. 0181-539 5522.

Grove Park Hospital
Marvels La SE12. 0181-857 1191.

Charing Cross Hospital
Fulham Palace Rd W6. 0181-846 1252.

National Hospital for   2 **A5**
Neurology and Neurosurgery
Queen Sq WC1. 0171-837 3611.

The National Health Service can send you free or at very low cost to one of their many convalescent homes by the sea or in the country – consult your hospital doctor.
King's Fund   4 **C2**
11-13 Cavendish Sq W1. 0171-307 2400. A directory for Greater London of places that offer convalescence, rehabilitation and other short-term care.
The London Clinic   1 **C6**
20 Devonshire Pl W1. 0171-935 4444. Top-notch, private.

Western Ophthalmic Hospital   1 **A6**
(St Mary's Hospital Teaching Group)
Marylebone Rd NW1. 0171-402 4211.

Royal National Orthopaedic   1 **D5**
Hospital
45-51 Bolsover St W1. 0171-387 5070.

Castlewood Day Hospital
25 Shooter's Hill SE18. 0181-856 4970.
London Hospital (St Clements)
2a Bow Rd E3. 0171-377 7953.
Maudsley Hospital
Denmark Hill SE5. 0171-703 6333. Also drug clinics and drug in-patient facilities. *24-hr walk-in emergency.*
Parkside Clinic
63-65 Lancaster Rd W11. 0171-221 4656. Referral by GP, social worker etc, from anywhere in the London area.
West Lambeth Community Care
NHS Trust
Church La SW17. 0171-346 5400. Drug in-patient facilities, geriatric unit.

Eastern Hospital
Homerton Gro E9. 0181-985 1193.
Guy's Hospital   5 **E4**
St Thomas St SE1. 0171-955 5000.
London Hospital (Whitechapel)
Whitechapel Rd E1. 0171-377 7000.
Middlesex Hospital   4 **D1**
James Pringle House, 73 Charlotte St W1. 0171-380 9141.
Newham District General
Glen Rd E13. 0171-476 1400.
Royal Free Hospital Marlborough
Clinic
Pond St NW3. 0171-794 0500.
Royal Northern Hospital
Holloway Rd N7. 0171-272 7777.
St Bartholomew's Hospital   5 **C1**
West Smithfield EC1. 0171-601 8888.
St Mary's Hospital   3 **E2**
Praed St W2. 0171-725 6619/20.
St Thomas' Hospital   5 **A6**
Lambeth Palace Rd SE1. 0171-928 9292.
University College Hospital   1 **F5**
Gower St W1. 0171-388 9625.

If you wish to donate blood, or to leave your organs for transplant or research purposes, these wishes must be recorded in writing on a donor card which should be carried at all times. For further information contact:

Dept of Health (DoH)   **5 C6**
Hannibal House, Elephant & Castle SE1. 0171-972 2000.

Blood

West End Donor Centre   **4 D2**
26 Margaret St W1. 0171-580 8772/3.

Eyes

Royal National Institute for   **4 C1**
the Blind
224 Great Portland St W1. 0171-388 1266.

Organs

Dept of Health (DoH)   **5 C6**
Anatomy Dept, Hannibal House, Elephant & Castle SE1. 0171-972 2000.

Public lavatories

Look out for signs in the streets directing you to the nearest public lavatories, or ask someone likely to be familiar with the area: police, traffic wardens, news-vendors or shopkeepers. All lavatories in this country are divided into separate areas for men and women except for the new cabin-style ones to be found in the street which are completely self-contained and therefore unisex. OPEN 24 hrs. Nearly all large stores, museums and national art galleries have lavatories, as do all pubs, restaurants and mainline stations, and the major ones – Euston, King's Cross, Paddington, Victoria and Waterloo – are OPEN 24 hrs. Some London Transport underground stations have lavatories. All public places must now provide access for the disabled wherever practicable and this includes lavatories; look for the wheelchair symbol.

Emergency and late-night help

Accidents: motor

When in an accident with another vehicle you must stop and exchange names, addresses and insurance details with the other party. There is no need to call the police to the scene of the accident unless a person is seriously injured, in which case dial 999 immediately. In the case of a person being injured but able to walk away, or where the other driver fails to stop, then this must be reported to the nearest police station within 24 hrs.

Bombs

If you see a suspicious looking package:
1 – **DON'T TOUCH IT**
2 – *Get people away from the area*
3 – *Inform personnel in charge of the premises*
4 – *Dial **999** and tell the police where it is*

Car breakdown

AA (Automobile Association)
Freephone breakdown service (0800) 887766. *24 hrs Mon-Sun.* You can call the AA out if your car breaks down, but you will have to join on the spot if you are not already a member.

National Breakdown
Freephone breakdown service (0800) 400600. *24 hrs Mon-Sun.* Non-members will pay more for rescue/recovery than members.

Olympic Breakdown Service
0171-624 8662. *24 hrs Mon-Sun.* An AA and RAC-approved recovery service covering the whole of London.

RAC (Royal Automobile Club)
Freephone breakdown service (0800) 828282. *24 hrs Mon-Sun.* You will need to be a member of the RAC.

Cash

Cash dispensing machines outside major branches of most banks operate 24 hrs. Ask your bank about obtaining the special card, and a list of branches with dispensers. There are now many places (in small shops, arcades, etc), open till late in the evening, which call themselves Bureaux de Change and will change travellers cheques. Some are quite unscrupulous and charge a very high commission for the service. It is always best to change money in a bank or well-known and established Bureau de Change. The following are open longer hours than usual.

Chequepoint 4 **E3**

All Chequepoint branches in central London are open until at least 23.00. The following are OPEN 24hrs: 220 Earl's Court Rd SW5 (6 **B2**), 0171-373 9515; 71 Gloucester Rd SW7 (6 **C2**), 0171-373 9682; Marble Arch W1 (4 **A2**), 0171-723 1005; 2 Queensway W2 (3 **C3**), 0171-727 1399.

London Gatwick Airport

Lloyds Bank (in Hilton Hotel) (01293 537559). OPEN 08.00-15.00 Mon-Fri. Midland Bank (Crawley) (01293 519122). OPEN 09.30-17.00 Mon-Fri.

London Heathrow Airport

Thomas Cook (0181-897 3351) in Terminal 1. OPEN 24 hrs. Travelex (0181-897 3501) in Terminal 3. OPEN 24 hrs in Arrivals, 06.00-22.00 in Departures.

Luton Airport

International Currency Exchange (01582 30700). OPEN Easter-Oct 24 hrs; Nov-Easter 05.30-23.00 Mon-Sun.

Your local police station keeps a list of chemists and doctors available at all hours. Or try:

Bliss Chemist 4 **A3**

5 Marble Arch W1. 0171-723 6116. OPEN 09.00-24.00 every day of the year.

Boots 4 **E3**

Piccadilly Circus W1. 0171-734 6126. OPEN 08.30-20.00 Mon-Fri, 09.00-20.00 Sat, 12.00-18.00 Sun.

Warman Freed

45 Golders Green Rd NW11. 0181-455 4351. OPEN 08.30-24.00 every day of the year.

For information on reporting lost or stolen cards see 'Money and business services'.

See under 'Homelessness' in the 'Social services' section.

Whether you are a visitor or a resident, in an emergency dial **999** and ask for the ambulance service, or make your own way to a casualty hospital (see 'Social ser-

vices'). If at all practicable, go to a doctor (your local police station keeps a list of doctors) as casualty hospitals are for serious emergencies only. Visitors to London can register as temporary patients. Free medical treatment is available to British citizens, EC nationals and visitors from other countries with reciprocal arrangements. All other foreign visitors will be required to pay for medical treatment.

Apply to the nearest police station. Lost property found in the street is usually taken there.

Air travel: lost property is held by each individual airline. For property lost in the main airport buildings enquire: British Airport Authority's Lost Property Office, London Airport, Heathrow, Middx. 0181-745 7727. OPEN 09.00-16.00 Mon-Sun.

British Rail: if you lose something on a train, contact the station where the train you were on terminates. They will be able to inform you whether your belongings have been recovered and, if so, where they have been taken.

London Transport: for enquiries about property lost on the underground or buses, call in person at the Lost Property Office, 200 Baker St W1 (1 **B5**) or apply in writing (forms available at any tube station). No telephone enquiries. OPEN 09.30-14.00 Mon-Fri.

Taxis: apply 15 Penton St N1 (2 **C3**). 0171-833 0996. Alternatively, contact your nearest police station.

Lost children: will be cared for by the railway police if lost on British Rail, or ask at the nearest police station if lost elsewhere.

Lost car keys: if you know the number of your key (keep a note of it somewhere in your wallet) the AA or RAC can probably help (phone numbers under 'Car breakdown') if a nearby garage or the police can't.

Lost dogs: may have been taken to Battersea Dogs Home, 4 Battersea Park Rd SW8 (7 **B5**). 0171-622 3626.

Lost passports: report the loss to the police and to your embassy/high commission.

Most London car parks are run by National Car Parks (NCP), which have distinctive yellow signs. Notice boards at the entrance give details of charges. Most parking meters and single yellow lines along London streets cease to be *applicable as from 18.30 Mon-Fri, 13.30 Sat and all day Sun; but do read the signs on the meters or affixed to nearby lamp posts which give times of operation. Parking on double yellow lines, on the pavement and double-banked parking is forbidden at all times, and you may emerge to find your car has been towed away or that a clamp has rendered it immobile. Collecting your car (or having the clamp removed) is costly and inconvenient (see 'Wheel-clamping and Impoundment'). TRACE (see address p243) give advice on loading/unloading goods, pavement parking and how to appeal against a parking fine.*

24-hr car parks:

Abingdon St SW1.	7	**E1**
Arlington St SW1.	4	**D4**
Audley Sq W1.	4	**B4**
Brewer St W1.	4	**D3**
Cadogan Pl SW1.	6	**F1**
Cambridge Circus WC2.	4	**E2**
Denman St W1.	4	**E3**
Dolphin Sq SW1.	7	**C3**
Park La W1.	4	**B4**
Pavilion Rd SW1.	6	**F1**
Semley Pl SW1.	7	**B2**
Upper St Martin's La WC2.	4	**F3**
Young St W8.	3	**C5**

City Petroleum 2 **D2**
316 Essex Rd N1. 0171-226 5991.
Chiswick Flyover Service Station
1 Great West Rd W4. 0181-994 1119.
Star Service Station 3 **B3**
7 Pembridge Villas W11. 0171-229 6626.

For a list of police stations see 'Social services'.

when you need a doctor or a chemist:
Each police station keeps a list of emergency doctors and chemists who are available at all hours.

when you need a garage:
Each police station keeps a list of local garages and the times they are open.

when you need a hotel:
They keep up-to-date information on hotels and boarding houses in the area, with prices – of course, they don't know if there are vacancies, but at least you'd have somewhere to try.

when you've been burgled:
Report any theft to the nearest police station immediately.

when you've lost property in the street:
It may have been handed in to them, or they will be able to give you a list of lost property offices for things lost in trains and taxis, etc.

when your car has been stolen:
Ring them up straight away – it may have been towed away by them for a parking infringement. Otherwise they will circulate its description and let you know if they get it back.

when your dog is lost:
It may have been taken to them at the station, in which case they will look after it for one night and then take it to the Battersea Dogs Home, 4 Battersea Park Rd SW8. 0171-622 3626.

when you're stranded:
If you've come to London from a provincial town and spent your return fare, they can take the name of someone in your home town who will deposit your fare at the local police station and then the London police will give you a travel warrant to get you home. (This applies to British residents only – all other nationalities should apply to their own embassy for repatriation.)

when you're locked out:
The police keep a list of local locksmiths or try the *Yellow Pages* for a *24-hr* service or a willing locksmith who will come out after hours.

if you are arrested:
Always keep calm and remain polite. You do not have to say anything in answer to any allegations that are made but it is sensible to give your name and address. Ask to phone your solicitor or phone Release 0171-603 8654 *(OPEN 24 hrs)* who will give you advice and get a solicitor if necessary. Appeals for legal representation, legal aid and bail can be made in court. *See under 'Legal aid'.*

There is a late-opening post office in London:
Post Office 4 **F3**
24-28 William IV St, Trafalgar Sq WC2. 0171-930 9580. *OPEN 08.00-20.00 Mon-Sat.*

See under 'Social services'.

The underground system closes down about midnight. However, night buses *serve London every night, with a greatly extended service to the suburbs. All majornight bus routes pass through Trafalgar Sq (4 **E4**) and they run about once an hour. See night bus map.*

For a list of 24-hr taxi and mini-cab companies, see 'Transport in London'.

Wheel-clamping and impoundment

If you are illegally parked or your vehicle is causing an obstruction, it may be wheel-clamped or towed away to a pound. In

either case you will have to pay a substantial fine to recover your car. If you get wheel-clamped, follow the instructions on the label attached to your vehicle. If the label is missing, phone 0171-747 4747 (24 hrs) to find out which authority to contact. This line is operated by TRACE (Tow Away, Removal & Clamping Enquiries, 1st Floor, New Zealand House, 80 Haymarket SW1). If your car is missing, call TRACE on the above number to find out whether it has been removed to a pound and which one, how to get there by public transport and how to pay the fine.

Transport in London

Public transport

London has a fairly comprehensive system of public transport with a good night service. There are three different services – London Transport which operates buses and the underground (tube), British Rail (BR) which operates overground trains, and Docklands Light Railway (DLR). The system is supposed to be integrated so that all three connect with each other wherever practicable, but bus and train timetables don't always coincide. To find your way around, use the underground and bus maps in this book. For enquiries about lost property on public transport see 'Emergency & late-night help'.

London Transport   4 **E6**
Travel Information Centre, 55 Broadway SW1. 0171-222 1234. Will answer queries about timetables and fares for buses and the underground. Also give journey planning advice. Automatic telephone call queueing system *24 hrs*. Other travel information centres at these underground stations: Euston, Heathrow, Liverpool Street, King's Cross, Oxford Circus, Piccadilly Circus and Victoria (British Rail station). For the latest update on the travel situation call Travel Check (*24 hrs*) on 0171-222 1200.

The underground

For the stranger to London, this is the simplest way of getting around. For journeys starting from the centre, tubes run *approx 05.30-00.15 Mon-Sat, 07.30-23.30 Sun*. Start *30 minutes* earlier if

coming from the suburbs or if you have to change; all tube stations have a notice showing the times of first and last trains. Fares are graduated according to zones and, for the regular traveller, weekly, monthly or annual Travelcards provide considerable savings. Travelcards can be used on the underground, DLR, buses and Network SouthEast (in relevant zones), and are sold at Travel Information Centres, British Rail stations, all underground stations and some newsagents. Keep your ticket to use in the exit machine at your destination. London Transport enforce £10 on-the-spot fines if you are found travelling without a valid ticket. Cheap day returns are available if you start your journey *after 09.30 Mon-Fri or any time Sat & Sun*.

Buses

Covering the whole of Greater London they are slower than tubes, especially in the rush hours, but more pleasant and you see so much more. They run *approx 06.00-24.00 Mon-Sat, 07.30-23.30 Sun*. First and last times of bus routes are indicated on bus stops but heavy traffic can prevent buses from keeping to these times. Fares are graduated, apart from a few flat-fare routes. Return tickets are not available. On some buses you pay the driver as you get on but others (including all those with the entrance at the back of the bus) have a conductor who collects the fares as the bus goes along. Both give change but do not like being handed notes, especially large ones. If you are waiting at a request stop (red) you must raise your arm to make the bus stop for you. Once on the bus, if you wish to alight at a red request stop, you must ring the bell once, in good time. At other bus stops, compulsory stops (white), this is not necessary. For night buses, see 'Transport' under 'Emergency and Late-night Help'. Consult *Buses for Night Owls*, available from LT and BR travel information centres.

Docklands Light Railway

Docklands Light Railway (DLR) is integrated with the underground and British Rail networks. It links Docklands with the City of London, Stratford and Greenwich, and extends to Beckton, serving the area between the Isle of Dogs and the Royal Docks. A direct shuttle bus to London City Airport is part of the network. The red, white and blue trains are computer-operated with a guard/ticket collector on board. There are excellent views from the high viaduct route over the stretches of water which form the Docklands. Trains run from *05.30-00.30 Mon-Fri, 06.00-00.30 Sat and 07.30-23.30 Sun (Beckton branch does not run at weekends)*. Docklander tickets give unlimited travel for one day on DLR only. All tickets, Travelcards and passes issued by London Transport and British Rail are valid on DLR provided they cover the correct zone. Tickets can be bought from DLR Information Centres at Tower Gateway and Island Gardens *09.30-17.00 Mon-Fri*, or from ticket machines at DLR stations; keep some coins handy. *For 24-hr travel information on DLR phone 0171-918 4000.*

British Rail trains

BR run inter-city trains all over Britain; Network South East which serves London and the suburbs. These trains generally run *06.00-24.00 Mon-Sat, 07.00-22.30 Sun*. There are some one-off trains during the early hours; check with your station to see if there is a suitable one. Fares on BR trains are graduated and cheap day returns are available except *Mon-Fri* on busy trains during rush hours *(approx 08.00-09.30 and 16.30-18.00)*. Many BR stations connect with the underground. Take British Rail's Thameslink service to get through London quickly – rom Luton Airport via West Hampstead and Blackfriars to Gatwick Airport, Brighton and Kent. Ask at any station for a timetable.

British Travel Centre 4 **E4**
12 Lower Regent Street W1. A booking centre for rail travel in Britain, rail and sea journeys to the Continent and Ireland, motorail and rail package holidays and tours.
British Rail Travel Centres
Bookings for all rail travel in Britain.
87 King William St EC4. 5 **E3**
14 Kingsgate Pde, Victoria St SW1. 7 **C1**

RAIL TERMINALS
Blackfriars 5 **C3**
Queen Victoria St EC4. Information 0171-928 5100. South and south-east London suburbs. Built in 1864, rebuilt 1977.
Cannon Street 5 **E3**
Cannon St EC4. Information 0171-928 5100. South-east London suburbs, Kent, E. Sussex. Built 1866; rebuilt with office block above in 1965. *CLOSED Sat & Sun.*
Charing Cross 4 **F4**
Strand WC2. Information 0171-928 5100. South-east London suburbs, Kent. Built 1864. Trains from here go over Hungerford Bridge.
Euston 1 **F4**
Euston Rd NW1. Information 0171-387 7070. Fast trains to Birmingham, Liverpool, Manchester, Glasgow, Inverness. Suburban line to Watford, Northampton. Originally designed by Robert Stephenson, but completely rebuilt in 1968.
Fenchurch Street 5 **F3**
Railway Pl, Fenchurch St EC3. Information 0171-928 5100. Trains to Tilbury and Southend. Built 1841.
King's Cross 1 **G3**
Euston Rd N1. Information 0171-278 2477. Fast trains to Leeds, York, Newcastle, Edinburgh, Aberdeen. Built by Lewis Cubitt in 1851, a more modern concourse was added some years ago. The clock on the tower was taken from the original Crystal Palace in Hyde Park.
Liverpool Street 5 **F1**
Liverpool St EC2. Information 0171-928 5100. East and north-east London suburbs, fast trains to Cambridge, Colchester, Norwich and Harwich harbour. Built 1874.
London Bridge 5 **E4**
Borough High St SE1. Information 0171-928 5100. South and south-east London suburbs, Kent, Sussex, East Surrey. First opened in 1836, expanded in 1839 and 1864.
Marylebone 1 **B5**
Boston Pl NW1. Information 0171-262 6767. Suburban lines to Amersham, High Wycombe, Banbury, Aylesbury. Last of the main-line terminals to be built, 1899.
Moorgate 5 **E1**
Moorgate EC2. Information 0171-278 2477. Suburban services to Welwyn

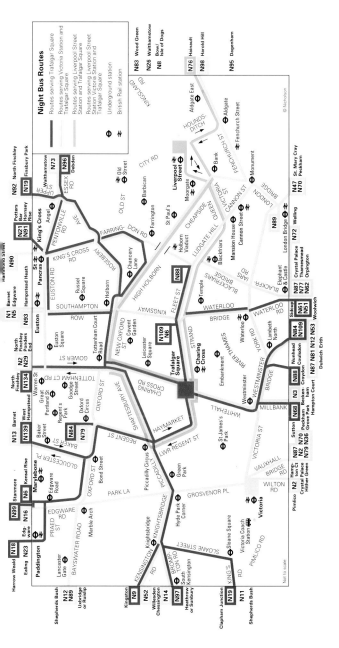

Garden City and Hertford. Constructed in 1904 as an underground station with tunnels to Drayton Park and thence overground. The tube tunnels are 16ft (4.9m) in diameter, the largest in London.

Paddington   **3 E2**

Praed St W2. Information 0171-262 6767. Fast trains to Bath, Bristol, Cardiff, Hereford, Swansea, Devon and Cornwall. Some 125mph services. Built in 1854 by Brunel, it was the London terminus of his Great Western Railway. The railway hotel, built by Hardwick, is a superb edifice in French Renaissance style.

St Pancras   **2 A4**

Euston Rd NW1. Information 0171-387 7070. Fast trains to Nottingham, Leicester, Sheffield, Derby; suburban to Luton, St Alban's, Bedford. An imposing Victorian Gothic glass and ironwork structure, it is more like a cathedral than a railway station with its 100ft (30.5m) high roof. Designed by Sir George Gilbert Scott and opened in 1868.

Victoria   **7 B2**

Terminus Pl, Victoria St SW1. Information 0171-928 5100. South and south-east London suburbs, Kent, Sussex, east Surrey. Fast trains to Brighton. Built in two parts; Brighton side in 1860, Dover side in 1862. Fast service to Gatwick Airport *(30-min journey)*. Every 15mins, 05.00-01.00; *less frequent through the night.*

Waterloo   **5 B5**

SE1. Information 0171-928 5100. Southwest London suburbs, west Surrey, Hampshire, Dorset. Fast trains to Portsmouth, Southampton, Bournemouth. Built 1848, partly modernised 1922. There is also a separate station, Waterloo (East), where all trains from Charing Cross stop. Waterloo International is the mainline terminus for channel tunnel services.

Green Line coaches

Enquiries: 0181-668 7261. Express buses run by London Country bus company. Most run from central London to outlying areas such as Windsor. The main departure point is Eccleston Bridge, Victoria SW1 (**7 B2**); others from Regent Street just north of Oxford Circus (**4 D2**). Three unique services: route 700 from Victoria to Windsor Castle, special express via M4 motorway; route 727 from Crawley via Gatwick & Heathrow; route 747 from Gatwick via Heathrow to Luton Airport. Services generally run *every hour.*

Coaches

Victoria Coach Station   **7 B2**

164 Buckingham Palace Rd SW1. 0171-

730 0202. The main provincial coach companies operate from here, travelling to destinations throughout Britain and the continent. Booking necessary.

Riverbus

Thames Commuter Services

Tavern House, Cannon Dri, Hertsmere Rd E14. 0171-537 4374. Service making use of London's great river. The riverbus travels from Festival Pier (**4 G4**) to Canary Wharf, stopping at London Bridge City Pier (**5 F4**), *07.30-09.30 every 15 mins Mon-Fri. CLOSED Sat, Sun & B.hols.* Return journey *16.45-19.00 every 15 mins.*

Taxis and mini-cabs

Taxis

The famous London black taxi cabs can be hailed in the street (some are now painted different colours and carry limited advertising, but are still bound by the same strict regulations); they are available for hire if the yellow 'taxi' light above the windscreen is lit. All these taxis have meters which the driver must use on all journeys within the Metropolitan Police District (most of Greater London and out to Heathrow Airport); for longer journeys the price should be negotiated with the driver beforehand. There is also a minimum payable charge which is shown on the meter when you hire the cab. Expect to pay extra for large luggage, journeys between 20.00-06.00, at weekends and B.hols. There are over 500 ranks throughout London, including all major hotels and British Rail stations. For your nearest rank, look in the telephone directory under 'Taxis', or try:

Computer-cab: 0171-286 0286. *(24 hrs).*
Dial-a-Cab: 0171-253 5000. *(24 hrs).*
Radio Taxicabs: 0171-272 0272. *(24 hrs).*

Mini-cabs

These cannot be hailed in the street, and in any case they are indistinguishable from private cars. Unlike the black cabs they are not licensed and neither do their drivers take the same stringent tests, but they are cheaper on longer runs. Essential to negotiate the price for any journey in advance. Your nearest mini-cab office is listed in Yellow Pages.
Below are listed some firms which OPEN 24 hrs:

Abbey Car Hire W2: 0171-727 2637.
Bartley Cars N5: 0171-226 7555.
Clover Cars W6: 0181-995 6000.

Greater London Hire N2: 0181-340 2450.
Hogarth SW5: 0171-370 2020.
Smart Cars E14: 0171-987 1888.

Cheaper and faster than black cabs, these are specially converted motorbikes with panniers and suitcase racks for luggage, driver-passenger intercoms and heated seats. Riders are all Institute of Advanced Motorists qualified or ex-Metropolitan Police. Operate 24 hrs throughout Greater London; minimum journey 3 miles (4.8km). Must be pre-booked outside 08.00-20.00.
Lee Addison Taxibikes   1 **E4**
35-37 William Rd NW1. 0171-387 8888.

Prices differ greatly from company to company and depend on the make of car and the season. There is a basic daily, weekly or monthly charge, sometimes inclusive of mileage, and you will also have to leave a deposit. Normally you will have to be over 21 and have held a licence, valid for use in the UK, for at least a year.
Avis Rent-a-Car   4 **B2**
8 Balderton St W1. 0171-917 6700. For bookings anywhere in London. *OPEN 07.00-20.00 Mon-Sun.* Worldwide reservations at Trident House, Station Rd, Hayes, Middx. 0181-848 8733.
Budget
0171-935 3518 or (0800) 181181 for your nearest branch in London. *OPEN 07.30-19.30 Mon-Fri, 07.30-15.30 Sat & Sun.*
Eurodollar
Warwick Pl, Uxbridge, Middx. (01895) 233300. Offices internationally. *OPEN 08.00-18.00 Mon-Sat.*
Godfrey Davis (Eurocar)   7 **C2**
Davis House, 129 Wilton Rd SW1. London bookings: 0171-834 8484. *OPEN 08.00-20.00 Mon-Sun.* Central reservations: 0181-950 5050. *OPEN 08.00-19.00 Mon-Fri, 08.00-13.00 Sat.*
Hertz Rent-a-Car
Radnor House, 1272 London Rd SW16. 0181-679 1799. Self or chauffeur driven. Branches throughout GB and the continent. *OPEN 08.00-18.00 Mon-Fri, to 17.00 Sat.*
Kenning   1 **G3**
1 York Way N1. 0171-833 3211. Self-drive cars. Branches throughout GB at airports and abroad. *OPEN 08.00-18.00 Mon-Fri, 08.00-14.00 Sat & Sun.*

International reservations on (01246) 208888. *OPEN 09.00-18.00 Mon-Fri.*
Sports Car Hire   6 **D2**
6 Kendrick Pl, Reece Mews SW7. 0171-589 8309. Morgan and Alfa Romeo Spyder for hire. *OPEN 09.30-19.00 Mon-Fri.*

Camelot Chauffeur Drive   4 **B5**
11-15 Headfort Pl SW1. 0171-245 9171. Jaguars, Mercedes, Daimler Limousines, Rolls Royces, Silver Spirits and Silver Spurs with liveried chauffeurs. Also saloons. *OPEN 07.00-24.00 Mon-Sat, 08.00-23.00 Sun. 24-hr telephone service.*
R & I Tours
R & I Tours, 823 Western Rd NW10. 0181-965 5333. Chauffeur driven Granada saloons and a wide range of vehicles from 12-49 seater. *OPEN 07.00-19.30 Mon-Fri. 24-hr telephone service.*

The bike offers an alternative and infinitely cheaper form of transport to the tube. Danger to health through breathing noxious fumes is not nearly as great as the benefit gained from the exercise of cycling and you can avoid parking difficulties. Test the experience for yourself by hiring before buying a bike, or contact the London Cycling Campaign (0171-928 7220) for information.
Bikepark   4 **F2**
Stukeley St WC2. 0171-430 0083. Raleigh mountain bikes for hire. Secure warehouse parking for 150 bicycles. Repairs.
On Your Bike   5 **F4**
52-54 Tooley St, London Bridge SE1. 0171-407 1309. Also at Lillywhites, 24-36 Regent St SW1 (4 **E3**). 0171-915 4101. Over 50 cycles available.

Greens
357 Hoe St, Walthamstow E17. 0181-520 1138.
Grey-Green Coaches
53-55 Stamford Hill N16. 0181-800 4549.
Heathrow Coach Centre
Sipson Rd, West Drayton, Middx. 0181-897 6131.
London Transport   4 **E6**
Tours & Charter Office, 55 Broadway SW1. 0171-222 5600.
R & I Coaches
12 Western Rd NW12. 0181-965 5333.

Index

NICHOLSON

KEY TO
MAP PAGES

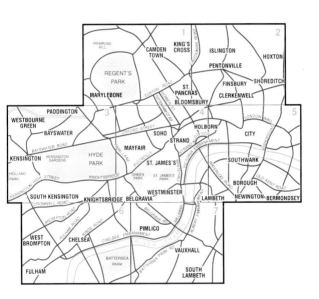

NICHOLSON
COMPUTER
MAPPING

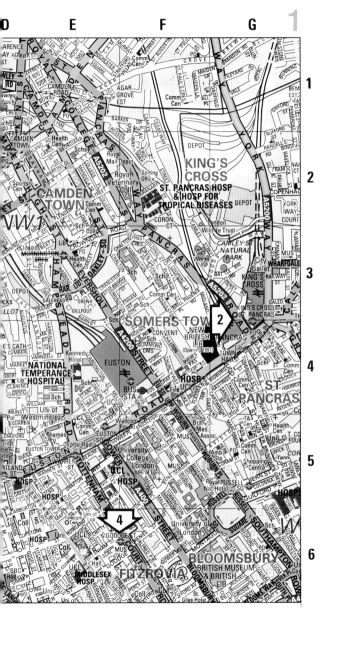

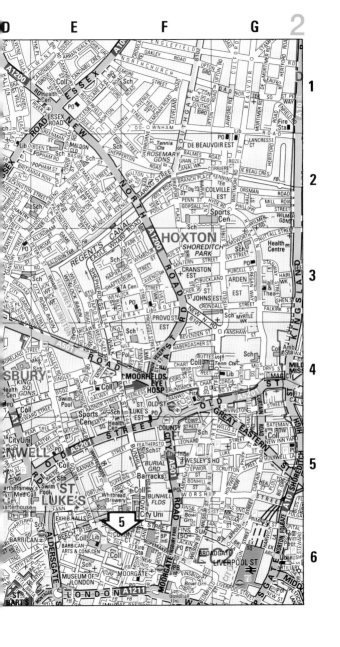

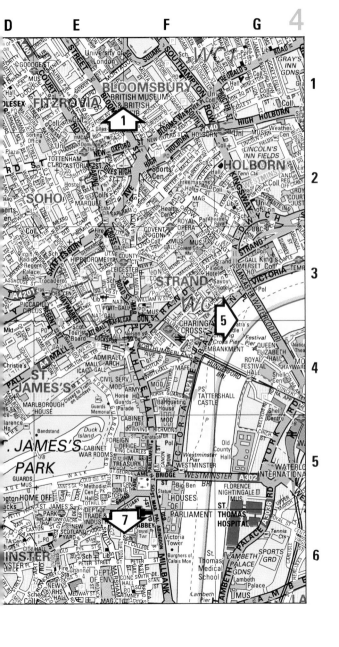

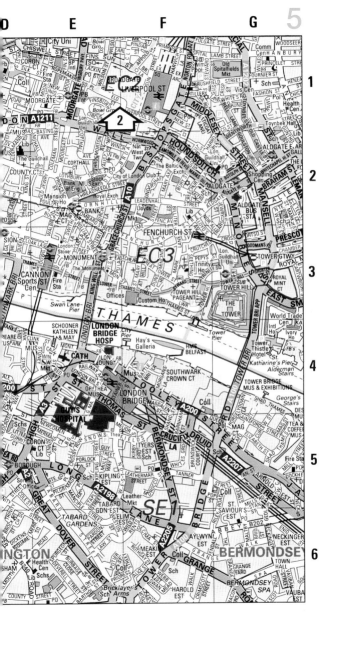

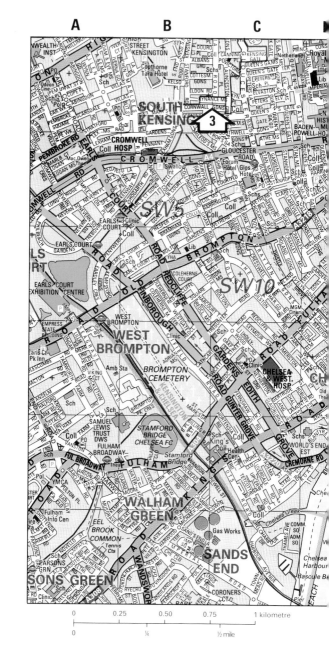

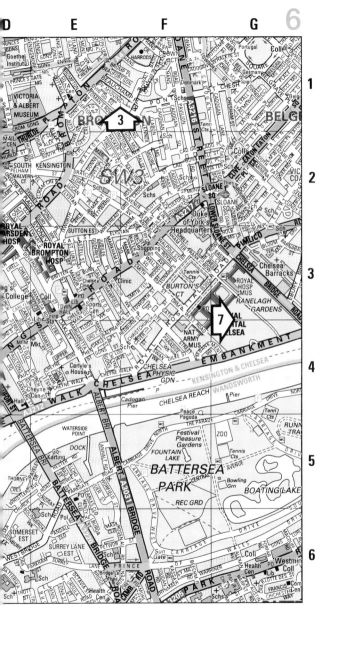

Blue numbers refer to double page maps.
Black letters and numbers refer to grid references on each map.

272

Street Index

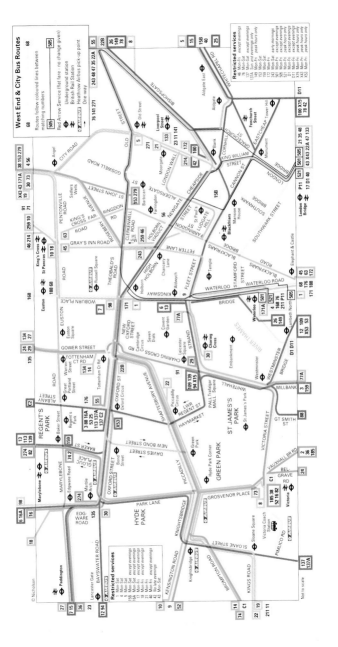

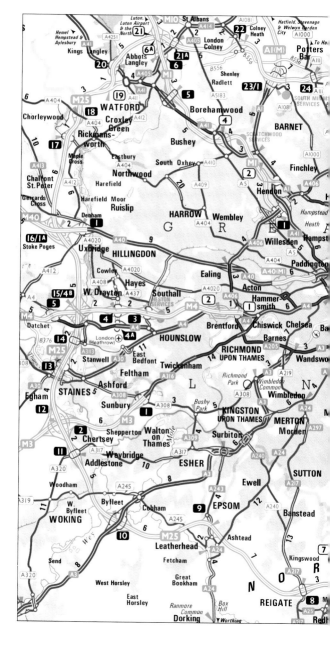

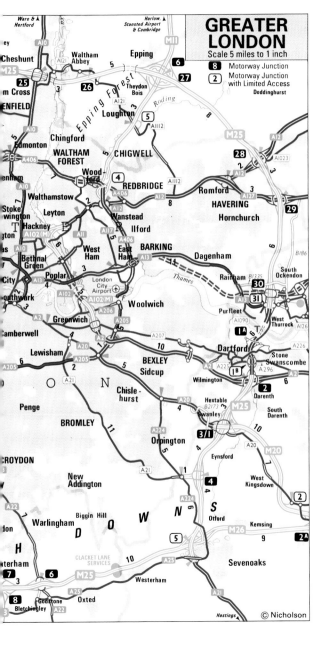

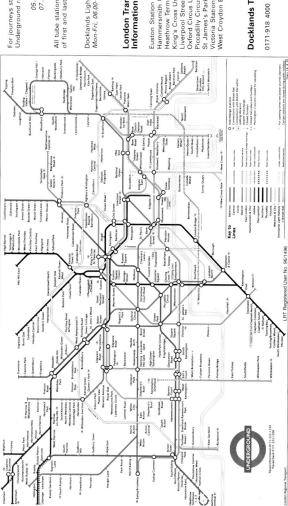

For journeys starting from central London, the Underground runs from

05.30–00.15 *Mon-Sat,*
07.30–23.30 *Sun.*

All tube stations have notices giving the times of first and last departures.

Docklands Light Railway runs from *05.30–00.30 Mon-Fri, 06.00–00.30 Sat & 07.30–23.30 Sun.*

London Transport Travel Information Centres:

Euston Station
Hammersmith Underground Station
Heathrow Terminals 1,3 & 4
King's Cross Underground Station
Liverpool Street Station
Oxford Circus Underground Station
Piccadilly Circus Underground Station
St James's Park Underground Station
Victoria Station
West Croydon Bus Station

Docklands Travel Information:

0171-918 4000